AF621617

KRÄMER'S EU ENVIRONMENTAL LAW

The new edition of this essential book details the present state of EU environmental law as it has developed over the last 50 years. The author was personally involved in its making and enforcement, having worked for more than 30 years in the environmental department of the European Commission. The book therefore provides unique insights into this complex field.

The book discusses in detail governance and other horizontal issues, such as competence questions, the division of power between the EU and its Member States, the individual right to a clean environment, and the integration of environmental requirements into other EU policies such as energy, transport, agriculture, fisheries, trade and tourism.

New chapters elaborate on the relationship between UK and EU law after Brexit (written by Christopher Badger) and on the global effect of EU environmental law and policy. Other chapters deal with climate change, biodiversity, water protection, air and noise pollution, products and waste. Implementation of EU law in the Member States and the prominent role of the EU Court of Justice with its more than 1,100 environmental judgments are discussed, as well as an overall assessment of EU law and policy in environmental matters and its perspectives to 2030 under the 8th EU environmental action programme.

At a time of globalisation, the book is indispensable reading for students, researchers and practising lawyers alike.

Krämer's EU Environmental Law

Ninth Edition

Ludwig Krämer
with
Christopher Badger

•HART•
OXFORD • LONDON • NEW YORK • NEW DELHI • SYDNEY

HART PUBLISHING

Bloomsbury Publishing Plc

Kemp House, Chawley Park, Cumnor Hill, Oxford, OX2 9PH, UK

1385 Broadway, New York, NY 10018, USA

29 Earlsfort Terrace, Dublin 2, Ireland

HART PUBLISHING, the Hart/Stag logo, BLOOMSBURY and the Diana logo are trademarks of Bloomsbury Publishing Plc

First published in Great Britain 2024

Copyright © Ludwig Krämer with Christopher Badger, 2024

Ludwig Krämer with Christopher Badger have asserted their right under the Copyright, Designs and Patents Act 1988 to be identified as Authors of this work.

All rights reserved. No part of this publication may be reproduced or transmitted in any form or by any means, electronic or mechanical, including photocopying, recording, or any information storage or retrieval system, without prior permission in writing from the publishers.

While every care has been taken to ensure the accuracy of this work, no responsibility for loss or damage occasioned to any person acting or refraining from action as a result of any statement in it can be accepted by the authors, editors or publishers.

All UK Government legislation and other public sector information used in the work is Crown Copyright ©. All House of Lords and House of Commons information used in the work is Parliamentary Copyright ©. This information is reused under the terms of the Open Government Licence v3.0 (http://www.nationalarchives.gov.uk/doc/open-government-licence/version/3) except where otherwise stated.

All Eur-lex material used in the work is © European Union, http://eur-lex.europa.eu/, 1998–2024.

A catalogue record for this book is available from the British Library.

Library of Congress Cataloging-in-Publication data.

Names: Krämer, Ludwig, 1939- author. | Badger, Christopher, author.

Title: Krämer's EU environmental law / Ludwig Krämer, Christopher Badger.

Other titles: EEC treaty and environmental protection | EU environmental law

Description: Ninth Edition. | Oxofrd [UK] ; New York : Hart Publishing, 2024. | Includes bibliographical references and index. | Summary: "The new edition of this essential book details the present state of EU environmental law as it has developed over the last 50 years. The author was personally involved in its making and enforcement, having worked for more than 30 years in the environmental department of the European Commission. The book provides therefore unique insights into this complex field. New chapters elaborate on the relationship between UK and EU law after Brexit (written by Christopher Badger) and on the global effect of EU environmental law and policy. The book is indispensable reading for students, researchers, and practising lawyers alike"— Provided by publisher.

Identifiers: LCCN 2024006586 (print) | LCCN 2024006587 (ebook) | ISBN 9781509974443 (hardback) | ISBN 9781509969074 (paperback) | ISBN 9781509969081 (Epub) | ISBN 9781509969098 (ebook)

Subjects: LCSH: Environmental law—European Union countries.

Classification: LCC KJE6242 .K729 2024 (print) | LCC KJE6242 (ebook) | DDC 341.7/62/094—dc21

LC record available at https://lccn.loc.gov/2024006586

LC ebook record available at https://lccn.loc.gov/2024006587

ISBN: PB: 978-1-50996-907-4
HB: 978-1-50997-444-3
ePDF: 978-1-50996-909-8
ePub: 978-1-50996-908-1

Typeset by Compuscript Ltd, Shannon
Printed and bound in Great Britain by CPI Group (UK) Ltd, Croydon CR0 4YY

MIX
Paper | Supporting responsible forestry
FSC® C013604

To find out more about our authors and books visit www.hartpublishing.co.uk. Here you will find extracts, author information, details of forthcoming events and the option to sign up for our newsletters.

PREFACE

This book on European Union environmental law is the result of 50 years of occupation with this topic. Indeed, in the early 1970s, as a young judge at the Landgericht Kiel (Germany), I was delegated to the European Commission in Brussels and worked, from its very beginnings, in the newly established environmental protection service, which later became the Directorate General for the Environment. Thus, I had the privilege to live through the evolution of Union environmental law from the first hour. As my delegation to the Commission continued until 2004, I was able to participate in the elaboration and monitoring of Union environmental law for decades. My parallel academic career was continued after 2004 and led me to lecture EU environmental law in some 50 universities and in six languages, while at the same time joining a European environmental organisation and publishing more than 350 articles and a number of books on Union environmental law.

European environmental law has evolved over these last 50 years in a spectacular manner, developing from a late-coming part of Union law into one of its most important and relevant sectors. In the majority of the EU Member States, it is the first source of national environmental law, which is derived almost 100 per cent from EU environmental provisions. There is no sector of the environment where EU law did not considerably influence the elaboration and application of national environmental rules.

The five big problems of the environment – the influence of climate change; the loss of biodiversity; pollution; the management of natural resources; and the fight against poverty – are global in nature, but also dominate environment-related discussions within the Union. In part, the Union developed structures, instruments and mechanisms to successfully react to these challenges. Examples are the very decision-making process at European level, with the right of legislative initiatives of the European Commission, majority decisions in most parts of environmental law, the surveillance of the application of Union law in Member States and sectoral successes, such as the emissions trading scheme for greenhouse gases, the Natura 2000 network for habitats, the treatment of urban waste water and the monitoring of chemicals (REACH).

In other areas of environmental law, the Union has been less successful. Despite harmonised or even uniform legal rules in almost all sectors of environmental law, vast differences in the state of the environment in Europe continue to exist. In particular, Southern and Eastern European states are often inclined to consider the protection of the environment because there was legislation from Brussels which asked them to do so. Indeed, the full and effective application of EU environmental law provisions in the 27 Member States remains the biggest legal problem which the EU environment faces. Another important problem of that law is the export of environmental protection provisions to third countries. The international agreements concluded by the EU on trade, fisheries, transport and in other sectors largely leave environmental issues to be solved by each partner of the agreement; the EU does not seriously try to export its environmental standards or address the global nature of environmental threats. Neither in the context of comprehensive trade agreements, such as with Canada or with New Zealand, nor in agreements with developing countries (the Cotonou Agreement, fisheries agreements) does it try to agree common standards for climate change, biodiversity or water management, or make serious efforts to improve the environmental situation. Also, the EU objective of eradicating poverty is not very actively pursued in its foreign environmental policy.

Within the Union, the requirement of Article 11 of the Treaty on the Functioning of the Union to integrate environmental requirements into the elaboration and application of the other Union policies is far from being systematically pursued. It is true that overfishing caused a number of measures to protect the – mainly EU – marine biological resources to be taken, and climate change called for the promotion of renewable energies. Yet, in most other EU policies and activities, considerations concerning the preservation, protection and improvement of the environment continue to play a marginal role. The fact that the environment has no voice all too often and too easily allows environmental concerns to be put aside and business to be continued as usual.

Without a corresponding political will, environmental law will not be able to ensure sustainable planet life for our children and grandchildren. Yet, I remain convinced that the full application of the existing rules, combined with a determination to comply with the Union's policy commitments – such as a high level of environmental protection, sustainability, open decisions close to the citizens and with their participation, zero greenhouse emissions by 2050, a serious restoration of nature, good quality of the Union's waters by 2027, a move towards zero air pollution, a circular economy, a serious and continuous fight against poverty – could bring lasting improvements to the EU, to its 27 Member States and to the planetary environment.

Fighting for a better environment presupposes the knowledge of the applicable rules. This book intends to deliver the legal tools for such a fight. If ever a young law student looks at it, he might remember the paraphrased statement by Bert Brecht: 'If you fight (for a better environment), you may lose. If you do not fight, you already lost.'

Legislation and jurisprudence were taken into consideration until the end of August 2023.

Chapter 13, on EU and environmental law and Brexit, was written by Christopher Badger, to whom I am much obliged and very grateful. He presents this complex and intricate issue with great skill and admirable knowledge.

I would also like to express my sincere thanks to the team from Hart Publishing, who made this book possible. My specific thanks go to Roberta Bassi, who seconded, encouraged and supported me throughout.

Ludwig Krämer
1 September 2023

CONTENTS

* Christopher Badger is the author of Chapter 13. All other chapters were written by Ludwig Krämer.

ABBREVIATIONS

ACEA	Association of European Car Manufacturers (Association des Constructeurs Européens d'Automobiles)
BAT	Best available technique
BREF	Best available technique reference
CAP	Common agricultural policy
CBAM	Carbon Border Adjustment Mechanism
CCA 2008	Climate Change Act 2008
CCC	Committee on Climate Change
CCS	Carbon capture and storage
CECA	European Coal and Steel Community
CETA	Comprehensive Economic and Trade Agreement
CFC	Chlorofluorocarbon
CEN	European Committee for Standardisation
CENELEC	European Committee for Electrical and Electronic Standardisation
CITES	Convention on International Trade in Endangered Species
CJEU	Court of Justice of the European Union
CO	Carbon monoxide
CO_2	Carbon dioxide
COM	Communication of the European Commission
COREPER	Committee of Permanent Representatives (Comité des Représentants Permanents)
CSR	Corporate social responsibility
dB, dB(A)	Decibels
Defra	Department for Environment, Food & Rural Affairs
DG ENV	Directorate General for Environment
EAFRD	European Agricultural Fund for Rural Development
EAGF	European Agricultural Guarantee Fund

EAP	Environmental Action Programme
EC	European Community
ECA	European Communities Act 1972
ECHA	European Chemicals Agency
ECLI	European Case Law Identifier
EEA	European Environment Agency
EEA Agreement	Agreement on the European Economic Area
EEC	European Economic Community
EECOSOC	European Economic and Social Committee
EFSA	European Food Safety Authority
EFTA	European Free Trade Area
EIA	Environmental Impact Assessment
Elni	Environmental Law Network International (Review)
EMAS	Environmental Management and Auditing System
EP	European Parliament
EPA	Environment Protection Agency (USA)
EPPS	environmental principles policy statement
ERDF	European Regional Development Fund
ETSI	European Telecommunication Standards Institute
EU ETS	EU Emissions Trading Scheme
EUWA	European Union (Withdrawal) Act 2018
EUWAA	European Union (Withdrawal Agreement) Act 2020
FLEGT	Forest Law Enforcement, Governance and Trade
GATT	General Agreement on Tariffs and Trade
GHS	Globally Harmonised System of Classification and Labelling of Chemicals
GMO	Genetically modified organism
HC	Hydrocarbon
HCFC	Hydrochorofluorocarbon
ICAO	International Civil Aviation Organization
IMO	International Maritime Organization

IMPEL	European Union Network for the Implementation and Enforcement of Environmental Law
ISO	International Organization for Standardization
IUCN	International Union for the Conservation of Nature
LIFE	Legal instrument for the environment
MARPOL	International Convention for the protection of pollution from ships
MMT	Methylcyclopentadienyl manganese tricarbonyl
Mtoe	Million tons of oil equivalent
NGO	Non-governmental organisation
NO_2	Nitrogen dioxide
NO_x	Nitrogen oxides
OECD	Organisation for Economic Cooperation and Development
OEP	Office for Environmental Protection
OJ C	Official Journal of the European Union, section communication
OJ L	Official Journal of the European Union, section legislation
OSPAR	Convention on the Protection of the Marine Environment of the North-East Atlantic
PBBs	Polybromated biphenyls
PCB/PCT	Polychlorinated biphenyls and triphenyls
PCP	Pentachlorophenol
PET	Polyethylenterephtalate
PFASs	Polyfluoroalkyl substances
PIC	Prior informed consent
PM	Particulate matter
POP	Persistent organic pollutant
PVC	Polyvinyl chloride
REACH	Registration, Evaluation, Authorisation and Restriction of Chemicals
REUL Act	Retained EU Law (Revocation and Reform) Act 2023
SAC	Special Area of Conservation
SCHEER	Scientific Committee on Health, Environment and Emerging Risks
SDG	Sustainable Development Goal

SEC	Staff Working Document of the European Commission
SO_2	Sulphur dioxide
SPA	Special protection area
SVHC	Substances of very high concern
SWD	Staff Working Document of the European Commission
TCA	EU–UK Trade and Co-operation Agreement
TEU	Treaty on European Union
TFEU	Treaty on the Functioning of the European Union
TIGRR	Taskforce on Innovation, Growth and Regulatory Reform
TiO_2	Titanium dioxide
TSIs	Technical specifications for interoperability
UK ETS	UK Emissions Trading Scheme
UN	United Nations
VAT	Value added tax
VOCs	Volatile organic compounds
WEEE	Waste electrical and electronic equipment
WHO	World Health Organization
WTO	World Trade Organization

TABLE OF CASES

TABLE OF PENDING CASES

TABLE OF REGULATIONS

TABLE OF DIRECTIVES

TABLE OF DECISIONS

TABLES OF OTHER MATERIALS

TABLE OF WTO CASES

TABLE OF UK CASES

Germany Cases

ECtHR Cases

EFTA Court of Justice Cases

TABLE OF UK LEGISLATION

1

Objectives, Principles and Conditions

I. The Environment in European Union Law

The European Union (EU) is an international organisation of, at present, 27 Member States, which have transferred part of their sovereignty to the EU. Its objectives are laid down in Article 3 of the Treaty on European Union. The Lisbon Treaty on European Union (TEU), which entered into effect on 1 December 2009,[1] fixes one of the objectives of the Union in Article 3(3) as 'a high level of protection and improvement of the quality of the environment'. In the same paragraph, sustainable development is fixed as one of the aims of the Union; both the protection of the environment and the sustainable development are also mentioned in Recital 9 TEU. The objectives of Article 3(3) TEU are completed by the specific environmental objectives in Article 191 of the Treaty on the Functioning of the Union (TFEU), which are a high level of protection, a prudent use of natural resources, a contribution to human health and the promotion of environmental protection at international level, in particular combating climate change. 1-01

Neither of these provisions, though, defines 'environment'; nor do the other provisions of the Treaties contain any definition. It follows from Articles 191(1) and 192(2) TFEU that the environment includes human beings, natural resources, land use, town and country planning, waste and water. These categories include practically all areas of the environment, in particular biodiversity and climate. The inclusion of issues concerning town and country planning underlines that the environment is not limited to natural elements, but also includes the man-made environment.

Article 177(2) TFEU provides for the setting up of a Cohesion Fund which shall provide a financial contribution to transport infrastructure projects of the trans-European networks and to the environment. Regulation 2021/1060 clarified that energy efficiency and renewable energy measures, the promotion of environmentally friendly production, and railway connections are considered environmental measures and capable of being (co-)financed by EU environmentally oriented funds.[2] Finally, Regulation 2020/852 laid down a framework for facilitating environmentally sustainable investments,[3] which was complemented by a Commission Regulation specifying the economic activities which could be considered environmentally sustainable.[4]

[1] [2008] OJ C115/1.

[2] Regulation 2021/1060 laying down common provisions on the different EU funds [2021] OJ L231/159.

[3] Regulation 2020/852 on the establishment of a framework to facilitate sustainable investment [2020] OJ L198/13. Art 2 no 1 clarified that the Regulation concerned *environmentally* sustainable investment.

[4] Commission Delegated Regulation 2022/1214 (2022) OJ L188/1 decided that under certain conditions, investments in nuclear energy and in gas should also be considered as environmentally sustainable.

1-02 When the section 'environment' was first included in the Treaty establishing the European Community (EC Treaty) in 1987, there was already extensive secondary European legislation adopted on the basis of three environmental action programmes and this was generally perceived as legislation on the environment. This secondary legislation covered water and air, noise and chemicals, nature conservation, waste and some measures of a general character. Furthermore, in June 1990, shortly before the commencement of the negotiations on the Maastricht Treaty on European Union, the Community Heads of State and Government adopted a 'Declaration on the Environment',[5] in which they proclaimed a right to a healthy and clean environment, including, in particular,

> the quality of air, rivers, lakes, coastal and marine waters, the quality of food and drinking water, protection against noise, protection against contamination of soil, soil erosion and desertification, preservation of habitats, flora and fauna, landscape and other elements of the natural heritage, the amenity and quality of residential areas.

It must be assumed that by using the concept 'environment' in this legal, political, economic and ecological context, the authors of the Treaties have given to the term the emphasis which it had at that time in EU law. The term 'environment' is thus very broad and includes economic, social and aesthetic aspects, the preservation of natural and archaeological heritage, and the man-made as well as the natural environment.

1-03 'Environment' in Articles 3 TEU and 4 and 191–93 TFEU is different from the 'working environment' used in Articles 114 and 153 TFEU, which obviously concerns the conditions at the workplace, such as air pollution, noise or accident prevention. The specific conditions of the workplace justify a different treatment of 'environment' and 'working environment', although, in the early 1970s, EU environmental policy did not make this distinction,[6] and some directives do not really differentiate between worker protection and environmental protection.[7] Working environment provisions now come under Article 114 or 153 TFEU, as the case may be.

Doubts were sometimes raised as to whether 'environment' also includes animal welfare. However, wild animals are part of the natural environment; thus, protection measures for wild animals – not only as a threatened species, but as living creatures – are environmental measures. The Amsterdam Treaty on European Union added a protocol to the EC Treaty, according to which the Union's policies on agriculture, transport, the internal market and research had to pay 'full regard to the welfare of animals'.[8] The TFEU took this up and inserted a new Article 13, which declared that, 'since animals are sentient beings', full regard had to be paid to the welfare requirements of animals. It is obvious, though, that this provision refers to domestic, not wild, animals and therefore does not contradict the interpretation given here. The Eighth Environmental Action Programme considered animal welfare law as part of food law, which would require a gradual adaptation of domestic animal welfare requirements to environmental objectives and principles.[9]

[5] European Council Resolution of 15 June 1990 (1990) *Bulletin of the European Communities* No.7 (July), para 1.36.

[6] See First Environmental Action Programme [1973] OJ C112/1 43.

[7] See Directive 2012/18 on the control of major-accident hazards involving dangerous substances [2012] OJ L197/1.

[8] [1997] OJ C340/110.

[9] Decision 2022/591 on an Eighth Environmental Action Programme [2022] OJ L114/22, Arts 2(2)(d) and 3(n).

The uncertainty of how to classify (wild) animal welfare became obvious when the Commission made a proposal for a directive on the protection of zoo animals. In view of a subsidiarity debate in Council, the Commission repealed this proposal and replaced it with a proposal for a recommendation. However, the Council rearranged the text so as to be mainly concerned with protecting animals as endangered species and, on that basis, adopted a directive in 1999.[10]

Geographically, the environment mentioned in the Treaty is not limited to the European Union's environment, as is clear from the mention of 'measures at international level and regional or worldwide environmental problems' in Article 191(1) TFEU. Consequently, the Union may – and did – take measures to protect the environment outside the territory covered by the Treaties, such as measures to protect the ozone layer, combat climate change, protect endangered species in the third world or ban the export of waste to non-industrialised countries. 1-04

The question of whether the Union should deal with matters of a purely local nature is something to be answered under the general principle of subsidiarity. In the past, the Commission has sometimes rejected requests to take initiatives on a specific environmental problem, arguing that such matters could be better solved at local or regional level; those questions concerned, for instance, noise from nightclubs and discotheques, bicycle facilities in urban areas or noise in the vicinity of airports. However, in order to ensure equal competition conditions within the Union while, at the same time, protecting the environment, the EU adopted, for example, detailed rules on the ambient noise level in the neighbourhood of airports.[11] Furthermore, it may well be argued that the quality of the (local) bathing waters, of drinking water or of urban waste water treatment are questions of purely local nature and should not, therefore, be regulated at Union level. The EU legislature has, in all three cases, decided that there should be EU-wide minimum standards, and no Member State ever invoked the subsidiarity principle in this regard. My own opinion is that the EU legislature has a large margin of discretion about whether a specific problem should be dealt with at EU level or not. I consider all three pieces of EU legislation compatible with the subsidiarity principle.

When, in 2006, the Commission made a proposal for a directive on the assessment and management of floods, some Member States suggested limiting this proposal to river basins which affected more than one Member State. However, this suggestion was rejected, probably because coastal floods were also included and because the management of such floods, including any financial assistance from the EU, would not be made easier; the directive which was adopted covered all types of floods.[12]

More generally, there is no EU environment distinguishable from any individual, local, regional or national environment. Therefore, the Union measures need not be and are not restricted to transfrontier environmental problems. Quite rightly, Article 5(3) TEU abandoned the notion of a 'transfrontier' dimension of a measure which was contained in Article 5 EC Treaty, and only refers to the 'scale' of the measure as one criterion among

[10] Directive 1999/22 relating to the keeping of wild animals in zoos [1999] OJ L94/24; for more details, see para 5-36.

[11] Regulation 598/2014 on the establishment of rules and procedures with regard to the introduction of noise-related operating restrictions at Union airports within a Balanced Approach [2014] OJ L173/65.

[12] Directive 2007/60 on the assessment and management of flood risks [2007] OJ L288/27.

others for assessing the application of the subsidiarity principle. As mentioned above, the definition of 'environment' is very wide as regards its content and its geographical extension, and includes human beings, fauna and flora, soil, water, air, climate, landscape, material assets and natural heritage.[13] Environmental law is the totality of the legal measures which try to prevent, protect and improve parts or all of the environment.

II. Genesis and Development of EU Environmental Law

1-05 The original Treaty establishing the European Economic Community of 1957 (EEC Treaty) did not contain any provision on the environment, environmental policy or environmental law. Subsequent to the discussions of the late 1960s, where the Club of Rome described the limits to growth, the European Commission announced in 1970 the necessity of establishing a Community action programme on the environment. In 1971, it submitted a first communication on Community environmental policy,[14] where it suggested the establishment of EU measures for the protection of the environment, recurring, if necessary, to the possibilities for action outlined in Article 308 EEC (now Article 352 TFEU). This communication was soon followed by a proposal for an environmental action programme.[15]

In 1972, the UK, Denmark and Ireland joined the Union. In the autumn of that year, the Heads of State and Government met for the first time, agreed on the necessity to take action on the environment and asked for an EU environmental action programme.[16] Since such a programme was already before the Council, discussions advanced relatively quickly. France in particular considered, however, that EU action should not be based on the EC Treaty provisions, but should instead take place in the form of intergovernmental co-operation, as the EEC Treaty did not contain an explicit competence provision. For this reason, the finally adopted programme was agreed in the form of a joint 'declaration' by the Community and by the representatives of Member States meeting in Council.[17] In the same way, the agreement to inform the Commission of national environmental measures which could have a direct effect on the functioning of the internal market was made in the form of a non-binding gentleman's agreement;[18] this policy continued throughout 1973 and 1974.[19]

1-06 The first legally binding instruments on environmental issues were adopted in 1975, based on Article 94 and/or 308 EEC (now Articles 115 and 352 TFEU). The choice of measures was determined both by the environmental action programme and by the necessity

[13] Enumeration from Directive 2011/92 on the assessment of the effects of certain public and private projects on the environment [2012] OJ L26/1, Art 3.

[14] Commission, 'First Communication on a Community Policy for the Environment' SEC(71) 2616 of 22 July 1971.

[15] [1972] OJ C52/1.

[16] Commission, Sixth General Report (1972) 8.

[17] [1973] OJ C112/1.

[18] [1973] OJ C9/1.

[19] See Agreement of 20 July 1974 to complete the 1973 agreement [1974] OJ C86/1; Resolution on energy and the environment [1975] OJ C168/2; Recommendation 75/436 on cost allocation and action by public authorities on environmental matters [1975] OJ L194/1; Resolution on a second group of air pollutants which are to be studied [1975] OJ C168/4; Resolution on adapting Community measures to technical progress [1975] OJ C168/5; Decision setting up a common procedure for an inventory of information sources on the environment [1976] OJ L31/8.

of selecting areas which did not come under the responsibility of the internal market or agricultural services of the Commission. This was the case in particular for measures in the areas of water and waste.[20]

The EEC Treaty was amended in 1987 to complete, by the end of 1992, the internal market.[21] Majority voting for internal market measures was introduced by inserting a new Article 95 (now Article 114) into the Treaty. And for the first time, a section was introduced for environmental measures (Articles 174–76, now Articles 191–93 TFEU). However, such measures had to be adopted unanimously. This led to considerable discussions on the legal basis for environmental measures, which the Commission and the European Parliament often wished to base on the pre-existing Article 114 EEC Treaty, while the Council and Member States preferred the present Article 192 TFEU.

When the Maastricht Treaty on European Union amended the EEC Treaty in 1993, renaming it the European Community (EC) Treaty, it introduced majority decisions in environmental matters (Article 192), though some matters remained subjected to unanimous decisions.[22]

The Amsterdam Treaty,[23] which entered into effect on 1 May 1999, introduced the co-decision procedure for environmental matters (Article 192(1)) and thus aligned this provision further to that of Article 114, though the unanimity clause for some areas (Article 192(2)) was not deleted. The Treaty of Nice, which came into effect on 1 February 2003, did not significantly change the provisions of Articles 191–93. Nor did the Lisbon Treaty bring changes to these provisions, except that environmental objectives were prominently inserted in Article 3 TEU; also, the fight against climate change was inserted into Article 191 TFEU as one of the objectives of EU environmental policy.

Following a referendum in 2016, the UK left the EU with effect from 1 January 2021 (Brexit), reducing the number of Member States to 27.

III. Sources of EU Environmental Law

The broad definition of objectives of EU environmental policy, as laid down in Articles 3 TEU and 191(1) TFEU, hardly leaves any area of environmental policy, as it is perceived in any one of the 27 Member States, outside EU competence. Measures to realise the objectives of the Union's environmental policy may be based on any relevant article of the TFEU, although Articles 191 and 192 remain the most relevant provisions. Thus, measures which concern agricultural aspects of environmental protection will normally be based on Article 43 TFEU; an example is Regulation 1107/2009 on the authorisation and marketing of plant protection products.[24] Measures on environmental aspects of transport 1-07

[20] See, in chronological order, Decision 75/437 to adhere to the Paris Convention on marine protection from land-based sources [1975] OJ L194/5; Directive 75/439 on waste oils [1975] OJ L194/23; Directive75/440 on surface water [1975] OJ L194/26; Directive 75/442 [1975] OJ L194/39 on waste; Directive76/160 on bathing water [1976] OJ L31/1.

[21] Single European Act [1987] OJ L169/1.

[22] Maastricht Treaty on European Union [1992] OJ C191/1.

[23] Amsterdam Treaty [1997] OJ C340/1.

[24] Regulation 1107/2009 [2009] OJ L309/1.

may be based on Article 91 TFEU; an example is Directive 99/62 on the charging of heavy good vehicles for the use of certain infrastructures.[25] The choice of the correct legal basis is important because the elaboration of the proposal, the participation of other Union institutions, the intensity of this participation (see Articles 293–94 TFEU) and the residual rights for Member States are different from one provision to another.

The rules of Articles 191 and 192 TFEU are not directly applicable: while, for instance, Article 34 TFEU states that 'quantitative restrictions on imports and all measures having equivalent effect shall … be prohibited between Member States', no similar formulation can be found in Article 191 or 192 TFEU stating that pollution is prohibited or that the polluter shall pay for pollution. Therefore, Articles 191 and 192 need to be operationalised and made precise by secondary legislation in order to become applicable for administrative bodies and courts or used for or against polluters.

The most relevant other provisions on which EU environmental measures can be based are: Article 114 TFEU, for measures aiming at the establishment and the functioning of the internal market; Article 43 TFEU, for agricultural and fisheries measures; Article 91 TFEU, for measures concerning transport; and Article 207 TFEU, for commercial measures. Environmental measures in the energy sector were in the past frequently based on Article 192 TFEU, as there was no specific chapter on energy policy in the EC Treaty; an example was Directive 2001/77 on the promotion of electricity produced from renewable energy sources in the internal electricity market.[26] Otherwise, Article 352 TFEU was used. The Lisbon Treaty introduced a new provision, Article 194 TFEU. This provision is now being used for energy-related environmental measures.[27]

The choice of the correct legal basis for an environmental matter will be further discussed below at paragraph 2-71ff, and the rights of Member States in chapter three.

1-08 International conventions to which the Union adheres are part of EU law, according to Article 216(2) TFEU. They rank below the primary law of the TFEU but above secondary legislation, and thus prevail over conflicting environmental directives or regulations.[28] However, the Court of Justice of the European Union (CJEU) only allows a provision of an international environmental agreement to be relied on in court when it is of direct effect.[29] When this is not the case, national courts are requested to do their best in order to give full effect to such a provision in national law (*effet utile*).[30] For itself, the Court has not yet accepted that it is under an obligation to apply the *effet utile* doctrine in such cases.

[25] Directive 1999/62 [1999] OJ L187/42.

[26] Directive 2001/77 [2001] OJ L283/33.

[27] See, eg Directive2012/27 on energy efficiency, [2012] OJ L315/1.

[28] See CJEU Case C-344/04 *IATA and ELFAA* ECLI:EU:C:2006:10, para 35: 'Article 300(7) EC [now Article 216(2) TFEU] provides that "agreements concluded under the conditions set out in this Article shall be binding on the institutions of the Community and on Member States". In accordance with the court's case-law, those agreements prevail over provisions of secondary Community legislation.'

[29] CJEU, Joined Cases C-401/12P and C-402/12P *Council and European Parliament v Milieudefensie and Stichting Stop Luchtverontreiniging Utrecht* ECLI:EU:C:2015:4; Joined Cases C-404/12P and 405/12P *Council and Commission v Stichting Natuur en Milieu and Pesticide Action Network Europe* ECLI:EU:C:2015:5.

[30] CJEU Case C-240/09 *Lesoochranárske zoskupenie* ECLI:EU:C:2011:125, para 50: 'it is for the national court, in order to ensure effective judicial protection in the fields covered by EU environmental law, to interpret its national law in a way which, to the fullest extent possible, is consistent with the objectives laid down in Article 9(3) of the Aarhus Convention'; see in the same way Joined Cases C-128/09-C-131/09, C-134/09 and C-135/09 *Boxus* ECLI:EU:C:2011:667.

The Union has adhered to a considerable number of international environmental agreements and to numerous protocols drawn up in pursuance of these agreements. All these agreements are so-called 'mixed' agreements: the competence for the subject matter regulated by the agreements was partly in the hands of the Union and partly in the hands of the Member States. Where exactly the line is drawn between the Union's responsibility and that of the Member States inevitably varies from one agreement to the other.

As decisions which are based on Article 192 TFEU and transpose environmental agreements into EU law have as a consequence that Member States may, under Article 193 TFEU, introduce more stringent provisions in that area at national level, such decisions can never establish an exclusive EU competence for the subject matter regulated by the agreement.[31]

In practice, an international environmental agreement only plays a significant role in the Union's law where the Union has adopted a directive or a regulation in order to transpose the content of the agreement into EU law. Where there is only a Council decision to adhere to an agreement, but no transposing secondary legislation, the Commission omits to enforce the content of the agreement against Member States. Member States are left at their discretion to ratify the agreement and to apply it. This practice is well established, although it clearly contradicts Article 17 TEU, which assign the task to the Commission to ensure that *all* EU law is applied within the Union.[32] Indeed, the European Union, by adhering to an international agreement, commits itself with regard to the other contracting parties to comply with the agreement's requirements throughout the territory of the Union, independently from the question whether the EU Member State in question has made, through its own ratification, a commitment that pertains to its national territory.

The Union has adopted an important number of pieces of environmental legislation in 1-09
the form of regulations, directives and non-binding recommendations. Their exact number depends on the classification of measures. Thus, for example, since at least the mid-1980s, standards for air emissions or noise levels from cars have been set and strengthened in order to better protect the environment; nevertheless, they were based on Article 115 or 114 TFEU, because the two basic directives on air and noise emissions from cars had been adopted, in the 1970s, as part of an EU programme for the elimination of technical barriers to trade in the internal market. The reason for recurrence to Article 114 TFEU is the existence of Article 193 TFEU: the car industry, EU institutions and probably also Member States have an interest in establishing uniform standards for cars and avoiding different national standards which create barriers to the free circulation of cars.

The different instruments will be further discussed at paragraph 2-31ff. Environmental action programmes have been regulated by Article 192(3) since the end of 1993; they are now adopted in the form of a legally binding decision.[33] This constitutes a significant difference to the five environmental action programmes which had been adopted between 1973 and 1993. These had been elaborated by the Commission and sent to the other EU institutions. The Council, together with governments from Member States, had normally approved their concept and approach in the form of a unanimously adopted

[31] See para 3-50, below, for concrete cases where the question of exclusive competence became relevant at EU level.

[32] Art 17 TEU: 'the Commission shall … ensure the application of the Treaties and of the measures adopted by the institutions pursuant to them'.

[33] See Decision 1600/2002 laying down the Sixth Community Environment Action Programme [2002] OJ L242/1.

(political) resolution, but had carefully avoided any statement saying that they adopted the programme as such.[34]

In future, the interpretation of the subsidiarity principle will be influenced by decisions under Article 192(3): where a decision under this provision explicitly provides for an EC measure on a specific item, it will normally not be possible to object to such an EU measure by invoking the subsidiarity principle – though much depends, of course, on the exact content of the measure. However, in practice, the Seventh and Eighth EU Environmental Action Programmes[35] were drafted in order to avoid any legal commitment of the EU legislature, in particular by not committing to any concrete action.

IV. Objectives of Environmental Policy

A. General Remarks

1-10 Article 3 TEU[36] fixes the general environmental objectives of the Union, which are completed by the specific objectives fixed in Article 191;[37] it is common understanding that the aims of Article 3(3) TEU are not an exhaustive enumeration.

The different objectives of the Treaties are not in a hierarchical order. The Union has to try to attain all its objectives. Should different objectives conflict in a specific case, then the EU institutions must try to find a compromise (see Article 7 TFEU). Conflicts – for instance, between the agricultural policy and the environmental policy – are frequent. Article 11 TFEU,[38] which was introduced by the Treaty of Amsterdam, does not lead to a different interpretation. Indeed, any such hierarchy would have needed clearer expression in the Treaty.

The different environmental objectives do not lead to concrete requirements for legislative action. It is not possible, for instance, to deduce from the requirement of a prudent use of natural resources the right to limit land use, eg for agricultural purposes. Nor are the objectives, in practice, enforceable. The possibility of an action under Article 265 TFEU against the Council or the Commission for not pursuing the environmental objectives is theoretical, since EU institutions have a very large discretion for taking – or not taking – action.

[34] See, eg Resolution of the Council and the Representatives of the Governments of the Member States, meeting within the Council of 1 February 1993 [1993] OJ C138/1: 'approve the general approach and strategy of the programme towards sustainability presented by the Commission'. Against the binding nature of the 5th Action Programme: CJEU Case C-142/95P *Rovigo v Commission* ECLI:EU:C:1996:325 (n 32).

[35] Decision 1386/2013 on a 7th EU Environment Action Programme [2013] OJ L354/171; Decision 2022/591 on an 8th Environment Action Programme (n 9).

[36] TEU (n 1) Art 3(3): 'The Union shall work for the sustainable development of Europe, based on … a high level of protection and improvement of the quality of the environment.'

[37] Art 191(1) TFEU: 'Union policy on the environment shall contribute to pursuit of the following objectives: – preserving, protecting and improving the quality of the environment; protecting human health; – prudent and rational utilisation of natural resources; – promoting measures at international level to deal with regional or worldwide environmental problems, and in particular combating climate change.'

[38] Art 11 TFEU: 'Environmental protection requirements must be integrated into the definition and implementation of the Union policies and activities, in particular with a view to promoting sustainable development.' An almost identical text had been inserted, in 1987, into an earlier version of the present Art 191(2.3) TFEU.

Union action shall *contribute* to achieve the different objectives, as is stated in Article 191 TFEU. Next to EU measures, national, regional, local or international measures exist to help reach the objectives. The responsibility and competence of the Union in environmental matters is thus shared with Member States, but is not exclusive. In specific cases, the environmental action programmes specify which action is to be undertaken in order to approach or even reach one or several objectives of the EU Treaties; nevertheless, the individual measures still need to be adopted by a formal EC instrument (see Article 288 TFEU), for which the relevant decision-making procedure under the different Treaty provisions must be followed.

B. Sustainable Development

The Amsterdam Treaty 1999 introduced the concept of sustainable development into EU law: the Preamble to the TEU, Article 3 of that Treaty as well as Article 11 TFEU mention this objective[39] without defining it. Article 2 of the Maastricht Treaty had already fixed 'sustainable growth' as one of the Community objectives, also without defining it. Both notions go back to a report which an ad hoc World Commission on Environment and Development, chaired by Gro Brundtland (Norway), had made in 1987 to the United Nations and which was entitled 'Our Common Future'. In that report, the need for economic development was emphasised which should, however, be 'sustainable'. Sustainable development was described as a 'development which meets the needs of the present without compromising the ability of future generations to meet their own needs', taking into account economic, social and environmental concerns. 1-11

However, even after 45 years of discussions, the precise meaning of the notion is still unclear. Like most legal authors, Boyle and Redgwell were rightly of the opinion that the term could not usefully be defined, and considered that a policy of economic growth which disregarded environmental considerations would not be sustainable.[40] This, though, was exactly what the Lisbon European Council did in 2000 when it fixed as an objective for the European Union to become, within 10 years, 'the most competitive and dynamic knowledge-based economy in the world, capable of sustainable economic growth with more and better jobs and greater social cohesion'.[41] In 2001, the Göteborg European Council tried to repair this (deliberate) omission by adding environmental aspects to the Lisbon declaration.[42]

In 2005, the Commission declared that sustainability of the EU policy required actions with regard to climate change, clean energy, public health, social exclusion, demography and

[39] Art 9 of the Recitals of TEU mentions that sustainable development is a 'principle'.

[40] A Boyle and C Redgwell, *Birnie, Boyle and Redgwell's International Law & the Environment*, 4th edn (Oxford, 2021) 45.

[41] Lisbon European Council, meeting of 23 and 24 March 2000, President's conclusions. Document 100/1/00.

[42] See Göteborg European Council, Presidency conclusions, 15 and 16 June 2001, nos 19 and 20: 'Sustainable development – to meet the needs of the present generation without compromising those of future generations – is a fundamental objective under the Treaties. That requires dealing with economic, social and environmental policies in a mutually reinforcing way. The European Council agrees a strategy for sustainable development which completes the Union's political commitment to economic and social renewal, adds a third, environmental dimension to the Lisbon strategy and establishes a new approach to policy making.'

migration, management of natural resources, global poverty and challenges to development.[43] This was followed by a declaration on guiding principles for sustainable development which the Council approved; these concerned environmental protection, social equity and cohesion, economic prosperity and the assuming of international responsibility.[44] And in June 2006, the European Council adopted a declaration on a strategy for sustainable development where it fixed seven objectives of sustainable development: (1) climate change and clean technologies; (2) sustainable transport, sustainable consumption and production; (3) conservation and management of natural resources; (4) public health; (5) social inclusion, demography and migration; (6) global poverty; and (7) the challenges of sustainable development. The European Council also fixed 10 leading principles and seven main challenges to be addressed. For each challenge, it fixed a number of actions to be taken by the EU institutions, though it carefully avoided giving them any legally binding form.[45]

In 2015, the UN General Assembly adopted 17 Sustainable Development Goals (SDGs), which were to be reached by 2030,[46] but which were not very precise as regards their legal and environmental content. In 2019, the EU Commission suggested a 'European Green Deal', which it saw as implementing the UN SDGs until 2030 and significantly improving the measures to fight climate change, reach climate neutrality by 2050, stop the loss of biodiversity and reach zero pollution.[47] It remains to be seen whether this Green Deal will extend beyond the present Commission's mandate, which ends in 2024.

In secondary legislation, 'sustainable development' was only rarely defined; as can be seen, such a definition is not really meaningful:

> Sustainable development means the improvement of the standard of living and welfare of the relevant populations within the limits of the capacity of the ecosystems by maintaining natural assets and their biological diversity for the benefit of present and future generations.[48]

Taken literally, nobody could comply with such requirements.

The basic difficulty of knowing which economic development is sustainable remains. It might well be argued that the use of nuclear energy, which leads to few greenhouse gas emissions but includes the generation of radioactive waste for which no safe disposal technology exists as yet and which will continue to be hazardous for thousands of years, most certainly affects future generations and is therefore not sustainable; this question is being heavily discussed under Regulation 2020/852.[49] Another example is the gradual, progressive contamination of groundwater, which often shows its effects only decades later, when the groundwater is used; from which moment should this contamination be considered

[43] Commission, COM(2005)37. See also Decision 1600/2002 (n 33) Recitals 6 and 7: 'A prudent use of natural resources and the protection of the global eco-system together with economic prosperity balanced social development are a condition for sustainable development. The Programme aims at a high level of protection of the environment and human health and at a general improvement in the environment and quality of life, indicates priorities for the environment dimension of the sustainable development strategy and should be taken into account when bringing forward actions under the strategy.'

[44] Commission, COM(2005) 218.

[45] Council, document 10917 of 26 June 2006.

[46] The 17 Sustainable Development Goals are enumerated in para 12-01.

[47] Commission, 'The European Green Deal' COM(2019) 640.

[48] Definition from Art 2 of Regulation 2493/2000 [2000] OJ L288/1; see also earlier Regulation 3062/95 [1995] OJ L327/9, Art 2(4).

[49] Regulation 2020/852 (n 3).

non-sustainable? Further examples are the disappearance of fauna and flora species, urbanisation and the construction of motorways. Under Regulation 2020/852, a private investment is considered environmentally sustainable when it substantially contributes to one of six environmental objectives,[50] does not significantly harm any of them and complies with certain minimum safeguards and Commission technical screening criteria.

Eurostat, the Commission's Statistical Office, publishes every two years a report on the European Union's sustainable development strategy which gives a large number of statistical data on economic, social and environmental issues.[51] Since 2019, these data have been arranged in chapters on the 17 SDGs. However, data on these issues and trends which may be deduced from them do not necessarily allow any conclusion on the state of the Union environment and its development towards sustainability.

In view of the contradictory and confusing use of the word 'sustainability', it is not 1-12
surprising that the Union practice shows an inflationary use of the expression 'sustainable' which is linked to very different activities – sustainable transport, sustainable tourism, sustainable use of energy or water, sustainable regional development, sustainable business, sustainable future, sustainable production and consumption – in order to give them a green tint;[52] contents are put into the notion of 'sustainability', which are later derived from it, and the notion is being increasingly used as a substitute for 'positive, favourable development', thereby losing all its environmental precision. Generally, it seems impossible to determine precisely if and when future generations will be able to meet their own needs. For example, the construction of the Via Appia some 2500 years ago affected the location of towns and villages; in the same way, any town siting and road construction today will affect future generations' rights to determine their own needs, ie their own town siting or road construction. The different provisions in the Treaty on sustainable development and their practical application thus give more of a guideline to policy action than any meaningful legal concept.

C. High Level of Protection

The objective of reaching a high level of environmental protection is now enshrined in 1-13
Article 3(3) TEU and is repeated in similar terms in Article 191(2.1) TFEU.[53] A similar provision is to be found in Article 114(3) TFEU.[54] None of these three articles specify what is a high level of protection; certainly, it is not the highest level one could think of.[55]

[50] These six objectives are: climate change mitigation; climate change adaptation; the sustainable use and protection of water and marine resources; transition for a circular economy; pollution prevention and control; the protection and restoration of biodiversity and ecosystems, see ibid Art 9.

[51] See the last report: Eurostat, *Sustainable Development in the EU*, 2022 edn (Luxemburg, 2022).

[52] The Sixth Environmental Action Programme, Decision 1600/2002 (n 33) used the word, in its different forms (sustain, sustainable, sustainability), not less than 64 times; the Seventh Environmental Action Programme, Decision 1386/2013 (n 35) used it 115 times and the Eighth Environmental Action Programme (n 9) still 31 times.

[53] Art 191(2.1) TFEU: 'Union policy on the environment shall aim at a high level of protection taking into account the diversity of situations in the various regions of the Community.'

[54] Art 114(3) TFEU: '(The Commission, in its proposals concerning environmental protection) will take as a base a high level of protection taking account in particular of any new development based on scientific facts. Within their respective powers, the European Parliament and the Council will also seek to achieve this objective.'

[55] See also CJEU Case C-444/15 *Italia Nostra Onius* ECLI:EU:C:2016:178, para 44: 'Whilst it is undisputed that Article 191(2) TFEU requires EU policy in environmental matters to aim for a high level of protection, such a

A high level could probably best be determined by looking at environmental standards which Member States that normally have a high standard of environmental protection (Denmark, the Netherlands, Sweden, Finland, Austria, Germany) have set; the practice of other industrial states with a recognised strong environmental policy, such as Switzerland or Norway, may also be considered. Policy declarations, resolutions and targets can be an important indicator, especially in areas where no standards have yet been set at national or international level, or where scientific uncertainty is great. As Article 3 TEU expressly declares improvement in the quality of the environment to be one of the objectives of Union policy, any measure aiming at a high level must therefore aim at improving the existing situation.

The specific reference to a high level of protection no longer permits the adoption of measures which only provide for the lowest common denominator of environmental protection and lets individual Member States, which are in favour of more stringent measures, adopt such measures at national level by virtue of Article 193 TFEU. Indeed, the high level is to be achieved by the Union as a whole, not by national measures. Article 191 TFEU clarifies that the interests of regions which are environmentally lagging behind shall be duly taken into account, allowing them to catch up; this again pleads for a high level, not the highest level, of protection.

A high level of environmental protection cannot be enforced in court. This follows from the fact that Articles 3 TEU and 191 TFEU refer to the environmental policy as a whole, not to the individual measure adopted under that policy; also, the policy has to 'aim at' a high level and can thus always argue that it is on its way towards attaining this. Epiney, who is of the opinion that the provision is legally binding and can be enforced, practically reaches the same conclusion by emphasising the wide discretion which the EC institutions have in interpreting the notion.[56]

1-14 In contrast to Articles 3 TEU and 191 TFEU, Article 114 TFEU requests Commission proposals to be made at a high level of environmental protection; thus, it refers to individual measures, not to the policy in general. Where a Commission proposal is not based on a high level of environmental protection, the European Parliament has a right of action against the Commission[57] under Article 263 TFEU. This follows from the procedural provisions of Articles 293 and 294 TFEU. Indeed, where the Commission has made a 'high level' proposal (case A), the Council can adopt that proposal, which lowers the protection, only by unanimity (Article 293 TFEU); however, where the Commission has made a 'low level' proposal (case B), the Council can finally adopt the proposal by a qualified majority at that lower level, since it does not amend the Commission's proposal. Where the European Parliament's opinion is of a high level and is concurrent with the Commission's proposal, the Council must decide unanimously (case A); where Parliament's high-level opinion does not concur

level of protection, to be compatible with that provision, does not necessarily have to be the highest that is technically possible. Article 193 TFEU authorises Member States to maintain or introduce more stringent protective measures.'

[56] A Epiney, *Umweltrecht der Europäischen Union*, 4th edn (Baden-Baden, 2019) 154, quoting extensively other German authors of the same opinion. Unclear J Jans and H Vedder, *European Environmental Law*, 4th edn (Groningen, 2011) 42.

[57] The Parliament has no such right against the Council, since Art 114(3) TFEU expressly provides that the Council shall only 'seek to achieve' a high level of protection.

with the Commission's low-level proposal, the Council may decide by majority (case B).[58] Thus, when the Commission makes a low-level proposal, Parliament's efforts to achieve a high level of protection may be more easily overcome by the Council.

These considerations are of a theoretical character. The European Parliament has so far never attempted such a case against the Commission; without doubt, this practice is also due to the difficulties of determining what is, in reality, a 'high level'. In all situations – under Articles 114 and 192 TFEU – that have occurred up to now, the practice of the Commission and the Council indicates that both institutions use the formula of a high level in its reversed order: whatever is proposed or adopted is considered to be a high level of environmental protection.

The 'sanction' for not proposing or adopting measures on a high level of environmental protection is Article 193 TFEU for measures under Articles 192 and 114(4)–(9) TFEU: in both cases, Member States may, under certain conditions, maintain or introduce more stringent national measures. In theory, one might argue that the lower the level of protection the Union measure is, the greater the pressure from Member States with a high level of protection becomes to opt out of the Union environmental measure and take or maintain national measures. In practice, though, economic operators rather push for lowering the high level also in Member States with more stringent measures than the Union, arguing that otherwise they would be at a competitive disadvantage. Recurring to Article 193 TFEU is thus in practice rare.

D. The Specific Objectives of Article 191(1) TFEU

The four specific objectives mentioned under Article 191(1) are rather detailed in their 1-15
description; but these details do not, in fact, add too much to the objective of protecting the environment. They clarify that the Union's protection measures are not limited to the Union's territory, which, in practice, these measures never were. Measures to protect human health[59] can, as the case may be, pursue an environmental, internal market, agricultural, consumer protection or public health objective, and may thus be based on Treaty provisions other than Articles 191–93. In the context of its examination of national legislative measures under Article 114(4–8) TFEU, the Commission does not accept that a national measure is based on health considerations, as that provision only allows considerations to protect the environment; this practice contradicts the provision of Article 191 TFEU, according to which environmental measures also aim at the protection of human health.[60]

'Natural resources' is a vague term: it probably covers the management of all resources which are found in the environment, fauna and flora, timber, minerals, air, water, soil, oil, natural gas and chemicals. Measures to prevent degradation or impairment of these resources,

[58] Jans and Vedder (n 56) 42 are of the opinion that a Commission proposal is not an 'act' in the sense of Art 263 TFEU, and thus cannot be tackled in court.

[59] The differences between 'health of humans' (Art 36 TFEU), 'human health' (Art 191, but also Art 169 TFEU) and 'public health' (title of Art 168 TFEU) have lost their legal precision; see also CJEU Case C-272/80 *Biologische Produkten* ECLI:EU:C:1981:312, where the Court referred to Art 30 EC (now Art 36 TFEU) as protecting 'public health'. See furthermore CJEU Case C-293/97 *Standley* ECLI:EU:C:1999:215, where the Court considered Directive 91/676 on the protection of water from nitrates pollution to be a directive which protects 'public health'.

[60] See ch 3.

such as accident prevention and the safe disposal of waste, are included in the term 'prudent and rational use'. Identifying the objective – eventually the main objective – of a measure is important, because it is one of the determining factors of the legal base for the measure; and the decision-making procedure, the content of the measure and Member States' residual rights and obligations vary according to the legal base applicable.

V. Principles of Environmental Action

A. General Remarks

1-16 Part one of the TFEU, Articles 1–17, is entitled 'Principles'. It fixes the basics of the TFEU, objectives, institutional and procedural rules, and a number of other provisions of a general character. As regards the environment, Articles 5 TEU on subsidiarity[61] and 11 TFEU on integration[62] are of relevance. To these general principles, Article 191(2.2) TFEU adds some specific environmental principles.[63]

It is doubtful whether all these different provisions have the same legal character. As regards the principles of Article 191(2.2) TFEU, they constitute, in my opinion, general guidelines for Union's environmental policy, but not binding rules of law which apply to each individual Union measure. They *allow* the taking of specific measures in favour of the environment, but do not *oblige* the EU institutions to take such measures. Therefore, they could only be enforced by the CJEU in very extreme cases where a systematic disregard of the principles in the policy is demonstrated.

1-17 This reasoning is contested. Some authors see the principles of Article 191(2.2) TFEU as binding rules of law, which have to be respected in each individual measure.[64] However, the wide discretion of Union institutions for taking measures could only lead to the illegality of a measure in exceptional cases because the principles had been disregarded. As can be seen, the practical results are not really very different.

The discussion on principles in environmental law and policy is, to a large extent, a spill-over from discussions which take place under the auspices of public international law. In that context, principles may play an important role in contributing to the shaping of international environmental law. However, it should not be forgotten that the essential part of public international environmental law is soft law, which is not really binding on the Member States. In contrast to that, EU law is binding and capable of fixing provisions that have binding force on Member States and on private persons. In the same way as, for example, the United Nations' Declaration on Human Rights remains of high value for the

[61] Art 5(3) TEU: 'Under the principle of subsidiarity, in areas which do not fall within its exclusive competence, the Union shall act only if and in so far as the objectives of the proposed action cannot be sufficiently achieved by the Member States, either at central level or at regional and local level, but can rather, by reason of the scale or effects of the proposed action, be better achieved at Union level.'

[62] Art 11 TFEU (n 38).

[63] Art 191(2.2) TFEU: '[Union policy] … shall be based on the precautionary principle and on the principles that preventive action should be taken, that environmental damage should as a priority be rectified at source and that the polluter should pay.'

[64] See the different contributions in R Macrory (ed), *Principles of European Environmental Law* (Groningen, 2004); L Krämer and E Orlando (eds), *Principles of Environmental Law* (Cheltenham, 2018).

international community but is of secondary importance in Europe, where the Council of Europe's Convention on Human Rights established binding, enforceable human rights, the environmental principles in the TFEU are less important for EU environmental law, which has developed a large number of binding provisions that materialise these principles for the actual, concrete situations.

The CJEU has in one case interpreted EU law in the light of one of the principles of Article 191(2.2) TFEU. In that judgment, the Court had to decide whether a Belgian ban for waste imports was compatible with the EU provisions on the free circulation of goods, although such waste imports from other Belgian regions were treated differently from imports of waste from other Member States. The Court found no discrimination in this case.[65] 1-18

In other cases, the Court frequently recurred to the formula that provisions of EU law could not be interpreted in such a way 'as to give rise to results which are incompatible with the general principles of Community law and in particular with fundamental rights'.[66] The question is whether the environmental principles of Article 191(2) TFEU are also such principles which EU legislation may not infringe. In my opinion, this is not the case. Rather, they constitute guiding principles for political or legislative decisions and are often used – as a sort of leitmotif – to explain or justify a decision which was taken. But they cannot really be used to declare an EU measure void with the argument that it contradicts one of these principles.

The judgment in the above-mentioned Case C-2/90 was given under the 1987 version of the present Article 191 TFEU, which referred to Community action rather than to Community policy. Under that provision, it could be argued that the principles of Article 191 TFEU referred to individual measures. By contrast, the present wording of that article considers the EU policy as a whole; it does not require that each individual EU measure take into account all the principles of Article 191(2.2) TFEU. Requesting that the principles of Article 191 apply to each individual EU measure would mean that numerous measures would contradict, for instance, the polluter-pays principle, since they do not contain any provision about it.[67]

Even where the principles of Article 191 TFEU are seen as general guidelines for EU policy only, they have some indirect legal significance. They place an obligation on the Union to base its policy on these principles and to plan policy and measures accordingly. Moreover, observance of these principles can play an important part in deciding, case by

[65] CJEU Case C-2/90 *Commission v Belgium* ECLI:EU:C:1992:310, para 34: 'in order to determine whether the obstacle in question is discriminatory, the particular type of waste must be taken into account. The principle that environmental damage should as a priority be rectified at source – a principle laid down by Art 174(2) E.C. for action by the Community relating to the environment – means that it is for each region, commune or other local entity to take appropriate measures to receive, process and dispose of its own waste.' See also Case C-157/96 *R v Minister of Agriculture* ECLI:EU:C:1998:191; Case C-180/96 *United Kingdom v Commission* ECLI:EU:C:1998:192, where the Court interpreted the prevention principle.

[66] CJEU Joined Cases 97/87, 98/87 and 99/87 *Dow Chemicals* ECLI:EU:C:1989:380, para 9.

[67] The judgment in Case C-2/90 (n 65) seems to have been influenced by some policy considerations which might explain some inconsistencies: the principle of Art 191(2.2) TFEU was applied to a national measure, although the article *refers* to EU policy; the Court did not examine whether the Belgian measure was proportional; the Court transformed the principle into a rule of law; it also justified its finding by reference to the Basel Convention on the shipment of hazardous waste, although the Union was, at the time of the judgment, not a member of that Convention, etc.

case, whether the objectives of Article 191(1) TFEU cannot be sufficiently achieved by the Member States and are therefore capable of being better achieved by the Union (subsidiarity, Article 5 TEU). Where, for instance, the Union takes a measure on environmental liability, it could invoke the prevention and the polluter-pays principle to justify the EU action against subsidiarity arguments; this example shows at the same time the limited usefulness of the principles, since Member States which oppose the measure could argue that the subsidiarity principle would not allow action to be taken at EU level.

The principles could also be used to justify the chosen legal basis – Article 192 TFEU or another provision – for a specific measure and its content,[68] and to interpret secondary EU legislation.

B. Subsidiarity

1-19 The subsidiarity principle,[69] which is now laid down in Article 5 TEU, was first inserted into the EEC Treaty in 1987, but in a different version and limited to environmental matters.[70] The Maastricht Treaty of 1993 repealed that provision and inserted a new Article 3b – the present Article 5 TEU – into the Treaty. The Amsterdam Treaty of 1997 added to this, as an annex to the EC Treaty, a 'Protocol on the application of the principles of subsidiarity and proportionality',[71] where, in 13 detailed points, rules were laid down on subsidiarity and proportionality. The Lisbon Treaty slightly reworded the principle, placed it at Article 5(3) TEU and also took over the Protocol. The style of this Protocol gives the impression that it was drafted less from the perspective of a European Union, but rather with the aim of containing as far as possible the 'threat' of European integration, which was perceived as reducing the amount of power that regional or national administration had up until then. Article 5 TEU and its Protocol were probably inspired by the old Article 130r(4) EC and a preceding draft from the European Parliament on a general Treaty on European Union.[72] It establishes a general rule for all Union activity, including on the environment.

It is not a rule of competence but a principle which concerns the exercise of that competence and predetermines the activity of the European Union;[73] as such, it has legal force. When taking action, EU institutions will have to demonstrate for each individual measure that the conditions of Article 5 TEU and its Protocol are actually complied with. They benefit, however, from a large amount of discretion on the question of what content a

[68] For the integration principle of Art 11 TFEU, see CJEU Case C-62/88 *Greece v Council* ECLI:EU:C:1990:153, para 20: '[the integration requirement which] reflects the principle whereby all Community measures must satisfy the requirements of environmental protection, implies that a Community measure cannot be part of Community action on environmental matters merely because it takes account of these requirements'.

[69] For this principle in general (without specific reference to the environment), see Commission, COM(93) 545; COM(94) 533; SEC(95) 580; SEC(96) 2; SEC(96) 7.

[70] EC Treaty, Art 130r(4) (1987 version): 'The Community shall take action relating to the environment to the extent to which the objectives referred to in paragraph 1 can be attained better at Community level than at the level of the individual Member States.'

[71] [1997] OJ C340/105.

[72] [1984] OJ C77/33, Arts 55 and 59.

[73] See also Commission, SEC(92) 1990.

measure would have. In practice, recitals of environmental acts regularly contain a clause saying that the legislative act in question respects the principle of subsidiarity.

The discussion on subsidiarity is ongoing at EU level, concentrating on the deregulation and simplification of legislation and of the possibility of the national parliaments and the Committee of the Regions to apply to the CJEU when they consider that an EU measure does not comply with the principle of subsidiarity. Political approaches were started in 1992, in the name of subsidiarity, to review existing environmental directives, where Member States felt obliged to undertake financial investments to clean the environment; this discussion has been particularly intense in the water sector. In contrast, there is hardly ever a discussion on subsidiarity when questions of EU funding for economically weaker regions are in question, where measures are considered which improve the competitivity of EU economic operators or where financial assistance for small- and medium-sized enterprises is discussed. 1-20

For the environment, much depends on the interpretation given to the requirement that the objective of environmental protection cannot be sufficiently achieved by Member States and can thus be *better* achieved at Community level. Probably the best illustration of the practical difficulties is the discussion in the Economic and Social Committee on the proposal for Directive 96/61 on integrated prevention and pollution control.[74] The Committee discussed the pros and cons of fixing Community-wide emission limit values for industrial installations and concluded:

> [T]he subsidiarity principle, properly understood, is not inconsistent with the establishment of limit values at European level. The high level of protection in the Community called for in the EC Treaty can only be achieved if European limit values are set.

A minority view of the Committee (eight members) stated in contrast to that:[75]

> [T]he subsidiarity principle, properly understood, is consistent with the establishment of limit values at Member State level. The high level of protection in the Community called for in the EU Treaty can only be achieved if Member State limit values are set and implemented.

It is not easy to establish general rules to show when environmental policy objectives can be better attained at EU level. Member States with an active environmental policy of their own may well think that measures at the level of individual Member States are a better solution. At present, there is a wide gap between the individual Member States' national environmental policies and regulations. Member States such as Denmark, the Netherlands, Sweden, Austria and Germany are far more convinced of the need for environmental protection measures than, for instance, Greece, Spain, Portugal, Italy, Cyprus, Slovakia or Poland – though the governmental approach to environmental issues also depends on the political party which is in power. In some Member States – Ireland, Greece, Portugal, Spain or the Member States which have acceded since 2004 – environmental legislation often consists of not much more than the transposition of measures which had previously been adopted at EU level. Consequently, action at EU level is often a means of ensuring that environmental measures are taken in *all* Member States. If, instead, it were left to the Member States to take action, it could not be ensured that all 1-21

[74] For this Directive, see para 4–45.
[75] [1995] OJ C195/54 and App II.

and not only some Member States would adopt provisions on that specific environmental problem. Even if they did, concepts, contents and timing would rarely coincide. Where Member States take action at different times, there is once again a danger for the Union as a whole of imbalances, distortions of competition and of trade patterns, the creation of new barriers to trade, etc.

Furthermore, river and sea water, air pollution, protection of fauna and flora species, climate issues, ozone layer protection, acidification, eutrophication and the management of products which have finished their useful lifetime (waste) cannot seriously be tackled at national level alone. In such cases, the efforts of one Member State would easily be frustrated by the passivity of another Member State. This also would have an effect on the location of industrial undertakings, employment and quality of life, for example. Therefore, the objectives of Article 191(1) TFEU can normally be attained faster and more effectively by and within the entire Union, ie for the EU ecosystem as a whole. This is the reason why EU legislative activities practically covers all areas of environmental protection.

It must also be borne in mind that some Member States find it difficult, if not impossible, to conceive and implement measures to provide effective protection for the environment in general, and for biodiversity in particular, since environmental protection measures are perceived as slowing down economic development. The negative effects of environmental impairment normally become more visible and therefore also politically more relevant when economic development is sufficiently advanced. Poverty is the biggest environmental pollutant; in Western Europe, there is an element of economic divide between the North and the South, to which new EU Member States of Central and Eastern Europe have to be added. In these countries, environmental awareness and readiness to act are distinctly less prevalent, due to differences in the public discussion of environmental matters, traditions – hunting, bull fighting, fox hunting – education, public and media sensitivity, administrative determination, law enforcement, political priorities, etc. EU discussions on where environmental protection can be better achieved may not leave these considerations aside, although this often happens in Germany, Hungary and Poland.

1-22 Precisely what 'better' means in Article 5 TEU is not at all clear; it could mean quicker, more effective, cheaper, more efficient, closer to the citizen (ie not too centralised), more democratic, more uniform, more consistent with measures in other parts of the industrialised world, or the global or the European Union, without these concepts being more precise.[76] It will, therefore, have to be decided on a case-by-case basis, considering all the facts, whether or not it is better to take measures at EU level in order to attain the Union's environmental objectives. The aim must be to protect and improve the quality of the environment in the whole Union. Due consideration must be given to the differences in the Member States' environmental legislation, the differing awareness of environmental issues, the environmental infrastructure in Member States, the risk that national protection measures might be differently timed or formulated, the danger of relocating industrial undertakings to countries with lower standards, the possible deflection of trade and the

[76] The European Parliament was of the opinion that the notions in Art 5 are deliberately vague in order to increase the legislative discretion of Union institutions, Resolution of 20 April 1994 [1994] OJ C128/190, fn 5.

potential changes in the competitive position within the Union and of the Union towards non-EU countries. The main concern is to improve the quality of the environment, to reach a high level of protection and to ensure sustainable development over the broadest possible area. Article 5 mentions the scale or effects of the proposed action as examples where objectives can be better achieved at Union level.

If one tries to apply all these theoretical issues to the debate as to whether there 1-23
should be EU legislation on, for example, environmental liability, the following aspects would also have to be considered: there is legislation on liability in all Member States, but this differs as to questions of liability for negligence or strict liability, burden of proof, protected assets and damages; there are differences as to the application of these provisions to damage to the environment itself; environmental damage is differently defined; *locus standi* varies; the number of cases decided by courts varies considerably; costs for economic operators are likely to increase, eg due to insurance premiums; the environmental problem is not one of accidental pollution, but the progressive accumulation of pollutants in the environment; many an impairment is caused by a multitude of polluters, not by a single one; where an economic operator respects existing legislation, he should not be liable for environmental impairment, etc. At the end of such a list of considerations, the conclusion cannot be other than that the question of whether there should be EU legislation on liability for damage to the environment or not and what content such legislation should have is a political one, not a legal one of subsidiarity.[77]

Another good example is the discussion on binding EU energy efficiency targets: Member States opposed such binding targets, arguing that under the principle of subsidiarity, questions on energy efficiency were of their competence. Others argued that in order to ensure efficient measures in all 27 Member States which contribute to the fight against climate change, EU action was necessary. The outcome of this discussion was finally determined by political, not legal, considerations.[78]

There are many other examples of the ambiguous nature of the subsidiarity principle: why should, under subsidiarity auspices, the Union be competent to ban the import of furs from third countries which do not prohibit leg-hold traps,[79] but not be competent to stop bull fighting, fox hunting or cock fighting? Why should there be common measures on air pollution in urban zones,[80] but not on the quality of bathing water in public swimming pools?

It is submitted that at the end of almost any discussion on a specific topic, the lawyer is placed in a position behind the policy-maker, who has to weigh political, economic, social, cultural, legal and environmental aspects as best he can: his decision usually remains a political decision. Probably for this reason, the CJEU is very reserved in discussing this principle: there is not one single environmental case where it discussed the validity of an EU act under the auspices of subsidiarity.

[77] See Directive 2004/35 on environmental liability with regard to the prevention and remedying of environmental damage (2004) OJ L143/56.

[78] In 2009, EU-wide binding measures were rejected by the Council. In 2012, the European Parliament and the Council adopted Directive 2012/27 on energy efficiency [2012] OJ L315/1. See now also Art 194 TFEU.

[79] See Regulation 3254/91 [1991] OJ L308/1.

[80] See Directive 2008/50 [2008] OJ L152/1.

C. Integration

1-24 The present Article 11 TFEU[81] had antecedents in the environmental chapter of the EC Treaty: the 1987 version of Article 174 contained a clause on integration,[82] which was formulated in such a way that it could, using the CJEU's doctrine of direct effect, be applied directly. The clause was considered both too precise and too vague, and was therefore replaced by a phrase that was similar to the one now used in Article 11 TFEU.[83] As it was felt that some other Union policies did not sufficiently integrate environmental considerations into their policies and measures, the discussion prior to the Amsterdam Treaty on European Union focused on the request to incorporate into the chapters on agriculture, transport, competition and so on a reference to environmental considerations. This was objected to by the sectors concerned as being too precise, and thus led to the removal and slight reformulation of the provision to the present Article 11 TFEU.[84]

The provision states that environmental considerations must be fully taken into account in the elaboration and implementation of other Union policies. It is based on the concept that environmental requirements and, subsequently, environmental policy cannot be seen as an isolated green policy which groups specific actions on the protection of water, air, soil or biodiversity. Rather, the environment is affected by other policies, such as on transport, energy or agriculture.[85] Article 11 TFEU therefore calls for a permanent, continuous 'greening' of all Union policies. As mentioned above, though, Article 11 TFEU does not allow priority to be given to environmental requirements over other requirements; rather, the different objectives of the Treaties rank at the same level and the policy must endeavour to achieve all of them; this is also the meaning of Article 7 TFEU.

The 'Union policies and activities' referred to in Article 11 TFEU are the different policies listed in Articles 3 and 4 TFEU. They include all activities of the Union under the TFEU. Policies under the Euratom Treaty are not included, as that is essentially a Treaty to promote the use of nuclear energy, so is not mentioned in Article 11 TFEU. In my opinion, the Union has, from the beginning, spent too much EU money on nuclear energy compared with expenses for renewable energy; Article 11 TFEU would allow a reversal of this policy if the political will existed to promote renewable energies. Again, this is a question of policy, not of law: there is no legal obligation to invest increased sums into the promotion of renewable energies.

1-25 'Environmental protection requirements' are first of all the different objectives laid down in Articles 3 TEU and 191(1) TFEU. Thus, the objectives of ensuring a sustainable development, of preserving, protecting and improving the quality of the environment, shall also have to be considered within the framework of other policies. The principles laid down in Article 191(2.2) TFEU also form part of environmental protection

[81] Art 11 TFEU (n 38).

[82] Art 130r(2.2) EEC Treaty (1987 version): 'Environmental protection requirements shall be a component of the Community's other policies.'

[83] Art 130r(2.3) EEC Treaty (1993 version): 'Environmental protection requirements must be integrated into the definition and implementation of other Community policies.'

[84] See also Arts 167 (culture), 168 (public health) and 169(2) (consumer protection) TFEU, which also contain a requirement of integration; however, these policies are not mentioned in Art 11 TFEU.

[85] Commission, COM(2019) 640 (n 47) s 2.1: 'To deliver the European Green Deal, there is a need to rethink policies for clean energy supply across the economy, industry, production and consumption, large-scale infrastrucure, transport, food and agriculture, construction, taxation and social benefits.'

requirements. Indeed, it does not make sense to apply the precautionary principle, under the environmental policy, and take action without the latest scientific evidence of a substance's harmfulness, and then take the opposite approach in the context of the internal market policy. The CJEU reached the same conclusion when applying the principle of preventive action of Article 191(2) TFEU to the BSE ('mad cow disease') case, which had no relationship whatsoever with environmental protection issues.[86] In Case C-428/07, it even went a step further, declaring that the present Article 11 TFEU had to be understood as inserting an environmental competence provision into the section on agricultural policy.[87]

In the same way, it would be contradictory to provide for preventive measures in environmental policy but not to do so in other policies, thus limiting EU action to remedial measures which try to repair the environmental damage. Indeed, the greatest damage to the environment is caused by transport, agriculture, energy, industrial development and other policies, not by measures taken within the framework of environmental policy.

1-26 The whole debate on how to classify a specific Union measure is rather futile: whether the protection of waters from nitrates of agricultural sources is a measure of agricultural or environmental policy should not have any influence on the measures which are to be taken. The same applies to a ban on asbestos fibres, the use of phthalates and pollution-abatement measures for cars, fuels or industrial installations. It seems rather old-fashioned to classify a specific measure as belonging to a specific policy: Article 11 TFEU contributes to progressively overcoming this artificiality. Therefore, its interpretation is wide: wherever a measure is taken under the TFEU, full consideration must be given to protecting the environment. This wide interpretation should not let us forget that environmental requirements should be taken into consideration at the formulation and implementation of *policies*, not of individual measures; it is true, however, that a specific policy is made operational by individual measures. It is therefore doubtful whether each individual measure in the internal market, agriculture or transport policy must take into consideration the environmental requirements; this appears too far-reaching. In any case, EU institutions have a very broad discretion in putting the principle of Article 11 TFEU into practice. Since Article 11, in contrast to its 1987 version, no longer states a fact but rather propounds the necessity of procedure for EU policy, its application in practice will depend almost entirely on the political will of EU institutions to make this provision operational. Again, only in extreme cases could it be argued that EU policies do not take into account environmental protection requirements in their definition and implementation. Normally, the wide discretion which is available under Article 11 TFEU would not make such an action successful.

[86] CJEU Case C-157/96 (n 65) paras 63–64; Case C-180/96 (n 65) paras 99–100: 'Where there is uncertainty as to the existence or extent of risks to human health, the institutions may take protective measures without having to wait until the reality and seriousness of those risks become fully apparent. That approach is borne out by Art 130 r(1) of the EC Treaty, according to which Community policy on the environment is to pursue the objective inter alia of protecting human health. Art 130r(2) provides that that policy is to be based in particular on the principles that preventive action should be taken and that environmental protection requirements must be integrated into the definition and implementation of other Community policies.'

[87] CJEU Case C-428/07 *Horvath* ECLI:EU:C:2008:458, para 29: 'Since requirements relating to environment protection, one of the essential objectives of the Community, must, according to Article 6 EC [now Article 11 TFEU] be integrated into the definition and implementation of … Community policies and activities, such protection must be regarded as an objective which also forms part of the common agricultural policy.' In the same sense, for transport policy, see CJEU Case C-440/05 *Commission v European Parliament and Council* ECLI:EU:C:2007:625, para 60.

To give some examples: to what extent transport policy promotes a European network of high-speed trains is a question for or against which a number of environmental and other arguments can be raised. The promotion of biomass for fuel by agricultural policy would save fossil fuels, but would at the same time promote monocultures and large-scale use of pesticides, and reduce biodiversity as well as food production. Other examples are provisions to ban aeroplane flights at night, the decommissioning of used platforms at sea, the development of a windfarm in or next to a natural habitat or the requirement for an environmental impact assessment in all cases where a project is co-financed with EU funds. The question to what extent such measures are to be taken is in all these cases of a political, not a legal, nature. The integration requirement of Article 11 TFEU does not provide for a useful solution to these problems.

To date, the CJEU has never discussed the question whether an EU act would have to be annulled because it did not take into consideration environmental requirements. Some legal writers are of the opinion that such a legal act would, as a matter of law, have to be annulled. An example is Regulation 1954/2003,[88] which gave the EU fishing fleet access to the waters around the Azores without even discussing the impact on the very vulnerable local ecosystems. The Azores brought a case to the General Court;[89] however, their application was considered inadmissible and their appeal was rejected.[90] In my opinion, the complete lack of even considering the environmental impact of the Regulation constitutes a breach of Article 11 TFEU and should have led to the annulment of the Regulation, had the action not been declared inadmissible beforehand.

D. The Precautionary Principle

1-27 The precautionary principle, now laid down in Article 191(2) TFEU, was inserted into Article 174(2) EC in 1993, while the prevention principle had already been present in the Treaty since 1987. The origin and content of the precautionary principle are unclear. Since no definition exists in the Treaties, the principle is open to broad interpretation. The CJEU defines the principle in settled case law as to mean 'that where there is uncertainty as to the existence of extent of risks, including risks to the environment, preventive measures may be taken without having to wait until the reality and seriousness of those risks become apparent'.[91] The principle was mentioned in the Declaration of the United Nations Conference in Rio de Janeiro in 1992[92] and is understood to allow[93] the taking of measures

[88] Regulation 1954/2003 [2003] OJ L289/1.

[89] General Court Case T-37/04 *Azores v Council* ECLI:EU:T:2008:236.

[90] CJEU Case C-444/08P *Azores v Council* ECLI:EU:C:2009:733.

[91] CJEU Case C-299/18P *Bayer CropScience v Commission* ECLI:EU:C:2021:367, para 80.

[92] Rio de Janeiro Declaration on Environment and Development, 16 June 1992, Principle 15: 'In order to protect the environment, the precautionary approach shall be widely applied by States according to their capabilities. Where there are threats of serious or irreversible damages, lack of full scientific certainty shall not be used as a reason for postponing cost-effective measures to prevent environmental degradation.' The reference to 'approach' rather than to 'principle' was due to US objections to the use of the word 'principle'.

[93] I would not go so far as to argue that, in certain cases, the precautionary principle *obliges* public authorities to act, though theoretically such a possibility might exist. No practical case is known where a court has judged that such an obligation existed.

also in cases where scientific or technical uncertainty exists as to the cause and extent of environmental or human health impairment.

Examples for the application of the precautionary principle are the taking of measures to ban or restrict the circulation of substances or products such as asbestos, cadmium and phthalates under Regulation 1907/2006 on chemicals, Regulation 1107/2009 on pesticides[94] or other provisions. Another example is climate change: the Union adhered to the United Nations' Convention on Climate Change, which undertakes to combat global warming, while the latest scientific evidence of man-made global warming – at least in the eyes of some – is still lacking.

Sometimes it is argued that the adoption of the precautionary principle requires a 1-28 scientific assessment of risks.[95] This argument seems to stem primarily from political efforts to reduce the field of application of this principle as far as possible; indeed, Article 191(2) TFEU does not contain any such condition, and the above-mentioned examples show the political character of these arguments: if a scientific risk assessment is necessary for precautionary measures, it would be necessary for any envisaged measure. However, such a requirement could only be introduced by way of legislation.[96]

Similar considerations apply to other requests to limiting the application of the precautionary principle to cases where there is the possibility of an extreme, irreversible hazard, where there is a need to adopt measures urgently or to limit it to provisional measures only. None of these conditions are found in Article 191(2) TFEU, which demonstrates the political rather than legal character of these arguments.

The CJEU applied the precautionary principle in the above-mentioned Cases C-157/96 and C-180/96,[97] though the English version referred to the prevention principle only, whereas the French and other language versions mentioned the precautionary *and* prevention principles. Of course, the Court did not request that the Commission, before pronouncing an export ban for British beef, should have made a risk assessment. The General Court considered the principle a 'general principle of Community law'.[98]

[94] Regulation 1907/2006 [2006] OJ L396/1; Regulation 1107/2009 [2009) OJ L309/1; for more details, see ch 6 below. Both Regulations explicitly mention the precautionary principle, though such a mentioning is not a condition for its application.

[95] See, eg Directive 1999/39 on baby food [1999] OJ L124/8, 4th recital: 'Whereas, taking into account the Community's international obligations, in cases where the relevant scientific evidence is insufficient, the precautionary principle allows the Community to provisionally adopt measures on the basis of available pertinent information, pending an additional assessment of risk and a review of the measure within a reasonable period of time.'

[96] See also CJEU Case C-343/09 *Afton Chemical* ECLI:EU:C:2020:419, where neither the Commission nor the Court considered a risk assessment to be necessary before the decision on the restriction of use of a chemical substance was taken.

[97] See n 65.

[98] General Court Joined Cases T-74/00, T-76/00 and others *Artegodan and others v Commission* ECLI:EU:T:2002:283, fn 184: 'the precautionary principle can be defined as a general principle of Community law requiring the competent authorities to take appropriate measures to prevent specific potential risks to public health, safety and the environment, by giving precedence to the requirements related to the protection of those interests over economic interests. Since the Community institutions are responsible, in all their spheres of activity, for the protection of public health, safety and the environment, the precautionary principle can be regarded as an autonomous principle stemming from the above-mentioned Treaty provisions. It is settled case-law that, in the field of public health, the precautionary principle implies that where there is uncertainty as to the existence or the extent of risks to human health, the institutions may take precautionary measures without having to wait until the reality and seriousness of those risks become fully apparent.'

The Commission adopted in the year 2000 a communication on the precautionary principle, where it stated:[99]

> [W]hether or not to invoke the precautionary principle is a decision exercised where scientific information is insufficient, inconclusive, or uncertain and where there are indications that the possible effects on the environment, or human, animal or plant health may be potentially dangerous and inconsistent with the chosen level of protection.

E. The Prevention Principle

1-29 It is unclear to what extent the prevention principle has content independent from the precautionary principle, although the history of the principles' insertion into the EC Treaty suggests there is none. Sometimes, prevention is associated with the certainty of risks, whereas precaution is linked to uncertain risks; however, this is not very helpful, nowhere is it laid down explicitly and it is not taken up by the CJEU. There seems to be no EU action which would be possible under the precautionary principle but not under the prevention principle – and vice versa. Since both principles are, in practice, almost always used together and there is no definition for either of them in the TFEU, the added legal value of one to the other is not visible; therefore, they should be used synonymously.[100]

The precautionary/prevention principle is of overriding importance in every serious environmental policy, since it allows action to be taken at an early stage. Measures are no longer primarily meant to repair damage or impairment after it has occurred: instead, measures are to be taken earlier, to prevent impairment or damage occurring. This also makes economic sense, since it is normally far more costly to clean up or remedy impairment after it has occurred – if any remedy is possible at all. Article 191(2) TFEU does not specify which form the preventive action should take: it is probably 'better' to produce goods without cadmium, but once cadmium-containing products are on the market – batteries, crates, window frames, etc – should they be recycled, burnt with or without energy recovery, or landfilled? No answer can be found in the prevention/precautionary principle.

F. Rectification of Damage at Source

1-30 The principle that environmental damage[101] should, as a priority, be rectified at source was inserted into the Treaty in 1987. It represents wishful thinking rather than reality. Indeed, to rectify environmental damage from cars – air pollution, land use, noise, traffic congestion, waste generation, etc – at source would mean that cars would have to be abolished or at the very least absolute priority be given to public transport, the price of fuel be increased in order to reduce the use of cars, restrictions on the making of cars – maximum

[99] Commission, 'Communication on the Precautionary Principle' COM(2000) 1.

[100] See also Cases C-157/96 and C-180/96 (n 65), where the CJEU based its reasoning on the supposition that, in order to combat the BSE disease, full evidence of the extent and seriousness of a risk was not required in order to take action on the prevention principle, but not on the precautionary principle.

[101] About half of the linguistic versions of the TFEU use the word 'damage', the other half 'impairment'.

fuel consumption, maximum speed etc – be imposed or other measures taken. This would have implications on production, employment and investments for which no country in the world seems to be prepared. The present technology of catalytic converters for cars is clearly an end-of-the-pipe technology, but it is not seriously challenged. Similar examples could easily be given for measures regarding climate change, waste generation, forest decline, acidification or marine pollution.

It is not clear what 'rectified' means. Certainly, as in all other cases, EU institutions have a large discretion as to what measures they wish to take, and the time span and content of these measures. Since environmental damage (impairment) often cannot really be completely rectified, it must be up to the legislature to decide how the damage, once it has occurred, can be minimised, how the environment can be restored – at the same or at a different place – and further damage be prevented.

As mentioned above at paragraph 1-18, the CJEU has justified a regional import ban on waste, amongst other arguments based on this principle, which leads, in the Court's opinion, to the necessity of disposing of waste as close to the place of waste generation as possible. In a similar case, the CJEU declared a German provision which required that the disposal of waste take place in Germany to be compatible with the Treaty since it 'reflects the pursuit of an objective which is in conformity with the principle laid down in Article 130r(2) of the Treaty that environmental damage should, as a principle, be rectified at source'.[102]

As stated, the judgment in the first case seems primarily motivated by considerations 1-31
about the division of responsibilities between the Union and Member States. It seems impossible to deduce a legal rule that 'waste shall be disposed of at the closest possible place' from the principle that is discussed here. Legal literature discusses whether the principle of rectifying damage at source does not lead to the European Union being required, in future, to adopt, as a priority, emission limit values rather than adopting or favouring quality standards.[103] EU practice, though, certainly prefers quality standards for air and water pollution.[104] This tendency has been more pronounced since 1991–92, when the EU debate on deregulation, subsidiarity and flexibility started.

Using the same reasoning as in the two waste judgments mentioned above, the CJEU could, in theory, state that the principle of rectification at source requires EU legislation to be based mainly on emission standards. Also, the Court could come to the conclusion that the catalytic converter approach, which EU law had adopted to minimise car emissions, was not compatible with this principle and that cars and fuels had to be developed which generate fewer pollutants. These examples demonstrate how far the reasoning could go if the principles of Article 191(2) TFEU were turned into legal rules – even leaving aside the point that at best they only constitute legal rules for Union, and not national or regional, provisions.

The conclusion is that this principle *allows* that EU provisions be established which deal with import or export bans on waste, but does not *require* the elaboration of such provisions. The principle allows EU emission limit values to be preferred over quality standards,

[102] CJEU Case C-422/92 *Commission v Germany* ECLI:EU:C:1995:125; the judgment referred to a time when EU secondary law did not yet contain a provision which dealt with the export or import of wastes for disposal. The judgment therefore dealt only with primary law. The relevant EU provisions were introduced in 1993.

[103] H Sevenster, *Milieubeleid en Gemeenschapsrecht* (Deventer, 1992) 111; Jans and Vedder (n 56) 48.

[104] See chs 7 and 8 below.

but it does not require that such an approach be taken: a ban on waste exports to non-EU countries[105] may be supported by this principle, but the principle does not impose such a ban. No Member State could bring the Council before the European Court if the Council were adopting other measures, though EU law would, under certain conditions, allow a Member State to stop exports of waste.[106]

G. The Polluter-Pays Principle

1-32 This principle was introduced into the Treaty in 1987, though it has existed at EU level since 1973.[107] Its linguistic versions are quite different: while the English version states 'the polluter should pay', there are several versions which affirm 'the polluter pays' or 'the polluter shall pay', and the German text talks of the principle of causation. As all versions are of equal value and the principle, as any other notion of EU law, must be interpreted autonomously by virtue of EU law and without recourse to national interpretations,[108] its content is difficult to determine: who is a polluter? A person who contaminates the environment or a person who exceeds existing limit values? Is a car driver a polluter, or the car manufacturer or the producer or importer of the fuel? Furthermore, who is to pay (or should pay) for the emissions or the damage that was caused? What about damage in another Member State or in a third country? Should car manufacturers or drivers also pay for the construction of roads? How much should be paid? Is an investment in cleaner technologies also a payment?

The questions demonstrate that the polluter-pays principle is first of all an economic principle and has to be understood as expressing the concept that the cost of environmental impairment, damage and clean-up should not be borne via taxes by society, but that the person who caused the pollution should bear those costs. Its transfer to the EU Treaties has led to all sorts of anomalies which have not much to do with law. First, hardly any Union text contains provisions on who shall pay for what or any other provision which puts the polluter-pays principle into practice: if the principle were legally binding and enforceable, this would be a systematic omission that could hardly be tolerated; however, no one as yet has invoked that principle and claimed damages.

1-33 Secondly, if the polluter and not the taxpayer had to pay for pollution, subsidies and state aids would not be in line with this principle and would have to be deleted. However, EU measures have from the very beginning accepted that undertakings and other economic operators may receive state aid and have set up general rules for such aid.[109] The same

[105] The principle of rectification at source gained some relevance in the waste sector, where it is called the self-sufficiency and proximity principle. See, eg Directive 2008/98 on waste [2008] OJ L312/3, Art 16(3): 'The [EU network of waste disposal and recovery installations] shall enable waste to be disposed of or … recovered in one of the nearest appropriate installations.' Stopping waste exports was considered in the Green Deal for Europe (n 47) s 2.1.3: 'The Commission is of the view that the EU shall stop exporting its waste outside the EU'; however, this consideration was not (yet) pursued.

[106] CJEU C-315/20 *Regione Veneto* ECLI:EU:C:2021:912. The case concerned non-hazardous mixed municipal waste.

[107] Recommendation 75/436 (n 19).

[108] See CJEU Case C-72/95 *Kraaijeveld* ECLI:EU:C:1996:404.

[109] See Recommendation 75/436 (n 19).

applies to EU environmental aid, which is given to Member States under the Structural Funds, the Cohesion Fund, LIFE+ and other budgetary titles. If the polluter-pays principle were a legally binding principle, the Cohesion Fund would certainly be partly incompatible with it since it also finances clean-up measures. However, no legal writer has ever claimed any enforcement of the polluter-pays principle with regard to state aids.

In reality, in all Member States and at EU level the clean-up of the environment is seen as a task for public authorities which exists independently from the question of whether a polluter can be identified and asked to pay for pollution. Such an identification is practically impossible in cases of groundwater or coastal water pollution, forest decline, soil erosion, desertification, climate change, smog in urban areas and numerous pollutions from past activities. Public authorities are thus the only ones who can ensure a clean-up or to take other remedial or preventive measures to stop continued contamination.

A rather sad illustration on the application of the polluter-pays principle is found in Directive 2004/35 on environmental liability.[110] The Commission proposal had suggested that in a case where the polluter of environmental damage could not be identified or was unable to pay, the Member States should be obliged to restore the impaired environment. The final version of the directive, invoking the polluter-pays principle, provides that in such cases no obligation exists to restore the environment. Thus, it is to be expected that in such cases the environment is normally not restored, and the high number of contaminated sites within the EU demonstrates that this is part of a deliberate policy.

The CJEU referred to the polluter-pays principle in particular in cases on waste law, where provisions in EU directives explicitly referred to this principle. The Court used the principle to concretise the responsibility of persons beyond the wording of the legislation, though its findings appear reasonable.[111] In Case C-534/13, the Court rejected the possibility of relying on the polluter-pays principle of Article 191 TFEU in order to take measures at national level against the owner of land that had been contaminated by a previous owner.[112] The Court declared that Article 191(2) TFEU only laid down the general environmental objectives for EU policy. Without secondary legislation which put the principles into concrete application, the polluter-pays principle could not be relied on either by individuals or by national public authorities. This judgment confirms the understanding which was defended in paragraph 1-32ff.[113]

On the whole, the polluter-pays principle *allows* EU institutions to adopt measures which charge persons who cause environmental pollution to bear the cost of pollution; however, this possibility would also be available to EU institutions without the principle being inserted in Article 191(1) TFEU: in its 2006 strategy for sustainable development, mentioned in paragraph 1-11 above, the European Council interpreted the polluter-pays principle as follows: 'Prices shall reflect the true societal costs of consumption and production and polluters should pay for the damage which they caused to human health and the environment.' This, indeed, is far away from a legally binding principle.

[110] Directive 2004/35 (n 77).

[111] CJEU Case C-1/03 *Van de Walle* ECLI:EU:C:2004:490; Case C-180/07 *Commune de Mesquer* ECLI:EU:C:2008/359; Case C-254/08 *Futura* ECLI:EU:C:2009:479; Case C-172/08 *Pontina Ambiente* ECLI:EU:C:2010:87.

[112] CJEU Case C-534/13 *Fipa Group* ECLI:EU:C:2015:140.

[113] See also, more generally, European Court of Auditors, 'The Polluter-Pays Principle: Inconsistent Approach Across EU Environmental Policies and Actions. Special Report 12/2021' (Luxemburg, 2021).

VI. Conditions for Action

A. General Remarks

1-34 Article 191(3) TFEU lists a number of conditions which EU environmental policy should take into account. This obligation refers to the policy as a whole, not to each individual measure adopted at EU level. The provision addresses all EU institutions and bodies. The words 'taken into account' indicate that the paragraph does not contain preconditions for EU actions, which is further clarified by the fact that no details are given as to which condition is to be attained, which level of regional development requires action (or derogations) or what data would be needed for action. No other sector of EU policy has such conditions laid down in the Treaty.

In EU practice, the four conditions play only a subordinate role. They are rarely mentioned in the recitals of legal texts; references to them are slightly more frequent in explanatory memorandums for legislative proposals. Their legal impact is hardly measurable except for the cost–benefit condition, which is used by economic operators to object to measures that would internalise the environmental costs or make the polluter pay.

B. Available Scientific Data

1-35 This criterion states the obvious: it only requires that account be taken of the available data. The Union need not even order its own studies before shaping its policy or taking individual measures, but may simply draw on the available data. Nor is there any need to provide scientific evidence that a specific measure would be effective, which is not really possible in any case. In particular, the precautionary/prevention principle allows action without definite scientific or technical proof being available. This principle would lose much of its force if unequivocal data had to be produced before any measure could be taken.[114] In order to improve information on the environment, the European Environment Agency was set up in Copenhagen[115] and has been operational since the end of 1993. The Agency has the task of collecting, processing and distributing information on the environment in order to improve knowledge of scientific and technical data.

It also has the task of publishing a report, at regular intervals, on the state of the EU environment.[116]

[114] For a case where a Member State (unsuccessfully) argued that not all available data had been taken into consideration, see CJEU Case C-128/17 *Poland v European Parliament and Council* ECLI:EU:C:2019:194.

[115] Regulation 401/2009 on the European Environment Agency and the European Environment Information and Observation Network [2009] OJ L126/13.

[116] Since 1977, the Union has published 10 reports on the state of the environment, beginning with European Environment Agency, 'State of the Environment, First Report' (Brussels/Luxembourg, 1977); the last two reports were 'SOER 2015 – The European Environment – State and Outlook' (Copenhagen, 2020); 'The European Environment – State and Outlook 2020' (Copenhagen, 2020). According to Art 5(4) of the Aarhus Convention on access to information, public participation in decision-making and access to justice in environmental matters, contracting parties shall publish a report on the state of the environment every three or four years. The Convention was ratified by the EU in Decision 2005/370 [2005] OJ L124/1. Its provisions prevail over secondary EU law, but the Agency ignores this and publishes its own reports every five years only.

C. Regional Conditions

The provision that the environmental conditions in the various regions of the Union be taken into account is a reminder that the environment within the European Union is by no means uniform, but that geographical, climatic, soil, water and other conditions vary greatly from one area to another. The provision does not require the taking into account of divergence; for this reason, some EU legislation contains specific derogations whilst other legislation does not. Where derogations are given, they are never directly applied to a specific region – though sometimes they are to small islands, mountainous areas or outermost regions – but instead to a specific Member State,[117] which well reflects the small direct influence that regions have in the decision-making procedure. Instead of giving a direct derogation for a Member State, EU legislation may provide for indirect derogations, eg for less sensitive or mountainous areas or small islands;[118] another form is to formulate a derogation which in practice applies to only one Member State in general terms, without naming the Member State.[119] 1-36

D. Potential Benefits and Charges

This condition reads 'advantages and charges of action or lack of action' in most EU languages but not in English, because it was thought, in 1987, when the provision was inserted, that 'costs and benefits' were equivalent to 'advantages and charges'. This is obviously not the case, at least not in the political debate, where discussion on the advantages and disadvantages of EU environmental measures has been reduced, de facto, to the economic costs and benefits of an EU measure for economic operators. Also, since economists have not yet developed a standardised method of how to calculate the environmental benefits of a measure in monetary terms, this debate is all too often reduced to the question of how much the envisaged measure will cost trade and industry. This development has been particularly evident in EU activity since the early 1990s, and most specifically in the measures to combat air pollution in the transport sector, where the Commission justified a number of derogations with nothing more than the argument that they were not 'cost-effective'. The advantages–charges factor suggests that the full range of short-, medium- and long-term measures be considered in an attempt to assess the effect of taking action or failing to do so. This consideration is not to be limited to economic aspects, but must include social, employment, ecological, human and other aspects. At the end of this appraisal, if doubts still persist as to whether the measures will be sufficiently effective, the precautionary or prevention principle comes into play, together with the express mandate of Article 191(1) 1-37

[117] Examples: Directive 88/609 on large combustion plants [1988] OJ L336/1, where Spain, Portugal and Greece obtained special derogations (no longer in force); see also para 8-31 below; Directive 94/62 on packaging and packaging waste [1994] OJ L365/10 (as amended), where 13 specifically named Member States obtained derogations; on this Directive, see also para 10-48.

[118] See, eg Directive 1999/31 on landfills [1999] OJ L182/1, which provides in Art 3(4) for derogations for small islands and isolated settlements.

[119] See, eg Directive 2008/98 on waste [2008] OJ L312/3, which contains in Art 16(1) a derogation for Czech waste incinerators and in Art 21(3) a derogation for the handling of waste oils in Italy – without naming these two states.

TFEU that the Union must aim at a high level of protection and must not only preserve, but also improve the quality of the environment.

The provision gives no details of the ways and means of taking account of the potential charges and advantages. In this respect, the political resolutions adopted by the Council and the decisions on the EU environmental action programmes under Article 192(3) TFEU become of importance: where the Union institutions approved or adopted a programme or a number of actions of environmental measures, this will normally be sufficient proof that, according to the best knowledge of the EU institutions, the advantages of a specific measure outweigh the disadvantages.

E. Economic and Social Development

1-38 The condition on the economic and social development of the Union as a whole and the balanced development of its regions is meant to reflect the less-developed Member States' concern that environmental protection provisions should not be imposed at the expense of economic growth. This criterion is so broadly drafted that it covers practically all economic and social development. Every EU-wide rule inevitably implies a degree of standardisation and harmonisation, and cannot, therefore, take account of every individual region. Similarly, the same scientific and technical data which demonstrate a need for action may not be available in every region; however, this cannot be a decisive factor in differentiating its legislation between regions and Member States. The Union also has the task of ensuring environmental improvement in all parts of the Union, although it is obvious that any specific measure will bring greater advantages for some regions than for others.

The Union institutions must weigh up all these factors and produce an overall assessment. Ultimately, it is up to the Council and the European Parliament to decide to what extent regional differences should lead to specific wording in the final texts adopted at EU level.

EU practice has never taken into consideration the situation of specific regions, but, as already mentioned, has from time to time given derogations to specific Member States – which, until 2004, mainly coincided with the so-called 'Cohesion Fund countries' (Greece, Spain, Portugal, Ireland) that were economically lagging behind. In the area of air pollution, one piece of legislation in 2001 fixed 'national emission ceilings', which laid down the specific quantity of allowed pollution emissions per Member State.[120] As can be seen, this concept has little to do with regional differences (which could be very great between Lombardy and Calabria, Catalunya and Estremadura, Hamburg and Thüringen, etc), but more to do with a certain renationalisation of environmental policy.

[120] Directive 2001/81 [2001] OJ L309/22; Directive 2016/2284 on the reduction of national emissions of certain atmospheric pollutants [2016] OJ L344/1.

2

Actors, Instruments and Decision-Making Procedures

I. Actors

EU environmental policy is conceived and elaborated by the EU institutions, with considerable input from national governments and other national actors. The EU institutions contribute to differing degrees to the making of EU environmental policy; Article 288 of the Treaty on the Functioning of the European Union (TFEU) provides for the legal instruments to carry out the Union tasks in the making of EU environmental law. Hereafter, the different actors will be described, followed by the instruments for the making of environmental law and the decision-making procedure. 2-01

A. The European Commission

The Commission has in particular the following tasks (see also Article 17 of the Treaty on European Union (TEU)): 2-02

- make proposals for new environmental legislation;
- ensure that the provisions of the EU Treaties and the measures taken by the institutions pursuant thereto are applied;
- formulate opinions and recommendations; and
- take decisions and 'participate in the shaping of measures' where the Treaty so provides.

(i) Administrative Structures

The Commission consists of 27 Commissioners – one for each Member State – appointed by the Council for five years.[1] The provision of Article 17(5) TEU, according to which the number of Commissioners should be reduced as of 2014, did not became operational, as the European Council guaranteed Ireland a post in order to influence an Irish referendum; as all the other Member States then requested the same treatment, the reduction was 2-03

[1] See Art 17(5) TEU: 'as from 1 November 2014, the Commission shall consist of a number of members, including its President and the High Representative of the Union for Foreign Affairs and Security policy, corresponding to two thirds of the number of Member States, unless the European Council, acting unanimously, decides to alter this number'.

abandoned. The President of the Commission is appointed by the Council acting in its composition of Heads of State or Government and with approval of the European Parliament.[2]

The Commission autonomously divides the general work among its members. Each ordinary member of the Commission has a private office, which consists of six members who assist him in his task.

The administrative services of the Commission consist of Directorate-Generals for the different areas (eg transport, agriculture and information); at present, there are some 30 Directorate-Generals, some of which are known as 'Services', eg the Legal Service. A General Secretariat organises the daily administration of the Commission and the Directorates-General. A member of the Commission may be responsible for several Directorates-General; conversely, one Directorate-General may, for different parts of its activity, be under the responsibility of several Commissioners. Overall, there is a staff of some 32,000 officials, among whom are a number of national officials on secondment with the Commission for up to three years and persons employed on a contractual basis. The Commission works in all the official languages – at present, 24 (Article 55 TEU) – though in daily practice English and French dominate.

2-04 Environmental matters are mainly, but not exclusively, the responsibility of the Directorate-General for Environment (DG ENV), which, between 2019 and 2024, is placed under the responsibility of the Lithuanian member of the Commission, Mr Virginijus Sinkevicius. After the establishment of a new Directorate-General for climate change issues, DG ENV comprised 492 officials in 2021; about half of these officials have a university education. The Directorate General for Climate Action, placed under the responsibility of Frans Timmermans (Netherland), has (in 2021) a staff of 285 persons.

The Commission's staff policy tries to ensure that officials change their jobs every three to five years. This policy, introduced under the influence of the UK, favours technocratic behaviour, not expert knowledge. Combined with strong incitements for striving for promotion – annual assessment, increased payment, power and prestige – this leads to officials' attitudes of 'his master's voice' rather than to conceiving policies, strategies, programmes and legislation which effectively protect the environment; this influence of staff policy is particularly strong for senior officials.

The 2022 budget – the overall EU budget was €169 billion – provided for environmental and climate expenses of about €23.5 billion, compared, for example, with €54 billion for agricultural policy and €36 billion for regional policy.[3] These figures, though, do not reflect the real situation, as numerous measures in the area of other EU policies – energy, agriculture, transport, fisheries, etc – also aim at protecting the environment or contribute to the fight against climate change. In 2020, about 20 per cent of the EU budget was aimed at environmental and climate action, and this percentage is intended to be increased to some 30 per cent by 2027.

The structure and working methods of the Commission continue to be considerably affected by the original aim of the EC Treaty to organise a common agricultural policy, to open up national markets and to realise the four fundamental freedoms of the EU Treaties: free movement of goods, services, capital and labour. Environmental policy, which started

[2] For details, see Art 17(7) TEU.

[3] [2022] OJ L45/1. The Commission's environmental and climate expenditures are listed at 809.

in the early 1970s without an express legal basis in the Treaty, was considered an 'illegitimate child', and this perception only gradually began to disappear when, in 1987, the Single European Act 'legitimised' it by inserting an environmental chapter in the Treaty; the economic crisis of 2008 put the environment again into a marginal position within the EU policies, in direct opposition to the demands of European citizens. It is true, though, that since then the awareness of climate change and its economic, social and environmental consequences have grown very considerably and have led to a reorientation of the EU's policy, culminating in 'The European Green Deal',[4] the promotion of renewable and sustainable energies, and attempts to stop biodiversity loss and reduce environmental pollution. The Russian aggression against Ukraine since February 2022 has not led to other priorities, but has strengthened this approach.

The Commission's environmental activity, orientated towards achieving the objectives laid down in Articles 3 and 191(1) TFEU, may be structured for the purpose of presentation into activities initiating new measures, activities of management and monitoring activities. Legal questions of monitoring activities will be discussed in detail in chapter twelve.

(ii) *Commission Initiatives*

Under the TFEU, the Commission has the exclusive right to initiate new environmental legal measures at EU level. As, in the early 1970s, when the European Union started an environmental policy, no explicit legal basis for environmental matters existed in the Treaty establishing the European Community (EC Treaty), it was considered opportune to lay down the objectives, principles and priorities of EU action in environmental action programmes. These different environmental action programmes constituted, at least in the past,[5] a frame for initiatives, but never put limits on such actions. Indeed, numerous proposals for directives or regulations which were made had never been previously announced by an environmental action programme, and initiatives which the action programmes announced were not necessarily presented by the Commission.[6] The action programmes are completed by annual working programmes, which the Commission publishes every year; the published version, however, only contains the most important new activities. Furthermore, each member of the Commission may have for their area of responsibility a work programme which directs the work of the administrative services. 2-05

Next to these general programmes, the Commission submits from time to time action programmes for specific sectors, such as groundwater and biodiversity, for which the environmental Directorate-General is, as for the general environmental action programme, the file-leading department. Under the Sixth Environmental Action Programme, the Union decided to develop thematic strategies for soil protection, urban environment, the

[4] Commission, 'The European Green Deal' COM(2019) 640; European Council, meeting of 12 December 2019, conclusions, EUCO 20/19.

[5] Since 1993, Art 192(3) TFEU has provided that general environmental action programmes are adopted in the form of a decision by the European Parliament and the Council jointly. See Decision 2022/591 on a General Union Environmental Action Programme to 2030 [2022] OJ L114/22 (Eighth Environmental Action Programme).

[6] An example of a legislative proposal which was not announced previously is Regulation 2020/741 on minimum requirements for water reuse [2020] OJ L177/32. An example of legislation which was announced, but not so far proposed, is a directive on construction and demolition waste, Decision 1600/2002 laying down a Sixth Environment Action Programme [2002] OJ L242/1, Art 8(2)(IV).

marine environment and some other sectors, which constituted, de facto, sectoral action programmes.[7] The Seventh and Eighth Environmental Action Programmes abandoned the adoption of thematic strategies for a specific sector.[8]

More general communications which the Commission submits are presented as Green Papers, White Papers or strategy papers, or else are given another name, without any specific difference between these communications; normally, they do not provide for specific legislative measures. Recent examples concern communications on circular economy,[9] biodiversity,[10] soils,[11] textiles[12] and solar energy.[13]

As requested by Article 11 TFEU – precursors of which have appeared in similar Treaty provisions since 1987 – other initiatives in other areas such as agriculture, industrial or regional policy or transport shall integrate the environmental requirements. Initiatives – programmatic initiatives or individual measures – are prepared by the Directorate-General responsible, generally with close participation from the environmental and other interested Directorate-Generals.

2-06 The Commission decides on all drafts as a college (ie all Commissioners decide on the drafts). This also leads to situations where the Commission does not dare to take action on proposals based on the majority of its members for fear of appearing disunited to the public. Examples are initiatives on climate change, where the Commission hesitated to decide on a 30 per cent reduction of greenhouse gas emissions until 2020, or a clear position on the safety of nuclear installations within the European Union, following the Japanese nuclear incident of March 2011. This clearly appears as lack of leadership in the eyes of the public.

In view of the shortage of staff in all its departments and the often considerable length of these (agriculture, industry, foreign trade or competition) drafts, it often remains only theoretical that a proposal, which has been developed for several months or even years by the file-leading department, can still be significantly amended by other departments. The general approach, the structure and most of the detailed provisions are de facto carried in the form proposed by the file-leading department and are only in exceptional cases put into question at the political level of the Commission. The shortage of staff thus makes it extremely difficult to integrate environmental requirements into other policies on an everyday basis. Indeed, identifying the specific environmental interest in the numerous discussions and preparatory meetings for decisions inside the Commission requires time, and human and financial resources and efforts, which the present DG ENV does not have at its disposal.

An Interinstitutional Agreement on better law-making of 2016 provided that 'the Commission will carry out impact assessments of its [legislative proposals and other

[7] Decision 1600/2002 (n 6).

[8] Decision 1386/2013 on a General Union Action Programme to 2020 'Living well, within the limits of our planet' [2013] OJ L354/171 (Seventh Environmental Action Programme); Decision 2022/591 (n 5).

[9] Commission, 'A New Circular Economy Action Plan for a Cleaner and More Competitive Europe' COM(2020) 98.

[10] Commission, 'EU Biodiversity Strategy for 2030. Bringing Nature Back to Our Lives' COM(2020) 380.

[11] Commission, 'EU Soil Strategy for 2030. Reaping the Benefits of Healthy Soils for People, Food, Nature and Climate' COM(2021) 699.

[12] Commission, 'EU Strategy for Sustainable and Circular Textiles' COM(2022) 141.

[13] Commission, 'EU Solar Energy Strategy' COM(2022) 221.

measures] which are expected to have significant economic, environmental or social impacts'.[14] No agreed method for making such assessments exists, and time pressure, political requirements or ambitions, lobby influence and similar aspects limit their usefulness. The economic and social value of the environment can often not be quantified and is thus not easily accessible to econometric determination – what is the economic value of a butterfly species, a woodlouse or a mosquito? In practice, therefore, the environmental aspects of these Commission impact assessments are not always credible and are sometimes used to impede or restrict environmental initiatives which are considered detrimental to economic interests. A recent example, where the Council found the Commission's impact assessment insufficient, is its Decision 2022/2572;[15] this decision referred to the Commission's proposal to significantly reduce the use of pesticides in agriculture, and the Council was of the opinion that a more thorough assessment was necessary.

Suggestions to take initiatives for new legislative measures come from all sources. The 2-07
Council and European Parliament may ask for this or that new proposal via resolutions, and the Council may, during the debate over or adoption of a Commission proposal, request another measure to be proposed or an existing proposal to be amended. The Commissioner responsible for the environment may wish a given new proposal to be developed or the environmental Directorate-General may take the initiative. From outside the EU institutions, the initiative for action might be suggested by Member States, it might stem from international activities such as existing or new environmental agreements, it might be proposed by lobby groups, researchers or environmental organisations, or it might have other origins. In all cases, however, the college of the Commission will have to formally decide on the text which is submitted to it by its administration before there can be any question of a Commission initiative.

Connected to the legislative initiatives is the possibility of the Commission to initiate new orientations for environmental policy. Examples of the past are the above-mentioned strategies or action plans. The extent to which such political initiatives are subsequently followed by policy reorientations or concrete actions by the Council and/or the Member States changes from one topic to another. Generally, political statements, including strategies, by the Commission, the Council or the European Parliament have little or no effect, unless they are later followed by binding legislative proposals and their adoption. This is explained by the fact that the European Union is not a state, and political interests and priorities in Member States are often too divergent to accept an integrated, joint environment policy.

(iii) Executive Activities

The Commission's task to initiate new environmental policies, strategies and indi- 2-08
vidual measures is perceived by the Commission itself as its most important task: management activities clearly rank lower. One of the reasons for this is the express provision in Article 192(4) TFEU, according to which it is the Member States which shall, as a rule, implement the measures decided at EU level. Since most of the Union's environmental legislation is adopted in the form of directives which are addressed to Member States

[14] Interinstitutional Agreement between the European Parliament, the Council of the European Union and the European Commission on Better Law-making [2016] OJ L123/1.

[15] Decision 2022/2572 [2022] OJ L331/6.

(Article 288 TFEU), it is up to the Member States to transpose these directives into national law and to ensure that their provisions are complied with. However, as an autonomous, proper obligation, the Commission has the task of ensuring that EU environmental directives and regulations are properly applied.[16]

2-09 Besides this, the Commission has a number of tasks attributed to it by the different environmental directives or regulations, which concern the administering of the 'Union *acquis*'. These tasks include:

The collection of national legislation which was adopted in pursuance of the EU provisions. Since European environmental legislation dates back to the mid-1970s and Member States' legislation is variously amended, renewed, replaced and often adopted at a regional level, sometimes even referring to non-environmental, more general legislation, precise knowledge about the state of environmental legislation within the European Union is at times difficult to obtain.[17] The Commission regularly mandates so-called conformity studies which examine the transposition of environmental directives by Member States. However, it refuses to disclose these studies.[18]

The collection and comparison of national reports on the transposition and implementation of directives and the publication of European implementation reports. Most European environmental directives and regulations provide for Member States to report regularly on the implementation measures adopted; the Commission is required to establish regular European reports. In view of the considerable deficiencies in national reporting and, subsequently, the Commission's reports, a directive was adopted in 1991 to streamline and improve the reporting.[19] However, this directive has not brought about the desired improvements and was later repealed. National and Commission reports normally continued to be published late or even not at all, their content was frequently incomplete and they did not comply with scientific or serious administrative standards. Judgments by the Court of Justice which blamed Member States for not submitting reports[20] had no visible effect.

The collection and comparison of national clean-up or other plans for specific sectors or plants. Several directives, for instance on air quality or nitrate concentrations in water, provide for clean-up programmes for regions which are contaminated or where pollutant levels are exceeded, or for industrial plants to adapt to new legal requirements. Other directives, such as on the protection of birds, or on water or waste management, provide for management plans.

Member States are regularly obliged to send such plans or programmes to the Commission, which shall align and occasionally also compare them in order to obtain greater coherence. The number of directives asking for planning measures has continuously

[16] Art 17 TEU. See also para 14-12.

[17] The Commission publishes on its website the titles of national legislation notified as implementation measures, but not the text of the national laws. For example, Member States sent to the Commission, as national implementation measures of Directive 92/43 on natural habitats and wild fauna and flora [1992] OJ L206/7, not less than 928 pieces of national legislation.

[18] On this, see CJEU Case C-612/13P *ClientEarth v Commission* ECLI:EU:C:2015:486.

[19] Directive 91/692 standardising and rationalising reports on the implementation of certain directives relating to the environment [1991] OJ L377/48. Repealed by Decision 2018/853 [2018] OJ L150/155.

[20] See, eg CJEU Case C-248/02 *Commission v Italy* ECLI:EU:C:2004:531; Case C-406/03 *Commission v Ireland* ECLI:EU:C:2004:664; Case C-191/04 *Commission v France* ECLI:EU:C:2005:393; Case C-61/07 *Commission v Luxembourg* ECLI:EU:C:2007:463; Case C-85/07 *Commission v Italy* ECLI:EU:C:2007:822.

increased since the early 1990s, although planning experience in conjunction with EU environmental law matters is anything but a success story. Indeed, the Commission has occasionally attacked Member States in court for not having drawn up or submitted plans or programmes. However, the Commission hardly ever evaluates or compares the national plans, tries to promote planning according to similar criteria or gives an overall assessment of the planning instruments, and in particular their monitoring, implementation and enforcement. In this way, plans give the wrong impression that they improve the protection of the environment, whereas this is often not the case.[21]

Exchange of experience concerning problems with the application of environmental measures. These comprise environmental acts which regularly ask Member States to plan improvements and clean-up, to promote or impose cleaner technologies and to reduce pollutant emissions; examples are directives on the prevention of industrial accidents,[22] on permits for industrial installations[23] or for environmental impact assessment.[24] Discussions during meetings take place on these questions, as well as on how provisions in a directive are transposed into administrative practice, as well as on co-operation in frontier regions or with administrations of another Member State. Often such exchanges between Member States' administrations are necessary or useful. They also allow a transfer of environmental know-how from one administration to another.

Information on new scientific and technical developments. EU directives age over time and might have to be adapted due to scientific and technical developments. Most of this exchange normally takes place in the different committees for adapting directives to scientific and technical progress.

Elaboration of implementation measures. Directives may require that the Commission deal with forms and formulae, establish lists and registers, collect data or take individual decisions on national derogating measures or other technical measures to ensure a smooth application of the legislation. On its own initiative, the Commission may find it necessary to issue guidance or interpretation documents, convey its understanding of specific legislative provisions and inform about its policy following judgments of the Court of Justice of the European Union (CJEU).

Administration of funds. The amount of EU funding for environmental measures, including in sectors such as energy, transport, climate change or research, has considerably increased over the years. These amounts are monitored according to specific regulations which lay out the legal basis for expenditure.[25] The Commission has to collect the national programmes or projects, assess them, select the most appropriate applications and decide on the Union's financial participation, and is assisted in this on a regular basis by a committee made up of representatives from Member States.

[21] See CJEU Case C-404/13 *ClientEarth v UK* ECLI:EU:C:2014:2382; Case C-323/15 *Commission v Italy* ECLI:EU:C:2013:2290; Case C-403/11 *Commission v Spain* ECLI:EU:C:2012:612.

[22] Directive 2012/18 on the control of major-accident hazards involving dangerous substances [2012] OJ L197/1.

[23] Directive 2010/75 on industrial emissions [2010] OJ L334/17.

[24] Directive 2011/92 on the assessment of the effects of certain public and private projects on the environment [2012] OJ L26/1.

[25] See, eg Regulation 2021/783 establishing a Programme for the Environment and Climate Action (LIFE) [2021] OJ L172/53; Regulation 2021/1056 establishing the Just Transition Fund [2021] OJ L231/1.

Exchange of data. Almost all EU decisions require that the Commission collect data on the state of the environment, such as data on air or water pollution and soil contamination. The Commission organises the networks, the co-operation required between different parties and the related practical questions. These tasks are progressively being transferred to the European Environmental Agency or the EU's Statistical Office, which, however, need assistance from the Commission, certainly in the beginning, combined, if necessary, with formal, binding decisions.

Participation in international discussions and negotiations. Where environmental issues are discussed at international level, the Commission, beyond participation in the elaboration of agreements, etc, co-ordinates and aligns the position of the Member States and tries to ensure that internationally the Union speaks with one voice.[26]

Information of the wider public. The Commission is not an administrative body that can remain distanced from discussions about the organisation of Europe and its environment. It has to inform about the state of the environment, its policy and its individual measures, and try to persuade, publicly, in committees or in bilateral meetings, policy makers, interest groups, environmental organisations, the media and the public of its proposals and the Union's decisions. For this purpose, press releases are made, speeches delivered, articles written, interviews granted, conferences, workshops or encounters organised and information placed on the website. In so doing, the Commission is fulfilling the objective which is outlined in Article 17 TEU: to promote the general interest of the Community in environmental issues.

(iv) The Environment Agency and Other 'Satellites'

2-10 During the last decades, a number of bodies have been set up to assist the Commission in its work. The most relevant of these are:

- The European Environment Agency was created in 1990,[27] but only became operational in 1993 due to Member States' disagreement on its seat, which was finally fixed in Copenhagen. The Agency has the task of collecting, processing and distributing information about the EU environment and publishing at regular intervals a report on the state of the environment. Its advice function is not limited to the Commission, but also extends to the other institutions and to Member States. It is headed by an executive director, who is appointed by the management board; this board is composed of Member States' representatives, two Commission representatives and two scientific experts appointed by the European Parliament. Non-EU states which are members of the Agency are also represented. The Agency has 33 countries as members and a further six, from the Balkans, as co-operating countries. It has a staff of about 200 persons, to which a network of about 2000 persons in member countries have to be added, and an annual budget of about €50 million.

[26] For more details, see Art 216 TFEU; ch 12.

[27] Regulation 1210/90 on the establishment of the European Environment Agency and the European Environment Information and Observation Network [1990] OJ L120/1, replaced by Regulation 401/2009 [2009] OJ L126/1.

When the Agency was created, there was much debate between the European Parliament and the Council over whether it should also have the function of enforcing the application of EU environmental law. A compromise was reached that provided that this question should be decided at a later stage. The amendment of the Agency's statute, adopted in 1999, does not contain anything on law enforcement;[28] as the European Parliament has no historic memory, it forgot its former request; at present, this question is no longer being discussed. Every five years, the Agency has to publish a report on the state of the environment in the European Union; this delay was shortened to four years by Regulation 1367/2006, which transposed the Aarhus Convention into EU law.[29] So far, the Agency has ignored this amendment.

- In 1993, a European Consultative Forum on the environment and sustainable development was set up by the Commission,[30] consisting of 32 members from business, local and regional authorities, environmental and consumer organisations, trade unions and general environmental experts. The Forum was consulted by the Commission on any problem of EU environmental policy. The impact of the opinions given by the Forum was rather limited, due mainly to its heterogeneous composition. In 2001, it was closed, because the Commission wanted to establish 'a sustainable round table which will report directly to the Commission's President'; this body was set up, but did not undertake any visible activity on environmental matters and died a silent death.[31]
- IMPEL. The Fifth Environmental Action Programme in 1992 announced the creation of an implementation network with the primary task of promoting the 'exchange of information and experiences and the development of common approaches at practical level, under the supervision of the Commission'.[32] This network was set up by Member States under the name European Network for the Implementation and Enforcement of Environmental Law (IMPEL). The driving force was the intention to avert requests for an EU environmental enforcement body, on the one hand, to give in particular to German Länder the possibility of influencing the making of EU environmental legislation. IMPEL was an informal body and acted as an inter-governmental, rather than an integrated EU, co-operation network. It tried to improve implementation of EU legislation and influence new Commission initiatives. In 2008, IMPEL transformed itself into an international association of environmental public authorities under Belgian law in order to obtain EU financing more easily. Overall, its impact is limited.
- In 2021, a 'European Scientific Advisory Board on Climate Change' was established.[33] It has 15 members, whose task it is to give scientific advice on climate change. The members are appointed by the European Environment Agency.

[28] Regulation 933/1999 amending Regulation 1210/90 [1999] OJ L117/1.

[29] Regulation 1367/2006 [2006] OJ L264/13, Art 4(4). As the Aarhus Convention, which was ratified by the EU by Decision 2005/370 [2005] OJ L124/1, provided for such a report every three to four years and prevails over secondary EU law, the four-year period is the correct one.

[30] Decision 93/701 [1993] OJ L328/53; amended by Decision 97/150 [1997] OJ L58/48.

[31] Decision 2001/704 [2001] OJ L258/20.

[32] Fifth Environmental Action Programme [1993] OJ C138/5, ch 9.

[33] Regulation 2021/1119 establishing a framework for achieving climate neutrality (European Climate Law) [2019] OJ L243/1, Art 3 and Art 12.

B. The European Parliament

2-11 The European Parliament has played a prominent role in initiating and strengthening environmental issues at EU level since the early 1970s. Its proposals and suggestions for institutional and administrative structures, for new initiatives or proposals were very often taken up by the Commission, although sometimes after some delay. One of the reasons for this impact is that the European Parliament also decides – along with the Council – on the Commission's budget and thus has subtle means of pressure at its disposal.

Parliament's opinions on proposals for directives or regulations, obviously considerably influenced by the very active Parliamentary Committee on Environment, Public Health and Food Safety and the European Green Party, may be summarised as follows:

- On general environmental questions or on horizontal legislation, Parliament constantly urges the Commission and the Council to do more and provide for even better environmental protection than the Commission has proposed. There seem to be few Commission environmental proposals where Parliament was of the opinion that they were too ambitious, too far-reaching or too protective. Parliament generally opposed soft law, environmental agreements or recommendations, environmental deregulation and other attempts to reduce environmental protection.
- Proposals of a more technical nature are only exceptionally challenged as to the approach chosen by the Commission. The amendments suggested concern the need for more and stricter environmental protection. Parliament not only looked for more progressive and efficient environmental legislation, but also pleaded for greater transparency in environmental matters, better access to information and greater participation of environmental organisations in the decision-making process.
- Parliament gradually managed to introduce environmental requirements into its opinions on proposals for legislative acts in agricultural and regional matters, the internal market or other policies, and in this it was more advanced than the Commission or the Council. This aspect is, however, influenced by the majority groups in Parliament: where these groups are conservative, environmental-minded opinions are more difficult to obtain.

2-12 Parliament's influence on the development of environmental legislation has been constantly increased over the years. Article 225(2) TFEU, introduced in the EC Treaty in 1993, gave, the majority of Parliament's component members the right to require that the Commission submit a proposal for a directive or regulation. The Lisbon Treaties, introducing the requirement that the Commission has to explain its position when it does not follow such a request, clarified that the Commission's monopoly of proposing legislation is not affected by Article 225. Parliament very rarely recurs to Article 225. In October 2020, it asked for a legislative proposal to deal with global deforestation issues,[34] which later became Regulation 2023/1115.

[34] European Parliament, Document EP_PE_TC1-COD(2021)336 of 11 April 2023, no 12.

Article 192(3) TFEU provides that general environmental action programmes be adopted by a joint decision of the Council and the European Parliament. Since a decision is 'binding in its entirety',[35] the Eighth Environmental Action Programme and future programmes will be binding. During the review of the Fifth and the discussions of the Sixth Environmental Action Programme, the European Parliament's objective therefore was to have concrete provisions laid down; it was the European Parliament that insisted on having the thematic strategies under the sixth programme adopted in the form of legally binding decisions, to have them submitted by the Commission by 2005 and to have an annual progress report on them. With regard to the Eighth Environmental Action Programme, the European Parliament suggested a considerable number of concrete actions to be undertaken, but later compromised with the Council and agreed to the adoption of an action programme without actions.[36]

The problem with Parliament's policy is that it has no historical memory. It quite often occurs that a conflict with the Council is postponed for some years; and when the matter is discussed anew, the Parliament – normally newly composed after elections – does not defend its previous position any more. For example, the Commission did not submit annual progress reports on the environmental thematic strategies, contrary to formal commitments – and the Parliament did not insist on this.

In the past, a considerable part of the Union's legislative activity which was subject to 2-13
the 'comitology' procedure (adaptation of existing provisions due to technical or scientific progress) of Article 202 EC Treaty was not accessible to the European Parliament, since the procedures for the some 250 different committees established by the Council[37] did not provide for its participation. Attempts in the 1990s to enable access of the European Parliament to the different technical committees did not prove successful, and though the 1999 and 2011 reviews of the procedure brought some improvement,[38] the overall situation remained unsatisfactory for the European Parliament.

Articles 290 and 291 TFEU try to simplify and clarify the procedure. A delegated act (Article 290 TFEU) now must be titled as such and may enter into force only if no objection has been expressed by the European Parliament (and the Council). At least in environment-related cases, such an objection by Parliament to a committee text has been extremely rare. It is not possible to see whether Article 290 TFEU has led to greater parliamentary influence on delegated or implementing decisions – which are regulated under Article 291 TFEU – in the environmental sector.[39]

The European Parliament does not attend meetings of the Council or of its working parties. Overall, its influence on the Council in the context of a specific legislative environmental act is limited for two main reasons: first, the Parliament had, until the coming into effect of the Amsterdam Treaty in May 1999, a mainly co-operative role; and second, its resolutions were not binding for the Council. As, since May 1999, the co-decision procedure

[35] Art 288 TFEU.

[36] European Parliament, Amendments adopted on 8 July 2022 to the proposal for an 8th environmental action programme [2022] OJ C99/315.

[37] Decision 87/373 [1987] OJ L197/33.

[38] Decision 1999/468 [1999] OJ L184/23; Regulation 211/2011 [2011] OJ L65/1.

[39] See also para 2-32.

of Article 294 TFEU applies in almost all cases, the legislative influence of Parliament has progressively increased, though it must be said that the detailed knowledge of the Parliament of a specific file is less good than that of the Council. On the other hand, the Council frequently discusses a proposal from the Commission before the European Parliament has given its opinion. These discussions often lead to a political consensus in the Council, which then waits for the opinion of Parliament before formally adopting its position. This Council practice, which is not limited to the environmental sector, at the very least contradicts the spirit of the EU Treaties, which is based on the idea that the opinions of Parliament, the Economic and Social Committee and the Committee of the Regions are available when the Council discussions begin – not after they have ended.

Over the last few years, the so-called 'trilogue' negotiations have gained in importance. These are meetings between the European Parliament, the Council and the Commission to negotiate a compromise text on a Commission legislative proposal; the non-public meetings might take place either before or after the Parliament has adopted its position. The compromise text of a trilogue is normally found more quickly than via the lengthy formal procedure under Article 294 TFEU. However, the trilogue process, though it is a legislative process, is not transparent,[40] and where it takes place before Parliament has laid down its own opinion, it has the consequence that the legislative proposal is not discussed in the plenary of the Parliament.

In the conciliation procedure of Article 294 TFEU, which is quite frequently used in environmental matters, the Council's position regularly prevails over that of the Parliament. The reasons for this are, in particular:

1. the Council secretariat plus the number of environmental attachés from each Member State have greater facilities to liaise with each other and with the different national governments to form an opinion on a specific compromise text;
2. while the Member States have officials at their disposal who have been experts of the specific file for years and know all the details of the previous Council discussions, the European Parliament and its secretariat do not have the same amount of expertise at their disposal, as the rapporteur, the rapporteur's assistant(s) and almost all the other deputies are normally in contact with the subject matter only during the two readings of the Commission proposal in Parliament; and
3. Parliament's capacity to organise the necessary European know-how at short notice is less than that of the Council.

Generally, these reasons reflect the dominant role which public administration plays in all Member States in the legislative standard-setting for the environment. The influence of the European Parliament is also hampered by difficulties in accessing its positions to different files: its positions are published in the Union's Official Journal about 12 months after their adoption; its written and oral questions and the answers by the institutions are hardy accessible at all; and it does not play a significant role in controlling whether the legislation which it co-decided is properly applied within the Union.

[40] See General Court Case T-540/15 *de Capitani v European Parliament* ECLI:EU:T:2018:167. The Council discloses the positions of the Parliament and of the Council at the beginning and end of the negotiations; the positions of the individual Member States during the negotiations are not accessible.

C. The EECOSOC; Committee of the Regions

The European Economic and Social Committee (EECOSOC) (Article 301 et seq TFEU) is thought to represent the different non-governmental interests within the Union, although representatives of the environment are not expressly mentioned in Article 302(2) TFEU; there are no considerations to making EECOSOC a sustainability committee by adding 'Environmental' in the title and ensuring a representation of environmental interests. The Committee of the Regions (Article 305 et seq TFEU) is composed of regional and local authorities. The Committee of the Regions may apply to the Court of Justice where it is of the opinion that an environmental measure interferes with its prerogatives (Article 263(3) TFEU) or is against the principle of subsidiarity.[41] 2-14

Article 13(4) TEU provides that the EECOSOC Committee and the Committee of the Regions both advise the Council, the European Parliament and the Commission. In reality, this advisory function is exercised by both committees only after the Commission has submitted a proposal or made a communication. Nor does the Commission consult these committees. The opinions of both committees in environmental matters have not yet reached the point of having any significant influence on the content of EU directives or regulations. This is also due to the fact that the members of the two committees do not feel bound by the official committees' opinions.

D. The Council

The Council, while formally one institution, meets under relatively specific configurations (eg Agricultural Council, Transport Council, Social Affairs Council). In environmental matters, the Council normally meets three times under each presidency – which changes every six months – twice formally in Brussels and once informally at a place which is determined by each presidency. At the informal meetings, issues of environmental policy or environmental strategy are discussed, without any decisions being taken. The ministers responsible for environmental matters have Council meetings in Brussels or in Luxembourg on agenda issues drawn up by the presidency. The Council meetings are not public except where the Council decides otherwise; so far, however, such public meetings, introduced after 1993, have been exceptional and have not dealt with essential matters. Nor does the Council organise public hearings. Position papers from lobby groups or other organisations are only rarely distributed within the Council or among Member States. Contacts with media or with representatives of vested interests are not organised by the Council, though there is a press release issued after each Council meeting: at best, meetings with the media are organised by individual Member States immediately before or after a Council meeting. Normally, however, such contact takes place in the capital of each Member State; the public is thus informed about a Member State's viewpoint in the Council or during the preparatory meetings by the Member State itself. 2-15

[41] Protocol No 2 on the application of the principle of subsidiarity and proportionality [2008] OJ C115 206, Art 8(2).

There is no possibility of compelling the Council to debate a proposal for a legislative act presented by the Commission. Therefore, by not discussing a Commission proposal, the Council can let the proposal become obsolete. An example is the Commission proposal for a directive on access to justice in environmental matters.[42] The Council did not discuss the proposal, but the official reasons for this are not known; probably, Member States were of the opinion that the matter did not come under EU competence. Also a Commission proposal for a directive to protect the soil[43] was only very briefly discussed by the Council; again, reasons of subsidiarity were invoked, though it is known that UK, Germany, Netherlands, Austria and France opposed the proposal.

2-16 Institutional co-operation between the Council and the Commission generally occurs as regards the organisation of work in Council working groups, since here the Commission has to explain and defend its proposals for legislation. This co-operation is, however, limited to organisational questions; if, when and how often Commission proposals are discussed in the Council and within the different Council working groups is decided by each Council presidency at its discretion. The Council working groups are normally composed of the environmental attachés of each Member State's Permanent Representation with the Union plus a Commission official; officials from Member States – normally from the environmental department – participate at the discretion of each Member State, mainly in cases where expert advice is needed. The meetings are presided over by an official of the Member State who holds the presidency.

Institutional co-operation between the Council and other institutions, in particular the European Parliament, practically does not exist in environmental matters, though the increasing number of co-decision procedures has progressively led, during the last few years, to more organisational contacts between the two institutions, in particular in view of avoiding a second reading of the Commission's proposal or even a conciliation procedure.[44]

In recent years, the Council, the European Parliament and the Commission have met more and more frequently in trilogue meetings. As mentioned, these meetings have the objective of avoiding a first or a second reading of a Commission legislative proposal in Parliament, or avoiding a conciliation procedure. The meetings are not public and very little information is made available on the content of the discussions. They contradict the principle of open, transparent discussions on legislation and, more concretely, the provisions of Article 294 TFEU – which is not at the disposal of the EU institutions.

E. The European Courts (CJEU and General Court)

2-17 No detailed description needs to be given of the role of the European Courts in ensuring that 'the law is observed' in the interpretation and application of the environmental Treaty provisions and secondary legislation (Article 19 TEU). The Courts have frequently tried to interpret existing legislation in a way which is favourable to the environment and

[42] Commission, COM(2003) 624; the Commission repealed this proposal in 2014; see also para 4–18.

[43] Commission, COM(2006) 232; this proposal was repealed by the Commission in 2014.

[44] See also, as rare examples, the *modus vivendi* between the European Parliament, Council and Commission concerning the implementation measures for acts adopted in accordance with the procedure laid down in Art 251 EC [1995] OJ C293/1; or the Interinstitutional agreement on better law-making of 2016 (n 14).

to formalise the concept of environmental law which has often been rather general and vague; generally, the CJEU is more open to environmental concerns than the General Court. Of course, there have been judgments which have been influenced by political considerations.[45] However, it is usual, also within the EU Member States, that judgments from a supreme court will also include policy considerations and are not given in a policy-free environment.

The division of work between the CJEU and the General Court is decided by the Treaty (Article 256 TFEU). At present, the General Court decides in particular on all applications from individual persons (Article 263(4) TFEU) and in competition matters.

For a number of reasons, the Commission does not automatically bring cases concern- 2-18
ing a breach of EU law before the CJEU. The Court has repeatedly stated that, under Article 258 TFEU, the Commission has the discretion as to whether it wishes to bring an action or not.[46] This may well be so, but in any case, the clear wording of Article 258 indicates that the Commission has no such discretion to begin infringement procedures or not against a Member State. Since, however, the CJEU has furthermore stated that the Commission cannot be obliged to begin procedures under that article,[47] the Commission's attitude of not beginning procedures under Article 258, and thus not bringing them before the CJEU either, remains unchallenged. In my opinion, the Court has, by this jurisdiction, established an area where public power is exercised without being controlled by the judiciary, which is to be regretted.

In matters of standing of individuals and non-governmental organisations (NGOs) in environmental matters (Article 263 TFEU), the Court adopts an extremely restrictive interpretation of the terms of Article 263 that a person or an NGO must be directly and individually concerned by an EU measure; as the protection of the environment is a general, not an individual, interest, this had the consequence that no environmental NGO has ever had access to the CJEU. Article 9(3) of the Aarhus Convention, which was ratified by the EU, did not make the Court change its position: while it stated that the national judge shall do everything possible in order to make Article 9 of the Convention have its full effect,[48] it refused to assume the same obligation for itself.[49]

One essential difference between the judgments given by the CJEU and those given by a national supreme court is that the Court of Justice's judgment is given in an area in which different legal cultures exist. Thus, for example, a judgment which states that one Member State has breached EU law because it has not submitted clean-up plans, not

[45] This seems to be the case, for instance, with Case C-252/85 *Commission v France* ECLI:EU:C:1988:202 on traditional hunting; Case C-302/86 *Commission v Denmark* ECLI:EU:C:1988:421 on a deposit and return system for bottles; Case C-2/90 *Commission v Belgium* ECLI:EU:C:1992:310 on import bans for waste; Case C-155/91 *Commission v Council* ECLI:EU:C:1993:98 on the legal basis for waste legislation; Case C411/17 *Inter-Environnement Wallonne* ECLI:EU:C:2019:622 on nuclear installations; Case C-594/18P *Austria v Commission* ECLI:EU:C:2020: 742 on state aid for Hinkley; Case C-565/19P *Carvalho v European Parliament and Council* ECLI:EU:C:2021:252 on climate change measures.

[46] CJEU Cases 416/85 *Commission v United Kingdom* ECLI:EU:C:1988:321; C-234/91 *Commission v Denmark* ECLI:EU:C:1993:910.

[47] CJEU Cases C-247/87 *Star Fruit Company v Commission* ECLI:EU:C:1988:58; C-371/89 *Emrich v Commission* ECLI:EU:C:1990:158.

[48] CJEU Case C-240/09 *Lesoochranárske zoskupenie* ECLI:EU:C:2011:125.

[49] CJEU Joined Cases C-401/12P to 403/12P *Council and European Parliament v Milieudefensie a.o.* ECLI:EU:C:2015:4.

reported on the implementation of a specific directive or not ensured that the quality of drinking water complies with the requirements of the Union's law is not normally accepted by the administration of all other Member States as obliging them to make sure that the same omission does not occur under their responsibility; and the national courts also often do not take the Court's jurisdiction into account in their daily judgments. In fact, Member States do not really pay too much attention to an environmental judgment that was given against another Member State – at least, where this would involve obligations for them. Implementation, application, monitoring and enforcement of EU environmental legislation is thus very different in the different legal cultures.

F. Non-institutional Actors

(i) Professional Organisations

2-19 The representation of vested interests at Union level is probably even greater than in most capitals of Member States, though the internal cohesion of European organisations is normally considerably looser than that of the national member organisations. Economic operators and their professional organisations discovered the common market, globalisation effects and the advantages of economies of scale a long time ago, and are also well aware that European Union trade needs EU legal provisions. Their influence on the shaping of European environmental law is considerable, although this is capable of being demonstrated only with difficulty. This influence is not so much exercised by legal papers which argue this or that rule as by influencing the strategic thinking inside the Commission administration. I estimate that, even with DG ENV, out of the 100 contacts or interlocutors which the Directorate-General has outside the national administrations, more than 90 represent vested interests. Such exchange of views is bound to have some long-term repercussions. The influence of vested interest groups appears to have increased in the last years, due to the economic crisis in Europe and the stronger orientation of the EU policy towards economic growth.

Since 2011, the European Parliament and the Commission have set up a Transparency Register, where lobby groups are registered. This register was made mandatory by an interinstitutional agreement, which the Council also joined.[50] Other EU bodies or organs may adhere to the Agreement. Registered persons or groups are requested to give some information on their finances and their activity and to respect a code of conduct for lobbyists.[51] In 2015, 7649 organisations were registered; in 2022, there were 12,425 organisations or persons.

Examples where vested interests in my opinion seem to have significantly influenced the EU policy of environmental law are: the abandoning of integrated emission limit values for industries or sectors of industries;[52] the abandoning, as a rule, of setting air or water

[50] Interinstitutional Agreement between the European Parliament, the Council of the European Union and the European Commission on a mandatory transparency register [2021] OJ L207/1.

[51] ibid Art 6 and annexes I and II.

[52] See para 4-45ff.

emission values from point sources at European level;[53] the omission to establish provisions for environmental taxes and charges at European level; the 15-year delay in fixing limit values for CO_2 emissions from cars;[54] the omission to formalise, in some binding form, the polluter-pays principle; active participation in industrial standardisation; the omission to heavily promote alternative energies and the strong financial support for a nuclear energy policy; and the omission to fix air quality standards for heavy metals.

(ii) *Environmental Organisations*

European environmental organisations suffer from a chronic shortage in manpower and financial resources which seriously affects their organisational structures. There is no overall European umbrella organisation which includes all environmental associations. In the mid-1990s, environmental organisations formed a loose co-operation group, Green 10, to pool their forces. Its members are: BirdLife International (European Office); Bankwatch Network; Climate Action Network Europe; European Environmental Bureau; European Federation for Transport and Environment; European Public Health Alliance; Friends of the Earth Europe; Greenpeace Europe; International Friends of Nature; and the World Wildlife Fund for Nature European Policy Office. 2-20

The Green 10 organisations frequently divide work priorities among themselves, according to their political preferences. Their joint activity is rather limited. With the exception of Greenpeace, they all obtain financial support from the Commission. However, the financial amount of that support is not fixed. The attributions to environmental organisations are decided yearly, on the basis of work programmes. It cannot be excluded that the financial support from the Commission also influences the respective organisations' actions and positions.

One might wonder whether it is time for environmental organisations to pool their limited personal and financial resources and form an EU institute for environmental organisations or a similar body. Their current diversity is an obstacle to professionalisation. For example, an association such as the European Environmental Bureau, the umbrella environmental organisation of some 140 national organisations, has a permanent staff of some 40 people in Brussels, but is thought to cover all facets of EU environmental policy and law. Other organisations are even smaller. All of the organisations mainly work to influence the opinions of the European Parliament and the public. Overall, the contribution of environmental organisations to EU environmental law is limited. Their best ally is public opinion, and where they do manage to highlight an issue in the public awareness and find access to the media, they may influence EU environmental policy and the content of some measures considerably. Also, in cases of catastrophes, such as the mad cow disease, accidents – the *Prestige* tanker accident 2002 or the *Aznalcollar* (Spain) accident 1998 – or scandals such as the Brent Spar platform incident 1995, contaminated food, PVC in toys or others, their ability to influence public opinion definitely influenced the EU legislature.

[53] See para 7-08ff.
[54] See para 8-29ff.

(iii) Individual Persons

2-21 The environmental provisions of the EU Treaties do not mention individual persons and, as mentioned, are not set out in such a way that, under the CJEU's doctrine of direct effect, they could be interpreted so that individual persons could invoke them in disputes with administrations or courts. The CJEU made a major effort in increasing the position of individual persons by declaring, in a landmark decision of 1991, that environmental measures which also aimed at the protection of human health were to be interpreted in a way that would allow individuals to invoke these rights in courts.[55] But neither the Commission nor environmental organisations or individual persons have ever pushed this line of thinking further, eg by making proposals for introducing a right of action for individuals or their associations against environmental impairment (Commission), by trying, via an established number of test cases in court, to explore the content and the limits of environmental rights for individuals (environmental organisations) or by trying to make operational a 'right to a clean environment', which is so often referred to by politicians.[56] And the CJEU refused to grant compensation to individual persons whose health was affected by air pollution levels which exceeded the limit values that had been laid down in EU legislation.[57]

EU institutions, and in particular the Commission, start from the premise that the protection of the environment is the task of the public administration – as if the (EU) administration were the owner of the environment; since, under this concept, the EU administration knows best what is desirable to preserve, protect or improve the quality of the environment, an individual person is rather perceived as a nuisance. This basic concept is the reason why access to environmental information at European level is so much less organised than access to environmental information at national level,[58] why there are no systematic hearings organised for the preparation of environmental legislation in order to overcome the structural imbalance between professional and environmental organisations and why environmental organisations and individuals are simply not given the possibility to contribute to the enforcement of EU environmental provisions. The EU does not wish to see the basic difference between an environmental action by a professional organisation and one by an environmental organisation: an environmental organisation tries to promote the general interest to protect the environment, whereas a professional organisation usually has in mind specific, vested interests, not the general interest.

The Lisbon Treaties introduced, in 2009, a right of citizens' initiative:[59] one million citizens who come from at least seven different Member States may invite the Commission to submit a legislative proposal to the other institutions. Until the end of 2022, about 100 such initiatives were started, one-quarter on environmental topics. A good part of the initiatives were held inadmissible by the Commission, because their subject matter did

[55] CJEU Cases C-361/88 *Commission v Germany* ECLI:EU:C:1991:224; C-237/07 *Janecek* ECLI:EU:C:2008:447.

[56] See para 4-01 below.

[57] CJEU Case C-61/21 *Ministère de Transition Écologique* ECLI:EU:C:2022: 1015.

[58] See, on the one hand, Directive 90/313 [1990] OJ L158/56 and Directive 2003/4 [2003] OJ L41/26, and on the other hand, Regulation 1049/2001 on access to documents held by EC institutions [2001] OJ L145/43.

[59] See Art 11(4) TEU.

not come under EU competence. Only nine initiatives obtained more than one million signatures but did not cause the Commission to initiate legislation. In view of the bureaucratic system which was put in place and the numerous financial, linguistic and administrative barriers which were erected, the efficiency of the whole system is questionable. A reform of 2019 tried to improve the system.[60]

The European Commission is to blame for not trying to mobilise private individuals who wish to ensure better protection of the environment by making people participate in environmental law-making and implemention. The EU citizenship, introduced by Article 20 et seq TFEU, is lacking concrete implementation measures in the environmental sector, where individual persons remain receivers of EU environmental law and policy rather than being given the status of instigators and participants.[61]

II. Instruments

A. Legal and Political Instruments

(i) General Remarks

The following presentation of instruments is limited to the TFEU; the terminology of the Euratom Treaty corresponds to it – except, of course, in the numbers of the articles. The CECA Treaty expired in July 2002 and no longer exists. 2-22

In environmental matters, a number of instruments have been developed which are not detailed in the central provision of Article 288 TFEU. The main reason for this evolution is the absence of an express chapter in the EC Treaty on environmental policy prior to 1987.

Regulations and directives can be adopted by the European Parliament and the Council jointly, by the Council alone or by the Commission. The Commission has a monopoly on initiating legislative measures in all such cases: environmental regulations and directives may only be adopted upon a proposal of the Commission.

The possibility to have directives and regulations adopted jointly by the European Parliament and the Council has only existed since 1993. As regards the environment, Articles 192(1) for environmental measures, 114 for measures which have significance for the internal market and 192(3) TFEU for the adoption of environmental action programmes provide for this joint adoption. In a number of cases, the Council alone adopts environment-related acts, in particular under Articles 192(2), 43(3), 113 and 207(3) TFEU. A qualified majority by the Council requires the agreement of 55 per cent of the Member States (ie at least 15 Member States) which comprise at least 65 per cent of the population of the Union.[62] It is important to underline that the Council can only amend a Commission proposal unanimously (Article 293 TFEU). 2-23

[60] Regulation 211/2011 [2011] OJ L65/1; repealed by Regulation 2019/788 on the European citizens' initiative [2019] OJ L130/55.

[61] As regards participation in decision-making, see para 4-14ff below.

[62] See Arts 16(4) TEU, 238 TFEU and Protocol 36 to the Treaties on transitional provisions [2008] OJ C115/322.

The Commission can adopt regulations or directives only where it has expressly been authorised to do so by the Treaty or by secondary EU law (Articles 290 and 291 TFEU). The delegation to adopt acts (Article 290 TFEU) is specific to each legislative act. The Commission may act according to the delegation, without being assisted by a committee – though, in practice, the Commission normally acts in concertation with a committee, as this way it obtains the opinion of Member States. The Parliament and the Council may object to a specific delegated act with the argument that it is ultra vires; in that case, the measure does not enter into effect.[63]

Where implementation powers are given to the Commission (Article 291 TFEU), the Commission is assisted by a committee composed of representatives of Member States and chaired by the Commission. The Commission shall submit a draft implementing act to the committee. Where the committee gives a negative opinion, the Commission shall not adopt the measure; where the committee gives a positive opinion, the Commission shall adopt the measure; and where the committee gives no opinion, the Commission may normally adopt the measure.[64]

Regulations, directives and decisions must 'state the reasons on which they are based' (Article 296 TFEU). This is the aim of the recitals which precede the different texts and give, in condensed form, the objectives of the legislative act and why the different provisions were adopted in this or that form. The CJEU uses the recitals for the interpretation of the provisions; the Court's interpretation is not too severe as regards their content,[65] though sometimes legal acts are voided because of a lack of reasoning.[66]

Regulations, directives and decisions are published in the Official Journal of the European Community, with the exception of those directives and decisions which are addressed to individual Member States or individual persons (Article 297 TFEU). Since 1 July 2013, only the electronic version of the Official Journal shall be authentic and shall produce legal effects.[67]

(ii) Regulations

2-24 In environmental matters, the Union mainly acts in the form of directives; regulations are exceptional. The latter are normally adopted when uniform provisions are sought, since regulations are of general application, are binding in their entirety and are directly applicable to all Member States (Article 288 TFEU). A first group is composed of regulations which set up a specific administrative structure, such as the European Environmental

[63] For details, see Art 290 TFEU. As regards the difference between delegated measures and implementation measures, see CJEU Case C-427/12 *Commission v European Parliament and Council* ECLI:EU:C:2014:170; Case C-65/13 *European Parliament v Commission* ECLI:EU:C:2014:2289.

[64] For details, see Regulation 182/2011 laying down the rules and general principles concerning mechanisms for control by Member States of the Commission's exercise of implementation powers [2011] OJ L55/13.

[65] See, on the one hand, CJEU Case C-528/16 *Confédération Paysanne* ECLI:EU:C:2018:583, and on the other hand, Case C-165/20 *Air Berlin* ECLI:EU:C:2022.42, para 55: 'the preamble to an EU act has no binding legal force and cannot be relied on either as a ground for derogation from the provision of the act in question or for interpreting that provision in a manner clearly contrary to their wording'.

[66] See, eg CJEU Case C-41/93 *France v Commission* ECLI:EU:C:1994:196; General Court Case T-105/95 *WWF v Commission* ECLI:EU:T:1997:26; CJEU Case C-378/00 *Commission v EP and Council* ECLI:EU:C:2002:42.

[67] Regulation 216/2013 on the electronic publication of the Official Journal of the European Union [2013] OJ L69/1.

Agency,[68] the financial instrument LIFE[69] or the Cohesion Fund.[70] Furthermore, there are measures which create committees, uniform procedures or structures; examples are the provision on organic agriculture,[71] the procedures for attributing an eco-label[72] and the eco-audit scheme.[73]

A second group is formed by regulations which transpose obligations of international environmental agreements into EU law. They mainly serve to organise international trade concerning products, waste, fauna and flora species. Examples are the regulations on ozone-depleting substances,[74] on the shipment of waste[75] and on trade in endangered species.[76] Also, the regulations on an import ban of whale products,[77] on the ban of leg-hold traps and the import of certain furs[78] and on the import or export of chemicals[79] belong to this category.

Regulations do not exist in the air and noise sectors, and there are only a few in the areas of nature protection, water, waste and chemicals. However, these last two sectors show a slowly increasing need for uniform provisions. The reasons for this might lie in the necessity of having uniform provisions vis-à-vis the international state or trade community, but also in the wish to avoid, within an internal market which is still developing, different provisions from one Member State to another that could lead to competitive distortions and changes in commercial relationships. 2-25

Although regulations are directly applicable in all Member States, not all provisions of environmental regulations have this direct effect. Several regulatory provisions require an action by Member States, such as the licensing and supervision of environmental auditors;[80] the authorisation of imports; the establishment of documents or certificates;[81] the designation of competent authorities; the supervision of plants, activities or transport; the establishment of reports; and the transmission of information to the Commission or to other Member States. In these cases, regulations seem to have more the content of a directive. Furthermore, not all provisions of a regulation are of a mandatory nature: thus, a provision such as 'Member States may apply the system provided for in Titles II and VIII within their jurisdiction'[82] is of a purely facultative character.

[68] Regulation 401/2009 (n 27).

[69] Regulation 2021/783 (n 25).

[70] Regulation 2021/1058 on the European Regional Development Fund and on the Cohesion Fund [2021] OJ L231/60.

[71] Regulation 2018/848 on organic production and labelling of organic products [2018] OJ L150/1.

[72] Regulation 66/2010 on the EU Ecolabel [2010] OJ L27/1.

[73] Regulation1221/2009 allowing voluntary participation by organisations in a Community eco-management and audit scheme [2009] OJ L342/1.

[74] Regulation 1005/2009 on substances that deplete the ozone layer [2009] OJ L286/1.

[75] Regulation 1013/2006 on shipments of waste [2006] OJ L190/1.

[76] Regulation 338/97 on the protection of species of wild fauna and flora by regulating trade therein [1997] OJ L61/1.

[77] Regulation 348/81 on common rules for imports of whales or other cetacean products [1981] OJ L39/1.

[78] Regulation 3254/91 prohibiting the use of leghold traps in the Community and the introduction into the Community of pelts and manufactured goods of certain wild animal species originating in countries which catch them by means of leghold traps or trapping methods which do not meet international humane trapping standards [1991] OJ L308/1.

[79] Regulation 649/2012 concerning the export and import of dangerous chemicals [2012] OJ L201/60.

[80] Regulation 1221/2009 (n 73).

[81] Regulation 338/97 (n 76), Art 8.

[82] Regulation 1013/2006 (n 75), Art 33(3).

2-26 No environmental regulation outlines details of sanctions which apply in case of non-respect of the regulation. For instance, the Regulation on the shipment of waste provides that Member States[83] 'shall lay down the rules on penalties applicable for infringement of the provisions of this Regulation and shall take all measures necessary to ensure that they are implemented. The penalties provided for must be effective, proportionate and dissuasive.'

The REACH Regulation on chemicals asks Member States to[84] 'lay down the provisions on penalties for infringement of the provisions of this Regulation and … take all measures necessary to ensure that they are implemented. The penalties provided for must be effective, proportionate and dissuasive.'

Whether the sanction is criminal, administrative or civil is left to the discretion of the Member States. The jurisprudence of the CJEU requires that national sanctions are proportional, dissuasive and deterrent, and correspond to sanctions which are laid down for similar cases under national law.[85]

(iii) Directives

2-27 Directives[86] are the most frequently used instrument in EU environmental policy. The degree of detail provided for in a directive is determined less by the concept of a 'directive' than by the need to attain the different objectives pursued. Thus, directives on harmonising motor vehicle rules quite often contain 50–80 pages of detailed rules, which outline all the details of the composition of products, test methods, etc.[87] Such detailed directives are frequent for products, but also exist in the agricultural sector. In contrast, environmental directives tend to be of a general nature. In particular, the debate over the last decades on subsidiarity and deregulation and the general loss of integration capacity of the Union has led to environmental directives which limit themselves to outlining general rules, framework provisions and basic requirements. Provisions on measuring methods and frequency, emission limit values, quantitative restrictions and other similar provisions are only laid down in exceptional cases. Whether this restriction is really capable of contributing to a high level of environmental protection is doubtful; such general provisions do not increase the added value of EU environmental law provisions and, furthermore, perpetuate differences in the level of protection among Member States: they allow the Member States to apply the EU provisions, if the political will to do so exists, but also allow them to avoid full application of such rules if the political will does not exist.

Directives address Member States and normally oblige them to reach a certain result. Private persons, undertakings or associations cannot be obligated by a directive; however, they can acquire rights from a directive in those cases where a provision in the directive is sufficiently concrete, precise and unconditional and where the Member State has not transposed that directive completely or correctly into national law (direct-effect doctrine).[88]

[83] ibid Art 50(1).

[84] Regulation 1907/2006 on the registration, evaluation, authorisation and restriction of chemicals (REACH) [2006] OJ L396/1.

[85] CJEU Case C-68/88 *Commission v Greece* ECLI:EU:C:1989:339.

[86] Art 288 TFEU: 'A directive shall be binding, as to the result to be achieved, upon each Member State to which it is addressed, but shall leave to the national authorities the choice of form and methods.'

[87] Directive 97/24 on three-wheel cars had a length of 454 pages in the Official Journal [1997] OJ L226/1. Such a length would not be imaginable for a directive on the environment.

[88] See further at para 14-27.

Member States have to transpose the provisions of a directive into national law. It is up to each Member State to decide whether this is done by an Act of Parliament or a regulation, whether the transposition measure is one piece of legislation or whether several regional or even local provisions are adopted. It is only relevant that the directive's provisions are transposed for the whole territory of the Member State. The transposing measure may be incorporated in one legal act; more frequently, however, the transposition is ensured by a number of legal measures, especially in Member States with a decentralised or federal structure. 2-28

Where the definition of a provision is relevant, such transposition also needs to include the definition in order to establish a common language.[89] For the other provisions, at the very least those which are capable of creating rights or obligations for private persons need to be transposed. In contrast, those which exclusively address the administration (for instance, requiring it to send reports to the Commission or to designate competent authorities) do not need to be transposed.

The provisions of directives which have been transposed into national law must be actually applied. This follows from the very nature of a directive, which obliges Member States to achieve a certain result. It is not enough to take all practical steps to reach the directive's objectives; indeed, the directive indicates to Member States which result is to be achieved, but does not leave it at their discretion as to whether they achieve the result or not. It was for this reason that the UK's argument that it had taken all reasonable steps to ensure clean drinking water was not heard before the CJEU: the Court requested that the requirements of the Drinking Water Directive be complied with.[90] 2-29

Amendments of directives follow the general rules. Normally, they are adopted by the same institutions which adopted the original directive; however, as pointed out, the Commission may be authorised, under Article 290 TFEU, to amend a directive, in particular to adapt it as a result of technical or scientific progress. Furthermore, the legal basis of a directive is determined by its objective and its content, not by the legal basis of a previous directive; thus, where an environmental directive, based on Article 192 TFEU, is amended by a directive which has a trade-related objective, Article 207 TFEU may become the appropriate legal basis for the amending measure, and the institution which adopts the amendment may be different.[91]

Legally, differentiations such as 'umbrella directive' or 'daughter directive' are not relevant. Such concepts only signal that the specific directive is placed in a more general context; however, each directive is to be interpreted by itself, albeit including possible references to other directives.

Directives do not become obsolete with time. Since they are legal acts, they need to be repealed expressly: in EU practice, this normally takes place with the adoption of a new directive. The agreement of the Council and the European Parliament will be necessary for any repeal.

[89] See, eg CJEU Case C-120/09 *Commission v Belgium* ECLI:EU:C:2009:802; Case C-648/13 *Commission v Poland* ECLI:EU:C:2016:490.

[90] CJEU Case C-337/89 *Commission v United Kingdom* ECLI:EU:C:1992:456; see also Case C-404/13 *Commission v United Kingdom* ECLI:EU:C:2014:2382.

[91] See, eg Regulation1420/1999 [1999] OJ L166/6, which concerned the shipment of non-hazardous waste and was based on Art 133 EC, though the original Regulation 259/93 on the shipments of waste was based on Art 175 EC.

(iv) Decisions

2-30 Decisions[92] are rather numerous in EU environmental policy. The most frequent types are decisions: to establish a committee or another body;[93] to grant financial assistance for environmental projects under the Cohesion Fund or the financial instrument LIFE; in the context of competition policy on agreements (Article 101 TFEU), the abuse of dominant positions (Article 102 TFEU) or state aid (Articles 107 and 108 TFEU); on details of putting into operation specific directives or regulations,[94] or establishing criteria for the attribution of an eco-label for specific product groups;[95] on the adherence of the Union to international (environmental) agreements; on environmental action programmes according to Article 192(3); and on Article 114(4) and (5) TFEU on the authorisation of more stringent national environmental measures.

(v) Recommendations

2-31 Commission or Council recommendations have no binding force (Article 288 TFEU). They play a limited role in EU environmental policy. Indeed, experience has shown that neither economic operators nor Member States are inclined to respect recommendations, and the example of international organisations – Organisation for Economic Cooperation and Development, Council of Europe, United Nations – which largely work with recommendations demonstrate the very limited effective influence of non-binding environmental measures.

The Council made environmental recommendations, among others, on cost allocation,[96] the cost of pollution control to industry,[97] the reuse of waste paper and the use of recycled paper,[98] and coastal zone management.[99] The Commission in particular made recommendations on birds,[100] environmental agreements,[101] the use of chlorofluorocarbons in industry,[102] the environmental footprint[103] and the speeding-up of permits for renewable.[104]

None of these recommendations, which, since 2009, are increasingly based on Article 292 TFEU, have had, as far as can be seen, any significant influence on European or national environmental policy or law.

[92] Art 288 TFEU: 'A decision shall be binding in its entirety. A decision which specifies those to whom it is addressed, shall be binding only on them.'

[93] See, eg Decision 76/431 setting up a committee on waste management [1976] OJ L115/73.

[94] See, eg Decision 2022/2462 establishing a list of ship recycling installations [2022] OJ L322/15.

[95] Under Regulation 66/2010 (n 72), eg Decision 2017/1216 establishing an eco-label for dishwashers [2017] OJ L180/31.

[96] Recommendation 75/436 [1975] OJ L194/1.

[97] Recommendation 79/3 [1979] OJ L5/28.

[98] Recommendation 81/972 [1981] OJ L355/56.

[99] Recommendation 2002/413 [2002] OJ L148/24.

[100] Recommendation 75/66 [1975] OJ L21/24.

[101] Recommendation 96/733 [1996] OJ L33/59.

[102] Recommendations 89/349 [1989] OJ L89/56, 90/437 and 90/438, [1990] OJ L227/26 and 30 (CFC).

[103] Recommendation 2021/2279 [2021 L 471/1.

[104] Recommendation 2022/822 [2022] L 146/132.

(vi) Communications

Communications, which are not expressly provided for in the TEU, are legally not binding.[105] They are sent from the Commission to another institutions, in particular the Council or the Parliament, and expose the Commission's position on a particular problem, indicate orientations and discuss options which the Commission considers possible. As the EU tries to avoid the adoption of environmental legislation, the number of communications on environmental matters has increased during the last years. 2-32

Communications appear under different headings, as strategies, Green or White Papers, reports or communications. Legally, there is no difference between them. Communications may be accompanied by a draft for a Council resolution, a directive or a regulation.

(vii) Action Programmes

EU environmental action programmes have been developed since the early 1970s, mainly in reaction to the fact that the EC Treaty did not provide for an express legal basis for environmental measures. When such specific provisions were introduced in 1987, the practice of action programmes was maintained. Action programmes were, legally, communications by the Commission to other EU institutions, which set out, for a period of four to five years, the objectives, principles and priorities of EU action which the Commission envisaged. The CJEU confirmed that the environmental action programmes did not contain legally binding or enforceable provisions.[106] Action programmes were followed by (political) resolutions by the Parliament and the Council. Between 1973 and mid-1998, five environmental action programmes were agreed at EU level.[107] Their main effect was essentially political. They achieved a large consensus among Member States on objectives and priorities of EU environmental policy, and since the majority of Member States did not have a structured national environmental policy, the measures agreed and adopted at EU level often influenced environmental policy within Member States. Since the end of 1993, environmental action programmes have to be adopted by way of a joint decision by the European Parliament and the Council (Article 192(3) TFEU), which is, of course, binding. 2-33

Action programmes under Article 192(3) TFEU must at least outline priority objectives for EU action, provide for measures to achieve these objectives and contain a time period within which the measures are taken. The right of initiative for such programmes rests with the Commission, and no other institution can oblige it to submit a programme.[108] 2-34

[105] In Case T-584/13 *BASF v Commission* ECLI:EU:T:2018:279, the General Court concluded that the Commission communication on the precautionary principle, COM(2000) 1, provided for a cost-benefit analysis to be made; the absence of such an analysis constituted a breach of EU law. This judgment appears to be wrong.

[106] CJEU Case C-142/95P *Rovigo* ECLI:EU:C1996:493.

[107] First Environmental Action Programme 1973–1976 [1973] OJ C112/1; Second Environmental Action Programme 1977–1982 [1977] OJ C139/1; Third Environmental Action Programme 1982–1986 [1983] OJ C46/1; Fourth Environmental Action Programme 1987–1992 [1987] OJ C328/1; Fifth Environmental Action Programme 1993–2000 [1993] OJ C138/5.

[108] Argument taken from CJEU Case C-347/97 *Commission v Belgium* ECLI:EU:C:1999:19.

EU action programmes may oblige the Commission to make proposals for specific measures, with the consequence, in the case of failure to do so, of an action – by the Council and also by the European Parliament – under Article 265 TFEU. It is true that the Commission normally has the monopoly for legal initiatives and cannot be compelled to make a proposal. However, primary and secondary law contain a number of exceptions to this rule,[109] and there is no provision in EU law which would oppose such an exception. In contrast to this, it does not seem possible to oblige, by virtue of a programme, the Council or even the Member States to adopt specific measures: in such a case, too concrete a content – such as that the use of certain substances or products will be banned from a specific date onwards – would contradict the form of an action programme; such measures would require a directive or a regulation, and would be adopted in respect of the procedures foreseen for those instruments.

The provision of Article 192(3) TFEU created new possibilities for the European Parliament to influence the legislative programme of the European Union and to see proposals for legislative measures presented. Parliament's interest must therefore be to have environmental action programmes as concrete as possible, whereas the interests of the Commission and the Council must be to keep the programme as general and loosely drafted as possible. This difference of interest was very notable in the Commission's proposal for a review of the fifth action programme and Parliament's position on it.[110] The final Decision on this review contained objectives and principles, but not actions.[111] This approach was repeated in the Seventh (2014–20) and Eighth Environmental Action Programmes (2022–30), which do not contain concrete actions.[112]

(viii) Resolutions

2-35 The Treaty does not contain any provision on resolutions. These are political statements adopted by the Council, with or without a proposal from the Commission. Following a consensus in the Council which is not laid down in writing, Council (environmental) resolutions are agreed upon unanimously; it is true that no vote is taken, but the Council redrafts the text until a consensus of all Member States is reached.

Resolutions often constitute the Council's reaction on a Commission communication concerning an environmental issue. However, the Council is not obliged to react to such communications. Where it adopts a resolution, this gives political or legal orientation to the Commission, the Parliament or private actors, without being legally binding for the Council. Also, the European Parliament adopts environmental resolutions either as a reaction to a Commission communication or on its own initiative. These resolutions are adopted by majority vote. Again, they are of a political, not legal, nature.

[109] See, eg Art 241 TFEU; an example in secondary law was Art 1(5) of Directive 91/689 on hazardous waste [1991] OJ L377/20, which requested the Commission to make a proposal on hazardous household waste; Directive 91/689 has now been repealed.

[110] Commission [1996] OJ C140/5; European Parliament [1996] OJ C362/112.

[111] Decision 2179/98 on the review of the Fifth Environmental Action Programme [1998] OJ L275/1.

[112] Seventh Environmental Action Programme (n 8); Eighth Environmental Action Programme (n 8).

(ix) Environmental Agreements

Environmental agreements were defined by the Commission as agreements, by which stakeholders undertake to achieve pollution abatement, as defined in environmental law, or environmental objectives set out in Article 191 TFEU.[113] 2-36

Such agreements are not mentioned in Article 288 TFEU. Since the Union may only act within the limits of powers conferred upon it (Article 5 TEU), agreements are not capable of regulating substantive parts of Community environmental policy, as this is reserved for the instruments listed in Article 288 TFEU. The European Parliament opposed the recourse to environmental agreements, which it understood as some form of commitment that was binding for the Commission or the Union.[114] It stated in particular that such agreements simply did not conform to the Parliamentary principle. As the European Parliament, the Economic and Social Committee and the Committee of the Regions have institutional rights and guarantees to take part in the EU decision-making procedures, environmental agreements, which set these rights aside, are not legally permissible. For this reason, the Commission declared in two communications that it could only make non-binding environmental agreements at EU level and even included this approach in the very definition of 'agreement'.[115] Further, in 2002, the Commission stated that 'environmental agreements are not negotiated with the Commission'.[116] Since then, environmental agreements have hardly been discussed any more.

Even with these basic concerns being left aside, procedures for the making of such agreements – who should negotiate in the name of the Union? – and the follow-up – how and by whom would the agreement be monitored, enforced, sanctioned and applied to free-riders, such as importers and third country producers? – are not clear; nor are they answered by the different Commission's communications or Parliament's resolutions.[117] Since Member States would have to monitor and enforce agreements, their participation in the negotiation procedure appears inevitable. However, it is then not clear where the advantage is with regard to a directive which is negotiated and decided in the Council and the European Parliament.

The core of the problem is the attempt to obtain a commitment from the legislature – at EU level mainly from the Commission, which has the right of initiating legislation – not to adopt binding legislation. In law, the legislature cannot bind itself in this way. Also, problems under competition policy – Articles 101 and 102 TFEU – are not really solved. 2-37

[113] Commission, 'Environmental Agreements at Community Level' COM(2002) 412 of 17 July 2002. Another definition is given in Art 3(12) of Directive 94/62 on packaging and packaging waste [1994] OJ L365/10: '"Voluntary agreements" shall mean the formal agreement concluded between the competent public authorities of the Member State and the economic sectors concerned, which has to be open to all partners who wish to meet the conditions of the agreement with a view to working towards the objectives of this directive.' Directive 2004/12 ([2004] OJ L47/26) inserted a new Art 3*bis*, according to which the directive's recycling targets could also be attained by voluntary agreements. As regards the most prominent 'agreement' at EU level – that on the reduction of CO_2 from cars – see also para 8-24ff.

[114] EP, Resolutions of 17 July 1997 [1997] OJ C286/254; 26 October 2000 [2000] OJ C197/433; 18 January 2001 [2001] OJ C262/236.

[115] Commission, 'Environmental Agreements' COM(96) 561; see also COM(2002) 412 (n 113); Council Resolution of 7 October 1997 [1997] OJ C321/6.

[116] Commission, COM(2002) 412 (n 113) 4.

[117] ibid; Commission (n 115); Council (n 115); EP (n 114).

Agreements among competitors may come under Article 101, even where public authorities participate in such agreements. As regards measures which have an impact on imports, international trade provisions may also be applicable.

Looking into the experience with environmental agreements in Member States, it seems that EU environmental agreements may contribute to the protection of the environment in those cases where legally binding measures are also effective; however, in those parts of the Union where environmental directives are almost or not at all effective, environmental agreements are not likely to have a greater effect.

2-38 EU legal policy tries to circumvent these obstacles: in the case of an environmental agreement on CO_2 emissions from cars, negotiations on what might be an acceptable offer from the car industry took place in the mid-1990s and at the end of the 1990s between the Commission and economic operators; the Council and Parliament were informed of the state of the negotiations, but did not participate. At the end of the negotiations, a statement and a recommendation were issued by the Commission to say that there was no need for binding measures at EU level, since there was a voluntary commitment by the car industry.[118] It should be noted, though, that the agreement was made not with the car manufacturers themselves, but with their industrial associations. Thus, when the Rover company later left the association, it was no longer bound by the agreement.

A second way consists in negotiations between the Commission and one or more professional organisations on an improvement in environmental performance. At the end of these negotiations, the European professional organisations make a unilateral commitment to the Commission. The Commission adopts a recommendation, based on Article 288 TFEU, which recommends that those environmental commitments be followed, which the professional organisation agrees to accept. An example of this model, which does not contain any form of 'agreement' (ie some form of a contract), is the use of detergents, on which the Commission made a recommendation in 1998.[119]

Underlying both types of environmental 'agreements' is the Commission's commitment not to make proposals for a directive or a regulation. The above-mentioned statement by the Commission that 'the Commission can never, by "acknowledging" such an engagement, forgo its right of initiative'[120] is legally quite correct. However, politically, an acknowledgment by the Commission is perceived by the economic actors as a commitment not to initiate legislation – which is, of course, what is intended.

The main difference to environmental agreements as they are negotiated and concluded, for example, in the Netherlands is that, on the one hand, the Dutch authorities themselves fix, by way of legislation/regulation or government decision, the result to be reached, whereas at EU level the result of an agreement to be reached is negotiated between the vested interest groups and the Commission. On the other hand, the obligation to regularly publish progress reports is normally much stricter and is much more strictly monitored by the Dutch public authorities.

[118] See also para 8-29ff.

[119] Recommendation 98/480 [1998] OJ L215/73; see also the recommendations on CFCs 89/349, 90/437 and 90/438 (n 102), which followed the same pattern, but became obsolete because of the evolution in the sector of ozone-depleting substances.

[120] Commission, COM(2002) 412 (n 113) 4.

As regards environmental agreements at national level, Member States are free to act as they consider appropriate. To what extent Member States might feel bound by any agreement that was produced at EU level and abstain from introducing legislation is a political decision. In 1996, the Commission made a communication and a recommendation on general aspects of the implementation of EU environmental legislation through national environmental agreements.[121] By the end of 2010, only four waste directives[122] contained a clause that allowed Member States to implement some of the directives' provisions by environmental agreements, for which a number of conditions were laid down. It seems that the statement in the Sixth Environmental Action Programme[123] that 'legislation remains central to meeting the environmental challenges and full and correct implementation of the existing legislation is a priority', later developments, in particular the 2019 Green Deal for Europe, and the growing awareness of the three big environmental challenges for the planet – climate change, biodiversity loss and pollution – led to a sort of tacit consensus that environmental agreements were not a promising path to pursue.

(x) Tripartite Contracts and Agreements

At the end of 2002, the Commission proposed the use of tripartite contracts and agreements at Union level.[124] Tripartite contracts were defined as contracts between the Union, a Member State and regional or local authorities 'in direct application of binding secondary Community law (regulations, directives or decisions)'; tripartite agreements were such contracts 'outside a binding Community framework'. In the case of tripartite contracts, an enabling clause in the legislative instrument is necessary, as is a clause in the contract that the Member State alone is responsible for the implementation of EU legislation. 2-39

In the environmental sector, tripartite agreements seem useful in particular in the area of local environmental issues such as coastal zone management, urban environment issues or questions of waste management, where legislation does not really reach. To what extent regions or local authorities will seize the opportunity to enter into a direct contractual relationship at EU level remains to be seen and might also depend on the availability of financial means. As of the end of April 2024, this instrument has never been used.

B. Instruments to Influence the Behaviour of Undertakings and Individual Persons

EU law contains a number of provisions which are aimed at influencing the behaviour of undertakings or individual persons towards a better environment. Since the great majority 2-40

[121] Commission, COM(96) 561 (n 115); Recommendation 96/733 (n 101).

[122] Directive 2000/53 on end-of-life vehicles [2000] OJ L269/34 Art 10(3); Directive 2012/19 on waste electrical and electronic equipment (WEEE) [2012] OJ L197/38 Art 24(3); Directive 94/62 (n 113); Directive 2006/66 on batteries [2006] OJ L266/9.

[123] Decision 1600/2002 (n 6) Recital 12.

[124] Commission, 'A Framework for Target-Based Tripartite Contracts and Agreements Between the Community, the States and Regional and Local Authorities' COM(2002) 709.

of EU environmental law is made in the form of directives, these provisions do not directly address private persons; instead, they normally address Member States and ask them to 'transmit' these messages, via their national provisions, to the addressees. The most important instruments that exist under EU environmental law are the following.

(i) Obligation of Notification

2-41 In a number of cases, natural or legal persons are obliged to notify the authorities of a Member State of a certain activity or practice. Thus, persons who intend to put new chemical substances on the EU market have to notify public authorities of their intention and submit certain documents referring to the tests of that substance: they may only put the substance on the market 60 days after that notification.[125] Where a chemical, whose use in the Union is prohibited or restricted, is to be exported to a third country for the first time, this intention must be notified 30 days before the export takes place; the intention behind this provision is to inform the third country ('prior informed consent' principle).[126] A notification obligation also exists for the contained use of genetically modified micro-organisms[127] and the deliberate release of genetically modified organisms;[128] sometimes in these two instances, however, the notification is followed by an express authorisation. Also, the production, processing and import of organic agricultural products must be notified.[129]

As regards installations, notification is required for any industrial activity during which certain chemicals are used or produced; the notification must inform the authorities of the substances and plant used, and possible risks of accidents.[130] Furthermore, malfunctions or breakdowns of the functioning of installations sometimes requires notification.[131]

All these obligations for information or notification are intended to inform the authorities responsible in due time, in order to allow them to take appropriate and, if necessary, preventive action.

(ii) Authorisation

2-42 Authorisation is organised in very different ways across Member States. It is thus usual for the EU legislature to limit itself to requiring that certain activities have an environmental authorisation[132] (sometimes the word 'permit' is used,[133] without there being any legal difference) and to setting out conditions for this authorisation.

[125] Regulation 1907/2006 (n 84); see further at para 6-24ff.

[126] Regulation 649/2012 (n 79); see also para 6-53ff.

[127] Directive 2009/41 on the contained use of genetically modified micro-organisms [2009] OJ L175/75.

[128] Directive 2001/18 on the deliberate release into the environment of genetically modified organisms [2001] OJ L106/1, Art 6 et seq.

[129] Regulation 2019/848 (n 71).

[130] Directive 2012/19 (n 122).

[131] See, eg Directive 2010/75 (n 23), Arts 8(2) and 37(2); Directive 2010/75 is a recast of Directive 2008/1 on integrated pollution prevention control [2008] OJ L24/8.

[132] See, eg Directive 2010/75 (n 23); Directive 76/464 on the discharge of pollutants into water [1976] OJ L129/23; this directive was repealed as of 2013; Directive 2006/118 on the protection of groundwater against pollution and deterioration [2006] OJ L372/19.

[133] See, eg Directive 2010/75 (n 23); Directive 2008/98 on waste [2008] OJ L312/3.

First, a number of new installations need an authorisation to operate. Directive 2010/75[134] has to some extent harmonised the permits and the conditions thereof, and Directive 2015/2193 extended this obligation to medium combustion plants.[135] The authorisation for discharges into water under Directives 76/464 on water discharges,[136] 2001/80 on large combustion plants,[137] 1999/13 on plants using organic solvents,[138] 78/176 on installations producing titanium dioxide[139] and 2000/76 on waste incinerators[140] were progressively integrated into the provisions of Directives 2010/75, which became a framework directive. In the waste sector, all installations which recover, collect, treat or dispose of waste need an authorisation.[141]

Authorisations are also needed to limit the impairment of the environment. Besides the discharge from installations as mentioned above, the artificial enrichment of groundwater may be mentioned,[142] or the discharge of waste water from urban waste-water treatment plants;[143] the discharge of sewage sludge into surface waters has been forbidden since 1998.[144] Product-related authorisations concern the placing on the market of pesticides[145] and biocides,[146] and the release of genetically modified organisms into the environment.[147] Also, the import and export of ozone-depleting substances[148] and of endangered species of fauna and flora[149] fall into this category. 2-43

There is no general rule on the conditions which accompany the authorisation. Early directives established very detailed conditions[150] which were, however, not really controlled. Directive 2010/75 also provides for detailed conditions, such as emission limit values or equivalent parameters, the best available techniques, measurement frequency and methodology, suitable requirements for controlling emissions and measures for other than normal operating conditions. However, the condition requirements are vaguely formulated and leave wide discretion to Member States.

In contrast to earlier directives, Directive 2010/75 does not provide for limited authorisations; it only requires that the authorisation be regularly reconsidered (Article 21). 2-44

[134] Directive 2010/75 (n 23).

[135] Directive 2015/2193 on the limitation of emissions of certain pollutants into the air from medium combustion plants [2015] L 313/1. Instead of a permit, the Member States may provide for a registration only.

[136] Directive 76/464 (n 132).

[137] Directive 2001/80 on the limitation of emissions of certain pollutants into the air from large combustion plants [2001] OJ L309/1.

[138] Directive 1999/13 on the limitation of emissions of volatile organic compounds due to the use of organic solvents in certain activities and installations [1999] OJ L85/1.

[139] Directive 78/176 on waste from the titanium dioxide industry [1978] OJ L54/19.

[140] Directive 2000/76 on the incineration of waste [2000] OJ L332/91.

[141] Directive 2008/98 (n 133).

[142] Directive 2006/118 (n 132).

[143] Directive 91/271 on urban waste water [1991] OJ L135/40, Arts 12 and 14.

[144] ibid Art 14.

[145] Regulation 1107/2009 concerning the placing of plant protection products on the market [2009] OJ L309/1.

[146] Regulation 528/2012 on the making available on the market and use of biocidal products [2012] OJ L167/1.

[147] Directive 2001/18 (n 128).

[148] Regulation 1005/2009 on substances that deplete the ozone layer [2009] OJ L286/1.

[149] Regulation 338/97 on trade in endangered species [1997] OJ L61/1.

[150] See, eg Directive 80/68 on the protection of groundwater against pollution caused by certain dangerous substances [1980] OJ L20/43, which required methods of discharge, essential precautions, monitoring arrangements and monitoring groundwater to be detailed. This directive has since been replaced by Directive 2006/118 (n 132).

The procedural requirements for authorisations are few and far between. Directive 2010/75 requires a written application with a number of minimal indications and a non-technical summary of the documentation (Article 12). The application has to be made available to the public for an appropriate length of time to enable it to comment. An environmental impact assessment is only required for certain specific projects and, since 2004, for spatial planning and programmes.[151] These Directives provide that the public must be given 'the opportunity to express an opinion' on the plan or project, which means that the affected person has a right to be consulted.

Directive 2010/75 furthermore provides that authorisation be made available to the public; most other directives concur with this requirement. No details are set out, and the requirement for checking on whether the conditions for authorisation continue to be complied with or not has been reduced in recent directives. Directive 2003/35 now introduces a right of the public concerned to participate in the authorisation of certain projects, plans and programmes.[152]

While Directive 76/464 and its subsequent different daughter directives outlined detail control requirements, Directive 75/440 on the quality of surface water[153] was even completed by a specific 'control' directive,[154] and the directives on air quality standards also contained detailed measurement and control provisions.[155] All water and air provisions in this regard are now substituted by more general provisions in the water and air quality framework directives,[156] which do not go into such fine detail. Directive 2010/75 introduced monitoring requirements for the installations (Articles 14 and 16) and the obligation for the authorities to periodically inspect the installations covered by that directive.

(iii) Interdiction and Obligation to Act

2-45 EU environmentally relevant interdictions have been pronounced essentially in the product-related legislation. The most important provision was Directive 76/769,[157] which was continuously amended to include further restrictions, but has now been replaced by the REACH Regulation on chemicals.[158] Besides that, every measure which fixes emission limit values, implicitly contains the interdiction on exceeding these values. Other

[151] Directive 2011/92 on the assessment of the effects of certain public and private projects on the environment [2012] OJ L26/1; Directive 2001/42 on the assessment of the effects of certain plans and programmes on the environment [2001] OJ L197/30.

[152] Directive 2003/35 providing for public participation in respect of the drawing up of certain plans and programmes relating to the environment [2003] OJ L56/17.

[153] Directive 75/440 concerning the quality required of surface water intended for the abstraction of drinking water in the Member States [1975] OJ L194/26. This directive has since been repealed.

[154] Directive 79/869 concerning the methods of measurement and frequencies of sampling and analysis of surface water intended for the abstraction of drinking waters in the Member States [1979] OJ L271/ 44. This directive has since been repealed.

[155] Directive 80/779 (SO_2 in the air) [1980] OJ L229/30; Directive 82/884 (lead in the air) [1982] OJ L378/15, Directive 85/203 (NO_x in the air) [1985] OJ L87/1. These Directives have since been replaced.

[156] Directive 2000/60 establishing a framework for Community action in the field of water policy [2000] OJ L327/1; Directive 2008/50 on ambient air quality and cleaner air for Europe [2008] OJ L152/1.

[157] Directive 76/769 relating to restrictions on the marketing and use of certain dangerous substances and preparations [1976] OJ L262/201. This directive has since been integrated into Regulation 1907/2006 (n 84).

[158] Regulation 1907/2006 (n 84).

interdictions and restrictions are found in numerous directives, such as the bans on certain heavy metals or other substances in products, on the discharge of sewage sludge into water[159] and on the non-authorised disposal of waste.[160] Most of these interdictions provided that the interdiction is disregarded in extraordinary circumstances. Occasionally, EU law itself authorises Member States to establish a ban.[161] General authorisation in this regard is found in Articles 114(4) and 193 TFEU.

Further elements exist in secondary law under the so-called safeguard clause: these clauses give the possibility of temporarily prohibiting a product even though it complies with EU requirements. Such a ban provokes an EU control procedure which ends either with an EU-wide prohibition or an invitation to the acting Member State to repeal its ban. Specific authorisations for Member States to issue bans exist for using sewage sludge where certain concentrations of heavy metals are exceeded[162] and for importing/exporting hazardous waste for disposal purposes.[163] EU environmental law only rarely provides for general national derogations of a ban. An example is the possibility of hunting certain birds in specified Member States.[164] Considerably more often, it happens that a Member State may grant a derogation of a ban on a case-by-case basis.

Obligations to act are also rather few and far between. They concern, for instance, 2-46
obligations to keep registers, to measure emissions, to hand over waste to an authorised undertaker, to discharge air emissions via a chimney, etc. Sanctions are never imposed: these are left to national legislation.

Directive 2010/75 sets out the 'general principles' for the operator of an installation that come under that directive;[165] these probably only have a placebo effect, because they are hardly enforceable and may be interpreted in many different ways. Also, Directive 2012/18 obliges the operator of a plant to take 'all necessary measures' to prevent accidents.[166]

Recent waste legislation started to introduce take-back obligations for cars and electrical/electronic equipment.[167] National take-back schemes are allowed and sometimes required by EU legislation.[168] Deposit and return systems are likewise possible at national level, but have not yet been imposed by EU legislation. Obligations to ensure financial security only exist for the shipment of hazardous waste to another state.[169] No insurance obligation exists against environmental impairment; the Directive on environmental

[159] Directive 91/271 (n 143).

[160] Directive 2008/98 (n 133).

[161] See eg Directive 2015/412 as regards the possibility for the Member States to restrict or prohibit the cultivation of genetically modified organisms [2015] OJ L68/1.

[162] Directive 86/278 on the use of sewage sludge in agriculture [1986] OJ L181/6, Arts 5 and 7.

[163] Regulation 1013/2006 (n 75).

[164] Directive 2009/147 on the conservation of wild birds [2010] OJ L20/7, Art 7(3) and annex II(2).

[165] Directive 2010/75 (n 23), Art 11: for instance, 'no significant pollution is caused'; 'energy is used efficiently'; 'the necessary measures are taken to prevent accidents and limit their consequences'.

[166] Directive 2012/18 (n 122) Art 5.

[167] Directive 2000/53 (n 122); Directive 2012/19 (n 122), where the obligation is limited to waste from electrical and electronic equipment (WEEE) other than that from private households. For such waste from private households, Member States only have to set up return systems, Art 5(2).

[168] Directive 2006/66 on batteries and accumulators (n 122); Directive 94/62 (n 113), Art 7; Directive 96/59 on the disposal of PCB/PCT [1996] OJ L243/31, Art 6.

[169] Regulation 1013/2006 (n 75).

liability left the question of whether there should be compulsory insurance for damage to the environment to national legislation.[170]

2-47 There is no obligation for an undertaking to mandate a person to look into environmental issues. Directive 82/501 contained the obligation for an undertaking coming under that directive to designate a specific person in charge of security and to implement the accident prevention and evacuation plans.[171] However, Directives 96/82 and 2012/18, which replaced Directive 82/501, deleted this provision altogether.

2-48 EU environmental law does not expressly require operators to take the supply of water, electricity or fuel from a specific place, or to deliver waste or waste water to a specific place or installation. However, such an obligation implicitly underlies the Directive on urban waste water.[172] Member States are free to make provisions for such an obligation, but not for waste which may be recovered. Obligations for remedial action, following an action that impaired the environment, were established by Directive 2004/35 on environmental liability.[173] An indirect obligation flows from Article 13 of Directive 2008/98 on waste[174] which ensures that waste disposal does not impair the environment; this provision requires the elimination of illegally disposed waste and the restoration of the impaired environment.[175] Regulation 1013/2006 obliges Member States to take back waste which has been illegally shipped to another Member State.[176]

Liability obligations currently only exist for damage caused by defective products;[177] Directive 85/374 also applies to damage caused by waste, although this is contested.[178] Directive 2004/35 on environmental liability does not contain any financial responsibility of a polluter to compensate a victim, but is limited to environmental restoration obligations under public law.

(iv) Information, Appeals, Warnings

2-49 EU environmental law and policy contain numerous addresses and appeals to citizens to behave in a way which is environmentally beneficial. A good example is the Council resolution on the Fifth Environmental Action Programme, where the Council declared that 'many current forms of activity and development are not environmentally sustainable' and that 'the achievement of sustainable development calls for significant changes in current patterns of development, production, consumption and behaviour'; this implied 'a sharing of responsibility at global, Community, regional, local and even personal level'.[179] It is impossible to measure the impact of such appeals.

[170] Directive 2004/35 on environmental liability with regard to the prevention and remedying of environmental damage [2005] OJ L143/56, Art 14.

[171] Directive 82/501 on accident prevention [1982] OJ L230/1; see also CJEU Case C-190/90 *Commission v Netherlands* ECLI:EU:C:1992:225.

[172] Directive 91/271 (n 143).

[173] Directive 2004/35 (n 170).

[174] Directive 2008/98 (n 133).

[175] CJEU Case C-365/97 *Commission v Italy* ECLI:EU:C:1999:544; Case C-196/13 *Commission v Italy* ECLI:EU:C:2014:2407.

[176] Regulation 1013/2006 (n 75).

[177] Directive 85/374 on product liability [1985] OJ L210/29.

[178] See also para 4-60ff.

[179] [1993] OJ C138/1.

Since 1992, the Union has tried to reorient consumers' and users' behaviour towards environmentally 'better' products by establishing an EU eco-label.[180] Since industry associations are not really in favour of a system that classifies some products to be better than others, work advanced very slowly, all the more as the system also had to compete with differing national systems; thus, its effects have so far been very limited.[181] The EU eco-audit scheme[182] had more success, though it had to compete with an international ISO-standard which is less ambitious.[183]

The Union never issued warnings against environmentally dangerous products. A recommendation to be careful with toys for small children that contain PVC with certain phthalates,[184] obviously aimed more at protecting health than the environment. Under Directive 2008/50,[185] Member States are obliged to warn the population at local level where certain levels of ozone concentration or of other pollutants are exceeded, a way to replace remedial action by warnings.

Generally, the effect of EU appeals and information is not significantly greater than that of corresponding national measures. It is correct that EU institutions have, at least in part, greater credit with the population in environmental matters; however, this is balanced by a greater distance towards the ordinary citizen.

(v) Financial Assistance

So far, no EU provision provided for financial advantages – such as a lower VAT – 2-50
of environmentally 'better' products. Member States oppose such rules, since environmental protection is of different importance in the different Member States, and they are afraid of competitive disadvantages. Thus, a Commission proposal to introduce a price differentiation between leaded and unleaded petrol and thereby accelerate the introduction of catalytic converters and lead-free petrol[186] was rejected: such differentiation was subsequently introduced at national level. In the same way the attempt failed to introduce general financial advantages for the introduction of cars with catalytic converters; the final compromise only allowed such encouragement for a limited period of time. Attempts in this direction seem to have been largely abandoned since then, also for the introduction of electric cars, though the idea of 'getting the prices right' continues to be mentioned. Attempts to introduce a reduced VAT tax for products which carry an EU eco-label were discussed, but finally not proposed by the Commission.

(vi) Subsidies

National subsidies (state aids) are prohibited (Article 107 TFEU) in principle, but in 2-51
practice are widespread in all Member States. The total amount of state subsidies in 2022

[180] Regulation 66/2010 (n 72).
[181] For more details, see para 6-55ff.
[182] Regulation 1221/2009 (n 73).
[183] For more details, see para 4-55ff.
[184] Recommendation 98/485 [1998] OJ L217/35.
[185] Directive 2008/50 on ambient air quality and cleaner air for Europe [2008] OJ L152/1.
[186] [1984] OJ C178/5.

for energy alone was €184 billion;[187] the amount of environmental aid – environmental protection and energy saving, as well as biodiversity conservation – is not known, in part because it overlaps with aid for agricultural, fisheries, transport and other activities. Since 1974, the Commission set up an EU framework for environmental aids.[188] The guidelines fix the framework within which the Commission normally considers environmental state aid compatible with the EU Treaties. Financial encouragements for consumers to acquire environmentally 'better' products do not fall into this scheme as long as the aid does not advantage individual undertakings.[189]

EU subventions are mainly granted under the Structural Funds and the Cohesion Fund,[190] and more recently, with regard to climate change, under the Innovation Fund and the Modernisation Fund, both of which have their origin in the consolidated Directive 2003/87.[191] The Structural Funds aim to improve the situation of economically disadvantaged regions, including rural areas (Article 174 TFEU). The Member States entitled to receive funds establish programmes which are approved by the Commission; the individual projects which come under these agreed programmes are then realised under the responsibility of the Member State. The priorities and the taking of environmental measures are largely left at the discretion of each Member State.

The Cohesion Fund co-finances individual projects in the environmental and transport sectors in those Member States where the gross national product lies below 90 per cent of the EU average. For the period 2021–27, it benefits Bulgaria, Croatia, Cyprus, the Czech Republic, Estonia, Greece, Hungary, Latvia, Lithuania, Malta, Poland, Portugal, Romania, Slovakia and Slovenia. The regional policy system, applicable since 2007, integrated the Cohesion Fund into the general Regional Fund System, which means that the sums which are made available are no longer earmarked for specific projects. Regional funds may thus also co-finance projects which contribute to the implementation of obligations under EU environmental law, such as the construction of sewers, waste-water treatment plants, waste disposal or recovery installations or nature protection projects; this is hardly completely compatible with the polluter-pays principle as laid down in Articles 191 and 192(5) TFEU. There are several other EU aid programmes, in particular in the sectors of energy, research and agriculture.

As mentioned, no fiscal advantages have so far been granted by EU measures. Likewise, there are as yet no EU rules on environmental charges.

(vii) Tradable Certificates, Bubbles

2-52 The concept of tradable permits comes from Anglo-Saxon legal systems; its introduction into EU law was due to commitments which the EU made in international agreements.

[187] Commission, 'Report on Energy Subsidies in the EU 2022' COM(2022) 642: €50 billion concerned fossil fuels, €78 billion non-fossil fuels and €7.2 billion nuclear energy.

[188] See Commission, Guidelines on State aid for climate change, environmental protection and energy 2022 [2022] OJ C80/10.

[189] ibid.

[190] See last Regulation 2021/1058 on the European Regional Development Fund and on the Cohesion Fund [2021] OJ L231/60.

[191] Directive 2003/87 establishing a system for greenhouse gas emission allowance trading within the Community [2003] OJ L275/32.

Environmental certificates are used as tokens, which, against payment, are issued by the public authorities and give the right to emit into the environment the quantity of pollutants indicated by the token. These certificates are tradable.

In 2003, the Union adopted a directive on tradable emission permits for greenhouse gases.[192] This directive was elaborated under the auspices of the Kyoto Protocol to the United Nation Convention on Climate Change,[193] which required, internationally, the introduction of tradable certificates by 2008. The EU system has been operational since the beginning of 2005. Undertakings which come under the directive – some 20,000 installations, which emit about 45 per cent of all CO_2 emissions – obtain an allowance for emitting CO_2 gas. Where they invest in cleaner technologies and/or reduce emissions, they may sell those allowances which they do not need any more. If, conversely, they need more allowances, they can buy them from other undertakings.

Under Regulation 1005/2009, producers of ozone-depleting substances have the possibility, granted by the Commission, of marketing specific quantities of ozone-depleting substances or to use the quantities themselves. Such rights may be transferred to other EU producers of the same substance; the Commission is to be informed of any such transaction.[194] The essential difference from certificates is the fact that this provision deals with a product for which limitations already exist and that the general objective of all these provisions is to progressively reduce and ultimately terminate the production of such substances.

The bubble concept requires, within a specific geographical area, that total pollution quantities are taken into account. Within this total quantity, the different emittors may emit differing quantities of pollutants. EU law provided for a bubble concept in Directive 2001/80 on emissions from large combustion plants,[195] where total quantities for sulphur dioxide (SO_2), nitrogen oxides (NO_x) and dust emissions were set for each Member State. These total quantities were to be reduced in two or three stages. It was left to Member States to distribute nationally the total quantities for emissions. In the meantime, this directive was integrated into Directive 2010/75.[196]

Furthermore, Directive 2016/2284 on national emission ceilings asked Member States to reduce, by 2030, air emissions of SO_2, NO_x, non-methane volatile organic compounds, ammonia and fine particulates ($PM_{2.5}$) by a certain percentage.[197] How Member States achieve this reduction target was left to them. As with the Directive on large combustion plants, the main problem with this directive is the monitoring of its application. It will hardly be possible for any national or EU body to monitor the application of the targets, or for the Commission to take any action under Article 258 TFEU. Indeed, the compilation of data to prove the non-respect of the obligations is much too complicated and is left in

[192] ibid; for more details, see para 9–14ff.

[193] See Decision 2002/358 concerning the approval, on behalf of the Community, of the Kyoto Protocol to the United Nations Framework Convention on Climate Change and the joint fulfilment of commitments thereunder [2002] OJ L130/1.

[194] Regulation 1005/2009 (n 74), Arts 3(10) and 4(5).

[195] Directive 2016/2284 on the reduction of national emissions of certain atmospheric pollutants [2016] OJ L344/1. This directive replaced Directive 2001/81 on national emission ceilings for certain air pollutants [2001] OJ L309/22.

[196] Directive 2010/75 (n 23).

[197] Directive 2001/81 (n 195).

the hands of the Member State in question. Therefore, where a Member State has the political will to comply with the requirements of Directive 2016/2284, it has at its disposal a sufficiently flexible instrument to do so. However, where this political will is absent, almost no means of enforcement are available.

A form of bubble concept was incorporated into the Agreement on the transit of the Alps between Austria and the European Union.[198] Trucks which crossed the Alps via Austria were charged with 'eco-points'; the number of points varied according to the truck's pollution emissions. Member States obtained a total number of carriages, which they had to distribute among the individual trucks. The total number of eco-points was to be reduced by 60 per cent during the 12-year period of the Agreement. This Agreement became incorporated in the Austrian Accession Treaty when Austria joined the European Union in 1995, but ended in 2003.

(viii) Targets

2-53 Beginning with the Fifth Environmental Action Programme of 1993, the EU environmental policy worked more and more with 'targets'. Targets (in French, 'objectifs') are normally numeric objectives to be reached within a specific time span, for example a 55 per cent reduction of greenhouse gas emissions by 2030. They may be binding[199] or non-binding,[200] and may be addressed at Member States or at the EU. Targets set by the European Council[201] are always non-binding targets, as the European Council does not exercise legislative functions (Article 15(1)TEU). Targets are frequent in the EU climate change policy.

EU targets are, in practice, not enforced. Contributing to this without doubt is that the measured results of such targets are known only after a delay of several months or even years, and that the evidence is not easy to establish, though the main reason is political: the Commission does not wish to take Member States to court with regard to their climate change policy. Thus, for example, when Spain increased its greenhouse gas emissions by more than 50 per cent until 2008 despite being allowed, under Decision 2002/358,[202] to increase it by only 15 per cent, the Commission turned a blind eye to this situation. Targets set for EU institutions could at best be enforced by a Member State, but Member States are not keen to do so. The conclusion is that even binding targets set by the EU are essentially of political, not legal, importance.

[198] Agreement between the European Economic Community and the Republic of Austria on the transit of goods by road and rail [1992] OJ L373/6; Regulation 3637/92 on a system of distribution of rights of transit (eco-points) for heavy goods vehicles with a laden weight of over 7.5 tonnes registered in a Member State transiting through Austria [1992] OJ L373/1.

[199] See, eg Directive 2009/28 on renewable energies [2009] OJ L140/16, Arts 1and 3(4): 'This directive … sets mandatory national targets. Each Member State shall ensure that the share of energy from renewable sources in all forms of transport in 2020 is at least 10% of the final consumption of energy in transport in that Member State.'

[200] See, eg Directive 2012/27 on energy efficiency [2012] OJ L315/1, Art 3(1): 'Each Member State shall set an indicative national energy efficiency target.'

[201] See, eg Regulation 2021/1119 (n 38), Art 4: 'the binding Union 2030 climate target shall be a domestic reduction of net greenhouse gas emissions (emissions after deduction of removals) by at least 55% compared to 1990 levels by 2030'.

[202] Decision 2002/358 (n 113).

III. The Decision-Making Procedure

A. Elaboration of a Legislative Act

(i) Commission Proposal

The Commission has, as mentioned, a monopoly on taking initiatives for environmental legal action, although there is a political obligation to take such initiatives under Article 192(3) TFEU.[203] It is at the Commission's discretion to decide what form, objective and content its proposal for a legislative act shall take and what preparatory work is undertaken. Normally, a comparative assessment of national legislation is made as well as one or several studies on the scientific, technical, economic and environmental aspects of a subject and estimations about the impact of the planned measures undertaken. Draft proposals are prepared by the technical units inside the Directorate-General responsible, not by a central 'drafting unit'. 2-54

Consultations with Member States at an administrative level generally start with the first draft of a directive, which is frequently accompanied by background documents which explain the approach chosen, indicate the options and raise other matters that might be of interest. Practice varies as to whether, at this stage of the drafting, a consensus is sought with other departments inside the Commission before a draft is sent to a wider audience.

Such discussions hardly ever take the form of bilateral discussions with Member States (which would take place in the different capitals rather than in Brussels): if they are undertaken, they are limited to particularly 'important' Member States and they are mainly made to consult on the approach to be taken or the strategy to be adopted. Multilateral discussions on draft proposals for environmental directives between the Commission's administration and Member States' officials always take place. These meetings are convened in Brussels on invitation by the Commission administration which chairs them. Officials from interested Commission departments participate. The invitation to these meetings is addressed to the Permanent Representation of Member States with the Union and asks them to designate experts to attend the meeting. The experts need not come from environmental administration or even administration at all. 2-55

As environmental law is often technical and has a limited number of national rules to take into consideration, only a few such multilateral meetings of experts are usually needed to reach an understanding of the subject matter. In areas where more general problems are touched upon, discussions inside the Commission and with Member States' experts may take a long time. Thus, while the Commission services drafted 23 texts for a proposal on environmental impact assessment[204] before the text could become an official proposal for a directive and be sent to the Council, the Directive on liquid beverage containers[205] had almost as many drafts.

Parallel to those meetings with governmental experts, discussions with organisations from trade and industry and environmental organisations take place. No systematic 2-56

[203] See para 2-42 ss.

[204] Directive 85/337 [1985] OJ L175/40; for more details, see para 4-33ff.

[205] Directive 85/339 [1985] OJ L176/18; see also para 10-48ff.

consultation is organised, although the Commission services prefer consultation with European organisations over national bodies or even individual companies. The sheer number of professional organisations guarantees them a greater chance of consultation than environmental organisations, which are under-represented at EU level and lack resources, know-how and expertise in successful lobbying. For several years, Internet consultation has become more and more frequent; it is almost exclusively done in English. The European Ombudsman considered that consultations which do not take place in all official EU languages constitute a case of maladministration from the side of the Commission; however, the Commission refused to change its practice.[206]

Since the beginning of 2003, the Commission has established an impact assessment process. An impact assessment is made for all new legislative proposals. This researches the economic, social and environmental implications of the proposal, including the examination of alternatives, of a zero alternative (not legislating), etc.[207] The impact assessment paper is made available to the public in the form of a Commission working document after the formal adoption of the legislative proposal by the Commission.[208]

At the end of the consultation and impact assessment process, a draft text is produced which the Directorate-General responsible takes to the Commission in order to start the formal adoption phase. The draft, together with an explanatory memorandum,[209] is sent to all interested Directorates-General and in all cases to the Legal Service with the request for approval. These bodies will often take different positions (which, of course, are also influenced by outside lobbying), so an attempt will be made to reach a compromise text. The revised text then goes into the approval procedure of the Commission itself. If necessary, attempts will be made at cabinet level to find a political compromise on any outstanding questions.

If the cabinet succeeds, the 27 Commissioners normally approve the draft by way of written procedure. Where the cabinet does not succeed or where the text is of political importance, the draft is discussed orally. A simple majority of Commissioners is needed to have a draft adopted as a formal Commission proposal. It may happen that a text is not capable of being approved by the Commission, though this is rather unusual in environmental matters.

The official Commission proposal for a directive or a regulation is published as a COM document, and only in exceptional cases in Part C of the Official Journal of the European Communities. The explanatory memorandum, which is not an integral part of

[206] European Ombudsman, *Annual Report 2013* (Strasbourg, 2014) 33.

[207] Commission, 'Communication on Impact Assessment' COM(2002) 276.

[208] The CJEU held that such impact assessments had to be disclosed to the public *before* the Commission adopts a legislative proposal, see Case C-57/16P *ClientEarth v Commission* ECLI:EU:C:2018:660.

[209] Internal Commission rules have largely standardised the content of the explanatory memorandum, though each text is adapted to the specific subject matter; as an example, the proposal for a regulation on nature restoration (COM(2022) 304) may be quoted, which contains the following headings: 1. Reasons for and objectives of the proposal; 2. Consistency with existing policy provisions in the policy area; 3. Consistency with other Union policies; 4. Legal basis; 5. Subsidiarity; 6. Proportionality; 7. Choice of the instrument; 8. Expert evaluations/fitness checks of existing legislation; 9. Stakeholder consultation; 10. Inception impact assessment; 11. Public consultation; 12. Stakeholder workshops; 13. Collection and use of expertise; 14. Impact assessment; 15. Regulatory fitness and simplification; 16. Fundamental rights; 17. Budgetary implications; 18. Implementation plans and monitoring evaluation and reporting arrangements; 19. Detailed explanation of the specific provisions of the proposal.

the proposal, is made available to the public in the form of an official COM document; in order to avoid lengthy translations, numerous details are put into a SEC (Secretariat) or SWD (Staff Working Document) document, which is normally also publicly available. The text of the proposed act is drafted in all official languages, while the explanatory memorandum is usually produced in only English, French and German.

(ii) European Parliament, EECOSOC and Committee of the Regions

The Commission's proposal is transmitted to the European Parliament and the Council, which passes the text on to the European Economic and Social Committee and the Committee of the Regions. The Parliament adopts a legislative resolution with textual amendments, the Committees give opinions on the text. These comments are prepared within sub-committees, under the responsibility of a rapporteur for the proposal, who is selected from the Committee's members. Commission officials attend committee meetings, answer questions and explain reasons for the options taken. Their position is marked by the necessity to 'defend', if possible, the Commission's proposal. 2-57

There is no standard practice for how the parliamentary rapporteurs assemble the necessary know-how to prepare their report and the draft opinion. Both are mostly prepared by means of informal contacts with persons or groups which are politically or professionally close to the rapporteur's political party or group; formal written consultation with groups or public hearings in the Parliament are exceptional and almost never take place in the other two bodies.

In Parliament, the Environmental Committee votes on the draft opinion and all amendments which were presented by members of the Committee. Other committees also deal with the proposal, according to their responsibilities. Thus, for example, the Commission's proposal for a directive on environmental liability was discussed in the Committee on Legal Affairs and Internal Market as the leading committee, the Environmental Committee, the Industry Committee, the Economic Affairs Committee and the Petitions Committee. All these committees may request amendments of the proposed text. The text which has been adapted by the leading committee then goes to Parliament's plenary, where again amendments to the draft opinion may be tabled. The opinion is voted upon and, after adoption, is published in the Official Journal. The committees' reports are published on the Internet.

Since 1979, when the European Parliament became elected by general elections, there has been agreement between the Commission and the Parliament that the Commission would take on board amendments suggested by the Parliament wherever possible. Obviously, such a vague clause, which raises difficulties in practice, does not satisfy Parliament, which is of the opinion that, as it is an elected body, all amendments to proposals should be accepted by the Commission. It sometimes uses procedural means (delays or refusals to vote, extensive discussions between the rapporteur and the Commission's services, or between the president of the Environmental Committee and the Commissioner for Environmental Issues) in order to compel the Commission to accept its amendments. The procedure in the Economic and Social Committee and the Committee of the Regions is similar; their adopted opinions, which generally do not contain precise drafting proposals, are also published in the Official Journal. 2-58

(iii) Procedure in the Council

2-59 At Council level, the Commission's proposal is first examined by a working group, which normally undertakes its work without having the opinion of the other institutions. The frequency of meetings depends on whether the presidency wishes to advance the proposal;[210] whereas some proposals are immediately taken up, others might wait for years or not be discussed at all. The working party starts with a general discussion and then passes through each individual article. After having revised the proposal and listed all the objections to its different provisions in detail, the working group's chair sends the text to the Committee of Permanent Representatives (COREPER). He may also do so when he wishes to receive political instruction on questions which the working group feels unable to solve. The report sent to COREPER contains the new text proposal, accompanied by remarks, reservations, suggested compromise solutions or declarations by Member States.

COREPER meets once a week and deals with practically all questions of EU policy. In environmental matters, COREPER tries to concentrate discussions on Commission proposals in one or two meetings which take place in preparation of Council meetings on environmental matters. After discussion of the environmental proposal as it emerged from the working group, the text is either sent back to the working group with further instructions or – where an agreement by the Council seems possible – it is sent to the Environmental Council for decision or for political guidance on basic issues. COREPER prepares the Council agenda, though the final decision on it is made by the presidency of the Council.

2-60 The Council may only take a decision where the opinions of the other institutions, in particular that of the European Parliament, have been given; and in all cases, the Council must decide unanimously where it amends a Commission proposal (Article 293 TFEU), though the Commission, wanting its proposal to be adopted, hardly ever refuses to agree to amendments in environmental matters. The Council's decision in environmental matters consists in the adoption of the Commission's proposal, where the Parliament has only a consultative function – mainly Article 192(2) TFEU in environmental matters and Article 43 TFEU in agricultural-environmental matters – or where Parliament has either not proposed amendments or the Council adopts all amendments proposed by the European Parliament.[211] In other environmental cases, the Council establishes its 'position'.[212]

Subsequently, the Council's position is submitted to the European Parliament for a second reading. If Parliament agrees to that position or does not reach a decision, the Council's position is formally adopted as the legislative act; if Parliament rejects the Council's position with an absolute majority, the proposal is rejected. If the Council agrees to all amendments

[210] As examples, Directive 96/59 on PCB/PCT (n 168) took eight years between the Commission's proposal and the adoption by the Council; in contrast, the proposal for Directive 96/61 on integrated prevention and pollution control, which now, after several amendments, has become Directive 2010/75 (n 23), was adopted within two years. The proposal which later became Directive 2016/2284 on air pollution was discussed in 24 working group meetings of the Council, 13 COREPER and four ministerial meetings, see CJEU Case C-128/17 *Poland v European Parliament and Council* ECLI:EU:C:2019:194, para 14.

[211] Art 294(4) TFEU.

[212] Art 294 TFEU uses the term 'position'. Before the entry into force of the Lisbon Treaty, this Council's position was called the 'common position', and this terminology continues to be frequently used.

which Parliament has proposed in the second reading, the legal act is so adopted. In practice, as mentioned in paragraph 2-22, the Parliament only very exceptionally succeeds in substantially changing the Council's position.

Where, after the second reading, divergences continue to exist, a Conciliation Committee is convened, which consists of 27 members of the Council and the same number of members from Parliament; the Commission participates, but is not a member as such. Also, the Commission is no longer to defend its own proposal, but has the obligation to try to find a compromise between the European Parliament and the Council. Where a compromise is reached, that compromise becomes the adopted legal act. Where no compromise is reached, the proposal is considered rejected. Details of this co-decision procedure, which has been the normal procedure in environmental matters since 1999, are laid down in Article 294 TFEU.

The co-decision procedure is complicated and can hardly be called a legislative procedure in which citizens have much input. It is marked by the effort to place more influence on the legislative procedure with the European Parliament, the only elected EU institution, without significantly reducing the decision-making power of Member States who meet in the Council. 2-61

In order to shorten the legislative procedure, the Council, the European Parliament and the Commission meet more and more frequently – the European Parliament estimated in about 70 per cent of all cases – in so-called 'trilogue' meetings. In such cases, normally only the Parliament's rapporteur and the shadow rapporteurs of the other political parties represent the Parliament.[213] The discussions during the trilogue meetings are not public. A compromise text is looked for concerning each of the Commission's provisions, Parliament's amendments and Member States' positions. Where a compromise text emerges from such meetings, before Parliament has given its opinion on a Commission proposal, the plenary of the Parliament will never discuss this proposal, but only the compromise text which emerges from the trilogue meeting and to which its representatives have already agreed. This procedure is not in compliance with Article 294 TFEU.[214]

The procedure of Article 294 TFEU is the normal procedure for decisions in environmental matters, as follows from Article 192(1) TFEU. However, since Article 11 TFEU requires that environmental requirements are taken into consideration when measures in other policy sectors are adopted, measures which aim at protecting or improving the environment need not necessarily be based on Article 192(1) TFEU. Rather, Article 192(2) or Article 191(4) for international environmental matters, Article 43 for agricultural matters, Article 90 on transport, Article 113 on taxation, Article 114 on the internal market, Article 207 on commercial matters or Article 188 TFEU on research may also be applicable.

Under Article 290 TFEU, the Commission may be empowered in a Union act to adopt non-legislative delegated acts 'to supplement or amend certain non-essential elements'. This delegation is, in environmental matters, normally linked to the condition that neither the European Parliament nor the Council objected within a fixed period.

Under Article 291(2) TFEU, the Commission may be empowered by a binding Union act to adopt uniform conditions for implementing that Union act. The initiative for such an

[213] Rule 70 of the Rules of Procedure of the European Parliament.

[214] See also General Court Case T-540/15 (n 40).

act lies with the Commission. Its proposal for an environmental implementation measure is submitted to a committee composed of Member States' representatives for examination.[215]

B. The Choice of the Legal Basis

(i) General Principles

2-62 The choice of a legal basis of a legislative act is of importance, as the decision-making procedure, and in particular the European Parliament's right to participate in the making of the decision, is different under different Treaty provisions. Furthermore, the rights of Member States to adopt legislation at national level after the adoption of the EU legislative measure vary.

The Council favours Article 192 TFEU in environmental matters, but does not hesitate, according to circumstances, to choose a double legal basis[216] or to take another legal basis than Article 192, in particular Article 114, 90 or 43 TFEU. Sometimes, such a decision also seems to be influenced by political considerations.

The CJEU stated at several occasions that the choice of the legal basis for an EU measure is not left at the discretion of the EU institutions, but has to be based on objective criteria, in particular the stated objective and the content of the measure.[217] Furthermore, the Court is of the opinion that where a measure pursues two objectives at the same time, which have exactly the same weight in a given context, preference has to be given to the legal basis that ensures greater participation of the European Parliament.

A situation that two policy objectives have exactly the same weight seems to be very exceptional. The relevant decision in this regard[218] was taken at a time when the European Parliament had greater participation rights under Article 114 TFEU (co-decision rights according to Article 294 TFEU) than under Article 192 TFEU (at that time, the co-operation procedure under Article 252 EC). These differences no longer exist. It seems impossible to base a legislative environmental act on both Articles 192 and 114 TFEU, as the residual powers of Member States under Articles 193 and 114(4–9) TFEU are different and a double legal basis would create considerable legal uncertainty. Consequently, and quite rightly, neither the Commission nor the Council has ever tried to base a legislative act on Articles 192 and 114 TFEU jointly.[219]

[215] See also para 2-32.

[216] See, eg Decision 94/800 on adhering to the Uruguay agreements (WTO provisions) [1994] OJ L336/1,which was based on (old) Arts 43, 54, 57, 66, 75, 84, 99, 100, 100a, 113, 235 EC Treaty; Decision 98/487 on an agreement with the United States on humane trapping methods for animals [1998] OJ L219/24, which was based on (old) Arts 113 and 100a EC Treaty. For a more recent example, see Decision 2017/37 on the signing of a trade agreement (CETA) with Canada [2027] OJ L11/1, which was based on Arts 43,91,100, 153, 192 and 207 TFEU.

[217] Case C-155/91 (n 45); Case C-187/93 *European Parliament v Council* ECLI:EU:C:1994:265; Joined Cases C-164/97 and C-165/97 *European Parliament v Council* ECLI:EU:C:1999:99.

[218] CJEU Case C-300/89 *Commission v Council* ECLI:EU:C:1991:244.

[219] See as an example Directive 2000/53 on end-of-life vehicles (n 122), which also contained a ban of certain substances in cars; this directive was based on Art 175 EC; however, see also Directive 2012/19 on waste electrical and electronic equipment [2012] OJ L197/38 and Directive 2002/95 [2003] OJ L37/19, which limited the use of certain substances in electrical and electronic equipment. While Directive 2012/19 was based on Art 192 TFEU, Directive 2002/95 was based on the present Art 114 TFEU.

However, in Case C-178/03, the CJEU stated that Regulation 304/2003 on the export and import of dangerous chemicals had to be based on the double legal basis of Articles 133 and 175 EC Treaty (now Articles 207 and 192 TFEU).[220] It considered, without further discussion, that the co-decision procedure of Article 251 EC Treaty (now Article 294 TFEU) should apply, though this procedure was foreseen in Article 175, but not in Article 133 EC Treaty. The Court did not discuss the question of Member States' residual rights; this is problematic, as Article 192 TFEU is followed by Article 193 TFEU, which gives Member States the right to maintain or introduce more stringent environment legislation, whereas Article 207 TFEU is not accompanied by any corresponding provision.

May a Member State, based on Article 193 TFEU, thus ban the export of a chemical, the export of which was not banned by the Union? It will be interesting to see how this dilemma is finally solved. I plead for an application of Article 193 TFEU in such a case, as this would strengthen environmental legislation. The solution which would better correspond to the structure of the Treaty, though, would have been to have opted for Article 207 TFEU as the only legal basis; indeed, Regulation 304/2003, which has now been replaced by Regulation 649/2012,[221] is a product-related measure and it makes more sense to use, for such product-related provisions, Articles 114 (internal market) and 207 (international trade) TFEU.[222]

Another option was chosen by Regulation 842/2006 on certain fluorinated greenhouse gases:[223] the Regulation was based on the EC Treaty 'and in particular, Article 175(1) thereof and Article 95 thereof in relation to Articles 7, 8 and 9 of this Regulation'. Thus, within one and the same legislative act, different legal provisions apply. This might help to a certain extent; however, provisions are also to be interpreted in their systematic content, which may require subtle ponderations about whether a Member State may deviate from the act's provision or not. It appears doubtful whether this differentiation will increase legal certainty. Such a twin legal basis was most recently used in 2023 for batteries.[224]

Where two or more objectives of an environmental measure have a different emphasis, 2-63
the CJEU applies the theory of the 'centre of gravity': it looks at the legislative measure as a whole, as well as at its different provisions. Where the measure primarily aims at the protection of the environment, Article 192 TFEU applies; where the main emphasis is placed on ensuring the free movement of goods, Article 114 TFEU is the appropriate legal basis, even in cases where the measure also aims, secondarily, at the protection of the environment.[225] Similar reasoning is applied when other Treaty provisions, such as Article 43 or 207, are considered against Article 192 TFEU.

[220] CJEU Case C-178/03 *Commission v Council* ECLI:EU:C:2006:4.

[221] Regulation 649/2012 (n 79).

[222] See also CJEU Case C-288/08 *Kemikalieinspektionen* ECLI:EU:C:2009:718, where the Court decided that a national ban on mercury exports was not compatible with EU secondary law. In my opinion, the Court wrongly interpreted EU law against the interests of the environment.

[223] Regulation 842/2006 on certain fluorinated greenhouse gases [2006] OJ L161/1.

[224] See Regulation 2023/1542 on batteries and waste batteries [2023] OJ L1191/1, which was based on Art 114 TFEU, except the chapter on the management of waste batteries, which was based on Art 192(1) TFEU. See also Regulation 517/2014 on fluorinated greenhouse gases [2014] OJ L150/195, which replaced Regulation 842/2006 and was based on Art 192 TFEU alone.

[225] CJEU Joined Cases C-164 and C-165/97 (n 217) para 14.

The Court summarised its jurisprudence as follows:[226]

> [I]t is necessary, in order to determine the appropriate legal basis, to consider whether the measures in question relate principally to a particular field of actions, having only incidental effects on other policies, or whether both aspects are equally essential. If the first hypothesis is correct, recourse to a single legal basis is sufficient … if the second is correct, it is insufficient and the institution is required to adopt the measure on the basis of both the provisions from which its competence derives … However, no such dual basis is possible, where the procedures laid down for each legal basis are incompatible with each other.

2-64 This theory seems to give good results in most cases. However, its concept raises a number of problems. Whether the main objective of a directive or a regulation is the protection of the environment or the achievement of the internal market and the free flow of goods is not at all clear. It is worth mentioning in this regard that the basic Directive on emission standards for cars was adopted as part of the EU programme to eliminate technical barriers to trade, ie with the objective of establishing a common market for cars.[227] The fact that a Member State presses for more stringent environmental standards for cars does not detract from the fact that the EU provision is primarily designed to maintain the free circulation of goods and to lay down stringent environmental standards to prevent a disturbance of the internal market. However, it may equally be the objective of an EU provision to take on board the motives of the environmentally conscious Member State and improve the quality of the environment. These reasons for an EU provision may be supplemented by others, such as protection of consumers, protection of the national or European motor industry, the attempt to restrict imports from third countries, or economic, transport or commercial policy reasons.

The introduction of EU car emission standards, which required the introduction of catalytic converters, was motivated by increased air pollution. This was the reason stated in the directives, which were partly an amendment of Directive 70/220 and partly independent directives;[228] mention was also made of internal market considerations – though in a very accessory way. Yet, all those directives were based on the present Article 114 TFEU.

2-65 Directive 91/173 on restrictions of the use of pentachlorophenol (PCP),[229] based on the present Article 114 TFEU, was constructed in a similar way: the Commission was notified by Germany of restrictions on the use of PCP. On its proposal, the Council adopted Directive 91/173, which severely restricted the use of PCP in the European Union, the directive stating that the main objective was to reduce the environmental and human health risk of PCP. Directive 2006/66 limited the content of dangerous substances in batteries and accumulators.[230] Its primary objective, as it appears in both the preamble and the text, was the reduction of dangerous substances in the environment; it was based on the present Article 192 TFEU, with the exception of Articles 4, 6 and 21, which were based on the present Article 114 TFEU. The Directive concerning the reduction of lead in petrol

[226] ibid.

[227] Directive 70/220 [1970] OJ L76/1. In contrast, Regulation 443/2009 on emission standards for CO_2 from cars [2009] OJ L140/1 was based on the present Art 192 TFEU.

[228] Directive 88/76 [1988] OJ L36/1; Directive 89/458 [1989] OJ L226/1; Directive 91/441 [1991] OJ L242/1; Directive 94/12 [1994] OJ L100/42.

[229] Directive 91/173 [1991] OJ L85/34.

[230] Directive 2006/66 (n 122).

and sulphur in diesel[231] was based on the present Article 114 TFEU, the Directive on the reduction of sulphur in diesel alone on the present Article 192 TFEU.[232] The restriction and ban of ozone-depleting substances was based on Article 192 TFEU,[233] though the regulation expressly stated that its main objective was the need to reduce the environmental and human health risks.

If one were taking the theory of the 'centre of gravity' seriously, all these directives would have had to be based on Article 192 TFEU alone, since their primary objective, as indicated in their recitals and as it appeared from their objective and content, was the protection of the environment. In particular, where a substance or a product is banned or its use restricted, it is almost never the case that the primary objective will be the functioning of the internal market.

The theory of the centre of gravity of a specific measure is not as clear as it might appear. 2-66
A good example is Case C-300/89,[234] relating to Directive 89/428 on the harmonisation of programmes for the reduction of waste from the titanium dioxide industry,[235] where both the Council and the Commission agents based their arguments before the CJEU on the primary objective of Directive 89/428. However, while the Commission agent saw the primary objective of the directive to be the creation of equal competitive conditions for the titanium dioxide industry and thus wanted to have the present Article 114 established as the correct legal basis, the Council agent saw as its primary objective the protection of the environment, and pleaded for the present Article 192 as the appropriate legal basis. The Court, in that specific case, did not concur with that theory at all, and decided, for other reasons, in favour of Article 114. Also, in Case C-178/03, the Commission, Council and Parliament disagreed on the centre of gravity of Regulation 304/2003; in that case, the Court decided that the double legal basis of Articles 133 and 175 EC Treaty – now Articles 192 and 207 TFEU – was the correct basis.[236]

The conclusion from all this is that the wording of the preamble and the articles of a 2-67
legal act cannot be decisive on their own, particularly as it is an EU institution – namely, the Council – which determines the wording of a legislative act in cases of a common decision together with the European Parliament. Recitals are normally adopted without much discussion. However, the Council is also obliged to respect the provisions of the Treaty; it cannot turn away from it just by arranging the wording of a legislative measure.

The relevant criterion must therefore be whether – independent from the wording of the measure – uniformity is necessary to achieve the Treaty's objective. Indeed, as follows from Article 26 TFEU, the European Union has the objective of achieving the free movement of goods and services as quickly as possible. This objective requires uniform rules. For this reason, EU instruments laying down common product standards must come under Article 114 TFEU. This provision also applies when the measure contains common provisions of a restrictive nature, such as bans, restrictions on use or maximum concentration levels. If such measures were based on Article 192 TFEU, the effect arising from

[231] Directive 98/70 [1998] OJ L350/58.
[232] Directive 1999/32 [1999] OJ L121/13.
[233] Regulation 1005/2009 (n 74).
[234] CJEU Case C-300/89 (n 218).
[235] Directive 89/428 [1989] OJ L201/56.
[236] CJEU Case C-178/03 (n 220).

Article 193 TFEU would be that the Union's objective of achieving free circulation of goods or, more generally, of completing the internal market would never be attained. The legal basis of a measure which affects the environment *and* the circulation of goods should therefore be chosen with a view to permitting achievement of both objectives, namely completion of the internal market (Article 26 TFEU) and improvement of the quality of the environment (Article 192 TFEU). The better provision for both these objectives is Article 114 and, for international measures, Article 207 TFEU. Since Article 11 TFEU requires that environmental requirements must be integrated into other EU policies, the choice of this legal basis is not really a risk for the environment.

The Council seems, at present, to apply Article 192 as a basis for harmonisation of product-related measures in cases where it does not wish to proceed to total harmonisation under Article 114. This approach neglects Article 26 TFEU, which expressly requires measures that lead to the achievement of the internal market. Article 26 TFEU is so clear and unambiguous that there is no room for having product-related measures adopted under Article 192 TFEU. Article 26 TFEU and, more generally, the whole Treaty are also binding on the Council. It should also be noted that Article 114 TFEU also allows the adoption of legislative acts which allow Member States to adopt or maintain more stringent protection measures; a recent example is Directive 2010/63.[237]

In conclusion, therefore, all product-related measures should, under the present TFEU, be based on Article 114 TFEU, with the exception of Article 43, which is *lex specialis* to Article 114, as appears from Article 38(2) TFEU.[238] For international product-related measures, Article 207 TFEU would be the appropriate legal basis.

(ii) Nature Protection

2-68 Nature conservation measures are a specific problem. Fauna and flora species are not products under the TFEU, as is obvious from Article 36 TFEU: if they were to be treated as products, their mentioning in Article 36, which constitutes an exception to Article 34 TFEU, would not be justified. It also appears from Article 114(4) TFEU that measures for the protection of the health and life of animals and plants are different from product-related measures: under certain conditions, Member States may take such measures, while they are not allowed to do so in order to protect products.

The Council has therefore quite rightly based nature protection measures on Article 192(1),[239] including provisions on trade in endangered species. Exceptions are Regulation 3254/91 on the ban of leg-hold traps and the import of certain furs from specified non-EU countries, which the Council based on the present Articles 192(1) and 207 TFEU jointly,[240] and Regulation 1007/2009, which introduced a ban on trade in seal products and was based on the present Article 114 TFEU.[241]

Measures on biotechnology also belong to nature conservation measures. Genetically modified organisms (GMOs) as well as genetically modified micro-organisms remain

[237] Directive 2010/63 on the protection of animals used for scientific purposes [2010] OJ L276/33.

[238] Art 38(2) TFEU: 'Save as otherwise provided in Articles 39 to 44, the rules laid down for the establishment and functioning of the internal market shall apply to agricultural products.'

[239] Prior to 1987, the Council had used Art 308 EC Treaty as the legal basis.

[240] Regulation 3254/91 [1991] OJ L308/1; see also para 5-34ff.

[241] Regulation 1007/2009 on trade in seal products [2009] OJ L286/36.

organisms (and micro-organisms), that is, living entities. The fact of basing the deliberate release of genetically modified organisms on Article 114[242] only indicates that the borderline between life and non-life has been lost. I would not find it shocking to have different provisions on biotechnology from one Member State to another, as the ethical and environmental opinions about this technology differ so widely within the Union. The situation is not fundamentally different from that of nuclear technology, waste incineration or the landing and take-off – the 'free circulation' – of the Concorde aeroplane, where each Member State decided whether or not it wanted to have this technology on its territory. In 2015, a directive allowed Member States to prohibit or restrict the cultivation of genetically modified organisms on their territory for reasons other than the protection of health or the environment; that directive was adopted on the basis of Article 114 TFEU, though it abandoned the idea of having uniform standards for the cultivation of GMOs.[243]

(iii) Waste

Another specific problem is the legal basis for waste measures. Wastes are physical objects, and as such are capable of being traded between Member States. International legislation has, in the last 30 years, differentiated between waste which is destined for recovery and waste which is destined for final disposal. The reason for this is that a buyer might have an interest in acquiring waste which has an economic value; by contrast, the owner of waste which is destined for disposal would normally be willing to pay for such a disposal, in order to get rid of the waste. 2-69

The CJEU decided that waste comes under the present Article 34 TFEU, whether it is recoverable or not.[244] The Court justified this decision by pointing out that waste was the subject of commercial transactions and that it was in practice impossible to differentiate between recoverable and non-recoverable waste. The Court added, however, that 'waste has a special characteristic. The accumulation of waste, even before it becomes a health hazard, constitutes a threat to the environment because of the limited capacity of each region or locality for receiving it.'

Although waste is a product, the Court held, in another judgment, that Directive 91/156[245] on waste was rightly based on Article 175 EC Treaty (now Article 192 TFEU).[246] In this judgment, the Court recurred to the theory of the 'centre of gravity', to the primary objective of the legislative act: it saw the directive as aiming primarily at the protection of the environment and only dealing in an ancillary way with aspects of the internal market. This choice of legal basis was further confirmed in Case C-187/93,[247] where the Court again recurred to the theory of 'centre of gravity' and held that Regulation 259/93 on the shipment of waste[248] was correctly based on the present Article 192 TFEU. 2-70

[242] Directive 2001/18 (n 128).

[243] Directive 2015/412 (n 161).

[244] CJEU Case C-2/90 *Commission v Belgium* ECLI:EU:C:1992:310: 'waste, whether recyclable or not, should be regarded as a product the movement of which must not in principle, pursuant to Article 30 EEC, be impeded'.

[245] Directive 91/156 on waste [1991] OJ L78/32.

[246] Case C-155/91 (n 45).

[247] CJEU Case C-187/93 *European Parliament v Council* ECLI:EU:C:1994:265.

[248] Regulation 259/93 [1993] OJ L30/1; this regulation was replaced by Regulation 1013/2006 (n 75).

The Council based directives on titanium dioxide waste[249] and on packaging and packaging waste[250] on Article 95 EC Treaty (now 114 TFEU). This approach seems to suggest that the Council considers Articles 192 and 114 as being equally capable of being used for product-related waste standards and that it chooses the legal basis according to the relative emphasis on free circulation or the protection of the environment as it is expressed in each directive. As mentioned, the Treaty provisions are not at the disposal of the Council and the obligation to complete the internal market as quickly as possible excludes having recurrence to Article 192 or 114 at the Council's discretion.

2-71 A closer look at Directive 94/62 illustrates the problem. Directive 94/62 is based on the present Article 114. Of the first 12 recitals, 10 deal with environmental objectives and two with environmental and internal market issues; not one recital deals exclusively with internal market issues. Article 1 indicates the objectives of the directive, stating as the first objective the protection of the environment.[251] Articles 9 and 10 provide for essential requirements which packaging has to comply with. Article 18 stipulates that packaging which satisfies the directive's provisions shall not be impeded from circulating within the European Union.

It is difficult to see how the main aim of this directive, according to its objective and content, could be the achievement of the internal market rather than the protection of the environment. All the Court's criteria plead for Article 192 TFEU as the legal basis.

2-72 Advocate-General Tesauro, in his Opinion on Case C-155/91,[252] held that waste directives concerning specific items of waste or waste from specific industrial sectors (such as batteries, packaging waste or waste from the titanium dioxide industry) should be based on Article 114 TFEU, since in such cases the competitive element of an act at EU level was dominant. In contrast, waste measures which tackle the problem of waste generally were to be based on Article 192 TFEU, since their primary objective was environmental protection.

It is not quite clear whether the CJEU implicitly adhered to that concept in Case C-155/91. The concept has the disadvantage that the impact of a 'general' directive or regulation on a specific sector of industry might be as great as the impact of a 'specific' directive: the borderline between general acts and specific acts is not at all clear, particularly if one remembers that, for instance, 'general' Directive 2008/98 is accompanied by Decision 2000/532, which contains a detailed list of wastes that come under that directive;[253] and that 'general' Regulation 1013/2006 on the shipment of waste contains a long list of waste, the shipment of which undergoes different control procedures or the export of which to third countries is banned.[254]

[249] Directive 89/428 (n 235).

[250] Directive 94/62 (n 113).

[251] ibid Art 1: '1. This directive aims to harmonise national measures concerning the management of packaging and packaging waste in order, on the one hand, to prevent and impact thereof on the environment of all Member States as well as of third countries or to reduce such impact, thus providing a high level of environmental protection, and, on the other hand, to ensure the functioning of the internal market and to avoid obstacles to trade and distortion and restriction of competition within the Community. 2. To this end this directive lays down measures aimed, as a first priority, at preventing the production of packaging waste and, as additional fundamental principles, at reusing packaging, at recycling and other forms of recovering packaging waste and, hence, at reducing the final disposal of such waste.'

[252] Case C-155/91 (n 45) Advocate Tesauro's Opinion, para 10.

[253] Decision 2000/532 (n 122). The decision was significantly amended by Decision 2014/955 [2014] OJ L370/44.

[254] Regulation 259/93 (n 248); see also para 10-36ff.

In conclusion, there is not yet a clear, convincing way to classify waste-related measures under either Article 192 or 114 TFEU. The Council favours Article 192, because of the existence of Article 193 and because that provision leads to less uniform EU legislation, leaving national administrations more leeway. The CJEU generally accepts this approach. It is to be expected that in future most waste legislation will be based on Article 192, also because the European Parliament no longer has more participation rights under Article 114 than under Article 192 and is thus unlikely to push for the application of Article 114.

(iv) Other Environmental Measures

Prior to the entry into force of the Lisbon Treaties, environmental-related energy measures were based on Article 192 TFEU. With the introduction of Article 194 TFEU, measures on renewable energies or energy saving are based on Article 194.[255] As Article 194 does not provide that Member States are allowed to adopt stricter environmental measures, a provision corresponding to Article 193 TFEU is often inserted in the individual directive or regulation.[256] 2-73

Standards for industrial installations, other production-related standards and environmental production standards concern air emissions or water discharges from installations, conditions for landfill sites and accident-prevention measures in industrial plants. Installations do not circulate freely within the Union, but the products produced in them do. Environmental standards for plants may have an impact on costs and affect the competitive position of a manufacturer. This is therefore relevant for the establishment and functioning of the internal market, which also includes competition that is free from distortion (Article 114(4)TFEU).[257] The risk of distortion of competition increases as environmental standards become more stringent, unless uniform provisions prevail throughout the Union. If the objectives 'completion of the internal market' and 'improvement of the quality of the environment' are to be attained simultaneously throughout the Union, provisions relating to production standards or to plants must be based on Article 114 TFEU.

The Council instead bases all production-related directives on Article 192 TFEU, and the Commission now follows the same line in its proposals. Underlying this decision is the concept that production standards within the Union should not, in principle, be harmonised, a decision which was taken implicitly when Directive 84/360 was substituted by Directive 96/61[258] and Directive 76/464 was repealed by Directive 2000/60.[259] The consequence is that the air or water emission standards vary from one steelworks to another, from one cement kiln to another or from one power plant to another within the European Union.

The present practice seems inconsistent. Different environmental standards for the production of goods will lead to different competitive situations; the more cost-intensive

[255] See, eg Directive 2010/31 on the energy performance of buildings [2010] OJ L153/13; Directive 2012/27 on energy efficiency (n 200).

[256] Directive 2010/31 (n 255), Art 1(3); Directive 2012/27 (n 200), Art 1(2).

[257] CJEU Case C-300/89 (n 218).

[258] Directive 96/61 [1996] OJ L257/26; this directive has since been replaced by Directive 2008/1 and then by Directive 2010/75 (n 23).

[259] Directive 2000/60 (n 156).

such standards are, the greater the competitive distortion becomes. It might be acceptable to have differences between one Member State and another of one or two per cent in the production costs, when the differences are due to different environmental standards. However, where such differences reach five, 10 or more per cent of the production costs,[260] these differences must be eliminated through the adoption of uniform standards, thus by measures based on Article 114. In other words, the dividing line between Articles 114 and 192 TFEU is not fixed once and for all: it is flexible, and the more stringent the environmental standards are – always bearing in mind the requirement of a high level of environmental protection – the more it is necessary to base the measure on Article 114.

2-74 Basing production-related environmental measures on Article 192 also bears the political risk that Member States who place low priority on environmental issues will inevitably try to ensure that standards fixed at EU level are low, arguing that Member States with a developed environmental policy could always, under Article 193, adopt more stringent protective measures. But a tendency towards lower EU environmental standards is bound to increase discrepancies within the Union and will thus be, from an environmental point of view, counterproductive. Indeed, even environmentally conscious Member States will be reluctant to adopt stricter measures, as this would lead to a competitive disadvantage of installations on their territory.[261] Finally, it should be mentioned that the debates at EU level on environmental standards such as air emissions or water discharges, or even on quality standards, never centre on the issue of how much pollution by the pollutant the environment can tolerate; the discussion instead focuses on the question of what standards can reasonably be imposed on the polluting industries or other polluters. This demonstrates that it is the competitive aspect – which comes under Article 114 TFEU – which is in question, not the protection of the environment – which comes under Article 192.

The Council's practice is in the meantime well established. The use of Article 192 is in Member States' and the affected industries' interests, though not necessarily in the interests of competition or the environment. However, as the environment has no voice, it cannot be expected that the present practice will change.

2-75 The Council's practice as to the choice of the legal basis might be summarised as follows:

1. Measures of a general nature are based on Article 192. Examples: access to information, environmental impact assessment, eco-audit, measures related to installations, environmental liability.
2. Nature conservation measures are all based on Article 192. Exceptions: bans on leghold trap and fur trade, Articles 192 and 207 TFEU; the ban on trade in seal products, Article 114.
3. Product measures are based on Article 114. Exceptions: authorisation for pesticides, Article 43; ozone-depleting substances, contained use of genetically modified micro-organisms, Article 192.
4. Water measures are all based on Article 192;
5. Air pollution measures are based on Article 192. Exceptions: emissions other than CO_2 emissions from cars and motorcycles, composition of petrol and gas, Article 114; emissions from aeroplanes, Article 90.

[260] In CJEU Case C-300/89 (n 218) these differences reached 20% of the production costs.

[261] Such a trend is already visible in the discussion on the introduction of a CO_2 tax at national level.

6. Product-related noise measures are based on Article 114. Exception: noise from aeroplanes, Article 90. Measures on measuring noise levels are based on Article 192.
7. Energy measures to fight climate change are based on Article 194.
8. Waste measures are based on Article 192. Exception: packaging and packaging waste, waste programmes from titanium dioxide industry, Article 114; batteries are based on Article 114, except the chapter on waste batteries, which is based on Article 192.

(v) Measures under Article 192(1) TFEU

Legal decisions – regulations, directives or decisions – under Article 192(1) are taken by the Council and Parliament jointly, according to the procedure in Article 294 TFEU. Consultation with the Economic and Social Committee and the Committee of the Regions is mandatory. When deciding, the Council and Parliament must be in possession of a proposal by the Commission. 2-76

Article 192(1) is completed by Article 192(5) TFEU, which was introduced in 1993. This provision has its origin in the idea, particularly stressed by the less wealthy Member States, that if the protection of the environment were in the general interests of the Union, then the Union should pay for such measures. The provision stipulates that the Council may, when it adopts a legislative measure, decide on either a temporary derogation for a specific Member State or a financial support from the European Union for that State. The following conditions must be fulfilled:

1. The EU measure must be adopted by a majority decision under Article 192(1) TFEU. This condition prevents a single Member State from vetoing the adoption of a Union measure until the Member State has obtained a temporary derogation or a financial assistance;
2. there must be a request from a Member State that costs are disproportionate. This condition leads to an examination of the request by the Council, ie by all other Member States, and the Commission; thus, trivial requests will more easily be detected; and
3. the costs must be deemed to be inappropriate for the public authorities. It is thus not the cost of the measure itself which will be examined, but rather the cost impact on public authorities; where these authorities have the possibility of charging private undertakings, and in particular where they can make the polluter pay, Article 192(5) TFEU is not applicable.

The Council decision, which needs a qualified majority, may consist of temporary derogations or financial support from the Cohesion Fund. The possibility of granting a temporary derogation to some Member States existed well before the Maastricht Treaty and was used in a number of cases. This provision demonstrates that non-compliance with environmental provisions brings an economic advantage to the non-complying Member State. 2-77

The financial support from the Cohesion Fund, which, under Article 192(5), is not limited to the Member States which are normally beneficiaries of the Cohesion Fund,[262] is not further specified. It may consist of a lump sum or regular payments over a longer period, or the financing of an investment programme.

[262] At present, and until 2027, Greece, Portugal, Estonia, Latvia, Lithuania, Poland, Czech Republic, Hungary, Slovakia, Slovenia, Cyprus, Malta, Romania, Bulgaria and Croatia.

Paragraph 5 is introduced by the words 'Without prejudice to the principle that the polluter should pay'. In view of this wording, it could well be argued that non-compliance with EU environmental legislation is a breach of the polluter-pays principle.

Until the end of 2022, Article 192(5) had not been applied even once by the Council.

(vi) Decisions on Programmes, Article 192(3)TFEU

2-78 Article 192(3) TFEU provides for co-decision majority procedures and also for the adoption of 'general action programmes setting out priority objectives to be attained'. The initiative for Article 192(3) lies with the Commission, which cannot legally be obliged to submit a proposal for a decision on an action *programme*.[263] An action programme may be limited to a specific sector of environmental policy; it need not cover the whole range of activities.[264]

(vii) Decisions under Article 192(2)TFEU

2-79 Article 192(2) provides for the adoption of some measures by unanimous decisions. The provision is an exception to Article 192(1) and must therefore be interpreted narrowly. The European Parliament, the Economic and Social Committee and the Committee of the Regions are only to be consulted; the Parliament has no right of deciding together with the Council.

Fiscal provisions. Provisions of a fiscal nature normally come under Article 113 TFEU, which expressly provides for unanimous decisions. Article 113 provides for harmonisation of fiscal legislation to the extent that it is necessary for the establishment and functioning of the internal market. Article 192(2) TFEU clarifies that fiscal measures are also permitted in order to achieve the objectives of environmental protection that are mentioned in Article 191(1) TFEU. Fiscal measures touch the core of national sovereignty. It is therefore understandable that Member States who did not accept majority decisions under Article 113 TFEU were not ready to accept such majority decisions for eco-taxes.

Since the provision only mentions the fiscal character of a measure, acts which provide for environmental charges, environmental fees or an environmental fund for covering damage of the environment do not come under Article 192(2) TFEU.[265] For a measure to come under Article 192(2), the fiscal content must be the primary objective of the EU measure. Environmental provisions on taxes which form an additional part of another set of rules that are not primarily of a fiscal nature may be the subject of majority decisions.[266] This was the reason for the Union to base its regulation on a carbon border adjustment mechanism on Article 192(1) TFEU; the mechanism is intended to increase the price of energy-intensive products at their importation into the Union, in order to compensate for the costs of the Union measures to fight climate change.[267]

[263] See also para 2-88.

[264] See, eg the proposal for a groundwater action programme [1996] OJ C355/178.

[265] P Pagh, *EU miljoeret*, 2nd edn (Copenhagen, 1996) 120; A Epiney, *Umweltrecht in der Europäischen Union*, 4th edn (Baden-Baden, 2019) 106.

[266] See, eg the tax provisions in the different directives on car emissions, para 4-65ff.

[267] Regulation 2023/956 [2023] OJ L130/52. The Regulation covers cement, electrical energy, fertilisers, iron and steel, aluminium and hydrogen.

Town and country planning and land use. The underlying concept of this provision is that Member States should themselves decide how they want to organise their territory. Therefore, measures for town and country planning and land use also have to be adopted unanimously. The provision in particular leaves infrastructural planning decisions to the autonomous decision of each Member State, since it gives to each state, via the unanimity requirement, a veto against EU planning decisions which affect its territory. It is consistent with this understanding that the provision of the TFEU which deals with planning measures for infrastructures also follows this approach: Article 172(2) TFEU concerns the planning of trans-European networks for transport, telecommunications and energy infrastructure; it provides for the elaboration of EU (non-binding) guidelines for such networks, which may be adopted only with the approval of the Member State concerned. However, the Union based its Directive 2014/89 on maritime planning on Articles 43, 100, 192(1) and 194 TFEU, apparently under the assumption that the provision of Article 192(2) TFEU only applied to terrestrial planning;[268] this appears incorrect. 2-80

Measures on environmental impact assessment for plans and programmes[269] do not concern town and country planning as such, but the way in which this planning is to be organised; such measures therefore come under Article 192(1).

The quantitative management of water resources or affecting, directly or indirectly, the availability of those resources. This provision was reformulated by the Treaty of Nice; the previous version of the Treaty only talked of 'management of water resources'. In Case C-96/98, the CJEU had, against the wording of the Treaty in all languages except Dutch and French, clarified that this older version only applied to the quantitative but not the qualitative management of water resources.[270] The Court based its interpretation on the objective of the provision, arguing that a measure concerning the quality of water would not affect the availability of the water resource. The Treaty of Nice followed this judgment. 2-81

Land use, with the exception of waste management. This provision was also reformulated by the Treaty of Nice. The earlier version had, as a supplementary exclusion, 'measures of general nature'. It is questionable whether this amendment changed the sense of the provision. 2-82

The objective of the exclusion is again to ensure that Member States keep responsibility if, where and in which dimensions they want to build, eg a new airport, a railway line, a port or another infrastructure project. This means, in practical terms, that, for instance, Directive 91/271 on urban waste water, which requests Member States to build waste-water treatment plants,[271] was rightly adopted not under Article 192(2), but under Article 192(1) TFEU: indeed, each Member State remains free to decide how many installations are to be built and where they are to be placed.

Whether Directives 2009/147[272] and 92/43[273] principally deal with 'land use' is doubtful. Indeed, both directives aim at the protection of species of fauna and flora, and provide for

[268] Directive 2014/89 establishing a framework for maritime spatial planning [2014] OJ L257/135, recital 17: 'If Member States apply terrestrial planning to coastal waters, this directive should not apply to those waters.'

[269] Directive 2001/42 (n 151).

[270] CJEU Case C-36/98, *Spain v Council* ECLI:EU:C:2001:64.

[271] Directive 91/271 (n 143).

[272] Directive 2009/147 on the conservation of wild birds [2010] OJ 20/7; this directive replaced Directive 79/409 on wild living birds [1979] OJ L103/1. Art 175(1) EC Treaty (now Art 192(1) TFEU) remained the legal basis.

[273] Directive 92/43 (n 17).

a number of measures in this regard. Directive 2009/147 asks Member States to designate a sufficient number of birds' habitats in order to allow for all those habitats together to form a 'coherent whole', and thus a European network of habitats. The individual decision of which habitat is to be designated is up to the Member States. Directive 92/43 requests Member States to establish lists of habitats which might form part of an EU-wide list of habitats. Again, the original choice is thus made by Member States, and specific provisions ensure that final, EU-wide designations of a habitat only occur with the agreement of the Member State in question. Furthermore, land use and changes thereof in designated habitats are not prohibited, though restrictive assessment criteria apply.

It follows from all this that habitat protection measures in both directives do not prohibit the land use in designated areas, and that the provisions for the balancing of interests in specific areas allow for a proportionate consideration of diverging interests. As the objective of both Directives is not the regulation of land or of habitats, but of fauna and flora protection, for which comprehensive provisions are made, the centre of gravity of both directives is not land use, but nature and biodiversity protection. Therefore, Article 192(1), not 192(2), TFEU is the correct legal basis.

2-83 *Energy matters*. Unanimous decisions are finally required for 'measures significantly affecting a Member State's choice between different energy sources and the general structure of its energy supply'. Measures which come under this provision are, for instance, measures which lead to the abandoning, for environmental reasons, of nuclear energy, or of lignite or coal that has too high a sulphur content. Also, an EU measure to ban the import of petrol from third countries and to rely primarily on nuclear energy throughout EU territory would need unanimity in the Council.

In contrast to this, the decisions to adhere to the United Nations Convention on Climate Change and to one of its protocols, the Paris Agreement,[274] were rightly based on Article 192(1), not 192(2), TFEU. Indeed, the Convention and the Paris Agreement neither impose specific measures which affect energy supply nor ask Member States to change their choice of energy sources. Finally, they do not impose the introduction of fiscal measures either, such as the introduction of an energy tax. What measures are taken at EU level in order to comply with the requirements of the Convention and the Agreement thus need to be decided by another measure, but this has not been prejudged by the decision to adhere to the Convention.

When the Union prepared for adherence to the Kyoto Protocol, a number of Member States were of the opinion that the Council decision would have to be based on Article 192(2), as the commitment to reduce greenhouse gas emissions by eight per cent from the 1990 figures by 2012 significantly affected their energy policy. Only when the environmental Commissioner threatened to submit this matter to the CJEU was the resistance abandoned and Article 192(1) accepted as the legal basis. As the reduction of eight per cent does not prescribe how it is to be achieved, there can be hardly any doubt that Article 192(1) was the correct legal basis for the Council decision.[275]

[274] Decision 94/69 to adhere to the Climate Change Convention [1994] OJ L33/11; Decision 2016/1841 to conclude the Paris Agreement [2016] OJ L282/1.
[275] Decision 2002/358 [2002] OJ L130/1.

In Case C-5/16, the CJEU was asked to decide whether Decision 2015/1814[276] had to be based on Article 192(1) or 192(2) TFEU.[277] The Court held that the aim and content of the measure in dispute were decisive, not its effects, as these were too uncertain. Article 192(1) was considered to be the correct legal basis.

While, in all cases concerning Article 192(2), the Council decides unanimously, it may decide in future to take majority decisions in this area. This provision is of a rather theoretical nature; indeed, it has existed in a different form[278] since 1987, but has not played any significant role: there has not been a single sector in which the Council has introduced majority decisions.

(viii) Decisions on International Co-operation (Article 191(4) TFEU)

Article 191(4) TFEU gives express competence to the Union to conclude international environmental agreements (conventions), which are then binding on the institutions of the Union and on Member States (Article 216(2) TFEU). Details are laid down in Article 218 TFEU. 2-84

Prior to the Lisbon Treaty, agreements were negotiated by the Commission. Article 218(3) TFEU now provides that the Council appoints a 'negotiator', which, if it is not the Commission, may be the Member State that holds the presidency of the Council. The Council may give, on the proposal of the Commission, but without the participation of the European Parliament, a negotiating mandate which is not published. During the negotiation period, the Commission continuously consults with a special Council committee composed of Member States' representatives. In practice, Member States also participate in the negotiation of environmental agreements at international level, since such agreements also come into the competence of Member States; in fact, during these negotiations, the influence of Member States – or at least some of them – is often greater than that of the Commission.

The question of whether decisions to adhere to an international environmental convention, agreement or protocol should be based on Article 191(4), 192(1) or even 207 TFEU was, for some time, answered differently by the Commission and the Council. While the Commission, following a Court judgment in Case C-268/94,[279] based its proposals on Article 191(4), the Council adopted the proposals on the basis of Article 192(1).[280] A clarification in this controversy was brought by Opinion 2/00 of the CJEU,[281] where the question at issue was on what basis the Council decision to adhere to the Protocol of Cartagena[282]

[276] Decision 2015/1814 concerning the establishment and operation of a market stability reserve for the Union greenhouse gas emission trading scheme [2015] OJ L264/1.

[277] CJEU Case C-5/16 *Poland v European Parliament and Council* ECLI:EU:C:2018:483.

[278] Between 1987 and 1993, all environmental measures under Art 192 TFEU had to be adopted unanimously.

[279] CJEU Case C-268/94 *Portugal v Council* ECLI:EU:C:1996:461; this case concerned the legal basis of Art 181 EC, which had the same wording as Art 174(4) EC Treaty (the present Art 191(4) TFEU).

[280] Decision 2002/628 [2002] OJ L201/48.

[281] CJEU Opinion 2/00 ECLI:EU:C:2001/664.

[282] Protocol on biosafety, specifically focusing on transboundary movement, of any living modified organism resulting from modern biotechnology that may have adverse effects on the conservation and sustainable use of biological diversity, setting out for consideration, in particular, appropriate procedures for advanced informed agreement [2002] OJ L201/50.

should be made. The Commission was of the opinion that Articles 207 and 191(4) TFEU constituted the appropriate legal basis, whereas the Council and Member States were in favour of Article 192(1) TFEU. The Court examined what the predominant purpose of the Protocol was and concluded that this was an environmental purpose. It excluded the application of Article 191(4) TFEU, as the Protocol did not merely establish 'arrangements for co-operation in environmental matters', but laid down precise substantive rules; this, it stated, required the Council decision to be based on Article 192(1) TFEU. In Case C-377/12, the Court held that an agreement with the Philippines on partnership and co-operation was to be based on Articles 207 and 209 TFEU alone, as transport, migration and environmental matters were only marginally touched upon in the agreement.[283]

As practically all international environmental agreements and the accessory protocols go beyond the fixing of arrangements for environmental co-operation, Article 191(4) TFEU may thus only be used in rather exceptional circumstances. Following the Opinion of the Court in Case 2/00, the Commission abandoned its idea to use, as a rule, Article 191(4) as a basis for decisions to adhere to international conventions.

(ix) Decisions Based on Other Treaty Provisions

2-85 As mentioned, EU acts affecting the environment may be based on Treaty provisions other than Articles 191 and 192 TFEU. This applies to those environmental provisions where the 'centre of gravity'[284] lies in a policy area other than environmental policy. The most relevant provisions are as follows.

Decisions in the agricultural sector (Article 43 TFEU). Article 43 provides that the Council, in working out and implementing the common agricultural policy, adopts legislation by a qualified majority. Numerous measures in agricultural policy affect air, soil, water, fauna, flora and the landscape. Examples include the use of fertilisers and pesticides, drainage and irrigation measures, land use, discharge of substances, animal waste, and the production and marketing of agricultural products. The objective of the rules adopted by virtue of Article 43 is the establishment of a common agricultural policy among Member States, which includes the production of uniform products and unified production and marketing conditions.

Since 1988, it has been accepted that measures under Article 43 may also protect human health.[285] Also in 1988, the CJEU had to decide on the relationship between Article 192 and Article 43, and concluded that the latter also included measures to protect the environment. The case concerned the ban on drift nets for fishing which the Council had established by Regulation 345/92.[286] Some fishermen contested the legality of that ban, arguing, amongst other things, that the regulations should also have been based on Article 192, which required, at that time, unanimous decisions. The Court held that Regulation 345/92's principal objective was the protection of living marine resources and that this was an

[283] CJEU Case C-377/12 *Commission v Council* ECLI:EU:C:2014:1903.

[284] See para 2-72.

[285] The landmark decision was CJEU Case 68/86 *United Kingdom v Council* ECLI:EU:C:1988:85. See also CJEU Case C-61/09 *Bad Dürkheim* ECLI:EU:C:2010:06, para 39: 'environmental protection, one of the essential objectives of the European Union, must be regarded as forming part of the common agricultural policy'.

[286] Regulation 345/92 [1992] OJ L42/15.

objective of the common fishery policy; thus, the appropriate legal basis was Article 43. According to the Court, the application of Article 192 was not necessary because environmental requirements had to be integrated into other policies anyway.[287]

As pesticides are authorised by Member States, their ban is also the competence of Member States, which might lead to different decisions within the Union. The active substances for pesticides are authorised by the EU;[288] their 'ban' is normally decided by the Commission, in the form of an implementing decision, not authorising a substance or not prolonging its authorisation. 2-86

Legal debate has taken place over which legal basis should apply to measures that protect forests against fire or against air pollution. The Council originally adopted such measures on the basis of Articles 37 and 308 EC Treaty,[289] as, in 1986, there were no environmental provisions in the Treaty. Amendments of 1989 were based on Articles 37 and 175 EC Treaty.[290] In 1997, the Council adopted further amendments, basing them exclusively on Article 37 EC Treaty.[291] However, the CJEU considered Article 175 (now Article 192 TFEU) to be the appropriate legal basis as it was of the opinion that the protection of forests against fire and atmospheric pollution was primarily an environmental measure and did not establish rules on the production and marketing of agricultural products.[292] This reasoning is all the more convincing if one considers that the Commission co-financed reforestation projects after fire damage under the Cohesion Fund – which may co-finance environmental, but not agricultural projects.[293]

Decisions in the transport sector. The common transport policy, Articles 90–100 TFEU, tries to set common conditions for transport within the Union and beyond; such conditions may have a very considerable impact on the environment. 2-87

Both Articles 91 and 100 TFEU now provide, as a rule, for majority decisions by virtue of Article 294 TFEU. For that reason, the most relevant question is whether Article 193 can be applied to measures adopted under Article 90; this question will be discussed below at paragraph 3-70ff.

Decisions regarding the internal market. Article 114 outlines the fulfilment of the objectives set out in Article 26 TFEU,[294] ie the progressive establishment of the internal market. Its wording clarifies that it can also be the legal basis for measures aiming at the protection of the environment. Indeed, finding the demarcation line between Articles 114 and 192 TFEU was one of the biggest legal problems of the past. The Amsterdam Treaty has brought the two provisions much closer to one another, so that only some differences continue to exist concerning the procedures and consequences of maintaining or introducing more stringent national environmental measures than those agreed at EU level. 2-88

[287] CJEU Case C-405/92 *Mondiet v Islais* ECLI:EU:C:1993:906.

[288] Regulation 1107/2009 concerning the placing of plant protection products on the market [2009] OJ L309/1. The Regulation was based on the present Arts 43, 114 and 168 TFEU.

[289] Regulation 3528/86 [1986] OJ L326/2.

[290] Regulation 1613/89 [1989] OJ L165/8.

[291] Regulation 307/97 [1997] OJ L51/9.

[292] CJEU Joined Cases C-164/97 and C-165/97 (n 217).

[293] See also Regulation 995/2010 laying down the obligations of operators who place timber and timber products on the market [2010] OJ L295/23, which was based on Art 192 TFEU.

[294] Art 26(2) TFEU: 'The internal market shall comprise an area without internal frontiers in which the free movement of goods, persons, services and capital is ensured in accordance with the provisions of the Treaties.'

The TFEU itself does not contain criteria for making a clear distinction between Articles 114 and 192. Article 114 wishes to achieve an internal market; Articles 191–93 are aimed at the protection of the environment at a high level; the provisions do not contain anything explicit that could be described as the 'free movement of goods'. On the contrary, Article 191 explicitly states that different measures are both possible and necessary to protect the environment at a high level.

As Article 114 is concerned with goods and services, provisions which affect trade in such goods and services should, as mentioned above, be allocated primarily to Article 114. Provisions which contribute to the attainment of one of the objectives specified in Article 191 should primarily be assigned to Article 192. As a consequence of the arguments on the choice of the legal basis given above, at paragraph 2-71ff the Council should have based the Regulation on ozone-depleting substances[295] and the Regulation on export and import of certain dangerous chemicals[296] on the present Article 114, since both deal with product standards.

2-89 *Decisions in the energy sector.* Decisions in the energy sector are now mostly taken on the basis of Article 194 TFEU, in particular as regards decisions on renewable sources of energy or on energy efficiency. Where climate-related energy decisions are taken, Article 192 seems to be preferred to Article 194. In order to tackle the EU-wide energy crisis of 2022, the Council – without participation of the European Parliament – adopted a regulation to accelerate the permitting of renewable energy installations.[297] The legal basis was Article 122 TFEU.

2-90 *Decisions on commercial matters (Article 207 TFEU).* Framework decisions in the area of commercial policy are taken by the European Parliament and the Council by a qualified majority (Article 207(2) TFEU). The Council alone decides, with a qualified majority, on the negotiation and conclusion of trade agreements with third countries or international organisations (Article 207(4) TFEU); the European Parliament does not participate. The provisions on commercial policy establish exclusive Community competence, which means that there is no longer Member States' commercial policy. In the past, however, the importance of Article 133 EC Treaty (the present Article 207 TFEU) for environmental issues was diminished as a result of differences about its meaning. Whereas the Commission considered Article 133 EC relevant for all commercial provisions and international agreements, the Council applied Article 133 EC only in those cases where the measure in question did not pursue any objective other than a commercial one. Thus, where a trade-related measure also aimed at the protection of the environment, Article 133 was, according to the Council, not relevant; other provisions applied instead, in particular Article 175. In practice, therefore, Article 207 TFEU is not applied to environmental matters, at least not without Article 192 TFEU being added.

The respective interpretations have been influenced by the fact that Article 133 EC Treaty (now Article 207 TFEU) gives exclusive competence to the Union (see Article 3(1e) TFEU), whereas, under Articles 191–93 TFEU, the competence is shared between the Union and Member States.

[295] Regulation 1005/2009 (n 74).

[296] Regulation 2455/92 [1992] OJ L251/13. This regulation was replaced by Regulation 649/2012 (n 79).

[297] Regulation 2022/2577 laying down a framework to accelerate the deployment of renewable energy [2022] OJ L335/36.

In recent times, the CJEU consistently applied its theory of 'centre of gravity' to the present Article 207 TFEU; for a long time, this had not been the case. Thus, in Case C-281/01,[298] the Court decided that Article 207 was the appropriate legal basis for the decision to conclude an agreement between the USA and the EC on the co-ordination of energy-efficient labelling requirements for office equipment. The Council had based its decision on the present Article 192.[299] The Court held that the 'predominant' objective of the agreement was to facilitate trade and therefore commercial policy promotion. In contrast to that, the Court decided that a decision to ratify the Cartagena Protocol on trade in genetically modified products would have to be based on the present Article 192,[300] as environmental considerations were predominant in this protocol. The Commission had argued in favour of the application of the present Article 207. 2-91

In view of these decisions, it is not likely that the Council practice will change quickly, especially as the Court had decided, as mentioned in paragraph 2-75, that, under certain conditions, the present Articles 207 and 192 TFEU could be the double legal basis, without discussing Member States' residual rights.[301]

Decisions on research matters. Article 188 TFEU provides that the European Parliament and the Council decide on research measures, such as the establishment of joint undertakings or any other structure for the execution of EU research, technological development and demonstration programmes, and on measures for the implementation of multi-annual research programmes. Multi-annual research framework programmes are adopted under Article 182 TFEU. 2-92

Thus, decisions on research and development programmes in the area of the environment are taken on the basis of Article 182. Article 192 does not apply since Article 179(3) TFEU has solved this potential conflict by stipulating that 'All Union activities under the Treaties in the area of research and technological development, including demonstration projects, shall be decided on and implemented in accordance with the provisions of this Title'.

(x) Decisions under the Provisions on Enhanced Co-operation

The Amsterdam Treaty had introduced a new form of decision-making, the so-called 'enhanced co-operation' procedure. This procedure, which was amended by the Treaty of Nice and the Lisbon Treaty, is laid down in both Article 20 TEU and Articles 326–34 TFEU. It is not limited to environmental matters. 2-93

The underlying rationale of the procedure is that some Member States might wish to advance more rapidly than the Union as a whole. Nothing currently prevents them from concluding a bilateral or multilateral international convention, which would then be governed by public international law and not constitute EU law – although, of course, such obligations would have to respect the Member States' obligations under the Treaty on European Union.

[298] CJEU Case C-281/01 *Commission v Council* ECLI:EU:C:2002:761.

[299] Decision 2001/469 [2001] OJ L172/1.

[300] CJEU Opinion 2/00 (n 281).

[301] See also Decision 2017/37 (n 216), where Art 192 and Art 207 TFEU, together with other provisions, were applied.

2-94 The flexibility provisions now offer a new possibility to those Member States that want to proceed more quickly: they may, under certain conditions[302] laid down in Article 20 TEU, make use of the institutions, procedures and mechanisms laid down by the Treaties.

For any such enhanced co-operation, the Member States in question need an express authorisation from the Council. The Council may only act on a proposal from the Commission, which has its own discretionary power to decide whether it wishes to submit a proposal to the Council or not.[303] The Council shall decide on the authorisation to co-operate by unanimity of those Member States which want to co-operate, after consultation with the European Parliament.

2-95 As regards the measure adopted under the enhanced co-operation procedure, all the relevant provisions of the Treaty apply. The question once so controversial under Article 293 EC Treaty (now repealed) – whether agreements adopted under that provision were part of EU law or were measures of public international law – is answered in the case of the flexibility procedure: they are EU law. Indeed, the Commission, which must make a proposal for an enhanced co-operation measure, has only the competence to propose measures that are mentioned in Article 288 TFEU, ie a regulation, directive or decision. As regards the enhanced co-operation procedure, the decision-making in the Council, the consultation of or the co-decision with the European Parliament, the transposition of the measure into national law, its monitoring by the Commission under Article 258 TFEU and the possible judicial control under Articles 19 TEU all follow EU law provisions. This leaves no room for the application of provisions of public international law. Article 20(4) TEU, however, provides that only the Member States which participate in the enhanced co-operation are bound by the measures adopted under that procedure, and that accession countries are not obliged to take them over when they accede to the Union.

2-96 In order to illustrate the impact of the flexibility provisions on the environment, the fictitious example of a directive on environmental standards for swimming pools may be given. Under Article 20(2) TEU, at least nine Member States could request the Commission to submit a proposal for such a directive. The Commission could then ask the Council to authorise the use of the 'institutions, procedures and mechanisms of the Treaty'. The Council would normally decide on this proposal by a qualified majority of the Member States which participate in the enhanced co-operation (Article 330 TFEU).

The procedure of substance has to be distinguished from the authorisation procedure. The Commission would make a proposal for a directive on water quality in swimming pools, following the institutional procedures of Article 192(1). The directive would be adopted by a qualified majority of those Member States that participate in the co-operation. If, later, another Member State would like to be party to the EU enhanced co-operation procedure, the provisions of Article 331 TFEU shall apply; the Council shall finally decide whether the conditions for such a participation are fulfilled.

Nothing would prevent the Commission, during its discussions in the Council on a proposal which was intended to cover all Member States, from submitting to the Council a proposal for authorising the enhanced co-operation procedure. Indeed, despite the

[302] See Art 329(1) TFEU: 'In the event of the Commission not submitting a proposal, it shall inform the Member States concerned of the reasons for not doing so.'

[303] Art 329 TFEU.

somewhat unclear wording of Article 329 TFEU,[304] the start of the procedure does not depend on the initiative of a majority of Member States. It is up to the Commission to ensure that the flexibility procedure does not put the coherence of the Union at risk.

Article 326 et seq TFEU do not provide for the elaboration of a proposal by Member States. Indeed, the reference to the Treaty provisions also has the consequence that the Council may only act upon a proposal from the Commission, as is also foreseen in Article 192(1). In particular, Article 293(1) TFEU provides that the Council may only unanimously amend a proposal from the Commission. This provision would be set aside if the Council could also decide upon a proposal from Member States. 2-97

In conclusion, co-operating Member States have the choice to either recur to forms of public international law or to establish, within the EU framework, EU law.

Since 1999, not a single case has occurred where, in environmental matters, a Member State asked for or suggested the application of the enhanced co-operation procedure. The chances of this situation changing in the future are small, though the enlargement of the Union might make general decision-making more difficult. Particular candidates for enhanced co-operation are provisions in the area of climate change. Politically, it is feared that a 'Europe at different speeds' would rather contribute to the disintegration of the Union as a whole.

[304] Art 329 TFEU: 'Member States which wish to establish enhanced cooperation between themselves … shall address a request to the Commission … The Commission may submit a proposal to the Council to that effect.'

3

Union Powers and Member State Powers

I. General Aspects on the Division of Competence in Environmental Matters

3-01 The objective of EU environmental policy and law is the preservation, protection and, overall, the improvement of the quality of the environment within the Union. This objective, however, is also that of Member States' environmental policy and law. The protection and preservation of the environment is a fundamental part of the general interests of the Union[1] and of Member States. Because it is in the general interest, the environment, like the non-commercial assets listed in Article 36 of the Treaty on the Functioning of the Union (TFEU), cannot be left unprotected: as long as the Union fails to take action on a given environmental issue, the Member States retain their powers to adopt provisions to protect and preserve the environment, provided that these measures are compatible with the general rules laid down in the EU Treaties. When the Union takes action, this by no means removes Member States' powers to take environmental measures, although such powers then no longer apply to the particular subject governed by EU legislation, insofar as this has been regulated.

Since the protection of the environment is in the general interests of the Union, the Union is 'competent',[2] ie responsible for taking legal provisions in order to protect it. In doing so, the European Union must, of course, take into consideration the principles which the Treaties provides for such action, in particular the subsidiarity principle.[3] According to Article 19 of the Treaty on European Union (TEU), it is the Court of Justice of the European Union (CJEU) which shall interpret EU law. Where an EU environmental legal rule conflicts with a national legal rule, EU law prevails, according to the established case law of the CJEU.[4] The reason for this is obvious: if the national legal rule prevailed, the EU legal provision would apply only in those Member States which had not taken legal measures at national level. Then, the EU legal rule would not be a rule which applied

[1] See CJEU Case C-240/83 *Procureur de la République v Assoc. de Défense de Brûleurs de Huiles Usagées* ECLI:EU:C:1985:59, para 13: 'environmental protection … is one of the Community's essential objectives'.

[2] The notion of 'competence' is used in Art 191(4) TFEU and, more generally, in Arts 3 and 4 TFEU.

[3] TEU, Art 4(a): 'competences not conferred upon the Union remain with the Member States'; Art 5(3): 'in areas which do not fall within its exclusive competence, the Union shall act only if and insofar as the objectives of the proposed action cannot be sufficiently achieved by the Member States, either at central level or regional and local level but can rather, by reason of the scale or effects of the proposed action, be better achieved at Union level'; Art 5(2): 'Under the principle of conferral, the Union shall act only within the limits of the competence conferred upon it.'

[4] CJEU Case 6/64 *Costa v ENEL* ECLI:EU:C:1964:66; Case 106/77 *Simmenthal* ECLI:EU:C:1978:49; Case C-213/89 *Factortame* ECLI: ECLI:EU:C:1990:257; 1991:50; Case C-493/17 *Weiss* ECLI:EU:C:2018:1000.

throughout the Union, but only in those parts of it where no national measures had been taken. Also, the EU measure could at any moment be reduced in its application by a subsequent national measure, which would create quite considerable legal uncertainty. Such legal uncertainty would also be created by differences over the question of whether or not the national measure really is applicable in a specific case or not. As the national law would mainly be interpreted by national courts, inevitable discrepancies would follow.

This understanding has been challenged by national constitutional courts. In particular, the German constitutional court argued that German constitutional law could not be interpreted by the CJEU on the basis of Article 19 TEU, but was the competence of the German constitutional court; this court could thus decide whether an EU provision was ultra vires, was contrary to German fundamental rights or was against the constitutional identity of Germany.[5] The Polish and Romanian constitutional courts argued in a similar way. This legal conflict cannot be solved, as the 'German identity' is laid in the German constitution and cannot even be changed by amendments of the constitution.

The conflict also had repercussions on environmental law. In Case C-121/21, Czechia brought a case against Poland under Article 259 TFEU, because the operation of a Polish lignite mine close to the Czech frontier led to land subsidence in Czechia and to the groundwater flowing into the mine, threatening the drinking water supply of some 10,000 people. Czechia asked, by interim measures, for the mine to be closed, which the CJEU ordered.[6] Poland refused to do so, arguing that this would be against the fundamental rights laid down in the Polish constitution, which prevailed over Union law. The CJEU then ordered Poland to pay €500,000 for each day of not complying with the closing order.[7] Poland refused the payments. Czechia finally got €45 million of compensation from Poland and withdrew its application.

The case illustrates well the consequences of diverging interpretations of EU law and the difficulties which arise when EU law does not prevail over national law.

In this author's opinion, EU law and policy cannot function in the same way as they did over the last 60 years unless, in the case of conflict, EU (environmental) law prevails over national law. From this, it follows that EU environmental law cannot be amended by subsequent national law. In other words, the rule *lex posterior derogat legem anteriorem* (the later legal provision prevails over the earlier provision) does not apply to the relationship between EU law and national law.

Both the Union and Member States are responsible, 'competent' or empowered to 3-02
take action on environmental issues. In view of the almost unlimited scope of the term 'environment' in the EU Treaties, this holds true for all environmental issues. Apart from the 'conservation of marine biological resources under the common fisheries policy' (Article 3 TFEU, exclusive Union competence), the Treaties assign no particular area of environmental legislation exclusively to the Union or exclusively to Member States. As can be seen from Article 193 TFEU, this similarly applies to subjects already covered by EU legislation. Consequently, the interrelationship between the Union's competence and that of the Member States is flexible, dynamic and complementary.

[5] German Bundesverfassungsgericht, judgment of 20 May 2020, 2 BvR 159/15.
[6] CJEU Case C-121/21R, *Czechia v Poland* ECLI:EU:C:2021:420.
[7] CJEU Case C-121/21R *Czechia v Poland* ECLI:EU:C:2021:752.

3-03 It follows from Article 5 TEU that EU environmental action is dependent on certain circumstances which have to be fulfilled. EU institutions themselves decide whether this is the case. In the case of dispute, the matter has to be decided by the CJEU, which has to ensure, under Article 19 TEU, that the provisions of the Treaty are respected.[8] The logical consequence of Article 5 TEU is that in cases where the Union has not taken action to protect, preserve or improve the quality of the environment, Member States are free to do so. Their competence to deal with environmental issues is unlimited. They can do whatever they wish in whatever form they wish to ensure environmental protection. Limitations to this right to protect – or not to protect – the environment stem from:

- Member States' own national rules, such as rules on local government and rules for regional responsibility in environmental matters;
- rules of international law, such as existing international agreements or other written or unwritten rules of international law; or
- rules of EU law.

The first two limitations are not dealt with in this book, which deals with EU law. As regards the third limitation, the EU Treaties themselves contain a number of provisions that limit the Member States' possibilities of action. These different limitations will be discussed below.

II. Member States' Measures in the Absence of EU Measures

A. National Environmental Measures that Affect Imports: Articles 34 and 36 TFEU

3-04 Article 34 TFEU provides that all 'quantitative restrictions on imports and all measures having equivalent effect shall be prohibited between Member States'; Article 35 TFEU mirrors this provision by stating that 'quantitative restrictions on exports, and all measures having equivalent effect, shall be prohibited between Member States'.

From these provisions, Article 36 TFEU makes an exception; this provision reads as follows:

> The provisions of Articles 34 and 35 shall not preclude prohibitions on imports, exports … justified on grounds of … the protection of health and life of humans, animals or plants … Such prohibitions or restrictions shall not, however, constitute a means of arbitrary discrimination or a disguised restriction on trade between Member States.

Article 36 TFEU thus does allow certain trade restrictions. The CJEU has declared, on a number of occasions, that Article 36 is an exception to the principle of Article 34 and

[8] Art 19 TEU: 'It [The Court of Justice of the European Union] shall ensure that in the interpretation and application of the Treaties the law is observed.'

must therefore be interpreted narrowly.[9] In particular, according to the established case law of the CJEU, the grounds for restricting trade by virtue of Article 36 constitute an exhaustive list and may not be extended.

The protection of the environment is not listed in Article 36 TFEU as a possible justification for restrictions to the free circulation of goods of Article 34. Therefore, only such national environmental measures that aim at the 'protection of health and life of humans, animals and plants' could be justified by Article 36. Such measures concern, for instance, provisions on banning or restricting the use of substances or products which are dangerous to health; measures to limit the presence of pollutants in drinking water or in the air; and measures to regulate the marketing of pesticides or biocides.

However, there are numerous environmental measures which cannot be considered 3-05
to protect the health and life of humans, animals or plants. Such measures include environmental labelling schemes, eco-management systems, environmental taxes and charges, measures to prevent the generation of waste, environmental impact assessment measures, deposit-and-return schemes, liability or information and education. For other measures, it is doubtful whether they can really be considered to protect health and life; such measures are, for instance, provisions to reduce the noise level of cars, the designation of fauna or flora habitats, emission limit values of installations and licensing procedures or measures to protect the ozone layer or to combat global warming.

The criterion that defines whether or not a measure aims at the protection of health or life is the relationship of the measure to health effects, ie its 'proximity' to health effects. Thus, the CJEU decided that the shipment of recoverable waste oils did not pose a threat to the life and health of humans that could justify the application of Article 36.[10]

Another example is the restriction on the use of chlorofluorocarbons (CFCs) and other ozone-depleting substances in order to protect the ozone layer. Damage to the ozone layer may increase skin cancer for humans and may have other health effects on humans, animals and plants. However, this possibility is remote and indirect. Therefore, national measures to restrict the use of ozone-depleting substances cannot really be justified on the basis of Article 36 TFEU. Likewise, the CJEU decided that the reduction of greenhouse gas emissions and the fight against climate change is an environmental problem, not a problem of human health.[11]

Fortunately enough, however, this problem of subsuming environmental measures 3-06
under Article 36 TFEU has lost its relevance. Indeed, the CJEU in 1979 adopted a landmark decision on Article 34.[12] The Court declared that, in the absence of EU legislation, a national non-discriminatory and proportional restriction on the free circulation of goods from other Member States had to be accepted to the extent that it was necessary to satisfy mandatory requirements such as the necessity for fiscal controls, fair trading practices and consumer protection, and added that there might be other mandatory requirements:

> [I]n the absence of common rules relating to the marketing of the products in question obstacles to free movement within the Community resulting from disparities between the national laws

[9] CJEU Case 29/72 *Marimex* ECLI:EU:C:1972:126; Case 113/80 *Commission v Ireland* ECLI:EU:C:1981:139; Case C-205/89 *Commission v Greece* ECLI:EU:C:1991:123.

[10] CJEU Case C-203/96 *Dusseldorp* ECLI:EU:C:1998:316, para 47.

[11] CJEU Joined Cases C-204/12 to C-208/12 *Essent* ECLI:EU:C:2014:2192.

[12] CJEU Case C-120/78 *Rewe v Bundesmonopolverwaltung* (*Cassis de Dijon*) ECLI:EU:C:1978:42.

> must be accepted insofar as such rules, applicable to domestic and imported products without distinction, may be recognised as being necessary in order to satisfy mandatory requirements recognised by Community law. Such rules must also be proportionate to the aim in view. If a Member State has a choice between various measures for achieving the same aim, it should choose the means which least restricts the free movement of goods.[13]

In 1988, the Court recognised that the protection of the environment was such a mandatory requirement which could justify restrictions on the free circulation of goods.[14] In this case, the Commission had attacked a Danish national measure which introduced a deposit-and-return system for drink containers. The Commission considered that the system could not be justified by Article 36 TFEU and that it was incompatible with Article 34. It was supported in its assessment by the Advocate General, but not by the CJEU.

3-07 As regards the application of Article 36, there was practically no dispute: it was not really possible to consider a deposit-and-return system as protecting the health or life of humans; Article 36 was therefore not discussed by the Court. Instead, the Court held that Denmark was entitled to introduce a deposit-and-return system, since such a system aimed at the protection of the environment, which was an objective of general Union interest. Denmark, according to the Court, was entitled to set up an efficient system of waste prevention and such a system required the introduction of a deposit-and-return scheme even though the practical circumstances might make it more difficult for non-Danish producers and traders to comply with the system.

The recognition of the protection of the environment as a mandatory requirement under Article 34 was confirmed in later Court judgments[15] without the Court sharply distinguishing between justification under Articles 36 (health grounds) and 34 (grounds to satisfy a mandatory requirement).[16] Thus, while national environmental measures may restrict the free circulation of goods on either of these grounds, the limits to such national measures follow from the Treaty provisions and from the limits drawn by the very detailed and sophisticated case law of the Court.

3-08 *Necessity*. The first problem is whether a Member State may adopt any trade-restricting measure to protect the environment which seems appropriate or whether it may only adopt measures which are 'necessary' or, in the Court's words, proportionate. The Court itself has contributed to this debate by not accepting, in Case 302/86, a Danish measure which obliged economic operators to use only authorised standardised containers. The Court stated:[17]

> It is undoubtedly true that the existing system for returning approved containers ensures a maximum rate of reuse and therefore a very considerable degree of protection of the environment.

[13] Wording from CJEU Case 302/86 *Commission v Denmark* ECLI:EU:C:1988:421.

[14] ibid.

[15] CJEU Case C-2/90 *Commission v Belgium* ECLI:EU:C:1992:431; Case C-131/93 *Commission v Germany* ECLI:EU:C:1992:315; Joined Cases C-204/12 to C-208/12 (n 11).

[16] See, eg CJEU Joined Cases C-204/12 to C-208/12 (n 11), paras 91 and 92: 'the use of renewable energy sources for the production of energy.is useful for the protection of the environment inasmuch as it contributes to the reduction in greenhouse gas emissions which are among the main causes of climate change that the EU and its Member States have pledged to combat … such an increase [in the use of renewable energy sources] is also designed to protect the health and life of humans, animals and plants, which are among the public interest grounds listed in Article 30 EC' [now Art 36 TFEU]. In the same sense, Case C-379/98 *PreussenElektra* ECLI:EU:C:2001:160, para 75.

[17] CJEU Case 302/86 (n 13) paras 20 and 21.

> Nevertheless, the system for returning non-approved containers is capable of protecting the environment.

This seems to indicate that the Court is of the opinion that a 'very considerable degree' of environmental protection is not necessary – or proportionate – and therefore not allowed; only a 'reasonable' degree of environmental protection – whatever that may be – is permitted. In other words, it is not a Member State which decides on the necessary degree of environmental protection, but EU law (as interpreted by the Court) which determines what is necessary (or proportionate). This proportionality is measured against the interest in free circulation of goods, as there is no other factor to consider.

The underlying principle of this approach is that EU law provides for the free circulation of goods, which is of paramount importance. Restrictions on the free circulation of goods are allowed only where they are necessary (proportionate); in other words, measures to protect the environment are possible where their importance is greater than that of the free circulation of goods. This leads to the conclusion that the free circulation of goods, in the event of any conflict with environmental (national) measures, will normally prevail, unless it can be proven that environmental interests are more relevant.

This conclusion, however, is not compatible with the division of competence for the protection of the environment. The protection of the environment is of general Union interest. It is expressly mentioned in Recital 9 and Article 3(3) TEU. Nothing indicates that it is less important than other objectives, in particular the free circulation of goods. On the contrary, the rule of Article 11 TFEU according to which environmental protection requirements must be integrated into the definition and implementation of all other policies is unique in the Treaties; nowhere in the Treaties is the same said of the free circulation of goods. Furthermore, Commission proposals in the area of the internal market must be based on a high level of environmental protection, and the European Parliament and the Council must try to achieve such a high level (Article 114(3) TFEU). This is the only provision in the TFEU which contains quality requirements for individual measures that are proposed by the Commission. Finally, Articles 114(4)–(8) and 193 TFEU allow Member States, once an EU measure has been taken, to maintain or introduce more protective environmental measures at national level. Article 114(5)–(8) applies only to environmental measures, not to all non-economic assets of Article 36, as is the case with Article 114(4) TFEU. 3-09

All these provisions clearly show the importance that the Treaties attach to the protection of the environment. In view of this importance, which has been growing continuously and achieved recognition in the different Treaty amendments of 1987, 1993, 1999 and 2003, it cannot be considered that only a reasonable degree of environmental protection is allowed to restrict the free circulation of goods. Rather, it is the Member States which decide on the amount of environmental protection which they wish to ensure.

There are two other arguments which plead against a limitation for environmental measures to 'reasonable' measures. First, Article 114(5)–(8) TFEU, which was introduced by the Amsterdam Treaty of 1997, outlined provisions for the Member States to introduce new environmental measures at national level once an EU harmonisation measure under Article 114(1) had been adopted. These measures are not limited to reasonable measures, as will be discussed below; rather, the criteria for the national measures are whether the measure constitutes an arbitrary discrimination or a disguised distortion of trade, or whether it hampers the functioning of the internal market. It is not consistent to ask for only reasonable 3-10 measures under Articles 34–36 where no EU measure exists, nor to ask for only reasonable measures under Article 114.

3-11 Second, the only instance which could decide what is proportionate is the CJEU – or, in the pre-litigation stage, the European Commission. But what criteria could be used, if there is no EU legislation? The EU Treaties give no clarification of what is reasonable or not.

To give a specific example: in the early 1990s, Denmark limited the noise level from electrical windmills that are used for energy production; the standards are stricter the closer the windmill is installed to residential areas. France protested against this measure, arguing that the sale and export of French windmills to Denmark would be hampered by the Danish measure. It seems obvious that nobody outside Denmark can really decide whether a noise level of 50 decibels is reasonable for the Danish environment and Danish citizens, or whether a noise level of 40 decibels is unreasonable. The environmental conditions are specific in each case. No element in the Treaty allows the establishment of EU criteria for such an assessment. As there is no EU legislation on windmills or on acceptable noise levels for citizens, EU law cannot decide what is reasonable or not in Denmark.

Similar reasons argue in favour of restrictions on the noise levels of pleasure boats to be allowed, which Sweden introduced in the early 1990s. In view of the thousands of lakes – independent of the endless miles of shoreline – with numerous small islands in Sweden, it would not be possible to allow the marketing of pleasure boats but to prohibit their use in all or in parts of Sweden if they exceed a certain noise level. Also, the level of permitted noise cannot, in the absence of EU provisions, be determined by a manufacturer or authorising body from another Member State – or by the Union. The Swedish problem was 'solved' by an EU directive of 1994, which fixed common noise levels for new boats but allowed Member States to adopt provisions concerning navigation on certain waters for the protection of the environment.[18]

3-12 Another example is the restriction on the use of Karlstad airport, which Sweden had banned for some noisy aeroplanes, although Directive 92/14[19] provided that these aeroplanes were allowed to be used until 2002. It is clear that not every aeroplane which circulates within the Union may use any airport that exists. Indeed, Member States implicitly regulate access to airports, for example by regulating the number and length of the runways, the size of the airports or the landing and take-off times. Where the neighbourhood is residential or is an ecologically valuable habitat, this may lead to the conclusion that specific aeroplanes may not use specific airports. The most obvious example is the supersonic aeroplane Concorde, which was not allowed to land at most EU airports. In the same way as it is possible to prohibit the use of certain roads by trucks – or, indeed, by cars generally – without impeding the free circulation of cars, it is possible to prohibit the use of certain airports by certain aeroplanes. It is not clear who else other than the Swedish authorities could determine whether the local environmental conditions at Karlstad make it

[18] Directive 94/25 relating to recreational craft [1994] OJ L164/15. That directive was replaced by Directive 2013/53 on recreational craft and personal watercraft [2013] OJ L354/90. Art 5 of this directive allows Member States to provide for restrictions, of navigation, in order to protect the environment, provided these restrictions are 'justified and proportionate'.

[19] Directive 92/14 on the limitation of the operation of aeroplanes covered by Part II, Chapter 2, Volume 1 of Annex 16 to the Convention on International Civil Aviation 2nd edn [1992] OJ L76/21. That Directive was repealed by Directive 2006/93 [2006] OJ L374/1.

necessary or not to restrict the landing or taking off of noisy aeroplanes at it. Directive 92/14 is not relevant, since aeroplanes which conform to that directive are allowed to use Swedish airports, except, perhaps, Karlstad airport.

The Commission based its decision against the Swedish restrictions at Karlstad airport not on Article 34 TFEU, but on secondary EU legislation, Regulation 2408/92 and Directive 92/14,[20] and decided that these provisions gave any air transport carrier a right to access any EU airport;[21] Sweden accepted this decision. If that secondary EU legislation indeed went so far (and I question this), the above-mentioned considerations, which start from the assumption that there is no EU legislation regulating this issue, are obsolete.

For restrictions in the free circulation of goods which affect human health and therefore come under Article 36 TFEU, the CJEU has already come to the same conclusion. In Case C-125/88,[22] the Court was faced with a Dutch measure concerning the use of a pesticide 'Improsol'; the question was whether such a national measure did not unduly restrict the free circulation of that pesticide, which was used in other Member States. The Court found that pesticides constituted 'significant risks to the health of humans and animals and to the environment', and then continued: 3-13

> It is therefore for the Member States, pursuant to Article 36 of the Treaty and in the absence of full harmonization in this matter, to decide at what level they wish to set the protection of the life and health of humans.

This judgment has been confirmed by several other judgments on pesticides and Member States' measures to restrict their use.

It is not really imaginable that the Member States themselves can set the degree of protection which they wish to ensure for measures to protect the environment which concern the health and life of humans, animals and plants (Article 36 TFEU) without respecting the proportionality requirement, whereas for measures to protect the environment which come under Article 34 TFEU, they are limited to proportionate measures.

The conclusion is that the freedom to set national environmental standards does not allow protectionist measures to be taken or measures to be taken which are not really necessary to protect the local, regional or national environment. These issues will be discussed below. It nevertheless remains that there are no specific, autonomous criteria for assessing whether national environmental measures are necessary (proportionate) or not. It is up to Member States to establish the degree of environmental protection at local, regional or national level which they consider appropriate. In this, however, Member States must take into consideration the state of science at international and EU level, such as the statements of the World Health Organization or the EU scientific committees; the greater the scientific certainty about the risk of a substance is, the more reduced is the discretion of the Member State. The attempts by the CJEU to limit this discretion by an extensive use of the proportionality principle are to be considered with caution. Indeed, the national legislature also has a large amount of discretion as to which measures to take in order to protect the environment and humans. The CJEU only can control the obvious exceeding of this discretion. 3-14

[20] Regulation 2408/92 [1992] OJ L240/8; Directive 92/14 (n 19).

[21] Commission, Decision 98/523 [1998] OJ L233/25.

[22] CJEU Case C-125/88 *Nijman* ECLI:EU:C:1989:401.

3-15 *Non-economic grounds.* The discretion of Member States is limited by the provisions of the Treaties. When establishing its jurisdiction on the mandatory requirements which justified, under Article 34 TFEU, a restriction on the free circulation of goods, the CJEU stated that such measures were not allowed to be discriminatory or disproportionate and had to be applied indistinctively to national and imported products. As can be seen, the two criteria of non-discrimination and proportionality are taken from Article 36(2) TFEU,[23] but apply both to measures which are examined under Article 36 and to measures assessed, under the *Cassis de Dijon* jurisdiction, under Article 34.

To these limits has to be added the proviso that Article 36 TFEU itself only refers to non-economic criteria, as can be concluded from Article 114;[24] this limitation also applies under Article 34 TFEU, as the CJEU has clarified: 'aims of a purely economic nature cannot justify barriers to the fundamental principle of the free movement of goods'. With this argument, the CJEU rejected an argument by the Dutch government that restrictions to the shipment of waste were necessary to enable a Dutch waste recovery installation to operate in a profitable manner with sufficient material at its disposal and to ensure it a sufficient supply of recoverable waste.[25]

3-16 *Discriminating measures.* A discrimination or, as Article 36(2) puts it, an arbitrary discrimination exists when goods from other Member States are subject to conditions which are, directly or indirectly, stricter than those on domestic goods. Since the CJEU also takes into consideration indirect discrimination, practically every national environmental measure will have to be weighed in the balance as to whether it factually leads to a different treatment of domestic or imported goods or not.

In Case 302/86,[26] the Commission had tackled the Danish deposit-and-return system by arguing that the mandatory use of reusable containers for drinks and beers indirectly discriminated against imported goods: reusable containers – mainly glass bottles – were considerably heavier in weight than containers made of plastic or other material. Therefore, the costs of transporting them to Denmark and, in their empty state, back to the country of origin, were higher than necessary and created indirect discrimination. If a foreign producer or trader wanted to avoid transport, it had to set up a deposit-and-return system of its own in Denmark, which would be costly.

The Court did not discuss questions of discrimination. Since it rejected the Commission's application, it must be presumed that it did not consider the increased transport costs or the difficulties involved in the setting up of a deposit-and-return system to be sufficiently relevant as to constitute indirect discrimination. In Cases C-309/02 and C-463/01, which concerned German legislation on packaging, the question whether the German mandatory deposit system constituted a discrimination was not discussed either.[27]

3-17 In Case C-2/90,[28] the Wallonian government's import ban on waste from other Member States was tackled by the Commission, which argued that waste from other Member States was not more harmful than waste generated in Wallonia. The Court

[23] See para 3-08 above.

[24] See Art 114(4), (5) and (10) TFEU.

[25] CJEU Case C-203/96 (n 10), para 44.

[26] CJEU Case 302/86 (n 13).

[27] CJEU Case C-463/01 *Commission v Germany* ECLI:EU:C:2004:797; Case C-309/02 *Radlberger* ECLI:EU:C:2004:799.

[28] CJEU Case C-2/90 (n 15).

rejected that argument. It held that waste, while coming under Article 34 TFEU, had special characteristics. As there was an obligation to dispose of waste as close as possible to the place where it was produced in order to transport waste as little as possible, which followed from Article 191(2) TFEU,[29] the different treatment between Wallonian waste and imported waste did not constitute, in the opinion of the Court, an arbitrary discrimination.

Another case, which was ultimately not decided by the Court as Denmark repealed its national legislation, was the Danish ban on metal cans for beer and some soft drinks, introduced in the early 1980s. The Commission had considered that this measure was taken in order to protect the (Danish) environment, and had therefore not attacked this ban before the CJEU; the attempts of the UK, as a third-party intervenor, to have this ban discussed in Case 302/86 failed for procedural reasons, since a third-party intervenor may not enlarge the object of litigation before the Court beyond the limits which the main applicant has established by its application.[30]

If it is correct that a Member State, in the absence of EU provisions, establishes itself the 3-18
necessary degree of protection of the environment which it wishes to achieve at national level, then it is in principle up to the Danish authorities to decide whether they wish to have metal cans in their environment. Such metal cans made from aluminium or steel take more natural resources to produce than glass or cardboard containers and are not reusable; they constitute litter in the environment when they are thrown away and reduce the efficiency of the reuse systems which a Member State may have set up.

In contrast to the Danish general ban, however, is an Irish draft regulation of 1988 which aimed at prohibiting metal cans, but only for beer. In this case, many of the environmental arguments in favour of such a ban were not really valid, since they would apply, in the same way, to metal cans for soft drinks. The Commission was therefore of the opinion that environmental reasons could not have been the cause for the Irish government to consider a ban on metal cans for beer, but that this ban constituted an attempt to reduce the import of British beer. Confronted with this argument, Ireland withdrew its draft regulation.

In Denmark, other soft drinks, such as iced tea, were allowed to be marketed in metal cans; also, of course, metal cans are used in Denmark for fruit and vegetable preserves and other food products. While fruit and vegetable containers might not really be comparable to drink containers, this is certainly the case with, for example, iced tea or chocolate drinks. It is thus very much a question of weighing up the different aspects of the Danish ban in order to come to a decision whether or not it is discriminating. Also, it should be pointed out that, in 1994, an EU Directive on packaging and packaging waste was adopted, which provides for the free circulation of packaging containers that comply with the requirements of this directive.[31] Any decision on the Danish ban would therefore take into consideration that directive and no longer consider only the article of the TFEU.[32] In view of this new

[29] See para 1–30.

[30] CJEU Case 302/86 (n 13).

[31] Directive 94/62 on packaging and packaging waste [1994] OJ L365/10; see also para 10-48.

[32] See CJEU Case C-24/21 *Regione Venezia* ECLI:EU:C:2022:526, para 61: 'It is settled case-law that, where a matter has been the subject of exhaustive harmonisation at EU level, any national measure relating thereto must be assessed in the light of the provisions of those harmonisation measures and not in the light of primary law.'

legislation, in 1999, the Commission appealed to the CJEU, and Denmark repealed its ban before a judgment was given.[33]

3-19 In 1993, the Netherlands set up a national Covenant on Tropical Hardwoods, which provided that, after 1995, only timber from sustainably managed forests was to be traded or processed in the Netherlands. The Covenant, an environmental agreement, was signed by the Dutch government, the timber trade and timber-processing industry, trade unions and environmental organisations. It was intended to introduce a Dutch approval mark in order to distinguish sustainably produced timber from other timber. Since the Covenant was actively supported and signed by the Dutch government, it must be considered a national public measure[34] and therefore be assessed under Article 34 TFEU.

The discrimination problem lies in the fact that the Covenant referred to timber imports from tropical timber only; other hardwood-producing countries, such as Canada and Russia (Siberia), were not covered. It is not really clear why this differentiation was made; environmental reasons require the same treatment in both cases. The Dutch Covenant therefore seems to be discriminatory. It must be mentioned, though, that it never became effective, because no agreement could be found on what constituted 'sustainable forest management'.

3-20 Some German Länder had adopted, in the 1980s, smog regulations, which provided for restrictions on the use of private cars in the case of smog. Cars equipped with catalytic converters could circulate during the first stage of a smog alert, whereas cars without a catalytic converter could not. The Commission stated that this measure discriminated against car producers from other Member States, since the EU provisions valid at that time had considered the emissions from cars to be equivalent, whether or not the cars were equipped with catalytic converters; any differentiation between cars with and without catalytic converters was thus discriminating. According to the Commission, foreign manufacturers were also more severely affected by the German measures than German producers.

In the 1980s, there was no EU legislation on smog and therefore Member States were free to decide on their own measures in the case of an extraordinary situation such as smog. Since cars with catalytic converters emit fewer pollutants than cars without such converters, and since all manufacturers were producing, at the time of the German measure, cars with catalytic converters, no discrimination can be seen in the smog regulations, which, in each case, were measures to deal with a temporary situation. When the Commission changed its policy in 1987 and began working towards EU emission limit values which required catalytic converter equipment, it ended the case against Germany.

In Case C-379/98, the Court examined whether a German measure to support the production of electricity from renewable sources of energy, but to limit the financial support to undertakings in Germany, was compatible with the present Article 34 TFEU. The Court did not discuss the question of discrimination of persons in other Member States, but held the German measure to be compatible with Article 34.[35]

These examples might show, in an assessment of whether a Member State's measure constitutes an arbitrary discrimination of products, how much depends on the concrete,

[33] CJEU Case C-246/99 *Commission v Denmark* ECLI:EU:C:2002:477.

[34] Private measures would have to be assessed against Arts 101 and 102 TFEU as to their compatibility with the TFEU.

[35] CJEU Case C-379/98 *PreussenElektra* (n 16); Case C-573/12 *Aalands Vindkraft* ECLI:EU:C:2014:2037.

specific circumstances of each case. This is confirmed by the jurisdiction of the Court, which appears to differentiate between measures that are discriminating and those that constitute arbitrary discrimination. Thus, in several cases, the Court accepted national discriminating environmental legislation which it considered to be environmentally oriented without discussing, in the majority of these cases, much of their discriminating character. This could mean that national measures which pursue a legitimate environmental objective may also be justified under Articles 34/36 TFEU where they discriminate against products from other Member States.[36] However, a detailed case-by-case analysis of each specific case is always necessary.

Disproportionate measures. The second requirement set up by the CJEU is the proportionality requirement, according to which it must be examined whether there are other measures available which restrict the free circulation of goods less severely than the measure which was taken. In practice, the proportionality principle is often merged with the necessity requirement discussed above: when a national measure is not necessary, it is disproportionate. 3-21

The proportionality requirement became relevant in Case C-131/93, where Germany had prohibited the import of living crayfish in order to protect the health and life of indigenous crayfish species.[37] The Court did not contest Germany's right to take such measures; however, it argued that Germany could have taken other, less restrictive steps, such as health controls for crayfish imports from other Member States, or licensing requirements for putting living crayfish into German waters. The Court also came to this conclusion because Germany had been rather generous in granting derogations from the import ban and shown that a licence system, together with strict conditions, did ensure sufficient protection.

In Case 302/86,[38] the Court considered the Danish measure to only allow approved drink containers to be part of the Danish deposit-and-return system to be incompatible with Article 34 TFEU; a Danish measure to allow some derogations for importers of small quantities was considered disproportionate. The Court did not explain what other, less restrictive, measures Denmark could have taken; its judgment is instead confined to the statement that 'a very considerable degree of protection of the environment' was not really necessary to protect the environment. This seems to have the hallmark of a political statement. 3-22

In Case C-2/90,[39] the Court did not discuss at all whether or not the Belgian measure to ban waste imports was disproportionate: as Belgium had argued that the measure was taken in order to react to a sudden increase in the importation of waste and as the judgment was given nine years after the taking of the measure, there would have been good reasons to discuss the proportionality requirement.

In its Decision 98/523,[40] the Commission considered the limitation of access to Karlstad airport to less noisy aeroplanes disproportionate, except as regarded a night curfew between 22.00 and 07.00 hours. The Commission argued, amongst other things, that the airport was situated in a sparsely populated area away from the city centre and that it accounted for a

[36] In this regard, see F Jacobs, 'The Role of the European Court of Justice in the Protection of the Environment' [2006] *Journal of Environmental Law* 185.

[37] CJEU Case C-131/93 *Commission v Germany* ECLI:EU:C:1991:290.

[38] CJEU Case 302/86 (n 13).

[39] CJEU Case C-2/90 (n 15).

[40] Commission Decision 98/523 on access to Karlstad airport [1998] OJ L233/25.

rather low traffic volume. The Commission requested that the Swedish authorities demonstrate the need to take the noise-restriction measures.

In Case C-320/03,[41] the Court had to decide on a regional Austrian legislation which prohibited, for environmental reasons, the transport of certain non-perishable goods on the Brenner Autobahn. The Court did not discuss the question of discrimination. It held that the Austrian measure was disproportionate because Austria had introduced it at extremely short notice and had not provided for possibilities to transport the goods otherwise.

3-23 There is a lot of discussion on questions of the burden of proof or the burden of evidence. However, this rule of procedure simply means that in a dispute attempts must be made from the Commission, other parties, private bodies and Member States to clarify the facts as far as possible. The more substantiated the arguments from one side are, the more detailed those from the other side have to be. Only at the end of this process, where factual aspects remain open, can there be a question of who is to have the burden to prove that a factual aspect has not been clarified.

It has already been pointed out that, under the EU Treaties, environmental protection reasons are not subordinated to considerations of free circulation of goods. In an assessment under Article 34 TFEU, whether the consideration of free circulation of goods or the protection of the environment prevails, Member States have an amount of discretion as to the degree at which level they wish to fix the protection of the environment. It is difficult to understand why a night curfew should comply with the principle of necessity and proportionality but a limitation on access to the airport to less noisy aeroplanes does not. This issue cannot be solved by shifting the burden of proof.

3-24 Also, how difficult the proportionality principle is to apply in practice may be demonstrated by the question of product bans. Member States have pronounced a considerable number of bans of products; besides those mentioned on metal cans (Denmark) or pesticides (Netherlands), one could mention the restriction on phosphates in detergents (Italy, 1988), the Austrian ban of polybromated biphenyls (PBBs), non-biodegradable plastic bags (some local authorities in Italy), lead capsules for alcoholic beverages (Germany, Netherlands), waste-shredding machines (Germany), lead-containing ammunition (Denmark, the Netherlands) and PVC (polyvinyl chloride) (Czechia, Spain).

The argument that a ban is not allowed where other means are available which are less restrictive of the free circulation of goods must not be overused. Indeed, as has been already mentioned, the CJEU had expressly recognised the right of Member States to ban pesticides which had not been the subject of EU secondary legislation.[42] It would theoretically always be possible to argue that a strict licensing system together with control and surveillance mechanisms would reach more or less the same result, but would be less restrictive than a total ban. The Court's jurisdiction to allow the complete ban of pesticides by Member States means in practice that the Court grants them a considerable amount of discretion to decide on what measures they consider appropriate. Following the same line of reasoning, the Court accepted that the fixing of noise emission limit values for aeroplanes was the most effective and most appropriate means of combating noise emissions from aeroplanes; indeed, investments in construction around airports are

[41] CJUE Case C-320/03 *Commission v Austria* ECLI:EU:C:2005:684.

[42] CJEU Case 125/88 (n 22).

normally very cost-intensive. Establishing noise emission limit values was therefore not disproportionate.[43]

This reasoning also applies to the German ban on waste-shredding machines, which the Commission accepted. Waste-shredding machines cut biological waste into small pieces, which are then disposed of together with ordinary waste water. German law provides that waste must first of all be recovered; this conforms to the EU waste hierarchy which is laid down in Directive 2008/98.[44] Disposing of waste by shredding it and discharging it into the sewer system contradicts this principle. Furthermore, the pipes for waste water would be clogged with the waste, filtering would become more difficult and costly, waste water treatment stations would incur increased costs, etc. It would therefore certainly be possible to prohibit waste disposal together with waste water without banning the shredding machines. In order to find out whether the marketing of waste-shredding machines might be prohibited as well, the import of such machines into Germany would have to be considered, as would the possibility of controlling the ban on using these machines and of disposing of the waste via the waste water flow. Since such a ban could probably never be effectively controlled, a ban on marketing shredding machines appears not to be disproportionate. 3-25

Italy, the UK, Denmark and Sweden took measures, in 1996–97, to prohibit the marketing of self-chilling cans. These are metal cans for drinks which contain hydrofluorocarbons (HFCs), a cooling gas, which is spread between the wall of the can and the drink in such a way that the can functions as a mobile mini-refrigerator, chilling the content of the can. 3-26

HFCs are greenhouse gases, used as a substitute for CFCs; they are considered, in global warming terms, to have a global warming potential of 11,700 (CO_2 has a global warming potential of 1).[45] In the mid-1990s, they were not yet regulated by international agreements or EU legislation, but were identified as greenhouse gases under the Kyoto Protocol (1998). Their extensive use would undermine efforts in other sectors to reduce CO_2 emissions and thus combat climate change. Therefore, national bans on HFCs or on products and equipment that contain HFCs are justified under Article 34 TFEU.

As regards an Italian ban of phosphates in detergents, it is not clear what less restrictive measure could reduce the eutrophication of rivers, lakes and coastal waters. The same applies to the Danish and Dutch ban on lead-containing ammunition, which aims at reducing the presence of lead in the environment. If Denmark and the Netherlands consider that there is too much lead in the environment, and that ducks and birds might eat that ammunition, then a ban appears appropriate since equally effective measures which restrict the free flow of goods less are not available.[46] The Commission did not take any legal action against these three Member States. Similar considerations apparently also influenced the Commission in the case of the ban of non-biodegradable plastic bags, which was also accepted.[47] In the

[43] CJEU Case C-389/96 *Aher-Waggon* ECLI:EU:C:1998:357.

[44] Directive 2008/98 on waste [2008] OJ L312/3, Art 4.

[45] See ch 9, fn 26.

[46] Commission Regulation 2021/57 [2021] OJ L24/19 only prohibited the 'lead in gunshots in and around wetlands'.

[47] An Italian judge had asked the CJEU whether such a ban was compatible with EU law, but omitted to ask about its compatibility with Art 34 TFEU. The Court therefore only assessed its compatibility with Directive 75/442 – now replaced by Directive 2008/98 (n 44) – and found no problem with this directive, Case 380/87 *Enichem v Cinisello-Balsamo* ECLI:EU:C:1989:318.

case of lead capsules for alcoholic beverages, the Union thought it appropriate to adopt EU regulations in order to provide for a complete EU-wide phasing-out of such capsules.[48]

3-27 In 1999, the Netherlands issued draft legislation which considerably restricted the use of chlorinated paraffins. This measure was a follow-up to a decision, taken within the framework of the Paris Convention of 1995,[49] aimed at progressively reducing paraffin in order to prevent marine pollution. The Commission did not object to this restriction on the free circulation of goods.

A similar case is the Austrian ban on PBBs. PBBs are suspected of causing serious health or environmental problems; however, definitive scientific evidence on the risk of PBBs has not yet been produced. The Commission considered that the Organisation for Economic Cooperation and Development had recommended, at international level, that the marketing and use of PBBs be stopped and decided to accept the Austrian ban. This example shows that in the case of conflict between the free circulation of goods (Article 34 TFEU) and environmental protection, the precautionary principle of Article 191(2) TFEU may apply and lead to preference being given to measures which aim at environmental protection.

As mentioned in paragraph 1-27ff, there are attempts, in particular from economic operators, to limit the application of the precautionary principle also as regards national measures, and to require, for its application, that there is a possibility of severe and irreversible hazard, that there is a need to adopt measures urgently and that national legislation is of a provisional nature only.[50] These attempts to reduce the application of the precautionary principle are legally unjustified, as they try to interpret this principle as containing aspects which it does not contain. The Austrian PBBs ban demonstrates well that Member States' discretion under the precautionary and proportionality principles is rather broad and wider than the attempts for a restriction from the side of economic interests.

3-28 In another case, Greece prohibited the import of diesel cars for private use, arguing that the heavy air pollution in Athens and Thessaloniki required such a measure. It seems obvious that a total import ban on private diesel cars in order to combat air pollution in two regions is disproportionate. Upon the request of the Commission, Greece amended its legislation and prohibited the use of diesel cars in Athens and Thessaloniki. Such a measure may be proportional if the air pollution in these two regions is primarily due to the use of diesel cars. However, it seems rather unlikely that the air pollution is caused more by diesel and petrol cars than, for example, by industrial emissions, other economic activities and household heating. Unless a significantly higher contribution of diesel cars' emissions is established, the restriction on the use of diesel cars, but not petrol cars, is discriminatory; furthermore, the measure as such is disproportional, since it appears that it is not capable of reaching the objective, ie the reduction of environmental pollution.

In 2014, discussions started in Paris to restrict the use of diesel cars, as they were blamed for the increase in the presence of nitrogen oxides (NO_x) beyond the limits permitted under Directive 2008/50.[51] This discussion, which turned on fiscal incentives to buy a non-diesel

[48] See, eg Regulation 3280/92 [1992] OJ L327/3.

[49] Paris Convention for the protection of the marine environment in the North-East Atlantic (OSPAR), see Decision 98/249 [1998] OJ L104/1; see also para 7-32ff.

[50] These restrictions find their origin in principle 15 on the precautionary 'approach' under the Rio Declaration on the Environment and Development of 1992.

[51] Directive 2008/50 on ambient air quality and cleaner air for Europe [2008] OJ L152/1.

car, to restrict access to the city for diesel cars and to increase taxation on diesel cars, failed to reach a conclusion.

In 1998–99, Denmark announced and adopted draft national legislation which intended to limit considerably the marketing in Denmark of lead and of products containing lead; these products were expressly listed in an annex to the legislation. Products which complied with EU directives were exempted from this ban. The essential question in this case is whether Denmark was entitled, in the absence of EU law, to decide that it does not wish to see lead in its environment. In my opinion, this is indeed the case, and it cannot be argued, in the name of proportionality, that less restrictive measures could be taken. The Commission did not object to the Danish legislation.

In 1998, Sweden prohibited the export of mercury-containing products, including dental amalgams, for reasons of human health and of environmental protection. The CJEU held[52] that this export ban was incompatible with Directive 93/42 concerning medical devices,[53] though this directive aims at the protection of human health, albeit not the protection of the environment. Article 34 TFEU would thus have allowed Sweden to maintain this export ban.[54]

In 2022, the Commission proposed a regulation to prohibit the placing on the Union market of products made with forced labour,[55] which was based on Articles 114 and 207 TFEU and which is currently still under discussion. It is hard to imagine politically that any national ban of such products would be tackled in the name of free circulation of goods, though the International Labour Organization estimated that there are about 800,000 people working under forced labour conditions in the Union.[56] Legally, the situation is more complicated, as such a ban could be followed by bans on the disregard of human rights, aggressive warfare (Russia's invasion in Ukraine) or minority treatment (China in Tibet). How such bans could effectively be enforced and applied is unclear. 3-29

Protecting the environment outside the national territory. It has been argued in legal texts that, under Article 34 TFEU, a Member State may take an environmental measure to protect the environment outside its own jurisdiction. However, the CJEU has not yet formally decided on this issue. The first argument which is relevant in this context is the fact that the requirements of environmental protection under the TFEU are not limited to the EU's territory. If the point of departure defended in this chapter is correct – that in the absence of EU measures, the task of ensuring environmental protection is with the Member States – it cannot seriously be argued that such measures are not allowed under Article 34 or 36 TFEU. Indeed, measures to combat climate change or to protect the ozone layer, tropical forests, elephants, whales, tigers or rhinos do affect the environment outside the EU territory – and yet have been taken by the Union without ever having seriously been 3-30

[52] CJEU Case C-288/08 *Kemikalieinspektionen* ECLI:EU:C:2009:718.

[53] Directive 93/42 concerning medical devices [1993] OJ L169/1.

[54] In 2008, the EU adopted Regulation 1102/2008 on the banning of exports of metallic mercury and certain mercury compounds and mixtures [2008] OJ L304/75, and in 2017 it adopted Regulation 2017/852 on mercury. This last regulation limited the use of dental amalgam to encapsulated amalgam. It indicated the intention to phase out dental amalgam by 2030 [2017] OJ L127/1, Art 10 and Recitals 21 and 22. As the Regulation was based on Art 192 TFEU, the Swedish ban would be allowed (Art 193 TFEU).

[55] Commission, 'Proposal for a Regulation on Prohibiting Products Made With Forced Labour on the EU Market' COM(2022) 453.

[56] Commision, SWD(2022) 439, 1.

questioned under Article 34.[57] In the absence, then, of any EU measures, this competence is with Member States.

The possibility of protecting the environment outside the national jurisdiction of a Member State finds its limits in the general Treaty provisions, in particular in Article 4(3) TEU, which lays down the principle of sincere co-operation.[58] Thus, the protection of the environment in another Member State will normally have to be left to that other Member State. However, each individual case will have to be weighed carefully. For instance, where a Member State decides to enact a national import ban on ivory in order to protect the African elephant,[59] this measure also affects the imports of ivory from other Member States. Nevertheless, this measure may be upheld under Article 34 where the principles of non-discrimination and proportionality have been respected.

A similar reasoning may apply for the protection of an endangered species that lives in another Member State. Normally, under Article 4(3) TEU, it would be up to that Member State to protect that species. However, there may be circumstances where such a measure is not taken for political, economic or other reasons. In such a case, another Member State may decide to take measures to protect the species. An example is the German ban of the mid-1980s on imports for products made from *Corallium rubrum*, a coral which lives in the Mediterranean Sea and from which jewellery is made in some Member States. Weighing the arguments, the Commission did not see in that import ban a breach of Germany's obligations under Article 34 TFEU.[60]

The CJEU has not accepted export restrictions which France and the Netherlands[61] had introduced for specific wastes and for which they had invoked, amongst other arguments, the necessity of protecting the environment in other Member States. The Court considered that nothing indicated that the other Member States did not or could not protect themselves and their environment. In Case C-203/96,[62] the Court considered illegal a Dutch provision which allowed the export of specific waste, unless the processing of that waste abroad was 'superior' to the processing of it in the Netherlands; the Court held that the treatment methodologies in both countries were equivalent, and that therefore the export restriction was not justified.

In Case C-169/89,[63] the Court decided that the Netherlands could not lawfully prohibit the marketing of a bird which had been legally marketed in the UK. The details of this judgment appear questionable, as the EU legislation expressly required the protection of *all* birds and constructed national hunting provisions as exceptions to that rule; however, this

[57] In Case C-284/95 *Safety Hi-Tech* ECLI:EU:C:1998:352, the CJEU assessed the validity of EU measures to protect the ozone layer against Art 34 TFEU, but found no breach of the Treaty provisions; see also para 9-37ff.

[58] Art 4(3) TEU: 'Pursuant to the principle of sincere cooperation, the Union and the Member States shall in full mutual respect, assist each other in carrying out tasks which flow from the Treaties … The Member States shall … refrain from any measure which could jeopardise the attainment of the objectives of this Treaty.'

[59] Regulation 2496/89 [1989] OJ L240/5 introduced an EU-wide import ban on ivory. However, a number of Member States had already decided, at national level, to introduce such a ban prior to the EU action.

[60] Since then, *Corallium rubrum* has been the subject of Community measures to restrict its trade, see Regulation 338/97 on the protection of species of wild fauna and flora by regulating trade therein [1997] OJ L61/1.

[61] CJEU Case 172/82 *Inter-Huiles* ECLI:EU:C:1983:69: 'The environment is protected just as effectively when the oils are sold to an authorised disposal or regenerating undertaking of another Member State as when they are disposed of in the Member States of origin'; Case 118/86 *Nertsfoederfabriek* ECLI:EU:C:1987:424; the case concerned poultry waste.

[62] CJEU Case C-203/96 (n 10).

[63] CJEU Case C-169/89 *Gourmetterie van den Burg* ECLI:EU:C:1990:227.

case will not be discussed here, since the judgment mainly dealt with the interpretation of Directive 2009/147 on the conservation of wild birds.

In 2007/08, Belgium and the Netherlands adopted legislation to prohibit the trade in seal furs and seal products. The measures also affect the trade with other EU Member States; they were envisaged to counteract the large-scale and frequently inhumane killing of seals which the Canadian government had authorised. Canadian seals are not an endangered species. Nevertheless, as measures to protect wild animal welfare are environmental measures (see paragraph 1-03 above), such measures could be justified under EU law as well under World Trade Organization (WTO) law. In order to preserve the unity of the EU market, the Union introduced legislation to prohibit trade in seal products for the whole of the European Union.[64] Appeals against the regulation were unsuccessful before the CJEU.[65] The WTO Appellate Body found, in 2014, that while the EU ban could, in principle, be justified for moral concerns regarding the welfare of seals, the two exceptions which the EU had provided for indigenous communities and for the sustainable management of marine resources were not justified and contradicted WTO law (Article XX(a) of the General Agreement on Tariffs and Trade).[66] The Union then adopted an amending regulation in order to adapt these exceptions to the WTO requirements; the ban of seal imports as such was maintained.[67]

In conclusion, Member States may, in the absence of EU provisions on specific prod- 3-31
ucts, take those measures to protect the environment against the risk arising from the products which they consider appropriate. However, Articles 34 and 36 TFEU and the very sophisticated and detailed case law of the CJEU require that a very careful assessment is made between the environmental advantage and the restriction of the free circulation of goods. Any national measure which restricts the circulation may constitute a discrimination against producers or traders from other Member States. The national measure must be capable of reaching the envisaged aim and not go beyond what is necessary to reach it (proportionality). The different criteria – arbitrary discrimination, proportionality, a non-economic objective – leave a considerable amount of discretion to the CJEU, which is the final place for deciding on the legality of the national environmental measure. Therefore, a case-by-case assessment which carefully considers all aspects of a national measure is necessary.

When a Union legislative act provides for total harmonisation on a specific matter, an act by a Member State is no longer assessed as regards Article 34 or 36 TFEU, but as to its compatibility with the Union legislative act.

B. National Measures Affecting Exports

Similar requirements apply to measures which concern the export of products. 3-32
Article 35 TFEU prohibits quantitative restrictions on exports as well as measures having

[64] Regulation 1007/2009 on trade in seal products [2009] OJ L286/36.

[65] General Court Case T-18/10 *Inuit Kanatami ao v European Parliament and Council* ECLI:EU:T:2011:419; CJEU Case C-583/11P *Inuit Kanatami v European Parliament and Council* ECLI:EU:C:2013:625.

[66] WTO, Document WT/DS400 and DS401/AB/R of 29 April 2014.

[67] Regulation 2015/1775 [2015] OJ L262/1.

an equivalent effect; Article 36 constitutes an exception also to this principle, and allows export restrictions for, amongst other things, reasons to protect the life and health of humans, animals or plants. The CJEU interpreted Article 35 in such a way that this prohibition 'concerns all national measures which have as their specific object or effect the restriction of patterns of exports and thereby … provide a special advantage for national products or for the domestic markets'.[68]

A frequent way of prohibiting waste exports is the requirement to deliver waste to specific (national) plants. The CJEU held that such an obligation constituted an indirect export ban and was therefore incompatible with Article 35.[69] The decision in Case C-422/92 stands in contradiction to these judgments: in that case, the CJEU declared that the requirement to dispose of waste generated in Germany only in that country was compatible with EU law.[70]

It should be noted that, on the one hand, waste is a product of a specific nature to which different provisions may apply.[71] On the other hand, in 2006, the Union adopted new and specific provisions on the shipment of waste within the Union which replaced previous provisions.[72] Under these provisions, Member States may oblige waste generators or holders to deliver their waste to specific plants, provided that the plant is for waste disposal. However, where waste is shipped for recovery to another Member State, it is not possible to prohibit the shipment by a provision which obliges the waste holder to supply it to a specific waste recovery plant. Such a provision contradicts Article 35 and the above-mentioned Regulation on waste shipments.[73]

In particular, in Germany, local authorities which have set up waste treatment (incinerators) or disposal installations often try to prohibit the export of municipal waste to other municipalities or abroad, establishing an obligation to deliver the waste to the local installation (*Anschluss- und Benutzungszwang*). Such measures are not compatible with Article 35 TFEU when waste is to be exported for recovery purposes.[74] Spanish waste legislation of 2012 provided that recyclable waste shall, as a priority, be offered to recycling installations within the Union. This provision is used by local administrations to put into public tenders the requirement of offering recyclable waste to Spanish or EU installations. Under the *Dassonville* formula of the CJEU,[75] such a provision undoubtedly constitutes an indirect restriction of exports and is therefore not compatible with Article 35.

Apart from waste issues, there has not yet been any Court decision to allow or disallow export restrictions for environmental purposes. In practice, therefore, the export ban for environmental purposes does not play a significant role.

[68] CJEU Case 172/82 (n 61).

[69] ibid; Case C-37/92 *Vanacker* ECLI:EU:C:1993:836; Case 118/86 (n 61).

[70] CJEU Case C-422/92 *Commission v Germany* ECLI:EU:C 1995:125; in that judgment, the Court did not expressly discuss Art 35 but examined the German legislation under Directive 84/631 on the shipment of waste [1984] OJ L326/31 (in the meantime repealed).

[71] See para 2-78.

[72] Regulation 1013/2006 on shipments of waste [2006] OJ L190/1.

[73] See, however, Directive 2008/98 (n 44) Art 16(1), where Member States were authorised to restrict imports of waste for recovery in order to protect their national incineration network.

[74] For more details, see para 10-39ff.

[75] CJEU Case 8/74 *Dassonville* ECLI:EU:C:1974:82 para 5: 'all trading rules … which are capable of hindering, directly or indirectly, actually or potentially' trade, were declared incompatible with Arts 34 and 35.

C. Measures under Other Policies

(i) Agricultural Policy

Since the entering into force of the Lisbon Treaty at the end of 2009, agricultural policy is no longer the exclusive competence of the Union; rather, the competence is shared (Article 4(2d) TFEU). Member States' measures in environmental matters that would affect the common agricultural policy and its legislation, which were forbidden in the past, are now permitted, provided they follow the general lines which were indicated above. 3-33

Thus, Member States may only take measures if the Union has not taken action; and such measures are under the permanent threat of being replaced by EU action. An example is the setting up of national criteria for organic farming and food therefrom: as the Union has now regulated this matter,[76] there is no competence for national measures in this area.

Measures which had been taken in the past include, in particular, the ban on certain agricultural pesticides. Since 1991, this subject has been regulated at EU level, presently by Regulation 1107/2009;[77] however, since the implementing provisions have not yet all been elaborated, the Union de facto accepts that Member States continue to maintain national bans or restrictions of the marketing or use of pesticides. Once the EU system is fully established, this practice will have to be abandoned.

Environmental measures which Member States may take under these restricted conditions concern, for instance, the handling of manure,[78] the limitation of the size of industrial feedstock installations, irrigation measures, action on the management of water resources and limiting the use of fertilisers or the number of cattle per km^2. As the Directive on the sustainable use of pesticides was adopted on the basis of the present Article 192 TFEU,[79] Member States have large possibilities to adopt more protective measures against pesticides (Article 193 TFEU).

(ii) Transport Policy

Transport policy (Articles 90–100 TFEU) has also become, under the TFEU, a common policy with shared competence (Article 4(2g) TFEU), though EU measures are less comprehensive than the common agricultural policy. For this reason, Member States have a much greater possibility of adopting environmental measures affecting transport. An important limitation, however, is Article 92 TFEU, which prohibits direct or indirect discrimination of carriers from other Member States. In 1992, the CJEU had to decide on a tax on the use of roads by heavy goods vehicles which Germany had introduced.[80] While 3-34

[76] Regulation 2018/848 on organic production and labelling of organic products [2018] OJ L150/1; for more details, see para 6-45.

[77] Regulation 1107/2009 concerning the placing of plant protection products on the market [2009] OJ L309/1; this regulation replaced Directive 91/414 [1991] OJ L230/51.

[78] CJEU Case C-254/13 *Orgacom ECLI*:EU:C:2014:2251: a tax on the import of manure into the Belgian region of Flanders discriminates non-Flemish traders and is therefore inadmissible.

[79] Directive 2009/128 establishing a framework for Community action to achieve the sustainable use of pesticides [2009] OJ L309/71.

[80] CJEU Case C-195/90 *Commission v Germany* ECLI:EU:C:1992:219.

this road tax was the same for all carriers, Germany had, at the same time, provided for a reduction in the motor vehicle tax to the same amount; thus, the charge of the tax on the use of roads only affected carriers from other Member States. The Court did not accept the German government's argument that the tax on the use of roads had an environmental objective because it was intended to increase the amount of goods transported by railway. Instead, it was of the opinion that there was no encouragement for German carriers to move to railway transport and that, therefore, the effect of the German measures contradicted Article 92 TFEU. The Court came to a similar result in Case C-205/98: Austria had raised, in 1995 and 1996, the toll rates for use of the Brenner motorway, but had provided that Austrian hauliers were charged less than foreign hauliers, who were thus, in the opinion of the Court, discriminated against.[81]

German legislation of 2015, which introduced an infrastructure use charge for all cars but at the same time reduced the tax for cars paid by German residents, had, in view of this case law, no perspective to be considered legal and was declared incompatible with Union law by the CJEU.[82]

Member States may therefore take, in the absence of EU measures, non-discriminatory environmental measures as regards, for instance, provisions on night flights at airports,[83] taxes or charges on the use of roads of all types of cars or provisions on ships. Since the Union has, so far, not taken many measures to integrate environmental requirements into the transport policy, Articles 90 et seq leave, in theory, large scope for national measures, although Member States do not seem inclined to make extensive use of this possibility.

(iii) State Aids

3-35 Under the TFEU, a state aid is a measure which provides a company or business with an economic or financial advantage, and is granted by the state or through state resources; it must favour certain undertakings or the production of certain goods, and it must affect the trade between Member States (Article 107 TFEU). State aids are in principle prohibited. The intention of granting state aid has to be notified to the Commission (Article 108(3) TFEU) in order to allow the assessment of its compatibility with the TFEU, as Article 107(2) and (3) TFEU allows state aid under certain conditions.

The connection with the Treaty's provision on competition needs to be underlined. Indeed, where consumers or users receive financial advantages to buy environmentally better products, there is normally no question of a state aid, since financial benefits are not given to particular undertakings.[84] Where this is the case, aid may be authorised where it is granted without discrimination and does not exceed 100 per cent of the extra environmental costs. Small amounts of aid – up to €200,000 per undertaking over a period of three years – are considered not to affect trade and need not be notified to the Commission.[85]

[81] CJEU Case C-205/98 *Commission v Austria* ECLI:EU:C:2000:493.

[82] CJEU Case C-591/17 *Austria v Germany* ECLI:EU:C:2018:504.

[83] On the interrelationship between aeroplane noise and environmental protection, see CJEU Case C-120/10 *European Air Transport* ECLI:EU:C:2011:556.

[84] See, eg CJEU Case C-379/98 (n 16). The case concerned price advantages which were granted to small German producers – mainly private persons – of renewable energy.

[85] Commission Regulation 1407/2013 on de minimis aid [2013] OJ L352/1.

The financial support of environmental organisations which manage habitats or other pieces of land (national parks, natural monuments etc) constitutes state aid, though such aid may normally be authorised.[86]

In the same way, financial assistance which is granted to every undertaking is not aid, but may be seen as such where the receiving companies are in competition with other companies that do not have access to this assistance. 3-36

In 1974, the Commission established guidelines for national aid with environmental objectives;[87] these have since been reviewed and published several times, most recently in 2022.[88] Legally, these guidelines are not rules of law, but a communication to Member States and the other institutions which indicates the criteria which the Commission uses to exercise its discretion for authorising national aids; they limit the Commission's discretion, as the Commission may not depart from them without reasons that are compatible with the principle of equal treatment.[89]

The basis for authorising national environmental aid is now Article 107(3c) TFEU;[90] however, in specific cases, Article 107(3a) or (3b) might be applicable. Under certain conditions, some environmental aid is block-exempted from notification and assessment by the Commission.[91]

The 470 paragraphs of the 2022 Guidelines list 14 categories of economic activities for which aid may be granted, for example on clean mobility, pollution reduction or the energy performance of buildings (paragraph 16). The intensity of the aid which is permitted varies, but may reach 100 per cent. The paragraphs differentiate very carefully between different undertakings, regional aspects or, for example, the innovative character of an activity, and explain for each possible aid its rationale, scope, incentive effects and impact on competition and trade (as well as the necessity of the aid and its proportionality). 3-37

Member States shall report annually on the environmental aid which they grant. The Commission publishes this information on the Internet.[92] These provisions thus open up a very large range of possibilities to financially assist undertakings which invest in clean technologies or otherwise improve the environment.

When it assessed, under earlier guidelines, the legality of a Spanish support scheme for indigenous coal, the General Court held that the Commission was not obliged, when it examined such aid, to examine whether the scheme was compatible with EU environmental

[86] General Court Case T-347/09 *Germany v Commission* ECLI:EU:T:2013:418.

[87] Beginning with Commission, *Fourth Report on Competition Policy* (Brussels, 1975) para 175.

[88] Commission, Guidelines on State aid for climate, environmental protection and energy 2022 [2022] OJ C80/1. The Guidelines are to be reviewed in 2027.

[89] CJEU Case C-397/03P *Archer Daniels Midland v Commission* ECLI:EU:C:2006:328, para 91: 'whilst rules of conduct designed to produce external effects as it is the case of the Guidelines [Guidelines on the method of setting fines in competition law, LK] which are aimed at traders, may not be regarded as rules of law which the administration is always bound to observe, they nevertheless form rules of practice from which the administration may not depart in an individual case without giving reasons that are compatible with the principle of equal treatment'.

[90] Art 107(3c) TFEU: '[The following may be considered to be compatible with the common market:] aid to facilitate the development of certain economic activities or of certain economic areas, where such aid does not adversely affect trading conditions to an extent contrary to the common interest.'

[91] Commission Regulation 651/2014 declaring certain categories of aid compatible with the internal market [2014] OJ L187/1.

[92] Commission, Guidelines 2022 (n 88), para 464.

law. The Court was of the opinion that the protection of the environment was not part of the internal market, and as the Spanish scheme was intended to be applied within the context of the internal market, it was irrelevant whether it complied with environmental protection provisions. The Commission might well start proceedings against Spain under Article 258 TFEU if it considers this necessary.[93] In view of Articles 3 TEU and 11 and 114 TFEU, and the extended jurisprudence of the CJEU, this judgment of the General Court appears to be wrong. Paragraph 33 of the 2022 Guidelines now states explicitly:

> If the supported activity or the aid measure or the conditions attached to it, including its financing method when it forms an integral part of the measure, entail a violation of relevant Union law, the aid cannot be declared compatible with the internal market.

(iv) Taxes and Charges

3-38 Member States' possibilities of adopting environmental taxes and charges are equally great. Their limitations are found in Article 110 TFEU; they apply only to goods, and any direct or indirect discrimination is prohibited. The very existence of these provisions show that national fiscal measures are not to be assessed under Article 34 TFEU. Indeed, Article 110 is *lex specialis* to Article 34.[94] The essential difference between the two provisions is that Article 110 prohibits discriminating taxation measures, but does not refer to disproportionate taxes; and as the primary function of taxes is to ensure income, there cannot be any question of environmental taxes only being allowed for non-economic reasons. Hence, Member States may fix taxes on whatever they wish and at whatever level they wish, as long as they do not discriminate against products from other Member States. No notification of a national measure to the Commission is necessary under Article 110.

Environmental taxes are generally divided into taxes in the energy or transport sector, with regard to pollution and concerning natural resources. By far the most frequent taxes are those in the energy sector. The CJEU is rather strict in assessing direct and indirect discrimination: for example, a tax on the first registration of (new or second-hand) cars which takes into consideration the age and the state of the car discriminates, because the tax on the purchase of non-imported second-hand cars is not influenced by such characteristics.[95] An environmental tax in the UK which provided for some exemptions for Northern Irish companies was considered to be discriminating against Irish companies.[96]

Denmark had fixed the registration tax on new vehicles at between 105 and 180 per cent of the net sales price. The Commission was of the opinion that this provision was incompatible with Article 110, since it impeded the free movement of goods. However, the CJEU decided that Article 110 only applied where tax measures were meant to protect domestic production; and since Denmark did not have a national car production industry,

[93] General Court Case T-57/11 *Castelnou v Commission* ECLI:EU:T:2014:1021; in the same sense, see Case T-158/99 *Thermenhotel Stösner v Commission* ECLI:EU:T:2004:2.

[94] CJEU Case 74/76 *Iannelli and Volpi* ECLI:EU:C:1977:81; Case C-78-83/90 *Compagnie Commerciale de l'Ouest* ECLI:EU:C:1992:118.

[95] CJEU Case C-402/09 *Tatu* ECLI:EU:C:2011:219.

[96] General Court Case T-359/04 *British Aggregates Association and others v Commission* ECLI:EU:T:2010:366.

there was no question of a breach of Article 110.[97] Article 34 could, in such a case, become applicable only where a tax is so high that the import of products from other Member States would be effectively barred. Even in such cases, a national tax may be compatible with Article 34, namely in those cases where a Member State has legitimate environmental or other grounds for raising such a tax. Where, for instance, a Member State would not like to see a Concorde aeroplane, a pesticide, metal cans or other products on its market or in its environment, it would be entitled, instead of prohibiting the use of that product, to levy a high, dissuasive tax on it.[98]

National eco-taxes, on CFCs, energy use, packaging, groundwater and so on, are to be examined initially under Article 110, not under Article 34. Besides the objective of creating income, they aim at influencing economic operators', users', consumers' and taxpayers' behaviour to reduce pollution, ensure prudent use of natural resources and encourage a preference for environmentally friendly products. In 1993, Belgium adopted legislation providing for an environmental tax on a number of products, in particular packaging for drinks, disposable cameras and razors, batteries, pesticides and paper. Products on which the tax was levied had to carry a distinctive sign, showing that they were eco-taxed. The CJEU considered the tax to come under Article 110;[99] however, since the distinctive sign was to be applied on the products, it directly affected the circulation of goods and had therefore to be assessed under Article 34. 3-39

In 1996, France informed the Commission of its intention to introduce tax exemptions for biofuels. The Commission at first refused to accept the French measures, since they advantaged French products and thus were in conflict with Article 110.[100] France then amended its legislation; the Commission was of the opinion that the new system eliminated the discrimination between the types of vegetable matter or crops which produce the biofuel and between French producers and those from other Member States. It therefore approved the system. However, the General Court considered the French measures incompatible with EU law, as they gave competitive advantages to French producers.[101]

At the request of a national court, the CJEU clarified that Union legislation on renewable sources of energy did not prevent Member States from putting a tax on, for example, wind turbines which were designed to produce electricity.[102]

A number of German local authorities taxed single-use packaging in order to promote reusable packaging. The Commission, seized with complaints from several economic operators, decided in 1996 that no infringement of the Treaty provisions was visible. In the meantime, these taxes were held to be incompatible with internal German law. In 1997, the Commission sent a communication to another institution in which it discussed environmental taxes and levies in the internal market.[103] The communication examined several aspects of eco-taxes, with the implicit intention of bringing as many 3-40

[97] CJEU Case C-47/88 *Commission v Denmark* ECLI:EU:C:1990:449.

[98] As regards metal cans, see para 3-18ff. Sweden had introduced a rather high tax for such cans, and while the Commission had tackled the Danish ban, it had not taken measures against Sweden.

[99] CJEU Case C-13/96 *Bic* ECLI:EU:C:1997:173.

[100] Decision 97/542 [1997] OJ L222/26.

[101] General Court Case T-184/97 *BP v Commission* ECLI:EU:T:2000:217, para 13: 'That decision was adopted without any communication being published in the Official Journal to allow interested third parties to submit their comments … the decision was not published in the Official Journal.'

[102] CJEU Joined Cases C-215/16, C-216/16, C-220/16 and C-221/16 *Elecday Carcelen* ECLI:EU:C:2017:705.

[103] Commission, COM(97) 9, [1997] OJ C224/4.

of the national taxes and levies under the control of Article 34 TFEU as possible. This is understandable since, with the progressive elimination of technical barriers to trade by Article 34, barriers with similar effect may result by virtue of the introduction of national taxes and charges.

Several Member States introduced taxes for plastic bags in order to reduce their use. The Commission accepted this and even encouraged Member States to take this or other measures to reduce environmental pollution by plastic bags.[104]

Since the mid-1990s, Germany has tried to promote alternative energies. National legislation obliged electricity companies to buy electricity from alternative energies produced in Germany at a fixed price which was determined by legislation, and to put the electricity into their grid. Presented with the question of whether this legislation was compatible with EU law, the CJEU decided[105] that the measures did not constitute state aid, as no public funds were made available to competitors. It also decided that, in view of the present state of integration of the electricity market, the German legislation did not contradict Article 34 TFEU. The discriminative character of the measure, which aimed at the promotion of German alternative energy but excluded electricity produced from alternative energy from other Member States, could not really be doubted. The only explanation for its decision, therefore, is that the Court considered the legislation to be a discrimination, but not an *arbitrary* discrimination. It is clear that such a differentiation can only be made by the Court – even though it does not increase transparency and legal certainty. In 2014, the CJEU confirmed its ruling of 2001, despite the development of the EU energy market in the meantime.[106]

Eco-taxes are a useful tool in the promotion of environmentally sound behaviour; they help to keep environmentally unwelcome products off the market.[107] Member States have always used taxes to influence the behaviour of economic operators or private persons; examples are the taxation of petrol and diesel, of spirits and cigarettes, water, electricity and heating. Examples of past eco-taxes are differential taxes for leaded and unleaded petrol, tax relief for nuclear energy, natural gas, lignite or coal, and landfill taxes.

III. Member States' Measures under Existing Union Legislation

A. General Aspects

3-41 As mentioned above, Member States' competence to deal with environmental measures does not end once the Union has adopted an environmental measure. However, it is 'superseded' by the EU measure, as far as the EU measure reaches. Member States'

[104] Commission, COM(2013) 761.

[105] CJEU Case C-379/98 (n 16).

[106] CJEU Case C-573/12 (n 35). See also, however, Case C-262/12 Vent *de Colère* ECLI:U:C:2013:851, where a national system was considered to imply State aid.

[107] See also European Environment Agency, *Environmental Taxes, Implementation and Environmental Effectiveness* (Copenhagen, 1996).

possibility of acting therefore depends both on the content of the EU legislative act, and on the legal basis of that legislative act.

In order to assess the legal content of an EU measure, it is important to examine exactly what the measure intends to cover. For instance, the EU measure might, for product standards, cover only the standards for those products which participate in the trade between Member States, but leave the standards for products which remain on the national market to Member States. EU terminology speaks, in such cases, of optional harmonisation, since Member States may decide to set up two different types of standards for products.[108] In contrast to this, total harmonisation exists where an EU measure intends to set standards for all products which are put into circulation within the Union, whether they cross a border or not.[109] Partial harmonisation only concerns some, but not all, products of a given type.[110] Minimum harmonisation sets standards at EU level, but leaves the possibility for Member States to fix more stringent requirements.[111] Combinations of these types of harmonisation are possible; thus, an EU directive may well fix standards for some products only (partial harmonisation), deal with all products that are on the EU market (total harmonisations) and leave Member States the possibility to adopt more stringent standards (minimum harmonisation).

The different approaches find their source in the EU Treaties themselves. Indeed, the TFEU provides for differences in Member States' rights according to the legal basis on which an EU environmental measure is grounded. For this reason, it is important to examine what the objective of a specific EU legislation is in order to determine the possibilities for Member States to legislate.[112]

As regards the possibility to examine whether a national measure complies with Union law, it is settled case law of the CJEU that where a Union legislative act constitutes a total (exhaustive) harmonisation of Member States' legislation, the national measure is not checked as to its compatibility with Articles 34 and 36 TFEU. Only when the Union legislation does not constitute a total harmonisation is compliance with these provisions required.[113]

B. Member States' Rights under Article 193 TFEU

Where an EU measure is based on Article 192 TFEU, the relationship between the Member States' and the Union's right to legislate is governed by Article 193.[114] The provision only refers to protective measures and it may thus be doubtful whether measures that 3-42

[108] Examples are the limit values for noise emissions from construction equipment, see para 8-46ff.

[109] Examples are the limit values for air emission from cars since 1988, see para 8-17.

[110] An example is Regulation 1102/2008 (n 54).

[111] Examples are standards for waste incineration plants, see para 10-32.

[112] See, eg CJEU Case C-329/95 *VAG Sverige* ECLI:EU:C:1997:256.

[113] CJEU Case C-24/21 *Regione Venezia* ECLI:EU:C:2022:526; for a case where the Union act had not realised a total harmonisation, see Case C- 573/12 (n 35).

[114] Art 193 TFEU: 'The protective measures adopted in common pursuant to Art 192, shall not prevent any Member State from maintaining or introducing more stringent protective measures. Such measures must be compatible with the Treaties. They shall be notified to the Commission.'

aim at preserving or improving the quality of the environment (see Article 191 TFEU) are also covered. However, such a differentiation would make no sense, all the more since no clear distinction can be drawn between protective, preserving and improving measures. 'Protective measures' must therefore be interpreted as including all measures adopted under Article 192, even where only the main objective of a measure – say, 55 per cent of it – is environmentally oriented and a considerable part – say, 45 per cent – is aimed at the achievement of internal market objectives.

Article 193 says nothing about the form which the EU provision under Article 192 must take. It is therefore irrelevant whether the provision is set out in a directive, a regulation or a decision – for instance, whether to adhere to an international agreement, whether the measure was adopted unanimously or by majority vote, or whether it was a partial, optional or total harmonisation measure.

3-43 Article 193 only allows *stricter* measures to be taken. Consequently, the Member States may not adopt different measures from those adopted by the Union. On the contrary: the more stringent national measure must follow the same direction and come closer than the Union to attaining the objectives of Article 191(1) TFEU. It is important that the rules adopted by the individual Member State are of the same type as the EU provisions, because then the Union and other Member States have the possibility of catching up and aligning with the more protective measure taken by one Member State, re-establishing in this way uniform legislation throughout the Union.[115]

3-44 For example, if the Union decides, in a measure based on Article 192, to halve the production and consumption of CFCs because of their ozone-depleting potential, any Member State may still propose an outright ban on the production and consumption of CFCs. However, it may not ban, on the basis of Article 193, the use of aerosol cans which contain CFC gas: this is not a more stringent protective measure, but another, different measure: an *aliud*. The legality of such a measure is therefore determined according to general Treaty provisions, in particular Articles 34 and 36 TFEU.

If the Union introduces a system of strict, unlimited liability for environmental damage but excludes the compensation of bodily injury, each Member State may impose strict liability and provide for the inclusion of compensation for bodily injury of individual persons. However, it may not provide for unlimited liability only for damage that was caused by negligence instead, since this is a different system. Nor could the Member State in that case argue that experience had shown that certain industrial activities too often give cause for environmental liability and then prohibit that specific industrial activity altogether.

When the Union introduced an eco-label for products and took a flower as its symbol, it expressly allowed Member States to maintain their national eco-label systems.[116] Without this express authorisation, Member States would not have been able, based on Article 193, to maintain their national systems. Indeed, the symbols as well as the selection and assessment criteria being different, these national systems are not 'more protective' systems under Article 193, but rather different systems.

[115] See also CJEU Case C-6/03 *Deponieverband Eiterköpfe* ECLI:EU:C:2005:222, where the Court required the national measure to pursue 'the same objectives'.

[116] Regulation 66/2010 on the Community eco-label [2010] OJ L27/1, Art 11 and Recital 15; see para 6-55.

A more protective system is a system which establishes stricter limit values for the emission of pollutants into the environment, which reduces emissions more quickly than the EU measure or which regulates, for emissions from an industrial plant, more pollutants than the EU measure.

3-45 The nationally more protective measures must be compatible with the Treaties. Consequently, they may not conflict with any provision of the Treaties, particularly with the provisions on the free circulation of goods or on undistorted competition. The measures must not constitute a means of arbitrary discrimination or a disguised restriction on trade between Member States (Articles 34 and 36 TFEU). Reference to the Treaties means, of course, reference to the interpretation given to the different Treaty provisions, by the CJEU in particular. Therefore, a national, more protective measure may neither be discriminatory nor disproportionate with regard to the objective that is pursued with it. Protectionism is still protectionism, even if the aim is to protect the environment.

3-46 'Treaties' refers also to secondary EU law, since this is based on the TFEU.[117] This theory was contested mainly by German writers who argued that otherwise the right to take more protective measures would be undermined by EU secondary legislation and become meaningless. However, this opinion did not take into consideration the fact that EU secondary legislation is also based on the Treaties. As regards Article 36 TFEU, it is settled CJEU case law – and in the meantime no longer contested – that this provision no longer applies where the Union has adopted secondary totally harmonising legislation – whether such EU measures were based on Article 114 or 192, or any other provision.[118]

Furthermore, it has already been discussed above[119] that the Council considers Articles 114 and 192 to be equally valid grounds on which to base environmental legislation and that it differentiates the legal basis, supported in this by the CJEU and the Commission, according to the 'centre of gravity' of a measure. This means that, for example, up to 49 per cent of a measure that is based on Article 192 may be provisions which deal with internal market issues. In such a case, Member States may also take more protective measures with regard to the provisions concerning the 49 per cent of the measures. An example is Directive 2000/53 on end-of-life vehicles,[120] which prohibited the use of certain heavy metals in new cars. Member States are, of course, allowed, under Article 193, to provide for further restrictions, under the condition that these measures are also justified under other Treaty provisions, in particular Articles 34 and 36 TFEU. In order to prevent Member States from taking such measures, the legislation on electrical and electronic waste was split up: the ban of heavy metals was regulated in Directive 2002/95, which was based on Article 114,[121] whereas the other provisions concerning such waste were regulated by Directive 2002/96, which was based on Article 192[122] and thus allowed to recur to Article 193. The opposite example is Directive 94/62 on packaging

[117] In this sense, see also EU Pagh, *Miljoeret* (Copenhagen, 1996) 242; contra A Epiney, *Umweltrecht in der Europäischen Union* 4th edn (Baden-Baden, 2019) 126, quoting other German authors.

[118] See n 92.

[119] See para 2-71ff.

[120] Directive 2000/53 on end-of life vehicles [2000] OJ L269/34.

[121] Directive 2002/95 on the restriction of the use of certain hazardous substances in electrical and electronic equipment [2003] OJ L37/19.

[122] Directive 2002/96 on waste electrical and electronic equipment (WEEE) [2003] OJ L37/24.

and packaging waste, which was based on the current Article 114.[123] In order to allow Member States to fix more demanding recycling targets than those provided for by the directive, Article 6(6) of the directive had to introduce an express provision allowing Member States to adopt more stringent targets.

3-47 The problem is of considerable practical importance. For example, Regulation 66/2010, based on Article 192, introduced an EU eco-label.[124] The EU criteria for attribution of an eco-label are set for product groups by EU decisions which are based on Regulation 66/2010 and, ultimately, on Article 192 TFEU. The specific decision to grant an eco-label for a specific product is taken at national level.[125] It seems an impossible idea to establish EU-wide criteria for specific product groups and then, when a producer asks a national authority to obtain the eco-label, inform them that the Member State in question has adopted more protective provisions so that they cannot obtain the eco-label. Such a solution would be all the more contradictory as the same producer could obtain the eco-label in another Member State that had not adopted such 'more protective measures', and could then circulate the product freely within the Union. Thus, within one and the same Member State, products could circulate with the same eco-label, but with different eco-criteria; this result is absurd.

Another example is the regulation on the shipment of waste, which is based on Article 192.[126] The Regulation established lists of non-hazardous and hazardous waste, for which different surveillance and control systems as regards shipments apply. Non-hazardous waste may be shipped practically without restriction. The question is whether Member States are allowed, under Article 193, to classify a non-hazardous waste as hazardous and then apply stricter controls to such shipments. I am of the opinion that this is not allowed.

A last example again concerns the shipment of waste. Regulation 1013/2006 differentiated, for hazardous wastes, between shipments that were made for disposal and shipments that were made for recovery purposes. While Member States may prohibit shipments of hazardous waste for disposal altogether,[127] they may object to shipments for recovery only in a number of specific cases which were listed in Article 12 of Regulation 1013/2006.

Article 12(1.g) allowed objections to shipments:

> [I]f the ration of the recoverable and non-recoverable waste, the estimated value of the materials to be finally recovered or the cost of the recovery and the cost of the disposal of the non recoverable fraction do not justify the recovery under economic and environmental considerations.

Could a Member State, invoking Article 193, also generally prohibit shipments of waste for recovery?

3-48 The answer must be in the negative. Indeed, there is no sense in differentiating between waste for disposal and waste for recovery at all if Member States could adopt provisions

[123] Directive 94/62 on packaging and packaging waste [1994] OJ L365/10.

[124] Regulation 66/2010 (n 116).

[125] For more details, see para 6-55.

[126] Regulation 1013/2006 on shipments of waste [2006] OJ L190/1; this regulation replaced Regulation 259/93 [1993] OJ L30/1.

[127] Regulation 1013/2006 (n 126) Art 11(1).

which would lead to an equal treatment of waste in both cases. Why should there be the necessity for very carefully considering environmental and economic aspects of a waste shipment under Article 12 of Regulation 1013/2006 if a Member State could ensure, as a general rule, that shipments of waste would be prohibited even if the weighing up of arguments showed that such a shipment was environmentally sound? Listing specific grounds for objecting to waste shipments in Article 12(1) and then admitting an unlimited number of supplementary objections does not really make sense.

This question was, under the previous Regulation on the shipment of waste, Regulation 259/93, submitted to the CJEU in Case C-203/96.[128] The Court found that neither Regulation 259/93 nor Directive 75/442 on waste[129] allowed the application of the principles of self-sufficiency and proximity to shipments of waste for recovery. However, it did not answer the question of whether Article 193 allowed such an application and thus whether Member States could go beyond Regulation 259/93 by invoking Article 193. Instead, it examined the grounds invoked by the Dutch government for its national measure which went beyond Regulation 259/93 and found that the justification – to ensure the continuity of supply of Dutch undertakings and increased risks for the environment by waste shipments – did not justify, in that specific case,[130] the restriction under Article 36 TFEU.

This judgment might well be claimed by both sides. Indeed, if a Member State could have recourse to Article 193 and generally object to waste shipments, an examination of whether such a restriction is contrary to Article 35 TFEU would not have been necessary. On the other hand, if the objections listed in Article 12(1) of Regulation 1013/2006 were exhaustive, should the Court have entered into an examination of supplementary objection grounds? 3-49

In my opinion, it should first of all be noted that the problem only appears as regards product standards, where the EU principle of free circulation of goods interferes. Indeed, where EU secondary legislation establishes limit values for emissions from installations or quality standards for concentrations of pollutants in water, there is general agreement that Member States may, on the basis of Article 193, set stricter provisions at national level.

As regards product-related secondary EU legislation, the solution lies in the necessity of reading the two criteria of Article 193 together – ie 'more protective measure' and 'compatible with the Treaty': any EU environmental legislation, including the legislation that is based on Article 192, must respect the provisions of Articles 34 and 36 – this is settled case law of the CJEU.[131] Thus, EU legislation also has to respect the principles of non-discrimination and proportionality,[132] although the EU legislature enjoys a large degree of discretion as to how to draft legislation in a specific case. The more the EU legislature has weighed up the different economic, ecological, social, political and other 3-50

[128] CJEU Case C-203/96 (n 10).

[129] Directive 75/442 as amended by Directive 91/156 [1991] OJ L78/32. This directive is now replaced by Directive 2008/98 (n 44).

[130] It is not clear why the Court entered into the discussion of this specific case, although it was a question which was put to the Court under the procedure of Art 267 TFEU.

[131] CJEU Case 15/83 *Denkavit Nederland* ECLI:EU:C:84:183; Case C-51/93 *Meyhui* ECLI:EU:C:1994:312; Case C-284/95 *Safety Hi-Tech* ECLI:EU:C:1998:352.

[132] The proportionality principle is also laid down in Art 5(4) TEU.

arguments in detail and has elaborated detailed, balanced and sophisticated provisions (such as decisions on eco-label criteria, waste lists, objection grounds), the more the principles of Articles 34 and 36 are 'filled up'; in a case of total harmonisation, there is thus no room left for the principles of Articles 34 and 36. Therefore, when a Member State, based on Article 193 TFEU, wants to take more protective measures, its legislative discretion is reduced in proportion to the concretisation which EU secondary legislation has given to the balance between environmental and economic interests in a specific situation. A national measure which deviates from the solutions set by EU secondary legislation would thus be disproportionate and therefore not compatible with the Treaties.

This means in the concrete case of waste shipments that Regulation 1013/2006 – and its predecessor, Regulation 259/93 – constitute total harmonisation measures as regards objects to waste shipments for recovery. Member States may not go further than Regulation 1013/2006 and invoke other grounds for objecting to shipments.

The problem has only been seen in practice in a few cases so far. Directive 87/416 allowed Member States to prohibit the use of leaded petrol, but required that the intention of such a ban be published and notified to the Commissions six months in advance.[133] Germany wanted, based on Article 193, to disregard the six-month delay and ban leaded petrol four months after notification. However, it finally accepted the Commission's request that the six-month delay be respected, which safeguarded the interests of producers, importers, traders and users of petrol and cars.

Another example is that of sewage sludge in agriculture. Directive 86/278 on protecting the environment and soil against the use of sewage sludge[134] fixed maximum permitted concentrations of some heavy metals in sewage sludge and in the soil. Where these concentration values are exceeded, the use of sewage sludge was prohibited. In view of the accumulation of heavy metals in the soil and the possible residues in food, Austrian and German regions prohibited the use of sewage sludge on or in soil altogether. In my opinion, such a measure is justified under Article 193 TFEU. Article 34 does not stand against this solution, as sewage sludge may nevertheless be traded within the Union. Under those national laws, it is only forbidden to use it on or in soil. And as sludge contains heavy metals, it must remain the decision of Member States to fix themselves the degree of protection which they want to apply to their soils.

When the Union introduced a greenhouse gas emissions trading scheme, it amended Directive 96/61 and provided that industrial installations which participated in the trading scheme were not obliged to apply, with regard to CO_2 emissions, the best available techniques.[135] The question is whether a Member State may, on the basis of Article 193 TFEU, introduce the requirement of using the best available techniques at national level. This is, in my opinion, the case. Each Member State is entitled to discriminate against its own national installations.[136] If the Council and the European Parliament

[133] Directive 87/416 [1987] OJ L225/33.

[134] Directive 86/278 on the use of sewage sludge in agriculture [1986] OJ L181/6.

[135] See now Directive 2010/75 on industrial emissions [2010] OJ L334/17, Art 9(1): 'Where emissions of a greenhouse gas from an installation are specified in Annex I to Directive 2003/87 in relation to an activity carried out in that installation, the permit shall not include an emission limit value for direct emissions of that gas, unless necessary to ensure that no significant local pollution is caused.'

[136] J Jans and H Vedder, *European Environmental Law*, 4th edn (Groningen, 2012) 108 appear to deny such a right of a Member State under Art 193. They hold that the EU legislature could make such a 'self-binding' commitment

wanted to provide for a total harmonisation, they should have based the legislation on industrial installations on Article 114 TFEU, instead of Article 192 TFEU.

Measures adopted under Article 193 must be notified to the Commission. There is no time limit for such notification and the measures need not be notified to the Commission in draft form; the Member State is also not obliged to wait for a certain period after the notification before adopting the measures. However, the situation is different where the national measure comes into the field of application of Directive 2015/1535.[137] Indeed, that directive provides that all product-related measures should be notified to the Commission in draft form in order to allow an examination of whether or not they could create new barriers to trade. Therefore, where a more protective measure could have an influence on Article 34 TFEU, the Commission must be notified of it in draft form. Under Directive 2015/1535, there is then a standstill period of at least three months during which the Commission and all other Member States may question the compatibility of the draft measure with Article 34 or secondary EU legislation. Omitting to notify the Commission of the draft makes the national provision unenforceable.[138] 3-51

Article 193 does not contain any procedural provisions for checking whether the national measure fulfils the conditions that are laid down in this provision. Where the Commission is of the opinion that a national measure is not a more protective measure, but a different one (an *aliud*), or where it believes that the measure is not compatible with primary or secondary EU law, it has, in the last instance, to recur to procedures under Article 258 TFEU. The same possibility is open to any Member States under Article 259 TFEU.

C. Member States' Rights under Article 114(4)–(8) TFEU

(i) General Aspects

Article 114(4)–(8) TFEU deals with the right of Member States to maintain existing or introduce new legislative measures where the Union has legislated on the legal basis of Article 114. 3-52

The present Article 114 was introduced into the Treaty in 1987 as Article 100a. Its paragraph 4 allowed Member States, in the case of decisions according to that provision and under certain conditions, to 'apply' diverging national legislation. The application of this provision left a number of questions open; they were finally solved by the Amsterdam Treaty, which brought Article 114 (4) and (5) TFEU into its present form and introduced Article 114(6), according to which the Commission had to take a decision under Article 114 within six months; otherwise, the national measure would be deemed to have been approved.[139]

to exclude such a possibility. This would mean that the legislature could make a commitment to prohibit the application of a provision of the EU Treaties.

[137] Directive 2015/1535 laying down a procedure for the provision of information in the field of technical regulations and of rules on Information Society services [2015] OJ L241/1.

[138] CJEU Case C-194/94 *CIA Security International* ECLI:EU:C:1996:172.

[139] For a case where the six-month delay had been exceeded, see General Court Case T-69/08 *Poland v Commission* ECLI:EU:T:2010:504.

The Amsterdam Treaty explicitly provided for the possibility for Member States to *maintain or introduce* national measures after the Union had adopted a measure under Article 114. This ended the extensive legal discussion on the former wording, whether 'apply' was to be understood as 'continue to apply' – this had always been the Commission's understanding – or was equivalent to 'maintain or introduce'. In 2003, the Commission resumed its practice under Article 114 in a communication.[140]

(ii) Maintaining National Legislation (Article 114(4))

3-53 For a Member State to maintain national environmental legislation, according to Article 114(4), despite EU legislation, a number of conditions must be fulfilled:

1. the Union must have adopted a harmonisation measure;
2. a Member State must deem it necessary to maintain its national legislation on grounds that relate to the protection of the environment;
3. the Member State notifies the Commission of these provisions, as well as of the grounds for maintaining them; and
4. the Commission approves of the national measures (Article 114(6)).

These different conditions will be examined one by one.[141]

3-54 *Adoption of a harmonisation measure.* The express inclusion of measures taken by the Commission clarifies that the adaptation of EU measures to scientific or technical progress or by other means of delegated or implementing acts (Articles 290 and 291 TFEU) may also lead to the right of Member States to maintain national legislation; such cases may well occur where technical annexes of directives are adapted to technical progress.

'Harmonisation measures' are measures adopted under Article 114 TFEU. Such a measure need not have been adopted by majority decision; even in the case of a unanimous decision, the right of a Member State to maintain its national legislation exists. It is not contradictory to vote in favour of an EU measure and then decide to maintain more stringent national legislation. Indeed, a Member State may well vote in favour of an EU measure because it wishes to see the level of environmental protection increased throughout the Union, even if the EU measure does not go as far as its own national legislation.

3-55 *Necessity of maintaining national legislation.* It is doubtful whether any national legislation may be maintained. These doubts stem from Article 114(7),[142] which demonstrates the aim of the Treaty legislature to ensure that uniform legislation applies throughout

[140] Commission, 'Communication Concerning Article 95 (paras 4, 5 and 6)' COM(2002) 760.

[141] The Commission adopted a number of environmental decisions concerning the application of Art 95(4) – the present Art 114(4) TFEU – in particular: Decision 99/831 (Netherlands – PCP) [1999] OJ L329/15; Decision 99/832 (Netherlands – creosote) [1999] OJ L329/25; Decision 99/833 (Germany – creosote) [1999] OJ L329/43; Decision 99/834 (Sweden – creosote) [1999] OJ L329/63; Decision 99/835 (Denmark – creosote) [1999] OJ L329/82; Decision 2000/509 (Belgium – organo-stannic compounds) [2000] OJ L205/7; Decision 2002/399 (Sweden – cadmium in fertilizers) [2002] OJ L138/24; Decision 2006/347 (Sweden – cadmium in fertilizers), [2006] OJ L129/19; Decision 2006/348 (Finland – cadmium in fertilizers) [2006] OJ L129/25; Decision 2006/349 (Austria – cadmium in fertilizers) [2006] OJ L129/31; Decision 2006/390 (Czech Republic – cadmium in fertilizers) [2006] OJ L150/17; Decision 2007/395 (Netherlands – paraffin) [2007] OJ L148/17.

[142] Art 114(7) TFEU: 'When … a Member State is authorised to maintain or introduce national provisions derogating from a harmonisation measure, the Commission shall immediately examine whether to propose an adaptation to that measure.'

the Union. Therefore, the EU measure shall, if at all possible, be adapted to that of the derogating Member State in order to ensure the continuous free circulation of goods in the Union's internal market.

These questions will be discussed below, when the Commission's options are examined for approving or refusing the Member State's maintaining of its national legislation. It is certain that a Member State may notify any national measure under Article 114(4); it is not necessary that the legislation is adopted at national level; regional measures may also be notified.[143]

Notification and justification of the national measure. The Member State which wishes to maintain its national legislation must formally inform the Commission of its intention to do so. There is no time limit for this notification; terms that require such notification to be addressed to the Commission within a specific time span after the adoption of the EU legislation or within the time span which was provided for in the EU measure for transposition into national legislation have not been retained. Usually, therefore, a Member State is free to notify the Commission when it seems fit to do so. 3-56

However, it is clearly in the self-interest of the notifying Member State to notify as early as possible. On the one hand, provisions of EU law prevail over national law and may have a direct effect, even where they are not transposed into national law; this means in practice that national law which is in conflict with an EU provision may not be applied – nor be enforced.[144] On the other hand, the notification puts into operation a six-month delay within which a decision on the national measure must be taken (Article 114(6)).

Finally, the CJEU decided[145] that a Member State may only apply national legislation which deviates from the EU harmonisation measure once it has received an approving decision from the Commission. It is doubtful whether this decision, which was taken at a time when the Treaty text did not yet differentiate in Article 114 between 'apply' and 'maintain/introduce', is of much relevance now. Indeed, it would constitute a considerable disturbance of economic operations and administrative practice if a Member State would have to suspend the application of national legislation which might have existed for years and wait for a Commission decision. The reasonable, and largely logical, consequence is therefore to consider the Court's statement remaining valid only for the cases of Article 114(5), ie for cases where new national legislation is introduced. Anyway, the uncertainty of the described legal situation suggests that the Member State has a strong interest in trying to obtain the Commission's decision as quickly as possible and before the transposition period for the harmonisation measure has ended. 3-57

The notifying Member State will also have to give the grounds for its decision to maintain national legislation. It has to indicate the factual and legal aspects in sufficient detail to allow the Commission to reach a decision on the notification within six months. The requirement of providing the grounds for the decision is new and constitutes, without doubt, a considerable supplementary burden for the notifying Member State.

[143] See, eg the legislation referred to in General Court Case T-366/03, *Austria v Commission* ECLI:EU:T:2005:247, which originated from the Land (region) Ober-Österreich. The appeal was rejected, Case C-439/05P *Austria v Commission* ECLI:EU:C:2007:510.

[144] CJEU Case C-41/93 *France v Commission* ECLI:EU:C:1994:196, para 30.

[145] See ibid para 30, Opinion of Advocate General Tesauro, para 9, who argued that this interpretation is the only one which is compatible with the supremacy of EU law and which avoids legal insecurity.

3-58 *Commission approval.* The Commission must 'approve' of the environmental measure; this wording of Article 114(6) is more precise than that of the previous version of the Treaty, which provided that the Commission should 'confirm' the national measure, since it is now – following the judgment in Case C-41/93, quoted above – clear that the approval must be made in the form of a decision under Article 288 TFEU.

Approval must be given if the national measure does not constitute a 'means of arbitrary discrimination or a disguised restriction on trade between Member States'. This wording is identical to that of Article 36(2) TFEU. Thus, the interpretation of Article 36(2) may be used to interpret this provision. Arbitrary discrimination or disguised trade restrictions are cases of abuse where a formally legitimate objective – the protection of the environment – is used to discriminate against goods from other Member States or to pursue protectionist goals.

3-59 To these two aspects – discrimination and trade restriction – which were already contained in the previous versions of Article 114, a third one has been added: the national measure 'shall not constitute an obstacle to the functioning of the internal market'.

It is clear that any national measure which is maintained, despite a harmonisation measure taken by the Union, constitutes an obstacle to the functioning of the internal market; the two bans on pentachlorophenol, in Germany and Denmark, on which the Commission had decided constitute a clear example, since products containing that substance were not allowed to circulate in those countries. It is thus not quite clear what the provision intends to achieve.

3-60 Where, for instance, the Union decides to create a uniform eco-labelling system throughout the Union, such a measure would have to be based on Article 114. Supposing that Germany then wanted to maintain its national eco-symbol, which is a blue angel, and not a flower, as is the EU symbol: could this be done by invoking Article 114(4)? The answer seems clearly to be in the negative. Indeed, it is possible to have either a system based on the flower or one based on the blue angel, but one cannot have both systems inside an internal market. In fact, the German system in this example would be a *different* system. Also, it is not clear what the environmental grounds would be which would make it 'necessary' to maintain the blue angel system; greater efficiency cannot be a valid ground, because the EU system is just meant to create an equivalent system. In conclusion, the maintaining of the blue angel system would be a different system, where the environmental grounds that would make its maintenance necessary are not visible.

Where the Union provides for certain limit values for noise emissions from coaches, any more stringent national limit value would, if properly enforced, create an obstacle to the free circulation of coaches and would thus have to be disallowed. This solution could be avoided where the Member State that wishes to maintain the more stringent national emission limit values would at least allow the circulation on its territory of coaches which are registered in other Member States and only occasionally circulate within the Member State with the more stringent values. This consideration demonstrates that the assessment of whether the maintaining of a national measure is necessary requires a detailed consideration of the pros and cons under internal market and ecological auspices. Sevenster[146] goes so far as to generalise this position: she is of the opinion that the necessity of considering

[146] H Sevenster, The environmental guarantee after Amsterdam: does the emperor have new clothes? *The Yearbook of European Environmental Law* 2000, 291.

whether the national measure constitutes an obstacle is a badly drafted expression of the proportionality principle.

In conclusion, the new addition to Article 114 does not mean that the national environmental measure may not, under any circumstances, constitute an obstacle to the free circulation of goods. It is only meaningful when it is completed by a word such as 'inadequate', 'inappropriate' or 'disproportionate'.[147] This would mean that, in each individual case, the Commission would have to weigh up the protection of the environment against the proper functioning of the internal market. Thus, a national measure must be proportional to the objective pursued by it; where a less restrictive measure is available, the Member State may be asked to recur to that measure even where this would mean a change in its national rules. Also, a measure that constitutes a significant obstacle to the functioning of the internal market and where the environmental advantage is not significant could be rejected by the Commission. 3-61

This interpretation would bring the principle of proportionality from Article 5 TEU into the assessment process of Article 114(6): while it is legitimate to protect the environment and not to see the national level of environmental protection lowered by a harmonisation measure from the Union, the national measure must not go beyond what is necessary to achieve appropriate environmental protection.

Procedure. The Treaty does not set a specific time period for the delay when the national measure has to be notified or approved. As mentioned, it would make sense to have it notified after the adoption of the EU measure but before the period for transposing the EU measure into national law has expired. However, it will be impossible not to approve a national measure exclusively with the argument that it was notified too late, though the CJEU has stated that the principle of sincere co-operation of Article 4(3) TEU obliges Member States to notify a national measure 'as soon as possible'.[148] 3-62

The Commission is required to decide on the national decision to maintain national legislation within six months of notification; in particularly complex cases, it may prolong this period by a maximum of six months more. This provision was introduced by the Amsterdam Treaty as a reaction to the fact that some national notifications under Article 114(4) had not been decided upon for several years.[149] It is not possible to prolong this delay, for instance, when the Commission argues that the Member State's decision has not been sufficiently argued. The Commission may then refuse to authorise the measure; but it may not ask for further documentation, evidence or other justification, since this would introduce supplementary conditions for the application of the six-month period, for which the Commission has no mandate in the Treaties.[150]

The time given for approval may appear short. It should be noted, however, that the legal and environmental situation in the different Member States has normally been discussed at EU level during the elaboration of the harmonisation measure. The subject matter of national legislation is thus not entirely new to the Commission.

The sanction for failing to decide within six months is tough: the national measure 'shall be deemed to have been approved'. The national measure has, in such a case, an effect on all 3-63

[147] In the same sense, see Commission, Decision 1999/831, para 23.
[148] CJEU Case C-319/97 *Kortas* ECLI:EU:C:1999:272, para 35.
[149] For an example, see Decision 2001/59 [2001] OJ L210/46.
[150] See General Court Case T-69/08 (n 139).

other Member States, as well as on all economic operators, even though they did not have the possibility of influencing the speed of decision-making within the Commission. Where a Member State is of the opinion that the Commission has made a wrong decision, either by approving or rejecting the national measure within six months or by letting the six-month period elapse, it may bring the matter before the CJEU directly (Article 114(8)). The procedure is governed by Article 263(2) TFEU if the action is directed against the Commission, or by Article 259 TFEU if the action is directed against another Member State. The two-month delay of Article 263(6) TFEU starts, in the case of the absence of a Commission decision within six months, at the end of the six-month period. As of the end of 2022, no Member State has ever taken such an action against another Member State or against the Commission.

Private operators may take action against the Commission under Article 263(4) TFEU if they are directly and individually concerned by the decision, for instance when their exports or imports are affected. They may also try to conform to the EU harmonisation measure and, where they see their trade affected, bring the matter before the competent national court and then ask for a preliminary ruling by the CJEU under Article 267 TFEU in order to have the Commission's decision checked.

(iii) Introducing New National Legislation

3-64 The provision of Article 114(5) clarifies that Member States may, under certain conditions, introduce new legislation in cases where the Union has adopted a harmonisation measure.[151] The possibility of introducing new measures exists only for measures relating to the environment and the working environment. The different grounds of Article 36 TFEU which allow Member States, under Article 114(4), to maintain existing more stringent national provisions may not be invoked for the introduction of new measures.

The conditions for introducing new national environmental measures are relatively strict. They are the following:

1. the new national measure must be based on new scientific evidence;
2. the problem must be specific to the Member State that wishes to introduce the measure; and
3. the problem must have arisen after the adoption of the harmonisation measure.

The three conditions must be fulfilled cumulatively. Their likely effect will make it very rare for a Member State to demonstrate the necessity to opt out of the common EU measure, although the acting Member State has a certain amount of discretion to assess whether the new situation requires the opting out of the EU measure ('deems it necessary'). Its decision is, in turn, assessed by the Commission and, in case of litigation, by the CJEU.

3-65 *New scientific evidence.* New scientific evidence may consist of studies, reports or other documentation showing that there is a real risk to the environment and that, therefore,

[151] Art 114(5) TFEU: 'if, after the adoption of a harmonisation measure by the European Parliament and the Council, by the Council or by the Commission, a Member State deems it necessary to introduce national provisions based on new scientific evidence relating to the protection of the environment or the working environment on grounds of a problem specific to that Member State arising after the adoption of the harmonisation measure, it shall notify the Commission of the envisaged provisions as well as the grounds for introducing them.'

it is necessary to introduce a more protective national measure. It is not easy to comply with this criterion. For instance, the fact that benzene, an additive in petrol, is carcinogenic has been known for years; thus, a Member State would not be allowed to lower the maximum admissible content of benzene in petrol below the level that was fixed by the Union. It might be argued that the cancer statistics which show the effects of benzene constitute 'new evidence'. This seems doubtful, though, in the end, acceptable; in any case such a discovery would not be specific to an individual Member State, but would concern the whole of the Union. For such cases, the new formulation of Article 114(3) suggests that the Commission make a new proposal for a harmonisation measure 'taking account in particular of any new development based on scientific facts'. To take another example: the continuing global climate problem would not justify a Member State introducing national standards for greenhouse gas emissions from cars which deviate from EU standards; again, this is not 'new' scientific evidence nor is the problem specific to one Member State alone.

Scientific evidence is new where the EU legislature was not able to take it into account at the moment of adopting the harmonisation measure. The word 'evidence'[152] will, also in the light of the precautionary principle, have to be interpreted broadly and will be considered to include data, the accumulation of existing studies which bring to light a specific problem and other factual aspects which allow the conclusion that there is the probability of environmental risks. It is not to be understood as requiring 'proof' of new risks or damage.

Specific problem. The condition that the problem must be specific to a Member State is 3-66
probably the most difficult to comply with. Indeed, since Article 114 refers to the internal market and thus mainly to product-related measures, it is difficult to imagine the effects of a product causing environmental problems that are specific to the national territory of a single Member State. Nor would the effect of a product on global warming, on the ozone layer, on water or on fauna and flora be sufficient, since, normally, all these effects affect more than one Member State.

In 2005, the Netherlands wanted to introduce legal requirements to reduce the emissions of particulates from diesel cars, in deviation from Directive 98/69. The measure would have required, under the present state of technical knowledge, diesel cars to be equipped with specific filters which were not required under EU legislation. The Commission accepted that the numerous studies which had been published on the problem constituted new scientific evidence. However, it compared the emissions of particulates in the Netherlands with those in other Member States and, furthermore, with the number of diesel cars in the Netherlands. It concluded that the health problems caused by diesel particulates were not specific to the Netherlands, but existed also in other Member States.[153] This decision is bitter and absurd, as health protection measures to save lives are prevented in one country because other countries were less active: overall, the annual number of premature deaths in the Union due to diesel particulates in the air is estimated to be more than 200,000.

[152] At least in some EU languages the word which is used has the connotation of 'findings', such as in Dutch (*gegevens*), German (*Erkenntnisse*), Portuguese (*novedades*) and French (*preuves*).

[153] On appeal, the CJEU quashed the Commission's decision for formal reasons: the Commission had not examined all the data that had been submitted by the Netherlands, Case C-405/07P *Netherlands v Commission* ECLI:EU:C:2008:613.

Filters for diesel cars have been available on the market for years, and are in particular offered by French car manufacturers. However, the Commission hesitated to propose amendments to the existing legislation and to prescribe their use, because, in the 1990s, it had agreed with the car industry a planned schedule for air pollution reduction: and then, in the name of law, it even prevented individual Member States to take measures.[154]

The Commission furthermore rejected a number of attempts by Member States to prevent the cultivation or placing on the market of genetically modified products, arguing that the national environment was not specifically different from the environment in other Member States. It was supported in this interpretation by the CJEU.[155] This matter was not solved by the adoption of Directive 2015/412,[156] as that directive only concerned the cultivation, but not the commercialisation, of genetically modified products.

3-67 *New problems*. The condition that the problem must have arisen after the adoption of the harmonisation measure may concern cases in which environmental effects of a specific problem become evident, such as a biocide, a pesticide or other chemical product which is suddenly shown to have caused serious environmental problems in a specific region. A simple change in the environmental policy in a Member State would not justify the introduction of new legislation. In the same way, this condition would not be fulfilled where an environmental problem – gradually or suddenly – appears before the adoption of the harmonisation measure and the Member State wishes to introduce opt-out legislation after the adoption of the harmonisation measure.

3-68 *Procedure*. The procedure for measures under Article 114(5), including the time delays, verification, approval or rejection of the national measure, is the same as in the case of the maintaining of a national measure (Article 114(4) TFEU). In the case of the introduction of new legislation, however, the standstill period stipulated by the CJEU will apply; thus, a Member State may only introduce its legislation after the Commission has approved of it. For the rest, reference is made to paragraph 3-62.

3-69 In Decision 1999/836,[157] the Commission rejected a German request to introduce new national legislation on the classification and labelling of certain hazardous chemicals. The Commission held that the scientific and technical grounds on which Germany had based its request had been discussed during the elaboration of the EU legislation in question, and thus did not constitute new evidence. The Court rejected the German appeal against the decision, arguing that Germany had not submitted 'new' scientific evidence.[158] By Decision 2001/570,[159] the Commission rejected another German request to introduce new national legislation on organo-stannic compounds that went beyond Directive 1999/51,[160] arguing again that Germany had not submitted new scientific evidence. The Commission maintained, amongst other things, that in the framework of Article 114(5) only human

[154] For further details, see para 8-29ff.

[155] Commission, Decision 2003/653 (Austria) [2003] OJ L230/34; Decision 2006/255 (Cyprus) [2006] OJ L92/14; Decision 2008/62 (Poland) [2008] OJ L16/17; Decision 2009/828 (Portugal) [2009] OJ L294/16; CJEU Case 439/05P (n 143).

[156] Directive 2015/412 as regards the possibility for Member States to restrict or prohibit the cultivation of genetically modified organisms (GMOs) in their territory [2015] OJ L68/1.

[157] Commission Decision 1999/836 [1999] OJ L329/100.

[158] CJEU Case C-512/99 *Germany v Commission* ECLI:EU:C:2003:40.

[159] Commission Decision 2001/570 [2001] OJ L202/37.

[160] Directive 1999/51 [1999] OJ L142/22.

health arguments related to the working environment were relevant. This opinion overlooked the fact that Article 191 TFEU explicitly states that environmental measures also aim to protect human health.[161] Furthermore, the concept of the 'centre of gravity' to determine the legal basis for a measure would exclude the mentioning of a human-health-related Treaty provision outside of Article 192 where the EU measure covers, for instance, 60 per cent environmental matters and only 40 per cent health protection issues. Refusing Member States in such cases recourse to Article 114(5), as the Commission suggests, cannot therefore be correct.

In Decision 2002/59,[162] the Commission approved for the first time the introduction of new national legislation under Article 114(5). This decision concerned a request by the Netherlands to ban creosote-treated wood. The Commission considered that detailed studies made in the Netherlands on the effects of creosote constituted new scientific evidence. It stated that the environmental concerns were *not* specific to the Netherlands, but it was of the opinion that the extent to which the problem existed in that country – which is rich in groundwater and surface water – allowed the conclusion that the conditions of Article 114(5) were complied with. The decision was apparently of a political nature.

D. Member States' Rights under Other Treaty Provisions

Where an EU environmental measure is based on Treaty provisions other than Article 192 or 114, it is doubtful whether Member States also have the possibility of maintaining or introducing stricter national environmental measures. This applies in particular to measures based on Articles 43 for agricultural policy measures, 91 or 100 for transport policy measures, 113 for tax measures or 207 TFEU for commercial policy measures. 3-70

German legal writers developed, in 1987, a concept according to which the EC Treaty contains a legally binding principle according to which environmental protection within the Union must be optimised. The reasoning was based on several provisions and principles of the Treaty, in particular the present Articles 192, 114(4) and 11 TFEU. The definition varies. Zuleeg, who later acted as a judge at the CJEU and who 'invented' that principle, defined it as 'the right of Member States to maintain or introduce more protection of the environment, even where the EU has adopted a measure to protect the environment'.[163] Other authors, while following Zuleeg in his approach, went even further; some declared that, in the case of conflict between environmental objectives and objectives under other policies, priority should be given to the environmental objective. Others even suggested that, for EU environmental measures, the Treaty provision which optimises environmental protection should be used as a legal basis, and this is usually Article 192.

For the question with which we are here concerned, the German writers suggested that, generally speaking, Member States be granted the rights to adopt more protective measures under Article 193 TFEU, whatever the legal basis was on which the EU measure had 3-71

[161] An example is Directive 98/83 on the quality of water intended for human consumption [1998] OJ L330/32. This directive was based on the present Art 192 TFEU, and was clearly aimed at the protection of human health.

[162] Commission Decision 2002/59 [2002] OJ L23/37.

[163] M Zuleeg, 'Vorbehaltene Kompetenzen der Mitgliedstaaten der Europäischen Gemeinschaft auf dem Gebiet des Umweltrechts' [1987] *Neue Zeitschrift für Verwaltungsrecht* 280 (author's translation).

been based. However, the legal concept is unconvincing. Indeed, it is not clear why the principle of optimising protection should just apply to environmental protection and not to the protection of human health, the respect of human rights and fundamental freedoms or any of the values which are mentioned in Article 36 TFEU. If ever the authors of the EU Treaties had it in mind to establish such a principle, they could have inserted it in the Treaties in one of the Treaty amendments in 1993, 1999, 2003 or 2009.

Furthermore, where a Union environmental measure in the sector of agricultural policy is based on Article 43 TFEU, it is not at all clear whether Article 193 is a more protective provision than Article 114(4) and (5), and hence which of these two provisions should apply. The concept of optimising environmental protection is incapable of explaining why Member States' residual rights have been organised differently under Articles 193 and 114, although there would have been the possibility of finding a single, optimising solution. Also, the concept is more motivated, it seems, by concerns about national powers to legislate than about environmental optimisation, since it cares little for those Member States which do not have an elaborated, consistent, national environmental policy.

As none of the Treaty provisions on which an environmental action can be based contain provisions similar to those of Articles 193 and 114, the conclusion must be that these provisions are exceptions to the general rule that EU measures cannot be derogated from by Member States unless EU law expressly so provides. Their application to measures which had been adopted by virtue of Article 43, 91, 113 or 207 TFEU is therefore not possible, all the more so since it would not be clear whether Article 193 or 114 should apply in a specific case. Article 11 TFEU is of no help either, as the possibilities which Member States have under Article 193 are not 'requirements'; if one were adopting another position, one would also have to consider Article 114 to be an environmental requirement – which, again, would raise the question of which article should apply in a given case. As discussed in paragraph 2-71 above, it will still have to be decided by the Court which are Member States' residual rights when an EU legislation was adopted on a double legal basis, such as Articles 114 and 192 (no such decision exists as yet) or Articles 207 and 192.

E. Member States' Rights under Safeguard Clauses

3-72 The safeguard clauses of both Articles 191(2) and 114(10) TFEU apply where secondary EU legislation expressly contains a provision which enables Member States to take safeguard measures. However, both provisions require a specific provision in secondary EU legislation; they do not directly give rights to Member States.

The specificity of safeguard clauses is that they allow Member States to object to the marketing or circulation of goods even in those cases where the products comply with the requirements which were laid down at EU level. This basic consideration leads to the consequence, expressed in the provisions of both Articles 191(2) and 114(10) TFEU, that the national safeguard measures may only be provisional, limited in time and subject to a decision by the Union as to its compatibility with EU law. In practice, safeguard clauses hardly play a role at all.

3-73 Safeguard clauses in EU secondary environmental legislation existed long before Articles 191(2) and 114(10) TFEU were introduced into the Treaty. A considerable number of EU directives or regulations contained safeguard clauses which allowed Member States to deviate, for health or environmental reasons, from EU standards. The conditions for having recourse to a safeguard clause were practically always the same:

- an express provision in the corresponding EU directive or regulation;
- a formal notification by a Member State that it had evidence that a product, while complying with the requirements of the directive/regulation, constituted a hazard for man or the environment, and that therefore the circulation of the product was restricted or suspended; and
- justification for the national decision taken.

The Commission then had to consult with the other Member States before taking a Union decision. Such a decision could consist of adapting the EU harmonisation measure to the requests of the notifying Member State, or informing the Member State that its safeguard measure was not justified and had to be abandoned.[164]

In the highly controversial area of genetically modified organisms, a number of Member States recurred to the safeguard clause and prohibited the marketing and/or cultivation of genetically modified plants even though the Commission had authorised them. The Commission did not take legal action against this obvious misuse of the safeguard clause but, rather, tried to find policy solutions.[165]

[164] See, eg Decision 90/420 [1990] OJ L22/49, informing Denmark that a specific substance which Denmark had declared carcinogenic by way of a safeguard measure was in reality not carcinogenic.

[165] For more details, see para 6-38ff.

4

Horizontal Measures

I. The Right to a Clean Environment

A. General Remarks

4-01 The Treaty on European Union (TEU) and the Treaty on the Functioning of the European Union (TFEU) do not contain a catalogue on fundamental rights. However, Article 6(1) TEU states:

> The Union recognises the rights, freedoms and principles set out in the Charter of Fundamental Rights of the European Union of 7 December 2000, as adapted at Strasbourg on 12 December 2007, which shall have the same legal value as the Treaties ...
>
> The Union shall accede to the European Convention for the Protection of Human rights and Fundamental Freedoms ...
>
> Fundamental rights, as guaranteed by the European Convention for the protection of Human rights and Fundamental Freedoms and as they result from the constitutional traditions common to the Member States, shall constitute general principles of the Union's law.

Prior to the adoption of the Lisbon Treaty, all Member States had adhered to the Convention for the Protection of Human Rights and Fundamental Freedoms; however, the European Union as such had not signed up to it, in particular for institutional reasons.[1]

Article 6 TEU provides that the EU should adhere to the European Convention on Human Rights and Fundamental Freedoms. A draft agreement was negotiated until 2014. However, when the Court of Justice of the European Union (CJEU) was asked for its opinion on that agreement, it raised a number of objections, arguing in particular that its function as the only arbiter on the interpretation of EU law would be impaired by decisions of the European Court of Human Rights.[2] These arguments appear largely unjustified, as the CJEU never accepted this kind of argument when raised by national supreme or constitutional courts. However, as the Court's opinion is binding on the other institutions (Article 218(11) TFEU), it has the effect of a veto and will have to be taken into consideration in future negotiations.

At the end of 2000, the European Parliament, Council and Commission proclaimed a Charter of Fundamental Rights of the European Union.[3] The Charter applies to the EU

[1] See CJEU, Opinion 2/94 on the accession of the EC to the European Convention on Human Rights ECLI:EU:C:1996:140.

[2] CJEU, Opinion 2/13 on the accession of the EU to the European Convention on Human Rights and Fundamental Freedoms ECLI:EU:C:2014:2454.

[3] Charter of Fundamental Rights of the European Union [2010] OJ C83/389.

institutions and bodies; it applies to Member States 'only, when they are implementing Union law' (Article 51(1) of the Charter), which means their legislative activity and judicial and administrative practices when fulfilling obligations under EU law. The Charter is not meant to create legal rights of citizens, but 'mak[es] these rights more visible'.[4] Its application within the Union is nuanced by a protocol and some declarations annexed to the Treaties.[5]

The discussion on a fundamental right to a clean environment at EU level had some antecedents. In 1989, the European Parliament adopted a resolution on fundamental rights and fundamental freedom which formulated that the preservation, protection and improvement of the quality of the environment was an integrative part of all Community policy.[6] In 1990, the Commission, in a contribution to the discussions on the Maastricht Treaty on European Union, suggested the insertion of such a right into the Treaty,[7] but remained unsuccessful. In 1997, the European Parliament adopted another resolution on the respect of human rights within the Union where it submitted for discussion a catalogue of about 150 provisions concerning fundamental rights.[8] As regards the environment, the Parliament abstained from formulating a provision that gave rights to individuals, and limited itself to confirming that the right to live included a responsibility for present and future generations and that public authorities should guarantee a healthy environment for everybody and grant the possibility to influence decisions on their environment. National legal provisions should be harmonised and sanctions for impairment of the environment should be strengthened according to the polluter-pays principle. Finally, Parliament asked that the export of all materials, food, drugs, etc which were forbidden to be marketed in the Union should be prohibited.[9] This resolution did not lead to any concrete consequences. 4-02

The Charter that was adopted at the end of 2000 did not create a right to a healthy environment. It limited itself to formulate, in Article 37: 'A high level of environmental protection and the improvement of the quality of the environment must be integrated into the policies of the Union and ensured in accordance with the principle of sustainable development.' 4-03

This provision is rather misleading, as it is not clear in what sense such a formula, which largely corresponds to Article 11 TFEU, creates 'rights'. The European Parliament, though, was satisfied with the Charter.[10]

In landmark decisions of 1991, the Court declared that air quality standards were to be adopted in the interest of protecting human health.[11] Therefore, a citizen must be entitled

[4] ibid, Preamble.

[5] Protocol 30 on the application of the Charter of Fundamental rights of the European Union to Poland and the United Kingdom [2008] OJ C115/313; Declarations no 2 [2008] OJ C115/337, no 53 [2008] OJ C115/355, no 61 [2008] OJ C115/358, no 62 [2008] OJ 115/358.

[6] European Parliament, Resolution of 12 April 1989 [1989] OJ C120/51, Art 24.

[7] Commission, 'Contributions to the Intergovernmental Conference' COM(90) 600 of 21 October 1990, Art 7: 'Every Union citizen shall have the right to enjoy a healthy environment and the obligation to contribute to protecting it. To this end, he shall have the right to information and the right to consultation where appropriate.'

[8] European Parliament, Resolution of 8 April 1997 [1997] OJ C132/31.

[9] ibid nos 161–64.

[10] European Parliament Resolution of 14 November 2000 [2001] OJ C223/74.

[11] CJEU Case C-361/88 *Commission v Germany* ECLI:EU:C:1991:224, para 16: 'the obligation imposed on the Member States to prescribe limit values not to be exceeded within specified periods and in specific circumstances … is imposed "in order to protect human health in particular". It implies therefore, that whenever the exceeding of the limit values could endanger human health, the persons concerned must be in a position to rely on mandatory

to ensure in court that the air-quality standards are actually complied with. This interpretation comes close to giving individuals who are affected by polluted air or water a right to clean air or water.[12] Unfortunately, though, environmental organisations and individual citizens hardly ever tested the potential and the limits of this jurisprudence in other cases, for example in waste cases. Thus, the judgments of 1991 are practically being ignored by the administration. A citizen initiative, based on Article 11 TEU,[13] which asked the Commission to formulate a right to water was rejected by the Commission in 2014.[14] A study of the European Economic and Social Committee (EECOSOC) of 2019, which proposed to give legal rights to nature,[15] found no echo with the other institutions.[16]

In 2022, the Eighth EU Environmental Action Programme asked the Commission and all Member States' public authorities to work towards 'advancing towards the recognition of a right to a clean, healthy and sustainable environment internationally', arguing that progressing towards such a right 'is an enabling condition for attaining the priority objectives of the 8th EAP'.[17] No explanation was given as to why such a right should just be promoted internationally and not within the Union.

The academic discussion on a fundamental right for a clean and healthy environment, which had started as far back as the 1970s, had soon made it clear that a meaningful enforceable substantial right to a clean environment could not be introduced into the constitutions of Member States or into primary EU law; where some constitutions had nevertheless tried, the contours of such a right remained unclear. The discussions therefore concentrated on formulating *procedural* rights to a clean environment, which consisted of three parts: the right of access to information on the environment; the right of participating in decision-making on the environment; and the right of access to the courts on environmental matters. Though the idea of a human right to a clean environment – albeit procedural – was not popular with the European Commission; some elements of those procedural rights were taken up in the context of the acts which transposed the requirements of the Aarhus Convention on access to information, participation in decision-making and access to justice in environmental matters. The Aarhus Convention[18] was signed and ratified (among others) by all 27 EU Member States.

rules in order to be able to assert their rights.' See also Case C-59/89 *Commission v Germany* ECLI:EU:C:1991:225. In 2008, the Court confirmed this jurisdiction, Case C-237/07 *Janecek* ECLI:EU:C:2008:447.

[12] See, however, CJEU Case C-61/21 *Ministère de la Transition écologique* ECLI:EU:C:2022:1015, where a right to compensation for health damage due to air pollution was refused.

[13] See Art 11 TEU and Regulation 211/2011 on the citizens' initiative [2011] OJ L65/1. An initiative must assemble one million signatures, from at least seven Member States. The administrative burden for such initiatives is too high.

[14] Commission, COM(2014) 177. The citizen initiative had the title: 'Water and sanitation are a human right. Water is a public good, not a commodity!'.

[15] EECOSOC, *Towards an EU Charter of the Fundamental Rights of Nature* (Brussels, 2019).

[16] Spain adopted legislation in 2021 to give legal rights to Mar Menor, a lagoon. However, the 'right' of the lagoon remained very vague and left essential legal questions open, such as: what about the conflict of rights between water and fish; between two trees (water, shadow etc); between farmers' rights and the lagoon? How far should such rights go? Who decides on the weighing of rights? Who monitors such rights of nature? How much investment by public bodies may be required?

[17] Decision 2022/591 on a general Union environment action programme [2022] OJ L114/22, Art 3(p) and Recital 28.

[18] Aarhus Convention of 25 June 1998 on access to information, public participation in decision-making and access to justice in environmental matters. The EU adhered to the Aarhus Convention by Decision 2005/370 [2005] OJ L124/1. The text of the Convention is reproduced in the annex to that decision.

B. Access to Information

(i) Member State Level

In 1990, the European Union adopted a Directive on the 'free access' to information on the environment.[19] Following the adoption of the Aarhus Convention in 1998, which the EU had signed, this directive was substituted by a new Directive on 'public access'.[20] This latter directive 'guarantees the right of access to environmental information' (Article 1) to any natural or legal person. The applicant does not have to prove an interest in the information or state the reason why they wish to obtain the information. The notion of 'environmental information' is very broad; it even includes 'the state of human health and safety, including the contamination of the food chain', which brings a good part of food legislation into the field of application of the directive. Nuclear elements are not expressly mentioned, with the exception of radioactive waste; however, as 'energy' is enumerated, information on nuclear energy, including permits, programmes, releases, etc, is covered by the directive. 4-04

The right of access to information is given against public authorities and all bodies that perform public functions; this includes transport or agricultural authorities, public research institutes, agencies, etc. The authorities need only supply information which is 'available', but are not obliged to start collecting information themselves; with regard to the earlier Directive 90/313, though, the obligation for active information to be disseminated by authorities has been increased considerably (Article 7). The authorities may charge reasonable costs for the supply of the information – but not for the refusal of it;[21] not all authorities had previously resisted the temptation to charge prices at a level that was deterrent for applicants. 4-05

Access to information may be refused in certain, explicitly enumerated circumstances (Article 4); with regard to the earlier directive, this catalogue has been enlarged and fine-tuned. Some of these exceptions are self-evident, such as documents which had been declared confidential by law, further information relating to international relations, public security or national defence. Others might be more difficult to interpret with precision; to these belong, in particular, the possibility to refuse access to 'unfinished documents or data', 'internal communications' or 'the course of justice'.

Reasons for refusing access to information must be given in all cases. Where information can be given in part, this must be done. Where the request for access to information was refused, there must be a possibility to address the courts (Article 6).[22] 4-06

As Directive 2003/4 placed access to information in the context of a human right, the right was given not just to citizens of the Union, but to everybody, including associations. The omission to require proof of a specific interest constituted for many local, regional or national administrations a change from traditional concepts in their relationships with citizens. Many authorities will need more time before they fully accept this concept; particular

[19] Directive 90/313 on the freedom of access to information on the environment [1990] OJ L158/56; see also Commission, 'Report on the Experience Gained in the Application of Directive 90/313' COM(2000) 400 of 29 June 2000.

[20] Directive 2003/4 on public access to environmental information and repealing Directive 90/313 [2003] OJ L41/26.

[21] CJEU Case C-217/97 *Commission v Germany* ECLI:EU:C:1999:395.

[22] See also para 4-18ff.

problems of this kind appeared in the 13 new Member States which joined the EU since 2004, though Directive 2003/4 is fully applicable also in these countries since their accession.

As with any fundamental right, the problem with the rights flowing out of the directive lie in their day-to-day application. Indeed, there have been numerous attempts not to grant access to information in individual cases. The most frequent issues concern simple omission to give an answer to an application, or wide interpretations of the exceptions, such as the concept of 'commercial and industrial confidentiality', the ability to conduct an enquiry of a criminal or disciplinary procedure or the argument that the decision-making process is not finished; and the threat of terrorism is now beginning to be used as a reason to refuse access to data on industrial emissions and similar information. Citizens rarely go to courts in order to enforce their rights; the Commission does not examine individual cases which are brought to its knowledge; rather, it refers complainants to the national judiciary.

(ii) Union Level

4-07 Directive 2003/4 is addressed to Member States and therefore does not apply to EU institutions. Based on a joint Code of Conduct,[23] the Council and the Commission[24] adopted in 1993/94 decisions concerning the access of the public to documents; almost all the other Community bodies and agencies subsequently adopted similar decisions. In 1997, the Amsterdam Treaty included a new Article 255 on access to EU documents in the EC Treaty (now Article 15(3) TFEU), which became effective in 1999.[25]

Subsequent to that, the Union adopted Regulation 1049/2001 on access to documents, which became effective at the end of 2001.[26] The regulation referred to the 'right of access' established by the present Article 15(3) TFEU and endeavoured to 'ensure the widest possible access to documents' (Article 1). The regulation was built on the content of Directive 90/313, but provided for more exceptions. In 2006, the Union adopted Regulation 1367/2006, which adapted EU law to the requirements of the Aarhus Convention.[27] It was marked by the Council's efforts to amend the original Regulation 1049/2001 as little as possible.

4-08 As they apply to a supranational organisation, it is normal that Regulations 1049/2001 and 1367/2006 have a number of specificities, the most relevant of which are the following:

1. Regulation 1049/2001 gives a right of access to documents to citizens of the Union and to residents: thus, a professor in Switzerland would not have a right of access to documents. Regulation 1367/2006 extends this right, in environmental matters, to everybody, in line with Directive 2003/4, which also gives a right of access to informa-

[23] Code of Conduct concerning public access to Council and Commission documents [1993] OJ L340/1.

[24] Decision 93/731 on public access to Council documents [1993] OJ L340/43; Commission Decision 94/90 on public access to Commission documents [1994] OJ L46/58.

[25] Art 15(3) TFEU: '1. Any citizen of the Union, and any natural or legal person residing or having its registered office in a Member State, shall have a right of access to documents of the Union institutions, bodies, offices and agencies, whatever their medium, subject to the principles and the conditions to be defined.'

[26] Regulation 1049/2001 regarding public access to European Parliament, Council and Commission documents [2001] OJ L145/43.

[27] Regulation 1367/2006 on the application of the provisions of the Aarhus Convention on access to information, public participation in decision-making and access to justice in environmental matters to Community institutions and bodies [2006] OJ L264/13.

tion to everybody.[28] In practice, though, the EU institutions give access to documents to any applicant.

2. The possibilities to refuse access to internal documents, suggested by the Commission,[29] was not retained by Regulation 1049/2001. In contrast to that, Directive 2003/4 allows Member States to refuse access to 'material in the course of completion or unfinished documents or data' (Article 4(1.d)).[30]
3. Except for the basic grounds for refusal – public security, defence and military matters, international relations, financial, monetary or economic policy and privacy – all other grounds for refusal must be balanced against the public interest in disclosure. This requires a case-by-case weighing of the different interests at stake. Regulation 1367/2006 provides in Article 6(1) that 'an overriding public interest in disclosure shall be deemed to exist where the information requested relates to emissions into the environment'. In other cases, the fact that the information relates to emissions into the environment 'shall be taken into particular account' when the environmental interests are weighed against other interests.
4. The Commission's proposal not to give access to letters of formal notice and to reasoned opinions under Article 258 TFEU was not accepted by the Council and the European Parliament when they adopted Regulation 1049/2001; the Commission now applies the exception 'inspections, investigations and audits' to refuse such access and is supported in this by the CJEU.[31] This exception is one of the areas where the CJEU held that there is a general presumption of the confidentiality of documents, the others being the review of state aid, documents produced during pending court proceedings and merger control documents.
5. The right of access to information on the environment exists, following the amendment in Article 3(2) of Regulation 1367/2006, with regard to all documents that are held by any 'Community institution or body'; this includes access to those documents of which the Member States or other persons are authors. The author of the document has to be consulted on a possible disclosure, though the EU institution has the final decision (Regulation 1049/2001, Article 4(4)).[32] Directive 2003/4 does not contain similar provisions.
6. Where access to documents is refused, the applicant must first ask for a confirmatory administrative decision (Regulation 1049/2001, Article 8). The applicant may address the General Court against that decision under Article 263 TFEU.

The CJEU declared that transparency and openness of EU legislative and administrative activities referred back to Article 1 TEU, according to which decisions had to be taken 4-09

[28] Directive 2003/4 (n 20) Recital 8: 'It is necessary to ensure that any natural and legal person has a right of access to environmental information held by or for public authorities without his having to state an interest.'

[29] Commission proposal for a regulation on access to documents [2000] OJ C177E/70.

[30] Directive 2003/4 (n 20) requests Member States to indicate, when material is in the course of completion, the estimated time needed for completion.

[31] See CJEU Joined Cases C-514/11P and C-605/11P *LPN and Finland v Commission* ECLI:EU:C:2013:738.

[32] The Commission interpreted Art 4(5) – 'A Member State may request the institution not to disclose a document originating from that Member State without its prior agreement' – as giving a right of veto to a Member State, and was supported in this by the General Court but not by the CJEU, see Case C-64/05 *Sweden v Commission* ECLI:EU:C:2007:802. For access to information on the environment, Regulation 1367/2006 (n 27) Art 6(3) now clarifies that the Commission has the final decision and that there is no veto right for Member States.

as openly as possible. They were thus fundamental principles of EU law and related to the democratic nature of the Union institutions.[33] The provisions of Regulations 1049/2001 and 1367/2006 thus had to be interpreted largely, and exceptions to the access to documents interpreted narrowly.

The practice of the Union institutions does not always comply with these decisions. There is a tendency not to disclose information which is considered to be sensitive. The following details may be given:

- The Council and the Commission are reluctant to disclose all documents which refer to the Union's legislative process. At present, the Council discloses, in the trilogue process,[34] the position of the Member States on the different provisions of a legislative text at the end of the negotiations; the different positions of Member States during the negotiations are not disclosed. The same applies to the negotiations of a legislative proposal in the Council working groups. The Commission publishes impact assessments of its legislative proposals once it has adopted them. The CJEU's decision that the impact assessment documents should be disclosed before a proposal is adopted, in order to allow the public to discuss the different possible options,[35] has not yet changed this practice.
- The Commission interpreted the exception that access to documents for 'the purpose of inspections, investigations and audits' may be refused extremely widely. It does not limit this exception to cases of criminal or disciplinary nature, as required by the Aarhus Convention. Other exceptions are also interpreted broadly; this has as a consequence that a considerable number of applications are being rejected, mainly because the decision-making process is not yet finished, there is a commercial interest invoked or the correspondence – in particular, internal emails – is considered not to be 'information on the environment'.
- The Commission also refused access to documents concerning comments which it made towards Member States in reaction of the notification of draft national legislation under Directive 2015/1535,[36] though there is no inspection or investigation visible, as the CJEU confirmed.[37]
- Regulation 1367/2006 did not take up an amendment which the European Parliament had suggested and which consisted in giving access to information on 'sustainable development' issues. The Council explained that 'sustainable development is outside the [Aarhus] Convention and not in line [with the present Article 192 TFEU] with regard to the objectives of environmental policy'.[38] At least this remark is revealing: according to the Council, sustainable development is not an element of environmental policy! This is in line with the efforts to promote, at EU level, the objectives on economic

[33] CJEU Joined Cases C-39/05P and C-52/05P *Sweden and Turco v Council* ECLI:EU:C:2008:374; Case C-57/16P *ClientEarth v Commisssion* ECLLI:EU:C:2018:660.

[34] On the trilogue, see para 2-69ff.

[35] CJEU Case C-57/16P (n 33).

[36] Directive 2015/1535 laying down a procedure for the provision of information in the field of technical regulations and of rules on Information Society services [2015] OJ L241/1.

[37] CJEU Case C-331/15P *France v Schlyter* ECLI:EU:C:2017:639.

[38] Council, Common Position 31/2005 [2005] OJ C264E/18, 25, no III.2.

> growth and social cohesion. But it is neither historically correct nor compatible with Articles 3(3) TEU[39] and 11 TFEU, which entered into force in 2009 and which are both based on the assumption that the environment is an integral part of sustainable development and that sustainable development cannot be reached without appropriate environmental protection.

Article 2(6) of Regulation 1049/2001 clarified that the provisions of the Aarhus Convention on access to information which are part of EU law prevail over the provisions of Regulation 1049/2001.[40] This is in line with settled case law by the CJEU.[41] The provisions on the exceptions to the right of information provided by the Aarhus Convention are considerably narrower than the exceptions provided for under Regulation 1049/2001: under the Aarhus Convention, authorities *may* refuse access when one of the exceptions applies; under Regulation 1049/2001, they *must* refuse access in such a case, at least where general interests are at stake. The Aarhus Convention does not provide for an exception to protect the 'financial, monetary or economic policy of the Union and of Member States' which Regulation 1049/2001 foresees.[42] Nor does it contain an exception of 'legal advice' which is foreseen in Regulation 1049/2001. The Aarhus Convention does allow the non-disclosure of information, but only in order to protect 'the ability to conduct an enquiry of a criminal or disciplinary nature', whereas Regulation 1049/2001 allows this exception in order to protect 'the purpose of inspections, investigations and audits'.[43] The Aarhus Convention also allows the protection of 'a legitimate economic interest where protected by national law'; Regulation 1049/2001 generally refers to the protection of 'commercial interests'. The Aarhus Convention requests the publication of a report on the state of the environment every three to four years; Regulation 1367/2006 fixed the frequency at four years, but the EU, following its Regulation 401/2009, publishes such a report every five years.[44] And the Aarhus Convention allows the protection of 'personal data relating to a natural person'; Regulation 1049/2001 provides for the protection of the 'privacy and the integrity of the individual, in particular in accordance with Community legislation regarding the protection of personal data'.

[39] Art 3(3) TEU: 'The Union shall establish an internal market. It shall work for the sustainable development of Europe based on balanced economic growth and price stability, a highly competitive social market economy, aiming at full employment and social progress, and a high level of protection and improvement of the quality of the environment. It shall promote scientific and technological advance.'

[40] Regulation 1049/2001 (n 26) Art 2(6): 'This regulation shall be without prejudice to rights of public access to documents held by the institutions which might follow from instruments of international law or acts of the institutions pursuant implementing them.'

[41] CJEU Case C-344/04 *IATA and ELFAA* ECLI:EU:C:2006:10, para 35: 'Article 300(7) EC [now Art 216(2) TFEU] provides that "agreements concluded under the conditions set out in this Article shall be binding on the institutions of the Community and on Member States". In accordance with the Court's case law, those agreements prevail over provisions of secondary Community legislation.'

[42] In Case T-362/08 *IFAW v Commission* ECLI:EU:T:2011:6, the General Court upheld a Commission to refuse disclosure of a document on the destruction of a natural habitat by the construction of a private airport on the grounds that the document served to protect Germany's economic policy. As this exception does not exist under the Aarhus Convention, the Court erred in referring to Regulation 1049/2001.

[43] The Commission also applies this exception to environmental letters of formal notice and reasoned opinions under Art 258 TFEU, though that procedure is not an enquiry of criminal or disciplinary nature.

[44] Regultion 401/2009 [2009] OJ L126/13, Art 2(h).

When it comes to the interpretation of the Aarhus Convention, the CJEU rather sides with the EU institutions and makes efforts to minimise the application of the Convention.[45]

The amendments brought to Regulation 1049/2001 by Regulation 1367/2006 and the Aarhus Convention did not significantly change the restricted practice of the EU institutions. The practice by the Commission and numerous agencies, and also, for example, by the European Investment Bank, continues to be marked by the effort to disclose as little information as possible. This is also evidenced by the omission of an active and systematic dissemination of environmental information, which is a substantive requirement of the Aarhus Convention (Articles 4 and 5) but is not seriously treated by the EU institutions, though Articles 11–13 of Regulation 1049/2001 and Article 4(1) of Regulation 1367/2006 deal with it. The general problem at EU level is that there is no European public opinion and not sufficient private groups or individuals who would try to progressively press the EU institutions and bodies to put into daily practice what the Aarhus Convention (Recital 17) describes as 'public authorities hold[ing] environmental information in the public interest', not in their own interests.[46]

C. Participation in Decision-Making

(i) Member State Level

4-10 EU involvement concerning participation in decision-making in environmental matters first dealt with participation in environmental impact assessment for specific projects which come under Directive 85/337.[47] Article 6 of this directive provided that where an impact assessment is made, the public must be informed; and the 'public concerned' must have the possibility of expressing its opinion on the project and its environmental impacts. The directive laid down in detail how this participation can be made operational[48] and its provisions aligned to the requirements of the Aarhus Convention.[49]

4-11 As regards permitting of industrial installations, Directive 2010/75 provided that, with regard to applications for permits for industrial installations, the decision on such an application and the results of the surveillance of emissions from industrial installations should be available to the public.[50] According to those provisions, the public shall have the possibility

[45] See CJEU Joined Cases C-514/11P and C-605/11 (n 32); Joined Cases C401/12P to 403/12P *Council and others v Milieudefensie and others* ECLI: ECLI:EU:C:2015: 4; Joined Cases C-404/12P and C-405/12P *Council and Commission v Stichting Natuur en Milieu and others* ECLI:EU:C:2015:5.

[46] See also European Parliament, Resolution of 11 March 2014 on public access to documents (A7-0148/2014-2013/2135/INI), which severely criticises the present practice by the Commission and the Council.

[47] Directive 85/337 on the assessment of the effects of certain public and private projects on the environment [1985] OJ L175/40, as amended by Directive 97/11 [1997] OJ L73/5.

[48] Directive 2011/92 [2012] OJ L26/1, Art 5(2): the operator must submit a non-technical summary of his examination of the impact and must report on the alternatives that were studied; a consultation with the nature protection administration is mandatory, whose opinion must be publicly available (CJEU Case C-321/96 *Mecklenburg* ECLI:EU:C:1998:300).

[49] Directive 2003/35 providing for public participation in respect of the drawing up of certain plans and programmes relating to the environment and amending with regard to public participation and access to justice Council Directives 85/337 and 96/61 [2003] OJ L156/17.

[50] Directive 2010/75 on industrial emissions [2010] OJ L334/17.

of commenting on applications for a permit. The public is, furthermore, to be informed of the results of surveillance of the installations.

As regards *plans and programmes*, Directive 2001/42 required an environmental impact assessment for plans and programmes that were likely to have significant environmental effects.[51] The directive covered such plans which lead, at a later stage, to projects that have to undergo an environmental impact assessment under annex I or II of Directive 2011/92 or under Articles 6 and 7 of Directive 92/43.[52] The impact assessment under Directive 2001/42 mainly consists in the elaboration of a written assessment and of extensive public consultation of such plans; it allows the public concerned the possibility to give its opinion on the plan in question.

The CJEU clarified that also national or regional legislation which contained 'a significant number of criteria and modalities for the permitting and realisation of projects that might have a significant impact on the environment' constituted 'plans' under that directive.[53]

Directive 2003/35[54] provided for participation of the public in the elaboration and updating of a number of expressly enumerated plans and programmes, in particular in the waste area.[55] And in water management, Member States have to promote the participation of the public in the elaboration, monitoring and updating of water management plans.[56]

However, it is clear that these different specific measures do not give a general right to individuals to participate in environmental decision-making. First, Directives 2011/92, 2010/75, 2000/60 and the different waste directives which are mentioned in Directive 2003/35 do not cover all decision-making in environmental matters. Rather, these directives concern some (larger) industrial installations and projects. Most medium-sized and small projects and installations are not covered by EU legislation but come, as regards environmental impact assessments and permits, under the responsibility of Member States. 4-12

Secondly, environmental decision-making not only deals with the permitting of projects and installations and the authorisation of plans and programmes: there are many other decisions which affect the environment, such as decisions on the authorisation of products and processes, management decisions, monitoring methods and processes, derogations and omissions to decide. These very diverse and different means of the administration which affect the environment have not been the subject of the Aarhus Convention, which is thus far from granting a general right of participation. In the same way, EU law does not provide for a *general* right of participation, but limits it to *certain* projects, plans and programmes. Also, EU law very generally speaks of the 'public concerned', which should be entitled to participate in the decision-making, but leaves the determination of the public

[51] Directive 2001/42 on the environment assessment of the effects of certain plans and programmes on the environment [2001] OJ L197/30.

[52] Directive 92/43 on the conservation of natural habitats and of wild fauna and flora [1992] OJ L206/7.

[53] CJEU Case C-24/19 *Nevele* ECLI:EU:C:2020:503; Case C-300/20 *Bund Naturschutz Bayern* ECLI:EU:C:2022:102.

[54] Directive 2003/35 (n 49).

[55] ibid annex I enumerates the following plans and programmes which are covered by its provisions: waste management plans, plans for the recycling of batteries, plans for reducing nitrate inputs into waters, plans for hazardous waste management, plans for packaging waste and plans for the improvement of air quality.

[56] Directive 2000/60 establishing a framework for Community action in the field of water policy [2000] OJ L327/1.

concerned in any specific case to the Member States. As it is obvious, for instance, that the 'public concerned' is different for the construction of a 1000 km motorway and for a waste incinerator, there is a necessity to determine beforehand what the 'public concerned' is. Furthermore, the question of how much time should be given for the participation process is not clear, and only exceptionally has EU law laid down obligations for the administration to give an account of what it has done with the opinions that were expressed during the participation process.[57]

4-13 Furthermore, the different directives do not specify how the opinion of the participating public is to be assembled (hearing, written submission, attributed time for oral representation) or how the administration shall manage the collected information: the best would probably be to require a written paper accompanying the final administrative decision which lists the results of the participation process and explains the reasons for the administration following or not following the opinion. Administrative practice in Member States at present shows little sign of improved citizens' participation. An Irish provision which charged citizens to pay a fee for participating in the decision-making on projects, plans and programmes was declared compatible with EU law by the CJEU;[58] in my opinion, this contradicts the character of the participation right as a fundamental right.

(ii) Union Level

4-14 In 2002, the Commission published two communications on public consultation[59] which were not limited to environmental issues. According to these communications, the consultation of interested groups should allow at least eight weeks for reception of responses to written public consultation and 20 working days' notice for meetings. However, the consultation principles referred to by these communications constitute internal instructions for Commission officials but do not create any rights to participate for the 'public concerned'. The Commission expressly stated that it was opposed to giving citizens the right to participate, as this would interfere with formal consultations which were taking place after the adoption of a proposal by the Commission; this remark alludes to the participation of the European Parliament, the EECOSOC and the Committee of the Regions in the legislative process. In contrast to that, there is no doubt that the Aarhus Convention requires contracting parties to give *rights* to citizens, not to create obligations for the administration only, though the Aarhus Convention is limited to projects, plans and programmes.[60]

Regulation 1367/2006, which intended to make the principles of the Aarhus Convention applicable at EU level, was adopted in 2006;[61] it endeavoured to give a right to participate in

[57] See now Directive 2010/75 (n 50) Art 24(2), concerning the information which has to be made available once a decision on a permit has been taken; see also para 4-40ff below.

[58] CJEU Case C-216/05 *Commission v Ireland* ECLI:EU:C:2006:706.

[59] Commission, 'Towards a Reinforced Culture of Consultation and Dialogue – Proposal for General Principles and Minimum Standards for Consultation of Interested Parties by the Commission' COM(2002) 277 and COM(2002) 704.

[60] Aarhus Convention (n 18) Art 1: 'In order to contribute to the protection of the right of every person of present and future generations to live in an environment adequate to his or her health and well-being, each Party shall guarantee the rights of access to information, public participation in decision-making and access to justice in environmental matters in accordance with the provisions of this Convention.'

[61] Regulation 1367/2006 (n 27).

EU environmental decision-making. The regulation defined plans and programmes relating to the environment as:

> plans and programmes
>
> which are subject to preparation and, as appropriate, adoption by a Community institution or body;
>
> which are required under legislative, regulatory or administrative provisions; and
>
> which contribute to, or a likely to have significant effect on, the achievement of the objectives of Community environmental policy, such as laid down in the Sixth Environment Action Programme, or in any subsequent general environment action programme.[62]

However, it also stated in the same provision: 4-15

> This definition shall not include financial, banking or budget plans and programmes, namely those laying down how particular projects or activities should be financed or those related to the proposed annual budget … or emergency plans and programmes designed for the sole purpose of environmental protection.

This provision clearly contradicts the provisions of the Aarhus Convention. This convention does not exempt any plans and programmes. There might be some wisdom in not including budget plans, as such plans do not 'relate to the environment' (Aarhus Convention Article 7). However, the exemption of financial or banking plans and programmes which lay down how particular projects or activities should be financed cannot be based on the Aarhus Convention when such plans relate to the environment. The provision mainly aims at exempting activities from the European Investment Bank, for which the TFEU provides that EU provisions on access to documents – not on participation rights – shall only apply where the bank is performing administrative tasks.[63] No reason can be found for an exemption of participation provisions. The same applies to the emergency plans of civil protection, though there has to be a line struck: it might be understandable to exempt emergency measures in the case of an actual disaster, such as an industrial accident or a flood catastrophe, where no time may be wasted to save humans or property; in such cases, participation normally would take too much time. Another question is, for example, the restoration plan or programme following a forest fire or a flooding: here, the same urgency does not exist and an exemption from participation is not justified.

EU plans and programmes are only those that are *required* under legislative, regulatory or administrative provisions. This wording is ambiguous. Indeed, for example, the Eighth Environment Action Programme constitutes a 'plan and programme', but Article 192(3) TFEU does not *require* the elaboration of EU environmental action programmes. Also, when the Commission decides to launch a programme to promote alternative energies, to promote human health in environmental matters or to co-finance model projects in coastal zone management, this is an initiative of the Commission itself, and there is no requirement laid down anywhere to elaborate such a plan or programme.[64] In such cases, the Commission does normally not ensure that the public participates in the

[62] ibid Art 2(e).

[63] Art 15(3) TFEU.

[64] In Case C-567/10 *Inter-Environnement Bruxelles* ECLI:EU:C:2012:159, and in subsequent settled case law, the CJEU held that a plan is also 'required' when the legislation provides details for its elaboration and content.

elaboration of the plan or programme. Generally, the Commission proceeds to consultations, not to a participation.

This becomes clear when Article 9(1) of Regulation 1367/2006 is considered.[65] Indeed, neither the 'Green Deal for Europe'[66] nor the urgency Regulation 2022/2577, which gave priority of renewable energy projects over nature protection interests,[67] or numerous other plans or programmes – in particular, in the area of climate change and at the borderline between energy and environment – were submitted to public participation. The provision of Regulation 1367/2006, Article 9(1) was and is more or less systematically ignored by the Union.

4-16 It is difficult to see what Regulation 1367/2006 means by 'participation': it limits itself to stating that the public shall have early and effective opportunity to participate during the preparation of the plans or programmes. It does not contain any indication of what the EU institution or body is to do with the information received from the public[68] and no general principles are laid down in the Regulation in this regard. In this way, Regulation 1367/2006 in practice declares 'participation' synonymous to 'consultation' – which it is not. The Aarhus Convention provides in this regard that the public shall be allowed to submit in writing or, as appropriate at a public hearing, its comments or opinions; that in the administrative decision due account is taken of the outcome of the participation; and that, after the decision has been taken, the text of the decision shall be made available to the public along with the reasons and considerations on which the decision is based (Article 6(7)–(9) Aarhus Convention). Participation is thus a bilateral concept, whereas consultation is unilateral: it leaves the administration free to decide what it wants to do with the information received through consultation, and no explanation is to be given to the consulted persons or bodies.

The transposition of the Aarhus Convention is thus only partial. This conclusion is all the more obvious as the consultations at EU level often take place in one language (English) or in English, French and German only – which is not an *effective* way of making citizens participate.[69] It is also true, though, that environmental organisations and citizens are not really claiming that their participation rights at EU level be made effective.

4-17 In the past, neither products nor production processes were authorised at EU level; rather, EU law normally determined which substances – heavy metals, chemicals,

[65] Regulation 1367/2006 (n 27) Art 9(1): ' Community institutions and bodies shall provide, through appropriate practical and/or other provisions, early and effective opportunities for the public to participate during the preparation, modification or review of plans or programmes relating to the environment, when all options are open. In particular, where the Commission prepares a proposal for such a plan or programme which is submitted to other Community institutions or bodies for decision, it shall provide for public participation at that preparatory stage.'

[66] Commission, COM(2019) 640.

[67] Regulation 2022/2577 laying down a framework to accelerate the deployment of renewable energy projects [2022] OJ L335/36.

[68] Council, Common Position (n 38): 'it should be left to institutions and bodies to determine how they want to take account of public participation results, on the basis of general principles laid out in the regulation.'

[69] See also European Parliament, Resolution of 14 December 2012 (2012/2676//RSP, P7_TA(2012)256): '[The European Parliament] urges the Commission to ensure that every EU citizen's right to address the EU institutions in any of the EU official languages is fully respected and implemented by ensuring that public consultations are available in all EU official languages, that all consultations are treated equally and that there is no language-based discrimination between consultations.' European Ombudsman, Decision of 4 October 2012 (640/2011/AN): 'public consultation should, as a matter of principle, be published in all official languages. Its failure to do so is an instance of maladministration.'

additives, etc – may be used in what quantities in products or which product emissions were allowed. The permits were then issued by Member States. From this general statement, dangerous chemical substances,[70] active substances for pesticides[71] and biocides[72] and genetically modified organisms (GMOs) or products[73] constitute exceptions, as it is now the Commission which grants authorisations in these areas; its decision is valid for all Member States. Originally, the Aarhus Convention was only concerned with projects, plans and programmes; however, in view of the politically sensitive nature of permits for GMOs, a clause was inserted in the convention that contracting parties should take care of participation in such GMO-permitting procedures (Article 6(11)). In 2005, the convention was modified in order to provide for participation also in GMO-permitting procedures.[74] The Council was of the opinion that this amendment did not require any changes of existing EU legislation and ratified the convention's amendment.[75] This appears legally wrong, because at least Regulation 1829/2003 on genetically modified food and feed[76] does not provide for any participation of citizens; under this regulation, an application for the release of GMO food or feed goes to the European Food Safety Authority (EFSA), which examines the application and is obliged to make the application available to the public. Then, members of the public may send observations (provided they know of the application). However, this has nothing to do with participation in the decision of the Commission on the application: EFSA's proposal for a decision is submitted to the Commission, which must decide on it within a specific time span. The public may comment on EFSA's opinion within 30 days,[77] but no public participation is foreseen.

Under general interpretation rules, it is not possible either that EFSA simply amends its practice and now follows the principles of Regulation 1367/2006. Indeed, according to the CJEU – which referred, of course, to situations in Member States – such a change would have to be laid down expressly in a legislative text in order to give legal security to the citizens. And it would appear that there is a contradiction between Regulation 1829/2003 and Regulation 1367/2006.

Nothing different applies in general cases of the deliberate release of GMOs. Article 9 of Directive 2001/18[78] provides for a consultation of the public, and Article 24 introduces the obligation to inform the public of applications and to allow it to comment to the Commission. Nothing is said about any participation rights of the public or on the subsequent treatment of the comments from the public.

[70] Regulation 1907/2006 [2006] OJ L396/1.

[71] Regulation 1107/2009 [2009] OJ L309/1.

[72] Regulation 528/2012 [2012] OJ L167/1.

[73] Directive 2001/18 on the deliberate release of genetically modified organisms into the environment [2001] OJ L106/1; Regulation 1829/2003 on genetically modified food and feed [2003] OJ L268/1.

[74] Aarhus Convention (n 18), Art 6*bis*: '1. In accordance with the modalities laid down in Annex I bis, each Party shall provide for early and effective information and public participation prior to making decisions on whether to permit the deliberate release into the environment and placing on the market of genetically modified organisms.'

[75] Decision 2006/957 [2006] OJ L386/46.

[76] See Regulation 1829/2003 on genetically modified food and feed [2003] OJ L268/1.

[77] It should be mentioned that EFSA's opinions in GMO matters are normally given more than five years after the initial application; 30 days is thus disproportionately short.

[78] Directive 2001/18 (n 73).

D. Access to Justice

(i) Member State Level

4-18 There are almost no EU provisions on access to national courts or to EU courts in environmental matters. The Commission's announcements in the Fifth Environmental Action Programme and the 1992 Working Programme[79] to submit a proposal for a general directive on access to justice was followed by a proposal for such a directive only in 2003.[80] However, this proposal was withdrawn in 2014.

EU provisions on access to justice to national courts in environmental matters exist in the following cases:

1. Where the right of access to environmental information under Directive 2003/4[81] was not respected (Article 6 of Directive 2003/4). Instead of giving access to a court and in conformity with the Aarhus Convention, Member States may provide access to an 'independent and impartial body established by law', whose decisions may become final and which are binding on public authorities. These provisions aim at allowing decisions to be taken by bodies such as an ombudsman, though it is doubtful whether the different environmental ombudsmen which exist in the different Member States really fulfil all the conditions laid down in the directive.
2. Where the right of participation in decision-making concerning an environmental impact assessment under Directive 2011/92 (Article 11) or a right to participate in decisions concerning permits for industrial installations (Directive 2010/75, Article 25) was not respected by an authority in a Member State.[82] Such a right to address courts implicitly existed already by virtue of these two directives. However, it is useful that the provisions in the two directives lifted any ambiguity concerning such a right.
3. Directive 2001/42 concerning an impact assessment for plans and programmes[83] does not contain a provision on access to justice, where consultation or participation concerning a plan or programme is refused. This question is left to national law: as the Aarhus Convention does not provide for access to justice in cases where the right of participation in the elaboration of plans and programmes is not respected – Article 7 of the Convention is not mentioned in its Article 9(2)[84] – Member States are free to regulate this question.
4. Where environmental damage was caused by one of the activities and under the conditions mentioned in Directive 2004/35 on environmental liability, a citizen or an environmental organisation may draw the attention of the public authorities to the damage and ask for remedial action. Where 'the request and the accompanying observations show in a plausible manner that environmental damage exists', the

[79] Fifth environmental action programme [1993] OJ C138/1, ch 9: 'Individuals and public interest groups should have practicable access to the courts.'

[80] See para 4-20.

[81] See para 4-04ff.

[82] Directive 2010/75 (n 50).

[83] Directive 2001/42 (n 51).

[84] Aarhus Convention (n 18) Art 7, on participation in plans and programmes, and Art 9, which only refers to Art 6.

administration will have to take a decision on that request. This decision may then be challenged in court in view of its procedural and substantial compliance with Directive 2004/35.[85]

Similar considerations to those of Directive 2001/42 apply with regard to Directive 2003/35, which also provides for the participation of 'the public' in the elaboration of certain plans and programmes under EC environmental legislation. Again, 'the public' is not defined. By virtue of Article 2(b), it is 'entitled' to participate. Directive 2003/35 does not indicate whether the public has access to the national courts in those cases where its entitlement is disregarded. However, it should be remembered that the Aarhus Convention contains, in Article 9(3), a general clause on access to courts[86] which also refers to access to the courts in cases of Article 7. As it is the declared objective of Directive 2003/35 to implement the Aarhus Convention,[87] and the Aarhus Convention intends to give rights to individuals, there is a right to look for judicial remedy for all those whose participation entitlement is not respected. The details of this right to access to the courts are determined by national law. 4-19

In 2003, the Commission made a proposal for a Directive on access to justice in environmental matters.[88] The proposal intended to put the relevant pillar of the Aarhus Convention into EU law. It suggested giving to environmental organisations a right of standing in courts where EU environmental law was breached. Environmental law was defined in a rather broad way. The proposal, which was based on the present Article 192 TFEU, was supported by the European Parliament, which wanted to strengthen it even further.[89] However, it met considerable objections in the Council from Member States, which were of the opinion that, under the principle of subsidiarity, access to national courts was their competence, and that the Union should not interfere in this area. They hardly discussed the proposal, which has, in the meantime, become obsolete and was withdrawn by the Commission in 2014. 4-20

In 2011, the CJEU clarified that the Aarhus Convention, including its Article 9(3), were part of EU law.[90] However, the Court declared that Article 9(3) was not directly applicable, because members of the public or environmental organisations only had access to the courts where they complied with the requirements that were laid down in national law. However, this reasoning, which was based on the words 'if any' in Article 9(3), did not (wish to) consider that 'if any' gives an option to the contracting parties to take national measures, but does not require them to do so. The Court continued by inviting the national courts to give the fullest possible effect to Article 9(3) with regard to standing of members of the public.

This decision was certainly also politically motivated. It would have been possible to declare the provision as having direct effect and giving standing to every member of the

[85] Directive 2004/35 on environmental liability with a view of prevention and remedying environmental damage [2004] OJ L143/56, Arts 12 and 13.

[86] Aarhus Convention (n 18) Art 9(3): 'In addition and without prejudice to review procedures referred to in paragraphs 1 and 2 above, each Party shall ensure that, where they meet the criteria, if any, laid down in its national law, members of the public have access to administrative or judicial procedures to challenge acts and omissions by private parties and public authorities which contravene provisions of its national law relating to the environment.'

[87] See the recitals of Directive 2003/35 (n 49).

[88] Commission, 'Proposal for a Directive on Access to Justice in Environmental Matters' COM(2003) 624.

[89] European Parliament, Legislative Resolution [2004] OJ C103E/626.

[90] CJEU Case C-240/09 *Lesoochranárske zoskupenie* ECLI:EU:C:2011:125; confirmed in Joined Cases C401/12P to 403/12P (n 45).

public until the Member State in question has laid down conditions to restrict such an *actio popularis*. The CJEU preferred to ignore that the burden of legislating was with the Member States and that it allowed them practically to take advantage of their own passivity to lay down specific conditions; in other cases on the direct effect, the Court had argued that a Member State should not be allowed to invoke its own omission to act and then oppose the direct effect of an EU provision.

The judgment means that, in each individual case, applicants will have to persuade local, regional or national courts of the wording, the objective and the spirit of Article 9(3) in order to obtain standing. As courts are, by nature, conservative, this means that, in practice, not much will be changing in the future. Article 9(3) will remain impressive in words, but not very relevant in practice. Also, it is not likely that the CJEU will change its opinion in the future, as it decided, in Case C-240/09, on the composition of a Grand Chamber (13 judges) which gives a particular weight to the judgment.

In order to reduce the impact of its judgment in Case C-240/09, the Court recurred increasingly to the help of Article 47 of the EU Charter of Fundamental Rights[91] and to the *effet utile* doctrine. In Cases C-664/15[92] and C-847/19,[93] it argued that Article 9(3) of the Aarhus Convention would lose its effect if national access to justice were not made effective, and that Article 47 of the Charter also required a system of effective access to justice. Therefore, national law had to be interpreted as widely as possible in order to allow individual persons and non-governmental organisations (NGOs) to have access to courts in environmental matters. Should such an interpretation not be possible, the national provisions, which prevented the access, would have to be set aside and access to courts ensured in this way.

(ii) Union Level

4-21 EU law gives natural or legal persons a right of access to the European courts where an EU measure is addressed to that person or where the person is directly and individually concerned by the measure.[94] This right was enlarged in 2009 by allowing access to the EU courts where a person was directly concerned by a regulatory act which did not require the taking of implementation measures.

As regards access to information, persons have a right under Regulation 1049/2001 to ask for access to documents. In such a case, the EU institution is obliged to formally respond to that person. Against this answer, access to the EU courts is possible as the applicant is addressed by the formal decision.

As far as participation in environmental decision-making at EU level is concerned, prior to the adoption of Regulation 1367/2006, there was only soft law which obliged Commission officials to involve individuals in measures which they are preparing. A breach of this

[91] Charter of Fundamental Rights of the European Union [2000] OJ C346/1, Art 47: 'Everyone whose rights and freedoms guaranteed by the law of the Union are violated has the right to an effective remedy before a tribunal.'

[92] CJEU Case C-664/15 *Protect* ECLI:EU:C:2019:987.

[93] CJEU Case C-873/19 *Deutsche Umwelthilfe* ECLI:EU:C:2022:857.

[94] Art 263(4) TFEU: 'Any natural or legal person may … institute proceedings against an act addressed to that person or which is of direct and individual concern to them, and against a regulatory act which is of direct concern to them and does not entail implementing measures.'

obligation did not lead to the possibility to recur to the application of Article 263(4) TFEU. Regulation 1367/2006, adopted in 2006, gave persons a right to participate in environmental plans and programmes which are elaborated at EU level (see paragraph 4-14ff). If this right was not granted, there was a possibility for the affected public to apply, under Article 263(4) TFEU, to the CJEU. The same applies, in my opinion, where the EU institutions and bodies only provide for consultation of the public instead of the public's full participation – and this difference requires a definition of the two notions. Participation clearly goes further than a mere consultation. It gives the participating persons a guarantee that their opinion is received, weighed and considered during the decision-making process and that the administration explains, once a decision has been taken, the reason it followed or did not follow the opinion which was issued.

As regards access to the European Courts in other areas, Regulation 1367/2006 introduced the possibility for environmental organisations to 'make a request for internal review to the Union institution of or body that has adopted an administrative act under environmental law or, in case of an alleged administrative omission, should have adopted such an act' (Article 10(1)). In such a case, a written reply was to be given within a specific time span. The environmental organisation then could institute proceedings before the CJEU 'in accordance with the relevant provisions of this Treaty' (Article 12). However, this possibility only existed with regard to 'an individual administrative act adopted under environmental law' (Article 10) – which in practice excluded Commission-delegated or -implemented acts and the majority of other acts. The CJEU refused to assess the compatibility of this approach with Article 9(3) of the Aarhus Convention, as it held that provision not to be directly applicable.[95]

The Council's Common Position, which was not changed by the final adoption of Regulation 1367/2006, expressly stated that 'the Common Position carefully sticks to the provisions contained in Articles 230(4) and 232(3) of the EC Treaty, which are sufficient to ensure compliance'.[96] In practice, the CJEU continued to apply the 'Plaumann' formula from 1965[97] to assess whether a person was individually concerned, and was likewise very restrictive in assessing whether that person was directly concerned.

The Compliance Committee, set up under the Aarhus Convention, considered that contracting parties of the Convention were not obliged to introduce an *actio popularis*. However, it was of the opinion that they were also not entitled to 'introduc[e] or maintain … so strict criteria that they effectively bar all or almost all environmental organisations from challenging acts or omissions that contravene national law relating to the environment'.[98] Consequently, the Compliance Committee found that the restrictive access to EU courts which was granted under Articles 263 and 267 TFEU was not in compliance with the requirements of the Aarhus Convention.[99]

[95] CJEU Case C-240/09 (n 90).

[96] Council, Common Position (n 38).

[97] CJEU Case 63/17 *Plaumann v Commission* ECLI:EU:C:1963:17: 'Persons other than those to whom a decision is addressed may only claim to be individually concerned if that decision affects them by reason of certain attributes which are peculiar to them or by reason of circumstances in which they are differentiated from all other persons and by virtue of these factors distinguishes them individually just as in the case of the person addressed.'

[98] Aarhus Convention Compliance Committee, Compliance by Belgium, Doc ACCC/C/2005/11 of 14 June 2005.

[99] Aarhus Convention Compliance Committee, Decision of 14 April 2011 in Case ACCC/C/2008/32. This decision was approved by the Meeting of the Parties to the Aarhus Convention. See also UN Economic Commission

Following controversial discussions at international level, Regulation 1367/2006 was amended.[100] The right to request an internal review was no longer limited to administrative acts, but opened to any non-legislative act.[101] Furthermore, the right to ask for an internal review was broadened for environmental organisations and newly introduced for individual persons; such a request had, however, to be supported by at least 4000 persons, coming from five different Member States.

Article 263(4) TFEU itself was not amended, though. This means that the CJEU's restricted interpretation of that provision is likely to continue. Indeed, at present, access to the European Courts is practically barred for environmental organisations and very largely also for citizens. There is not a single case where an environmental organisation has been given standing in environmental cases so far – except, of course, under the provisions on access to information. The Court is extremely restrictive in its interpretation in this regard.[102]

Furthermore, the internal review procedure is not sufficient to comply with the requirements of Article 9(3) of the Aarhus Convention, in particular because no possibility is foreseen for action to be taken against private persons that do not respect EU environmental law. Furthermore, it follows from Article 9(4) of the Aarhus Convention, which requires the procedure under Article 9(3) to 'provide adequate and effective remedies, including injunctive relief as appropriate, and be fair, equitable, timely and not prohibitively expensive', that Article 9(3) intends to introduce court procedures, not internal review procedures, by the same body that adopted or should have adopted the incriminated measure. A review by the same body is neither fair nor equitable, and no injunctive relief is foreseen.

Finally, the internal review procedure and the restrictive interpretation of Article 263(4) TFEU in environmental matters are, in my opinion, also not compatible with Article 47 of the Charter, which requires 'effective' judicial remedies.

II. Environment-Related Market Measures

A. Sustainable Activities (Taxonomy)

4-22 The European Green Deal of 2019[103] led to increased Union activities to promote sustainable finance. In 2020, the Union adopted, on the basis of Article 114 TFEU, a regulation on sustainable investment,[104] with the objective of harmonising the criteria for whether an economic activity qualified as environmentally sustainable. According to Article 3, this

for Europe, Economic and Social Council, Findings and recommendations of the Compliance Committee with regard to communication ACCC/C/2008/32(part II) concerning compliance by the European Union, ECE/MP/PP/C1/2017/7.

[100] Regulation 2021/1767 amending Regulation 1367/2006 [2021] OJ l 356/11. See also Commission, C(2017) 2616, a notice on access to justice; COM(2020) 643 on possibilities to improve access.

[101] The Aarhus Convention does not apply to legislative acts.

[102] See Case CJEU C-321/95P *Greenpeace v Commission* ECLI:EU:C:1998:153; see also para 14-43ff.

[103] Commission, 'The European Green Deal' COM(2019) 640.

[104] Regulation 2020/852 on the establisment of a framework to facilitate sustainable investment [2020] OJ L198/13.

was the case when the economic activity contributed substantially to one of the following environmental objectives (Article 9): climate change mitigation; climate change adaptation; sustainable use and production of water and marine resources; the transition to a circular economy; pollution prevention and control; and protection and restoration of biodiversity and ecosystems.[105] Furthermore, the activity had to avoid significant harm to any of those objectives,[106] and be carried out in compliance with a number of guiding principles of the United Nations, the Organisation for Economic Cooperation and Development and the International Labour Organization, as well as with technical provisions of the Union.

The Commission elaborated a list of economic activities which were considered sustainable,[107] but limited that list to activities which contributed to the mitigation of or adaptation to climate change. This list of 349 pages was completed by another Commission measure, which declared that, under certain conditions, nuclear energy and fossil gas activities were also 'sustainable'.[108] The inclusion of nuclear energy activities was particularly controversial because of the high technological risk (accidents, terrorist or warfare attacks) and because of the unresolved problem of nuclear waste handling. As regards fossil gas, its classification as sustainable contradicts to some extent the efforts to promote renewable sources of energy.

In order to promote sustainable financing, the Union adopted, again on the basis of Article 114 TFEU, an official European green bonds standard.[109] In order to call their financial instrument 'European Green Bond', investors must comply with the criteria and conditions laid down in the proposal, which is at present under discussion with the other Union institutions.

B. Environmental Reporting

Directive 2022/2464, based on Articles 50 and 114 TFEU, introduced an obligation for 4-23
some large and medium-sized undertakings to report on the impact of their activity on sustainable matters.[110] 'Sustainability matters' were defined as environmental, social and human rights and governance factors. The information shall be included in the undertaking's management report. It shall also refer to the undertaking's measures to contribute to restricting the overall global temperature to 1.5°C beyond pre-industrial levels and to contribute to reaching climate neutrality by 2050, and to the undertaking's activities related to fossil fuels.

[105] These objectives were further elaborated in Arts 10–15.

[106] Regulation 2020/852 (n 104) Art 17 further specified what constituted a 'significant harm'.

[107] Commission Delegated Regulation 2021/2139 establishing the technical screening criteria for determining the conditions under which an economic activity qualifies as contributing substantially to climate change mitigation or climate change adaptation and for determining whether that economic activity causes no significant harm to any of the other objectives [2021] OJ L442/1.

[108] Commission Delegated Regulation 2022/1214 [2022] OJ L188/1. An application by a member of the European Parliament who considered that such a far-reaching decision should rather have been adopted by the European Parliament and the Council was held inadmissible, as the applicant was not directly concerned with the Regulation, General Court Case T-628/22 *Repasi v Commission* ECLI:EU:T:2023:353.

[109] Regulation 2023/2631 on European Green Bonds and optional disclosures for bonds markets as environmentally sustainable and for sustainability-linked bonds", [2023] OJ L 2023/2631, 30 November 2023.

[110] Directive 2022/2464 as regards corporate sustainability reporting [2022] OJ L322/15.

Directive 2014/95 had already obliged certain large undertakings to report on the impact of their activities on, among others, the environment.[111] A Commission proposal of 2022 suggested imposing on certain large undertakings the obligation to prevent, mitigate and bring to an end any adverse human rights and environmental impacts of their own activities, those of their subsidiaries and those of companies with which they held an established business relationship – that is, their global value chain.[112] The undertakings shall publish annually a statement on their implementation of these provisions. Environmental adverse impacts were described as non-compliance with specific provisions of seven international environmental agreements which had all been concluded by the Union.[113] This rather controversial proposal is at present being discussed within the Union.

On the basis of Article 114 TFEU, the Commission proposed a directive to stop unfair environmental claims and other unfair commercial practices in marketing and product labelling.[114] The proposal intended to amend existing consumer directives and prohibit unsubstantiated generic environmental claims, such as 'eco-friendly', 'green', 'ecological', biodegradable', 'carbon neutral' or 'climate neutral'.[115] The Commission is currently undertaking discussions with the Union institutions.

The whole Union activity to reorient economic activities and financial investments towards sustainable activities, including environmental reporting and commercial practices, was developed rather recently, as a follow-up to the Green Deal of 2019. The different measures are not always coherent and consistent with regard to size of affected undertakings, content of activities, reporting details, etc, and it remains to be seen whether they will lead, in the coming years, to 'greener' activity of undertakings, investors and market participants.

III. Funds

A. General Remarks – Environmental Fund

4-24 The Union has not set up a general environmental fund. Attempts to introduce such a fund failed in the beginning of the 1980s. In 1987, a clause was inserted into the present Article 192(5) TFEU that, as a rule, 'Member States shall finance … the environment policy'. The reasons for this basic decision were more political than legal. Title XVIII TFEU (Articles 174–78) mentions economic and social cohesion; however, it is not clear why this title does not read 'Economic, social and environmental cohesion', which would parallel the objective

[111] Directive 2014/95 as regards disclosure of non-financial and diversity information by certain large undertakings and groups [2014] OJ L330/1.

[112] Commission, 'Proposal for a Regulation on Corporate Sustainability Due Diligence' COM(2022) 71.

[113] The violations proposed concern the Biodiversity Convention (see para 5-02) Art 10(b); CITES Convention (para 5-23) Arts III–V; Convention on Mercury (para 6-22) Arts 4(1), 5(3) and 11(3); the POP Convention (para 6-23) Arts 3(1) and 6(1); the Convention on the Import and Export of Chemicals (para 6-53) annex II; the Montreal Protocol (para 6-23), on the production and consumption of prohibited substances; the Basel Convention on the Shipment of Waste (para 10-37) Arts 1 and 4(5) and annex VII.

[114] Commission, 'Proposal for a Directive as Regards Empowering Consumers for the Green Transition Through Better Protection Against Unfair Practices and Better Information' COM(2022) 143.

[115] ibid Recital 9.

of 'sustainable development' of Article 3(3) TEU. Indeed, if one looks at the three pillars of sustainable development, the Union has established funds for both economic (Agricultural Fund, Article 40(3) TFEU; Regional Fund, Article 176(1) TFEU; Cohesion Fund, Article 177(2) TFEU) and social problems (Social Fund, Article 162 TFEU), but not for environmental problems. One might well reflect whether, under the auspices of the Union, this basic decision remains justified: for damage caused by the sea transport of petrol and by nuclear accidents, systems are set up under public international law which provide for funding solutions in order to ensure that, in every case, the damage caused to the environment is compensated, at least as far as the system – which operates under the considerable influence of multinational companies – reaches.

The absence of an EU fund for the environment would be less dramatic if, at the level of Member States, financial means were made available to address the environmental problems. This, however, is almost never the case and the result is that environmental damage is frequently not repaired or compensated. The infrastructural inferiority of environmental protection with regard to the protection of economic and social interests – the environment does not vote and has no voice – becomes all the more visible by this constellation. As the environment disappears in silence, the issue raises only a limited amount of concern.

In substance, a fund for the environment would have a potentially great number of 4-25
areas to cover, such as aspects of climate change, renewable energies, contaminated land remediation, environmental catastrophes, biodiversity and natural habitat protection and monitoring, awareness-raising for environmental matters, clean technologies and implementation of environmental legislation.[116] The problem of a fund for the environment is that Member States might cede to the temptation and ensure environmental protection only to the extent that EU finances are made available. This was the main reason why, in the 1980s, the creation of an EU fund was rejected.

Weighing all the pros and cons of a fund, it seems more appropriate to use the different existing funds to support the protection of the environment. The reason for this is that the environment cannot hope to be protected 'on its own'. Rather, environmental concerns must be integrated into all kinds of human and economic activities, such as energy, leisure and transport, and the corresponding EU policies (Article 11 TFEU). 'Greening' other policies seems, in the long term, a more promising approach to achieve environmental objectives than letting environmental policy try to fight for its own fund, which would always have insufficient resources. Financial instruments which concentrate on specific environmental aspects, such as habitat protection or environmental catastrophes, will continue to be necessary. The sheer amount of financial means that would be necessary for the protection, preservation and improvement of the quality of the environment at a high level – these are the requirements of Article 191 TFEU – will exceed the means of any environmental fund that could be set up.

Following a major flood in parts of the Union in 2002, the Union decided to establish an EU solidarity fund.[117] The fund is to intervene in cases of 'major disasters, mainly natural

[116] A Commission study of 2003 estimated that about €110 billion would be necessary to ensure the application of existing legislation in the accession countries, and in spring 2004 the Commission published a study which indicated that the habitat network Natura 2000 set up under Directives 79/409 and 92/43 (see para 5-10ff) would cost between €3.4 and 5.7 billion per year till 2013, see Commission, COM(2004) 431.

[117] Regulation 2012/2002 establishing the EU solidarity fund [2002] OJ L311/3.

disasters' which have serious repercussions on living conditions, the natural environment or the economy. To trigger use of the fund, the damage shall normally exceed €3 billion. Next to flooding, one might think, in the area of the environment, of droughts, forest fires, major industrial disasters or pipeline incidents. The overall amounts which are available under the funds are rather limited.

B. Structural Funds and the Cohesion Fund

4-26 In the context of EU regional policy, financial support in the form of structural funds are made available to Member States for agricultural, social and regional concerns. The present planning period lasts until 2027.[118] Environmental measures are in particular financed or co-financed by the European Regional Development Fund (ERDF) and the Cohesion Fund.[119] The Cohesion Fund has the task of financing, in addition to some transport activities,

> a greener, low-carbon transitioning towards a net zero carbon economy and resilient Europe, by promoting clean and fair energy transition, green and blue investment, the circular economy, climate change mitigation and adaptation, risk prevention and management and sustainable urban mobility.

Exactly the same task is given, among other tasks, to the ERDF, which has the general objective of reducing disparities between regions in the EU.[120] As other funds also finance environmental objectives, the amount which is available for environmental tasks cannot be specified – all the more so as it is up to the Member States themselves to ensure there is an appropriate balance between the Cohesion Fund's investments for the environment and for transport.[121]

Under the regional policy, programmes for the different measures are elaborated by Member States, which follow the priority objectives that have been laid down at EU level. These programmes are approved in some form by the Commission, which has, however, neither sufficient time nor sufficient personal resources to make a serious assessment. The individual projects are then decided by Member States.

For the coming years, Regulation 2021/1060 has indicated the possibility of financing measures on energy efficiency, renewable energy, adaptation to climate change, drinking water, water and waste water management, industrial and commercial waste management and clean urban infrastructure.[122] Funding for the prevention of risks, including the development and implementation of plans to prevent and cope with natural and technological risks, and sustainable tourism is mentioned in chapter twelve.

[118] See Regulation 2021/1060 laying down common provisions on the European Regional Development Fund, the European Social Fund Plus, the Cohesion Fund, the Just Transition Fund and the European Maritime, Fisheries and Aquaculture Fund [2021] OJ L231/159.

[119] Regulation 2021/1058 on the European Regional Development Fund and the Cohesion Fund [2021] OJ L231/60.

[120] Regulation 2021/1060 (n 118) Arts 5 and Art 3(1)(a).

[121] Regulation 2021/1058 (n 119) Art 6(1).

[122] Regulation 2021/1060 (n 118) annex I, positions 38–86.

How much of the sums available is spent on the construction of roads or other infrastructure projects and how much is spent on the environment is, as mentioned, decided by the Member States. Long-term effects of the regional policy – impacts of motorway construction or other infrastructure projects – on the state of nature, such as biodiversity or land use, are difficult to assess, as many other factors play a role. However, it seems obvious that many infrastructure and other projects in Member States which would never have been realised without the support of EU funds are detrimental to the protection of the environment. Environmental organisations have often tried to stop such projects – though normally without success.[123] The influence of such organisations on the elaboration of national plans under the structural funds is very limited.

The Cohesion Fund,[124] established under Article 177(2) TFEU did not work with 4-27
programmes until 2007; rather, it made money available for specific transport and environmental projects in countries which have a gross national product per capita of less than 90 per cent of the EU average. As of 2007, the Cohesion Fund follows the model of the other funds: Member States which benefit from the Cohesion Fund elaborate programmes and then obtain sums to implement those programmes. Which projects are then co-financed is up to the Member States.

The Cohesion Fund shall not co-finance the construction or the decommissioning of nuclear power plants;[125] the reduction of greenhouse gas emissions from activities covered by Directive 2003/87; housing, except for promoting energy efficiency or renewable energy use; the investment in airport infrastructure, unless related to environmental protection; landfills; or fossil fuel activities.[126]

The Member States that benefit from the Cohesion Fund between 2021 and 2027 are Bulgaria, Croatia, Cyprus, Czech Republic, Estonia, Greece, Hungary, Latvia, Lithuania, Malta, Poland, Portugal, Romania, Slovenia and Slovakia.

Regulation 2021/1060 provided in Article 8 that all projects which were co-financed with EU money must be 'legal and regular'.[127] However, the Union normally relies on the affirmation of the national authorities that a project conforms to EU environmental legal provisions. Local groups and environmental organisations often protest, arguing, for example, that no environmental impact assessment had been made before an infrastructure project was started. However, Article 97 of Regulation 2021/1060 enumerates the situations in which the Commission may suspend payments to a Member State; and non-compliance with applicable EU (environmental) law does not figure in this provision. This means in clear terms that the Commission would have to start proceedings under Articles 258 TFEU when a Member State does not comply with EU environmental law;[128] but the Commission

[123] See, eg the facts underlying CJEU Case C-325/94 *An Taisce* ECLI:EU:C:1996:293; Case C-321/95P (n 102); Case C-355/08P *WWF UK v Council* ECLI:EU:C:2009:286; General Court Case T-403/07 *Apiculteurs v Commission* ECLI:EU:T:2008:469.

[124] Regulation 2021/1058 (n 119).

[125] See, however, Decision 2022/182 for the general Union budget 2022 [2022] OJ L45/1, where Titles 1203 and 1204 provide for decommissioning contributions of the Union budget for Lithuania, Bulgaria and Slovakia (based on their Accession Treaty) and the EU Joint Research Centre. The total sum for 2022 was €173 million.

[126] ibid Art 7.

[127] Regulation 2021/1060 (n 118) Art 74. See also Art 9(4): 'The objectives of the Funds shall be pursued in full respect of the Union environmental acquis.'

[128] For an example of such a (lengthy) procedure, see CJEU Case C-385/13P *Italy v Commission* ECLI:EU:C:2014:2350.

would not be allowed to retain funds when, for example, a motorway is being built without an environmental impact assessment.[129] The underlying idea of the present provisions is presumably that protesters should go to the national court. However, there would be some value in a legislative provision that the Union taxpayer's money should only serve to finance projects which are in compliance with the Union legislation.

C. Other Funds

4-28 In 2021, the Union set up the Just Transition Fund,[130] destined to help territories which face serious socio-economic challenges deriving from the transition process towards the Union's 2030 target for energy and climate. Some 20 per cent of the presently available sum of €10 billion was earmarked for Poland, 13 per cent for Germany and 11 per cent for Romania, the three leading coal- and lignite-producing and using Member States. In 2023, the Union adopted, on the basis of Articles 91, 192(1), 194 and 322 TFEU, a Social Climate Fund.[131]

Specific provisions apply to agriculture. The Union set up a European Agricultural Guarantee Fund (EAGF) and a European Agricultural Fund for Rural Development (EAFRD), which both finance agricultural activities.[132] Member States are required to establish strategic plans which lay down the conditions under which payments to farmers may be made. The Union provisions of 2021 were clearly influenced by the Green Deal for Europe and endeavour to induce farmers to apply more environmentally favourable practices. The strategic plans shall provide an obligation for farmers who wish to obtain financial support from the Union to comply with some Union environmental legislation (conditionality),[133] though important parts of Union acts – in particular on groundwater, dangerous substances in water, waste water, the reduction of ammonia emissions, sewage sludge, all waste legislation, including animal waste, and invasive alien species[134] – are not referred to. Compliance with the conditionality provisions is entirely in the hands of Member States, which have to establish a control system that includes administrative

[129] See also Regulation 2021/1060 (n 118), which limited itself to advising (reluctantly) on the possibility of suspending payments in order to protect the financial interests of the Union, but did not mention (non-)compliance with existing Union law at all.

[130] Regulation 2021/1056 establishing the Just Transition Fund [2021] OJ L231/1.

[131] Regulation 2023/955 establishing a Social Climate Fund, (2023) OJ L 130/1.

[132] Regulation 2021/2115 establishing rules on support for strategic plans to be drawn up under the common agricultural policy (CAP Strategic Plans) and financed by the European Agricultural Guarantee Fund (EAGF) and the European Agricultural Fund for Rural Development (EAFRD) [2021] OJ L435/1; Regulation 2021/2116 on the financing, management and monitoring of the common agricultural policy [2021] OJ L435/187.

[133] Regulation 2021/2116 (n 132) Arts12, 31 and 70; see also Recitals 41 and 42. The Union acts which were mentioned in Art 12 and annex III were Directive 2000/60 on water [2000] OJ L327/1; Directive 91/676 on nitrates in water [1991] OJ L375/1; Directive 2009/147 on birds [2010] OJ L20/7; Directive 92/43 on habitats [1992] OJ L206/7; Regulation 1107/2009 on pesticides [2009] OJ L309/1; Directive 2009/128 on the use of pesticides [2009] OJ L309/71; Regulation 2016/1141 on invasive alien species [2016] OJ L189/4.

[134] The following acts were not mentioned: Directive 2006/118 on groundwater [2006] OJ L372/19; Directive 2008/105 on dangerous substances in water [2008] OJ L348/84; Directive 91/271 on waste water [1991] OJ L135/40; Directive 2016/2284 on (among others) ammoniac emissions [2016] OJ L344/1; Directive 86/278 on sewage sludge [1986] OJ L181/6; Regulation 1069/2009 on animal waste [2009] OJ L300/1.

penalties for cases of non-compliance; they shall inform the Commission of any irregularities which have occurred in the payment system. A publication of that information is not foreseen.

The Maritime, Fisheries and Aquaculture Fund,[135] based on no less than 11 provisions of the TFEU, has the objective of supporting activities which are mentioned in its title. Regulation 2021/1139 promoted the 'sustainable blue economy', which has to be in conformity with the UN Sustainable Development Goals and with EU environmental legislation which lays down a number of general environmental objectives.[136] No 'conditionality' was foreseen. Member States have to report 'serious' cases of non-compliance to the Commission, which may then suspend payments.

The precise sums which are made available by the different funds for the realisation 4-29
of environmental objectives cannot be indicated. For a start, it depends on the definition of 'environmental' objective or activity: should nuclear research, the activities of the Commission's Joint Research Centre or waste handling be considered as coming under this terminology? Everybody agrees that agricultural, fisheries, industrial, commercial or financial activities should be 'sustainable'. Yet, the vagueness of this term largely allows 'business as usual' to continue. Declarations according to which this or that percentage of the Union budget are spent on achieving environmental objectives are therefore of a political, not legal, nature.[137]

Overall, the Union funds' policy is tending increasingly in the direction of Member States receiving lump sums and spending them at their discretion, being loosely fenced in by the national priority programmes which they fix and which are only slightly controlled and then approved by the Commission. This trend makes the financing of environmental policies and projects increasingly dependent on the political rank that environmental policy has within the different Member States. And as the environment does not vote in elections, this rank is not high in many Member States. For a politician who wants to be re-elected, it is much more popular to build a new road than a waste water treatment installation, to protect farmers and hunters rather than the soil and the birds. European funds' development policy is quite problematic for the European environment.

D. LIFE – Financial Instrument for the Environment

Following earlier measures to support environmental projects in the Mediterranean, 4-30
Baltic and North Sea regions, a financial instrument, LIFE, was created in 1992 in order to support some environmental activities in Member States and beyond. Between 1992 and 2021, some 5500 projects were financially supported. For the period 2022–27, under the new LIFE Regulation,[138] €5.43 billion is available for four sub-programmes, on nature and

[135] Regulation 2021/1139 establishing the European Maritime, Fisheries and Aquaculture Fund [2021] OJ L247/1.

[136] ibid Art 2 no 15 and Art 14.

[137] See, eg European Court of Auditors, 'Special Report 9/2022: Climate Spending in the 2014–2020 Budget – Not as High as Reported' (Luxemburg, 2022). The Court of Auditors stated that, while the Commision argued that 20.1% of the 2014–20 budget was spent on climate change, its own calculations gave a percentage of 13% only. The Commission's calculations were too high by €72 billion.

[138] Regulation 2021/783 establishing a programme for the environment and climate change [2021] OJ L172/53.

biodiversity (€2.14 billion), circular economy (€1.35 billion), the transition to clean energy (€977 million) and climate change (€947,000).[139] Beneficiary countries are the EU Member States, countries in the different stages of accession to the EU, countries which are partners of the EU neighbourhood policy and those which adhered to the European Environment Agency – more than 35 countries overall. Under the environment programme, in particular, pilot and demonstration projects are co-financed.

A critical look at this regulation must begin with the sums that are made available for the protection of nature and biodiversity. The (missed) policy target of the Union was to stop the loss of biodiversity by 2010; the target to stop the loss by 2020 was also missed. In 2011, the Commission estimated the annual need for protecting Natura 2000 areas at €5.8 billion (27 EU Member States); in 2023, this figure was estimated at €10.1 billion annually.[140] Even if one takes the lower figure and considers it to be exaggerated, the shortfall of the amount Regulation 2021/783 provides – about €2.14 billion for six years, which is to be divided by some 35 countries – remains enormous. It is likely that the Commission will argue in future that Member States should provide for the financing of nature protection measures under the regional policy and other funds, while Member States will argue that it is LIFE which has to finance the protection of nature and biodiversity. The loser is the environment. It must also be pointed out that the protection of nature and biodiversity cannot be limited to the designated habitats of EU interest, the Natura 2000 network.

There are other problems with LIFE. Member States take great care to ensure that every Member State gets a fair share of the available sums. Thus, it is not necessarily the best project that is supported. Article 18 of Regulation 2021/783 mandates the Commission to adopt two multi-annual work programmes (four years and three years) where priorities for specific projects are set. The method of project approval via comitology-like procedures has in the past led to some concerted practices among Member States. Also in the past, there was a limited pilot effect of the specific project that was co-financed: the innovative measures were not easily made operational across the whole of the Union. In 2013, the Court of Auditors concluded in a report on the environmental component of LIFE+ (2007–13) 'that, overall, the LIFE environment component was not operating effectively because it was not sufficiently well designed and implemented'.[141]

IV. Planning and Land Use

A. Town and Country Planning; Land Use

4-31 Article 192(2) TFEU provides that measures concerning town and country planning and land use require unanimous adoption in the Council. The provision thus parts from the

[139] For LIFE+ (2007–13), where €2.1 billion was made available, the EU Court of Auditors observed: 'This is a modest budget for an ambitious objective: to contribute to the development, updating and implementation of EU environmental policy and legislation.' Court of Auditors, 'Special Report 15/2013: Has the Environmental Component of the LIFE Programme Been Effective?' (Luxemburg, 2013).

[140] Commission, SWD(2011) 1573; 'Investment Needs and Priorities for Natura 2000 and Green Infrastructure' SWD(2023) 99/10.

[141] Court of Auditors, Special Report 15/2013 (n 139); see also the much less critical Commission, 'Report on the Final Assessment of LIFE (2007–2013)' COM(2013) 478.

idea that such measures may also be adopted at Union level, though questions of subsidiarity are of particular relevance here. So far, though, almost no such measures have been taken. The Commission issued some communications which concern basic aspects of town and country planning,[142] the urban environment,[143] integrated coastal zone management[144] and wetlands.[145] On coastal zone management, the European Parliament and the Council adopted a recommendation which gives guidelines for an 'environmentally sustainable, economically equitable, sociable responsible and culturally sensitive management of coastal zones'.[146] Despite these words, the individual recommendations are of a very general nature and not really operational. And a look at coastal zones in the Union shows that the recommendation was largely ignored, the most obvious example being the destruction of the Spanish coast by construction.

In 2014, the Union adopted, on the basis of Articles 43, 100, 192(1) and 194 TFEU, a directive on maritime planning.[147] In this author's opinion, the directive should have been adopted unanimously (Article 192(2) TFEU), as it deals with country planning. Also, the Union competence under the subsidiarity and proportionality principles is doubtful.

In execution of Decision 1600/2002 on the Sixth Environmental Action Programme, the Commission published in early 2006 a thematic strategy – ie a sectoral action programme – on the urban environment[148] which addressed in particular problems of transport in urban agglomerations. Concrete actions on implementing the strategy were almost completely lacking. Under the regional policy, some pilot projects were supported financially, greater co-operation among agglomerations was promoted and awareness campaigns were initiated. In general, though, problems of the urban environment are much too large and too diversified to be handled at EU level. 4-32

The Seventh Environmental Action Programme[149] wanted to 'ensure' that by 2020 'a majority of cities in the Union are implementing policies for sustainable urban planning and design, including innovative approaches for urban public transport and mobility, sustainable buildings, energy efficiency and urban biodiversity conservation'. The programme indicated what would be necessary to reach this objective, but made no suggestions whatsoever for how to get there. The Eighth Environmental Action Programme was silent on local or regional town and country planning.[150]

Article 13 of the Directive on the prevention of major accidents[151] required Member States to ensure that the objectives of preventing major accidents and limiting the

[142] Commission, 'Europe 2000: Perspectives of Future Town and Country Planning of the Community' COM(90) 544; Commission, 'Europe 2000: Outlook for the Development of the Community's Territory' COM(91) 452.

[143] Commission, 'Green Paper on the Urban Environment' COM(90) 218; Council Resolution of 28 January 1991 [1991] OJ C33/4; see further Court of Auditors, Special Report on urban environment in the European Union [1994] OJ C383/1; Commission, 'Urban Development in the European Union' COM(97) 197.

[144] Commission, 'Integrated Coastal Zone Management' COM(2000) 547.

[145] Commission, 'The Wise Use and Conservation of Wetlands' COM(95) 189.

[146] Recommendation 2002/413 concerning the implementation of integrated coastal zone management [2002] OJ L148/24.

[147] Directive 2014/89 establishing a framework for maritime spatial planning [2014] OJ L257/135.

[148] Decision 1600/2002 laying down the sixth environment action programme [2002] OJ L242/1, Art 7(2.g); Commission, COM(2005) 718.

[149] Decision 1386/2013 [2013] OJ L354/171, s 95.

[150] Decision 2022/591 [2022] OJ L114/22.

[151] Directive 2012/18 on the control of major-accident hazards involving dangerous substances [2012] OJ L197/1.

consequences of those accidents were taken into account in their land-use policies. In the long term, there will have to be appropriate distances between establishments which come under Directive 2012/18 and residential areas, areas of public use and areas of natural value and interest. The implementation of these provisions is to be ensured by consultation procedures. Industrial accidents in Enschede (the Netherlands) and Toulouse (France) in 2000 demonstrated the necessity of such measures, though it is rather difficult to relocate industrial installations once they have been built too close to urban agglomerations or newly built residential areas. In practice, Article 13 of Directive 2012/18 is hardly enforceable. When Frankfurt Airport wanted to enlarge, work was held up in 2004/05 because a chemical plant was located exactly where the new runway was proposed to be sited. After years of negotiations, the plant was relocated.

Apart from these few measures, the different communications – including the Seventh Environmental Action Programme – have aimed at focusing attention on some specific aspects of development within the Union or showing the environmental problems of specific areas, rather than determining legal measures for town and country planning or land use.[152] Indeed, these measures do not announce or propose any new legal measures to contribute to the solutions of problems. Rather, they have to be viewed alongside the Union's policies which affect planning and land use, in particular regional, transport and agricultural policy. Sometimes the communications also serve to start a discussion on whether EU financial assistance for some specific topics should be envisaged, notably within the framework of the structural funds. Also, measures concerning the protection of the architectural and natural heritage of the European Union[153] are increasingly coming under the provisions on culture of Article 167 TFEU.[154]

B. Environmental Impact Assessment

(i) Projects

4-33 *Member State level.* A Directive on the assessment of the effects of certain public and private projects on the environment was adopted in 1985, substantially amended in 1997, consolidated in 2011 and again amended in 2014.[155] According to that directive, public authorities, before they grant a permit (development consent) for a specific public or private project, shall make an assessment of the direct and indirect effects which the project may have on humans and the environment; environmental factors, which are mentioned, are the

[152] See, eg Commission, 'The Urban Agenda of EU Policies – Key Features of an EU Urban Agenda' COM(2014) 490; Commission, 'New European Bauhaus' COM(2021) 573; Commission, 'Upgrading Cohesion Policy – Flexible Assistance to Territories (FAST-CARE) – to Address the Consequences of Russian Aggression' COM(2022) 324/2.

[153] See Recommendation 74/65 on the protection of the architectural and natural heritage [1975] OJ L21/22; Resolution of the Council and of Member States meeting in Council on the conservation of the European architectural heritage [1986] OJ C320/1; Decision 1194/2011 establishing an EU action for the European heritage label [2011] OJ L303/1.

[154] Decision 228/97 on an action programme for the conservation of cultural heritage [1997] OJ L305/11; Commission, *Europe's Cultural and Natural Heritage in Natura 2000* (Luxemburg, 2018); Commission, *European Framework for Action on Cultural Heritage* (Luxemburg, 2019).

[155] Directive 85/337 (n 47); Directive 97/11 (n 47); Directive 2011/92 (n 48); Directive 2014/52 amending Directive 2011/92 [2014] OJ L124/1.

population and human health, biodiversity, land, soil, water, air, climate, landscape, material assets and cultural heritage. Specific procedural provisions were laid down for such an assessment, such as the requirement for the developer to submit factual information on the project and its likely impact, as well as measures to reduce negative impacts, the participation of administrative bodies dealing with nature protection and the possibility for the public concerned to express an opinion. The administrative decision on the application shall take into consideration all these comments.

For a first group of projects, listed in annex I to Directive 2011/92, such as large refineries, large power stations, radioactive waste disposal installations, motorways, lines for long-distance railway traffic, larger airports, an environmental impact assessment always has to be made. For a second group of projects (annex II), an impact assessment has to be made where the project is likely 'to have significant effects on the environment by virtue, in particular, of its nature, size or location' (Article 2). Member States have a large amount of discretion in deciding whether a project has such a significant impact or not. However, the CJEU has considerably narrowed down this discretion, by requiring de facto that, for any project that is (objectively) likely to have a significant impact on the environment, an environmental impact assessment is necessary.[156] The public is to be informed of the project, and the 'public concerned' has a right to participate in the permitting procedure (Article 6).

Commission attempts in the 1980s to have an environmental impact assessment made for any project co-financed by EU funds failed, as the main Member States involved – from Southern Europe – successfully argued that this would be discriminatory. This was not convincing, since the taxpayers in the different Member States which contribute to the funds are certainly entitled to be assured that their money is properly used.

Directive 2011/92 has been implemented in all Member States, albeit with considerable delay in some states; however, not all legislation conformed to the directive's requirements and the Court sometimes had to make a statement on the non-conformity of national legislation years later.[157] A particular problem is the practical application of the directive: even after a number of years of the directive's application, a large number of the complaints, petitions and infringement procedures under Article 258 TFEU deal with Directive 2011/92.[158] The main concerns are the policy decisions to realise a project independently from its, potentially very negative, impact on the environment; the exclusion of annex II projects from an impact assessment; the poor quality or incomplete nature of the impact assessment; the commencement of work on the project before the end of the impact assessment procedure; the attempt to break down a project into several parts, each of which is below the financial threshold or is without significant impact, whereas the cumulated effects of the whole project would be significant (slicing);[159] and omissions to

[156] CJEU Case C-435/97 *WWF* ECLI:EU:C:1998:418; Case C-72/95 *Kraaijeveld* ECLI:EU:C:1996:404; Case C-43/92 *Commission v Germany* ECLI:EU:C:1995:260; Case C-301/95 *Commission v Germany* ECLI:EU:C:1998:493; Case C-392/96 *Commission v Ireland* ECLI:EU:C:1998:431.

[157] CJEU Case C-50/09 *Commission v Ireland* ECLI:EU:C:2011:109; Case C-115/09 *Trianel* ECLI:EU:C:2011:289; Case C-177/09 *Poumon Vert Hulpe* ECLI:EU:C:2011:738; Case C-182/10 *Solvay* ECLI:EU:C:2012:82; Case C-244/12 *Salzburg Airport* ECLI:EU:C:2013:203; Case C-137/14 *Commission v Germany* ECLI:EU:C:2015:683; Case C-576/16 *Commission v Poland* ECLI:EU:C:2018:356.

[158] Commission, Monitoring the application of Community law 13th report [1995] OJ C250/1, 175; 17th report (1999) [2001] OJ C30/1, 45; 19th report, COM(2002) 324, 45.

[159] This slicing is not allowed under the directive, see CJEU Case C-2/07 *Abraham* ECLI:EU:C:2008:133; Case C-531/15 *Strasswalchen* ECLI:EU:C:2015:79.

properly consult the public concerned.[160] The transboundary effects of a project, under Article 7 of the directive, are to be discussed and settled in an intergovernmental co-operation procedure. This is not compatible with the right of the public concerned – even when that public lives in a neighbouring country – or with Articles 3(9) and 6 of the Aarhus Convention, which give the right to participate to persons concerned independently of their domicile.

4-34 Directive 2011/92 has undoubtedly influenced the development of permitting procedures in all Member States by imposing the taking into consideration of environmental aspects on this procedure. In a number of regions, it was possible to limit and reduce the almost total discretion given to local or other authorities to decide on a project.

The main problems of the directive are:

- its loose drafting and the large discretion given to administrations often lead to the non-application of some of its principles;
- the directive does not oblige a developer to study or have studied alternatives to the project;[161]
- the administration is not in any way obliged to avoid and/or minimise the negative effects of a project on the environment, but may grant development consent where serious negative effects are to be expected;[162]
- no regular national reports and no Commission report on the application of the directive are foreseen;[163] and
- the directive does not provide for consequences when an environmental impact assessment has not been made. This leads to large differences. While, for example, in the UK the planning consent would be void and the whole procedure would have to start anew where an environmental impact assessment had not been made, German courts considered the omission to make an environmental impact assessment an administrative error which is only relevant where it can be proven that the impact assessment would have led to another decision. CJEU decisions clarified that the complete omission of an impact assessment as well as a significant procedural error made the permit procedure defective. The Court also clarified that the burden of proof that an impact assessment would have led to another decision regarding a project may not be placed on the applicant.[164]

[160] See the cases mentioned in n 159; CJEU Case C-396/92 *Bund Naturschutz Bayern* ECLI:EU:C:1994:307.

[161] See Directive 2011/92 (n 48), which provided in Art 5(3) and annex IV, fn 2 that the developer has to submit, together with his application, 'an outline of the main alternatives studied by the developer'. However, this clause is generally understood in the sense that the developer is not obliged to study alternatives; only where he has done so must he submit information on them. Under the Espoo Convention, which has also been concluded by the EU (see para 4-39), the developer of a project which has an impact on another state must examine 'reasonable alternatives'. This provision is binding on EU Member States.

[162] A good example is CJEU Case C-43/10 *Acheloos* ECLI:EU:C:2012:560, where the CJEU sent the decision on whether the project to divert the river Acheloos was compatible with EU law back to the Greek authorities.

[163] Directive 2011/92 (n 48) only provided in Art 11(3) that the Commission shall publish an implementation report five years after the adoption of the directive. This report was published in 1993 (COM) (93) 28 of 2 April 1993. The Commission occasionally published further reports, at an interval of about 5–8 years, see COM(2003) 334; COM(2009) 378.

[164] CJEU Case C-72/12 *Altrip ECLI*:EU:C:2013:712; Case C-463/11 *L v M* ECLI:EU:C:2013:247.

The amendments brought to Directive 2011/92 by Directive 2014/52 concerned in particular the screening procedure, ie the examination whether an annex II project shall be subject to an impact assessment, as well as the question of the scope and the details of the impact assessment report which the operator has to deliver (scoping procedure).

Directive 92/43[165] required an 'appropriate assessment' for projects which are to be realised within a protected habitat. If the project may have a significant adverse effect on the site or on the fauna or flora living therein, it will normally not be realised unless the exceptions of Article 6(4) of Directive 92/43 are applied – or if, for renewable energy projects, the emergency provisions of Regulation 2022/2577[166] allow its realisation. This is different to Directive 2011/92, which allows the realisation of a project even though the impact assessment shows negative effects on the environment. 4-35

As Article 6 of Directive 92/43 does not contain procedural rules, procedural requirements for the impact assessment under Directive 92/43 are in practice very similar to those under Directive 2011/92.[167] The CJEU held that a project that had to undergo an impact assessment under Directive 2011/92 also always had to undergo an assessment under Directive 92/43.[168]

Union level. The Commission does not itself authorise projects which are realised at national level. There are thus no provisions at EU level corresponding to those of Directive 2011/92. There was considerable discussion about whether there should be an EU assessment before the Commission agrees to co-finance Member States' projects. This idea was rightly rejected, as it could lead to two environmental impact assessments being made and there is no reason to duplicate these assessments, which are expensive and time-consuming. The problem would probably be smaller if Member States were required to make such an assessment for all projects that are co-financed by an EU budget and if the Commission systematically checked whether a necessary national environmental impact assessment was made. 4-36

The European Investment Bank requires the application of Directive 2011/92 when it co-finances a project within the EU. For projects outside the EU, where no legislation on environmental impact assessments might exist, it takes EU legislation as a base – without it being clear whether it systematically asks for an environmental impact assessment.

(ii) Plans and Programmes

Member State level. Directive 2001/42[169] requested Member States to make an environmental impact assessment for plans and programmes which were likely to have significant environment effects. Plans and programmes for which such an impact assessment was always necessary were listed in Article 3(2); this requirement was, however, limited to 4-37

[165] Directive 92/43 on the conservation of natural habitats and of wild fauna and flora [1992] OJ L206/7.

[166] Regulation 2022/2577 (n 67) Art 3: 'the planning, construction and operation of plants and installations for the production of energy from renewable sources shall be presumed as being in the overriding public interest when balancing interests in the individual case, for the purposes of Art 6(4) of Directive 92/43'.

[167] CJEU Case C-441/17 *Commission v Poland* ECLI:EU:C:2018:235; Case C164/17 *Grace and Sweetman* ECLI:EU:C:2018:593; Case C-411/17 *Inter-Environnement Wallonie* ECLI:EU:C:2019:622.

[168] CJEU Case C-293/17 *Cooperatie Mobilisation* ECLI:EU:C:2018:882.

[169] Directive 2001/42 (n 51).

plans or programmes which were required,[170] and they formed the basis for subsequent project-related environmental impact assessments.[171] For plans and programmes which determine the 'use of small areas of local level' and minor amendments to existing plans and programmes, an assessment was only necessary where Member States determined that they were likely to have significant environmental effects; a general exemption of small areas was, however, not allowed.[172] For other plans which 'set the framework for future development consent of projects', Member States should determine whether they were likely to have such effects, either through case-by-case examination or according to specific types of plans and programmes. Plans for national defence, civil emergency and financial or budget plans or programmes were not covered by the directive.

The definition of 'environment assessment' is different from that under Directive 2011/92. Under Directive 2001/42, it means 'the preparation of an environment report, the carrying out of consultations, the taking into account of the environment report and the consultations in decision-making and the provision of information on the decision' that is finally taken. The environment report must describe and evaluate the likely environmental impacts and reasonable alternatives. Consultation[173] must take place early and at any time before the adoption of the plan or programme or its submission to the legislative procedure. It must include consultations on the draft plan and on the environmental report. The public which is to be consulted includes those people affected, or likely to be affected, by or having an interest in the decision, 'including relevant non-governmental organisations, such as those promoting environmental protection'.

A national or regional legislative act constitutes a plan or programme when it contains 'a significant body of criteria and detailed rules' for the permitting and realisation of projects.[174]

4-38 Once a decision on the plan or programme has been taken, (i) the public that was consulted shall be informed and (ii) the relevant plan or programme and a statement must be made available, summarising how environmental considerations were taken into consideration, as well as the results of the consultation and 'the reason for choosing the plan or programme as adopted'. The directive also covered plans and programmes that were co-financed under the EU structural funds, although the wording is not entirely clear in this regard.[175] The directive tried to ensure that public discussions on the environmental effects of plans and programmes take place and it may be hoped that this progressively benefits the

[170] The CJEU held that a plan or programme is 'required' when there exists in national law a particular legal basis which authorises the adoption of a plan or programme and the procedure for preparing it, even if that adoption was not mandatory, CJEU Case C-56/10 *Inter-Environnement Bruxelles* ECLI:EU:C:2012:159; Case C-321/18 *Terre wallonne* ECLI:EU:C:2019:424.

[171] Directive 2001/42 (n 51) Art 3(2): 'an environmental assessment shall be carried out for all plans and programmes, (a) which are prepared for agriculture, forestry, fisheries, energy, industry, transport, waste management, water management, telecommunications, tourism, town and country planning or land use which set the framework for future development consent of projects listed in Annexes I and II to Directive 85/337, or (b) which, in view of the likely effect on sites, have been determined to require an assessment pursuant to Article 6 or 7 of Directive 92/43'.

[172] CJEU Case C-295/10 *Valciukene* ECLI:EU:C:2011:608.

[173] Directive 2001/42 uses the words 'participation' and 'consultation' synonymously. For the difference between these notions, see para 4-16ff.

[174] CJEU Case C-300/20 *Bund Naturschutz Bayern* ECLI:EU:C:2022:102, para 60.

[175] Directive 2001/42 (n 51) Arts 3(9), 11(3) and 12(4).

environment. The necessity to explain why a specific solution for a plan was taken might also reduce the administrations' discretion, which, in some parts of the Union, is in need of more democratic procedures. It is problematic, though, whether enough interested persons will participate in the impact assessment and how an interested public or an environmental organisation will be able to assess the environmental impact of any such plan.

National plans which were adopted without an environmental assessment must in principle be annulled by the national courts.[176] National legislation may also not foresee that a plan which was adopted without a proper environmental impact assessment nevertheless remains valid.[177]

Union level. In the context of the International Convention on Environment Impact Assessment in a Transboundary Context, signed in Espoo (Finland) in 1991 and which the EU joined in 1993,[178] a protocol was signed in May 2003 in Kiev (Ukraine) which provided for a strategic environmental assessment of plans and programmes; the protocol was signed by all EU Member States and by the Union itself. The protocol's content is very similar to that of Directive 2001/42.[179] 4-39

The Council approved the protocol in 2008.[180] The problem of the protocol's application to the EU institutions is whether there are plans or programmes elaborated by the EU institutions – not just co-financed by them, as these remain Member States' plans and programmes – that would come under the field of application of the protocol. This is undoubtedly the case. Indeed, already the different thematic strategies which were elaborated under the Sixth Environmental Action Programme[181] fulfilled the conditions of Article 2(5) of the protocol. Other plans and programmes which exist and which will be covered by the provisions of the protocol are plans for energy saving and programmes in the agricultural sector, on trans-European networks under Articles 170 et seq TFEU, on standardisation, etc. The Commission communications on the Green Deal for Europe,[182] on the circular economy, on food from farm to fork,[183] on a biodiversity strategy till 2030,[184] on the Eighth Environmental Action Programme[185] and numerous other plans, programmes or strategies also constitute 'programmes related to the environment'. However, no environmental impact assessment was made for any of these plans or programmes. As access to the CJEU is not possible for individuals or environmental organisations – they are not directly and individually concerned by such plans or programmes – this practice is not sanctioned.

(iii) *Policies and Legislation*

Member State level. There are no specific EU provisions which require Member States to make (environmental) impact assessments of national policies or legislation before 4-40

[176] CJEU Case C-41/11 *Inter-Environnement Wallonie* ECLI:EU:C:2012/103.
[177] CJEU Case C-463/11 (n 164).
[178] Decision of 15 October 1996. The decision appears never to have been published.
[179] On that directive, see para 4-37ff.
[180] Decision 2008/871 [2008] OJ L308/33; the protocol is published on p 35.
[181] See para 2-42ff.
[182] Commission, COM(2019) 640.
[183] Commission, COM(2020) 381.
[184] Commission, COM(2020) 380.
[185] Commisssion, COM(2020) 652.

such policies or legislations are adopted. The above-mentioned Aarhus Convention mentions public participation in policies and legislations, but in a form of soft law which does not provide for an obligation of contracting parties to take implementation measures (Article 8).

A certain form of consultation obligation for national legislation is created by EU law, not, however, for environmental purposes, but for economic or technical ones. Directive 2015/1535,[186] which was based on Articles 114, 337 and 43 TFEU, aims at the removal or reduction of any barriers which national legislation might create to the free movement of goods. It requested Member States to notify the Commission of draft product-related legislation. Where a restriction on use or a ban of a substance or a product was in question, the Member State was asked to add 'if available', data on production and substitution products, as well as, 'in appropriate cases', the conclusions of a risk evaluation made in accordance with the principles of chemical legislation. The national draft measure is sent to all other Member States and the notifying Member State may adopt the draft measure only after a standstill period of three months following notification. Where the Commission or another Member State indicates that the draft measure may create barriers to the free movement of goods, the standstill period is extended to six months. Where the Commission indicates its intention to propose a legally binding Community measure or where there is already a proposal on the subject matter in question before the Council, the standstill period is 12 months.

4-41 Where a Member State adopts a national measure without having complied with the procedure under Directive 2015/1535, the national provision is unenforceable on economic operators and national courts are obliged not to apply the national provision in question.[187] This 'sanction', which follows from the direct effect of the directive's provisions,[188] is very effective, since penalties, fines or other sanctions which were pronounced under the national provision could not be enforced either. Directive 2015/1535 affects numerous environmental measures[189] and has de facto replaced a standstill agreement in environmental matters which was adopted in 1973 in the form of a gentlemen's agreement.[190] The decisive criterion for the directive's application is whether the national measure may, directly or indirectly, influence the free circulation of goods; EU environmental considerations do not really come into this assessment, and hardly any weighing of the different interests takes place. With this proviso, measures which fix air or water quality standards normally do not come within the field of application of Directive 2015/1535. Likewise, nature protection measures and provisions on the storage of products or on the establishment and operation of industrial installations are not normally affected either.

The public is not consulted during this procedure, though it may be assumed that Member States which are informed of draft legislation of another Member State will consult

[186] Directive 2015/1535 (n 36).

[187] CJEU Case C-194/94 *Security International v Signalsson* ECLI:EU:C:1996:172.

[188] See para 14-27ff.

[189] In 2014 and 2015, out of 1382 national draft regulatory measures that were notified by Member States, 158 might be qualified as environmental measures. Commission, COM(2017) 788.

[190] Agreement of the Representatives of the Governments of the Member States meeting in Council on information for the Commission and for the Member States with a view to possible harmonisation throughout the Communities of urgent measures concerning the protection of the environment [1973] OJ C9/1; amended [1974] OJ C86/2.

their economic operators to see whether there is a potential impact on the free circulation of goods. The Commission considered the procedure to come under the 'investigation' exception of Regulation 1049/2001[191] and tried not to grant access to the comments which are made under the procedure of Directive 2015/1535, but was stopped in this by the CJEU, which saw no case for investigation in such cases.[192]

Union level. The interinstitutional agreement on better regulation provided that the Commission should make an assessment of its legislative proposals and other measures, which are expected to have significant economic, environmental or social impacts.[193] The Parliament and the Council may make such assessments on their own if they find this appropriate.[194] 4-42

The Commission's impact assessments focus on the examination of the existence, scale and consequences of a problem and on the question of whether Union action is needed, and, where possible, address the 'cost of non-Europe'. The impact assessment examines, possibly with the help of studies, the impact of a project, and provides for consultation with interested parties and relevant experts, including consultations on ethical and political issues. The results of the assessment, which also have to include an assessment of alternatives, are laid down in an assessment report, which forms a basis for the Commission's decision on the proposal. The assessment report is made available by the Commission once it has formally adopted the proposal.[195]

In practice, the European Parliament and the Council do not make impact assessments of their own. This did not prevent the Council requesting the Commission, on the basis of Article 241 TFEU, to make a better impact assessment concerning its proposal to reduce the use of pesticides in agriculture.[196]

The Commission practice since 2003 shows the limited added value of the assessments. The main issue of the examination is the cost of the planned measure for economic operators. In the area of agriculture, internal market, industry and regional policy, the impact assessment procedure often just rubber-stamps political decisions which have been taken elsewhere; here, the environmental impact is rarely examined and assessed in any detail. In contrast, most proposals in the environmental sector are very strictly scrutinised as to their impact on vested interests – frequently in the name of 'better regulation' – and then watered down or completely rejected before they even reach the Commission's decision-making level. The methodology of making the impact assessments is not laid open. Frequently, the options which are examined are pre-determined by the result which the Commission wishes to obtain.

To take some concrete examples: Regulations 1300/2013 and 1303/2013, on the Cohesion Fund and the Regional Fund respectively,[197] were the subject of a single impact

[191] See Regulation 1049/2001 (n 20) and para 4-07ff.

[192] CJEU Case C-331/15P *France v Schlyter* ECLI:EU:C.2017:639.

[193] Interinstitutional agreement between the European Parliament, the Council of the European Union and the European Commission on better law-making [2016] OJ L123/1, ss 12–18.

[194] ibid s 15.

[195] CJEU Case C-57/16P *ClientEarth v Commission* ECLI:EU:C.2018:660 held that at least impact assessments for legislative proposal had to be published before a Commission decision on a proposal was taken, in order to allow the public to discuss all alternatives.

[196] Decision 2022/2572 [2022] OJ L331/6. The Commission proposal was made under COM(2022) 305.

[197] Regulation 1300/2013 on the Cohesion Fund [2013] OJ L347/281; Regulation 1303/2013 on common provisions for several funds [2013] OJ L347/320.

assessment which considered shifting the EU support in a different way.[198] However, the impact assessment did not examine the effects of these structural funds on the environment within the EU, even though this impact is enormous; an examination of the likely environmental impact of the two regulations would require detailed studies which the Commission is neither able nor ready to finance and for which often there is not the time either. Also, the Commission proposal to allow Member States, under certain conditions, to restrict the cultivation of GMOs on their territory was not based on an impact assessment.[199] In the same way, Council Regulation 2022/2577 on urgency permitting procedures for renewable energy projects underwent no impact assessment.[200]

Such examples could be multiplied. The impact assessment requirement, though acceptable in its theoretical concept, thus turned in practice into an instrument of environmental deregulation. This is further strengthened by the fact that the impact assessment is made, under the political responsibility of the Commission's President, by the Secretariat General. In this way, the Secretary General can easily signal to the different departments that this or that legislative proposal is unwelcome and would receive a stiff reception with the Secretariat General. Examples in the past are the proposals for a directive on access to justice or on soil protection, or considerations to have a directive on biodiversity elaborated. The assessment process thus strengthens centralising activities inside the Commission, a tendency which is not favourable to the protection of the environment.

Following the Better Regulation Agreement, the Commission increasingly recurred to ex post impact assessments, which were called 'assessment', 'evaluation', 'implementation', etc. These evaluations tried to evaluate whether a legislative act was effective, efficient, coherent and consistent, and had an added Union value. Such an ex-post evaluation does not seem to exist for national legislation. Such an evaluation would give valuable insights in particular into factual aspects, such as Member States' legislative measures, delays, complaints, gaps in the Union act or new developments. However, the Commission's evaluations of Union's environmental acts are often not self-critical and do not centre on the environment, though they remain an important tool for assessing their impact.

V. Industrial Installations

A. Corporate Environmental Responsibility

4-43 Since 2001, the Commission has published four communications on corporate social responsibility (CSR).[201] It expressly stated that the responsibility of companies not only included social, but also environmental matters. The main signal of the Commission

[198] Commission, SEC(2011) 1138.
[199] Commission, COM(2010) 375.
[200] Regulation 2022/2577 (n 67).
[201] Commission, 'Green Paper: Towards a European Framework for Corporate Social Responsibility' COM(2001) 366; Commission, 'Communication Concerning Corporate Social Responsibility' COM(2002) 347; see also Council Resolutions [2002] OJ C86/1 and [2003] OJ C39/3; Commission, 'Implementing the Partnership for Growth and Jobs: Making Europe a Pole of Excellence on CSR 136' COM(2006) 136; Commission, 'A Renewed EU Strategy 2011–2014 for Corporate Social Responsibility' COM(2011) 681.

was that it did not intend to provide for any binding legislation in this regard, but that it expected companies to assume their responsibility on a voluntary basis. In line with the neo-liberal tendencies which the Commission pursued since the beginning of the twenty-first century, the change of the definition of corporate social responsibility is remarkable: while in 2001, the Commission defined CSR as ' a concept whereby companies integrate social and environmental concerns in their business operations and in their interaction with their stakeholders on a voluntary basis', the definition of 2011 now reads: '[CSR is] the responsibility of enterprises for their impacts on society'. In this way, the term 'environment' was removed from the definition.[202] It is true, though, that the Union policy pursued under the Green Deal for Europe since 2019 largely reaffirmed the economic importance of environmental issues.[203]

As companies within the Union are submitted to legislative requirements with regard to their emissions, waste generation and treatment, waste water requirements, etc, the corporate environmental responsibility aims in particular at EU companies that are active in developing countries. I would consider it normal that no EU-based company anywhere in the world would dispose of its waste in other places than authorised landfills, even if the political, economic and environmental situation in the host country does not require or enforce such behaviour; in the same way, a company should not discharge its waste water into rivers, lakes or coastal waters without prior treatment, wherever its installation is located; it should respect human and workers' rights, and take adequate measures to prevent industrial accidents. There are many examples of this kind. However, whether voluntary measures are really sufficient to make companies follow basic environmental protection standards is doubtful. An international convention on corporate social-environmental responsibility appears necessary and, pending EU binding measures with regard to EU companies' environmental behaviour, wherever they act, highly desirable. A first step in this direction would be the adoption of the Commission proposal for a directive on corporate sustainability due diligence.[204] The proposal provides for 'rules on obligations for companies regarding … environmental adverse impacts with respect to their own operations, the operations of their subsidiaries and the value chain operations carried out by entities with whom the company has an established business relationship' (Article 1). The proposal is currently being discussed by the other Union institutions.

B. Permitting

Directive 76/464[205] provided that EU-wide emission limit values for the industrial discharge of some dangerous substances into the water were to be fixed, based on the 'best technical means available'. As regards air emissions from industrial installations, Directive 84/360 stipulated that permits should be issued to new installations to prevent 4-44

[202] The Commission adds, but outside the definition, 'To fully meet their corporate social responsibility, enterprises should have in place a process to integrate social, environmental, ethical, human rights and consumer concerns into their business operations', Commission, COM(2001) 366 (n 201).

[203] See also para 4-16ff.

[204] Commission, COM(2022) 71 (n 112).

[205] Directive 76/464 on pollution caused by certain dangerous substances discharged into the aquatic environment of the Community [1976] OJ L129/23, Art 6(1). This directive ceased to exist in 2013.

air pollution, based on the best available technology not entailing excessive costs; for existing installations, Member States had to 'implement policies and strategies, including appropriate measures, for the gradual adaptation of existing plans … to the best available technology'.[206]

The putting into operation of the principle of introducing the best available technology largely failed, among other reasons, because no consensus was reached as to which technology, in a given case, was the best available. Under Directive 76/464, the EU-wide emission standards were fixed by way of a political compromise, not by having recourse to an analysis of the application of the best available technology. Furthermore, Member States were allowed to use EU quality standards instead of emission limit values.[207] Under Directive 84/360, technical notes were elaborated and published to determine what constituted, for specific sectors of industry, the best available technology. However, these notes did not have any significant impact, since they had no binding legal force, and it was neither controlled nor publicised whether they were complied with or not. Neither directive, therefore, led to a significant change in the technologies used in industrial installations. Furthermore, Member States did not really favour uniform emission standards for industrial installations, but rather proposed a non-harmonised approach within the Union.

4-45 In an attempt to accommodate this concern, while improving the present situation and deregulating, decentralising and taking into consideration the subsidiarity principle of the EC Treaty, the Council adopted Directive 96/61 concerning integrated pollution prevention and control,[208] which became applicable for new installations in 1999; existing installations have had to comply with its requirements since 2007. In 2008, this directive was replaced by Directive 2008/1, which, in turn, was replaced by Directive 2010/75.[209] Directive 2010/75 concerned some 52,000 large industrial and agro-industrial installations, the categories of which were listed in its annex I. It also covered large combustion plants, waste incineration and co-incineration installations, activities using organic solvents and finally installations producing titanium dioxide; these activities were regulated, until 2010, by different specific directives. Directive 2010/75 was thus a real framework directive on industrial emissions. It entered into effect in 2013, though the entry into effect of several provisions was postponed until 2014, 2016 and, for large combustion plants under certain conditions, even 2020 (Article 32).

For some time, the Commission had also pursued the idea of a similar, though less stringent, directive for smaller industrial installations. In 1997, environmental ministers of Member States concluded that, from an environmental point of view, there was no reason to apply environmentally less stringent standards to small enterprises,[210] but it took the Union

[206] Directive 84/360 on the combating of air pollution from industrial plants [1984] OJ L188/20, Arts 4 and 13.

[207] Directive 76/464 (n 205) Art 6.

[208] Directive 96/61 concerning integrated pollution prevention and control [1996] OJ L257/26.

[209] Directive 2008/1 concerning integrated pollution prevention and control [2008] OJ L24/8; Directive 2010/75 (n 50).

[210] President's conclusions, informal meeting of EU Environmental Ministers, Amsterdam, 18–20 April 1997, para 3: 'Environmental requirements should be related to the nature and magnitude of environmental pollution and not to the size of the enterprise. Therefore, in principle similar requirements should apply to larger and smaller enterprises.' The conclusions are not published. The reference is taken from M Pallemaerts, *Toxics and Transnational Law; An Inquiry Into the Effectiveness of International and European Community Environmental Law* (Oxford, 2003) 337.

until 2015 before it adopted, as a measure to fight climate change, a directive on medium combustion plants (between 1 and 50 MW thermal input).[211] Transition periods extend until 2030.

Despite its rather ambitious title, Directive 2010/75 essentially laid down framework rules for the national permitting systems with regard to large industrial installations. It provided that, as a rule, emission limit values were to be fixed in the individual permits. These permits must include emission limit values for pollutants which were likely to be emitted from the installation into water, air or land. The emission limit values 'shall be based on the best available techniques'. A technique is available when it is

> developed on a scale which allows implementation in the relevant industrial sector, under economically and technically viable conditions, taking into consideration the costs and advantages, whether or not the techniques are used or produced inside the Member State in question as long as they are reasonably accessible to the operator.[212]

Thus, the best available technique depended also on economic considerations. Furthermore, the conditions in the permit on emissions into the environment may be less strict than according to the best available technique, and may take into consideration the geographical location, the local environmental conditions and the technical characteristics of the installation concerned.[213]

The requirement to use the best available techniques does not exist for the emission of greenhouse gases when the installation participates in the EU emission trading scheme;[214] the reason for this is that it was considered impossible to ask installations to use the best techniques and at the same time give them the possibility to buy rights for emitting more greenhouse gases than the best technique would allow. This provision, though, is not able to eliminate Member States' rights under Article 193 TFEU to fix such emission limit values for greenhouse gases at national (or local) level or even in individual permits, as a directive cannot amend the TFEU.[215] Article 8 is thus mainly a policy concession made.

In order to find the best available techniques, the Commission, under Directive 2010/75, 4-46
has to organise an exchange of information with Member States, the industry sectors concerned and environmental organisations. This exchange is to take place in a forum. The opinion of the forum shall be taken into account for the drafting of a 'best available technique reference document', which shall contain, among others, emission limit values for the sector concerned (Article 13).[216] Such documents – called BREFs (Best Available Technique Reference Document) – are elaborated by a bureau which is part of the Commission's Joint Research Centre and is based in Sevilla. Working groups, composed of experts from industry, administrations, research institutes and NGOs, prepare these documents. At present,

[211] Directive 2015/2193 on medium-sized combustion plants [2015] OJ L313/1. According to the Commission, that directive concerns some 143,000 installations.

[212] Directive 2010/75 (n 50) Art 3(10).

[213] ibid Art 15(4).

[214] ibid Art 8.

[215] This opinion is, obviously, heavily contested.

[216] Art 11(6) of Directive 2010/75 provides that the BREF document shall be published after the adoption of BAT conclusions. This provision contradicts the provisions on access to environmental information, in particular those of the Aarhus Convention, see para 4-04ff above.

BREFs are produced only in English and are published on the Internet. By 2021, 17 BREFs had been produced for different industrial sectors.[217]

On the basis of the BAT (Best Available Technique) reference document, a committee, composed of Member States and the Commission, adopts the so-called 'BAT conclusions',[218] which are legally binding and contain, among others, 'the emission levels associated with the best available techniques' (Article 3.12). The BAT conclusions adopted so far are so general in nature that it is difficult to consider them legally binding – and it appears that they are not enforced anyway.

4-47 The fixing of binding emission limit values in the individual permits had led, under Directive 2008/1, to different emission limit values being fixed for the same type of industrial installation, according to its location, economic situation (costs and benefits) and other circumstances. The possibilities for the competent authorities in the Member States to deviate from the BAT conclusions in this regard and fix less stringent requirements have been made more difficult, but continue to exist. Therefore, the situation did not change much under Directive 2010/75. For example, two cement kilns five miles apart might still have different emission limit values fixed in their permits.[219] Also, the bargaining on less stringent conditions for emission limit values for the location of new installations probably increased, since the installations can threaten to look for another location with more favourable permit conditions. The words of Recital 3 of Directive 2010/75, that the chosen approach 'will also contribute to the achievement of a level playing field in the Union by aligning environmental performance requirements for industrial installations', are somewhat wishful thinking, as long as the different emission limit values are not fixed EU-wide.

Instead of fixing emission limit values for individual installations, Member States may also provide for 'general binding rules', provided they achieve the same results (Articles 6 and 17). This possibility, which was inserted into the text especially at the request of Germany, is of limited assistance; indeed, competition among industrial installations within the Union and its internal market is likely to be effective not only within the individual Member States, but also across national frontiers.

Member States must send to the Commission 'representative data on emissions' and on the emission values which were fixed (Article 72); the frequency and other details of reporting are decided by comitology decisions.[220] The Commission shall, every three years, submit a report on the implementation of the directive which also assesses the need for setting minimum requirements for EU-wide emission limit values and is accompanied, 'where appropriate', with a legislative proposal (Article 73).

[217] Commission, 'Report on the Implementation of Directive 2010/75' COM(2021) 793, s 4; see also Commission, 'Evaluation of Directive 2010/75' SWD(2020) 181; Commission, 'Evaluation of Directive 2010/75' SWD(2022) 111.

[218] See Commission Implementing Decisions on best available techniques: 2019/2010 [2019] OJ L312/55 (waste incinerators); 2021/2326 [2021] OJ L469/1 (large combustion plants); 2022/2110 [2022] OJ L284/69 (ferrous metal processing industries); 2022/2508 [2022] OJ L325/112 (textile industry); 2022/2427 [2022] OJ L318/157 (chemical industry).

[219] For example, the air emission limit values for cement kilns laid down in Decision 2013/63 [2013] OJ L22/25 go from 1 to 2; the air emissions limit values for ferrous metal processing industries (Decision 2022/2110, n 218) go from 1 to 20 according to the pollutant.

[220] See Commission Implementing Decision 2012/119 on rules concerning guidance on the collection of data [2012] OJ L63/1; Commission Implementation Decision 2018/1135 [2018] OJ L205/40.

The main concerns about Directive 2010/75 and its application are that industry very largely writes the BREF documents itself, making sure that the best technique is not too strict. Furthermore, the application of the directive by the national, regional and local permitting authorities is not effectively monitored and controlled. The Commission implementation reports remain rather general and contain a considerable amount of political optimism.[221] In particular, the Commission does not request that data on the permitted and the actually released pollutant emissions be made available to the public without explicit request,[222] which contradicts its general obligation to ensure an 'active and systematic' disclosure of environmentally relevant information.

A Commission study of 2021 identified the following five areas where Directive 2010/75 could be improved from an environmental point of view: (1) the directive was not as effective as it could be; (2) it did not sufficiently support innovative technologies; (3) it did not sufficiently contribute to reducing the use of hazardous chemicals, or to increasing resource efficiency and the circular economy; (4) it was not effective in reducing greenhouse gas emissions; and (5) it did not include some highly polluting sectors, such as cattle farming, aquaculture, extraction of oil and gas, mining, battery production, ship building and dismantling, and, furthermore (outside the thresholds of the directive), textiles, smithies and landfills.[223]

In 2006, the EU set up a European Pollutant Release and Transfer Register,[224] which 4-48
was largely aligned to the installations that were covered by the present Directive 2010/75. It required Member States to report, for some 29,000 individual industrial installations, emissions into the air and water of some 90 pollutants; releases to land and noise emissions were not part of the Register. The emission data are regularly published, though with considerable delay, as Member States only have to report to the Commission every three years. However, it seems that no consequences are drawn from the published data; in particular, environmental organisations, local authorities and individuals have not yet linked the available data on emissions to the (non-)use of the best available techniques by a specific installation – an approach which had been very successful in the USA, where the Environment Protection Agency approaches the most polluting installations in order to look for commonly agreed improvements. The fact that Member States have to report to the Commission only once every three years makes any active involvement by the Commission or the European Environment Agency practically impossible; the digital age should make more frequent reporting very feasible. However, the interest of the European or national public in the Register appears to be limited.

The Commission concluded that Regulation 166/2006 was fit for purpose.[225] This optimism is not shared here.

To what extent Directive 2010/75 and its predecessors, 96/61 and 2008/1, will lead to 4-49
a high level of protection of the environment as a whole, an objective which is announced

[221] Commission, 'Implementation Reports' COM(2017) 727 and COM(2021) 793.

[222] Commission, Implementing Decision 2018/1135 (n 220).

[223] Commission, *Assessment of Options for the Revision of the Industrial Installations Directive* (Luxemburg, 2021) 23ff.

[224] Regulation 166/2006 concerning the establishment of a European Pollutant Release and Transfer Register [2006] OJ L33/1.

[225] Commission, 'Refit Evaluation of Regulation 166/2006' SWD(207)710.

several times in Directive 2010/75,[226] will have to be seen; since 1996, the date of adoption of Directive 96/61, progress has been limited in this regard. It is to be welcomed that all installations covered by Directive 2010/75 must have a permit and that this permit must fix emission limit values; also, the provisions of the directive are significantly stricter than those of Directive 2008/1.

Directive 2010/75 does not provide that there be at least a central (national or Union) register for all permits and the conditions fixed in these permits, although such a register should be easy to set up in the digital age. Individuals or environmental organisations could themselves set up a register of permits and conditions, since the decision on a permit, the reasons for setting the emission limit values and a considerable amount of other information must be made available to the public (Article 24). However, environmental organisations and institutes do not appear to have the organisational capacity for such a private register.

C. Specific Industrial Sectors

4-50 At the launch of EU environmental policy in the 1970s, there was a general consensus on the necessity of regulating environmental emissions from specific industrial installations in order to stop environmental pollution at source.[227] Although the general usefulness of this concept was confirmed in 1987,[228] it did not lead to many concrete results.

Titanium dioxide (TiO2). In 1978, the Council adopted Directive 78/176 on waste from the titanium dioxide industry,[229] which was followed by a Directive on monitoring of TiO_2 installations[230] and another on the uniform reduction of waste discharges from such installations.[231] The origins of these directives go back to discharges of waste in the early 1970s from a Montedison factory at Scarlino (Italy) into Mediterranean waters, which caused concern in Corsica and led to discord between Italy and France.

Directive 78/176's main aim was the progressive reduction of pollution caused by waste from the TiO_2 industry. The manufacture of TiO_2, which is a white pigment used principally in paints, normally results in a larger quantity of waste than of product.

The implementation of the different directives raised problems and was poorly monitored by the Commission. The Commission was incapable of checking the actual discharges, and soon abandoned the attempt to have regular national reports and an EU-wide horizontal report on waste from the TiO_2 industry. The progressive reduction of the discharge of TiO_2 waste into sea and coastal waters was influenced more by debate from international agreements, the North Sea conferences and in particular by the technological possibility of recycling TiO_2 waste, which has progressively developed over the past 20 years.

[226] See, eg Directive 2010/75 (n 50) Arts 1, 3(10), 15(4), and 73.

[227] See First Environmental Action Programme [1973] OJ C112/1, 20, where measures for the paper and pulp industry, the iron and steel industry and the manufacture of TiO_2 were announced and measures for the chemical, leather, food and textile industries were envisaged.

[228] See Fourth Environmental Action Programme [1987] OJ C328/1, no 3.4.

[229] Directive 78/176 on waste from the titanium dioxide industry [1978] OJ L54/19.

[230] Directive 82/883 on procedures for the surveillance and monitoring of environments concerned by waste from the titanium dioxide industry [1982] OJ L378/1.

[231] Directive 92/112 on procedures for harmonising the programmes for the reduction and eventual elimination of pollution caused by waste from the titanium dioxide industry [1992] OJ L409/11. This directive took nine years between its proposal and adoption.

In 2010, the provisions of the three directives were incorporated into Directive 2010/75. TiO_2-producing installations need a permit, but are not obliged to apply the best available technique. Instead, the discharge of solid waste into waters was prohibited, and limit values were fixed for air and water emissions. These emission limit values differ according to the technical process being used (sulphate or chloride process), a clear sign that it is the economic concerns that prevail, not the environmental ones.

Other industrial sectors. In 1975, the Commission submitted a proposal for a Directive on the reduction of water pollution caused by wood pulp mills.[232] The proposal limited itself to proposing emission limit values for some pollutants. Since the UK and some other Member States were opposed to the fixing of EU-wide limit values for emissions into the environment, the proposal was not discussed in the Council and has in the meantime become obsolete. A Commission announcement on a Directive concerning environmental pollution by the paper industry[233] was not followed by concrete action. 4-51

A sector-oriented approach was partly used with the adoption of 'daughter' directives for Directive 76/464,[234] such as discharges by the chlor-alkali electrolysis industry. However, these directives all provided for quality objectives as well as for emission limit values, thus allowing Member States not to follow the sector-oriented approach. In 1991, legislative initiatives for 'daughter' directives under Directive 76/464 were stopped.

In other parts of environmental policy, sectoral approaches have been seen in air pollution, where legislation on large combustion plants was adopted in 1988 and confirmed in 2001.[235] It is noticeable that the 2001 Directive repeated emission reduction targets for 1998 and 2003, which were thus already outdated when the directive entered into effect; the reason for this erroneous approach was the objection, in particular by France, to having new targets fixed for large combustion plants. France preferred to see such plants coming under a system which required 'best techniques' instead of precise emission targets, as was later introduced in Directive 2008/1. In 2010, the provisions on large combustion plants were incorporated into Directive 2010/75. Emission limit values for sulphur dioxide, nitrogen oxides, carbon monoxide and dust were maintained, according to the type of installation and the fuel used. Very extensive transition periods and derogations were also fixed for installations which used indigenous coal or fuel and could not, therefore, respect the emission limit values.

Emissions from waste incinerators were originally grouped in several directives, later combined in a single piece of legislation, as the objective was to limit the emissions into air and water, whether they came from installations for municipal or for hazardous waste.[236] In 2010, these provisions were incorporated into Directive 2010/75. Waste incinerators and co-incineration installations need a permit. Directive 2010/75 maintains the system of emission limit values for such installations. A permit is also required for waste disposal facilities.[237]

[232] Commission, Proposal for a directive [1975] OJ C99/2.

[233] See Written Questions 1491/91 (Van Hemeldonck) [1992] OJ C242/4; Case E-2849/95 *De Coene* [1995] OJ C109/11.

[234] See, eg Directive 82/176 on limit values and quality objectives for mercury discharges by the chlor-alkali electrolysis industry [1982] OJ L81/29.

[235] Directive 88/609 [1988] OJ L336/1; Directive 2001/80 on large combustion plants [2001] OJ L309/1; see also para 8-30ff.

[236] Directive 89/369 [1989] OJ L163/32; Directive 89/429 [1989] OJ L203/50; Directive 94/63 [1994] OJ L365/24; Directive 2000/76 on waste incinerators [2000] OJ L322/91.

[237] Directive 1999/31 on the landfill of waste [1999] OJ L182/1.

4-52 Safety measures for nuclear installations that come under the Euratom Treaty are regulated by Decision 99/819/Euratom, by which the Union adhered to the International Convention on Nuclear Safety, and Directive 2009/71.[238] While Recital 3 of Directive 2009/71 recognised that the provisions of Articles 31 and 32 Euratom Treaty, on which the directive was based, aim at protecting workers, the general public *and the environment* against risks of nuclear installations, there was not a single provision in the directive which concerned the protection of the environment. Generally, the directive was extremely general. It asked Member States to ensure a high level of nuclear safety, recognising that Member States had already done so to a very large extent. No provisions on the participation of the public in the authorisation procedure of nuclear installations were foreseen. No measures on accident prevention – for example, on the model of Directive 96/82 (now Directive 2012/18), providing for internal and external emergency plans – were foreseen. The only concrete measure introduced was the requirement to set up a competent national authority which was responsible for the nuclear safety of installations – a measure which all Member States that had nuclear installations had already put in place. Member States were responsible for ensuring a high level of safety of nuclear installations, but Directive 2009/71 underlined that the primary responsibility in this regard rested with the licence holders. The added value of this directive to nuclear safety is unclear.

Following the nuclear accident in Fukushima (Japan) in 2011, Directive 2009/71 was amended, as a stress test had revealed that necessary safety measures had not been implemented for years.[239] The new directive provided for the effective independence of the regulatory authority and a functional separation of its tasks from those of any other nuclear or energy-related authority (Article 5). The safety of nuclear installations was constantly to be improved, when this was 'reasonably possible' (Article 6). At least every 10 years, the national regulatory frame should undergo an international peer review. The statement in Recital 5 of the directive that decisions on nuclear safety were exclusively a national responsibility appears wrong, in view of the considerable transboundary impact on humans and the environment which a nuclear accident within the EU would have.

Unless there is a new policy approach in the future, the sector-oriented approach can now be considered to be no longer pursued as a central part of EU environmental policy. Rather, the trend is going in the direction of fixing permit requirements, asking for the use of best available techniques and fixing, where unavoidable, emission limit values at Union level. This does not exclude regulating specific activities by way of fine-tuned provisions, in particular to make a specific technology more acceptable to the public. An example of this approach is the safety measures for mining activities being regulated in Directive 2006/21 after several severe environmental accidents had occurred in the EU.[240] Another example is the Directive on carbon capture and storage, which was adopted in the context of the EU climate change policy and had the objective of promoting this technology for coal-fired and other conventional power plants.[241]

[238] Commission Decision 99/819/Euratom [1999] OJ L318/20; the Convention was published on p 21. Directive 2009/71/Euratom establishing a Community framework for the nuclear safety of nuclear installations [2009] OJ L172/18.

[239] Directive 2014/87/Euratom [2014] OJ L317/35.

[240] Directive 2006/21 on the management of waste from the extracting industries [2006] OJ L102/15; see also para 10-58.

[241] Directive 2009/31 on the geological storage of carbon dioxide [2009] OJ L140/114; see para 9-33.

Directive 2013/30 on offshore gas and oil extraction[242] was adopted following a serious accident of the Deep Horizon oil platform in the Gulf of Mexico. The main content of the directive dealt with the prevention of accidents; emissions and discharges were not dealt with in detail. The directive required that the activities it covered be authorised. These activities were to be controlled by independent verifiers. The European Agency for Maritime Safety was to assist the Commission in monitoring the activities. The directive entered into effect in 2015. 4-53

Though the definition of offshore oil and gas activities included the decommissioning of platforms (Article 2(4)), no specific provisions on the decommissioning were included in the directive. After the Brent Spar saga of 1995–98 – where Shell had to abandon its plans to sink the Brent Spar platform in the North Sea due to heavy public protests, and had instead to decommission it on land – there was more or less a consensus that all offshore structures should, at the end of their useful life, be decommissioned on land; however, no legal provisions for this consensus were laid down for all Union waters. In 1998, the OSPAR Convention on the protection of the North-East Atlantic adopted a decision to prohibit the disposal of disused offshore installations in water, but provided for possibilities of derogation.[243] In 2019, the UK announced its intention to use the derogation possibilities and leave the footings of several oil platforms in the sea. The Union objected to that intention, as did several EU Member States. Discussions went on; however, since Brexit, the final decision is to be taken by the UK alone, as Decision 98/3 does not provide for an absolute interdiction.

No legislative measures have yet been taken on gas or oil pipelines.

Asbestos. Asbestos has been the subject of EU legislation since the early 1980s, when the use of a large number of asbestos fibres which were classified as carcinogens was restricted. This legislation is based on the present Article 114 TFEU. Though several Member States decided on a total ban of asbestos fibres, the Commission did not take action against them. Instead, it prepared for a larger ban at EU level, which finally was adopted in 1999.[244] As regards asbestos which is already on the market and in the environment, Directive 87/217 tried to establish integrated provisions.[245] Member States must use the best available technology not entailing excessive costs and take general measures to reduce asbestos emissions into the air – where a general emission limit value of 0.1 mg/m^3 is fixed – and the water; here, a complete recycling of waste water is required, unless this is 'economically not practicable', which makes this provision unenforceable. Measures shall also be taken during the demolition of asbestos-containing buildings and the transport of the waste, as well as in its disposal. Because of the directive's loose drafting and the absence of constant monitoring of its application in and by Member States, its real impact is limited. In 2022, the Commission announced new legislation for an asbestos-free Union, concentrating on asbestos at work, asbestos present in buildings and asbestos waste.[246] 4-54

[242] Directive 2013/30 on the safety of offshore oil and gas operations [2013] OJ L178/66. See also Commission, 'Report on the Assessment of Implementation of Directive 2013/30' COM(2021) 732; see in particular SWD(2021) 269.

[243] OSPAR, Decision 98/3: '2. The dumping, and the leaaving wholly or partly in place, of disused offshore installations within the maritime area, is prohibitied. 3.By way of derogation from para 2, if the competent authority of the relevant Contracting Party is satisfied that … an alternative disposal. is preferable to reuse or recycling or final disposal on land, it may issue a permit.'

[244] Directive 1999/77 on asbestos [1999] OJ L207/18.

[245] Directive 87/217 on the prevention and reduction of environmental pollution by asbestos [1987] OJ L85/40.

[246] Commission, COM(2022) 488.

D. Environmental Auditing

4-55 In 1993, after a rather short discussion, the Council adopted a regulation which established a voluntary system of eco-auditing for industrial installations.[247] In 2001 and 2009, the system was revised and opened up to any form of organisation – administrations, universities, funds, etc – which wishes to improve its environmental performance (the Eco-Management and Audit Scheme, EMAS).[248] An organisation that intends to participate in the scheme for its sites – whether one site at a time or all together – must establish an environmental policy for that site which must respect all existing environmental provisions and provide for continuous improvement of the environmental performance. The site must be submitted to an environmental review, which concerns such environmental conditions as water and energy use and waste treatment. The organisation then has to develop an environmental programme for all its activities on the site in order to reach its policy objectives and must ensure that measures necessary to realise the programme are taken at management level. The site shall be audited, either by auditors belonging to the organisation or by external auditors.

Finally, the organisation has to report (make an environmental statement) on its activity and its policy programme, strategy and management system. This report is validated by an independent, accredited verifier and published; following that, the site is listed in a register. The organisation is allowed to declare its participation in the EMAS scheme in its correspondence and papers – though not on products, or in product advertising and packaging.

Although participation in the scheme is voluntary, an organisation which decides to join in must comply with all the requirements of EMAS. The EMAS scheme is at present operational in all Member States. As at the end of 2022, some 4000 organisations with more than 12,500 sites – mostly of industrial installations, as, until 2001, the system was open only to industrial installations – were registered.

About 40 per cent of all organisations are small and medium-sized companies, though the costs of participation are sometimes significant. Ideas to have less stringent requirements for small companies have not been pursued. For the participating organisation, there are clear advantages in participation, in particular better motivation of personnel, improved competitiveness and, generally, better environmental performance. Furthermore, credit institutes and insurance companies have started to make their intervention dependent on the existence of an auditing scheme.[249] Some governments of Member States have started to adapt their control system of companies to whether or not they take part in EMAS, or to relieve them from reporting or other obligations.[250]

4-56 At international level, EMAS is competing with ISO 14001, an environmental management standard, developed since 1996 by the International Organization for Standardization (ISO). This voluntary standard differs from EMAS in particular in that it applies worldwide and it also refers to products, not only to sites. Furthermore, there is no necessity for an

[247] Regulation 1836/93 allowing voluntary participation by companies in the industrial sector in a Community eco-management and audit system [1993] OJ L168/1.

[248] Regulation 761/2001 [2001] OJ L114/1; Regulation 1221/2009 on the voluntary participation by organisations in a Community eco-management and audit scheme [2009] OJ L342/1.

[249] For an evaluation of EMAS, see Commission, COM(2017) 355.

[250] On incentives for EMAS-registered organisations, see also Commission, SEC(2010) 59.

organisation to make an initial examination of its environmental impact and to comply with all environmental legislation, a requirement that exists under EMAS. EMAS also requests the registration of companies or organisations by public authorities, provides for a strong involvement of the workers, contains stricter requirements on the measurement and evaluation of the environmental performance, includes the examination of direct and indirect impacts on the environment, asks for continuous improvement of such performance, and allows multi-annual comparability within and between organisations. Finally, the publication of an environmental statement is not necessary under the ISO standard; the organisation need not respect transparency as regards its environmental performance.[251]

The Commission recognised some elements of ISO 14001 to be equivalent to EMAS.[252] Thus, an organisation may use ISO 14001 as a first step towards adherence to EMAS and thereby avoid duplication of work.

Generally, EMAS is seen as an effective tool where an organisation tries to improve its environmental performance; its impact on the competitiveness of companies appears limited. Companies which adhere to the system sometimes feel, though, that their efforts are not sufficiently rewarded by the EMAS system, for instance by some sort of rebate during the permitting or operating process. As the ISO system is less ambitious, less demanding, less expensive and less exposing, but almost as capable as EMAS to be used for image purposes, the ISO system is favoured by economic operators.

E. Accident Prevention

In 1976, a serious industrial accident occurred in Seveso (Italy), where dioxin was emitted into the air; some 600 people had to be evacuated from their homes and about 2000 were treated for dioxin poisoning. Subsequently, the Union drew up and adopted, in 1982, a Directive on accident prevention from industrial installations.[253] Following two major accidents, in Bhopal (India – 1984), where more than 2500 people were killed, and Basel (Switzerland – 1986), where a massive pollution of the Rhine occurred, this directive was amended twice, in 1987 and 1988.[254] A complete revision then took place in the early 1990s; this led to the replacement of Directive 82/501 by Directive 96/82.[255] In 2012, a new Directive on accident prevention (Seveso III) was adopted.[256] 4-57

The structure and concept of Directive 82/501 were largely maintained. Directive 2012/18 aimed at preventing major industrial accidents which involve dangerous chemicals, and at limiting the consequences of such accidents. It concerns installations where dangerous chemicals are present in quantities that are laid down in an annex. The operator of the installation has to produce a safety report which gives details of the establishment, the dangerous chemicals present, major risks for accidents and the management systems which are available. This last requirement was justified by the fact that 'analysis of the major

[251] On the comparison between EMAS and ISO 14001, see Commission, SWD(2017) 253, 108.
[252] Commission Decision 97/265 [1997] OJ L104/37.
[253] Directive 82/501 on the major accident hazards of certain industrial activities [1982] OJ L230/1.
[254] Directive 87/216 [1987] OJ L85/36; Directive 88/610 [1988] OJ L336/14.
[255] Directive 96/82 [1997] OJ L10/13.
[256] Directive 2012/18 [2012] OJ L197/1.

accidents reported in the EU indicates that the majority of them are the result of managerial and/or organisational shortcomings'.

4-58 Establishments must furthermore have an internal emergency plan and must inform the public authorities in such a way that the public authorities are able to draw up an external emergency plan. Persons inside and outside the installation who are likely to be affected by an accident must be informed of the safety measures and of the requisite behaviour in the event of an accident. After an accident, the operator has to provide comprehensive information to the authorities on the accident and on the measures taken to prevent a recurrence. Directive 2012/18 also provided for detailed rules on the inspection of the establishments by competent authorities, which is a rather innovative provision in environmental law. Also, it introduced national and EU reporting provisions, which did not exist before.

A Commission report of 2021 reported 518 major accidents in the Union between 2000 and 2018 (28 EU Member States), about 25 accidents per year.[257]

4-59 Directive 2012/18, which affected about 11,000 installations (27 EU Member States), does not cover pipelines, of which there is an estimated 150,000 km for gas transmission, 35,000 km for oil and 10,000 km for chemicals. It also does not cover: transport activities; military establishments; hazards created by ionising radiation;[258] mines; quarries; boreholes; and landfills. Since the directive was based on Article 192 TFEU, Member States are, of course, free to extend its application to such installations, but have not made use of that possibility. Following spectacular accidents linked to mining activities in Aznalcollar (Spain – 1988) and Baia Mare (Romania – 2000), the directive was amended in order to include risks arising from storage and processing activities in mining in its scope of application.[259]

Overall, the system which was set up by Directive 82/501 and was improved and fine-tuned by Directive 2012/18 seems to work well, though it is obviously not possible to assess the exact impact of the prevention measures. The EU accident prevention scheme set up by the directives was taken over by a number of third countries and was at the origin of the International Convention of Transboundary Effects of Industrial Accidents of 1992 to which the Union and its Member States adhered.[260]

The prevention of accidents was also the main objective of Directive 2013/30 on offshore gas and oil activities, which was adopted after the Deep Horizon accident of 2010 in the Gulf of Mexico.[261] In contrast, a Commission announcement of an accident prevention initiative for nuclear installations, made shortly after the nuclear accident in Chernobyl,[262] was not followed by action, nor was any action taken after the Fukushima accident of 2011.

VI. Environmental Liability

4-60 The efforts of the Union to tackle issues on environmental liability took about 30 years to mature. As regards damage caused by waste, the Commission submitted proposals in

[257] Commission, COM(2021) 599.
[258] This clause means that nuclear installations which process dangerous chemicals are covered by the directive.
[259] Directive 2003/105 [2003] OJ L345/97.
[260] Decision 98/685 [1998] OJ L326/1.
[261] Directive 2013/30 on safety of offshore oil and gas operations [2013] OJ L178/66.
[262] Fourth Environmental Action Programme (n 228) paras 4.3.8 and 4.6.4.

1976, 1983 and 1989,[263] but none of these proposals were adopted. Whether damage caused by waste comes under Directive 85/374 on product liability[264] is doubtful. In my opinion, this should be the case, as waste material is deliberately 'produced' and put into circulation. Regulation 2027/97 concerned the liability of air companies in cases of accidents, but only dealt with personal injury and economic loss, not with environmental damage.[265]

Subsequent to the Sandoz accident in Basel (Switzerland) in 1986, the Council asked the Commission to consider whether it was appropriate to introduce an EU system on environmental liability. In pursuance thereof, the Commission submitted, in 1993, a Green Paper on environmental liability.[266] The European Parliament organised a hearing on the Green Paper and then asked, under the present Article 225 TFEU, for a proposal for a directive to be drawn up.[267] In 2000, the Commission published a White Paper on the question, with options for future legislation.[268] In 2002, the Commission made a proposal for a directive on 'environmental liability with regard to the prevention and remedying environmental damage', which the Council and Parliament adopted in 2004, 10 days before the accession of 10 new Member States to the Union. The directive applied to biodiversity, water and land (soil) damage, but not to air damage. It became effective on 30 April 2007, and only concerned damage which was caused after that date.[269]

Directive 2004/35 constituted a relatively drastic departure from the classical concept of environmental liability and from the Commission's White Paper. Indeed, while liability normally parts from the idea that a person who suffers bodily injury or economic damage will try to get compensation from the wrongdoer by way of a civil law action, the directive does not deal with this civil law damage, but leaves legislation on this 'traditional damage' (Recital 11) to Member States' law: 'This directive does not apply to cases of personal injury, to damage to private property or to any economic loss and does not affect any right regarding these types of damages.'[270] 4-61

The directive only dealt with environmental damage.[271] Where such damage occurs, it is the public authorities which shall ensure the restoration of the environment. The Commission's proposal had placed the task of restoration on the public authorities, starting from the concept that the environment is a public, not private, interest issue; and as the public authorities were mandated to protect, preserve and improve the quality of the environment, the primary task of restoring the impaired environment should be incumbent on them.[272] However, the Council did not like this suggestion and amended it.

[263] Commission [1976] OJ C194/2; [1983] OJ C186/3; [1989] OJ C251/3, amended [1991] OJ C192/6.

[264] Directive 85/374 on the approximation of laws, regulations and administrative provisions of the Member States concerning liability for defective products [1985] OJ L210/29; amended by Directive 1999/34 [1999] OJ L141/20.

[265] Regulation 2027/97 on liability of air companies in case of accidents [1997] OJ L285/1.

[266] Commission, Greenbook on remedying environmental damage [1993] OJ C149/12.

[267] European Parliament [1994] OJ C149/6.

[268] Commission, 'White Paper on Environmental Liability' COM(2000) 66.

[269] Directive 2004/35 on environmental liability with regard to the prevention and remedying of environmental damage [2004] OJ L143/56.

[270] Directive 2004/35, Recital 14; see also Art 3(3).

[271] Note that in continental Europe, 'damage' normally supposes that there is a damaged person; it is thus considered to be a civil law notion.

[272] Directive 2004/35 (n 270) Art 2(1): '"environmental damage" means: (a) damage to protected species which is any damage that has significant adverse effects on reaching or maintaining the favourable conservation status of

The final text invoked the polluter-pays principle on several occasions and placed the obligation of restoration on the polluter (Article 8). Where the public authorities voluntarily restored the environment without having an obligation to do so, they may ask for recompense of the money which they extended from the polluter; however, where the polluter does not pay because it has gone out of business, is insolvent or cannot be identified, there is no obligation on the public authorities to compensate, contrary to the Commission's proposal. This means that in such cases it is likely that the environment is not restored.

4-62 Directive 2004/35's concept needed a number of qualifications, as environmental impairment is ubiquitous. The following limitations to the obligation of restoration were therefore introduced:

1. Not every environmental impairment is to be restored, but only damage expressly mentioned in the directive;[273] air pollution is excluded, as air contamination sooner or later leads to depositions on the ground – acidification of the soil, damage to fauna and flora, etc (Recital 4). Also, the most serious environmental accidents of the past – nuclear accidents and marine pollution by hydrocarbons from tanker accidents – were excluded from the directive, with the argument that international conventions covered these aspects. However, the international conventions do not provide for restoration of the impaired environment; also, the sums which are available under their systems are not sufficient. Damage caused by genetically modified products such as seeds, is included, because the concept starts from the impaired environment, and the deliberate release of GMOs is expressly mentioned as one of the sources of pollution (annex III, no 11).
2. Diffuse pollution, that is, pollution caused by a multiplicity of polluting sources, is excluded. Indeed, this diffuse pollution is everywhere and it was considered that an inclusion of such pollution would overcharge the public authorities' budgets, all the more as recourse against a specific polluter would not be possible.
3. The implementing legislation of Member States shall decide whether polluters who comply with the conditions laid down in a permit shall be liable to compensate public authorities for the restoration of the environment or not.[274] Such a clause would practically introduce polluters' liability for negligence, as exceeding the conditions of a permit is normally due to a deliberate or negligent action.

such habitats or species … (b) water damage, which is any damage that significantly adversely affects the ecological, chemical and/or quantitative status and/or ecological potential, as defined in Directive 2000/60/EC … (c) land damage which is any land contamination that creates a significant risk to human health being adversely affected as a result of the direct or indirect introduction, in, on or under land, of substances, preparations, organisms or micro-organisms. "Damage" means a measurable adverse change in the natural resource or measurable impairment of a natural resource service which may occur directly or indirectly.'

[273] ibid Art 4(5): 'This directive shall only apply to environmental damage or to an imminent threat of such damage caused by pollution of a diffuse character, where it is possible to establish a causal link between the damage and the activities of individual operators.'

[274] ibid Art 8(4.a): 'The Member States may allow the operator not to bear the cost of remedial actions taken pursuant to this directive where he demonstrates that he was not at fault or negligent and that the environmental damage was caused by: (a) an emission or event expressly authorised by, and fully in accordance with the conditions of, an authorisation conferred by or given under applicable national laws.'

4. Member States shall also decide whether they allow the defence for development risks which intend to limit economic operators' liability in areas of new technologies, in particular for damage caused by biotechnology products (state-of-the-art defence).[275]
5. Finally, it is up to Member States to decide whether or not they provide for a compulsory financial security system in the cases covered by the directive (Article 14).

At the time, Member States were not able to agree on a solution for or against such compulsory insurance. Since then, however, Bulgaria, Portugal, Spain, Greece, Hungary, Slovakia, Czechia and Romania have all introduced such a mandatory system.

Leaving aside the differences of opinion among Member States and the heavy opposition 4-63
of economic operators to any liability system, the concept of compensating for environmental damage seems too far removed from environmental needs.[276] In short, the environment is sick, rather than suffering from specific accidents, pollutions or catastrophes. The liability concept which stems from compensating for physical injury was extended to economic loss and later to damages for pain and suffering, but adapts only with difficulty to the progressive deterioration or legalised contamination of the environment and the disappearance of species.

This is the reason why, so far, national environmental liability legislation has had only limited success. Directive 2004/35's approach to setting up a system which places the restoration of environmental damage in the centre is a step in the right direction. The future will show whether this direction will be pursued; as neither the environment nor future generations have a lobby or a voice, realism rather than optimism with regard to the effective benefit to the environment – the ultimate objective of environmental legislation – is appropriate.

The directive enumerated in annex III those operational activities of which the operator may be held strictly liable if they cause environmental damage. This annex lists a number of (mainly dangerous) activities which are regulated by Union acts. As Union legislation covers in particular large installations, many small or medium-sized companies do not come under the scope of application of Directive 2004/35 unless they act negligently, as the directive includes liability for negligent actions (Article 3(1.b)).

The directive does not cover oil pollution damage or damage caused by the transport of dangerous substances by sea or inland waterways, which are legislation of the Member State concerned (Article 4(2) and annex IV), nor does it cover nuclear damage (Article 4(4) and annex V).

The overall impression of the directive is that it has a rather limited field of application.[277] It aims more at the restoration of the environment after an industrial accident – with the exception of the most important cases, ie oil transport and nuclear accidents – than from it just being sick (ie suffering from normal wear and tear).

[275] ibid Art 8(4.b): 'The Member States may allow the operator not to bear the cost of remedial actions … where he proves … that the damage was caused by: (b) an emission or activity or any manner of using a product in the course of an activity which the operator demonstrates was not considered likely to cause environmental damage according to the state of scientific and technical knowledge at the time when the emission was released or the activity took place.'

[276] For another way of proceeding, see Commission, 'Proposal for a Regulation on Nature Restoration' COM(2022) 304.

[277] See also CJEU Joined Cases C-379/08 and C-380/089 *ERG* ECLI:EU:C:2010:127; Case C-534/13 *Fipa Group* ECLI:EU:C:2015:140. In both cases, the directive was held to be inapplicable.

Between 2007 and 2021, 1225 cases of the directive's application were notified to the Commission (EU-26); five Member States (Austria, Croatia, Czechia, Malta, the Netherlands) signalled that no case which came under the directive had occurred, while Poland (695 cases) and Hungary reported the bulk of cases. Waste management operations and the handling of dangerous chemicals were the most frequently affected sectors. The Commission gave as reasons for the great disparities of application in Member States ('patchwork') the framework character of the directive, its use of vague terms such as 'significant damage'[278] or 'favourable conservation status', the existence of optional defences, the ambiguity of key concepts and definitions, and the existence of pre-directive national liability legislation which Member States preferred to continue to apply.[279] Overall, these and other aspects, such as the absence of regulating the burden of proof, which works in favour of the polluter, ensures the directive neither leads to some sort of unified or harmonised system in the Union nor reaches the objective of a high level of environmental protection.

Under Article 12 of the directive, natural or legal persons may request public authorities to undertake restoration activities and may, under certain conditions, apply to a court for a decision. Between 2007 and 2013, 43 such requests were introduced – including 20 in Germany, nine in Ireland, four in Spain[280] – which, for 26 Union countries (minus Croatia and the UK), is a demonstration that the directive's mechanism is not a success.

The European Parliament adopted a resolution recommending numerous improvements of the directive with the aim, among others, of turning it into a regulation.[281] The Commission itself evaluated the directive[282] and commissioned a detailed study on it by a private law firm,[283] but had taken no steps to revise it by June 2023.

4-64 There have been a number of attempts at international level to introduce liability for environmental damage, which, however, essentially concern traditional damage (physical damage and economic loss). These efforts concern in particular:

- A protocol under the Basel Convention on the shipment of hazardous waste.[284] This protocol was elaborated in 1999 and covers personal injury and economic loss caused by hazardous waste. The Union adhered to the Basel Convention, but has not yet signed the protocol. No Member State has ratified the protocol, which has not yet entered into force.
- A protocol, signed in 2003 in Kiev under two international conventions, which deals with liability that is caused by industrial accidents on international watercourses.[285] The protocol covers traditional damage and, in a supplement, the restoration of the impaired environment. The Union did not sign the protocol as

[278] In 2022, the Commission published Guidelines providing a common understanding of the term 'significant damage' [2022] OJ C118/1, a rather unusual way of proceeding with definitions.

[279] Commission, 'Evaluation of Directive 2004/35' SWD(2016) 121, 34–38. See also Commission, 'Implementation Reports' COM(2010) 581 and COM(2016) 204.

[280] Commission, SWD(2016) 121 (n 279) 34.

[281] European Parliament, Resolution of 20 May 2021 on the liability of companies for environmental damage, TA-2021-0259.

[282] Commission, SWD(2016) 121 (n 279).

[283] V Fogleman, 'Facilitating Enforcement of the ELD by Competent Authorities' (Brussels, 2022).

[284] Basel Protocol on liability and compensation 1999.

[285] Protocol on liability and compensation for damage caused by the transboundary effects of industrial accidents on transboundary waters.

it is not clear how the dividing line between this protocol and Directive 2004/35 on environmental liability has to be drawn.

- A protocol on damage caused by GMOs, adopted in 2010 under the Cartagena Protocol on Biological Safety. The protocol applies to damage 'resulting from living [genetically] modified organisms which find their origin in a transboundary movement'. It requests a link of causation between the damage and the wrongful act, but otherwise provides for strict liability. The EU signed up to the protocol,[286] but considered that no measures were necessary to transpose it into Union law.

VII. Taxes and Charges

Environmental taxes are taxes that are based on a physical unit of something that has a proven, specific negative impact on the environment.[287] Most environmental taxes in the Member States – there are no Union environmental taxes – are on energy, followed by transport, pollution and resources. 4-65

The First Environmental Action Programme of 1973 pleaded in favour of economic instruments in the shaping of environmental policy.[288] Subsequent programmes repeated the usefulness of developing economic instruments, and the Fourth Environmental Action Programme was the first to mention that, besides legal 'command and control' provision taxes, charges and tradable pollution permits could also be an appropriate instrument for improving or preserving the quality of the environment from GMOs.[289] In order to combat climate change, the Commission submitted a proposal in 1991 for the EC-wide introduction of a combined CO_2 energy tax.[290] The proposal was based on Articles 93 and 175(2) EC Treaty (now Articles 113 and 192(2) TFEU), which both require unanimous decisions in the Council. This unanimity could not be reached, since a number of Member States, in particular the UK, opposed for reasons of principle the adoption of provisions on taxes and charges at EU level. The Commission therefore amended its proposal so that Member States remained free to decide whether they wanted to introduce a CO_2 energy tax; but where they so decided, they had to comply with the conditions fixed in the proposal.[291] This proposal, which again required unanimous acceptance in the Council, was not adopted either. It is now outdated, though reflections on the introduction of fiscal measures at EU level continue in the context of discussions on climate change.

[286] Decision 2013/86 on the conclusion of the Nagoya–Kuala Lumpur Supplementary Protocol on Liability and Redress to the Cartagena Protocol on Biosafety [2013] OJ L46/1.

[287] Regulation 691/2011 on European environmental economic accounts [2011] OJ L192/1, Art 2.

[288] First Environmental Action Programme (n 227) 31: 'careful analysis should be made of the economic instruments which can be used in the context of an environmental policy, their various functions, the advantages and drawbacks of using them, their relative effectiveness with regard to the objectives in view and their compatibility with the rules of cost allocation'.

[289] Fourth Environmental Action Programme (n 228) no 2.5.1. See also the very vague formulation in the Eighth Environmental Action Programme (n 150) Art 3(v), according to which the Union should make 'the best use of environmental taxation'.

[290] [1992] OJ C196/1.

[291] Commission, COM(95) 172.

In view of the obvious difficulties linked with this proposal, the Commission has not made any other proposals for the introduction of an eco-tax. Scattered in directives or regulations are references that taxes or charges will be fixed at EU level;[292] however, those provisions have not introduced such taxes, nor have they had any other legal effect or restricted the possibility of Member States deciding to introduce their own eco-taxes or charges. A Commission communication on 'Environmental Taxes and Charges in the Single Market' also had no visible impact.[293]

In 2023, the Union adopted a regulation on a 'carbon border adjustment' for certain goods.[294] It intended to avoid the issue that the efforts of the Union to reduce its greenhouse gas emissions were offset by increasing emissions outside the Union through a relocation of production ('carbon leakage') or through increased imports of more carbon-intensive products. The regulation was based on Article 192(1) TFEU (majority decision). It concerned cement, electricity, fertilisers, iron and steel, aluminium and hydrogen.

4-66 Taxes and charges play a considerable role in the environmental policy of Member States. Since they aim to influence, via pricing, the economic behaviour of economic operators, local or regional authorities and private persons, as well as their competitiveness and market position, the Union cannot remain unconcerned about developments at national level. Therefore, EU measures with regard to national eco-taxes are aimed at limiting their use, in order to prevent them from influencing the circulation of goods.

The most obvious example of attempts to limit national tax initiatives are the provisions in the automobile sector. When the catalytic converter for cars was introduced, the Netherlands and Germany in particular considered encouraging the introduction of cars with catalytic converters by means of tax incentives. The objection of other Member States that were afraid of a competitive disadvantage finally led to a provision which has since become standard for car emission directives:[295]

> Member States may make provision for tax incentives for the vehicles covered in this directive. Such incentives shall meet the provisions of the Treaty as well as the following conditions:
>
> - they shall apply to all domestic car production and to vehicles imported for marketing in a Member State and fitted with the equipment allowing the European standards to be met in 1992 to be satisfied ahead of time; they shall cease upon the date set in Article 2(3) for the compulsory entry into force of the emission values for new vehicles;
> - they shall be of value, for each type of vehicle, substantially lower than the actual cost of the equipment fitted to meet the values set and of its fitting on the vehicle.

In 2005, the Commission made a proposal for a directive to restructure car taxes on the basis of the annual circulation of the car, in order to make passenger car taxes more CO_2-efficient.[296] This proposal, which was based on the present Article 113 TFEU and therefore

[292] See, eg Directive 94/62 on packaging and packaging waste [1994] OJ L365/10, Art 15: 'Acting on the basis of the relevant provisions of the Treaty, the Council adopts economic instruments to promote the implementation of the objectives set by this directive. In the absence of such measures, the Member States may, in accordance with the principles governing Community environmental policy, inter alia, the polluter-pays principle, and the obligations arising out of the Treaty, adopt measures to implement those objectives.'

[293] Commission, COM(1997) 9.

[294] Regulation 2023/956 establishing a carbon border adjustment mechanism [2023] OJ L130/52.

[295] Text from Directive 89/458 [1989] OJ L226/1, Art 3.

[296] Commission, COM(2005) 261.

required unanimity for its adoption, would abolish the registration tax for cars and instead increase the circulation taxes; these would take into account the CO_2 emissions from cars. As the Council had not adopted this proposal by the end of 2014, the Commission withdrew it in 2015.

Another example for the interplay between national and EU rules is Directive 2003/96, which replaced Directive 92/81.[297] This directive, based on Article 113 TFEU, introduced a minimum rate of taxation on electricity and energy products. The minimum rates were differentiated according to the use of the products. As the directive required unanimity, it contained a long list of possibilities for Member States to apply reduced rates for specific uses; and Member States may exempt electricity produced from alternative energies altogether. The directive prolonged the possibility for 11 of the then 15 Member States – the exceptions being Sweden Denmark, Greece and the Netherlands – to apply reduced tax rates for the use of waste oils in production installations such as cement kilns or steel or power plants, though such a practice openly contradicted the requirements of Directive 75/439,[298] which imposed a priority for the regeneration (recycling) of waste oils. However, in the past, the Commission had not taken action against the national fiscal practices. In order to ensure consistency of EU law, Directive 75/439 was repealed altogether – to the advantage of economic operators, but to the detriment of the environment.[299] 4-67

Following the European Green Deal of 2019, the Commission proposed, in 2021, a new Directive on the taxation of energy products and electricity,[300] based on Articles 113 and 192(2) TFEU. Its three objectives were to better align the energy tax provisions to the Union objectives of climate change and climate neutrality by 2050, to give better incentives, in the internal market, to invest in clean, non-fossil energies and to continue to ensure income for the budgets of Member States. The proposal is presently being discussed by the other Union institutions.

A typical example of the Union's approach to taxes and charges is to be found in the Water Framework Directive.[301] It provides in Article 9 that 'Member States shall take account of the principle of recovery of the costs of water services, including environmental and resource costs'. However, it then continues: 'Member States in so doing have regard to the social, environmental and economic effects of the recovery as well as the geographic and climatic conditions of the region or regions affected.' This means in clear terms that Member States should provide for rules according to which the user of water shall pay for that use. However, the added phrase allows every Member State to maintain its own system of water charges, with the argument that social, environmental and economic considerations, as well the geographical situation of the affected regions, so require.[302] 4-68

[297] Directive 2003/96 restructuring the Community framework for the taxation of energy products and electricity [2003] OJ L283/51, replacing Directive 92/81 on the harmonisation of the structures of excise duties on mineral oils [1992] OJ L316/12.

[298] Directive 75/439 on used oils [1975] OJ L194/31; amended by Directive 87/101 [1987] OJ L42/43.

[299] Directive 2008/98 on waste [2008] OJ L312/3.

[300] Commission, 'Proposal for a Directive Restructuring the Union Framework of Energy Products and Electricity' COM(2021) 563.

[301] Directive 2000/60 establishing a framework for Community action in the field of water policy [2000] OJ L327/1.

[302] Moreover, in Case C-525/12 *Commission v Germany* ECLI:EU:C:2014:2202, the CJEU clarified that Art 9 did not require a Member State to take all services into consideration.

5

Biodiversity

5-01 Nature conservation measures within the Union were, until about the mid-1980s, influenced by the fact that the majority of Member States were of the opinion that nature protection came in their exclusive competence. Since environmental legal acts had to be taken unanimously prior to 1987, this attitude considerably influenced the number and the content of the measures adopted; indeed, Member States favoured the negotiation and conclusion of international conventions. Another consequence was that all nature conservation measures that the Council was ready to adopt were based on Article 308 of the Treaty establishing the European Community (now Article 352 of the Treaty on the Functioning of the Union (TFEU)).

When the present Articles 191–93 TFEU were introduced into the Treaty in 1987 to give an explicit environmental competence to the Union which included nature conservation, matters changed only gradually. The main reasons for this were: that Member States were very keen to keep their responsibility in land use planning matters, which they saw as being at least partly threatened by EU nature conservation measures; that transfrontier management of wildlife and nature protection was hardly practised; and that national and EU enforcement mechanisms for nature conservation measures were structurally too weak to properly enforce the different provisions, let alone initiate new measures.

The Union has accepted since 2019 that biodiversity loss, together with climate change and pollution, constitute the biggest environmentally challenges both Union-wide and globally. The most recent assessment of the biodiversity in the EU is the 2020 Report from the European Environment Agency (EEA), *State of Nature in the EU*.[1] This report is based on Member States' information concerning the implementation of Directive 2009/147 on birds[2] and Directive 92/43 on habitats, fauna and flora species,[3] but not on other nature-related Union acts. There is no general Union legislation on biodiversity.

I. General Measures

A. International Conventions

5-02 The Union signed up to a number of international agreements which aim, as a general objective, at the protection of nature or of parts of it. For the majority of these agreements,

[1] European Environment Agency, *State of Nature in the EU: Results From Reporting Under the Nature Directives 2013–2018* (Copenhagen, 2020) Report 10/2020.

[2] Directive 2009/147 on the conservation of wild birds [2010] OJ L20/7. This directive replaced Directive 79/409 [1979] OJ L103/1.

[3] Directive 92/43 on the conservation of natural habitats and of wild fauna and flora [1992] OJ L206/7.

however, the Union did not make secondary laws to implement them. In law, an international agreement to which the Union adheres becomes part of Union law (Article 216(2) TFEU) – at least, where the area covered by the agreement comes into EU competence – and is thus also binding for those Member States which have not ratified the agreement.[4] As regards the hierarchy, the provisions of the agreement rank between primary and secondary EU law, which means that they prevail on Union regulations and directives. The application and enforcement of the provisions of the agreement are shared between the Union and its Member States, according to their internal repartitioning of competence.

In practice, no application or enforcement of international environmental agreements to which the Union adheres takes place at the EU level unless it adopts a regulation or directive to implement its provisions; in particular, the Commission does not 'ensure' that the legal provisions of the international measure are applied, as Article 17 of the Treaty on European Union (TEU) requires. Rather, the Commission leaves it to Member States to apply the provisions of the agreement. The EU institutions apply a provision of an international environmental agreement only in those cases where the provision is sufficiently precise and concrete (direct effect).[5] Individual persons or environmental organisations may likewise rely on the provision of an international environmental agreement only when the provision is sufficiently precise and unconditional; the Court is quite restrictive in this regard.[6] And in cases initiated by individuals, the Court does not look at the *effet utile* of a provision of an agreement.

As a consequence, the decision to adhere to an international environmental agreement without adopting secondary Union law to implement it does not bring any added value to the protection of the environment.

The following environmental agreements, to which the Union adhered, belong to this group of conventions on nature conservation:

- Bonn Convention of 23 June 1979 on the conservation of migratory species of wild animals;[7]
- Canberra Convention of 20 May 1980 on the conservation of Antarctic marine living resources;[8]
- Salzburg Convention of 7 November 1991 on the protection of the Alps;[9]
- Rio de Janeiro Convention of 5 June 1992 on biological diversity;[10] and
- Paris Convention of 17 June 1994 on combating desertification.[11]

Biodiversity Convention. After adhering to the Convention on Biological Diversity, the 5-03
Union adopted a communication on an EU strategy for biological diversity.[12] No specific

[4] See CJEU Case C-213/03 *Pêcheurs de l'Etang de Berre* ECLI:EU:C:2004:464; Case C-239/03 *Commission v France* ECLI:EU:C:2004:598.

[5] See CJEU Joined Cases C-401/12P to C-403/12P *Council v Milieudefensie and others* ECLI:EU:C:2015:4.

[6] See ibid; CJEU Case C-240/09 *Lesoochranárske zoskupenie* ECLI:EU:C:2011:125.

[7] Decision 82/461 [1982] OJ L210/10.

[8] Decision 81/691 [1981] OJ L252/26.

[9] Decision 96/191 [1996] OJ L61/31.

[10] Decision 93/626 [1993] OJ L309/1.

[11] Decision 98/216 [1998] OJ L83/1.

[12] Commission, COM(98) 42.

legislative measures were announced; instead, the objectives of the strategy were to be reached within the context of the different ongoing EU activities.[13] In 2006, the Commission published a communication identifying a number of possible measures, but limiting itself largely to suggest measures at national level.[14] When it turned out, in 2010, that the loss of biodiversity had not stopped, the Commission adopted a new communication, on the basis of which the Council concluded that by 2050 EU biodiversity and the ecosystem services the EU provides should be protected and that the biodiversity loss should be halted by 2020.[15] Again, no specific measures were suggested.

The Commission recognised that more needed to be done to integrate the biodiversity considerations into other sector policies, to make the necessary funding available and to fill the existing policy gaps.[16] It did not, however, consider suggesting a framework legislation on biodiversity which could, among other things, transpose the requirements of the conventions mentioned above into EU law, incorporate the provisions of the Council of Europe Landscape Convention, make available the necessary funding and put into binding legal rules the biodiversity targets which had been agreed under the auspices of the Biodiversity Convention – including by the Union and its Member States – in Nagoya, Japan in October 2010 (the Aichi Targets). The model for putting such precise, binding targets agreed at international level into EU law was the commitments to reduce greenhouse gas emissions laid down in the Kyoto Protocol of 1997 and Decision 2002/358.[17]

When it turned out, in 2015, that biodiversity loss would not be halted by 2020,[18] a new biodiversity strategy was adopted.[19] In its diagnosis, the Commission was quite clear:

> [N]ature is in a state of crisis. The five main direct drivers for biodiversity loss – changes in land and sea use, overexploitation, climate change, pollution and invasive alien species – are making nature disappear quickly … In the last four decades, global wildlife population fell by 60% as a result of human activities. And almost three quarters of the Earth's surface have been altered, squeezing nature into an ever-smaller corner of the plant.

The commitments suggested till 2030 were considerable.[20] The problem is that these commitments are not necessarily those of the Council or the Member States.[21] The Commission

[13] See also Commission, 'First Report on the Implementation of the Convention on Biological Diversity by the European Community' (Luxembourg, 1998); the fifth Union report was submitted in 2014. The sixth Union report, due by the end of 2018, had not yet been submitted in February 2023.

[14] Commission, COM(2006) 216; see also Commission, 'The 2010 Assessment of Implementing the EU Biodiversity Action Plan' COM(2010) 548 concerning the assessment of implementing this Action Plan.

[15] See Commission, COM(2010) 4; Council, 'Conclusions of 15 March 2010' Doc 7536/10 of 16 March 2010. See also Commission, COM(2010) 548 (n 14); Commission, SEC(2010) 1164.

[16] Commission, COM(2010) 548 (n 14).

[17] Decision 2002/358 [2002] OJ L130/1; Decision 1386/2013 on a 7th Environmental Action Programme [2013] OJ L354/171, s 20.

[18] Commission, COM(2015) 478; Commission, SWD(2015) 187. See also Commisssion, State of nature report, COM(2015) 219.

[19] Commisssion, 'EU Biodiversity Strategy for 2030 – Bringing Nature Back Into Our Lives' COM(2020) 380.

[20] ibid s 2: legally binding restoration targets; the decline in pollinators is reversed; use of pesticides is reduced by 50%; 25% of agricultural land is under organic farming management; three billion new trees are planted; significant progress in the remediation of contaminated soil sites; 25,000 km of free-flowing rivers are restored; 50% reduction of Red List species threatened by invasive alien species; reduction of use of fertilisers by 20%; cities with at least 20,000 inhabitants have an ambitious urban greening plan; no chemical pesticides are used in sensitive areas; the negative impacts of fishing and extraction activities are substantially reduced; the by-catch of species is eliminated or reduced.

[21] See an example at para 6-34 concerning the use of pesticides.

submitted a proposal for a regulation on the restoration of nature, suggesting the elaboration of national restoration plans, their management and their review every 10 years.[22] The plans were to be assessed by the Commission. The Commission justified the proposal, which is at present being discussed by the other Union institutions, with the argument, among others, that Aichi Target no 15[23] – 'by 2020 … restoration of at least 15% of degraded ecosystems' – had not been achieved by the Union.

A Commission-sponsored study estimated in 2022 that between 2014 and 2020, the Union had spent €85,098.8 billion overall on 'biodiversity'; the expenses in 2020 were €13.6 billion, 8.3 per cent of the total EU budget.[24]

Convention on migratory species. Apart from the measures taken under Directives 5-04
2009/147 on birds and 92/43 on habitats and species, the Union did not take any measures directed specifically at migratory species.

Alpine Convention. Under the Alpine Convention, a number of protocols were adopted. The Union adhered to the protocols on mountain farming, tourism, energy, soil protection and transport,[25] but not to those on spatial planning and sustainable development, nature protection and landscape conservation, and mountain forests. In the Transport Protocol, the contracting parties committed themselves to 'refrain from constructing any new, large-capacity roads on transalpine transport' (Article 11), which would stop the construction of motorways. No specific Union acts were adopted.

Antarctic Convention. The Union did not adopt specific measures.

Desertification Convention. The European Court of Auditors stated in 2018 that between 2008 and 2017, the area of the Union which was threatened by desertification had increased from 1.68 million km^2 to 1.859 million km^2, ie by more than 10 per cent. The Court argued that, while desertification was increasing, 'there is no EU-level strategy on desertification and land degradation'.[26] The Commission replied that new legislative measures for soil protection would be proposed; these had not been tabled by June 2023.

B. Forests

Forestry is not part of the Common Agricultural Policy, as trees and forestry products 5-05
do not normally come under the notion of 'agricultural products'. When the Council tried to integrate forestry measures into the Common Agricultural Policy by basing such measures on the present Article 43 TFEU, the Court of Justice of the European Union (CJEU) opposed this and declared the measures in question to be part of the EU environmental policy.[27]

[22] Commission, 'Proposal for a Regulation on the Restoration of Nature' COM(2022) 304.

[23] See Biodiversity Convention, 'Decision X/2: The Strategic Plan for Biodiversity 2011–2020 and the Aichi Biodiversity Targets' Doc UNEP/CBD/COP/DEC/X/2 of 29 October 2010.

[24] Institute for European Environmental Policy and Trinomics, *Biodiversity Financing and Tracking* (Luxembourg, 2022) 26.

[25] Decision 2006/516 [2006] OJ L201/31 (tourism soil protection and energy); Decision 2006/655 [2006] OJ L271/11 (mountain farming); Decision 2013/332 [2013] OJ L177/13 (transport).

[26] See Court of Auditors, 'Combating Desertification in the EU: A Growing Threat in Need of More Action' (2018) Special Report 33/2918.

[27] CJEU Joined Cases C-164/97 and C-165/97 *European Parliament v Council* ECLI:EU:C 1999:99.

The Commission adopted forest strategies in 1998,[28] 2013[29] and 2021.[30] The strategies tried to persuade in particular the owners of private forests, estimated at some 16 million, to ensure they practised sustainable forest management, based on the fact – mentioned in the 2021 strategy – that only about 49 per cent of forests in the Union were in good environmental condition. Apart from the intention to plant three billion new trees by 2030,[31] the 2021 strategy mainly indicated ways to obtain financial support from Union funding sources (agricultural funds) and possibilities to improve forest management.

No specific Union measures were taken with regard to forest fires. The Commission set up the European Forest Fires Information System, which publishes an annual report on forest fires in Europe, Middle East and North Africa.[32] A Commission publication made some recommendations on forest fire prevention.[33]

In order to fight illegal logging, the Union adopted, in 2005, a regulation on the establishment of a Forest Law Enforcement, Governance and Trade (FLEGT) licensing scheme for imports of timber into the EU.[34] The regulation provided for the conclusion of non-binding, voluntary agreements with identified partner countries which 'place a legally binding obligation on a partner country to implement the licensing scheme'. Under these agreements, only the import of 'legally' harvested timber into the Union was allowed, that is, timber which complied with the national legislation or standards in force. The regulation tried to progressively reduce the import of illegally logged timber, as it was estimated that between one-third and one-half of tropical timber imports into the Union stemmed from illegal logging. However, whether bilateral agreements – by the end of 2022, agreements were concluded with Ghana, the Republic of Congo, Cameroon, Liberia, the Central African Republic, Vietnam and Indonesia, and negotiations with a number of other countries were ongoing – can be enforced in the wood-exporting country is not clear; also, the export, for example, of Indonesian timber to China which then produces wood products and exports them to Europe would not be covered by such agreements. Until 2023, only Indonesia had put into operation a national licensing system corresponding to the requirements of Regulation 2173/2005. Large timber-exporting countries – Russia, Brazil, Malaysia – showed no interest in joining the Union system. The Commission estimated that about one-third of imports of timber into the Union from partnership countries continued to be illegal and concluded generally that the system 'only had a limited impact on preventing illegal deforestation and/or reducing illegal logging globally'.[35]

In 2010, the Union adopted a regulation to prohibit the placing on the EU market of illegally harvested timber and timber products, in order to reduce illegal logging.[36] The

[28] Commission, COM(98) 649.

[29] Commission, 'A New EU Forest Strategy for Forests and the Forest-Based Sector' COM(2013) 659.

[30] Commission, 'New EU Forest Strategy for 2030' COM(2021) 572; see also Commission, 'Guidelines on Closer-to-Nature Forest Management' SWD(2023) 284.

[31] See also Commission, 'The 3 Billion Tree Pledge' SWD(2021) 651; Commission, 'Guidelines on Biodiversity-Friendly Afforestation, Reforestation and Tree Planting' SWD(2023) 61. By 30 June 2023, 11.35 million trees had actually been planted in the EU.

[32] Commission, *Last Report: Forest Fires in Europe, Middle East and North Africa 2021* (Luxembourg, 2022).

[33] Commission, *Land-Based Wildfire Prevention* (Luxembourg, 2020).

[34] Regulation 2173/2005 on the establishment of a FLEGT licensing scheme for imports of timber into the European Community [2005] OJ L347/1.

[35] Commission, SWD(2021) 328, 25.

[36] Regulation 995/2010 laying down the obligations of operators which place timber and timber products on the market [2010] OJ L295/23.

operators had to apply due diligence measures in order to ensure that timber and timber products come from legally harvested wood. The regulation became fully operational in 2013. It did not cover all wood-based products and, furthermore, considered that timber in countries with which a voluntary agreement under Regulation 2173/2005 had been concluded was legally harvested. While some third countries changed their forestry legislation to align with the Union regulation, illegal logging and deforestation continued globally.[37] A fitness check of the regulation showed only limited positive results.[38] Earlier attempts by the Union to make available specific financial support measures to protect forests in third countries[39] were discontinued.

In 2019, the Commission adopted a communication on the world's forests[40] and proposed, as a follow-up, on the basis of Article 192 TFEU, a regulation which was adopted in 2023[41] with the objective of curbing deforestation and forest degradation in third countries which was provoked by EU consumption and production. The regulation concerned the production of cattle (meat), cocoa, coffee, oil palm, rubber, soya and wood. In order to place such products on the Union market or export them from the Union, operators would have to make a 'due diligence' statement (consisting of the collection of information on the commodity and a risk assessment) and ensure that their products were 'deforestation-free'[42] and were produced according to the legislation of the country of production. Thus, the provisions moved away from the requirement that the products had been produced 'legally' and introduced a requirement of a 'sustainable' production. Consequently, the regulation repealed Regulation 995/2010, because of its explicitly recognised ineffectiveness at curbing illegal logging in third countries and illegal trade in timber;[43] most of its provisions had entered into effect by of June 2023.

C. Land Use and Soil Protection

There are no general EU measures which directly concern soil protection, although agricultural measures generally may have an impact on land use.[44] A regulation from 1992, several times amended and replaced,[45] provided for financial assistance to farmers who 5-06

[37] The Commission mentioned as positive examples Australia, South Korea, Japan and China, SWD(2021) 328, 24; at the same time, it stated that illegal harvesting continued to be far-spread, in Brazil, Russia, Ukraine, Myanmar and a number of African countries.

[38] Commission, Minimising the Risk of Deforestation and Forest Degradation Associated With Products Placed on the EU Market' SWD(2021) 326.

[39] Regulation 3062/95 [1995] OJ L327/9; Regulation 2494/2000 [2000] OJ L288/6.

[40] Commission, 'Stepping Up EU Actions to Protect and Restore the World's Forests' COM(2019) 352.

[41] Regulation 2023/1115 on the making available on the Union market and the export from the Union of certain commodities and products associated with deforestation and forest degradation [2023] OJ L150/206.

[42] ibid Art 2, no 13: '"Deforestation-free" means (a) that the relevant products contain, have been fed with or have been made using, relevant commodities that were produced on land that has not been subject to deforestation after 31 December, 2020, and (b) in the case of relevant products that contain or have been made using wood, that the wood has been harvested from the forest without inducing forest degradation after 31 December, 2020.'

[43] ibid Recital 32.

[44] The Commission's communication on sustainable agriculture [1999] OJ C173/2 indicated that some 156 million hectares of soil were suffering from water or wind erosion and that soil erosion was increasing (pt 2.3).

[45] See the final version of Regulation 1307/2013 establishing rules for direct payments to farmers under support schemes [2013] OJ L347/608. This regulation was amended 18 times.

voluntarily agree to substantially reduce the use of fertilisers or pesticides, to use organic farming methods, to set aside land – for at least 20 years – for environmental purposes or to pursue other ways of environmentally acceptable farming practices.

In the Seventh Environmental Action Programme, the EU considered measures on land use to be necessary in the areas of habitat and ecosystem protection and restoration, management of the countryside, management of landscapes, sustainable forest management, the fight against soil erosion and remediation of contaminated sites.[46] Measures on a sound use of pesticides were presented in the form of a communication (thematic strategy) in 2006.[47] It suggested in particular that Member States establish national plans to reduce the risks of pollution from pesticides. In environmentally friendly areas, the use of pesticides was to be limited and other accompanying measures were proposed. Following this, in 2009, a directive was adopted which obliged Member States to adopt national action plans for the use of pesticides and to set up targets for the reduction of the use of pesticides; some accompanying measures also aimed to progressively reduce the use of such products,[48] but they had a limited effect.[49]

In 2009, a regulation[50] was adopted concerning the placing of pesticides on the market. Under this regulation, the EU adopts a list of active substances which may be used in pesticides. Pesticide products, which may only contain authorised active substances, then need a national authorisation in order to be put on the market (Article 28). By not authorising active substances, dangerous pesticides are progressively eliminated, though the procedure works very slowly.

In 1995, the Commission launched an Integrated Coastal Zone Management Demonstration Programme.[51] This programme, however, only explored ways for effective management; it did not affect decisions on land use, which are taken at the Member State level. In 2001, it was followed by a recommendation with a similar limitation.[52]

In 2006, the Commission presented, in the form of a communication, a thematic strategy on the urban environment[53] which had the ambitious aim of improving the environmental performance and quality of urban areas, where three-quarters of the EU population live. The communication provided for integrated management of urban areas, sustainable transport, the exchange of best practices and similar measures. The Seventh Environmental Action Programme suggested that the EU should, by 2020, 'enhance the sustainability of the Union's cities'.[54] The announced agreement on a set of criteria to assess the environmental performance of cities, the improvement of information on and better access to the financing of measures to improve urban sustainability, the sharing of best practices between cities and

[46] Decision 1386/2013 (n 17), ss 17–28.

[47] Commission, 'Communication on a Thematic Strategy on the Sustainable Use of Pesticides' COM(2006) 372.

[48] Directive 2009/128 establishing a framework for Community action to achieve the sustainable use of pesticides [2009] OJ L309/71.

[49] Commission, 'Evaluation of Directive 2009/128' COM(2020) 204. See also para 6-34.

[50] Regulation 1107/2009 concerning the placing of plant protection products on the market [2009] OJ L309/1; see also para 6-33.

[51] Commission, COM(95) 511; Commission, 'Progress Report' COM(97) 744.

[52] Recommendation 2002/413 concerning the implementation of Integrated Coastal Zone Management in Europe [2002] OJ L148/24.

[53] Commission, 'A Thematic Strategy on the Urban Environment' COM(2006) 718.

[54] Decision 1386/2013 (n 17) Art 2(1)(h).

the development of a common understanding of how to improve urban environments was never realised. The Eighth Environmental Action Programme was also more than vague.[55]

These general and non-committing indications leave, in practice, everything to Member States and to cities. In 2021, the Commission set up the 'Green City Accord', where cities could commit to achieving, until 2030, significant progress in air quality, water protection, biodiversity conservation and moves towards a circular economy, as well as noise reduction. Progress was to be measured against a number of indicators and regular reports were to be published. No specific funds were made available for this initiative. Other initiatives – the Green Capital Award, Green Leaf Award – also aimed at inciting local authorities to become 'greener', without legal implications.

It is clear that the progressive ban of uncontrolled discharges into rivers, lakes or coastal 5-07
waters also contributes to the protection of land. The location of industrial installations or infrastructure measures is decided by Member States at their discretion; eventual negative impacts on the environment, demonstrated, for instance, by an environmental impact assessment,[56] do not restrict this right.

Directive 2009/147[57] required Member States to classify the most suitable territories as special protection areas for some particularly threatened bird species. Within these areas, they had to take 'appropriate steps to avoid pollution or deterioration of habitats or any disturbances affecting the birds, insofar as these would be significant'.[58] In individual cases, this may lead to restrictions of the use of land: in Case C-355/90,[59] the construction of roads and other infrastructure measures within a birds' habitat was declared incompatible with Article 4 of Directive 2009/147; that specific habitat had not been classified under that provision even though it should have been. In Case C-44/95,[60] the UK had classified an area under Article 4, but had exempted a specific part, since it considered that at a later stage this part could be needed for the extension of a nearby commercial port. The CJEU held that this was not allowed, although it did not discuss whether the port extension was compatible with the designation of the habitat.

A similar provision to Article 4 of Directive 2009/147 was introduced in Article 6 of Directive 92/43.[61] However, in reaction to Court jurisdiction, which was considered too restrictive,[62] a provision was inserted that, despite its negative effects, a measure could be carried out 'for imperative reasons of overriding public interest'.[63] This provision considerably facilitated the carrying out of measures even in a classified habitat, in particular in the light of the Commission's wide interpretation and loose handling of Article 6(4). The CJEU

[55] Decision 2022/591 on an 8th Environmental Action Programme [2022] OJ L114/22, Art 3(ad).

[56] See more closely para 4-33ff.

[57] Directive 2009/147 (n 2).

[58] ibid Art 4(4).

[59] CJEU Case C-355/90 *Commission v Spain* ECLI:EU:C:1993:331 (*Santona*); in the same sense, for a case under Directive 92/43, see Case C-340/10 *Commission v Cyprus* ECLI:EU:C:2012:143.

[60] CJEU Case C-44/95 *RSPB* ECLI:EU:C:1996:287 (*Lappel-Bank*); see also Case C-57/89 *Commission v Germany* ECLI:EU:C:1991:89 (*Leybucht*).

[61] Directive 92/43 (n 3) Art 6(2): 'Member States shall take appropriate steps to avoid, in the special areas of conservation, the deterioration of natural habitats and the habitats of species as well as disturbance of the species for which the areas have been designated, insofar as such disturbance could be significant in relation to the objectives of this directive.'

[62] CJEU Case C-57/89 (n 60).

[63] Directive 92/43 (n 3) Art 6(4).

continued to allow only a restricted application of Article 6 of Directive 92/43,[64] though the new urgency Regulation 2022/2577[65] is likely to further facilitate the realisation of energy projects also in protected natural habitats.

The protection of habitats, granted by Directives 2009/147 and 92/43, also applies when activities outside a habitat have an effect within such areas.[66] As regards, more generally, areas other than identified habitats, Directive 92/43 invited Member States to 'encourage the management of features of the landscape which are of major importance for wild fauna and flora' (Article 10); the directive mentioned rivers, field boundaries, ponds and small woods as examples. This invitation was no more than a recommendation to Member States. The Union has not yet taken any steps to adhere to the Council of Europe Convention on Landscapes, which was signed in Florence in 2000.

5-08 Directive 2008/98[67] prohibited the abandonment, dumping or uncontrolled management of waste. The CJEU clarified that this provision also included the obligation to clean up the land, when an unauthorised discharge of waste had taken place.[68] The Court, though, did not discuss the borderline between the obligations flowing out of EU waste law and the contamination of land by waste materials that had been discharged on land prior to 1977, when EU waste legislation became applicable, or prior to the accession of new Member States. In my opinion, such waste discharges are not covered by the clean-up obligation.

Directive 86/278[69] prohibited, under certain conditions, the use of sewage sludge on certain land, in particular where there are overly high concentrations of heavy metals, on grassland or forage crops, on soil in which fruit and vegetable crops are growing and on ground for the cultivation of fruit and vegetable crops which are normally eaten raw.

5-09 There are no specific EU provisions for protecting the soil against soil erosion,[70] although EU funds may assist national measures. Following an announcement in the Sixth Environmental Action Programme on measures concerning the protection of soil,[71] a first communication, identifying the main problems of the soil within the Member States, was published in 2002.[72] This was followed by a further communication and a proposal for a directive on soil protection in 2006.[73]

The proposal for a directive was based on Article 192(1) TFEU, as the Commission considered that it dealt with the protection of the environment and not with land use. It identified the following nine main aspects of the soil degradation process: erosion; organic matter decline; contamination; salinisation; compaction; soil biodiversity loss; sealing; landslides; and flooding. With the exception of flooding, for which the Commission had proposed a separate directive, it suggested that Member States identify areas at risk and

[64] CJEU Case C-258/11 *Grace and Sweetman* ECLI:EU:C:2013:220; Case C-521/12 *Briels* ECLI:EU:C:2014:330.

[65] Regulation 2022/2577 laying down a framework to accelerate the deployment of renewable energy projects [2022] OJ L335/36.

[66] See, eg CJEU Case C-404/09 *Alta Sil* ECLI:EU:C:2011:768.

[67] Directive 2008/98 on waste [2008] OJ L312/3, Art 36. This directive repealed Directive 75/442 and its later version (Directive 2006/12).

[68] CJEU Case C-378/13 *Commission v Greece* ECLI:EU:C:2014:2405; Case C-196/13 *Commission v Italy* ECLI:EU:C:2014:2407.

[69] Directive 86/278 on the protection of the environment and in particular of the soil, when sewage sludge is used in agriculture [1986] OJ L181/6, Arts 5 and 7.

[70] Commission, '12.7% of Europe Is Affected by Moderate to High Erosion' SWD(2021) 323, 10.

[71] Decision 1600/2002 on a 6th Environmental Action Programme [2002] OJ L242/1, Art 7(2c).

[72] Commission, 'Towards a Thematic Strategy for Soil Protection' COM(2002) 179.

[73] Commission, COM(2006) 232.

draw up national programmes. Also of considerable interest was the proposal to establish a national inventory of contaminated sites and to progressively start remediation work.

The Council discussed the legislative proposal on soil protection on several occasions. However, a blocking minority of Member States (Germany, France, Austria, the Netherlands and the UK) opposed any legislative measure on soil protection at EU level, for reasons of subsidiarity. These Member States had existing national legislation on soil; the other 22 Member States pronounced themselves in favour of a Union act. As there were no signs that these attitudes would change in a foreseeable future – though it is not contested that EU regional, agricultural and transport policies contribute to the problems of soil in practically all Member States – the Commission withdrew its proposal in 2014, while the Seventh Environmental Action Programme called for more measures to protect soil.[74] In 2012, the Commission adopted guidelines on soil sealing.[75] Under the European Green Deal, a new strategy for the protection of soil was adopted and legislative measures to protect the soil were announced.[76] In 2023, the Commission proposed a directive on soil monitoring and contaminated sites.[77] The proposal asked Member States to establish soil districts and to monitor and assess the health and resilience of soils. Furthermore, Member States were requested to establish a register of contaminated and potentially contaminated sites; any clean-up measures were almost entirely left at the discretion of Member States. The proposal, based on Article 192(1) TFEU, is at present being discussed by the other Union institutions.

Any land use measure by the Union would have to be adopted by virtue of Article 192(2) TFEU, which requires unanimous decisions. In legal texts, it is sometimes argued that this provision also applies to amendments of Directives 2009/147 and 92/43. However, both directives concern general measures which give a specific status to land, but do not directly deal with the use of the land. Indeed, land use is not outlined in a specific way by either directive. Their correct legal basis is therefore Article 192(1) TFEU.

D. Habitat Protection

The Commission stated in 1999 that: 5-10

> Pollution from transport, industry and agriculture continues to threaten natural areas and wildlife … Pressure is coming from the changes in how we utilise land … The building of

[74] 7th Environmental Action Programme (n 17) ss 23 and 25: 'The degradation, fragmentation and unsustainable use of land in the Union is jeopardising the provision of several key ecosystems, threatening biodiversity and increasing Europe's vulnerability to climate change and natural disasters. It is also exacerbating soil degradation and desertification. More than 25% of the Union's territory is affected by soil erosion by water, which compromises soil functions and affects the quality of freshwater. Soil contamination and sealing are also persistent problems … Every year more than 1000 km^2 of land are taken for housing, industry, transport or recreational services … The Union and its Member States should also reflect as soon as possible on how soil quality issues could be addressed using a targeted and proportionate risk-based approach within a binding legal framework. Targets should also be set for sustainable land use and soil.'

[75] Commission, SWD(2012) 101.

[76] Commission, 'Pathway to a Healthy Planet for All. EU Action Plan: Towards Zero Pollution for Air, Water and Soil' COM(2021) 400; Commission, 'EU Soil Strategy for 2050. Reaping the Benefits of Healthy Soils for People, Food, Waste and Climate' COM(2021) 699; Commission, SWD(2021) 323.

[77] Commissson, 'Proposal for a Directive on Soil Monitoring and Resilience (Soil Monitoring Law)' COM(2023) 416.

> new roads, houses and other developments is fragmenting the countryside into ever-smaller areas, making it harder for species to survive. All the trends suggest that the loss of open countryside to development will continue in the future … As habitats are degraded or lost, wildlife is frequently under pressure or even the threat of extinction.[78]

(i) Birds' Habitats

5-11 In 1979, the Union adopted Directive 79/409 on the conservation of wild birds,[79] following considerable public pressure in favour of such a measure; in 2009, this directive was renumbered as Directive 2009/147.[80] The directive aimed at comprehensive protection of *all* wild birds within the Union and outlined detailed provisions, in particular on hunting, capturing and trading of birds. Member States were required to take necessary measures 'to preserve, maintain or re-establish a sufficient diversity and area of habitats' for all birds (Article 3) by the creation of protected areas, or biotopes, and the upkeep, management and re-establishment of biotopes. For particularly threatened bird species, listed in annex I to the directive, they were asked to classify habitats as special protection areas for the conservation of these species (Article 4). The different designated habitats were to form a 'coherent whole',[81] which met the protection requirements for birds all over the Union. Inside these special protection areas, appropriate conservation measures had to be taken. When a habitat objectively qualified as a special protected area but was not so designated by a Member State, the CJEU could declare it a Special Protection Area (SPA).[82]

5-12 The provision of Article 3 has not apparently led to any significant change at national level; the provision was scarcely monitored by the Commission, though it undoubtedly has a legally binding content; in only one case has the CJEU found that Article 3 had not been respected by a Member State.[83] As regards Article 4, the designation of SPAs advanced only slowly. While Directive 79/409 required the classification to be completed by 1981, designations still continue today. They now comprise an area of 527,000 km^2 on land and 305,000 km^2 at sea (27 EU Member States);[84] the exact number of designated areas is unknown, as numerous areas have also been designated as habitats for species under Directive 92/43.

In 2010, the Commission indicated that the designation of areas was 'largely completed' for Belgium, Denmark, Germany, Estonia, France, Italy, Luxemburg, Malta, the Netherlands, Poland, Portugal and Finland.[85] Since then, the Commission has not disclosed any further information on implementation. However, the designation of SPAs is now more or less completed for all Member States.

[78] Commission, 'Directions Towards Sustainable Agriculture' COM(1999) 22 [1999] OJ C273/2, pt 4.1.

[79] Directive 79/409 (n 2).

[80] ibid.

[81] ibid Art 4(3); the French and German texts talk of a 'coherent network', which is certainly more precise.

[82] CJEU Case C-355/90 *Commission v Spain* ECLI:EU:C:1993:331.

[83] CJEU Case C-117/00 *Commission v Ireland* ECLI:EU:C:2002:366. See generally Commission, *Information sur l'application de la directive 79/409/CEE* (Brussels, 1990) 35 et seq; Commission, 'Report on the Application of Directive 79/409 (1993–1995)' COM(2000) 180; Commission, 'Report on the Application of Directive 79/409 (1996–1998)' COM(2002) 146.

[84] Commission, *Natura 2000 and Biodiversity Newsletter* No 51 (February 2022) 8.

[85] Commission, *Natura 2000 Newsletter* No 28 (June 2010) 6.

In a number of cases, the Commission tried to ensure the habitat status of specific zones through legal proceedings, where it was of the opinion that Member States had not fully complied with their obligations. These procedures are rather time-consuming, in particular where the dispute has to be decided by the CJEU.[86] The Commission announced in 2002 that it was developing a strategy to initiate general infringement proceedings, rather that beginning proceedings on a site-by-site basis.[87] This strategy had the practical consequence that the Commission did not bring any more cases before the CJEU.[88]

A Commission's fitness check of 2016 concluded that Directive 2009/147 had largely reached its objectives.[89] Practically the same conclusion was drawn in a Commission publication of 2019,[90] though both publications did not discuss in detail the evolution of birds' habitats. The Commission's implementation reports for the periods 2008–12 and 2013–18 discussed the birds and the habitats directive together, thus avoiding discussing trends and tendencies for birds' habitats.[91]

(ii) Natural and Fauna and Flora Habitats

Habitats are also protected by virtue of the provisions of Directive 92/43.[92] This directive protects over 200 different types of natural habitats of particular ecological value,[93] which are listed in its annex I; furthermore, it requires that habitats for those fauna and flora species listed in annexe II be designated by Member States. The procedure of designating these habitats is slightly different from that of Directive 2009/147: first, Member States have to establish national lists of sites which are important for the conservation of natural habitat types or of habitats for fauna or flora species. Out of these national lists, the Commission, in agreement with the Member State concerned, establishes a list of sites of EU importance.[94] Member States then have six years to designate the sites on this list as Special Areas of Conservation (SACs), which form, together with the habitats for birds, 'a coherent European ecological network,' called Natura 2000. 5-13

The national lists had to be drawn up by June 1995. In April 1996, five Member States had transmitted complete national lists, two others partial lists. In 1999, the Commission warned Member States that if they did not transmit adequate lists for the setting up of the

[86] See, eg CJEU Case C-57/89 (n 60); Case C-355/90 (n 82); Case C-44/95 (n 60); Case C-166/97 *Commission v France* ECLI:EU:C:1999:149; Case C-96/98 *Commission v France* ECLI:EU:C:1999:580; Case C-374/98 *Commission v France* ECLI:EU:C:2000:670.

[87] Commission, '19th Report on Monitoring Application of Community Law (2001)' COM(2002) 324, no 2.8.6.

[88] Between 2010 and the beginning of 2023, the Commission brought only two cases before the Court, one on the incorrect transposition of Directive 2009/147, Case C-192/11 *Commission v Poland* ECLI:EU:C:2012:44, and the other for not designating an SPA, Case C-97/17 *Commission v Bulgaria* ECLI:EU:C:2018:285. There were three or four cases where questions of habitats of Directive 2009/147 were raised together with Directive 92/43.

[89] Commission, 'Fitness Check of the EU Nature Legislation (Birds and Habitats Directives)' SWD(2016) 472.

[90] Commission, *The Birds Directive: 40 Years Conserving Our Natural Heritage* (Luxembourg, 2019).

[91] Commission, 'Report for the Period 2007–2012' COM(2015) 219; Commission, 'The State of Nature in the European Union; Report on the Status and Trend in 2013–2018 of Species and Habitats Protected by the Birds and Habitats Directives' COM(2020) 635.

[92] Directive 92/43 (n 3); Commission proposal [1988] OJ C247/3; European Parliament Opinion [1991] OJ C75/12; Economic and Social Committee Opinion [1991] OJ C31/25.

[93] See also Commission, 'Interpretation Manual of Environmental Habitats' (April 2013) http://ec.europa.eu/environment/nature/legislation/habitatsdirective/docs/Int_Manual_EU28.pdf.

[94] See CJEU Case C-117/03 *Dragaggi* ECLI:EU:C:2005:16: the protection under Art 6 of Directive 92/43 begins when the Commission has established a list of sites of Union interest.

Natura 2000 network, the Commission might not be able to evaluate and co-finance plans and programmes under the structural funds; accordingly, it might not be able to allot the corresponding financial means to Member States.[95] Though this warning raised an outcry, particularly in Germany, together with a number of CJEU judgments it had the effect that the lists of sites under Article 6 of Directive 92/43 arrived more regularly. In particular, the German *Länder* abandoned their fundamental opposition to the directive.

5-14 By the beginning of 2023, the Commission had published (updated) EU lists for the bio-geographical areas of the Macaronesia (Azores, Madeira and Canary Islands), Alpine (mountain), Continental, Atlantic, Boreal, Mediterranean, Steppic, Pannonian and Black Sea regions.[96] Overall, the 27 Member States had designated, by early 2022, 27,852 areas (bird areas and marine areas included), covering 1,358,125 km^2, 18.14 per cent of their area.[97] The Commission did not disclose information about whether the Member States had proceeded to classify SACs at national level.[98] Following a judgment by the CJEU, according to which Directive 92/43 also applied to the marine environment,[99] Member States progressively also designated marine habitats, though much less than terrestrial habitats. The largest parts of the national terrestrial areas were designated by Slovenia (38 per cent of its territory) Croatia (37 per cent), Bulgaria (35 per cent), Cyprus (30 per cent) and Slovakia (30 per cent); the smallest parts were designated by Denmark (8 per cent), Latvia (12 per cent), Sweden (12 per cent) and Lithuania, France, Finland and Ireland (each 13 per cent).

The designation of protected areas under Directives 2009/147 and 92/43 is, as of mid-2023, now well advanced. Yet, in its biodiversity strategy for 2030, the Commission declared the existing Natura 2000 to be not sufficiently large.[100] At present, 26 per cent of the Union land is protected: 18 per cent under Natura 2000 and eight per cent under national provisions. A total of 11 per cent of the EU seas are protected: eight per cent under Natura 2000 and three per cent under Member States' provisions. According to the Commission, by 2030, 30 per cent of the land area and 30 per cent of the sea area should be protected. This suggestion is at present being discussed by the other Union institutions, along with the Commission's proposal for a regulation on the restoration of nature.[101]

[95] CJEU Case C-329/96 *Commission v Greece* ECLI:EU:C:1997:333; Case C-83/97 *Commission v Germany* ECLI:EU:C:1997:606; Commission, 'Monitoring Application of Community Law – 15th Report 1997' [1998] OJ C250/1, 178.

[96] Commission Decision 2019/15 (Steppic region) [2019] OJ L7/1; Decision 2023/239 (Pannonian region) [2023] OJ L36/99; Decision 2023/242 (Black Sea region) [2023] OJ L36/299; Decision 2023/240(Macaronesian region) [2023] OJ L36/140; Decision 2023/243 (Alpine region) [2023] OJ L36/304; Decision 2023/238(Atlantic region) [2023] OJ L36/1; Decision 2022/231 (Continental region) [2022] OJ L39/19; Decision 2023/241 (Mediterranean region) [2023] OJ L36/384; Decision 2023/245 (Boreal region) [2023] OJ L36/723.

[97] Commission, *Natura 2000 and Biodiversity Newsletter* No 51 (February 2022) 8. As there might be an overlapping with the percentages which were given for bird areas, these figures may not be accumulated with those given in para 5-12.

[98] See, however, CJEU Case C-290/18 *Commission v Portugal ECLI*:EU:C:2019:629; Case 849/19 *Commission v Greece* ECLI: ECLI:EU:C:2020:1047, which held that these Member States had not taken measures to protect the designated habitats. Similar cases against Germany (Case C-116/22), Bulgaria (Case C-85/22) and Ireland (Case C-444/21) were pending in June 2023. The Commission mentioned that either the conservation objectives were not correctly established or additional measures to protect the sites were needed in Austria, Belgium, Denmark, Estonia, Germany, France, Greece, Finland, Czechia, Italy, Hungary, Latvia, Lithuania, the Netherlands, Malta, Slovenia and Slovakia; Commission, 'Environmental Implementation Review 2022' COM(2022) 438, s 3.2.

[99] CJEU Case C-6/04 *Commission v United Kingdom* ECLI:EU:C:2005:626.

[100] Commission, COM(2020) 380 (n 19).

[101] Commission, COM(2022) 304 (n 22).

One of the main reasons for the considerable delay in the setting up of national lists was the provision of Article 6(2) of Directive 92/43, which requested Member States to avoid 'the deterioration of natural habitats and the habitats of species as well as disturbance of the species for which the areas have been designated, insofar as such disturbance could be significant in relation to the objectives of this directive'.

Although this provision was completed by the above-mentioned provision of Article 6(4), the CJEU established criteria for the declassification of an SAC,[102] and even though the Commission decisions showed a wide interpretation of this exemption, there was considerable concern at local level in many Member States that, once a site came under Directive 92/43, economic or leisure activities would be severely restricted. Under pressure from hunters, fishermen, farmers and other groups, France even went so far, in the summer of 1996, as to freeze work on its national list for several months, arguing that it was neither clear who would finance the management measures of the habitats[103] nor exactly what activities would be forbidden within a habitat. Some months later, France reversed this decision.

The question of what is allowed and what is not allowed in a Natura 2000 habitat is a most intricate one.[104] (Bird) hunting in a habitat is often accepted – although heavily contested by environmental organisations. Other, more relevant, economic measures, such as irrigation, urbanisation and road construction, are often undertaken within habitats without systematic compliance with the conditions of Article 6 of Directive 92/43. Article 6(4) allows the realisation of projects within a protected area provided there is no alternative, an impact assessment is made and the project is necessary for 'imperative reasons of overriding public interest'. Member States decide when this is the case. The Commission shall be informed of any compensatory measures; however, this information is not at all regular and the Commission does not seriously enforce Article 6(4).

The main instrument used to financially support habitats is LIFE,[105] which, for the period 2021–27, was given €2.143 billion to finance its sub-programme 'nature and biodiversity'. This amounts to some €300 million per year, destined for some 35 countries (EU Member States plus accession countries and neighbouring countries). It should be remembered that the Commission, based on information from Member States, estimated the annual financial need to be €10.225 billion.[106]

Generally, economic development prevails over conservation, and cases where the development of a project has been stopped because of the existence of a habitat or a threatened species are extremely rare in the Union. The Commission attempted twice to have a rule adopted that all projects supported by Union funding[107] should, before development consent is given, be preceded by an environmental impact assessment; however, the Council twice rejected this approach.[108] Directive 2001/42 provided that any plan (though not a project!) which might significantly affect a designated natural habitat or a bird habitat must

[102] CJEU Case C-301/12 *Cascina Tre Pini* ECLI:EU:C:2014:214; Case C-281/16 *Hoekschewaard* ECLI:EU:C:2017:774.

[103] Commission, 'Monitoring the Application of Community Law, 17th Report' COM(1999) 53.

[104] See as examples CJEU Case C-308/08 *Commission v Spain* ECLI:EU:C:2010:281; Case C-2/10 *Eolica Franchini* ECLI:EU:C:2011:502.

[105] Regulation 2021/783 [2021] OJ L172/53.

[106] Commission, 'Investment Needs and Priorities for Natura 2000 and Green Infrastructure' SWD(2023) 99.

[107] Directive 2011/92 on the assessment of the effects of certain public and private projects on the environment [2012] OJ L26/1.

[108] Commission proposal for directive 92/43 [1988] OJ C247/7, Art 10; Commission proposal for directive 97/11 [1994] OJ C130/8; the Council's decision is found in Directive 97/11 [1997] OJ L37/5, Recital 10.

be preceded by an environmental impact assessment. Finally, in 2022, Regulation 2022/2577 was adopted, which more or less provides that energy projects from renewable energies should have priority over the protection of habitats or species.[109]

5-15 The dilemma is that, on the one hand, it is hardly possible to transform Natura 2000 areas into nature museums, where no change may take place; this is the reason why local people or authorities so often oppose the designation of a habitat. On the other hand, the Commission itself stated[110] that almost everywhere in Western Europe habitats and nature protection sites are shrinking slowly, but dramatically, due to road and other infrastructure construction, urbanisation, intensive farming activity, irrigation, and holiday and leisure activities.[111]

So far, there are only a few implementation reports, which are of limited informative value as regards the legal questions of transposition and application of Directive 92/43.[112] The Commission showed a growing disinterest in the practical application of the legislation to specific cases and concentrated on transposition of legislation and on the designation of habitats. Fortunately, though, the CJEU has taken on a very considerable role in defending the degree of protection given by Directive 92/43 against attempts of reducing this protection in favour of vested interests.[113]

With all the delays and difficulties in designating habitats and conserving them, Directives 2009/147 and 92/43 constitute the first serious attempt in Western Europe to conserve nature protection sites. As such, they go far beyond what individual Member States had done at national level in this area. The experience of 40 years of application of measures to protect birds and other species, which has neither led to sufficient designation of habitats and adequate conservation measures nor generally stopped the shrinking of individual habitats, does not promote optimism. In Western Europe, which is a small area that is densely populated, with great economic activity and an impressive transport and energy infrastructure network, nature is in retreat because it conflicts with demographic and economic evolution. For this reason, in almost all cases where economic interests in building a bridge, a port, an airport, a motorway or a new high-speed train clash with the environmental interests of preserving a habitat, the environmental interests lose. The application of Directive 92/43 did not significantly change this situation, all the more as the Commission apparently neglects problems of specific, individual habitats:[114]

> [B]iodiversity loss and the degradation of ecosystems continue at an alarming rate, harming people, the economy and the climate. The EU has so far failed to halt the loss of biodiversity. The outlook for biodiversity and ecosystems is bleak and shows that the current approach is not working.[115]

[109] Regulation 2022/2577 (n 65).

[110] Commission, 'Communication on Rational Use and Conservation of Wetlands' COM(95) 189 of 29 May 1995; repeated in COM(2020) 380 (n 19) and COM(2022) 304 (n 22).

[111] Perhaps the most eloquent example is the French habitat Camargue, which lost, between 1942 and 1984, about 1000 hectares per year of its natural surface, see A Tamisier, *Camargue, milieux et paysages évolution de 1942 à 1984* (Arles, 1992).

[112] Commission, COM(2003) 845, COM(2009) 358, COM(2015) 219 and COM(2020) 635. See also European Environment Agency (n 1).

[113] From 1994 up to the end of 2022, the CJEU delivered about 80 judgments on the interpretation of Directive 92/43.

[114] On the application of Directive 92/43, see generally A García Ureta, *EU Biodiversity Law. Wild Birds and Habitats Directives* (Zutphen, 2020); C Born and others, *The Habitats Directive in Its EU Environmental Law Context* (London, 2015).

[115] Commission, COM(2022) 304 (n 22).

Habitats of wild flora and fauna species are also protected under Article 4 of the Berne Convention on the Conservation of European Wildlife and Natural Habitats of 1979, to which the Union adhered by a decision of 1981.[116] However, as is explained above,[117] the Commission does not monitor the application of international conventions to which the Union has adhered, but leaves their application entirely to Member States. 5-16

A specific problem is that of (habitats of) species which are protected under the Berne Convention but not under Directive 2009/147 or 92/43; an example of this is the badger. Supposing a Member State were infringing the obligation adequately to protect the badger's habitat: would this constitute a breach of the Union's obligations under the Convention? In my opinion, by adhering to an international convention, the Union undertakes to ensure that the convention is respected all over the EU territory. EU Member States are obliged, under Article 4 TEU, to take all measures necessary to allow the Union to respect this obligation; the obligation even exists where a Member State itself is not a contracting party of the convention, and the Commission has the obligation to ensure, under Article 17 TEU, that Member States fulfil their obligations. The problem is, though, that the Commission is not willing to pursue such cases, and members of the public normally do not have the standing to bring such cases before the CJEU.

The opinion which is defended here was supported by the Aarhus Convention Compliance Committee in 2012. The case concerned Ireland not properly applying Article 7 of the UNECE Convention on Access to Information, Public Participation in Decision-making and Access to Justice in Environmental Matters (Aarhus Convention). At the time of the decision, Ireland had not ratified the Aarhus Convention, but the EU had. The Compliance Committee decided that the EU had breached its obligations under the convention, as it had not taken the necessary measures to ensure that the provisions of the convention were properly applied and enforced in Ireland.[118]

Directive 78/659[119] tried to protect the habitats of fish. Member States were asked to designate fresh waters to support fish life. For these waters, they had to establish programmes which had to ensure that the waters corresponded to the specific quality requirements laid down in the directive. A similar approach was followed by Directive 79/923 for shellfish.[120] 5-17

Both directives completely failed to reach their objective.[121] The main reasons were that Member States were also allowed to designate waters which already complied with the requirements so that no clean-up programme was necessary. Furthermore, the number of waters which were to be designated was not fixed, which led several Member States to designate only very few waters; a decision by the CJEU stipulating that Member States had to designate and clean up waters throughout their territory[122] did not lead to substantial changes. Finally, the Commission did not monitor the application of these directives closely.

[116] Decision 82/72 [1982] OJ L38/1.

[117] See para 5-02.

[118] Aarhus Convention Compliance Committee, 'Findings and Recommendations in Case ACCC/C/2010/54, adopted on 29 June 2012' Doc ECE/MP.PP/C.1/202/12.

[119] Directive 78/659 on the quality of fresh waters needing protection or improvement in order to support fish life [1978] OJ L222/1.

[120] Directive 79/923 on the quality required of shellfish waters [1979] OJ L281/47.

[121] See for the factual details in Commission, *Quality of Fresh Water for Fish and of Shellfish Water; Summary Report on the State of Application of the Directives 78/659 and 79/923* (Luxembourg, 1995) EUR 14118.

[122] CJEU Case C-322/86 *Commission v Italy* ECLI:EU:C:1988:385.

Both directives were repealed, in 2013, by Directive 2000/60,[123] which intended to take over the attainment of the objectives of these directives, though it deals with water quality, not with habitat protection.

II. Protection of Threatened Species

A. Fauna and Flora Species

5-18 There is no Union list of threatened or endangered species. The International Union for Conservation of Nature (IUCN), a non-governmental organisation, establishes global red lists for endangered fauna and flora species, which are widely recognised as reliable. Its regional office for Europe extrapolates these data for the EU, which are made public as the 'European Red List'. However, the fact that IUCN's lists are not based on official, public data limits their impact on policy-makers and the public.

The Birds Directive (Directive 2009/147) protects all birds which live in Europe; some birds, listed in annex I, need more protection, whereas other birds may be hunted, and thus apparently are meant to be less protected. Endangered species are marked by an asterisk in the Habitats Directive, though no specific measures as regards their conservation are laid down. Furthermore, the Habitats Directive (Directive 92/43) lists in annex II species which need the designation of habitats. Annex IV lists species which need 'strict' protection; Articles 12 and 13 specify what is meant by this term.[124] Species which are mentioned in annex V may be the subject of management measures, thus apparently might be less well protected; possible management measures are mentioned in Article 14 of the directive.

The lists of species in the Habitats Directive have not been amended since 1992, ie more than 30 years. As regards the Birds Directive, the only amendment concerned the cormorant, which was removed from annex I due to the pressure of fishermen and aquaculture operators.[125]

5-19 Directive 92/43 established in its annexes a general system of protection for European endangered species, which it listed in Latin only;[126] these lists cover about 1380 animal and plant species other than the some 460 bird species protected under Directive 2009/147; the accession of 13 new Member States since 2004 had led to enlargement of the lists. As Directive 92/43 was based on Article 192 TFEU, Member States may provide for other species to be protected at national level. The deliberate capture or killing, disturbance, taking eggs or deterioration or destruction of breeding sites or resting places of fauna species were prohibited. For some particularly endangered species, Member States must provide for supplementary measures, for example to prevent the unintentional capture or

[123] See Directive 2000/60 establishing a framework for Community action in the field of water policy [2000] OJ L327/1, Art 22(2).

[124] See also Commission, Guidance document on the strict protection of animal species of Community interest under the habitats Directive [2021] OJ C496/1.

[125] Commission Directive 97/49 [1997] OJ L223/9.

[126] Directive 92/43 (n 3) annex II: animal and plant species of Community interest whose conservation requires the designation of special areas of protection; annex IV: animal and plant species of Community interest in need of strict protection; annex V: animal and plant species of Commuity interest whose taking in the wild and exploitation may be subject to management measures.

killing (Article 12). Derogations from the protection rules were possible, under relatively loosely drafted provisions (Article 16). Reports on the derogations granted had to be sent to the Commission every two years; however, the Commission satisfied itself in all cases with the information transmitted, and never started proceedings where no report had been submitted and where only incomplete or vague information had been made available. Composite reports were prepared by outside contractors and were not helpful, due to their late production and the fact that the Commission did not assume any responsibility for the report.[127] It is surprising to find that, under Directive 92/43, the Commission's comments on the national derogations have only to be submitted to the Committee, and not published (Article 9(2)).[128] The implementation reports of the Commission[129] showed that some Member States just enumerated their protection legislation, and did not report on the concrete measures which they undertook to protect endangered species; probably, in most cases, Member States satisfied themselves with the adoption of legal requirements without trying to make them effective.

The problems with the designation and management of habitats under Directive 92/43 are so considerable that hardly any measures to ensure the protection of individual species were taken, apart from measures for big animals such as bears or Mediterranean seals, measures which were then financed under LIFE.[130] Reacting to complaints from individuals, the Commission took a few cases to court: to protect the sea turtle on Greek islands, the viper in Greece, the wolf in Finland and Slovakia, the corn crake in Austria, the hamster in France, the grass snake in Cyprus and the harbour porpoise in the UK.[131] Apart from disputes about the hunting of wolves, no problem of hunting or taking a species from the wild was taken up by the Commission.

The status of species following the Member States' reports for the period 2013–18 was as follows: 27 per cent had a good conservation status, 42 per cent had a poor status and 21 per cent a bad status; for 10 per cent, the status was unknown.[132] Of the species with an unfavourable (poor or bad) status, 35 per cent showed further deterioration with regard to the previous reporting period, 28 per cent were stable, 6 per cent had an improving status and for 31 per cent the trend was unknown.[133]

[127] The latest report available in early 2023 deals with derogations 2017 and 2018, thus four years later: Commission, *2017–2018 Composite Report on Derogations According to Article 16 of Directive 92/43* (Brussels, 2021.

[128] See also Commission, Eighth report on monitoring application of Community law (1990) [1991] OJ C338/1 220, where the Commission stated that the reports on the derogations under Directive 79/409 were so general that they did not allow any control.

[129] See n 127.

[130] Overall, between 1992 and 2018, LIFE co-financed over 1800 nature projects, spending three billion euros. 6000 Natura 2000 areas and 1340 species of wild fauna and flora (without birds) benefited from such support, see Commission, 'LIFE Programme' www.switchtogreen.eu/the-life-programme/.

[131] CJEU Case C-135/04 *Commission v Spain* ECLI:EU:C:2005:374 (wood pigeon); Case C-518/04 *Commission v Greece* ECLI:EU:C:2006:183 and Case C-504/14 *Commission v Greece* ECLI:EU:C:2016:847(sea turtle); Case C-342/05 *Commission v Finland* ECLI:EU:C:2007:341, Case C-647/17 *Tapiola* ECLI:EU:C:2019:851 and Case C-88/19 *Alianta* ECLI: ECLI:EU:C:2020:458 (wolf); Case C-117/00 *Commission v Ireland* ECLI:EU:C:2002:366 (red grouse); Case C-209/02 *Commission v Austria* ECLI:EU:C:2004/61 (corn crake); Case C-383/09 *Commission v France* ECLI:EU:C:2011:369 (hamster); Case C-340/10 *Commission v Cyprus* ECLI:EU:C:2012:143 (grass snake); Case C-669/16 *Commission v United Kingdom* ECLI:EU:C:2018:846 (harbour porpoise); Case C-661/20 *Commission v Slovakia* ECLI:EU:C:2022:496 (capercaillie).

[132] European Environmental Agency (n 1).

[133] ibid 58.

B. Birds

5-20 Directive 2009/147, which protects all living birds – over 460 species – in the Union, lists in annex I some 200 particularly threatened bird species which require special protection measures. The most important of these measures are the designation of special protection areas under Article 4[134] and the taking of conservation measures within these areas. The list of threatened bird species has constantly been increased, in particular due to the subsequent accessions to the Union of Greece, Spain, Portugal, Austria, Finland and Sweden, then of the 13 new Member States in 2004, 2007 and 2013.

Directive 2009/147, however, protects not only threatened birds, but all wild birds within the Union; the reason for this overall protection was most likely the fact that 'a large number of wild birds … are declining in number'.[135] The directive thus provided for restrictive measures, such as restrictions of hunting times, or prohibitions on killing or capturing birds or taking eggs. Furthermore, it banned a number of means for large-scale or non-selective capture or killing of birds (snares, limes, hooks, mirrors, explosives, nets, traps or motor vehicles). Derogations are possible 'where there is no other satisfactory solution' (Article 9).

5-21 Directive 2009/147 meant to improve the conditions of birds in Western Europe. This also implied a considerable change in people's habits. Apart from the designation of birds' habitats, the different provisions, including hunting provisions, proved difficult to enforce.[136] In particular, in, but not restricted to, France, Spain, Italy and Malta, hunting is perceived as a *right* by hunters, farmers and others. When Malta acceded to the Union in 2004, it even obtained a transition period for allowing bird hunting by means that are normally forbidden under Directive 2009/147. National hunting provisions often did not correctly transpose the directive;[137] hunting seasons were generously allowed and little restricted. To what extent the hunting of migrating birds, which Article 7(4) of the directive expressly forbids, has really been reduced, in particular in Southern Europe – nobody can argue that it has stopped in reality – is unknown.

[134] See para 5-12ff.

[135] Directive 2009/147 (n 2) Recital 2.

[136] CJEU Case C-297/85 *Commission v Belgium* ECLI:EU:C:1987:339; Case C-262/85 *Commission v Italy* ECLI:EU:C:1987:340; Case C-412/85 *Commission v Germany* ECLI:EU:C:1987:370; Case C-236/85 *Commission v Netherlands* ECLI:EU:C:1987:436; Case C-252/85 *Commission v France* ECLI:EU:C:1988:202; Case C-169/89 *Gourmetterie van den Burg* ECLI:EU:C:1990:227; Case C-334/89 *Commission v Italy* ECLI:EU:C:1991:13; Case C-345/92 *Commission v Germany* ECLI:EU:C:1993:110; Case C-435/92 *Association des Animaux v Préfet Maine et Loire* ECLI:EU:C:1994:110; Case C-149/94 *Ministère public v Vergy* ECLI:EU:C:1996:37; Case C-202/94 *VD Feesten* ECLI:EU:C:1996:39; Case C-10/96 *Ligue belge des oiseaux* ECLI:EU:C:1996:504; Case C507/04 *Commission v Austria* ECLI:EU:C:2007:427; Case C-293/07 *Commission v Greece* ECLI:EU:C:2008:706; Case C-259/08 *Commission v Greece* ECLI:EU:C:2009:13; Case C-164/09 *Commission v Italy* ECLI:EU:C:2010:672; Case C-192/11 *Commission v Poland* ECLI:EU:C:2012:44.

[137] See the different cases on national hunting rules: CJEU Case C-339/87 *Commission v Netherlands* ECLI:EU:C:1998:285; Case C-288/88 *Commission v Germany* ECLI:EU:C:1990:202; Case C-157/89 *Commission v Italy* ECLI:EU:C:1991:22; Case C-435/92 (n 136); Case C-118/94 *WWF v Veneto* ECLI:EU:C:1996:86; Case C-79/03 *Commission v Spain* ECLI:EU:C:2004:782; Case C-344/05 *Commission v Finland* ECLI:EU:C:2005:770; Case C-221/04 *Commission v Spain* ECLI:EU:C:2006:329; Case C-60/05 *WWF v Lombardia* ECLI:EU:C:2006:378; Case C-503/06 *Commission v Italy* ECLI:EU:C:2008:279; Case C-76/08 *Commission v Malta* ECLI:EU:C:2009:536; Case C-164/09 *Commission v Italy* ECLI:EU:C:2010:672; Case C-557/15 *Commission v Malta* ECLI:EU:C:2018:477; Case C-161/19 *Commission v Austria* ECLI:EU:C:2020:290; Case C-217/19 *Commission v Finland* ECLI:EU:C:2019:291; Case C-900/19 *One Voice* ECLI:EU:C:2021:211.

In 1994, the Commission gave in to the pressure from (French) hunting interests and suggested an amendment of the directive's hunting provisions which would have prolonged hunting seasons,[138] but this was stopped by the European Parliament and the Council. In 1998, the French Parliament adopted legislation which extended the hunting period for birds into the time of migration and breeding, in deliberate and open defiance of Directive 2009/147. In 1999, France was condemned by the European Court of Human Rights because some of its hunting provisions were in conflict with the individual right of property. And in 2000, the CJEU gave a judgment on the French hunting rules[139] which once more stated that they were not compatible with EU rules. In 2004, hunters and environmental organisations signed, on the initiative of the Commission, an agreement on 'sustainable hunting'. Since then, the Commission has practically stopped taking action against Member States' hunting legislation or practice.

Generally, implementation of the Birds Directive was slow. Before 2012, the Commission 5-22
had to take court action, because national legislation did not fully comply with the directive, and until 2015, the Commission had only published five of the composite reports which it should have published every three years under Article 12(2) of the Birds Directive, limiting these reports largely to reproducing Member States' comments, without analysing and assessing the situation itself. As a consequence, the reporting period was prolonged to six years and the task of reporting was transferred to the European Environmental Agency.[140]

According to the most recent report of 2020, 47 per cent of the bird populations in the Union have a good conservation status, 20 per cent a poor status and 19 per cent a bad status, while for 14 per cent the status is unknown. The trends are positive (increasing) for 23 per cent, stable for 28 per cent, fluctuating for two per cent, negative (decreasing) for 30 per cent and unknown for 17 per cent. The main factors influencing these figures were the conversion of agricultural land, drainage, leisure activities, unsustainable forest practices and illegal killing[141] and hunting.[142] The Union's LIFE programme supported measures aiming at the protection of more than 460 bird species.[143]

The conclusion, after 40 years of operation of Directive 2009/147 and its predecessor directive, Directive 79/409, is that they have undoubtedly had positive effects. Directive 2009/147's legally binding provisions, which contrast markedly with international conventions, which are considered as soft law and are neither enforceable nor enforced, have alerted administrations concerned and have influenced public opinion and researchers, and

[138] Commission [1994] OJ C100/12.

[139] CJEU Case C-38/99 *Commission v France* ECLI:EU:C:2000:674; see also Case 252/85 *Commission v France* ECLI:EU:C:1988:202; Case C-900/19 (n 137).

[140] See most recently European Environmental Agency (n 1).

[141] A Brochet et al, 'Preliminary Assessment of the Scope and Scale of Illegal Killing and Taking of Birds in the Mediterranean' (2016) 26 *Birdlife Conservation International* 4; A Brochet et al, 'Illegal Killing and Taking of Birds in Europe Outside Mediterranean Countries: Assessing the Scope and Scale of a Complex Problem' (2019) 29 *Birdlife Conservation International* 12 gave the following figures of annually illegally killed birds in EU Member States: Austria, 3500; Belgium, 60,200; Bulgaria, 37,700; Cyprus, 5.6 million; Czechia, 12,800; Denmark, 31,300; Estonia, 6300; Finland, 7600; France, 522,000; Germany, 100,000; Greece, 704,000; Hungary, 14,600; Ireland, 3200; Italy, 5.6 million; Latvia, 2300; Lithuania, 3100; Malta, 108,000; the Netherlands, 13,200; Poland, 18,400; Portugal, 82,400; Romania, 99,700; Slovenia, 8000; Slovakia, 5700; Spain, 254,000; Sweden, 58,600.

[142] Brochet et al, 'Preliminary Assessment' (n 141) 14. The European Environmental Agency (n 1) 70 stated that annually at least 52 million birds were hunted in the Union.

[143] Commission, 'LIFE Programme' (n 130).

caused them to seriously consider the state of birdlife in Europe. Habitats have been designated and concern for ensuring the survival of the different species of birds has been raised. No international convention was capable of achieving similar results, not least because the Commission acted and continues to act as a co-ordination and enforcement body. The problems of applying the directive are the same as those applying to nature conservation and to biodiversity generally: the overall decline of birds has not yet been stopped in Western Europe.

C. Pollinators

5-23 Following an international publication in 2016,[144] the Commission published, in 2018, a first communication on EU wild pollinators,[145] which highlighted the dramatic decline in the occurrence and diversity of wild pollinators (bees, some species of flies, hoverflies, butterflies, moths, beetles, birds, bats and others). It identified habitat loss, the use of pesticides in agriculture and the occurrence of invasive alien species as the main causes of this decline and suggested an action plan to increase knowledge and awareness of the problem, and to fight the causes of the decline. A devastating report of the European Court of Auditors clarified in 2020 that the 2018 communication had not led to changes in practice, in particular not in the agricultural sector and as regards the use of pesticides.[146]

The soft measures which had been proposed by the Commission met little opposition. However, when the Commission presented a legislative proposal[147] to reduce, by 2030, the use of pesticides in agriculture by 50 per cent and to restrict the use of pesticides in certain sensitive areas, it obtained a rather angry (agricultural) Council reaction, which considered that the Commission's impact assessment of its proposal – a 322-page paper[148] – had not sufficiently examined the impact on food production in the EU, food prices, small farms, etc.[149] This reaction also echoed the dispute of pesticides containing neonicotinoids – substances harmful to bees – where the European Food Safety Authority (EFSA), in 2013, had provided for new tests of pesticides which took account of their impact on bees; about half of the Member States opposed the adoption of the EFSA guidelines and/or recurred to the bypassing of the ban of three neonicotinoid substances which the Commission had previously imposed.[150] By the end of 2023, the Council were still unable to agree on EFSA's proposal.[151]

[144] IPBES (Intergovernmental Science-Policy Platform on Biodiversity and Ecosystem Services), *Assessment Report on Pollinators, Pollination and Food Production* (Bonn, 2016).

[145] Commission, COM(2018) 395.

[146] European Court of Auditors, *Protection of Wild Pollinators in the EU – Commission Initiatives Have Not Borne Fruit. Special Report 15/2020* (Luxembourg, 2020).

[147] Commission, 'Proposal for a Regulation on the Sustainable Use of Plant Protection Products' COM(2022) 305.

[148] Commission, SWD(2022) 170.

[149] Decision 2022/2572 requesting the Commission to submit a study complementing the impact assessment of its proposal and to propose follow-up actions, if appropriate in view of the outcomes of the study [2022] OJ L331/6.

[150] Commission Implementing Regulation 485/2013 [2013] OJ L139/12; Implementing Regulation 2018/783 to 785 [2018] OJ L132/31, 35 and 40. For details, see European Court of Auditors (n 146) 33–37, Commission, COM(2021) 261, 9s.

[151] CJEU Case C-900/19 (n 137). On the general issue of banning neonicotinoids, see CJEU Case C-499/18P *Bayer CropScience* ECLI:EU:C:2021:367; Case C-514/19 *Union des industries de la protection des plantes* ECLI:EU:C:2020:803; Case C-162/21 *Pesticide Action Network* ECLI:EU:C:2023:30.

The Commission reported on the progress in the protection of pollinators[152] and adopted, in 2023, an updated action plan for pollinators, which again focused largely on soft law measures.[153]

Generally, the following statement appears pertinent to biodiversity protection by the Union even today:[154]

> The absence of a political will, the lack of financial resources, the predominance of traditional interests over ecological interests, outdated systems of criminal law, the inability of environmental associations in many Member States to bring court actions, and the ambiguity of the applicable legal provisions are just a few of the undermining the application of harmonised EC rules. It comes as no surprise that despite the number of laws that now exist with respect to nature conservation, and the many positive impacts that they had, these positive steps are falling short of preventing Noah's Ark to sink.

D. Trade Restrictions

Internationally, the trade in endangered species is regulated by the Convention on International Trade in Endangered Species of Fauna and Flora (CITES), which covers some 30,000 species of animals and plants.[155] CITES was, in the beginning, only open to states, not to international institutions. A 1983 amendment of the convention, which would enable the Union to adhere, only entered into force in 2013.[156] The Union then adhered to the Convention in 2015.[157] However, the Union had applied the provisions of that Convention within the EU since 1982. The last update was in 1997.[158] This Regulation 338/97, which was aligned to many of the decisions by the CITES institutions,[159] is the main instrument of the Union to fight illegal trade in animals and plants. The Council now publishes the position the Union should adopt with regard to any proposed CITES decisions, as well as the statements made by the Union during the CITES Conference.[160] 5-24

Regulation 338/97 only deals with conservation measures. Provisions in earlier regulations and also in the Commission's proposal for Regulation 338/97,[161] which aimed at dealing with questions of public safety and animal welfare, were removed from the final version of the regulation, which led, at the same time, to the taking of Article 192 TFEU as a legal basis, rather than Articles 114 and 207 TFEU, as proposed by the Commission. The regulation treated the Union as a single territory. It introduced a differentiated system of

[152] Commission, COM(2021) 261.

[153] Commission, COM(2023) 35.

[154] N de Sadeleer, 'EC Law and Biodiversity' in R Macrory (ed), *Reflections on 30 Years of EU Environmental Law* (Groningen, 2005) 369.

[155] CITES Convention of 3 March 1973 [1982] OJ L384/8.

[156] The so-called Gaborone amendment of 30 April 1983.

[157] Decision 2015/451 [2015] OJ L75/1.

[158] Regulation 338/97 on the protection of species of wild fauna and flora by regulating trade therein [1997] OJ L61/1; this regulation replaced Regulation 3626/82 [1982] OJ L384/1.

[159] See, eg Commission Regulations 1320/2014 [2014] OJ L361/1; 2016/2029 [2016] OJ L316/1; 2017/127[2017] OJ L21/1; 2017/160 [2017] OJ L27/1; 2019/2117 [2019] OJ L320/13; 2021/2280 [2021] OJ L473/1.

[160] See, eg Decision 2022/2569 on the position to be taken on behalf of the EU at the 19th meeting of the Parties to CITES [2022] OJ L330/186. Council, 'Publication of Statements Made' Doc 5508/23 of 20 January 2023.

[161] [1992] OJ C26/1.

protection. Annex A contained all endangered species which were under the total protection of the CITES Convention, along with a number of other species which were considered threatened under the stricter criteria of the regulation. Trade in these species for primarily commercial purposes was prohibited; only very narrow possibilities for derogation existed. The Commission's proposal generally to prohibit any possession of species listed in annex A was not accepted by the Council.

Annex B contained species which were not actually threatened by trade; however, trade in these species should take place under strict conditions in order to avoid them becoming threatened. Again, the regulation went considerably beyond the requirements of the CITES Convention. Importing these species into the Union required an import licence from the country of destination, which must be presented at the time of importation.

5-25 The import of species listed in annex C of Regulation 338/97 into the Union was subject to the presentation of an import notification rather than a licence. Finally, annex D included species that were not threatened, but were imported into the Union in such quantities that an import notification was considered necessary.

Under Articles 4(6) and 19(2) of Regulation 338/97, the Commission may, under certain ecological conditions, restrict the introduction of certain specimens of species into the Union because of reasons in the country of origin, such as excessive killing or loss of habitats. The amendments to the annexes of the regulation were drawn up by way of a committee procedure, which allowed a speedy reaction to decisions of the contracting parties to the CITES Convention.

Trade transactions which are covered by CITES mainly concern imports. In 2012, some 100,000 such import transactions were reported by Member States, while only 225 exports took place.[162] Illegal trade in endangered species is high; the EU often serves as a transit region.

In 2016, the Commission adopted an action plan against illegal wildlife trafficking,[163] which, it estimated, had more than doubled since 2007 and had created an annual benefit for organised crime of €8–20 billion. The action plan identified a number of shortcomings of the existing structure to fight wildlife trafficking[164] and fixed three main priorities: prevent wildlife trafficking and tackle its root causes; ensure better implementation; and strengthen global partnership. The mixed results of the action plan led to the adoption of a renewed plan in 2022, which repeated the three above-mentioned priorities and added a fourth priority: strengthening the legal and policy framework against wildlife trafficking.[165] Priority was given to prevent trade in wild-sourced reptiles, amphibians, birds, glass eels, African elephants, rhinoceros and pangolins, and medicines/supplements containing

[162] United Nations Environment Programme, 'Analysis of the 2012 EU Annual Reports to CITES' euanalysis/2012.unep.wcmc.org/overview-of-eu-trade. The 10 mostly imported commodities in 2012 were: live plants; plant leaves; plant stems; reptile skins; small leather products; plant wax; plant roots; timber; live corals; and raw corals.

[163] Commission, COM(2016) 87; Commission, 'Progress Report' COM(2018) 711; Commission, 'Evaluation of the Effects of the Plan' SWD(2022) 354.

[164] Commission, SWD(2022) 354: uneven implementation of existing rules; low awareness of problems with wildlife trafficking; insufficient capacities throughout the enforcement chain; co-ordination and information-sharing within Member States; low capacity to fight organised wildlife crime; limited co-operation among Member States and with third countries.

[165] Commission, COM(2022) 581.

illegally harvested wild plants.[166] The protection of African elephants and rhinoceros had already been identified as priorities by the Council,[167] and the Union had adopted, since the mid-1970s, several measures to restrict trade in ivory.[168]

Trade restrictions on seals, which are not an endangered species, will be discussed below, at paragraph 5-33. The trade restrictions with regard to timber and timber products, mentioned above,[169] also have the purpose of protecting tropical forest species. 5-26

The Commission indicated that it had, up to 2016, spent more than €500 million on nature protection measures in Africa.[170] These measures were not, however, aimed at the targeted protection of specific species (elephants, rhinoceros). Indeed, the Union did not aim at the protection of specific species outside trade restriction measures.

E. Invasive Species

In 2014, the EU adopted a Regulation on invasive alien species.[171] Under this regulation, a species is considered alien when it is introduced, by human intervention, outside its natural range. It is considered to be 'invasive' when its adverse impacts are found to threaten biodiversity or the ecosystem services the EU provides (Article 3). Invasive alien species may have 5-27

> severe impacts on native species and the structure and functioning of ecosystems, through the alteration of habitats, predation, competition, the transmission of diseases, the replacement of native species throughout a significant proportion of range and through genetic effects by hybridisation. Furthermore, invasive alien species can also have a significant adverse impact on human health and the economy.[172]

The Commission was asked to establish a Union list of invasive alien species, based on scientific evidence, a risk assessment and a consideration of the cost impact. Article 5 provided for an import, trade, use etc ban for such species. Regional and national invasive alien species were subject to specific provisions of information and co-operation.

Member States may inform the Commission of invasive alien species in order to have them included in the Union list, which shall be regularly updated. Member States were further requested to adopt an action plan in order to identify the pathways of the introduction of invasive alien species. They then had to set up a national surveillance and control system. Whenever they detected invasive alien species that are not yet present in their country or are at an early stage of invasion, they had to notify the Commission. They then shall adopt eradication measures within three months. For invasive alien species that were already established or widely spread, they had to set

166 ibid annex, no 2.
167 Council Decision 2022/2569 [2022] OJ L330/186, no 14.
168 See Commission, Guidance on worked specimens under the EU wildlife trade regulations, C/2017/3108 [2017] OJ C154/15; Revised Guidance document: EU regime governing trade in ivory, C(2021) 7169 [2021] OJ C528/19.
169 See para 5-05.
170 Commission, SWD(2022) 354, 9.
171 Regulation 1143/2014 on invasive alien species [2014] OJ L317/35.
172 ibid Recital 3.

up a management system. National emergency measures may be taken under certain conditions. All Union or national measures were subject to scientific advice and had to take the cost of the envisaged measure into consideration. Regulation 1143/2014 does not apply to genetically modified organisms or to species 'which change their natural range without human intervention, in response to changing ecological conditions and climate change' (Article 2).

The Union list was published in 2016 and enlarged in 2017, 2019 and 2022.[173] At present, it includes 47 animal species and 41 plants. In view of the fact that the regulation estimated the presence of some 12,000 alien species in the EU, 10–15 per cent of which were thought to be invasive (Recital 1), the effectiveness of the regulation will only be able to be assessed in the future.[174]

F. Other Measures

5-28 Among the other measures to be mentioned, capturing methods for capturing animals should be particularly noted. Directives 2009/147 and 92/43 both contain a specific annex prohibiting the use of large-scale or non-selective capturing methods, though they have been unable to stop completely the use of such means within the Union, in particular for bird hunting. As regards the capturing of animals with leghold traps, see paragraph 5-34 below.

Regulation 2019/1241,[175] which replaced a number of earlier legislative acts, prohibited the use of a certain number of fishing practices, such as the use of toxic, stupefying or corrosive substances, electric current, explosives, pneumatic hammers, towed devices for harvesting corals and – with some exceptions – any type of projectile. These restrictions also apply to Union vessels fishing in international waters or in waters of third countries.[176] Furthermore, it prohibited having on board driftnets of more than 2.5 km in length (or, in the Baltic Sea, any driftnet).[177] The reason for this ban was the non-selective character of capturing with driftnets, which may reach 100 km in length; the problem first appeared at global level, when dolphins were captured during the fishing of tuna. Besides this problem, the use of driftnets leads to overfishing and has contributed to the serious depletion of fish resources worldwide and in EU waters. Regulation 2019/1241 also regulated the mesh size and other technical aspects, and restricted the use of some other nets for the capture of certain fish, but it provided for numerous exceptions and derogations, which made the provisions relatively easy to circumvent.

[173] Commission Implementing Regulations 2016/1141 [2016] OJ L189/4; 2017/1263 [2017] OJ L182/37; 2019/1262 [2019] OJ L199/1; 2022/1203 [2022] OJ L186/10.

[174] The Commission's report on the implementation of the regulation, COM(2021) 628, held an assessment to be premature. It considered positively that the regulation had established a Union-wide coherent framework, that the Union lists were relevant for Member States and that information, transparency and awareness of problems caused by invasive alien species had improved.

[175] Regulation 2019/1241 on the conservation of fisheries resources and the protection of marine ecosystems through technical measures [2019] OJ L198/105.

[176] ibid Art 7.

[177] The Member States' enforcement systems did not function well, see CJEU Case C-429/07 *Commission v France* ECLI:EU:C:2009:131; Case C-556/07 *Commission v France* ECLI:EU:C:2009:153; Case C-249/08 *Commission v Italy* ECLI:EU:C:2009:672; yet, a proposal of the Commission to have driftnets generally prohibited, COM(2014) 265, was not adopted.

III. Animal Welfare

A. Animal Welfare and the EU Treaties

Animal welfare concerns animals as living beings. It tries to protect animals independently from the question of whether a species is endangered or not. It is obvious that such a concept is strongly influenced by ethical, religious and similar considerations. The EU Treaties treat animals differently from goods, as appears clearly in Article 36 TFEU, which allows restrictions for the free circulation of goods in order to protect the life and safety of animals and plants; furthermore, trade measures for animals are based on Article 192 TFEU or, in agricultural matters, on Article 43, rather than on Article 114 TFEU. 5-29

At EU level, the idea that animals could or should have rights of their own, or that trees should be important in their own right, has never seriously been discussed: such considerations appear too distant from the anthropocentric concept of nature, in particular in Roman law Member States. A mention of consideration for animals in the Fourth Environmental Action Programme in 1987 did not lead to the development of a coherent approach.

Attempts by animal welfare groups, supported in this also by the European Parliament,[178] to have a specific provision on animal welfare inserted into the EU Treaties, were only successful in 2009. At the conclusion of the Maastricht Treaty, a declaration was made by the Intergovernmental Conference that animal welfare aspects should be taken into consideration in the context of some EU policies.[179] The Amsterdam Treaty on European Union added a protocol to the Treaty,[180] which provided that EU policy should take animal welfare fully into consideration in its policies on agriculture, transport, internal market and research.[181] In 2009, this provision was included in the TFEU, where animals were called 'sentient beings'.[182] It is not quite clear why environmental policy was not also enumerated. 5-30

Wild animals are part of the natural resources; measures to protect them, to provide for their welfare when captured and so on are environmental measures. Indeed, the preservation and protection of natural resources is not limited to protecting endangered species, but applies to all natural resources. Measures regarding wild animals, even where they do not belong to an endangered species, therefore come under Articles 191–93 TFEU. This approach was recognised in 1999, when the Union adopted a directive on the keeping of wild animals in zoos, based on Article 192 TFEU,[183] though it was explicitly mentioned that

[178] 4th Environmental Action Programme 1987–1992 [1987] OJ C328/1, no 5.1.9: 'An improvement in the quality of life also entails respect for animals in the Member States and in the Member States' dealings with the rest of the world. The regular debates concerning the hunting of seal pups should not conceal the many questions raised by the exploitation of animals in Europe: the use of animals for experiments, factory farming, trading in animals and the processing of animals for consumption. The Commission will examine all possible steps which it can take in this connection.'

[179] See European Parliament, Resolution of 21 January 1994 [1994] OJ C44/206; the European Parliament in particular wanted animals to be no longer called, within the context of agricultural policy, 'agricultural products'.

[180] [1992] OJ C191/1, Declaration no 12.

[181] [1997] OJ C340/110.

[182] Art 13 TFEU: 'In formulating and implementing the Union's agricultural, fisheries, transport, internal market, research and technological development and space policies, the Union and the Member States shall, since animals are sentient beings, pay full regard to the welfare requirements of animals, while respecting the legislative or administrative provisions and customs of the Member States relating in particular to religious rights, cultural traditions and regional heritage.'

[183] See para 5-36.

this directive intended to protect (endangered) species of animals, not individual animals. However, it is obviously erroneous to consider all animals in zoos to be specimens of endangered species.

I would not classify domestic animal welfare measures as environmental measures. The agricultural provisions of the Treaties are *leges speciales* to the environmental provisions. It is certain, though, that the EU agricultural and transport animal welfare measures need considerably strengthening in order to ensure adequate animal welfare.

5-31 The main legal problem is that the rules of international trade, established by the General Agreement on Tariffs and Trade (GATT) and the World Trade Organization (WTO), are generally interpreted as prohibiting measures which restrict trade because of the production methods – or, as regards wild animals, capturing methods – used. Debate about these issues is not very thorough, as the examples of products made by working children or those produced in jail demonstrate; indeed, trade in such products may be prohibited under GATT/WTO rules. As further discussed below, though, the WTO accepted, in 2014, an EU ban on trade in seals as justified on moral grounds, though seals are not an endangered species.

The discussion on environmentally sustainable production methods – an example is the consideration of import restrictions for tropical wood that does not stem from sustainable production – has only just started. In the early 1990s, the Union began to take measures in order to prevent possible conflicts with the WTO or trading partners which might end in formal WTO proceedings.[184] This explains why the full implementation of animal welfare measures is often delayed.

B. Tests with Animals

5-32 Directive 2010/63[185] limited the use of animals for experimental or scientific purposes, in particular in order to avoid unnecessary experiments and to avoid pain, distress and lasting harm. The directive is based on Article 114 TFEU, but allows Member States to maintain stricter measures at national level (Article 2). It laid down detailed provisions on the authorisation of animal testing, the persons responsible for experiments, the keeping of animals, the establishments, etc; detailed guidelines for accommodation and care of animals are annexed to the directive. Particular restrictions apply to endangered animals and great apes.

Whether the directive applies when animals are used to 'produce', for instance, a secretion, blood or antibodies was doubtful and, since 1986, this question has been answered differently by Member States. The limitation of animals to use for experimental or other scientific purposes (Article 3(1)) and the limitation of 'procedures' to basic, translational or applied research with specific aims (Article 5) indicate that Directive 2010/63 does not allow animals to be used for such production purposes.

Animals may not be used where another scientifically satisfactory method or testing strategy is available (Article 4). Endangered species and non-human primates may normally

[184] See also paras 5-33 and 12-14ff.

[185] Directive 2010/63 on the protection of animals used for scientific purposes [2010] OJ L276/33; this directive replaced Directive 86/609 [1986] OJ L358/1.

not be used for scientific purposes (Articles 7 and 8); animals taken from the wild may not be taken either, though national authorities may grant derogations (Article 9).

Since 1994, the Commission has published reports on statistical data concerning the practical application of Directive 86/609, the predecessor of Directive 2010/63.[186] The figures in these reports are not comparable, as the number of EU Member States changed and the statistical methods used for calculations were amended. The report of 2020, which covers the year 2017, only gave rather general data. According to that report, there were about 12.6 million animals used for scientific or experimental purposes, compared with 12 million animals in 2008. Mice (10.5 million, or 83 per cent of the animals used), zebra fish (696,000, or seven per cent) and rats (568,000, or five per cent) were the most used animals. No great apes were used.[187] 5-33

The Union adhered to the Council of Europe Convention for the protection of vertebrate animals used for experimental and other scientific purposes in 1998.[188]

In 1993, the Directive on cosmetic products[189] was amended with a view to banning, as of 1 January 1998, cosmetic products containing ingredients or combinations of ingredients tested on animals.[190] This date was subsequently extended several times, eventually becoming effective in 2013.[191]

Regulation 1907/2006 on chemicals[192] contained specific provisions in order to reduce and avoid the duplication of testing on vertebrate animals and even imposed, under certain conditions, the sharing of test studies.[193] Provisions with the same objective are contained in the regulations on pesticides and biocides.[194]

C. Seals

Beginning in 1982, the killing of baby seals, particularly in Canada, attracted considerable attention from the Western European media. The European Parliament asked for an import ban on baby seal furs[195] and environmental organisations urged action. Although the Council strongly doubted the possibility of banning imports of baby seal furs,[196] it finally adopted such an import ban for two years.[197] After an initial prolongation to four years, the 5-34

[186] Commission, COM(95) 195; COM(1999) 191; COM(2003) 19; COM(2005) 7; COM(2007) 675; COM(2010) 511.

[187] Commission, COM(2020) 15 and SWD(2020) 15.

[188] Decision1999/575 [1999] OJ L222/29; the convention is published in the annex to this decision.

[189] Directive 93/35 [1993] OJ L151/32.

[190] See Directive 76/768 on cosmetic products [1976] OJ L262/169, Art 4(1.i) as amended by Directive 93/35 (n 189) and Directive 2000/41 [2000] OJ L145/25.

[191] See now Regulation 1223/2009 on cosmetic products [2009] OJ L342/59, Art 18.

[192] Regulation1907/2006 [2006] OJ L396/1.

[193] ibid Recitals 33 and 47 and Art 26ff.

[194] See Regulation 1107/2009 on pesticides [2009] OJ L309/1, Art 62; Regulation 528/12 on biocides [2012] OJ L167/1, Art 62: 'In order to avoid animal testing, testing on vertebrates for the purposes of this Regulation shall be undertaken only as a last resort. Testing on vertebrates shall not be repeated for the purposes of this Regulation.'

[195] European Parliament, Resolutions of 11 March 1982 [1982] OJ C87/87 and [1982] OJ C267/47.

[196] Resolution of 5 January1983 [1983] OJ C14/1; France, the UK, Belgium, Denmark and Greece were reported to have opposed measures, since these would be motivated by purely moral motives.

[197] Directive 83/129 concerning the importation into Member States of skins of certain seal pups and products derived therefrom [1983] OJ L91/30.

import ban was further extended, in 1989, for an undetermined time.[198] The directives did not argue that seals are an endangered species. For that reason alone, the only justification for the import ban on furs and other seal products were the killing methods which were used, thus animal welfare considerations.

Since 2002/03, Canada has allowed the hunting and killing of several million seals per year that were not considered to be endangered species. In reaction to that, Belgium and the Netherlands adopted national legislation which prohibited the trade in seal products, pointing to the fact that such a ban has been effective in the USA for decades and that Mexico had introduced a similar ban in 2005. Several other Member States considered similar action. In view of this, the Commission proposed a regulation banning trade in seal products, which the European Parliament and the Council adopted in 2009.[199] Canada and Norway submitted the matter to the WTO, arguing that this was an unjustified barrier to the free trade in products. Their application was rejected, as the WTO considered the EU measures justified on public moral grounds.[200] The EU lost on a few minor points, but amended the Seals Regulation in order to bring it fully into line with the WTO requirements.[201] Canadian groups also attacked the regulation before the CJEU, but without success.[202]

This clarifies that such a ban is, for animal welfare reasons, compatible with Article 36 TFEU, as well as with the corresponding WTO/GATT rules. Indeed, public opinion in the Union does not accept the methods which are used in Canada for the hunting of seals, which frequently lead to the skinning of live animals. Public morals and animal welfare considerations cannot be the same all over the world; it must be thus a decision for each individual state – or, in this case, the European Union – whether it considers public morals to be affected or not.

D. Leghold Traps

5-35 Regulation 3254/91 prohibited, as of 1995, the use of leghold traps within the Union.[203] Leghold traps, which hold the leg of a captured animal until the hunter arrives or until the animal dies, are considered non-selective[204] and cruel (not 'humane'). Bans or restrictions on the use of leghold traps are in use in about 60 states all over the world.[205]

[198] Directive 85/444 [1985] OJ L259/70; Directive 89/370 [1989] OJ L163/37.

[199] Regulation 1007/2009 on trade in seal products [2009] OJ L286/36.

[200] WTO Document WT/DS 400 and DS 401/AB/R of 29 April 2014. The relevant provision of the WTO/GATT Agreement reads: 'Article XX: Subject to the requirement that such measures are not applied in a manner which would constitute a means of arbitrary or unjustifiable discrimination between countries where the same conditions prevail, or a disguised restriction on international trade, nothing in this Agreement shall be construed to prevent the adoption or enforcement by any contracting party of measures (a) necessary to protect public morals.'

[201] Regulation 2015/1775 [2015] OJ L262/1.

[202] CJEU Case C-583/11P *Inuit Katanami and others v European Parliament and Council* ECLI:EU:C:2013:625.

[203] Regulation 3254/91 prohibiting the use of leghold traps in the Community and the introduction into the Community of pelts and manufactured goods of certain wild animal species originating in countries which catch them by means of leghold traps or trapping methods which do not meet international humane trapping standards [1991] OJ L308/1.

[204] According to figures quoted by the European Economic and Social Committee (EECOSOC), Opinion of 26 April 1990 [1990] OJ C168/32, no 1.6.3, about 10% of animals caught in leghold traps are caught unintentionally.

[205] Written Question 1936/88 (Zarges) [1989] OJ C255/15.

While this ban is undisputed, the Commission had – subsequent to a petition of 272 Members of the European Parliament – proposed and the Council had adopted an import ban on the furs of 13 animal species (beaver, otter, coyote, wolf, lynx, bobcat, sable, raccoon, muskrat, fisher (*Martes pennanti*), badger, marten and ermine) from those countries which continued to use leghold traps.[206] The import ban was to come into effect in 1995;[207] the Council expected that by then internationally 'humane trapping standards' would be agreed.

However, this was not the case. In particular, the USA, Canada and Russia heavily opposed the import ban, arguing that it was contrary to the rules of the GATT/WTO and disadvantaged indigenous populations. In view of this, the Commission proposed, in December 1995, to replace the import ban by a mandate to be given to the Union in order to negotiate an agreement with third countries on humane trapping standards.[208] The Council agreed to negotiations. An agreement with Canada and Russia was reached in 1997, and another with the USA in 1998.[209] The agreements provided essentially for the fixing of some trapping standards and the phasing out, within four years, of some leghold traps for two species, without containing a legally enforceable commitment. In substance, the Union thus abandoned its import ban with regard to these three countries. Regulation 3254/91 has not yet been amended. Thus, for other third countries, the import ban entered into effect in 1997.[210] 5-36

In 2004, the Commission proposed a directive in order to implement the two international agreements.[211] However, the European Parliament rejected the proposal with its absolute majority, arguing that the proposal intended to consider the actual practice of Canadian, US and Russian trappers as 'humane' trapping methods, without having made scientific research as to less painful trapping methods. The proposal is thus politically dead.

E. Animals in Zoos

5-37 In 1991, the Commission proposed a directive on the keeping of animals in zoos, of which there are about 1000 within the Union.[212] Following the extensive discussion on subsidiarity and deregulation which followed the signing of the Maastricht Treaty on European Union in 1991, the proposal was listed, by the Edinburgh summit meeting of the European Council and under pressure from the UK, as one of the instruments for which

[206] The Commission's proposal [1989] OJ C134/5 did not contain a ban on leghold traps, since such a ban had been proposed in the Directive on habitats [1988] OJ C247/3; since it thus only contained an import ban, it was based on Art 207 TFEU. The Council Regulation was based on Arts 207 and 192 TFEU.

[207] Subsequently, there was a controversy whether the ban did indeed become effective. Art 3(1) of Regulation 3254/91 stipulates: 'The introduction into the Community of the pelts … shall be prohibited as of 1 January 1995, unless the Commission [states that in a third country leghold traps or inhumane trapping methods are forbidden]'. This wording indicates, in my opinion without any legal doubt, that the ban became effective as of 1 January 1995, since the Commission has not made any such statement.

[208] [1996] OJ C58/17.

[209] Decision 98/142 [1998] OJ L42/40 (Canada and Russia); Decision 98/487 [1998] OJ L219/24 (USA); the Decisions were based on Arts 207 and 114 TFEU; see also European Parliament [1998] OJ C210/31, which had rejected the agreements.

[210] See Decision 97/602 [1997] OJ L242/64; see also Written Question E-294/98 (Pollack) [1998] OJ C223/160.

[211] Commission, COM(2004) 532.

[212] [1991] OJ C241/14.

the subsidiarity clause should apply; this meant that the Union should leave the matter to Member States to deal with. The Commission thus withdrew its proposal and replaced it with a proposal for a Council recommendation which contained detailed guidelines on the accommodation and care of animals in zoos.[213]

The European Parliament and EECOSOC both pleaded in favour of a directive. The Council first agreed unanimously on a common position concerning a recommendation. However, upon the instigation of the UK, which completely changed its position of 1992 at the Edinburgh summit, it changed the principal objective of the instrument to make it an instrument for the conservation of biodiversity; the detailed rules on accommodation and care of animals were deleted. Zoos were mainly considered to have a role in the conservation of biodiversity, though it was obvious to everybody that the animals kept in zoos were not all endangered. Zoos had to have a permit and were to be regularly inspected by the national competent authorities. On this basis, a directive was adopted in 1999 based on Article 192(1) TFEU.[214] It is remarkable, though, that the Commission does not monitor its application. The Commission published a document of good practices of zoos.[215] A report of 2018 on the evaluation of Directive 1999/22 was essentially based on information from 14 Member States and thus of limited usefulness. It concluded (of course) that the directive was fit for purpose.[216]

[213] Commission, COM(95) 619.

[214] Directive 1999/22 on the keeping of wild animals in zoos [1999] OJ L94/24.

[215] Commission, *EU Zoos Good Practices* (Luxemburg, 2015).

[216] Commission, 'Evaluation of Directive 1999/22' SWD(2018) 455.

6

Products

I. General Questions

There is no consistent and coherent EU policy on products. Most of the product-related measures adopted meant to establish common rules for the establishment and functioning of the internal EU market and thus enable the free circulation of goods. Aspects of health, safety, consumer protection and, at a later stage, environmental protection were not systematically tackled at EU level but, rather, were left to be regulated at Member State level; however, common rules progressively became necessary in order to ensure a level playing field. The so-called 'new approach' to product standards' harmonisation, introduced in the 1980s by a Council Resolution,[1] where EU legislation only fixes the essential requirements for a product, leaving the details to industrial standardisation by European standardisation organisations, has not changed this situation. Indeed, these 'essential requirements' normally referred to health and safety aspects of a product, not its impact on the environment. The Regulation on general product safety refers to the 'safety and health of persons', and only concerns environmental risks 'inasmuch as it poses a risk to the health and safety of consumers'.[2] And legislation on the protection of workers at the working place is limited to that area, but has no general application.[3] 6-01

In a judgment of 2009, the Court of Justice of the European Union (CJEU) held that, as regards mercury, references to 'health' also included environmental concerns. Thus, where the Union had regulated health aspects of products containing mercury, Member States were barred from adopting measures at national level which concerned the environmental aspects of mercury.[4] This judgment, which has remained isolated, ignored the dividing line which primary and secondary EU law draws between the protection of health and safety on the one side, and the protection of the environment on the other side. As Regulation 2023/988[5] does not deal with environmental safety, Member States are, in this author's opinion, entitled to regulate such issues.

A Regulation on the market surveillance of products asked Member States to establish market surveillance authorities which had to ensure that only those products which

[1] Council Resolution of 7 May 1985 [1985] OJ C136/1.

[2] Regulation 2023/988 on general product safety [2023] OJ L135/1. This regulation replaced earlier legislation, in particular Directive 2001/95 [2002] OJ L11/4. Sometimes, acts on specific products include a reference to the protection of the environment; see, eg Directive 2014/90 on marine equipment [2014] OJ L257/146; Directive 2009/48 on toys [2009] OJ L170/1, annex II.

[3] For details, see on the EU product policy approach Commission, The 'Blue Guide' on the implementation of EU product policy 2022 [2022] OJ C247/1.

[4] CJEU Case C-288/08 *Kemikalieinspektionen* ECLI:EU:C:2009:718.

[5] Regulation 2023/988 (n 2).

complied with harmonised Union legislation – that legislation was enumerated in an annex – were placed on the Union market.[6] Where a Member State was of the opinion that a product presented a risk to humans or to the environment, it had to take appropriate and proportionate corrective measures. Several provisions intended to ensure co-ordination and collaboration between the national authorities.

6-02 Scientific advice on chemical substances and products is made available by the European Chemicals Agency (ECHA), which was set up under Regulation 1907/2006[7] and which also advises on biocidal products.[8] The European Food Safety Authority (EFSA)[9] advises on food and feed, pesticides and genetically modified organisms (GMOs). Furthermore, since 2015, the Commission is advised on the environmental aspects of its product policy by a Scientific Committee on Health, Environment and Emerging Risks (SCHEER), which replaced earlier scientific committees.[10] SCHEER gives, on request, scientific advice to the Commission and may also draw its attention to a specific or emerging problem for which the request for scientific advice might be opportune. For example, in 2021, requests for an opinion concerned possible health effects of the exposure to electromagnetic fields and environmental quality standards for priority substances under the Water Framework Directive.[11]

The Joint Research Centre at Ispra (Italy), originally set up under Article 8 of the Euratom Treaty to promote nuclear research, developed into a technical and scientific research body to support the Commission's policy.

6-03 Product policy inevitably affects health and safety, consumer protection and environmental impairment, aspects which cannot clearly be dissociated from each other. EU efforts concentrate on the attempts to find a balance between health and safety of humans on the one hand and the free circulation of goods, their export and import on the other. Environmental concerns play a secondary role. The fact that substances or products – in the form of emissions, goods, wastes, residues, etc – exist everywhere in the environment and present considerable risks to biodiversity, soil, fresh and marine waters or buildings has not led to the setting up of a product policy which is less anthropocentric and more integrated.

The Commission's attempt to launch an 'integrated product policy'[12] did not really contain what the title promised. The Commission defined integrated product policy 'as an approach which seeks to reduce the life cycle environmental impacts of products from the mining of raw materials to production, distribution, use and waste management'.[13] This approach was thus limited to trying to integrate environmental requirements into product-related aspects. The Commission favoured non-binding instruments under this approach,

[6] Regulation 2019/2010 on market surveillance and compliance of products [2019] OJ L169/1.

[7] Regulation 1907/2006 on the registration, evaluation, authorisation and restriction of chemicals (REACH) and setting up a European Chemcials Agency [2006] OJ L396/1.

[8] Regulation 528/2012 concerning the making available on the market and use of biocidal products [2012] OJ L167/1.

[9] The EFSA was set up under Regulation 178/2002 laying down the general principles and requirements of food law, establishing the European Food Safety Authority and laying down the procedures in matters of food law [2002] OJ L31/1.

[10] Commission Decision C(2015)5383 establishing scientific committees in the field of public health, consumer safety and the environment.

[11] Directive 2000/60 establishing a framework for Community action in the field of water policy [2000] OJ L327/1.

[12] Commission, 'Green Paper on Integrated Product Policy' COM(2001) 68; Commission, COM(2003) 302.

[13] Commission, COM(2001) 68 2.

and in 2005 and 2006 published the results of two pilot projects, on mobile phones and teak garden chairs; there was no further follow-up on either of these projects. Since then, the whole discussion on integrated product policy has largely come to a standstill.[14]

In the context of its policy for a green deal for Europe,[15] the Commission announced a 'strong and coherent product policy framework that will make sustainable products, services and business models the norm'.[16] In pursuance thereof, the Commission adopted a recommendation on the life cycle assessment method to quantify the environmental impacts of products[17] and proposed, on the basis of Article 114 of the Treaty on the Functioning of the Union (TFEU), a regulation 'establishing a framework for setting eco-design requirements for sustainable products',[18] which built on the assumption that up to 80 per cent of products' environmental impacts are determined at the design stage.[19] The proposal listed a number of sustainability requirements, the details of which were to be further elaborated by the Commission in delegated acts.[20] The very detailed proposal, which would imply, for the next five years, costs for the Commission alone of €106 million,[21] is at present being discussed by the other Union institutions.

Generally, the Union tries to avoid regulating products directly, but influences production and placing on the market through emission limits, provisions on substances, additives or other indirect measures. A good example of this policy is PVC (polyvinyl chloride), a plastic product. Vinyl chloride is a known carcinogen and the additives which influence PVC's properties – phthalates, lead, cadmium in particular – are also considered dangerous to human health and the environment. The Union partly regulated the additives,[22] but has never directly regulated PVC.

More important perhaps than the conceptual differences are the concrete actions which 6-04
are undertaken. Almost all depend on the political determination to bring the concept of sustainable product policy, which replaced the concept of integrated product policy, into reality. An important principle in this concept is the substitution principle, which the EU Sixth Environmental Action Programme described as follows:[23] 'Chemicals that are dangerous should be replaced by safer chemicals or safer alternative technologies not entailing the use of chemicals, with the aim of reducing risks to man and the environment.'

[14] Commission, 'Report on the State of Implementation of Integrated Product Policy' COM(2009) 693; Commission, 'An Integrated Industrial Policy for the Globalisation Area; Putting Competitiveness and Sustainability at Centre Stage' COM(2010) 614.

[15] Commission, COM(2019) 640.

[16] Commission, 'A New Circular Economy Action Plan. For a Cleaner and More Competitive Europe' COM(2020) 98, s 2.1. See also Commission, 'A New Industrial Strategy for Europe' COM(2020) 102.

[17] Commission Recommendation 2021/2279 on the use of the Environmental Footprint methods to measure and communicate the life cycle environmental performance of products and organisations [2021] OJ L471/1.

[18] Commission, COM(2021) 142.

[19] Commission, COM(2020) 98 (n 16) s 2.1.

[20] Commission, COM(2021) 142 (n 18) Arts 1 and 4. These proposed requirements are: durability and reliability; reusability; upgradability, reparability, maintenance and refurbishment; the presence of substances of concern; energy use and resource efficiency; recycled content; remanufacturing and recycling; the carbon and environmental footprint; and the expected generation of waste materials.

[21] ibid annex.

[22] See, eg Regulation 1907/2006 (n 7) annex XVII, nos 23 (cadmium), 51 (phthalates) and 63 (lead); Commission Regulation 2023/923 on the lead content of PVC [2023] OJ L123/1.

[23] Decision 1600/2002 laying down the Sixth Community Environmental Action Programme [2002] OJ L242/1, Recital 25 and Art 7(1). Such a commitment is, however, *not* repeated in Decision 1386/2013 on a general Union environment action programme to 2020 [2013] OJ L354/171.

Though the principle's application is limited, in this context, to chemicals, its application is much broader and, it is submitted, applies to all products.[24] The substitution principle is also expressed in Regulation 528/2012 on biocidal products[25] and in Directive 2011/65, which limits the use of certain dangerous substances in electrical and electronic equipment and which provides that substances other than those mentioned in the directive shall be regulated in view of their substitution by environmentally more friendly substances, as soon as sufficient scientific information is available.[26]

In 2001, a judgment of the CJEU showed strong sympathy for the substitution principle in environmental law.[27] Regulation 1907/2006 on chemical products, REACH (see paragraph 6-24ff, below), tried to make the substitution principle one of the cornerstones of the new system on chemicals.[28]

Also, Regulation 1107/2009, concerning the placing on the market of pesticides and biocides, provided for recurrence to the substitution principle.[29] In 2015, the Commission published a list of 77 active substances of pesticides that were candidates for substitution; in 2020, it added seven substances to that list, and in 2022 deleted 47 from it.[30] The exact number of substances which were actually substituted is not published; environmental organisations argue that practically no substitutions have taken place. The very fact that an active substance is on a candidate list for substitution does not necessarily have a direct effect, but may only influence the authorisation procedure of products containing such substances.[31]

The integrated or sustainable product policy approach at EU level had never mentioned the substitution principle as one that would be guiding action in this area. It is not clear either yet which other principles apply and whether there will be any attempt to systematically address environmental issues caused by products. In my opinion, a sustainable product policy must base itself, in particular, on the following four principles:

1. The substitution principle, according to which substances of concern (carcinogens, etc) should not be used in products where substances that are less dangerous for humans or the environment are available.
2. The precautionary principle, according to which the absence of scientific certainty does not prevent the taking of action where a presumption of a risk to humans or the environment exists.
3. The minimisation principle, according to which a product should have the smallest possible adverse impact on humans and the environment.
4. The principle of producer responsibility, according to which the producer shall be responsible for the product from the selection and choice of the raw materials to when it has finished its useful lifetime and becomes waste.

[24] See also CJEU Case C-473/98 *Toolex* ECLI:EU:C:2000:379.

[25] Regulation 528/2012 (n 8).

[26] Directive 2011/65 on the restriction of the use of certain dangerous substances in electrical and electronic equipment [2011] OJ L174/88, Recitals 16 and 18 and Art 5. This directive replaced Directive 2002/95 [2003] OJ L37/19.

[27] CJEU Case C-473/98 (n 24); see also CJEU Case C-389/19P *Commission v Sweden* ECLI:EU:C:2021:131.

[28] Regulation 1907/2006 (n 7).

[29] Regulation 1107/2009 concerning the placing on the market of plant protection products [2009] OJ L309/1.

[30] Commission, Implementing Regulation 2015/408 [2015] OJ L67/18; Implementing Regulation 2020/1295 [2020] OJ L303/18; Implementing Regulation 2022/1252 [2022] OJ L191/41.

[31] See Regulation 1907/2006 (n 7) Art 55; General Court Case T-350/15 *Copper Task Force v Commission* ECLI:EU:T:2016:265.

Efforts to formulate an EU product policy are also hampered by the fact that products (goods) are the subject of trade, and EU-wide and international efforts are dominated by the attempt to ensure free trade in goods. Free trade in goods should therefore only be restricted where the risk assessment for substances or products demonstrates an unacceptable risk to health or the environment. Where such a risk assessment also includes a cost–benefit analysis, the objective is no longer to minimise the adverse impact of products on humans and the environment, but rather to minimise the impact of environmental measures on trade in goods.

The attempts to minimise the environmental impact on the free circulation of goods involved requested Member States, before adopting any product-related legislation that might affect the free circulation of goods, to transmit their draft legislation, together, 'if available', with a risk analysis, to the Commission and to all other Member States.[32] For chemicals, Regulation 1907/2006 now requires producers and importers to deliver the results of safety tests to the ECHA, which means that they have to make a sort of impact assessment; the difference to the previous legislation is that it is no longer the public authorities which have to test the safety of chemicals.[33] This is the consequence of the general understanding that risk assessment was slow and resource-intensive, and did not allow the system to work efficiently and effectively.[34] In the past, the Commission had committed itself to carrying out risk assessments and adequate analyses of the costs and benefits prior to any proposal or adoption of a regulatory measure affecting the chemical industry.[35] 6-05

This policy of requiring that any action on the restriction of use of a substance is preceded by a risk assessment contradicts the precautionary principle of Article 191 TFEU, which asks EU institutions to act even in cases where there is scientific uncertainty as to the harmfulness of a substance to humans or the environment. In case of doubt, these principles suggest EU action, so that, in the case of an error, free trade is affected rather than human health or the environment: where a product or a substance is suspected to be dangerous, it is appropriate to act and not to wait for definitive scientific evidence. 6-06

It is comforting that in the past, the Commission itself has not systematically provided for a risk assessment on specific substances, in particular in those cases where public opinion was concerned about the risks of a substance for humans or when Member States took action to restrict the use of a substance. Cases dealt with since 1997 where the results of a risk assessment were not available before EU legislative action was started concern phthalates,[36] asbestos,[37] greenhouse gases,[38] ozone-depleting substances,[39] the restriction of heavy metals in cars[40] or in electrical and electronic equipment,[41] the measures taken in reaction to the accident of *The Prestige* tanker off the Spanish coast in November 2002[42]

[32] Directive 2015/1535 laying down a procedure for the provision of information in the field of technical regulations and of rules on Information Society services [2015] OJ L241/1, Art 5(1).

[33] Regulation 1907/2006 (n 7).

[34] See in more detail para 6-24ff.

[35] Commission, 'White Paper on Chemical Policy' COM(1998) 88, no 2.1.

[36] See para 6-24ff.

[37] See para 4-54.

[38] See para 9-04ff.

[39] See paras 6-23 and 9-37.

[40] Directive 2000/53 on end-of-life vehicles [2000] OJ L269/34.

[41] Directive 2011/65 (n 26).

[42] See Commission, 'Report on Actions to Deal with the Effects of the Prestige Disaster' COM(2003) 105.

or cadmium in batteries and accumulators.[43] Requesting a risk analysis and a cost–benefit analysis in all cases neglects the fact that the environment suffers from the presence of too many pollutants. Accident prevention and remediation procedures are very important for the environment; however, the primary aim of any environmental policy should be to prevent environmental impairment and therefore to reduce the placing of environmentally hazardous substances into the environment.

The CJEU, in its judgment in Case C-180/96, confirmed the possibility for preventive action without putting as a condition that a risk assessment or cost–benefit analysis must be undertaken beforehand.[44] Nothing else can apply to the protection of the environment, especially as the CJEU, in its above-mentioned judgment and in later decisions, expressly referred to the necessity of preventive action, as laid down in Article 191(2) TFEU.

It is to be expected that the battle will continue between supporters of a wide application of the precautionary and prevention principles in order to promote an active, environmentally sound EU product policy and supporters of the unhampered circulation of goods who try to introduce risk analyses, life-cycle assessments and cost–benefit calculations into any such decision-making, limit precautionary measures to provisional action, etc. This discussion will be of particular importance in the context of the increasing number of free trade agreements which the EU has concluded or intends to conclude with South Korea, Vietnam, Canada, Japan and other countries.

II. Composition and Marketing of Products

6-07 There are only a few EU provisions on the making of products. It is general EU policy that a certain technology for products should not be prescribed in order to reach environmental results and that EU legislation should set targets (results) to be achieved, such as emission limits, and leave it to manufacturers how to achieve these results. Obviously, this principle applies more to machinery than to other products. Indeed, chemical legislation does provide, via the establishment of lists of substances that may or that may not be used in a product, for direct influence on the product; an example is the sector of pesticides, where EU legislation is setting up a list of active substances that may be used in pesticides, while leaving the composition of the pesticides to the producer.[45] Also, the legislation on end-of-life vehicles and on electrical and electronic products which prohibits the use of certain heavy metals in these products belongs to this category.[46]

In contrast to that, the Union has never applied the principle of Article 191(2) TFEU, according to which environmental impairment should be rectified at source, to its general product-related legislation. For example, it did not request cars to be equipped, from a certain time onwards, with catalytic converters, but rather fixed emission limit values that, at the time when they were fixed, could only be reached when a catalytic converter was used.

[43] Directive 2006/66 on batteries and accumulators and waste batteries and accumulators [2006] OJ L266/1.

[44] CJEU Case C-180/96 *United Kingdom v Commission* ECLI:EU:C:1998:192; see also European Parliament Resolution of 20 October 1998 [1998] OJ C341/31 on endocrine disruptors.

[45] See para 6-33ff.

[46] See Directive 2000/53 (n 40); Directive 2011/65 (n 26).

In the same way, it is unthinkable that EU legislation would ever require cars to be built in a way that they cannot run quicker than 100 km/h or that they use no more than 3 l of petrol per 100 km; at least this last legislation is partly in force in California. Within the Union and in Germany, France, Italy, etc, the car industry is much too influential to ever accept such legislation.

In 2005, the Council and Parliament adopted Directive 2005/32 on the ecodesign of energy-using products, which was updated in 2009 by Directive 2009/125.[47] The latter directive was based on Article 114 TFEU; it was part of the Union's policy to fight climate change by increasing energy efficiency. It provided for measures at EU level to reduce energy consumption of products, relying to a considerable degree on self-regulation, industrial standardisation, etc. As a first step, stand-by losses and products that offer a high potential for cost-effective reduction of greenhouse gas emissions, such as heating and water heating equipment, electric motor systems lighting, domestic appliances, office equipment, consumer electronics and heating–ventilating–air conditioning systems were tackled. The instruments used were Commission regulations, adopted in the form of comitology decisions. Voluntary agreements by producers and industrial standards which should, according to Directive 2009/125, be preferred to regulatory measures played only a very minimal role: economic operators appeared to be too afraid of free-riders and third country producers who would not be subjected to voluntary provisions, and preferred the legal certainty offered by legislative acts. Though the directive allowed other issues of ecodesign to be tackled, such as water consumption, noise levels or material use, it was clarified in the recitals that the (only) priority would be to reduce the emission of greenhouse gases.[48]

At the end of 2005, the Commission published a communication on a thematic strategy for the sustainable use of natural resources.[49] The communication underlined the necessity of life-cycle thinking for products, from raw materials to the waste stage. The objective was to reduce the environmental impact of using natural resources. The measures announced mainly addressed Member States and did not anticipate the promotion of legally binding instruments to ensure 'ecologically sound and sustainable product design'. The Commission expressly clarified that it had no intention of phasing out bad materials for the making of products. Nor were any binding instruments proposed to prevent waste generation.[50] Overall, the strategy[51] was not really a strategy, but a – rather superficial – description of the situation and the expression of hope that something would change in the future. And the strategy was not followed by concrete action. As mentioned above, it was only in 2021 that the Commission proposed, in the context of its objective to promote a circular economy, a regulation to considerably broaden the ecodesign approach.[52]

[47] Directive 2005/32 [2005] OJ L191/29; in 2009, this directive was replaced by Directive 2009/125 establishing a framework for the setting of ecodesign requirements for energy-related products [2009] OJ L285/10.

[48] Directive 2009/125 (n 47) Recital 14: 'Although a comprehensive approach to environmental performance is desirable, greenhouse gas mitigation through increased energy efficiency should be considered a priority environmental goal, pending the adoption of a working plan.'

[49] Commission, COM(2005) 667.

[50] ibid.

[51] Commission, 'Communication: Taking Sustainable Use of Resources Forward: A Thematic Strategy on the Prevention and Recycling of Waste' COM(2005) 666.

[52] See para 6-03.

6-08 Environmental directives and regulations have established some lists of substances or products[53] that were considered dangerous for the environment, frequently taking inspiration from international environmental agreements.

As regards water discharges, Directive 76/464, which, in 2006, was codified as Directive 2006/11, created a blacklist of substances and products, which were selected because of their toxicity, persistence and bioaccumulation; a second list was fixed for those substances which have 'a deleterious effect on the aquatic environment'.[54] For list I, a priority list of 129 substances was then agreed, which should be regulated by Community emission standards;[55] these measures were brought to a halt in 1991, after only 17 substances had been regulated. Under Directive 2000/60,[56] which repealed Directive 76/464 by 2013, a list of hazardous substances was established in 2001 which were to be further examined in view of a prohibition to discharge them into waters.[57] This list included substances such as atrazine, benzene, naphthalene, pentachlorophenol and simazine, as well as groups of substances such as cadmium, mercury, nickel, lead and their compounds. In 2008, a directive fixed environmental water quality standards and pollution controls for the substances of the 2001 list as well as for eight new substances, and abandoned the objective of prohibiting their discharge.[58] A new directive of 2013 brought further amendments and prolonged the date for compliance until 2021 and 2027.[59] A decision of 2015 introduced, for the first time, a watch list for substances for which Union-wide data gathering appeared necessary; this watch list is regularly updated.[60] The Renewed Drinking Water Directive also provided for a watch list.[61]

For air pollutants, Directive 84/360 on air emissions[62] contained another list of pollutants the emissions of which were to be limited; no indication was given as to how these substances had been selected. The pollutants were not tackled systematically. This list was practically replaced by another list of air pollutants which was laid down in Directive 96/62 on ambient air quality and for which air quality standards were to be elaborated;[63] on pollutants in general, Directive 96/61 – replaced in 2008 by Directive 2008/1 and in 2010 by Directive 2010/75 – on integrated prevention and pollution control laid down a list for air and water pollutants which were emitted by industrial installations.[64]

[53] EU terminology is not consistent. Sometimes, the word 'substances' is used, where clearly a preparation, ie a mixture or composition of two or more substances, is meant.

[54] Directive 76/464 on pollution caused by certain dangerous substances discharged into the aquatic environment of the Community [1976] OJ L129/23, in particular Art 6 and annex, list I; codification of Directive 76/464 by Directive 2006/11 [2006] OJ L64/52.

[55] Council Resolution of February 1983 [1983] OJ C46/17. For details on the monitoring of Directive 76/464, see para 7-05.

[56] Directive 2000/60 (n 11).

[57] Decision 2455/2001 establishing the list of priority substances in the field of water policy [2001] OJ L331/1.

[58] Directive 2008/105 on environmental quality standards in the field of water policy [2008] OJ L348/84.

[59] Directive 2013/39 [2013] OJ L226/1.

[60] Commission Implementing Decision 2015/495 [2015] OJ L78/40. At present, Commission Implementing Decision 2022/1307 applies, which contains 26 substances [2022] OJ L197/117.

[61] Directive 2020/2184 on the quality of water for human consumption [2020] OJ L435/1; Commission Implementing Decision 2022/679 on a watch list [2022] OJ L124/41; the list contains two substances.

[62] Directive 84/360 on the combating of air pollution from industrial plants [1984] OJ L188/20; for more details, see para 8-02ff.

[63] Directive 96/62 [1996] OJ L296/55; this directive was replaced in 2008 by Directive 2008/50 on ambient air quality and cleaner air for Europe [2008] OJ L152/1.

[64] Directive 96/61 on integrated pollution prevention and control [1996] OJ L257/26; Directive 2008/1 on integrated pollution prevention and control [2008] OJ L24/8; Directive 2010/75 on industrial emissions [2010] OJ L334/1.

The Stockholm Convention on Persistent Organic Pollutants, which was signed in 2001 by the European Union and all its Member States and which was transposed into EU law by way of (at present) Regulation 2019/1021, provided for a list of persistent organic polluting substances (POPs) which are, in principle, banned.[65]

All these lists had no direct influence on product-related provisions adopted at EU level, but were, rather, aimed at framing EU policy for the limitation of the emission of pollutants into the environment. The EU institutions did not take them as binding either, but were quite loose in working according to the frame which was set by them.

Restrictions concerning the composition of products had been mainly – but by no means exclusively – inserted into Directive 76/769,[66] which, up to mid-2006, had been amended more than 30 times; this directive has since been replaced. The restriction of chemicals was regulated under the REACH Regulation for chemical substances and included in its annex XVII.[67] 6-09

Most initiatives for introducing EU-wide restrictions came from Member States, which introduced bans or restrictions of substances or products in order to protect humans or the environment. This then initiated the restriction procedure at EU level, since the Commission wished to preserve the unity of the internal market, which requires uniform product standards. It is likely that in future the majority of initiatives to restrict the use of substances will still come from Member States; only gradually will the new ECHA assume a leading role and propose restrictions based on the safety assessments that it receives.

There are only very limited possibilities to provide for interim EU-wide measures that take a substance or a product from the market. When, in 2000, the Commission was of the opinion that six phthalates presented a risk in children's toys and published a proposal for a directive to have the use of these phthalates restricted, it had to recur to Directive 92/59 on general product safety,[68] which allowed for interim measures to be taken for a period of three months. As the Commission's proposal on phthalates was eventually adopted in 2005,[69] the interim measures had been prolonged more than 10 times.[70]

A. Detergents

The first provisions that regulated the composition of products concerned those products where diverging national provisions risked the creation of barriers to the free circulation of goods. Thus, from 1973, a directive prohibited the placing on the market of detergents 6-10

[65] Regulation 2019/1021 [2019] OJ L169/1. See also Decision 2006/507, by which the EC adhered to the Stockholm Convention [2006] OJ L209/1; the text of the Stockholm Convention is reproduced there at p 3. See also para 6-36.

[66] Directive 76/769 relating to restrictions on the marketing and use of certain dangerous substances and preparations [1976] OJ L262/201.

[67] Regulation 1907/2006 (n 7); see in particular Commission Regulation 552/2009 [2009] OJ L164/7, which transferred the restrictions of Directive 76/769 into annex XVII of Regulation 1907/2006.

[68] Directive 92/59 on general product safety [1992] OJ L228/24.

[69] Directive 2005/84 [2005] OJ L344/40. These restrictions are now found in Regulation 1907/2006 (n 7) annex XVII, no 52.

[70] Directive 2001/95 (n 1) Art 13 in the meantime prolonged the validity of a Commission interim measure to one year.

which were less than 90 per cent biodegradable;[71] since that directive had to be adopted unanimously and no real consensus was reached as to whether a percentage of 80 or 90 per cent should apply, a compromise was found that the detergent could be placed on the market as long as the harmonised test methods showed that it was biodegradable by 80 per cent.[72]

In 2005, a completely new regulation on detergents was adopted which replaced the existing legislation[73] and dealt with the biodegradability of all surfactants in detergents, not only that of anionic and non-ionic surfactants. Regulation 648/2004 provided for the use of different test standards, which may be used alternatively, as obviously no consensus on the use of a single standard existed. The biodegradability must normally be 60 per cent (five test methods, annex IIIA) or 70 per cent (two other test methods, annex IIIB). Where this biodegradability was not reached, the producer may ask for a derogation, which may, under certain conditions, be granted by the EU Commission (comitology procedure), provided the biodegradability did not exceed 80 per cent (annex II).[74] In order to reduce the eutrophication of waters, Regulation 259/2012, amending Regulation 648/2004, limited the content of phosphates and phosphorous compounds in consumer detergents.[75]

A detailed evaluation of Regulation 648/2004 by the Commission revealed minor environmental problems, such as the absence of provisions on nanomaterials and microplastics, insufficient provisions concerning the presence of substances of concern and some labelling incoherences.[76] A Commission proposal of 2023 to update the provisions on detergents[77] is at present being discussed by the other Union institutions.

B. Fuels

6-11 The combustion of fuels releases pollutants that contaminate the environment – the damage caused by one tonne of sulphur dioxide was estimated in 1997 at €4000.[78] Measures concerning the composition of fuels have concentrated on the reduction of pollutants. As Member States had different perceptions of environmental problems, it is not surprising that such differences reappeared when fuels were regulated.

EU legislation started with regulating the sulphur content of gas oil, which was fixed between 0.5 and 0.8 per cent in 1975.[79] In 1987, a general level of 0.3 per cent was introduced.[80] However, Member States were allowed to require the use of gas oil with a

[71] Directive 73/404 on the approximation of the laws of the Member States relating to detergents [1973] OJ L347/51.

[72] Directive 73/405 on the approximation of the laws of the Member States relating to methods of testing the biodegradability on non-ionic surfactants [1973] OJ L347/53; subsequently, Directives 82/242 [1982] OJ L109/1 and 82/243 [1982] OJ L109/18 completed the provisions for testing methods.

[73] Regulation 648/2004 on detergents [2004] OJ L104/1.

[74] As to the equivalence of results, see Regulation 648/2004 (n 73) annex IIIB: 'It should be noted that the pass criterion of at least 70 percent of these methods is to be considered as equivalent to the pass criterion of at least 60 percent referred to in the methods listed in point A.'

[75] Regulation 259/2012 [2012] OJ L94/16.

[76] Commission, 'Evaluation of Regulation 648/2004' SWD(2019) 298.

[77] Commission, 'Proposal for a Regulation on Detergents and Surfactants' COM(2023) 217.

[78] Commission, COM(1997) 88 44.

[79] Directive 75/716 [1975] OJ L307/22.

[80] Directive 87/219 [1987] OJ L91/19. This directive was based on the present Art 115 TFEU.

sulphur content of 0.2 per cent in regions with high pollution or 'where damage to the environment or to the national heritage caused by total sulphur dioxide emissions requires' a sulphur content lower than 0.3 per cent. In 1993, Directive 93/12, based on the present Article 114 TFEU, introduced a level of 0.2 per cent sulphur as of the end of 1994 and 0.05 per cent as of the end of 1996; the directive stated expressly that this was necessary in order to reach the emission limit values fixed in other EU provisions.[81] Then, a directive of 1999 fixed the maximum permissible sulphur content in gas oil at 0.2 per cent as of 1 July 2000 and at 0.1 per cent as of 1 January 2008.[82] Member States were allowed to use, until 2013, gas oil with a sulphur content between 0.1 and 0.2 per cent if the quality standards of Directive 80/779 were respected and the emissions did not lead to an exceedance of the critical quantities in other Member States. Furthermore, Spain (for the Canary Islands), France (for its overseas departments), Greece and Portugal (for Madeira and the Azores) were allowed, for an unspecified time, to use gas oil with a higher sulphur content than 0.2 per cent.

As regards heavy fuels which are used in particular by ships, the Commission 6-12
published, in 1997, figures according to which most sulphur dioxide emissions in the Union stemmed from the burning of coal (62.9 per cent), heavy fuel (18.4 per cent), gas oil/diesel (7.0 per cent) and refinery fuels (6.5 per cent).[83] As part of the EU strategy to combat acidification, Directive 1999/32 reduced the sulphur content of heavy fuel oils to 1 per cent as of 2003. However, Member States obtained the possibility of allowing the use of heavy fuels with a sulphur content of up to 3 per cent under certain conditions. Directive 2005/33, based on Article 114 TFEU, amended Directive 1999/32.[84] It fixed the sulphur level of heavy fuels at 1 per cent as of 1 January 2003 (thus retroactively!) and that of marine fuels for ships which sail under the flag of a Member State or use Member States' ports at 1.5 per cent. However, this last restriction applied only to the Baltic Sea and the North Sea. A further directive, of 2012, limited the sulphur content of marine fuels generally to 3.5 per cent in sulphur oxide emission control zones – the Baltic Sea and North Sea – to 1.0 per cent.[85] The Union thus clearly wanted to let sea transport provisions prevail over environmental considerations and leave the decision of generally limiting the sulphur content of marine fuels to the international maritime organisations. For inland waterway vessels, the sulphur content was fixed at 0.1 per cent as of 2010, with some exceptions for some Greek vessels.

Directive 2016/802, which replaced numerous previous legislative acts, fixed the maximum content of sulphur dioxide in heavy fuels at 1 per cent by mass, for gas oil at 0.1 per cent by mass and for marine fuels at 3.50 by mass. In Union waters, the maximum allowed content was fixed, as of 2020, at 0.50 per cent by mass.[86]

Member States were for a long time divided on the lead content of petrol. Directive 6-13
78/611[87] fixed the lead content to 0.4 g/l, but allowed Member States to lower this level down to 0.15 g. Until 1986, Ireland was allowed to apply a level of 0.64 g.[88] In the early

[81] Directive 93/12 on the sulphur content of certain liquid fuels [1993] OJ L74/81.

[82] Directive 1999/32 [1999] OJ L121/13.

[83] Commission, COM(91) 154.

[84] Directive 2005/33 [2005] OJ L191/59.

[85] Directive 2012/33 on the sulphur content of marine fuels [2012] OJ L327/1.

[86] Directive 2016/802 relating to a reduction in the sulphur content of certain liquid fuels [2016] OJ L132/58.

[87] Directive 78/611 [1978] OJ L197/19.

[88] The reason for this split standard was that Germany had already introduced, as of 1976, a standard of 0.15 g and was not prepared to go back on this decision.

1980s, campaigns on reducing the lead content in the air – for health reasons in the UK, for environmental reasons (Waldsterben – the problem of dying forests) in Germany – led the European Council to ask for the introduction of lead-free petrol,[89] which was adopted in March 1985, almost a record time.[90] Directive 85/210 required Member States to 'take the necessary measures to ensure the availability and balanced distribution within their territories of unleaded petrol from 1 October 1989' (Article 3). Unleaded petrol was defined as petrol that contained less than 0.013 g of lead per litre, leaded petrol as containing between 0.15 and 0.40 g of lead per litre. Directive 98/70, which finally replaced Directive 85/210, prohibited the marketing of leaded petrol as of 1 January 2000, though exceptions were possible and actually granted.[91] That directive also fixed the benzene content at 1.0 per cent and contained a number of other specifications for unleaded petrol.

6-14 Directive 2009/28 required that, by 2020, the share of energy from renewable sources in all forms of transport was at least 10 per cent of the final consumption of energy in transport.[92] However, when Directive 2009/28 was repealed by the over-sophisticated Directive 2018/2001,[93] this requirement was not repeated. Member States were, instead, requested to adopt strategies, plans and measures to enable the Union to reach, by 2030, a share of renewable energies of at least 32 per cent in the gross final consumption of energy; in 2022, the Commission announced that it would propose to have this share increased to 45 per cent.[94] No percentage share of biofuels was fixed.[95] Applications to the CJEU in order to have forestry biomass excluded and fuel from palm oil included in the definition of renewable energy have so far remained without success.[96]

The different provisions mentioned do not concern the composition of fuel in general. There are numerous substances that are added to fuels in order to influence their quality (antioxidants, biocides, icing or corrosive inhibitors, etc), which may later enter the environment, in the form of emissions. A new Article 8a of Directive 98/70, inserted by Directive 2009/30, asked the Commission to establish for the first time, by 2012, a test methodology for metallic additives. The additive MMT was restricted in use (6 mg/l).[97]

[89] See (1993) 6 *Bulletin of the European Communities* 1.5.15.

[90] Directive 85/210 on the approximation of the laws of the Member States concerning the lead content of petrol [1985] OJ L96/25.

[91] Directive 98/70 relating to the quality of petrol and diesel fuels [1998] OJ L351/58, Art 3: 'No later than 1 January 2000, Member States shall prohibit the marketing of leaded petrol within their territory.'

[92] Directive 2009/28 on the promotion of the use of energy from renewable sources [2009] OJ L140/16. This directive was based on the present Art 192 TFEU and, as regards the sustainability criteria of biofuels, their verification and calculation, on the present Art 114 TFEU.

[93] Directive 2018/2001 on the promotion of the use of energy from renewable sources [2018] OJ L328/82. Art 2, no 1 defined 'renewable energy' as 'energy from renewable non-fossil sources, namely wind, solar (solar thermal and solar photovoltaic) and geothermal energy, ambient energy, tide, wave and other ocean energy, hydropqwer, biomass, landfill gas, sewage treatment plant gas and biogas'.

[94] Commission, 'EU Solar Energy Strategy' COM(2022) 221 3.

[95] Directive 2018/2001 (n 93) Art 2, fns 24 and 32 defined biofuels as fuels from biomass. 'Biomass' was declared to be 'the biodegradable fraction of products, waste and residues of biological origin from agriculture, including vegetal and animal substances, from forestry and related industry, including fisheries and aquaculture as well as the biodegradable fraction of waste, including industrial and municipal waste of biological origin.'

[96] CJEU Case C-297/20P *Sabo a o v European Parliament and Council* ECLI:EU:C:2021:24; Case C-402/20P *Santiga v Commission* ECLI:EU:C:2021:872.

[97] For MMT, see also CJEU Case C-343/09 *Afton Chemicals* ECLI:EU:C:2010:419.

C. Cars

There are almost no EU environmental provisions on the making of cars. However, numerous provisions exist that decide on the air emissions from cars, although it is left to car manufacturers to decide how they intend to comply with the emission standards – whether they install a catalytic converter, use an electromotor or another engine with a low consumption of fuel and thus generate only low emissions. The installation of defeat devices in cars which have an impact on its air emissions has been prohibited since the year 2000.[98] Several car manufacturers nevertheless secretly used such defeat devices, arguing that this was necessary to protect the motor. All such arguments were rejected by the CJEU, but it took years to reach this conclusion.[99] 6-15

A future ban on using petrol- or diesel-driven cars will be pronounced not by a prohibition on constructing such cars, but by imposing emission limit values which may only be complied with by electric cars. Another example of the discretion left to car manufacturers is the noise levels of cars: these are fixed in the form of emission limit values, but do not require the use of particular materials, designs or tyres, etc, in order to comply with them.

Sometimes the different objectives pursued in the car sector contradict each other. Thus, a reduction of the weight of cars, which would lead to less fuel consumption, might contradict the objective of increased safety of passengers. The increased use of plastic materials, which make a car lighter, could make the recycling of end-of-life vehicles more difficult. The use of aluminium in cars involves a material that is produced in a very polluting way, etc. 6-16

The Union has never considered imposing certain product standards on cars, such as a maximum fuel consumption, the use of certain materials or fuels, or an in-built speed limitation for cars. Directive 2009/125 on the ecodesign of energy using products,[100] which allows the Union to provide for design requirements, could also, in theory, apply to cars and lead to provisions imposing a certain design; however, as the climate change situation is not yet perceived to be serious enough, this consideration remains purely theoretical, and cars are expressly exempted from the provisions of that directive. Tax provisions which are, so far, purely national,[101] do not differentiate according to the car emissions or fuel consumption, though in most countries, diesel fuel is taxed lower than petrol in order to indirectly subsidise the transport and agricultural sectors.

The Directive on end-of-life vehicles[102] contained an article on waste prevention, but suggested measures for promotion and encouragement as regards car design and production, recycled materials and hazardous substances in cars; another provision provided for a ban of the use of lead, mercury, cadmium and hexavalent chromium, though a number

[98] Directive 1999/96 on air emissions from vehicles [1999] OJ L 44/1, annex 6.2.1. Regulation 715/2007 on type approval for motor vehicles with respect to emissions from light passenger cars and commercial vehicles (Euro 5 and Euro 6) [2007] OJ L171/1, Art 5(2).

[99] CJEU Case C-693/18 *CLVC* ECLI:EU:C:2020:1040; Case C-128/20 *GSMB Invest* ECLI: ECLI:EU:C:2022:570; Case C-134/20 *Volkswagen* ECLI:EU:C:2022.571; Case C-145/20 *Porsche and Volkswagen* ECLI:EU:C:2022:572; Case C-873/19 *Deutsche Umwelthilfe* ECLI:EU:C:2022:857; Case C-100/21 *Mercedes-Benz* ECLI:EU:C:2023:229.

[100] Directive 2009/125 establishing a framework for the setting of ecodesign requirements for energy related products [2009] OJ L285/10.

[101] The Commission had proposed, in 2005, to tax cars according to the CO_2 emissions, COM(2005) 161. As no agreement could be reached in the Council, it withdrew this proposal in 2015.

[102] Directive 2000/53 (n 40).

of derogations were foreseen. Finally, the directive provided for cars to be 85 per cent recyclable by 2015, which again will have an impact on the composition of cars – provided the directive is properly applied and monitored.

D. Packaging and Plastic Products

6-17 The production and waste management of packaging in the EU has an estimated total turnover of €370 billion.[103] Directive 94/62 on packaging and packaging waste[104] provided for a reduction of the total metal content of four heavy metals – cadmium, lead, mercury and polyvalent chromium – in three steps by the year 2001. The directive did not fix methods for the measuring of this content. Specific requirements for the composition of packaging were not laid down. There was, however, an interesting combination of the new approach system for product harmonisation and environmental requirements: Member States were obliged to accept on their markets all packaging that complied with the essential requirements of Directive 94/62, which were laid down in annex II. These included the provision that 'packaging shall be designed, produced and commercialised in such a way as to minimise its impact on the environment when packaging waste or residues from packaging waste management operations are disposed of' and that packaging 'shall be so manufactured that the presence of noxious and other hazardous substances and materials … is minimised with regard to their presence in emissions, ash or leachate when … packaging waste are incinerated or landfilled'. These provisions would easily allow a Member State, which so wishes, to prohibit PVC packaging, restrict the use of aerosols or provide for other restrictions on the use of packaging; however, this would raise difficulties, since Directive 94/62 is based on Article 114 TFEU, which aims at ensuring the free circulation of packaging. Anyway, in practice, these provisions did not have any significant impact on packaging.

6-18 The Comité Européen de Normalisation (European Committee for Standardisation, CEN; see paragraph 6-56) was charged with elaborating European standards for the essential environmental requirements for packaging. As the CEN standards did not correspond to Directive 94/62's requirements, but were drafted in a rather loose and vague way, the Commission initially refused, under the procedure of the present Directive 2015/1535,[105] to recognise four of them as harmonised EC standards[106] – which would have meant that compliance with the CEN standards created a presumption of compliance with the directive's requirements. CEN then re-presented the same standards some time later, and this time got the EU's approval, as the environmental enthusiasm had diminished in the meantime.

In 2013, the Commission proposed amending Directive 94/62 in order to allow Member States to reduce the number of light plastic carrier bags.[107] Member States should be able to tax such bags to prohibit them altogether, or take other appropriate measures. The Commission justified its proposal with the environmental problems caused by such bags,

[103] Council, Working Document 9226/23 of 16 May 2023, 2.

[104] Directive 94/62 on packaging and packaging waste [1994] OJ L365/10. An ex-post evaluation of this directive is found in Commission, SWD(2014) 209.

[105] Directive 2015/1535 (n 32).

[106] Commission Decision 2001/524 [2001] OJ L190/21.

[107] Commission, COM(2013) 761.

of which it declared about eight billion were littered. Directive 2015/720 did not go that far.[108] Instead, it provided for the possibility of Member States to either reduce the overall average consumption of such bags or to ensure that bags were not made available free of charge at the point of sale of goods; very light bags could be exempted altogether. Also, a directive of 2018, again based on Article 114 TFEU, which asked Member States to 'encourage' the increase in the share of reusable packaging without imposing measures, and which limited itself to general provisions on the reuse and recycling of packaging and packaging prevention, did not lead to significant reductions in packaging.[109] Then the Commission proposed a new regulation on packaging. It held greater harmonisation to be necessary. The new regulation should contain measures to ensure that all packaging was reusable or recyclable, and that it addressed the presence of heavy metals in packaging, provided for a recyclable content in plastic packaging and dealt with compostable packaging and the minimisation of packaging.[110] The proposal is at present being discussed by the other Union institutions. As can be seen, the Union has not really dared, so far, to prohibit certain forms of (plastic) packaging, and has thus accepted that the volume of packaging will continuously increase.[111]

Directive 2019/904 prohibited the placing on the market of some single-use plastic products (cutlery, plates) and some products made from expanded polystyrene, because of their high presence in waste materials.[112] Member States were also requested to reduce their consumption of other single-use plastics – cups for beverages and some food containers. And for the very first time, that directive imposed a specific share of recycled material in a product: specifically, a share of recycled plastic for beverage bottles other than glass or metal bottles, applicable from 2030 onwards (for PET bottles, from 2025 onwards).[113] The Union did not go so far as to prohibit certain plastic materials altogether.

E. Substances of Concern in Other Products

The Union has regulated the composition and marketing of a considerable number of products, in particular to ensure the establishment and functioning of the internal market. 6-19
These included foodstuffs, animal feeding stuff, pharmaceuticals, cosmetics, textiles, toys, pesticides, fertilizers, drinking water, batteries, packaging, paints and varnishes, construction material and footwear, not to mention non-consumer goods such as ships, aeroplanes and office equipment. Scattered amongst these provisions are provisions that prohibit or restrict the use of this or that substance. Examples are as follows. Directive 2006/66[114]

[108] Directive 2015/720 as regards reducing the consumption of light plastic carrier bags [2015] OJ L115/11.

[109] Directive 2018/852 [2018] OJ L150/141.

[110] Commission, COM(2022) 677. See also Commission, SWD(2022) 384 on the impact assessment of the proposal.

[111] The Commission (ibid) 1 stated that 40% of plastic material and 50% of paper in the Union was used for packaging and that 36% of municipal waste was composed of packaging. For figures concerning the increase in packaging, see ibid 5.

[112] Directive 2019/904 on the reduction of the impact of certain plastic products on the environment [2019] OJ L155/1.

[113] ibid Art 6(5)(a).

[114] Directive 2006/66 (n 43).

prohibited the use of certain batteries where the mercury levels fixed in the directive were exceeded. Lead carbonates and lead sulphates could not be used in paints,[115] though some derogations were allowed for the restoration of works of art and historic buildings.[116] Mercury, arsenic or organostannic compounds[117] may not be used to prevent the fouling by micro-organisms (plants or animals) of boats, in fish or shellfish farming and in the preservation of wood.[118] Cadmium and its compounds were banned from use as colourants or stabilisers for different products; also, cadmium plating was forbidden in a number of expressly defined products.[119] Nickel was prohibited for use in products which come into contact with the human skin.[120] The use of cadmium, mercury, lead and hexavalent chromium was prohibited in cars and in electrical and electronic equipment,[121] as was the use of polybromated biphenyls and diphenyls also in electrical and electronic equipment.[122] The different provisions each contained a number of exceptions, derogations or transition provisions.

6-20 As can be seen, the restrictions are anything but systematic. Most of the provisions concern heavy metals, in particular lead, mercury or cadmium. In recent times, substances that deplete the ozone layer or lead to the emission of greenhouse gases are also regulated. It is true that a small number of products, such as polychlorinated biphenyls (PCBs)[123] and asbestos,[124] were forbidden by the Union, mainly in reaction to national bans. However, the phase-out periods were extremely long.

6-21 So far, there have been only two attempts to systematically tackle the problem of dangerous substances in products; these were the attempts to regulate cadmium and mercury. The first environmental action programme (1973) designated cadmium, together with other substances, as a substance that should be examined as a priority, because of its toxicity and its effects on human health and the environment.[125] The Council confirmed in 1975 that an examination of the effects of cadmium on water was already ongoing and asked for an examination of air emissions of cadmium.[126] In 1981, the Commission asked the Consultative Scientific Committee on the Toxicity and Ecotoxicity of Chemical Compounds for an opinion on cadmium, and it recommended the reduction of cadmium emissions wherever possible.[127]

In 1987, the Commission sent a communication to the Council, in which it listed 20 directives which limited the use of cadmium, suggested an action programme consisting of

[115] Directive 76/769 (n 66).

[116] As regards lead, see also Written Question E-0837/96 (Muscardini) [1996] OJ C297/35.

[117] For these substances, see Written Question 1139/89 (Adam) [1990] OJ C328/4.

[118] Directive 76/769 (n 66) nos 19, 20 and 21.

[119] ibid no 24.

[120] ibid no 28.

[121] Directive 2000/53 (n 40).

[122] Directive 2011/65 (n 26).

[123] As regards PCBs, Directive 76/769 (n 66) prohibited their marketing in 1983. However, Directive 96/59 on the elimination of PCB/PCT [1996] OJ L243/31 provided for the final elimination of these materials till 2010.

[124] Asbestos was partly prohibited in the EU by Directive 83/478 [1983] OJ L263/33, which amended Directive 76/769 (n 66); in 1999, Directive 1999/77 [1999] OJ L207/18 introduced an almost total ban.

[125] First Environmental Action Programme [1973] OJ C112/1, 13.

[126] Resolution of 24 June 1975 [1975] OJ C168/4.

[127] Scientific Consultative Committee on the Toxicity and Ecotoxicity of Chemical Compounds, opinion of April 1981, published in *Activity Report 1979–1983*, EUR 9246 (Luxembourg, 1984) 37.

nine points to eliminate cadmium from the environment[128] and announced that it would, within two years, submit proposals for all nine points. The Council approved the strategy.[129] In 1991, the Council adopted a directive to reduce the content of cadmium as a colourant, stabiliser or surface coating for a number of products,[130] and this directive was to be reviewed 'at regular intervals' – though this was never done.

Nevertheless, the Commission considered it necessary to include cadmium and its different compounds in its priority lists for existing chemicals,[131] which were established under Regulation 793/93[132] and which were designed to assess the effects of substances on man and the environment. This assessment, for which Belgium was in the lead, started in 1996 and was completed in 2008. The Commission adopted a recommendation on cadmium which had a very limited content – resuming 35 years of attempts to reduce the presence of cadmium in the environment.[133] 6-22

The main source of the presence of cadmium in the environment is the cadmium content of fertilisers that are used in agriculture. EU law does not contain limit values for cadmium concentrations in fertilisers, but the national legislation of the three acceding Member States at the time – Sweden, Austria and Finland – did. The Accession Treaty therefore provided that this legislation could be maintained for four years; in the meantime, a re-examination of the EU provisions would take place. In 2003, the Union adopted new legislation on fertilisers, which again did not provide for a limit on cadmium;[134] this act was repealed in 2019.[135] Another new regulation again granted Austria, Sweden and Finland, along with the Czech Republic, the possibility to continue to apply their limitations. Overall, this transition period had thus existed for more than 25 years. This sequence of events shows that a systematic EU approach to cadmium simply does not exist.[136]

Thanks to international initiatives, things went better for mercury restrictions. In 2005, the Commission presented, at the request of the Scandinavian countries, a communication for a strategy to reduce the emissions of mercury.[137] The strategy listed more than 20 actions that should be taken at EU level to reduce the use and emissions of mercury, including banning its export by 2011. This latter was finally decided, for a number of mercury-containing products, in 2008.[138] Subsequently, further restrictions on the use of mercury in measuring devices were adopted,[139] and other restrictions were inserted in the

[128] Commission, 'Environmental Pollution by Cadmium. Proposal for an Action Programme' COM(87) 165.

[129] Resolution of 25 January 1988 [1988] OJ C30/1.

[130] Directive 91/338 amending, for the tenth time, Directive 76/769 [1991] OJ L186/59.

[131] See Regulation 143/97 [1997] OJ L25/13, nos 2 and 3.

[132] Regulation 793/93 evaluation and control of the risks of existing substances [1993] OJ L84/1.

[133] Commission Recommendation 2008/446 [2008] OJ L156/22; the reference to the Belgian risk assessment is found in [2008] OJ C149/6. See also General Court Case T-456/11 *ICdA v Commission* ECLI: EU:T:2013:594.

[134] Regulation 2003/2003 on fertilisers [2003] OJ L304/1; see also, by way of example, the derogation granted to Sweden, Decision 2006/347 [2006] OJ L129/19.

[135] Regulation 2019/1009 laying down rules on the making available on the market of the EU fertilising products [2019] OJ L170/1, Art 3(2).

[136] Some restrictions for cadmium are listed in Regulation 1907/2006 (n 7) annex XVII, no 23. However, that list is not complete, as cadmium restrictions are also found in other Union acts.

[137] Commission, COM(2005) 20; reviewed in Commission, COM(2010) 723.

[138] Regulation 1102/2008 on the banning the exports of metallic mercury and certain mercury compounds and mixtures and the safe storage of metallic mercury [2008] OJ L304/75.

[139] Directive 2007/51 restricting the use of mercury in measuring devices [2007] OJ L257/13.

Chemicals Regulation;[140] the storage of metallic mercury in landfills was also regulated[141] and the mercury content in batteries reduced.[142] The ratification of the Minamata Convention on Mercury of 2013 by the Union[143] led to a comprehensive Regulation on mercury, which addressed the production, import and export of mercury-containing products and other uses, including the prohibition of the use of dental amalgam in bulk form, the largest mercury use in the Union; only pre-closed encapsulated forms were allowed to be used.[144] In 2020, the Commission announced a proposal in 2022 to prohibit dental amalgam altogether, which it submitted in 2023.[145] The use of dental amalgam was to be banned as of 2025, unless the use was considered strictly necessary by the dental practitioner; and the export of dental amalgam was to be prohibited.

Horizontal provisions on other substances of concern, such as endocrine disruptors, carcinogens or bioaccumulative, persistent or toxic substances, were not adopted. Also, the action plan on zero environmental pollution[146] provided for measures to limit the concentration of pollutants in the environment – quality standards – and on the use of products, but not on the systematic elimination of substances of concern in products. Restrictions on the use of such substances take place under Regulation 1907/2006 on chemicals, mainly on a case-by-case basis. The Commission announced that, for the chemical sector, it would more frequently resort to a 'generic approach', which consists in a process to restrict certain chemicals on the basis of their hazardous characteristics, regardless of whether there is an actual risk present.[147] An example is the request from four Member States (Denmark, Sweden, the Netherlands and Germany) plus Norway from the beginning of 2023, which asked the ECHA to take the necessary measures in order to ban all per- and polyfluoroalkyl substances because of their negative environmental effects (persistency, risk to human health). Such a ban would affect thousands of these synthetic chemicals. Any decision, though, would not be taken before 2024.

F. Products Containing Ozone-Depleting Substances

6-23 In order to protect the ozone layer, the Union adopted a number of measures as regards ozone-depleting substances.[148] Internationally, the Montreal Protocol[149] deals with about

[140] Commission Regulation 847/2012 amending annex XVII of Regulation 1907/2006 [2013] OJ L253/1. The mercury restrictions are listed under nos 18 and 18a.

[141] Directive 2011/97 [2011] OJ L328/49.

[142] Directive 2013/56 amending Directive 2006/66 [2013] OJ L329/5.

[143] Decision 2017/939 [2017] OJ L142/4.

[144] Regulation 2017/852 on mercury [2017] OJ L137/1, Art 10. This regulation repealed Regulation 1102/2008 (n 138).

[145] Commission, COM(2023) 395.

[146] Commission, 'Pathway to a Healthy Planet for All. EU Action Plan to Reach Zero Pollution for Air, Water and Soil' COM(2021) 400; Commission, 'First Implementation Report' COM(2022) 378.

[147] Commission, 'Chemicals Strategy for Sustainability. Towards a Toxic-Free Environment' COM(2020) 667. See also Commission, 'EU's Beating Cancer Plan' COM(2021) 44, 12; Commission, 'Commission Fitness Check for EU Chemical Legislation (except REACH)' SWD(2019) 199.

[148] For more details, see para 9-37ff.

[149] Montreal Protocol of 16 September 1987 on substances that deplete the ozone layer; it was adhered to by the EU by Decision 88/540 [1988] OJ L297/8.

100 such substances, but only indirectly touches the question of products that contain ozone-depleting substances.[150] It is true, though, that Article 2(11) of the protocol allows contracting parties to 'take more stringent measures' than those required by the protocol. These provisions, incidentally, also apply to 'products produced with, but not containing' ozone-depleting substances.

The Montreal Protocol was transposed into EU law by Regulation 1005/2009,[151] which banned, with some exceptions, the production, trade and export of ozone-depleting substances and went in part beyond the protocol by limiting trade and use of products and equipment containing such substances, for example in air-condition installations, refrigerators and fire extinguishers. In 2022, the Commission proposed a regulation to update Regulation 1005/2009.[152]

G. Chemicals (REACH)

Chemicals, in the form of substances, preparations, pesticides, fertilisers, pharmaceuti- 6-24
cals, cosmetics and food additives, are extensively regulated at EU level, since for all these products uniform rules are necessary – from the industry's point of view – to establish a common market. Pharmaceuticals, cosmetics and food additives will not be discussed in this book, since they primarily concern health issues and environmental elements are only peripheral. EU legislation on substances and mixtures of substances is based on Article 114 TFEU and tries to achieve total harmonisation; this means that national legislation on chemicals that diverges from existing EU provisions is, in principle, not allowed.[153]

EU legislation on chemicals has been introduced periodically since 1967. It was based on directives which differentiated between substances and preparations on the one hand,[154] on chemicals which were on the EU market before 1981 and those which were put on the market later (new substances) on the other hand.[155] Existing substances were allowed to be used freely until they were examined by the EU, whereas new substances had to undergo an EU-approval procedure before they were allowed to be placed on the market. Restrictions on the use of chemicals were mainly introduced at the initiative of individual Member States, and then generalised by an EU directive.[156]

Overall, the system was considered successful for new substances, as these had to undergo a risk assessment before they could be marketed.[157] In contrast, the system for

[150] Art 4(3) of the Montreal Protocol provides for rules to be elaborated which prohibit the import of products containing ozone-depleting substances from states that are not party to the protocol; Art 9(1b) invites research and development of alternatives to products that contain ozone-depleting substances.

[151] Regulation 1005/2009 on substances that deplete the ozone-layer [2009] OJ L286/1; this regulation replaced the earlier Regulation 2037/2000 [2000] OJ L244/1. For an assessment of the EU and the global efforts to reduce the emissions of ozone-depleting substances, see Commission, SWD(2019) 406.

[152] Commission, COM(2022) 151.

[153] For a good example on the discussion about total harmonisation, see CJEU Case C-473/98 (n 24).

[154] Directive 67/548 on the classification, labelling and packaging of dangerous substances [1967] OJ 196/1; Directive 1999/45 relating to the classification, packaging and labelling of dangerous preparations [1999] OJ L200/1.

[155] Directive 79/831 [1979] OJ L259/10.

[156] Directive 76/769 (n 66); each restriction of a substance required an amendment of this directive.

[157] Directive 93/67 laying down the principles for assessment of risks to man and the environment of substances notified in accordance with Directive 67/548 [1993] OJ L22/79; the Commission guidance document on the

existing substances was found to be too complicated. By 2005, only some 3500 substances had been properly regulated, while some 100,000 substances were registered as being on the EU market. Attempts to accelerate the procedure[158] remain unsuccessful.

6-25 In 2001, the Commission published a White Paper on the strategy concerning a future chemical policy.[159] The ensuing discussions led, in 2006, to the adoption of the so-called REACH Regulation.[160]

REACH provided that all chemical substances which were manufactured or imported into the EU in quantities of one tonne per year or more had to be registered with the ECHA (Article 6). This also applied to producers or importers of a substance which had already been registered by another person, in order to avoid giving an economic advantage to free-riders. Registration was also necessary for substances which were contained in products, provided the substance was present in those products in quantities of more than one tonne per year and was intended to be released under normal or reasonably foreseeable conditions of use (Article 7). Where a dangerous substance was present in a product 'above a concentration of 0.1% by weight' (Article 7(2)(b)), the producer or importer had to notify the ECHA.[161] Several persons putting a substance into circulation could do this in common (Article 11) and, in order to avoid the duplication of vertebrate animal testing, a new registration was possible by referring to an earlier registration, without the consent of the earlier registrant, provided the costs were shared (Article 27). A substance which was not registered could not be placed on the market (Article 5).

6-26 A registration had to be accompanied by detailed information on the substance and its characteristics, its use and the quantities which were put on the market, and a report on the safety assessment (Article 14). This safety report constituted the risk assessment, which, before 2006, had been the responsibility of the public authorities and was now the responsibility of the registrant. The ECHA had to examine the completeness of the information which was submitted. If it did not require more information or otherwise object, the substance could be placed on the EU market (Article 21); the Agency did not have the power to take provisional measures in order to stop the marketing of a substance.

The evaluation of the registered substance – in particular with regard to the safety report – was made by a Member State on the basis of a rolling action plan established by the Agency (Articles 44–47). The responsible Member State had to submit its conclusion to the Agency, which then informed the Commission, the other Member States and the registrant.

6-27 The ECHA then had to decide how to classify the substance in question. Substances that were carcinogenic, mutagenic, toxic for reproduction, persistent, bioaccumulative or toxic, or very persistent or very bioaccumulative, were listed in annex XIV.[162] The consequence

making of a risk assessment, 'Technical Guidance Document in Support of Commission Directive 93/67 on Risk Assessment for New Notified Substances and Commission Regulation 1488/94 on risk assessment for existing substances' (Luxembourg, 1996), had a length of 700 pages. Until the end of 2005, some 3000 new substances had been notified and classified.

[158] Regulation 793/93 on the evaluation and control of the risk of existing substances [1993] OJ L84/1.

[159] Commission, COM(2001) 88.

[160] Regulation 1907/2006 (n 7).

[161] It was disputed whether the 0.1% referred to the product as a whole (eg a car) or whether it referred to a component of a product (eg the brakes of a car). The CJEU decided in favour of the component, Case C-106/14 *FCD and FMB* ECLI:EU:C:2015:576.

[162] For details, see Art 57 of Regulation 1907/2006 (n 7).

of such a classification was that the placing on the market and use of the substance was prohibited after a certain date, unless an authorisation was granted (Articles 57–59). The producer or importer had to apply for an authorisation and submit the relevant information. Committees for risk assessment and socio-economic analysis which were set up by Regulation 1907/2006 were consulted on the application. The Commission then made a decision using a comitology procedure. An authorisation to use a substance was normally only granted where it was shown that the socio-economic benefits outweighed the risk to human health or the environment and if there were no suitable alternative substances or technologies (Article 60(4)). The authorisation was also subject to a time-limited review.

Articles 68–73 REACH dealt with the restriction of use of chemicals. When the Commission (Article 69) or a Member State (Article 70) was of the opinion that a substance posed an 'unacceptable risk' to human health or the environment, it may ask the ECHA to prepare a dossier and suggest restrictions; under certain conditions, the ECHA may also act on its own initiative. The committees on risk assessment and socio-economic analysis had to give an opinion. The final decision was again taken by the Commission by way of the comitology procedure.

It should be noted that not all the substances which are banned or restricted by EU legislation are assembled in annex XVII to the REACH Regulation. Rather, other restrictions are contained in different regulations and directives, scattered throughout EU law.[163]

The putting into operation of the REACH Regulation advanced slowly. The ECHA, situated in Helsinki, was quite absorbed by the registration of chemicals and their evaluation. It developed a rather limited number of its own initiatives to restrict the use of substances or place them in annex XIV, in order to submit them for an authorisation. 6-28

Up to the end of 2022, Regulation 1907/2006 was amended 71 times. Between 2007 and 2022, 18 substances were added to annex XVII; in 22 other cases, the existing restrictions were amended. During the same period, 59 substances were inserted into annex XIV as needing an authorisation.

In 2013, the Commission published a first report on the implementation of Regulation 1907/2006 and of Regulation 1272/2008.[164] It showed itself satisfied with the effectiveness of both instruments and did not see the need to suggest major amendments to the REACH legislation. A second report of 2018 identified some weaknesses in the legislation, such as the considerable non-compliance with the registration documentation requirements by industry, the need to simplify and accelerate the authorisation procedure, the effective implementation and enforcement of the restrictions, and the relationship with other Union legislation.[165] Overall, though, the Commission was satisfied with the functioning of the REACH legislation.

The evaluation concerning the coherence with other Union legislation on chemicals asked for a number of improvements to be made to the legislation regarding:

- the self-assessment of chemicals of concern by industry, which did not always work well;
- the improvement of knowledge on exposure of the environment to hazardous chemicals;
- a better application of the precautionary principle;

[163] See, eg Regulation 1223/2009 on cosmetic products [2009] OJ L342/59; Regulation 2019/1021 (n 65).
[164] Commission, COM(2013) 49; Commission, SWD(2013) 25.
[165] Commission, COM(2018) 116; in particular, see Commission, SWD(2018) 58.

- a better understanding of the impact of hazardous chemicals on the environment, biodiversity and the resilience of ecosystems;
- a better understanding of the impact of hazardous chemicals in products, and on the combined effects of several chemicals; and
- an improvement in the provisions on endocrine disruptors and an acceleration of the substitution of hazardous chemicals.[166]

6-29 Following work at global level, under the auspices of the United Nations, the Globally Harmonized System of Classification and Labelling of Chemicals (GHS) was agreed in 2002, which was influenced by the less environment- and consumer-friendly system used for the transport of goods. The EU amended its earlier system, which had been established by Directive 67/548,[167] and aligned it to the new GHS system. The classification of a substance – whether it was toxic, dangerous, explosive, etc – was regulated in Regulation 1272/2008.[168] Manufacturers and importers had to classify substances and mixtures, before placing them on the market (Article 4). Any supplier – including manufacturers and importers – had to label and pack the substance or mixture according to its classification. Regulation 1272/2008 fixed in detail the classes and degrees of risks; it was then, in principle, up to the manufacturer or importer to classify their product according to these risks. The classification decision had to be notified to the ECHA, which had to verify it for correctness and keep an inventory of the classifications received (Articles 40–42). The self-classification by the manufacturer/importer was particularly necessary for mixtures, as there were no lists of substances which are included in mixtures.

6-30 Some substances are subjects of a Union-wide classification which may also take place at the request of a Member State, a manufacturer or an importer. In such a case, the Commission decides on the harmonised classification by way of the comitology procedure, on the basis of preparatory work by the ECHA. This classification is then binding on everybody. Annex VI to Regulation 1272/2008 contains, on about 1000 pages, the list of substances which are the subject of harmonised classification. That list is regularly updated; at the same time, the regulation was aligned to amendments which were introduced, at global level, to the GHS system.

The labelling requirements for chemicals are discussed in para 6-51 below.

6-31 Regulation 1907/2006 is based on the precautionary principle.[169] This allows the public authorities to ban or restrict the placing on the market or use of a substance which is suspected to present a risk to humans or the environment without having to wait until the full evidence has demonstrated such a risk. The regulation has made use of this principle in several cases. For example, the burden of proof that a chemical substance was safe to be used was laid on the manufacturer/importer, who has to submit, together with the registration, data on the possible hazards of the substance and the risk management measures which

[166] Commission, COM(2019) 264; Commission, SWD(2019) 199.

[167] Directive 67/548 (n 154).

[168] Regulation 1272/2008 on the classification, labelling and packaging of substances and mixtures [2008] OJ L353/1.

[169] See Regulation 1907/2006 (n 7) Art 1(3): 'This regulation is based on the principle that it is for manufacturers, importers and downstream users to ensure that they manufacture, place on the market or use such substances that do not adversely affect human health or the environment. Its provisions are underpinned by the precautionary principle.' As regards the precautionary principle, see also para 1-27ff.

must be taken in order to allow the safe use of the substance. Furthermore, a substance may be restricted in use or even be banned altogether where the authorities have sufficient evidence of a possible risk. In taking a restriction decision, the authorities benefit from a very wide discretion, which may only be overruled by the EU courts when there is a manifest error, a misuse of powers or a manifest exceeding of the limits of discretion.[170]

An expression of the precautionary principle is also found in the requirements that:

- without data, substances may not be placed on the market;[171]
- substances which are carcinogenic, mutagenic or toxic for reproduction may not be supplied to the general public, because of their intrinsic hazard, without the necessity of evidence that they constitute an actual risk (Articles 57 and 58); and
- manufacturers or importers of substances of very high concern must submit specific supplementary information, without the public authorities being required to prove the existence of a risk.

The limits linked to the application of the precautionary principle became evident with the Union's handling of endocrine disruptors. These are substances that adversely affect the health of humans or animals by altering the functioning of the hormonal system. The Commission published several communications on such substances,[172] but did not present any proposals on the identification and management of endocrine disruptors, in part because industry and third countries were strongly opposed to such a horizontal approach. The Commission accepted that Union legislation on pesticides and biocides contained provisions on endocrine disruptors[173] but other legislation did not, and that some Member States – France, Denmark – acted at national level, thus putting in question the internal market.

In 2013, negotiations started between the EU and the USA on a Transatlantic Trade and 6-32
Investment Partnership Agreement, which also intended to cover the free trade of chemicals; these negotiations were eventually abandoned, but the influence of the USA on global developments with regard to chemicals' regulations remains very important. In the USA, the precautionary principle does not apply, which means that the approach to regulation is somewhat different from the EU approach: a manufacturer is normally not obliged to convey information to the public authorities on a substance which he markets. The authorities may only ask for such information in order to ascertain whether an actual risk exists when they already have sufficient information about a potential risk of that substance.[174] The authorities must also have similar suspicions that a chemical poses a risk before they

[170] See CJEU Case C-288/13P *Rüttgers v* ECHA ECLI:EU:C:2014:2176, settled case law.

[171] See Regulation 1907/2006 (n 7) Art 5: 'substances on their own, in preparations or in articles shall not be manufactured in the Community or placed on the market unless they have been registered in accordance with the relevant provisions of this Title where this is required.'

[172] Commission, COM(1999) 706; Commission, COM(2018) 734; Commission, 'Fitness Check on Endocrine Disruptors' SWD(2020) 251.

[173] On this, see Commission, SWD(2016) 211.

[174] See US Toxic Substances Control Act 15 USC §2601 et seq (1976), s 5: 'If the Administrator finds that the manufacture, distribution in commerce … of a chemical substance or mixture. may present an unreasonable risk of injury to health or the environment. the Administrator shall by rule require that testing be conducted on such substance or mixture with respect to the health and environmental effects for which there is an insufficiency of data and experience.'

may take any regulatory action to restrict the production or use of the substance.[175] In practice, this burden for public authorities is so high that, since the adoption of the US chemical legislation in 1976 and until 2018, only five substances have been subject to restrictions in the USA, and none of them have been in the last 20 years.[176]

H. Pesticides and Biocides

6-33 Pesticides in EU terminology are subdivided into agricultural (plant protection products) and non-agricultural (biocides) pesticides. As regards agricultural pesticides, of which some 25,000 are thought to be on the market, Regulation 1107/2009 deals with the authorisation for their placing on the market;[177] pesticide residues on and in food and feed are regulated in a separate regulation.[178]

Regulation 1107/2009, based on Articles 43, 114 and 169 TFEU, regulated the placing on the market of plant protection products. The regulation differentiated between products that have to be authorised by the individual Member States and the active substances for such products, which are authorised by the Union. An agricultural pesticide may only be authorised to be placed on the market if it contains an active substance that is listed – and is thus authorised EU-wide – in Regulation 1107/2009. The regulation fixed a number of conditions for the authorisation of pesticides, such as the requirement that the pesticide may not have unacceptable effects on plants, does not have damaging effects on the health of humans or animals or on groundwater, or does not have unacceptable effects on the environment in general.

The authorisation of a pesticide is valid for the Member State for which it was requested. For the recognition of the pesticide in another Member State, the regulation divided the Union in three biogeographical zones: North, Centre and South.[179] When the recognition is asked for a Member State of the same zone, this recognition has to be given, subject to some exceptional situations. For the authorisation in another zone, a new authorisation has to be requested.

Active substances are assessed, as regards their effects, by an EU mechanism. Applicants must submit detailed dossiers and a comprehensive risk assessment, which are examined and assessed, on the basis of a Member State's report, by the Standing Committee on Plant Health;[180] after a positive decision, the substance is registered in an annex to Regulation

[175] ibid s 6: 'If the Administrator finds that there is a reasonable basis to conclude that. a chemical substance or mixture presents … an unreasonable risk of injury to health or the environment, the Administrators shall by rule apply (restriction provisions).'

[176] See V Buonsante, 'Regulatory Coherence in the Transatlantic Trade and Investment Partnership Agreement: The Case of Chemicals' [2014] *Elni Review* 39; Commission, SWD(2018) 54, 57.

[177] Regulation 1107/2009 (n 29).

[178] Regulation 396/05 on maximum residue levels of pesticides in and on food and feed of plant and animal origin [2005] OJ L70/1. By the end of 2022, this Regulation had been amended 197 times.

[179] See Regulation 1107/2009 (n 29) annex I: the North zone comprises Denmark, Estonia, Latvia, Lithuania, Finland and Sweden; the Centre zone comprises Belgium, Czech Republic, Croatia, Germany, Ireland, Luxembourg, Hungary, the Netherlands, Austria, Poland, Romania, Slovenia and Slovakia; and the South zone comprises Bulgaria, Croatia, Greece, Spain, France, Cyprus, Malta and Portugal.

[180] This committee was set up by Decision 76/894 [1976] OJ L340/25.

1107/2009, together with any restrictions of use, expiry dates for the authorisation, etc.[181] The withdrawal or non-renewal of an authorisation or the refusal to approve an active substance is organised by Commission implementing regulations.[182] As mentioned above, active substances which qualify as persistent organic pollutants are the subject of explicit prohibitions under Regulation 2019/1021.[183]

The lists of approved active substances of Regulation 540/2011 indicated, in early 2023, 154 substances which had been examined and then approved under Regulation 1107/2009, but also 354 substances which were 'deemed' to be approved – and thus allowed to be used in pesticides – as they had been approved under the less stringent requirements of Directive 91/414. These figures demonstrate the slow progress in making Regulation 1107/2009 operational.[184]

The conditions for use are generally rather vague: for example, it mentions, as regards glyphosate, a widely used active substance:

> only uses as herbicide may be authorised … For the implementation of the uniform principles … the conclusions of the review report on glyphosate and in particular Appendices I and II thereof, shall be taken into account. In this overall assessment, Member States must pay particular attention to the protection of the groundwater in vulnerable areas, in particular with respect to non-crop uses.

Such information may be of very limited use for farmers or households who use glyphosate. Scientific concern that glyphosate might be carcinogenic did not move the Commission to prohibit its use. A citizen initiative of 2017 to have the substance banned was answered negatively,[185] and in 2023 its authorisation was prolonged for a further 10 years. In this case, the scientific uncertainty thus works in favour of the glyphosate producer. At the same time, the case demonstrates the excessive length of procedures.

The labelling of pesticides is regulated by a Commission implementing regulation,[186] which also provides standard phrases for specific risks to humans, animals or the environment (annex II) and for safety precautions (annex III).

In 2009, a directive was adopted, based on Article 192 TFEU, on the sustainable use of 6-34 pesticides which required Member States to adopt National Action Plans in order to reduce risks and dependence on pesticides (Article 4) and to provide for integrated pesticide management (Article 14) and compulsory training of distributors and professional users.[187] Implementation of that directive was poor and hardly enforced by the Commission.[188]

[181] Commission Implementing Regulation 540/2011 containing the list of active substances [2011] OJ L153/1. By the end of 2022, this regulation had been times amended 401.

[182] See, eg Commission Implementing Regulation 767/2013 on bifertranol [2013] OJ L214/5; Regulation 1022/2011 on cyclanilide [2011] OJ L270/11.

[183] Regulation 2019/1021 (n 65).

[184] See also Commission, 'Evaluation of Regulation 1107/2009 and of Regulation 396/05' COM(2020) 208; Commission, SWD(2020) 87.

[185] Commission, C(2017) 8414.

[186] Regulation 547/2011 as regards labelling requirements for plant protection products [2011] OJ L155/176.

[187] Directive 2009/128 establishing a framework for Community action to achieve the sustainable use of pesticides [2008] OJ L309/71.

[188] The implementation reports by the Commission itself were rather devastating; see Commission, COM(2017) 587; Commission, COM(2020) 204. Their conclusions were confirmed by the European Court of Auditors, *Sustainable Use of Plant Protection Products. Limited Progress in Measuring and Reducing Risks* (Luxembourg, 2020).

Yet, when the Commission presented its strategy for a toxic-free Europe, which would imply a reduction in the use of pesticides, compared to 2005, by 50 per cent in 2030[189] and proposed a regulation with concrete measures,[190] the Council considered that the impact of such measures on the competitivity of farmers had not sufficiently been taken into account and asked for more documentation.[191]

6-35 Regulation 528/12, which replaced an earlier directive, deals with the authorisation and use of non-agricultural pesticides (biocides); it is based on Article 114 TFEU.[192] The regulation concerns pesticides such as disinfectants, preservatives, pest-control products, anti-foulants and insecticides – overall, some 15,000 products. These products were grouped in 22 product types (annex V). The regulation built on Regulation 1907/2006 on chemicals and Regulation 1107/2009 on pesticides. Considerable monitoring tasks were delegated to the ECHA, established under Regulation 1907/2006.

Regulation 528/12 contained a list of active substances which may be used in biocidal products. These substances were authorised at Union level. The authorisation for a biocidal product is normally granted by Member States (Article 29 et seq). The manufacturer may, however, under certain conditions, apply for an EU authorisation which would be valid in the whole of the Union (Article 41 et seq). The regulation also contained detailed provisions for the mutual recognition of national authorisations (Article 32 et seq) on products that were treated with biocides, on the information which has to accompany any application and on the labelling of biocides.

The Commission's implementation report[193] of 2021 showed that the system set up by Regulation 528/2012 does not function properly. Since the adoption of the Regulation 528/2012, only 179 active substances have been approved, while 474 active substances remain to be assessed, but were, according to Regulation 528/2012, allowed to be used in biocidal products. Seven active substances were not approved. Overall, the Commission estimated that 35 per cent of the necessary work under the regulation had been completed.

I. Persistent Organic Pollutants

6-36 At international level, an agreement was concluded to restrict the use of POPs, which persist in the environment and accumulate in living organisms. The Union adhered to the Stockholm Convention and adopted legislation, which was progressively extended and sharpened, and which went in part beyond the international requirements, in Regulation 850/2004.[194] In 2019, the regulation was updated and made significantly more transparent in Regulation 2019/1021.[195] This regulation provided for the prohibition to produce, place on the market or use of some 25 pollutants (annex I), for relevant reductions of seven other

[189] Commission, 'Towards Zero Pollution for Air, Water and Soil' COM(2021) 400.

[190] Commission, 'Proposal for a Regulation on the Sustainable Use of Plant Protection Products' COM(2022) 305; Commission, SWD(2022) 170.

[191] Decision 2022/2572 [2022] OJ L331/6.

[192] Regulation 528/2012 on biocidal products [2012] OJ L167/1; this regulation replaced Directive 98/8 [1998] OJ L123/1.

[193] Commission, COM(2021) 287; Commission, SWD(2021) 178.

[194] Regulation 850/2004 on persistent organic pollutants [2004] OJ L158/7.

[195] Regulation 2019/1021 on persistent organic pollutants [2019] OJ L169/45.

substances (annex III) and for waste management measures for a series of them (annex IV). Member States have reporting and clean-up obligations which are, however, not closely monitored. For example, in numerous countries, disused pesticides containing POPs are still lying around, contaminating the environment and constituting a risk for human health. In Spain, there is about 150,000 tons of one single insecticide, Lindane, now classified in annex I, lying around; the overall remnants in the Union are estimated at more than one million tons.[196] Member States and the responsible industries are in particular deterred from dealing with it due to the high costs of elimination.

J. Products from Biotechnology

EU legislation on biotechnology and products derived from biotechnology, which started in the mid-1980s, is scattered, because, especially in the areas of agriculture and food on the one hand and of pharmaceuticals on the other, numerous directives fix specific provisions for certain products; these provisions are not presented here, since they concern the sectors of agriculture, consumer protection, health or industrial policy. As regards the environment, two basic directives, on the contained use of genetically modified micro-organisms[197] and the deliberate release of GMOs,[198] were adopted in 1990; the latter directive was substituted, in 2001, by Directive 2001/18.[199] A third directive, on the legal protection of biotechnological inventions, was adopted in 1998, after 10 years of discussion at EU level.[200] This directive is based on Article 114 TFEU. It provides for the protection of such inventions by national patent law of Member States and completes these provisions with a number of common rules. Furthermore, the Union adopted legislation on GMOs in food and feed,[201] and the transport of GMOs.[202] 6-37

Directive 2009/41 on the contained use of genetically modified micro-organisms[203] was based on Article 192 TFEU. It defined micro-organisms as any microbiological entity, cellular or non-cellular, capable of replication or transferring genetic material; this definition shows that the directive deals with living beings, which, for economic reasons, are treated as chemicals. The directive divided contained-use operations into those which are for teaching, research, development or non-industrial or non-commercial purposes and which are of small scale (type A operations) and other (type B) operations. Before an installation is used, a notification has to be made to the competent authorities, which describes the work, the scale of the operation and an 'assessment of the contained uses as regards the risks to human health and the environment that may occur'. The amount of information to be notified depends, furthermore, on the types of micro-organisms and the operations to be carried out. If new aspects become known which might affect the risk, this information

[196] J Vijgen, *The Legacy of Lindane HCH Isomer Production* (Amsterdam, 2006).

[197] Directive 90/219 on the contained use of genetically modified micro-organisms [1990] OJ L117/1; in 2009, this directive was codified under number 2009/41 [2009] OJ L175/75.

[198] Directive 90/220 [1990] OJ L117/15.

[199] Directive 2001/18 on the deliberate release of genetically modified organisms [2001] OJ L106/1.

[200] Directive 98/44 [1998] OJ L213/13.

[201] Regulation 1829/2003 on genetically modified food and feed [2003] OJ L268/1.

[202] Regulation 1946/2003 on the transboundary movement of genetically modified organisms [2003] OJ L287/1.

[203] Directive 2009/41 (n 197).

must also be conveyed. Also, information on any accident – 'any incident involving a significant and unintended release … which could present an immediate or delayed hazard to human health or the environment' – that has occurred has to be given to the authorities.

6-38 The competent authorities must examine the completeness of the information received. In certain cases, operations may not begin before consent is given; in other cases, a waiting period of 60–90 days must be respected. The authorities may impose conditions for the operations to be carried out, may provide a consultation of 'groups or the public' and may generally take all measures that they consider necessary.

Since, in particular, economic operators had considered several provisions of the original Directive 90/219 too restrictive – including the 'small scale' requirement – a major amendment of the directive was adopted in 1998.[204] The different procedures were simplified; notably, the procedures for the risk assessment of the operation were specified in more detail, and the number of micro-organisms that come into the lower categories of risky organisms was considerably increased. Directive 2009/41 maintained these simplifications.

Directive 2001/18,[205] which was based on Article 114 TFEU, dealt with the deliberate release into the environment of GMOs and of products containing them. The directive replaced Directive 90/220, which had been in force since 1990 and had two sections, on experimental releases of GMOs and on the release of products. Its application had led to more than 1000 experimental releases and some 30 releases of products containing GMOs.[206]

A crisis in the application of Directive 90/220 developed in 1996.[207] The Swiss company Novartis had applied, in France, for the authorisation to market genetically modified maize (Bt-maize). France examined the dossier that accompanied the application and considered that the risk assessment, which was part of the dossier, allowed the placing on the market of the maize. It thus sent the application with a favourable opinion to the European Commission, which transmitted the dossier to the other Member States. The Commission shared France's opinion and therefore submitted a corresponding proposal to the Committee set up under Directive 90/220. However, the great majority of the Member States (13 out of the then 15 Member States) were of the opinion that the risk assessment did not allow the placing on the market; they held that further research was necessary. Under the committee procedure of Directive 90/220, an opinion of the Committee which differed from the Commission's proposal needed unanimity; and this unanimity could not be reached as France sided with the Commission. The dossier then went to the Council, which again needed, under the present Article 293 TFEU, unanimity in order to amend the Commission's proposal. As France sided once more with the Commission, the fact that 13 Member States favoured a rejection of the application was of no help. Under the committee procedure, the dossier therefore went back to the Commission, which decided to give a positive opinion to the application.[208]

This decision led to strong reactions from the Member States. A number of them adopted national provisions, which prohibited the placing on the market of the maize, invoking a

[204] Directive 98/81 [1998] OJ L330/13.

[205] Directive 2001/18 (n 199).

[206] Commission, COM(1998) 85.

[207] Parts of the events are described in CJEU Case C-6/99 *Greenpeace France* ECLI:EU:C:2000:148, in particular in the Advocate General's Opinion.

[208] Commission Decision 97/98 [1997] OJ L31/69.

safeguard clause of Directive 90/220. As all Member States had expressed concern about the procedure and had stopped submitting new proposals to the Commission, and as, at the same time, there was 'growing concern on the part of the general public … with … this new technology', the Commission did not take legal action against the Member States. Under this standstill, no further applications under Directive 90/220 were made, discussed or decided at EU level. Rather, the elaboration of amendments to Directive 90/220 was prepared. When the Commission suggested making these amendments, Parliament and Council agreed that it would be better to have a completely new directive; this finally led to the adoption of Directive 2001/18. This directive became effective in October 2002; in 2003/2004, the standstill on the placing of new GMO-containing products on the market ended, at the same time as the new legislation on genetically modified food and feed entered into effect.[209]

Directive 2001/18 distinguished between releases for 'any other purpose than the placing on the market' – thus, in particular, releases for research, development or experimental purposes – and the placing on the market of GMOs 'as or in products'. A deliberate release for 'other purposes' must be notified in advance to the competent authority of the Member State in which the release is to take place, and be accompanied by a technical dossier. This dossier must in particular contain information on the GMO, the conditions of release and the receiving environment, a plan for monitoring, information on control, remediation methods, waste treatment and an environmental risk assessment, for which detailed provisions are laid down. The competent authority must, within 90 days, decide in writing on the application, provided the dossier is complete; the authorisation procedure is thus purely national. However, where the competent authority is of the opinion that sufficient experience has been obtained with such a release, it may ask the release to be admitted EU-wide. In this case, all other Member States become involved in the decision. The public 'and, where appropriate, groups' (Article 9) shall be consulted on deliberate releases. Furthermore, the public shall be informed of all 'other-purposes' releases. 6-39

Where GMOs are placed on the market 'as or in products', again the applicant has to submit a notification to the competent authority where the product is to be placed on the market for the first time. The application and a summary of the accompanying dossier are immediately transmitted to the other Member States and the Commission. The notification shall contain extensive information and documentation, in particular on the GMO, indications for use and handling, the environmental risk assessment, data on results from research and development releases, the conditions for placing on the market and a monitoring plan, as well as a proposal for packaging and labelling the product. The competent authority must react to the notification within 90 days. Where it decides that it has sufficient information to indicate that a GMO release would not be a risk to humans or the environment, it shall send the dossier to the European Commission, together with an assessment report and an indication whether or not the GMO product should be placed on the market. The other Member States, who also receive the dossier, and the Commission may ask for further information; they may also comment on the application or present reasoned objections to the placing on the market of the GMO (product). The summary of the notified dossier and of the assessment report must be made available to the public. Comments from the public shall be circulated among public authorities.

[209] See para 6-38.

Where objections are raised, the Commission is obliged to consult the relevant EU Scientific Committee.[210] The Commission may also consult a committee that it has set up with a view to obtaining advice on the ethical implications of biotechnology. The Commission shall then elaborate a proposal for a decision, which is submitted to the Committee that was set up under Article 30 of Directive 2001/18. Where the Committee agrees with the Commission proposal, the Commission takes the decision. Where the Committee does not give an opinion or disagrees, the Commission's proposal is referred to the Council, which has three months to decide. If the Council opposes the proposal with a qualified majority, the Commission shall re-examine it, re-present it anew to the Council and present a modified proposal or a legislative proposal. Where the Council does not raise objections, the Commission adopts its proposal and sends the dossier back to the Member State that first received the notification. That Member State finally authorises the placing on the market of the GMO (-product).

6-40 In order to further mitigate concerns of consumers and public opinion, the Council adopted a regulation on novel food,[211] which required food products that contain GMOs to be authorised EU-wide or – where the risk is less great – notified to the national authorities and to bear a corresponding label, insofar as differences to normal food products can scientifically be detected. Furthermore, Commission Regulation 1813/97[212] and Council Regulation 1139/98[213] fixed supplementary labelling requirements for the labelling of food and food additives that were produced with the help of GMOs.[214]

Regulation 1829/2003 on genetically modified food and feed[215] also applied to GMOs used for cultivation (as seeds) to produce food or feed, which thus no longer come under Directive 2001/18.[216] For these products, it deviated considerably from Directive 2001/18. Applications under this regulation are now to be made to the EFSA, seated in Parma; Member States play only a marginal role in the authorisation procedure. It is the EFSA which evaluates the application and gives an opinion on it to the Commission. The Commission decides by a comitology procedure whether to authorise the placing of the product on the market.

The participation of the public is not ensured.[217] And it is not surprising that the 'club'-attitude of the EFSA and the considerable secrecy surrounding the decision-making process have raised considerable suspicion with public opinion in Europe, which remains – including the majority of farmers – sceptical with regard to the new technology. Almost all authorisations that have been given since the end of the standstill (moratorium) in 2000 have been given under the new procedure of Regulation 1829/2003, and not under Directive 2001/18. Thus, although the World Trade Organization (WTO), which had examined the procedure under Directive 2001/18, condemned the Union for practising a moratorium and not authorising GMO products any more, this did not raise concerns within the Union.[218]

[210] On this committee, see para 6-02.

[211] Regulation 258/97 on novel food and novel food ingredients [1997] OJ L43/1; see also Commission Regulation 1813/97 [1997] OJ L257/7.

[212] Commission Regulation 1813/97 [1997] OJ L257/7.

[213] Regulation 1139/98 [1998] OJ L159/4.

[214] See also Commission Regulations 49/2000 [2000] OJ L6/13 and 50/2000 [2000] OJ L6/15.

[215] Regulation 1829/2003 (n 201).

[216] ibid Recital 34 and Arts 16(7) and 18(3)(c); see also CJEU Case C-58/10 *Monsanto* ECLI:EU:C:2011:553.

[217] On participation in the decision-making procedure for authorising GMO products, see para 4-17.

[218] WTO Case DS 291 *USA v European Union*, Panel Report of 29 September 2006.

By the end of 2022, the Commission had authorised the placing on the market of 90 genetically modified plants (soya, maize, cotton, rape and sugar beet).

Regulation 1946/2003 dealt with the transboundary movement of GMOs,[219] following a requirement of the Cartagena Protocol on Biosafety. The Union adhered to the Cartagena Protocol itself,[220] the CJEU having confirmed, at the request of the Commission, that Article 192 and not Article 191(4) and/or 207 TFEU was the appropriate legal basis for that decision.[221] The regulation was based on the principle of prior informed consent, in order to promote trade in GMO products.

In 2015, Directive 2001/18 was amended on the basis of Article 114 TFEU; in particular, a new Article 26b was inserted into the directive,[222] which reads: 6-41

> [A] Member State may adopt measures restricting or prohibiting the cultivation in all or part of its territory of a GMO, provided that such measures are in conformity with Union law, reasoned, proportionate and non-discriminatory and, in addition, are based on compelling grounds such as those related to: (a) environmental policy objectives; (b) town and country planning; (c) land use; (d) socio-economic impacts; (e) avoidance of GMO presence in other products; (f) agricultural policy objectives; (g) public policy ... Those grounds shall, in no case, conflict with the environmental risk assessment carried out pursuant to this directive or to Regulation (EC No 1829/2003).

The Member State concerned shall send a draft of its measure to the Commission and wait during a standstill period of 75 days for (non-binding) Commission comments before it adopts the measure.

Recitals 14 and 15 of Directive 2015/412 underline that the grounds which may be invoked by Member States to take restriction or prohibition measures must be 'distinct from and complementary to' the risk assessment which was made under EU GMO legislation. Such environmental measures could be (Recital 14)

> the maintenance and development of agricultural practices which offer a better potential to reconcile production with ecosystem sustainability, or maintenance of local biodiversity, including certain habitats and ecosystems, or certain types of natural and landscape features, as well as specific ecosystem functions and services.

Examples of socio-economic impacts are high costs, impracticability or impossibility of implanting coexistence, small islands or mountain zones, the diversity of agricultural production or the need to ensure seed and plant-propagating material purity; cultural traditions are also mentioned by way of example.

The underlying consideration of these provisions was that health and environment aspects were already harmonised at EU level. This approach, though, appears inconsistent: objections against the planting of GMO seeds are based just on health or environmental concerns: even where such plants might impair organic agricultural production, the concern is one of health. Indeed, consumers buy organic food because they consider it to be less treated with chemicals, produced in an environmentally more friendly way, etc.

[219] Regulation 1946/2003 (n 202).

[220] Decision 2002/628 [2002] OJ L201/48.

[221] CJEU Opinion 2/00 ECLI:EU:C:2001:664.

[222] See Directive 2015/412 amending Directive 2001/18 as regards the possibility for Member States to restrict or prohibit the cultivation of genetically modified organisms (GMOs) in their territory [2015] OJ L68/1.

Out of 27 Member States, 18 made use of Directive 2015/412 and prohibited or restricted the cultivation of GMO plants on their territory (the most notable exceptions being Spain and Portugal, where cultivation of GMO plants currently takes place). Compliance with WTO provisions on free trade appears doubtful. The correct way to address the concerns of numerous Member States would have been to suggest either that the legal basis for the EU legislation be changed and that Article 192 TFEU become the legal basis, allowing Member States to recur to Article 193 TFEU and completely prohibit GMO plants (or GMO animals), or insert the provisions of Article 193 TFEU into the existing EU legislation, which is possible even where the legislative act is based on Article 114 TFEU.

In 2018, the CJEU held that only organisms obtained by the use of techniques or methods of mutagenesis, which had conventionally been used in a number of applications and had a long safety record, were excluded from the field of application of Directive 2001/18.[223] Thus, the so-called CRISPR method, which enabled much more precise genetic modification of organisms, was covered by the directive's provisions. Many scientists strongly opposed this approach, as they disliked in particular the requirement to make an environmental risk assessment; they argued that the CRISPR method did not allow the distinction between conventional and CRISPR-based modifications. However, this argument neglects the fact that Directive 2001/18 explicitly requested an indication in the notification which made the method used for the modification transparent;[224] moreover, the possibility to patent innovations in this area speaks rather in favour of a differentiation between GMO and non-GMO plants. In July 2023, the Commission gave in to the pressure and proposed exempting 'new genetic techniques plants' (NGT plants) from the field of application of Directive 2001/18.[225] The proposal is at present being discussed by the other Union institutions. The main controversy concerns the question of whether this approach, which is argued to be more precise, more controllable and more predictable, justifies the amendment of the legislation.

6-42 The 20 years of discussion on the placing of genetically modified products on the market of the Union have thus led to a strong centralisation of the permitting procedure. As the Union is not a state, many of the democratic safeguards which exist at Member State level have disappeared or been reduced at EU level, such as full access to the scientific data which accompany the application, a public discussion of the necessity and opportunity to authorise the placing of the product on the market, of the health and environmental risks linked to this placing on the market, etc. Opinion polls show continued public hostility to the use of genetically modified food, feed and seeds, not to mention animals – though much less to medical and industrial uses. An increasing concern is that of the cross-fertilisation of organic farming products by GMO farming, which would make organic farming – the relevant EU provisions provide that organic farming must be GMO-free – impossible.

[223] CJEU Case C-528/16, *Confédération paysanne ao* ECLI:EU:C:2018:583. In 2023, the CJEU nuanced its position with regard to certain in vitro techniques, allowing them to be, under certain conditions, exempted from Directive 2001/18, see Case C-688/21 *Confederation paysanne II* ECLI:EU:C:2023:75.

[224] Directive 2001/18 (n 199) annex III, A and B.

[225] Commission, COM(2023) 411; the impact assessement is contained in Commission, SWD(2023) 412. NGT plant 'means a genetically modified plant obtained by targeted mutageneis or cisgenesis or a combination thereof, on the condition that it does not contain any genetic material originating from putside the breeders' gene pool that temporarily may have been inserted during the development of the NGT plant' (Art 3 no 2 of the Commission proposal COM (2023) 411).

The health risk of GMO products does not seem beyond suspicion, if one considers long-term effects, plant resistance, allergy issues and the uncertainty of animal tests. It is not clear why genetic modification technology should be introduced: it is made for industrial agriculture, brings limited benefits to farmers in the Union, who already produce too much food, does not constitute a solution to world hunger – which is mainly a problem of distribution, not of production – and favours patents on life to the benefit of industrial companies. The environmental problem with GMOs is that once they are released into the environment, they cannot be taken back. GMO products in agriculture seem to require an increased rather than decreased use of pesticides, because plants and pests become resistant to the new, genetically modified plant. Also, the coexistence of GMOs with organic food production is impossible over the long term. From that angle, the public request to err on the side of caution is more than understandable. However, it seems that, in view of the worldwide development and expansion of this new technology – in particular, in agriculture, food and pharmaceuticals – the large-scale introduction of genetically modified organisms into the environment is no longer reversible unless new data demonstrate beyond doubt the long-term adverse health and environmental effects.

The difference in approach between public opinion which is afraid of, and therefore opposed to, biotechnology and economic operators and EU public authorities which favour it and try to press this technology on the market cannot be solved simply by requiring labelling for GMO products, at least not until the Union introduces a 'GMO-free' label – which the Commission has rejected so far. A label that informs consumers of the presence of GMOs which is meant to allow consumers to make an informed choice will have little or no effect in many situations (hotels, restaurants, catering, food aid), apart from the fact that labels are frequently not read. The placing on the market of agricultural GMOs in developing countries is not in the general interests of those countries and their economic development, as it rather increases economic dependence on industrialised countries.

Overall, GMO technology in Union agriculture seems to be superfluous, is profitable to few, promotes industrial agriculture and bears risks for humans and the environment.

III. Environmental Labelling

The Union has developed a considerable number of labels which refer to environmental 6-43
aspects of products[226] without forming a consistent and coherent whole. There are two main groups of labels:

1. environmental quality labels, which present the environmental performance or the environmentally 'good' composition of products and which intend to incite buyers and users to make an informed choice, preferring the environmentally 'better' product; and
2. labels which warn of the environmental risks and dangers of a product.

[226] See also the definition of the International Standardization Organization for environmental labels: 'A logo or a symbol attached to a product which is awarded by a third-party, agency or non-governmental organisation and which is based on multiple criteria and lifecycle analysis.' A second type of eco-label includes claims of single attributes, such as 'energy efficient'.

A. Quality Labels

(i) Eco-labelling

6-44 In 1992, the Union adopted a regulation on an eco-label award scheme with the aim of promoting products which have a reduced environmental impact during their entire life cycle and which give better information to consumers/users. The system was revised in both 2000 and 2010, but not significantly modified.[227]

Participation in the scheme is voluntary. The scheme consists of an eco-logo – a flower with a corolla of petals in the form of the 12 EU stars surrounding an 'E' – and is granted to products which satisfy certain environmental criteria. These criteria are fixed at EU level for specific product groups, while the attribution of the label to the individual product is decided by the competent authorities of each Member State. The regulation fixes selective criteria, and organises the consultation with interest groups and other relevant matters for the functioning of the scheme.

In the follow-up of the deregulation move of 1992, economic operators tried to see the system privatised, but met with stiff opposition from the Council, led by the UK and Denmark.[228] Nevertheless, the system had difficulties to overcome in order to succeed. Indeed, it met from the very beginning with the opposition of economic operators' associations, who opposed the idea that some 15, 20 or 30 per cent of products of a specific product group should be allowed to bear an official label which qualified these products to be 'better' and allowed their producers to be 'frontrunners'. Such objections were formed at national level in countries that were afraid of competition from other Member States, but finally reached EU level. Furthermore, procedures for determining criteria for product groups were long-lasting and complicated; products were not allowed to contain hazardous substances (Article 6(6)); and consumers barely knew about the eco-logo, so producers did not have much to gain from using it, even though it was not inexpensive. National eco-label systems, in particular the Blue Angel in Germany and the Green Swan in Scandinavia, were well established, better known and accepted, and quicker at producing results.

Finally, third countries – first of all the USA, but also Brazil – complained that the scheme created barriers to international trade. Typical controversies concerned questions such as whether the use of recycled paper in toilet paper and other papers should be rated as environmentally favourable: wood-exporting countries were, of course, not of this opinion. The USA was of the opinion that, if criteria concerning the production methods were taken into consideration, this would mean that the Union wanted to impose its production standards on third countries. In contrast, EU producers were of the opinion that production or social standards in third countries were not adequately taken into account and that this privileged imports.

6-45 Following a review of the scheme, the Commission suggested phasing out national and regional eco-labels for product groups which were covered by the EU scheme; introducing a graded system that would allow products to obtain one, two or three flowers, depending on how environmentally superior they were; and transferring responsibility for fixing the

[227] Regulation 66/2010 on the EU eco-label [2010] OJ L27/1; this regulation replaced Regulation 1980/2000 [2000] OJ L237/1; the original regulation was Regulation 880/92 [1992] OJ L99/1.

[228] Environmental Watch, 7 October 1994, 1.

ecological criteria for the different product groups to an independent body.[229] All these proposals were rejected. The coexistence of the EU scheme with national eco-label schemes was solved by allowing the coexistence of the two systems for one and the same product.

By mid-2015, criteria for some 33 product groups had been established,[230] 2000 licences had been granted and 42,000 products had received the EU eco-label – still a very small number, though a considerable increase compared to 2010, when 1073 had the eco-label. Denmark even turned away from the EU system and back to the Scandinavian eco-label system, while not fewer than 13 Member States set up national eco-labelling schemes – though often with limited success. The status of the EU eco-label scheme is still very uncertain; neither economic operators nor environmental or consumer groups are enthusiastic about it. The label is not well known and has not really reached consumer awareness;[231] producers complain about a lack of recognition by public authorities, for example by reduced tax, reduced inspections or other advantages when they use the eco-label. Decisions to develop eco-labels for hotels[232] and camping sites[233] could make the label better known, provided it is used to attract tourists.[234]

(ii) Organic Farming

Agricultural products which come from specific ecological production – the conditions of which have been very meticulously laid down in order to avoid abuses and, at the same time, make life for traditional farmers easier – must bear the label 'organic farming'.[235] In 2020, about 9 per cent of land in the Union was farmed organically; the share of organic products in the total Union consumption is not known.[236] Products from third countries may bear the statement 'organic product' where the production methods have expressly been recognised as being equivalent to the requirements of Regulation 2018/848.[237] The Union label for organic production – 12 stars forming the shape of a leaf on a green background – is not well known, partly because the agricultural policy tries to favour traditional farming and make life for organic farmers as difficult as possible. In 2020, the Commission proposed a number of measures to increase the share of organic production to 25 per cent by 2030.[238] Negative reactions from the agricultural sector quickly followed.[239] 6-46

[229] [1997] OJ C114/9.

[230] Commission, 'Fitness Check for Regulation 1221/2009 (EMAS) and Regulation 66/2010' SWD(2017) 253.

[231] See also Commission Decision 2006/402 establishing the EU eco-label working plan [2006] OJ L162/78, which was relatively ambitious.

[232] Commission Decision 2017/175 on tourist accommodation services [2017] OJ L28/9.

[233] Commission Decision 2009/564 on campsite services [2009] OJ L186/36.

[234] By mid-2015, 98 hotels in the EU had acquired the eco-label, more than half of them in Italy; see ec.europa.eu/ecat.

[235] Regulation 2018/848 on organic production and labelling of organic products [2018] OJ L150/1. This regulation replaced Regulation 834/2007 [2007] OJ L189/1. The labelling details were fixed by Commission Regulation 889/2008 [2008] OJ L250/1.

[236] Commission, *Organic Farming in the EU. A Decade of Organic Growth* (Brussels, 2023).

[237] At present (end of 2022), equivalence of organic production with Union provisions is recognised with regard to 14 countries: Chile, Switzerland, the UK, Argentina, Australia, Canada, Costa Rica, India, Israel, Japan, New Zealand, Korea, Tunisia and USA; see Commission, COM(2022) 728.

[238] Commission, 'A Farm to Fork Strategy for a Fair, Healthy and Environmentally-Friendly Food System' COM(2020) 381; Commission, COM(2022) 305.

[239] Decision 2022/2572 (n 191).

(iii) Energy Consumption

6-47 The EU discussion on the labelling of energy consumption of electrical household appliances started about 30 years ago. However, attempts to obtain solutions via industrial standardisation and voluntary agreements with manufacturers failed. This led the Union to develop, since 1992,[240] environmental labels for electrical or electronic household appliances, which are somehow too narrowly called energy labels: indeed, the labels indicate, according to industrial standards or other provisions fixed in the annexes to Directive 92/75 and in a graphically fixed scheme, the energy and water consumption, performance and noise level.

In 2017, a regulation was adopted on the energy labelling of products[241] which was based on Article 194(2) TFEU; it replaced a directive of 2010 and applied to all new energy-related products (except means of transport), such as washing machines, televisions and air conditioners. The detailed labelling requirements were subsequently elaborated for each type of product by Commission delegated regulations.[242] They consisted of green, yellow or red arrows, ranging from A to G according to the energy efficiency, which measures the annual energy consumption. Previous attempts to introduce labels with classes A+, A++ and A+++ were in principle abandoned, as the vast majority of products had progressively reached the A+ classes. The intention now is to have the A+ classes reserved for products with energy from renewable sources.[243] Generally, a rescaling of the labels shall take place every 10 years, in order to incite improved products. The Court of Auditors found that the efforts of energy labelling to save energy were reduced by considerable regulatory delays and significant cases of non-compliance by manufacturers and retailers.[244]

A separate, but similar regulation was adopted on the energy efficiency of tyres;[245] the label shall also contain information on the noise level and on the wet grip (snow grip).

(iv) Fuel Consumption of Cars

6-48 Directive 1999/94, based on Article 192 TFEU, introduced a requirement that all new passenger cars at the point of sale bear a label on the official fuel consumption and average CO_2 emissions.[246] Also, a guide on fuel economy and CO_2 emissions had to be made available to consumers at the point of sale, free of charge, but 'on request' only (Article 4). Extending the labelling requirement in future to used cars was under consideration (Recital 6), but has since been abandoned.

[240] Directive 92/75 on the conservation of energy and other resources by household appliances [1992] OJ L297/16.

[241] Regulation 2017/1369 setting a framework for energy labelling [2017] OJ L198/1. This regulation replaced Directive 2010/30 [2010] OJ L153/1.

[242] See, eg Commission Delegated Regulation 2019/2014 on household washing machines and household washers-dryers [2019] OJ L315/29. Commission, COM(2022) 723 contains a list of all adopted delegated regulations, which is continuously being updated.

[243] Regulation 2017/1369 (n 241) Recital 17.

[244] European Court of Auditors, 'Special Report 1/2020: EU Action on Eco-design and Energy Labelling: Important Contribution to Greater Energy Efficiency Reduced by Significant Delays and Non-compliance' (Luxembourg, 2020).

[245] Regulation 2020/740 on the labelling of tyres with respect of fuel efficiency and other parameters [2020] OJ L177/1.

[246] Directive1999/94 [1999] OJ L12/16.

Such a label is not really capable of making the consumer change their intentions and buy a car that consumes or emits less, as there is no yardstick against which the consumer can measure possible economies. The label requirement was mainly introduced at the instigation of the car industry, which wanted to be seen as contributing to the fight against climate change. There is general consensus in the meantime that the directive did not reach its aims.[247]

(v) Recyclable Packaging

Under Directive 94/62 on waste and packaging waste,[248] the Commission made a proposal for the marking of reusable or recyclable packaging.[249] The symbols consisted of different round circles. The proposal attempted to create new, EU-specific symbols. As economic operators, however, oriented themselves increasingly to the US system for labelling of packaging, which is also promoted via international standardisation organisations, the Commission's proposal received a cool reception. The Council did not discuss it and the European Parliament suggested instead taking over symbols that had been developed by different sectors of the packaging industry. The proposal is now obsolete. 6-49

(vi) Forest Label

In view of the disappearance of tropical rain and other forests, discussions have continued for a considerable amount of time about the creation of a label for wood which indicates that the wood comes from sustainable forestry. The EU has indicated on several occasions its commitment to such a label. In decisions taken in the context of the EU eco-label scheme, one of the criteria for paper products was that the wood must stem from sustainable forestry. So far, however, no internationally recognised label for such sustainable forestry exists. The Union has not developed such a label. Attempts in the Netherlands to impose such a label failed because no agreement could be found as to what exactly sustainable forestry meant. At present, illegal logging continues to be practised in numerous countries, without trade in wood products being affected. The Regulation on timber and timber products did not introduce a label to inform users and consumers that the timber was legally harvested.[250] 6-50

(vii) Blue Flag for Beaches

The Blue Flag is a certification granted by a private, globally operating organisation, the Foundation for Environmental Education. The Blue Flag award is given when the water and beach quality, or the quality of marinas and boat tourism, complies with the Foundation's 6-51

[247] See also the same conclusions, though hidden in diplomatic language, in Commission, 'Evaluation of Directive 1999/94' SWD(2016) 270.

[248] Directive 94/62 (n 104).

[249] [1996] OJ C382/10.

[250] Regulation 995/2010 laying down obligations of operators who place timber and timber products on the market [2010] OJ L295/23.

quality requirements. The award is granted annually. It has nothing to do with Union law and policy regarding bathing waters.

B. Warning Labels

(i) Chemicals

6-52 Directive 67/548[251] on dangerous chemical substances was amended in 1979 to include a label 'hazardous to the environment'. The label consisted of a symbol showing a dead fish beached beside a dead tree, both in black, on a yellow-orange background; the symbol was accompanied by phrases on the special risks (R-phrases) and the safe use of the substance (S-phrases). By the end of 2007, some 200 substances had been labelled with the 'hazardous to the environment' symbol. This seems quite a small number. However, some 1000 substances from petrol refining, such as aromatic hydrocarbons, naphtha, extracts and distillates, which are classified 'toxic', did not bear this label, though they appear to be dangerous for the environment. The reason for this was that a substance that was labelled 'toxic' need not also be labelled 'hazardous to the environment' (Article 23 of Directive 67/548). The same was true for substances where the indication 'may cause cancer' was obligatory.

In 2008, this labelling system was significantly amended by a new regulation, which adapted the EU labelling scheme to the United Nations Global Harmonized System of Classification and Labelling of Chemicals (GHS), which itself was considerably influenced by the global labelling scheme for the transport of goods.[252] The new regulation ignored the fact that the risks for the consumer/user and for the environment are very different during the transport of a product and during its use in the home, in the garden, at the workplace or in agriculture. The most significant change in the new system is the abandoning of the yellow-orange background of the label, which was replaced by a rhombus with a white background, sometimes surrounded by a red frame. The new label is much less visible. The pictogram – where it is required – is accompanied by signal words ('danger' or 'warning'), and by hazard statements and precautionary statements which are standardised by Regulation 1272/2008. The hazard statements and precautionary statements are limited to indicating risks to the aquatic environment and to the ozone layer; all other R-phrases referring to the environment were deleted. The pictogram 'hazardous to the environment' only appears for the aquatic environment; the risk to the ozone layer is symbolised by a pictogram showing an exclamation mark. The number of environment-related S-phrases (precautionary statements) was strongly reduced.

Pesticide labelling is not included in the present labelling requirements for dangerous mixtures. The labelling of pesticides is regulated by Commission Regulation 547/2011.[253] No pictograms are foreseen. The label must indicate the concentration of the active substance and contain standard phrases for special risks to humans and the environment (annex II), as well as standard phrases for safety precautions (annex III). The labelling of

[251] Directive 67/548 (n 154).
[252] Regulation 1272/2008 (n 168).
[253] Commission Regulation 547/2011 [2011] OJ L155/176.

biocidal products follows the provisions of Regulation 1272/2008 for chemicals, but also requires the indication of the presence of nanomaterials.[254]

(ii) Separate Collection

Directive 2006/66 on batteries[255] contained a symbol indicating 'separate collection' of batteries, which consisted of a crossed-out wheeled bin, accompanied by an indication of which heavy metal was involved (Hg for mercury, Cd for cadmium or Pb for lead). This symbol was to be placed on batteries only, and indicated that they were subject to separate collection and should not be put in a normal waste bin. The same symbol was used in Directive 2012/19 to indicate that electrical and electronic products had to be collected separately.[256] 6-53

(iii) Products Containing GMOs

In order to meet public concern within the Union regarding the placing on the market of products that contain GMOs, the Union adopted a regulation[257] that required food labels to indicate that the food contained GMOs; however, this requirement only applied to those cases where differences between such food products and normal food products could be scientifically detected. Since this label neither covered all products nor all products that contained GMOs – estimations indicate that 90 per cent of all food products are not covered by the labelling requirements – it will not allow consumers systematically to avoid such products. The large-scale introduction of GMOs cannot be stopped by such a measure; at best, it will be slowed down. Requests from environmental and consumer organisations to introduce a 'GMO-free' label – this would be perceived as a quality label, not as a warning label – have so far been rejected by the Union. Based on a recital of Regulation 1830/2003,[258] a number of Member States have introduced such a label at national level, without the Commission taking action against them. 6-54

IV. Imports and Exports of Products

There are no general provisions on the import and export of products. In particular, the Union has no general provision which provides that a product which is banned from or severely restricted on the Union market should not be exported, either to any third country or at least to any non-industrialised country. Rather, the Union follows international trends, which are based on the principle that any country should decide for itself whether it wishes to have certain substances or products on its market or not. International agreements thus 6-55

[254] Regulation 528/2012 (n 8) Art 69.

[255] Directive 2006/66 (n 43).

[256] Directive 2012/19 [2012] OJ L197/38.

[257] Regulation 1830/2003 concerning the traceability and labelling of genetically modified organisms and of food and feed products produced from genetically modified organisms [2003] OJ L268/24.

[258] ibid Recital 11: 'It is necessary to ensure that consumers are fully and reliably informed about GMOs and the products, foods and feed produced therefrom, so as to allow them to make an informed choice of product.'

follow the principle of 'prior informed consent' (PIC): prior to the first export, the importing state is to be informed of the existence of the ban or the restrictions that exist in the exporting country. Then it has to decide whether to allow the import.

If one takes asbestos products as an example: what reasons may exist for asbestos fibres, which are known to cause cancer, to be banned within the Union but to only undergo the PIC procedure when they are exported to Africa or Asia? In my opinion, the PIC principle does not offer sufficient protection to humans and the environment in the developing countries, where administrative controls are often insufficient. The EU policy should rather provide that, as a rule, any substance or product that is banned or severely restricted in use within the Union shall have the same restriction when it is exported to non-industrialised countries.

The Union, however, follows a different approach. In 2002, it decided to ratify the Rotterdam Convention of 1998 on the PIC procedure related to the export and import of chemicals,[259] which had been elaborated under the auspices of the Food and Agricultural Organisation and the United Nations Environment Programme. Regulation 649/2012[260] replaced earlier regulations and was based on both Articles 192(1) and 207 TFEU.[261] Annex 1 of the regulation listed different groups of chemicals and pesticides which were subject to the notification procedure. The three parts of annex 1 differentiated them according to the amount of information which had to accompany the notification. Part 1, comprising some 250 substances (as at the end of 2022), required information to be conveyed on the identity of the substance, the type of restriction which existed and other necessary information. Part 2 only required the indication of the identity of the substance. An exporter who intended to export for the first time a chemical coming under the regulation had to inform the competent authority of the Member State where they were established at least 35 days before the export was due to take place and 15 days in advance each year thereafter. The competent authority had to check whether the information was complete and then inform the ECHA of the export, which had to ensure that the importers receive notification at least 15 days prior to the first shipment. Annex V contained a list of 32 substances and products the export of which was banned. This list included in particular the persistent organic pollutants covered by Regulation 2019/1021.[262] Article 3 of Regulation 2017/852 provided, furthermore, an export ban of mercury and mercury compounds, in accordance with the international Minamata Convention.[263] For imports into the Union, the regulation provided for the Commission's comitology decisions for the whole of the Union where a Member State was notified by a third country of a substance or product that was banned in that third country (Article 13).

It is doubtful whether these measures are sufficient. Indeed, administrations in third countries do not always seem to be able fully to assess the impact of chemicals that are to be imported. Also, the World Health Organization estimated that every year a considerable number of persons suffer acute unintentional poisoning as a result of the misuse of

[259] Decision 2003/106 [2003] OJ L63/27.

[260] Regulation 649/2012 concerning the export and import of hazardous chemicals [2012] OJ L201/60.

[261] On the double legal basis, see CJEU Case C-178/05 *Commission v European Parliament and Council* ECLI:EU:C:2007:317.

[262] Regulation 2019/1021 (n 65).

[263] Regulation 2017/852 (n 144).

pesticides; no figures exist for environmental damage caused by chemicals the use of which is banned or restricted within the Union.

V. Industrial Standardisation

Environmental requirements for products – as for processes – may be fixed by legislative regulation, such as for emissions from cars. They may also be fixed by industrial technical standards, which are elaborated by private standardisation organisations and the result of which is a technical indication for some product characteristics. 6-56

Industrial standards are, by definition, not mandatory. Legally, they constitute a recommendation of their authors to the manufacturer to follow the indications laid down in the standard. Their degree of recognition depends on the readiness of producers to apply the standard. Public authorities often support the application of standards, for instance by providing in legislation that standards must be complied with or by not laying down specifications in regulations but referring to (private) standards, etc.

At EU level, there are no specific EU standardisation organisations. Rather, the three organisations CEN, CENELEC and ETSI that exist are international bodies which, right from their beginnings, have gone beyond the borders of the Union. All three organisations have close relations with national standardisation bodies on the one hand, and with international bodies on the other, which include arrangements to avoid the duplication of work.

CEN was created in 1961 and is located in Brussels. Its members are national standards institutions of Western European countries and, since 1992, it also has associate members in the form of organisations that represent economic and social interests at European level and which fulfil certain conditions as regards representativity and objectives. About half of CEN's budget is provided for by EU funds. 6-57

CENELEC (Comité Européen de Normalisation Electrotechnique; European Committee for Electrotechnical Standardization) began its work in the early 1960s. It has been located in Brussels since 1972. Its members are national electro-technical committees. It elaborates standards in the area of electrical and electronic equipment; roughly one-third of its budget is provided by the Union. About three-quarters of all CENELEC standards are parallels of international electro-technical standards.

ETSI (European Telecommunications Standards Institute) was created in 1988 for the telecommunications sector.

Industrial standardisation is of growing importance for environmental issues in the Union, since it opted, in the early 1980s, for a 'new approach' to the approximation of national legal rules,[264] by which the Council intended to limit legislative harmonisation to the adoption of the essential safety requirements (or other requirements in the general interest) with which products put on the market must conform; other parts of a product or services sector would be assured by voluntary standards that were elaborated by industrial standardisation organisations, Yet, the problem of how industrial standards can be made greener has not 6-58

[264] The definition of 'new approach' was first used in Commission, COM(85) and Council Resolution of 7 May 1985 On a new approach to technical harmonisation and standards [1985] OJ C136/1.

yet been solved. Indeed, at national level, public authorities normally participate in working groups on the elaboration of technical standards. Their representatives may bring environmental general interest aspects into the discussion and influence discussions on finding the balance between economic and environmental (general interest) aspects. Where they do not succeed, they may suggest governmental regulation on the subject covered by the standard.

At Union level, the representatives of economic operators in CEN and CENELEC write the standards more or less alone and are hardly influenced by environmental organisations, which are too weak and financially feeble to be much more than a figleaf.[265] Commission officials do not normally participate in the CEN or CENELEC working groups; written comments do not appear to have a significant influence, and the threat of regulatory action at Union level is not very convincing.

A number of product-related directives have been elaborated since the mid-1980s according to the new approach.[266] However, the essential requirements laid down in these directives have practically never dealt with environmental issues. Thus, the impact of these directives on the environment has been limited: indeed, since the protection of the environment is also an essential requirement of EU policy,[267] the omission of the regulation of environmental issues in the context of essential requirements at EU level means that Member States were free to adopt environmental measures at national level as regards these products.

6-59 The only environmental directive adopted under the new approach was Directive 94/62 on packaging and packaging waste.[268] This directive, which was based on Article 114 TFEU, contained an annex which laid down vaguely formulated essential requirements for packaging. Thus, packaging had to be:

- so manufactured that the packaging volume and weight is limited to the minimum adequate amount to maintain the necessary level of safety, hygiene and acceptance for the packed product and for the consumer;
- designed, produced and commercialised in such a way as to permit its reuse or recovery, including recycling, and to minimise its impact on the environment when packaging waste or residues from packaging waste management operations are disposed of; and
- manufactured so that the presence of noxious and other hazardous substances and materials is minimised with regard to their presence in emissions, ash or leachate when packaging or residues are incinerated or landfilled.

In 2014 and 2022, Commission assessments led to the conclusion that Directive 94/62 had not stopped the increase in packaging and that there was 'underexploited prevention–reuse–recycling and too much incineration and landfill'.[269] One of the main reasons was the poor

[265] This comment is not meant to depreciate the valuable work of ECOS, the Environmental Coalition on Standardization, which represents environmental interests in CEN and CENELEC.

[266] In particular, Directive 73/23 on low-voltage equipment [1973] OJ 77/29; Directive 87/404 on pressure vessels [1987] OJ L220/48; Directive 87/378 on toy safety [1987] OJ L187/1; Directive 89/106 on construction products [1989] OJ L40/12; Directive 89/392 on the safety of machines [1989] OJ L183/9; Directive 90/396 on appliances burning gaseous fuels [1990] OJ L196/15; Directive 92/42 on new hot-water boilers fired with liquid or gaseous fuels [1992] OJ L167/17; Directive 94/62 on packaging and packaging waste [1994] OJ L365/11).

[267] CJEU Case 240/83 *Procureur de la République v Association de Défense de Bruleurs* ECLI:EU:C:1985:59.

[268] Directive 94/62 (n 104).

[269] Commission, SWD(2022) 384, 6; Commission, SWD(2014) 209.

design of the essential requirements, and the fact the industrial standardisation was not able to achieve Union-wide harmonisation. Therefore, the Commission proposed a regulation on packaging instead of a directive, and so diverged from the 'new approach' law-making. In the environmental sector, this new approach does not appear to have a future.

In 2012, the Union adopted a regulation to improve the rules on co-operation with the 6-60
three above-mentioned standardisation organisations and to officialise the strong financial support which these organisations had received annually from the Commission.[270] The organisations were requested to elaborate an annual work programme and 'encourage and facilitate' (Article 5) the participation of environmental organisations and other stakeholders in their work. Public authorities were encouraged to participate at national level in the work of standardisation organisations (Article 7); a corresponding provision for the Union level does not exist. The Commission had to elaborate an annual work programme for standardisation with priorities regarding its work and shall seek to concert the priorities with the private organisations. These Commission work programmes are published, though not regularly. The Commission strategy for standardisation until 2030 is mainly concerned with the global leadership of EU standardisation, which the Commission sees threatened by global competitors. As a matter of urgency, the Commission declared a need for environmental standards on the recycling of critical raw material, the roll-out of the clean hydrogen value chain and low-carbon cement.[271]

[270] Regulation 1025/2012 on European standardisation [2012] OJ L316/12.

[271] Commission, 'An EU Strategy on Standardisation. Setting Global Standards in Support of a Resilient, Green and Digital EU Single Market' COM(2022) 31, 2; Commission, 'The 2022 Annual Union Work Programme for European Standardisation' C(2022) 546.

7

Water Protection

I. European Union Water Policy and Law

7-01 EU water policy and law is about 45 years old. It was fixed, in the beginning, on two objectives: on the one hand, it set quality requirements for specific water uses, such as surface waters, groundwater, bathing or drinking water; on the other hand, it tried to limit discharges of pollutants into the waters. In 1988, an inter-ministerial meeting on water policy endeavoured to lay down the principles of a more coherent water policy;[1] however, the objectives identified at this seminar only very partially materialised.

The European Council, when it met in Edinburgh in December 1992, tried to start a deregulation process, fixed a number of orientations for EU policy and invited the Union to simplify, consolidate and adapt EU environmental legislation.[2] Nowhere was this statement taken more seriously than in the water sector, probably also because the UK, which had presided over the Edinburgh Council, had just received a judgment from the Court of Justice of the European Union (CJEU) which obliged it to make considerable investments in cleaning up drinking water.[3] Subsequent to this Council, and on the repeated insistence of the European Parliament,[4] the Commission published a communication in 1996 on the 'European Community Water Policy'.[5] This communication fixed as the objectives of the EU water policy:

- a secure supply of drinking water;
- sufficient quality and quantity of water resources to meet other economic requirements;
- to protect and sustain the good ecological state and functioning of the aquatic environment and meet the water needs of wetland and terrestrial ecosystems and habitats; and
- the management of water so as to prevent or reduce the impact of floods and droughts.

7-02 These objectives obviously referred to fresh and coastal water rather than, for instance, oceans. They were targeted to meet, first of all, human needs. The communication stated that the 'environmental quality objectives approach' and the 'emission limit values approach' were complementary and not contradictory. It continued by stating that quality objectives could either fix common parametric values applicable in all Member States or could be

[1] The conclusions of this seminar were never published; a short report is found in [1988] *Bulletin of the European Communities* para 2.1.175; the Council adopted a resolution on the follow-up of the seminar [1988] OJ C209/3.

[2] See (1992) 12 *Bulletin of the European Communities* 18.

[3] CJEU Case C-337/89 *Commission v United Kingdom* ECLI:EU:C:1992:456.

[4] See in particular European Parliament, Resolution of 23 October 1996 [1996] OJ C347/80.

[5] Commission, COM(96) 59.

expressed in a form such that common criteria for the establishment of parameters and values were fixed at EU level, but that the values were established at national level in order 'to allow flexibility to adapt to the very different environmental conditions in different parts of the Community'. The Commission clearly indicated that it preferred this approach.

The European Parliament was of the opinion that the communication failed in its objective to present a coherent overall concept and requested that the review of water policy should in no way lead to a lowering of standards; as a minimum, the fixing of strict and uniform emission standards was necessary.[6]

The first EU water directives and other measures were regularly based on Articles 100 and 235 of the Treaty establishing the European Community (EC Treaty), which later became Articles 115/114 and 352 of the Treaty on the Functioning of the Union (TFEU), and were adopted with unanimity.[7] Despite the existence of environmental action programmes from the early 1970s, the adoption of these directives did not follow a political strategy; rather, the directives were adopted where political or legal opportunities existed. They were often drafted by non-lawyers, and perceived more as guidelines than as legally binding requirements for Member States and water administrations. The Commission did not look closely into questions of their legal implementation or practical application. 7-03

In 1987, the present Article 192 TFEU became the legal basis for all environmental matters, including those on the protection of waters. Such measures continued to demand unanimous decisions, until the Maastricht Treaty introduced, in 1993, majority decisions into Article 192 TFEU. This amendment of the Treaty, however, brought some uncertainty as to the correct legal basis for EU water legislation. Indeed, while Article 192(1) provided for majority decisions, Article 192(2) provided for unanimous decisions by the Council for measures concerning 'the management of water resources'. And while Article 192(1) introduced the co-decision procedure with the European Parliament under the present Article 294 TFEU,[8] Article 192(2) limited the role of the European Parliament to a consultative function.

The different interpretations on the delimitation between Article 192(1) and (2) as regards water measures were solved by a judgment from the CJEU.[9] This judgment concerned Decision 97/825, by which the Union had adhered to the Convention on Co-operation for the Protection and Sustainable Use of the River Danube;[10] the Council had based that decision on the old Article 130s(1) EC Treaty – now Article 192(1) TFEU. Spain was of the opinion that the decision should have been based on Article 192(2), as it concerned the management of water resources, and applied to the CJEU. The Court found that only the Dutch version of Article 192(2) used the word 'quantitative', but that the French version also used expressions which signalled that the quantitative management of water was in question. The Court then referred to the purpose and general scheme of the provision and 7-04

[6] European Parliament, Resolution of 23 October 1996 (n 4); see also Economic and Social Committee [1996] OJ C30/5; Committee of the Regions [1997] OJ C34/30.

[7] Directive 75/440 on the protection of surface waters for the abstraction of drinking water [1975] OJ L194/6; Directive 76/160 on the quality of bathing water [1976] OJ L31/1; Directive 78/659 on fresh water supporting fish life [1978] OJ L222/1; Directive 79/923 on shellfish water [1979] OJ L281/47.

[8] Between the entry into force of the Maastricht Treaty in 1993 and the Amsterdam Treaty in 1999, Art 192(1) provided for the co-operation procedure according to Art 252 EC Treaty.

[9] CJEU Case C-36/98 *Spain v Council* ECLI:EU:C:2001:64.

[10] Decision 97/825 [1997] OJ L342/18.

concluded that Article 192(2) was limited to quantitative aspects of water management; this judgment conformed to the overwhelming opinion in legal literature. Two weeks after this judgment, the Treaty of Nice was signed which amended Article 192(2). Unanimity is now required where a measure concerns *quantitative* aspects of water management. As of mid-2023, the Union has not adopted any water measures based on Article 192(2) TFEU.

II. The Water Framework Directive

7-05 As regards the reduction of pollution of waters, a framework directive was adopted in 1976 which fixed the principle of emission limit values for pollutants;[11] exceptionally, Member States were allowed to recur to concentration limits (quality standards). Subsequently, Union-wide emission limit values and quality standards were fixed for 17 substances[12] out of a list of 129 candidate substances.[13] However, this activity came to a standstill in the early 1990s, in particular because of the controversy between the UK, a strong defender of the fixing of quality standards but not emission limit values, and the rest of the EU; that controversy was all the more intense, as the adoption of secondary EU legislation required unanimity.

In its efforts to give greater coherence to measures on water protection while following the trend towards deregulation and the abandonment of precise provisions, the Commission submitted a proposal in 1994 for a directive on the ecological quality of water.[14] The proposal suggested maintaining a good ecological water quality for all surface water in the Union. Member States were to identify the sources of pollution and to fix objectives in order to reach this good ecological quality. They were then to elaborate integrated programmes to reach those objectives. The proposal met with little enthusiasm in the European Parliament, which continued to press for a more coherent approach to water policy.[15] The Commission, however, accepted this request and presented, on the one hand, a communication on water policy[16] and, on the other hand, a proposal for a directive 'establishing a framework for Community action in the field of water policy'.[17] This proposal was adopted in 2000 and came into effect at the end of 2003.[18] It progressively phased out several directives concerning water quality[19] and, furthermore, Directive 76/464 and its daughter directives, which had regulated the 17 substances mentioned above.

[11] Directive 76/464 on pollution caused by certain dangerous substances discharged into the aquatic environment of the Community [1976] OJ L129/23.

[12] The substances were mercury, cadmium, HCH (lindane), carbon tetrachloride, DDT, pentachlorophenol, aldrin, dieldrin, endrin, isodrin, hexachlorobenzene, hexachlorobutadiene, chloroform, 1,2-dichloroethane, TRI, PER, trichlorobenzene.

[13] Council, Resolution of 7 February 1983 [1983] OJ C46/17.

[14] [1994] OJ C222/6; Commission, 'Explanatory Memorandum' COM(93) 680.

[15] European Parliament, Resolution of 23 October 1996 (n 4).

[16] See n 5.

[17] [1997] OJ C184/20; Commission, 'Explanatory Memorandum' COM(97) 49; amendment of the proposal [1998] OJ C16/14 and [1998] OJ C108/94.

[18] Directive 2000/60 establishing a framework for Community action in the field of water policy [2000] OJ L327/1.

[19] Directive 75/440 (n 7); Directive 78/659 (n 7); Directive 79/923 (n 7).

Directive 2000/60 aimed at the protection of surface waters, groundwaters and coastal waters, but did not cover marine waters. Article 1 fixed five objectives:

1. prevention of further deterioration and protection, and enhancement of aquatic and terrestrial ecosystems;
2. promotion of sustainable water use, based on long-term protection of available water resources;
3. enhanced protection and improvement of the aquatic environment through the progressive reduction of discharges and the cessation or phasing-out of discharges, emissions and losses of priority hazardous substances;
4. progressive reduction of groundwater pollution; and
5. mitigation of the effects of floods and droughts.

Directive 2000/60 requested Member States to organise their waters – including ground- 7-06
water and coastal water – according to river basin districts.[20] Where a river basin covered the territory of more than one Member State, it had to be assigned to an international river basin district (Article 3(3)); where non-EU countries belong to a river basin – for example, the Rhine or the Danube – Member States were asked to 'endeavour to establish appropriate co-ordination'. The river basin administration shall ensure the application of the directive's rules in the river basin; for 'international river basin districts the Member States concerned shall together ensure this co-ordination'.

These provisions thus obliged, in regionalised or federal countries, the water administration to organise itself in administrative units – districts – which it had not set up until then. Also, the obligation to form a joint administration in international river basin districts constituted an interference with political or administrative autonomy that met – for instance, in German regionalised legal literature – some concern. However, these provisions had a number of precedents: Directive 91/271 obliged Member States to build specific waste water treatment installations;[21] and Directive 85/337 on the environmental impact assessment obliged Member States to co-operate in those areas where transfrontier elements of environmental protection were in question. This obligation to administrative co-operation flows from Article 10 EC Treaty – at present Article 4(3) of the Treaty on European Union (TEU) – which establishes the basic principle that Member States have to co-operate. In the last instance, one might ask what the Union is really about if there was not even the possibility to organise environmental protection measures – which are, by nature, not limited by a national frontier – according to reasonable objective criteria such as river basins.

Article 4 of Directive 2000/60 fixed environmental objectives separately for surface 7-07
waters, groundwater and protected areas. The legal requirements were to prevent the deterioration of waters and to reach 'good' surface water (groundwater) status of 'good' ecological potential and 'good' water chemical status. Under certain conditions, Member States may aim to achieve less stringent environmental objectives for specific bodies of water which are so strongly affected by human activity that the achievement of the normal objectives is infeasible or disproportionately expensive (Article 4(5)). And Member States were declared to be 'not in breach of this directive' when certain new sustainable human development

[20] Art 2(13) of Directive 2000/60 (n 18): 'river basin means the area of land from which all surface run-off flows through a sequence of streams, rivers and, possibly, lakes into the sea at a single river mouth, estuary or delta'.

[21] Directive 91/271 concerning urban waste-water treatment [1991] OJ L135/40.

activities or new modifications of the water body occurred (Article 4(7)). The objectives had to be achieved 'at the latest' by 2015, though Member States were allowed to prolong this date unilaterally until 2027 (Article 4(4.c)). In the meantime, the Union itself tacitly accepted that the directive's objectives had to be reached by 2027 only.

The directive defined what is 'good' by reference to criteria that were laid down in its annex V. This meant in practice that each river basin plan fixes the water quality which is to be achieved under the directive, though the criteria of annex V may lead to some alignment between river basins. Also, the question of whether a water had a high, good or moderate status, whether a water was to be classified as good, poor or bad – all classifications introduced by the directive – depended on the decisions taken within the water management bodies and could thus vary from one water basin to another.

In order to reach the objectives of the directive, Member States had to establish, by 2009, a programme of measures for each river basin district,[22] for which a considerable number of conditions were set in the directive (Article 11). Such programmes had to be updated every six years. Furthermore, for each river basin district, a river basin management plan had to be produced and again updated every six years (Article 13(1)).[23] Member States were only obliged to produce such a plan for districts that were entirely situated within their territory. For international districts, Member States had to co-ordinate such plans among each other and, where third countries were involved, they had to 'endeavour to produce a single river basin management plan' (Article 13(4)). The 'public' had to have the possibility to comment on the elaboration, review and updating of the river basin management plan (Article 14). For groundwater, the adoption of a specific directive was foreseen; this directive was adopted in 2006.[24]

7-08 In order to reduce water pollution, Article 16 provided that EU measures would be taken for specific pollutants or groups of pollutants. These measures aimed, for priority hazardous substances, 'at the cessation … [or] phasing-out of discharges, emissions or losses' (Article 16(1)). For this purpose, a list of priority substances had to be fixed at EU level. These substances then had to undergo a risk assessment or targeted risk assessment.[25] For priority substances, EU measures for the control of the progressive reduction of discharges, emission, limits or losses were foreseen (Article 16(6)). Discharges, emissions and losses should be completely stopped within a period which 'shall not exceed 20 years' after the EU decision on priority hazardous substances (Article 16(6)). Annex X to Directive 2000/60 identified 22 priority hazardous substances to be stopped by mid-2023.

At the end of 2001, the Union adopted a list of priority substances.[26] The list contained 33 substances or groups of substances, out of which 25 were identified as priority hazardous substances. In 2008, a Union directive fixed quality standards for the 33 substances, and for eight other substances which had already been regulated at EU level; at the same time, it repealed several earlier directives which had fixed emission limit values.[27] The new

[22] This obligation was, for international river basin districts, limited to the territory of each Member State.

[23] See the progress report with regard to the seond set of River Basin Management Plans 2016 to 2021, Commission, 'European Overview – River Basin Management Plans' SWD(2021) 253.

[24] Directive 2006/118 on the protection of groundwater against pollution and deterioration [2006] OJ L372/19.

[25] A targeted risk assessment focuses solely 'on aquatic ecotoxicity and on human toxicity via the aquatic environment'.

[26] Decision 2455/2001 establishing the list of priority substances in the field of water policy [2001] OJ L331/1.

[27] Directive 2008/105 on environmental quality standards in the field of water policy [2008] OJ L348/84.

directive asked Member States not to exceed certain concentrations of the substances in water. It did not refer to the objective of Article 16, which had intended to progressively, and at the latest within 20 years, phase out all discharges of priority hazardous substances into waters,[28] and thus took away from public authorities, and in particular from affected industries, the obligation to reduce and progressively phase out discharges into waters of the priority hazardous substances. Neither the European Parliament, which had successfully fought to insert Article 16 into Directive 2000/60, nor the public protested seriously enough against this change (U-turn) in policy, which largely went unnoticed.

In 2013, an amendment of Directive 2008/105 revised some of the previously fixed quality standards and introduced new quality standards in the form of maximum allowable concentrations for 45 substances, mainly pesticides, industrial chemicals and metals.[29] Where quality standards were amended, Member States had time until the end of 2021 to comply with them; where new quality standards were fixed, Member States had to comply with them by 2027.

Directive 2008/105 also established a watch list for substances that might become a concern for human health or the environment, but for which not enough data were available. The substances may remain on the list for a maximum period of four years. Taking measures to restrict their use or fix concentration values required new decisions. The last watch list, of 2022, contained nine substances.[30]

Furthermore, Member States had to take measures to control emissions into the EU waters, including an inventory of all discharges. The authorisations for the emission of priority substances were to be given by the Member States; the emission values should be based either on existing or future EU legislation or on best available technologies. Compliance with the quality standards was considered to be a problem of Member States, so was not monitored at Union level. In 2022, the Commission proposed a further amendment of Directive 2008/105 in order to complete the existing quality standards and include new substances of concern. The Commission admitted that the national measures adopted by virtue of annex II had led to 'too large variations in pollutants and quality standards' and proposed measures to better monitor the water quality in the Union.[31]

Several Member States were late in transposing Directive 2000/60 into their national law. 7-09
The Commission took action against Belgium, Finland, France, Germany, Italy, Luxembourg, the Netherlands, Portugal and the UK;[32] further, the CJEU held that Belgium, Germany, Italy, Luxembourg and Portugal were in breach of their obligations.[33] The Commission

[28] Directive 2000/60 (n 18), Art 16(1) and (6).

[29] Directive 2013/39 [2013] OJ L226/1.

[30] Commission, Implementing Decision 2020/1161 [2020] OJ L257/32.

[31] Commission, COM(2022) 540; Commission, SWD(2022) 543.

[32] Commission, SEC(2005) 1055, 11.

[33] CJEU Case C-33/05 *Commission v Belgium* ECLI:EU:C:2005:790; Case C-67/05 *Commission v Germany* ECLI:EU:C:2005:791; Case C-32/05 *Commission v Luxembourg* ECLI:EU:C:2006:749; Case C-85/05 *Commission v Italy* ECLI:EU:C:2006:33; Case C-118/05 *Commission v Portugal* ECLI:EU:C:2006:35. See also the later judgments Case C-264/07 *Commission v Greece* ECLI:EU:C:2008:69; Case C-85/07 *Commission v Italy* ECLI: ECLI:EU:C:2007:522; Case C-516/07 *Commission v Spain* ECLI:EU:C:2009:291; Case C-351/09 *Commission v Malta* ECLI:EU:2010:815; Case C-297/11 *Commission v Greece* ECLI:EU:C:2012:228; Case C-223/11 *Commission v Portugal* ECLI:EU:C:2012:379; Case C-366/11 *Commission v Belgium* ECLI:EU:C:2012:316; Case C-403/11 *Commission v Spain* ECLI:EU:C:2012:612; Case C-151/12 *Commission v Spain* ECLI:EU:C:2013:690; Case C-525/12 *Commission v Germany* ECLI:EU:C:2014:2202; Case C-648/13 *Commission v Poland* ECLI:EU:C:2016:490; Case C-556/18 *Commission v Spain* ECLI:EU:C:2019:785.

found, in 2007, that transposition of the directive was poor[34] and mentioned that significant transposition problems existed in 19 of the then 27 Member States. Since then, it has limited its action against Member States to cases of incomplete or incorrect transposition of Directive 2000/60 into the national legal order (including the lack of adopting plans), but has not taken up cases where the directive was not or not correctly applied in practice. Nor has it published studies which led on practical applications and did not disclose any other relevant information.

The rather disappointing post-evaluation report of the Commission admitted that the Commission had focused on formal and procedural aspects of applying Directive 2000/60,[35] and that it relied mainly on the Member States' reports concerning the implementation of the river basin management plans. By 2018, 15 years after the directive came into force, only 40 per cent of the Unions surface waters were in good ecological status and 38 per cent in good chemical status.[36] No significant progress was being observed.[37] The requirement of a complete phasing out of discharges of priority hazardous substances into water, laid down in Article 4(1)(a)(iv) of Directive 2000/60, was not discussed.

Article 4(1)(a)(i) of Directive 2000/60 requested Member States to 'prevent deterioration of the status of all bodies of surface waters'. It did not indicate, though, from when this prohibition of deterioration applied: 2000 (the date of adoption of the directive), 2003 (the date of its final transposition into national law), 2008 (the beginning of monitoring of surface water according to Article 8) or 2012 (the date of the beginning of measures according to Article 12). Nor did the directive define what exactly 'deterioration' meant or how significant it must be; a transitory deterioration does not appear relevant (see Article 4(6)).

The Commission did not take action against any Member State with regard to the prohibition of deterioration, but the CJEU clarified the meaning of 'deterioration' in a number of preliminary rulings, underlining in particular that the deterioration provision was a legal requirement which was applicable in each individual case and was not just a planning objective.[38] The reports on the evaluation of the Union's waters[39] did not report on the respect of this obligation.

7-10 The directive did not clarify whether the good surface status of waters was an objective which Member States shall have to reach or an orientation which Member States should endeavour to reach;[40] this last understanding was the point of view of the Netherlands, without the Commission protesting. Furthermore, while Article 4(1)(a)(ii) indicated that the good surface water status shall be achieved 'at the latest 15 years' after 2000, Article 4(4) allowed this delay to be extended, 'for the purposes of phased achievement', by a further

[34] Commission, COM(2007) 128.

[35] Commission, 'Fitness Check of the Water Framework Directive and the Floods Directive' SWD(2019) 439, 119.

[36] ibid 19. The figures were taken over from European Environment Agency (EEA), *European Waters. Assessment of Status and Pressures 2018* (Copenhagen, 2018).

[37] EEA (n 36) 32 and 47.

[38] CJEU Case C-461/13 *BUND* ECLI:EU:C:2015:433; Case C-664/15 *Protect* ECLI:EU:C:2017:987; Case C-535/18 *Land NRW* ECLI:EU:C:2020:391; Case C-525/10 *France Nature* ECLI:EU:C:2022:350. See also Case C-346/14 *Commission v Austria* ECLI:EU:C:2016.322.

[39] See nn 23 and 35.

[40] In the meantime, the CJEU clarified that the objectives of Art 4 constituted legal requirements, CJEU Case C-461/13 (n 38).

12 years overall. Soon after the adoption of Directive 2000/60, the UK and the Netherlands signalled that the achievement of a good surface water status by 2015 would be too expensive, and prolonged the delay until 2027; other Member States and the Commission tacitly followed. The CJEU, though, clarified in the above-mentioned decision in Case C-461/13, that the provisions of Article 4 constituted legal requirements, not only policy considerations.

The Directive did not clarify what would happen if the good surface water status was not achieved by 2027. This vagueness considerably reduces the relevance of the directive.

Artificial and heavily modified bodies of water were subjected to less stringent requirements according to Article 4(1)(a)(iii). The definition of such bodies (Article 2, nos 8 and 9) was not precise. As the designation of such bodies was put in the hands of Member States, they may reduce their obligations by designating more waters as artificial or heavily modified; at present, about half of the Union's surface water bodies come under this provision.[41]

Member States had to adopt river basin management plans by the end of 2009 and to 7-11
update them every six years. A Commission map showed that, by March 2011, Belgium (Wallonia and Brussels), Cyprus, Greece, Portugal, Slovenia and Spain had not yet adopted management plans. Belgium, Greece, Portugal and Spain were subsequently found to be in breach by the CJEU.[42] In 2015, the Commission published a progress report on the implementation of Directive 2000/60. The data were given only in general terms, so that the reader could not find out which Member States were in compliance or in default.[43] Attached to this report were analyses of the management plans of Belgium, Croatia, Greece, Portugal and Spain which described in detail the general characteristics, deficiencies and omissions of the different river basin management plans in these countries.[44] This report, as well as later reports of 2019 and 2021, concentrated on administrative/governance question, but did not give details on the concentration of pollutants in water.

Over the next years, this comprehensive directive will strongly influence water manage- 7-12
ment within the enlarged Union and – in particular via the river basin concept – beyond. As numerous provisions of Directive 2000/60 are very loosely drafted,[45] the question of whether the directive's objectives will be reached by 2027 (they should, in principle, have been reached by 2015!) will depend on the political will and the determination of the relevant administrations to work for the improvement of water quality rather than monitoring the status quo. It is true that Member States decided a joint implementation plan for the directive,[46] but its monitoring lacks any transparency and democratic control, and its

[41] Commission, SWD(2019) 439 (n 35) 119.

[42] CJEU Case C-297/11, Case C-223/11 Case C-366/11 Case C-403/11)(all n 33).

[43] Commission, The Water Framework Directive and the Floods Directive: actions toward the 'good status' of EU water and to reduce flood risks, COM(2015) 120.

[44] Commission, SWD(2015) 52–56. The Report on Spain (SWD(2015) 56) had a length of 90 pages.

[45] A good example is Art 9 of the Directive It asks Member States 'to take account of the principle of recovery of the costs of water services, including environmental and resource costs', but allows them 'in so doing have regard to the social, environmental and economic effects of the recovery as well as the geographic and climatic conditions of the region or regions affected'. It is difficult to see in these provisions more than a policy recommendation addressed to Member States. See also CJEU Case C-525/12 *Commission v Germany* ECLI:EU:C:2014:2202 and generally European Environmental Bureau: *10 years of the Water Framework Directive A toothless tiger?* (Bruxelles, July 2010).

[46] Common strategy on the implementation of the Water Framework Directive (2000/60) as agreed by the Water Directors under Swedish Presidency, May 2, 2001; http://ec.europa.eu/environment/water/water-framework/objectives/pdf/strategy.pdf [Accessed April 8, 2011].

implementation is more than uncertain. And the Commission does not enforce compliance with the directive's requirements.

By 2022, the Commission had published six reports on the implementation of Directive 2000/60,[47] where it showed itself prudently optimistic about the progressive implementation of the directive, though it did not hide the necessity for more measures: 'the distance to be covered to full compliance with the Water Framework Directive's objectives is still considerable'.[48] Directive 2000/60 appears to serve as a framework for monitoring waters, but it does not really matter whether the fixed targets are reached by 2015, 2021 or 2027.[49] Overall, Directive 2000/60 appears more to provide for the monitoring of the status quo ('business as usual') than progressively improving water quality. The political will of each individual Member State and of the Commission to ensure its full application is not evident.

III. Groundwater

7-13 Some provisions for the quality of groundwater were laid down in Directive 2000/60. Directive 2006/118, which repealed an earlier directive, went into further details.[50] It asked Member States to ensure a good chemical status of groundwater, in particular by fixing quality standards for nitrates (50 mg/l) and active substances of pesticides (01 µg/l per pesticide, 0.5 µg/l for all pesticides) (annex I). Where necessary, Member States should establish quality standards (threshold values) for the specific pollutants listed in annex II, for which no Union-wide quality standards appeared necessary. Member States alone had to ensure the respect of any such threshold values. Furthermore, Member States were requested to ensure a good quantitative status of groundwater and to avoid its deterioration. On a voluntary basis, Member States agreed to observe some pollutants on a Union watch list, in order to see whether they might require some future action. Groundwater was to be considered as of 'good' quality where the quality standards and threshold levels were either not exceeded or were exceeded only under the conditions that were laid down in the directive. No date was fixed by when its requirements had to be achieved.

A 2019 evaluation of Directive 2006/118, based very largely on reports by Member States, showed that 74 per cent of the groundwater had reached a good chemical status, 89 per cent had a good quantitative status, 24 per cent had a poor chemical status and 9 per cent had a poor quantitative status; detailed figures on nitrates or pesticides were not made available.[51] The report identified the chemical sector as a sector where the directive could be improved. Indeed, the fixing of threshold values for national territories or for (some) river basin districts had led to considerable differences, which could not be

[47] Commission, COM(2007) 128; COM(2009) 156; COM(2013) 670; COM(2015) 120; COM(2019) 95 and COM(2021) 970. The reports are rather general: see for example COM(2021) 970 16: 'Most of the Member States have made some progress in identifying the gaps to good status.'

[48] Statement of 2021 in Commission, COM(2021) 970 16.

[49] This conclusion is also to be drawn from Commission, COM(2015) 120 (n 43).

[50] Directive 2006/118 on the protection of groundater against pollution and deterioration [2006] OJ L372/19. This directive replaced Directive 80/68 [1980] OJ L20/43. It was amended by Commission Directive 2014/80 [2014] OJ L132/53.

[51] Commission, SWD(2019) 439 (n 35) 20; EEA, *Europe's Groundwater – a Key Ressource Under Pressure* (Copenhagen, 2022). The results were based on Member States' information.

explained by national or regional particularities.[52] It must rather be presumed that the values were fixed at a level which could easily be achieved. Details in respect of the values for the annex I substances were not published either by the Commission or by the EEA. In 2022, the Commission suggested amending the directive in order to improve the situation.[53]

IV. Water Scarcity and Reuse

Climate change is likely to increase the frequency of droughts in the EU, not only in Southern Europe, but also in Central and Northern Europe. No concrete measures have been taken by the EU so far. Furthermore, problems are also to be anticipated in the management of water scarcity,[54] which mainly occurs in Southern Europe. Directive 2000/60 did not address this problem.[55] A good example of this problem was the Spanish National Hydrological Plan of 2001, which was adopted by parliamentary procedure and which provided for the transfer of about 1.05 billion m^3 of water per year from the Tajo and Ebro rivers to southern Spanish regions which lacked water. The Plan included the construction of some 900 dams, the destruction of a considerable number of natural habitats and wetlands, and other considerable interferences into more traditional water management and infrastructures; it met with considerable resistance from 'water exporting' regions, environmental groups and others, which pleaded for desalination of seawater, while the 'water importing' Spanish regions generally favoured the Plan. General or specific environmental impact assessments had not been undertaken. When the government in Spain changed in 2004, the plan to transfer Ebro water was abandoned – though many of the envisaged infrastructure projects had, in the meantime, been completed. The plan might be reanimated in future, when the government changes again. It was not subjected to any Union intervention. 7-14

It is remarkable that EU water law played hardly any role in the attempt to find, in this or similar cases,[56] an adequate balance between economic interests and environmental concerns, a problem which will become more acute with climate change in Europe. The Commission has limited itself to publishing reports on water scarcity and droughts, and indicating measures which might be taken at national or Union level.[57] It reported in 2011 that Cyprus, Czechia and Malta declared having continuous problems with water scarcity; France, the Netherlands, Romania and Sweden had local scarcity problems. France, Hungary, Portugal, Spain and the UK indicated that their rainfall was lower than the long-term annual average, while Austria, Belgium, Estonia, Ireland, Luxembourg and Slovakia declared that they had no scarcity or drought problems. Since then, the situation might have

[52] The Commission reported that in 2004, the national threshold values for heavy metals showed differences of up to 1:1500, eg 1:1300 for arsenic, 1:1200 for cadmium and 1:500 for mercury, Commission, SEC(2010) 166, annex III.

[53] Commission, COM(2022) 540.

[54] Water scarcity exists where the abstraction of water exceeds the available water quantities.

[55] Directive 2000/60 (n 18) provided in annex VI, part B that Member States were entitled to adopt measures concerning the reuse of waters. However, this possibility already existed by virtue of Art 193 TFEU.

[56] See the underlying facts of CJEU Case C-43/10 *Acheloos* ECLI:EU:C:2012:560 and Joined Cases C-514/11P and 605/11P *LPN and Finland v Commission* ECLI:EU:C:2013:738.

[57] Commission, COM(2007) 414; Commission, COM(2008) 875; Commission, COM(2011) 133; Commission, 'Report on the Review of the European Water Scarcity and Drought Policy' COM(2021) 672.

changed: in 2022, Austria, Bulgaria, Cyprus, Greece, Portugal, Slovenia and Spain, with the support of Belgium and Hungary, addressed the Union to ask for renewed efforts to improve drought management at Member State and Union level.[58] The Commission's agricultural guidelines recognise the possibility for state aid in case of floods, but not in case of drought or water scarcity.[59]

In 2020, the Union adopted Regulation 2020/741, mainly in order to fight water scarcity and the consequences of climate change.[60] The regulation, based on Article 192 TFEU, concerned waste water which stemmed from urban waste water treatment plants acting under Directive 91/271.[61] Such waste water, which complied with the minimum requirements laid down in annex II to the regulation, could be used for irrigation purposes in agriculture; Member States were also allowed to extend its use for industrial, leisure or environmental purposes.

Member States were entitled to decide that it was 'not appropriate to reuse water for agricultural irrigation'. However, they then had to 'duly justify' this decision to the Commission (Article 2). This means that any obligation for farmers to reuse waters depends on the decision of their Member State to make such reuse mandatory.

The regulation was to be applied as of June 2023. It is thus too early to evaluate its effectiveness.

V. Floods

7-15 Following a series of floods, mainly in Central Europe, the Union adopted, in 2007, a Directive on the assessment and management of flood risks.[62] The directive was based on Article 192(1) TFEU; a suggestion by the UK to limit its field of application to transboundary river basins was rejected by the majority of Member States in the Council. The directive covered inland and coastal waters. It mainly provided for three measures by Member States: (i) the making of a preliminary flood risk assessment. This assessment was to be made for each river basin and had to describe the factual situation, the likelihood of future floods and a forecast of their estimated consequences. Where the assessment concluded that no potential significant flood risks existed, Member States had no further obligation; (ii) for basins districts with a potential significant flood risk, Member States had to elaborate flood risk maps in order to increase public awareness, orient investments and strategies, and support planning; and (iii) for these basin districts, flood risk management plans were to be elaborated by the end of 2015, for which some orientations were laid down in the directive.

A Commission evaluation of the directive concluded in 2019 that all Member States had improved their administrative structures to manage flood risks, but that it was not yet possible to assess whether it had actually reduced the number and seriousness of floods.[63]

[58] Council, Document 13769/22 of 22 October 2022.

[59] Commission, Guidelines for State aid in the agricultural and forestry sectors and in rural areas, C(2022) 9120, para 323, 60.

[60] Regulation 2020/741 on minimum requirements for water reuse [2020] OJ L177/32.

[61] On Directive 91/271 (n 21), see para 7-27ff.

[62] Directive 2007/60 on the assessment and management of flood risks [2007] OJ L288/27.

[63] Commission, SWD(2019) 439 (n 35) 123 and 36. Also Commission, 'European Overview – Flood Risk Management Plans' SWD(2021) 254, concentrated on administrative/governance issues, but did not contain any

Between 2012 and 2018, Member States reported around 2700 significant flood events; no reliable data exist for comparison with previous events.[64] The Commission called for better co-ordination between measures under the Floods Directive and the Water Framework Directive, but did not propose any concrete measures.[65]

VI. Drinking Water

Directive 80/778, adopted in 1980, limited the presence of undesirable substances in drinking water.[66] The directive fixed maximum admissible concentrations for 62 substances in drinking water and gave non-mandatory guide values for some of them; Member States had to take the necessary measures to ensure compliance with the concentrations. At the request of the UK government, which had argued that Directive 80/778 only requested Member States to take 'all practicable steps' to comply with the directive's standards, the CJEU stated expressly that Member States were not only obliged to make an effort, but were obliged to reach the specific result that was required by the directive.[67] The directive introduced, for the first time, objective standards for drinking water in all EU Member States, oriented investments and led to a considerable, though slow, improvement in drinking water quality. 7-16

Since there were difficulties in complying with the directive's requirements, considerable pressure was put on the Commission to lower the standards, in particular as regards pesticides, where the agrochemical industry and agroindustry were particularly active. In 1995, the Commission made a proposal for replacing Directive 80/778 with a new directive, which the Council adopted in 1998.[68] 7-17

Directive 98/83 provided that drinking water, at the point of entry into the domestic distribution system, must be wholesome and clean. This was the case when the water was: free from micro-organisms, parasites and substances which may, in numbers or concentrations, constitute a potential danger to human health, and when the requirements of some 28 parameters, laid down in annex I(A) and (B), are respected. Annex I(C) contained a list of 20 indicator parameters for which the Member States need only fix parameters for monitoring purposes; this annex included, among others, aluminium, ammonium, chlorides and coliform bacteria. When these parameters were exceeded, Member States had to consider whether this posed any risk to human health; if that was the case, they had to take remedial action.

In 2020, Directive 98/83 was replaced by Directive 2020/2184.[69] This directive updated the list of substances of concern by deleting and adding some substances and amending the allowed maximum concentration of other substances.[70] Member States were allowed to

assessment, whether the plans and other measures that had been adopted, had actually succeeded in limiting the frequency and intensity of flood events and reducing damage.

[64] Commission, 'European Overview, 2nd Preliminary Flood Risk Assessments' SWD(2021) 971, 20.

[65] ibid; similarly Commission, COM(2015) 120.

[66] Directive 80/778 relating to the quality of water intended for human consumption [1980] OJ L229/11.

[67] CJEU Case C-337/89 (n 3).

[68] Directive 98/83 on the quality of water intended for human consumption [1998] OJ L330/32.

[69] Directive 2020/2184 on the quality of water intended for human consumption [2020] OJ L435/1; Commission, 'Fitness Check of Directive 98/83' SWD(2016) 428; Commission, 'Proposal for Directive 2020/2184' COM(2017) 753; Commission, Impact Assessment of That Proposal' SWD(2017) 449.

[70] The added substances were bisphenol A, chlorate, chlorite, haloacetic acids, microcystin, total per- and polyfluoroalkyl substances (PFASs) and the sums of PFASs and uranium; these substances had to be monitoried as of 2026.

increase the allowed maximum concentration 'in duly justified circumstances' for a period of up to three years ('derogation'). They had to inform the affected population, but inform the Commission only when they prolonged the derogation, which was allowed for another three years; the possibility of granting a third derogation, allowed under Directive 98/83, was deleted. Directive 2020/2184 also dealt with materials in contact with drinking water (Articles 11 and 12) and introduced a risk-based approach to the monitoring of drinking water (Article 7). Article 16 contained some vague provisions on access to drinking water for all, which is a problem in some parts of the Union.[71]

General reports to the Commission on the implementation of Directive 2020/2184 were not foreseen. However, the EEA was tasked with establishing, 'on a regular basis', a Union-wide overview of the application of the directive, though it was not specified, how the EEA would obtain the necessary information; the Commission was given a mandate to fix details for such overviews (Article 18(3) and (4)). Also, the Commission was asked to establish a watch list for possible candidates for future quality standards – pharmaceuticals, endocrine-disrupting compounds and microplastics were named (Article 13(8)) – and evaluate the directive in 2035(!). All citizens in the Union were entitled to receive, at least once a year, information on the quality of their drinking water, its price, the volume consumed and a comparison with the average household consumption (Article 17).

7-18 In 2013, a directive fixed parametric values for radioactive substances (radon, tritium and their indicative doses) in drinking water.[72] Member States were asked to set up a system to monitor the presence of such substances in drinking water. Where the levels indicated in the directive were exceeded, Member States were asked to examine whether there was a risk to human health. If that were the case, they had to take appropriate measures.

Also in 2013, a citizen initiative, started under Article 11(4) TEU and assembling more than 1.6 million signatures, asked the Commission to recognise water and sanitation as human rights. In its official reaction, the Commission treated the request as if it concerned drinking water. It enumerated all legal, financial and political measures taken in the past with regard to water, but carefully avoided recognising access to drinking water and sanitation as human rights.[73]

VII. Bathing Water

7-19 In 1975, the Council adopted, on the basis of Articles 94 and 308 EC Treaty (now Articles 115 and 352 TFEU), a Directive on the quality of bathing water,[74] which fixed, for coastal and freshwater zones, quality requirements for bathing waters. Imperative or guide

For benzopyrene (0.010–010 μg/l) boron (1.0–1.5 μg/l) and selenium (10–20 μg/l), the allowed concentrations were increased; for chromium (50–25 μg/l, but only from 2035 onwards) and lead (10–5 μg/l, but only from 2035 onwards), the allowed concentrations were reduced.

[71] Commission, SWD(2017) 449, 10 indicated that in Romania, only 57% of the population was connected to a public water supply.

[72] Directive 2013/51/Euratom [2013] OJ L296/12. The CJEU held that Art 31 of the Euratom Treaty constituted the correct legal basis for this directive, Case C-48/14 *European Parliament v Council* ECLI:EU:C:2015:91.

[73] Commission, COM(2014) 177.

[74] Directive 76/160 on the quality of bathing water [1976] OJ L31/1.

parameters were fixed for a number of pollutants. Member States were given 10 years to comply with the directive's requirements. During its years of existence, the directive has caused a significant improvement in bathing-water quality. Contributory factors have been: the publication of annual reports which 'named and shamed' non-complying local bathing waters; that a private organisation had launched a 'blue flag' campaign,[75] which identified high-quality bathing waters and beaches; and finally that, in general, the data on bathing-water quality found their way into tourism prospectuses, advertising campaigns, etc. This also caused local authorities to publish data, invest in water improvement and make specific efforts to comply with the directive's requirements.

In 1994, the Commission made a proposal to replace Directive 76/160 with a new directive.[76] It justified this by the need to take into account subsidiarity questions and scientific and technical progress, and the need to simplify the text. The proposal was not discussed in the Council. For that reason, the Commission published a communication and, based on the reactions to it, a proposal for another new directive, which was adopted in 2006.[77] The directive was based on Article 192(1) TFEU. 7-20

The notion of bathing water concerned water where public authorities expected a large number of bathers, having regard to past trends and to existing infrastructure for services. Waters in swimming pools and waters for therapeutic purposes were not covered. Contrary to requests which were made during the consultations, the directive did not extend its scope of application to areas concerning such recreational use of waters as surfing, kayaking, etc. The number of parameters which were to be sampled of Directive 76/160 was reduced from 19 to two – intestinal enterococci and *Escherichia coli*.[78]

Directive 2006/7 did not provide that bathing waters must comply with certain quality requirements. Rather, it required Member States to make a 'bathing water quality assessment'. This quality assessment was to be made at the end(!) of the bathing season, and had to take the average results of the just finished and four preceding bathing seasons into consideration. The bathing water was then to be classified as 'excellent', 'good', 'sufficient' or 'poor'. The maximal concentrations for the two parameters were differentiated in annex IA, with average methods of calculation ensuring that the results remain positive. Member States must sample the water quality by means of taking at least four samples per bathing water season, plus one sample before the season starts. Short-term pollutions – up to three days – could be ignored, provided Member States identified the source of the pollution and addressed the issue. Where a water was of 'poor' quality, it nevertheless complied with the directive provided Member States pronounced a prohibition to bathe or gave advice not to

[75] On the 'blue flag' campaign, see Written Question P-1667/02 *Carnéro Gonzalesz* [2002] OJ C301E/208. The Commission indicated in its answer that, since 1998, it no longer participated in the activities of the private body in awarding blue flag, nor did it grant financial assistance.

[76] Commission [1994] OJ C112/3; Commission, COM(94) 36.

[77] Directive 2006/7 concerning the quality of bathing water [2006] OJ L64/37.

[78] The levels are, for intestinal enterococci per 100 ml, in coastal waters: 100 for excellent quality, 200 for good quality and 185 for sufficient quality; in inland waters: 200 for excellent quality, 400 for good quality and 330 for sufficient quality. For *Escherichia coli* in 100 ml: coastal waters: 250 for excellent quality, 500 for good quality and 500 for sufficient quality; in inland waters: 500 for excellent quality, 400 for good quality and 330 for sufficient quality. The fact that the values for sufficient quality are occasionally stricter than for good quality is explained by the different calculations of the average of the sampling. Where the sampling exceeds the level of 'sufficient', the water is of 'poor' quality.

bathe. Only where the water was classified 'poor' for five subsequent bathing seasons had a permanent prohibition to bathe to be decided.

7-21 The EEA and the Commission report annually on the quality of bathing waters. The last report, for 2021,[79] reported that about 21,500 bathing waters were covered. Of these, 84.8 per cent were of excellent quality – ranging from 97.4 per cent in Austria to 44.5 per cent in Poland – while 1.5 per cent (332 bathing waters) were of poor quality. The five countries with the highest percentage of bathing waters with excellent water quality were Austria, Malta, Greece, Croatia and Cyprus; the lowest percentages were noted in Latvia, Estonia, Hungary, Slovakia and Poland.

Directive 2006/7 increased the flexibility for local authorities very considerably and made it almost impossible for citizens and environmental organisations to get reliable information on compliance issues. The initial classification of waters and the possible changes during the bathing season cannot be properly controlled and enforced by others than the (local) administrations themselves. The average quality over five seasons is of very limited informational value for the next bathing season. The small number of samples required is inadequate for bathing waters where several thousands of people bathe. It is to be expected that the directive's application will lead to reports with very good results without the environmental quality of the bathing waters necessarily having significantly improved.

VIII. Nitrates in Water

7-22 Directive 91/676, adopted in 1991 and based on Article 192 TFEU, tried to protect waters against pollution by nitrates and thereby to combat eutrophication.[80] It was one of the first directives to provide for measures against pollution from agricultural activities. 'Waters' were not defined and thus referred to fresh water as well as coastal and marine waters. Member States had to designate vulnerable zones in their territories according to criteria fixed by the directive; the decisive criterion was whether the nitrate content of the water exceeded or risked exceeding 50 mg/l or whether the waters were eutrophic. For these vulnerable zones, Member States had to establish action programmes, for which the directive fixed some measures, amongst which were the necessity of prohibiting the use of certain fertilisers during certain periods and restricting the amount of livestock manure applied to the land per year to not more than 170 kg/ha of nitrogen, though some transitional periods were allowed.

7-23 Furthermore, Member States had to establish a code of good agricultural practice 'to be implemented by farmers on a voluntary basis' with the objective of reducing nitrate pollution, for which the directive gave a number of possible ('should contain') provisions. Member States had to report on the implementation every four years, from which the Commission had to publish a summary report.

Member States had to transpose the directive into national law by the end of 1993. Spain, Italy, Spain again, the UK, Luxembourg, Italy again, Germany, France, the Netherlands,

[79] EEA, *Bathing Water Quality in 2021* (Copenhagen, 2022).

[80] Directive 91/676 concerning the protection of waters against pollution caused by nitrates from agricultural sources [1991] OJ L375/1.

Ireland and Belgium were condemned by the CJEU for not having correctly transposed or applied the directive or for not having sent plans, data or reports.[81] On average, Member States took the necessary measures to transpose the directive with a delay of five years.[82]

In 2021, the Commission found that 36 per cent of rivers, 32 per cent of lakes, 31 per cent of coastal waters and 81 per cent of marine waters were eutrophic, mainly due to nitrate inputs from agriculture, which was responsible for 50–80 per cent of such inputs; the Baltic Sea was eutrophic at 97 per cent.[83] Thirty years after the adoption of Directive 91/676, this is indeed a depressing result. In contrast to Directive 91/271 on urban waste water, the Commission did not seriously try to enforce Directive 91/676. Over the years, it granted Member States some 30 derogations from the 170 kg/ha requirement, sometimes for the whole of the Member State's territory, and for several Member States (Denmark, Ireland, the Netherland) for decades. In order to improve this situation, effective application of the directive would constitute the most efficient way – and is, at the same time, the biggest problem, as it would mean that agricultural interests would have to be tackled.

The core environmental question is whether the directive's objective to have the number of cattle reduced in vulnerable zones, where the permitted levels of nitrate are exceeded, should be enforced so that the output of nitrogen per hectare does not exceed 170 kg. This appears not to be the case so far. Denmark, Germany, Ireland, the Netherlands and the UK had derogations granted by the Commission for the whole of their territory, and Belgium and Italy for some of their regions. These derogations were regularly renewed: thus, for example, Denmark has had this derogation since 2002. France, where serious nitrate problems exist, particularly in the waters of Brittany, and which was found to have infringed Directive 91/676 three times,[84] has regularly invoked the social problems linked to a full application of the directive. The Commission did not take action under Article 260 TFEU against France, even though the nitrate levels in the water there did not decrease between 2008 and 2019,[85] nor against Germany, which was found in breach in 2018[86] and has not ensured full compliance since; the only Member State so far against whom an action under Article 260 TFEU has been taken is Greece.[87] The Commission has preferred to grant derogations or to remain passive, rather than to enforce the directive against all Member States. The cases which it submitted to the CJEU did not address this core question, but touched on aspects of minor importance.

[81] CJEU Case C-71/97 *Commission v Spain* ECLI:EU:C:1998:455; Case C-195/97 *Commission v Italy* ECLI:EU:C:1999:100; Case C-274/98 *Commission v Spain* ECLI:EU:C:2000:206; Case C-293/97 *Standley* ECLI:EU:C:1999:215; Case C-266/00 *Commission v Luxembourg* ECLI:EU:C:2001:151; Case C-127/99 *Commission v Italy* ECLI:EU:C:2001:597; Case C-161/00 *Commission v Germany* ECLI:EU:C:2002:170; Case C-258/00 *Commission v France* ECLI:EU:C:2002:400; Case C-322/00 *Commission v Netherlands* ECLI:EU:C:2003:532; Case C-396/01 *Commission v Ireland* ECLI:EU:C:2004:136; Case C-221/03 *Commission v Belgium* ECLI:EU:C:2005:573.

[82] Commission, 'Implementation of Directive 91/676' COM(2010) 47.

[83] Commission, 'Implementation Report of Directive 91/676' COM(2021) 1000, 5 and 6. The report carefully avoided assessing the results of the 30 years of existence of the directive.

[84] CJEU Case C-258/00 (n 81); Case C-193/12 *Commission v France* ECLI:EU:C:2013:394; Case C-237/12 *Commission v France* (C-237/12) ECLI:EU:C:2014:2152.

[85] Commission, SWD(2021) 1001, part 18/38, 323.

[86] CJEU Case 543/16 *Commission v Germany* ECLI:EU:C:2018:481.

[87] CJEU Case C-298/19 *Commission v Greece* ECLI:EU:C:2020:133.

IX. Discharges from Industrial Installations and Ships

7-24 The EU measures on emissions, including water discharges, from the titanium dioxide industry have already been discussed.[88] As regards water discharges from hazardous waste incinerators, the Commission proposed a directive where it suggested emission limit values for a total of 15 pollutants, which it later withdrew.[89] Generally, however, the sector-oriented approach, where emission limit values are fixed for a specific industrial sector, was abandoned with the adoption of Directive 96/61,[90] which requested the application of the best available technique. This policy change, however, created a problem, since Directive 96/61, which has since been replaced by Directive 2010/75 on industrial emissions,[91] only applied to certain large industrial installations, whereas water contamination depends on the quantity of discharges, which may also stem from cumulated emissions from smaller plants.[92]

Directive 2010/75 required the fixing, by the public authorities of the Member States, of emission limit values in the individual permits for installations that come under the directive. The pollutants covered were those 'likely to be emitted from the installation in significant quantities, having regard to their nature and their potential to transfer pollution from one medium to the other (water, air and land)'. Special attention was to be given to fixing emission limit values for 13 'main polluting substances', listed in annex II.[93]

In 2023, the CJEU held that a derogation from the requirement of using the best available technique under Directive 2010/75 was not allowed when the quality objectives of Directive 2008/50 on air pollution would be exceeded.[94] This judgment is also relevant with regard to the quality objectives that were fixed for waters in Directive 2008/105;[95] it is true, though, that these quality objectives are much less precise than those of Directive 2008/50, and neither the requirements of Directive 2008/105 nor those of Directive 2010/75 are carefully monitored.

7-25 Legally speaking, the discharge of waste is no different from any other discharge into water; the terminology 'dumping' stems from international agreements which wanted

[88] Directive 2008/105 (n 27).

[89] Commission [1998] OJ C13/6.

[90] Directive 96/61 [1996] OJ L257/26. In 2008, this directive was replaced by Directive 2008/1 [2008] OJ L24/8.

[91] Directive 2010/75 on industrial emissions [2010] OJ L334/17.

[92] Directive 2015/2193 on the limitation of emissions from certain pollutants into the air from medium combustion plants [2015] OJ L313/1 only refers to air emissions.

[93] Directive 2010/75 (n 91) annex II (water pollutants): (1) organohalogen compounds and substances which may form such compounds in the aquatic environment; (2) organophosphorous compounds; (3) organotin compounds; (4) substances and preparations which have been proved to possess carcinogenic or mutagenic properties or properties which may affect reproduction in or via the aquatic environment; (5) persistent hydrocarbons and persistent and bioaccumulable organic toxic substances; (6) cyanides; (7) metals and their compounds; (8) arsenic and its compounds; (9) biocides and plant protection products; (10) materials in suspension; (11) substances which contribute to eutrophication (in particular, nitrates and phosphates); (12) substances which have an unfavourable influence on the oxygen balance (and can be measured using parameters such as BOD (biological oxygen demand) and COD (chemical oxygen demand), etc); and (13) substances which are listed in annex X to Directive 2000/60 (this provision concerned 45 substances).

[94] CJEU Case C-375/21 *Za Zemyata* ECLI:EU:C::2023:173.

[95] Directive 2008/105 (n 27).

to give a specific definition to the discharge of waste from ships and called this practice dumping. Under EU waste legislation, the discharge of waste needs an authorisation; thus, Member States may authorise the discharge of waste into waters at their discretion.[96]

In 1976, the Commission made a proposal on the dumping of waste at sea; it made another proposal in 1985.[97] However, these proposals were not extensively discussed in the Council, since Member States preferred to see questions of marine pollution discussed in the context of international agreements, rather than at EU level. Waste dumping from ships is now prohibited by Directive 2008/98 on waste.[98]

Identical considerations apply to the discharge of ships themselves and of offshore installations. At the end of their useful lifetime, offshore installations become waste. Their discharge into waters thus follows the same rules. After the Brent Spar incident – in 1995, an oil company had tried to sink a rig in the North Sea, but had abandoned its plans after massive public protests in some (northern) EU Member States – the Commission considered the elaboration of a directive on the decommissioning of offshore installations. However, it abandoned these plans in view of the resistance from Member States; the decommissioning of offshore installations was then addressed within the framework of the OSPAR Convention; an OSPAR decision prohibits the decommissioning at sea, but allows for exceptions.[99] 7-26

In 2006, France wanted to send its aeroplane carrier *Clemenceau* to South Asia in order for it to be dismantled there. As the ship contained some quantities of asbestos, it was, legally speaking, hazardous waste, the export of which is prohibited under EU waste legislation (see paragraph 10-36ff below). Nevertheless, France pursued its action. When Egypt refused the transit of this hazardous waste through the Suez Canal, it obtained development aid from France and forgot its objections. Then Greenpeace activists entered the ship during its passage through the Suez Canal and protested against the shipment. At the same time, the French Conseil d'Etat confirmed that the transport in question was clearly a shipment of hazardous waste. In view of the public protests, the French President ordered the ship to return to France. This single case stands out, though European tankers and other commercial ships are regularly shipped to South-East Asia in order to be dismantled and shredded, under appalling social and environmental conditions. A recent regulation on ship dismantling tries to address the dismantling problems in general.[100]

In some parts of the Union, end-of-life fishing vessels were regularly discharged into the sea. Whether this practice continues is not known. There are no specific Union provisions on end-of-life fishing vessels and their disposal or recycling, so Directive 2008/98 on waste, which prohibits the dumping of waste at sea, applies. Directive 2019/904, which was aimed at the reduction of marine litter, only refers to 'fishing gear containing plastic', and not to plastic fishing vessels.[101]

[96] Directive 2008/98 on waste [2008] OJ L312/3.

[97] [1976] OJ C40/3; [1985] OJ C245/23.

[98] See Directive 2008/98 (n 96) Art 36: 'Member States shall take the necessary measures to prohibit the abandonment, dumping or uncontrolled management of waste.'

[99] See para 10-15.

[100] Regulation 1257/2013[2013] OJ L330/1; for more details, see para 10-38.

[101] Directive 2019/904 on the reduction of the impact of certain plastic products on the environment [2019] OJ L155/1.

X. Waste Water

7-27 In 1991, the Union adopted a Directive on urban waste water,[102] based on Article 192(1) TFEU. The directive aimed to reduce the pollution of surface waters with nutrients, in particular nitrates and phosphates from urban waste water and some industrial waste waters, and thus to combat eutrophication. It applied to domestic waste water, and the mixture of this water with industrial waste water and/or run-off rainwater. The directive required Member States to provide, by the end of 2005, a sewerage system for all agglomerations consisting of more than 2000 people; agglomerations of more than 15,000 people had to be equipped with such a system by the end of the year 2000. The Member States which joined the Union since 2004, obtained, at their request, transition periods. The directive was the only environmental directive which asked Member States to proceed to the construction of some infrastructure.

Before the waste water enters such a collecting system, it must undergo at least secondary (biological) treatment; this requirement was to be complied with by the end of 2005, and by the year 2000 for agglomerations of more than 15,000 people. Furthermore, Member States had to designate sensitive areas for which more stringent treatment requirements were to apply; such areas are waters that are found to be eutrophic; areas that are intended for the production of drinking water and could contain more than 50 mg of nitrates per litre; and areas where more than secondary treatment was necessary to comply with the directive. Member States were also allowed to designate their whole territory as a sensitive area. They could also consider certain areas as less sensitive areas (marine waters), for which less stringent requirements applied. The discharge of sludge from treatment installations into waters had to be phased out by the end of 1998.

Member States had to establish programmes for the implementation of Directive 91/271 and to publish, every two years, situation reports on the disposal of urban waste water and sludge. Overall, it was estimated that about 40,000 water treatment plants were to be constructed or renewed for the some 23,000 agglomerations that were covered by the directive; to this had to be added the construction of sewerage systems.[103]

7-28 Directive 91/271 had to be transposed into national law by mid-1993. By the end of 1994, only Denmark, France and Luxembourg had done so.[104] In 1996, the CJEU condemned Greece, Germany and Italy for not having transposed the directive into national law;[105] Belgium and Italy were also condemned for not having provided for waste water treatment for Brussels and Milan,[106] as were a number of other Member States for incorrect transposition or application, or for not co-operating with the Commission in implementing the directive.

The most recent implementation report by the Commission[107] indicated that 95 per cent of all waste waters in the Union were collected; for 88 per cent, the required secondary

[102] Directive 91/271 (n 21); amended by Commission Directive 98/15 [1998] OJ L67/29.

[103] European Court of Auditors [1998] OJ C191/1, paras 3 and 5.

[104] Commission, 12th report on monitoring application of Community law (1994) [1995] OJ C254/1 [1995] OJ C254/1, 128.

[105] CJEU Case C-161/95 *Commission v Greece* ECLI:EU:C:1996:152; Case C-297/95 *Commission v Germany* ECLI:EU:C:1996:500; Case C-302/95 *Commission v Italy* ECLI:EU:C:1996:502.

[106] CJEU Case C-236/99 *Commission v Belgium* ECLI:EU:C:2000:374; Case C-396/00 *Commission v Italy* ECLI:EU:C:2002:261.

[107] Commission, '10th Report on the Implementation of the Urban Waste Water Directive' COM(2020) 452.

treatment was effectuated, and for 86 per cent, a stricter treatment was made.[108] However, these general figures did not show that compliance particularly lagged behind in Central and Eastern Europe.[109] In 2010, 19 years after the directive's adoption, only 11 of the then 27 capitals of the Member States complied with the directive's requirements for big cities: of the 16 capitals that did not comply, Brussels, Sofia, Nicosia, Prague, Riga, Dublin, Rome, Tallinn, Luxembourg, La Valetta, Warsaw, Lisbon and London did not satisfy the requirements of waste water treatment;[110] in 2016, this was the case for Dublin, Bucharest, Sofia, Copenhagen, Prague, La Valetta and Ljubljana.[111] The Commission estimated that between 1990 and 2010, €152 billion had been invested in urban waste water infrastructure; necessary overall investments for construction and maintenance by 2030 were estimated to be between €230 and 253 billion.[112]

Unlike for Directive 91/676, where the Commission was not very serious about monitoring the implementation, the Commission took action against Member States for systematic infringements of Directive 91/271.[113] The CJEU held that infringements had been committed by Belgium (three judgments), France (four judgments), Greece (four judgments), Italy (five judgments), Portugal (four judgments), Spain (five judgments), Finland, Germany, Ireland, Luxembourg and Sweden (one judgment each).[114] Belgium, Luxembourg, Greece (twice), Portugal, Spain and Italy were even brought before the CJEU under Article 260 TFEU for not having complied with a first judgment, and were fined.[115] The only Member State of the countries that joined the Union since 2004 to be found in breach of Directive 91/271 was Cyprus.[116]

In 2022, the Commission proposed an amendment to the directive, which is presently being discussed by the other Union institutions.[117] The proposal intended to include agglomeration of more than 1000 persons into the collection and treatment system of the directive, reduce pollution from rainwater and ensure a more systematic reduction of nitrogen, phosphorous and micro-pollutants.

Overall, it appears that the attempt to enforce the application of Directive 91/271 is more successful than the working with derogations and the tolerating of non-compliance as under Directive 91/676.

[108] ibid.

[109] Commission, SWD(2020) 145: the different data for collection, secondary treatment and more stringent treatment were, for Bulgaria, 51%, 38% and 21%; Ireland, 100%, 51% and 23%; Malta, 100%, 0% and 0%; Romania, 15%, 9% and 9%; Slovenia, 62%, 29% and 24%; and Hungary, 72%, 71% and 73%.

[110] Commission, SWD(2013) 298.

[111] Commission, SWD(2020) 145.

[112] Commission, SWD(2020) 700, 131.

[113] Apart from the judgments mentioned in n 106, see CJEU Case C-526/09 *Commission v Portugal* ECLI:EU:C:2010:734; Case C-220/10 *Commission v Portugal* ECLI:EU:C:2011:558; Case C-343/10 *Commission v Spain* ECLI:EU:C:2011:260; Case C-565/10 *Commission v Italy* ECLI:EU:C:2012:476; Case C-23/13 *Commission v France* ECLI:EU:C:2013:723; Case C-85/13 *Commission v Italy* ECLI:EU:C:2014:251.

[114] Commission, SWD(2020) 700, 131–44.

[115] CJEU Case C-533/11 *Commission v Belgium* ECLI:EU:C:2013:659; Case C-576/11 *Commission v Luxembourg* ECLI:EU:C:2013:733; Case C-167/14 *Commission v Greece* ECLI:EU:C:2015:684; Case C-557/14 *Commission v Portugal* ECLI:EU:C:2016:471; Case C-328/16 *Commission v Greece* ECLI:EU:C:2018:98; Case C-205/17 *Commission v Spain* ECLI:EU:C:2018:606; Case C-251/17 *Commission v Italy* ECLI:EU:C:2018:358.

[116] CJEU Case C-248/19 *Commission v Cyprus* ECLI:EU:C:2020:171.

[117] Commission, COM(2022) 540.

XI. Oceans and Rivers

A. Oceans

7-29 Though the EU environmental policy also aims to contribute to the solution of global or regional environmental problems (Article 191 TFEU), it has not developed a consistent policy to address the protection of the marine environment. Directive 76/464 on discharges of pollutants into Union waters and its daughter directives[118] were never monitored as to their actual application. Even in those directives, though, the Union has, in its political and legal activity, only considered the seas adjacent to EU territory, in particular the North Sea, the Baltic Sea and the Mediterranean Sea, and to a lesser extent the Atlantic Ocean. A different approach as regards the environment was only taken in the context of the Common Fisheries Policy, where the Community also took an interest in fish – the 'natural resources' – in the West African Atlantic, the Caribbean Sea and the Antarctic waters; the marine waters were also dealt with within the framework of the Common Transport Policy.

In 2002, the Union set up a Maritime Safety Agency, which had, among others, the task of preventing and responding to pollution from ships and to pollution from oil and gas installations at sea;[119] the Agency's environmental activity consisted mainly in the publication of annual reports on maritime incidents (including pollution). In 2006, the Commission published a communication on an EU maritime policy.[120] The title explained the ideas behind the communication, which did not announce concrete measures.

7-30 In 2002, the Commission published a communication on the protection for the marine environment.[121] Following that, the Commission made a second communication on the marine environment in 2005[122] and suggested a directive on the marine environment, which was adopted in 2008 and was the very first act to address environmental issues of marine waters.[123] The directive aimed at achieving good environmental status of the marine environment by 2021. It limited itself to fixing objectives and principles, but omitted to provide for concrete measures. It established European Marine Regions as management units which happened to coincide with the areas covered by the three regional water conventions of Oslo/Paris (OSPAR, North East Atlantic), Helsinki (Baltic Sea) and Barcelona (Mediterranean Sea). The Black Sea Region was mentioned in the directive, but only marginally, as the Union is not a contracting party of the Bucharest Convention on the Protection of the Black Sea; that convention is only open to ratification by Member States.

[118] Directive 76/464 (n 11).

[119] Regulation 1406/2002 establishing a European Maritime Safety Agency [2016] OJ L208/1.

[120] Commission, 'Towards a Future Maritime Policy for the Union: A European Vision for the Oceans and Seas' COM(2006) 275.

[121] Commission, 'Towards a Strategy to Protect and Conserve the Marine Environment' COM(2002) 539 of 2 October 2002.

[122] Commission, 'Thematic Strategy on the Protection and Conservation of the Marine Environment' COM(2005) 504.

[123] Directive 2008/56 establishing a framework for Community Action on marine water quality in the field of Marine Environmental Policy (Marine Strategy Framework Directive) [2008] OJ L164/19. Commission Directive 2017/845 [2017] OJ L125/27 amended its annex III concerning good environmental status criteria. See also Commission Decision 2017/848 laying down criteria and methodological standards on good environmental status of marine waters and specifications and standardised methods for monitoring and assessment [2017] OJ L125/43.

Directive 2008/56 was based on an ecosystem approach, which means a strategy for the integrated management of land, water and living resources; such an approach differs from current approaches, which usually focus on single species, sectors, activities or concerns, and considers the cumulative impacts of the different sectors.[124] The directive required Member States to develop, for each Marine Region, a Marine Strategy, which had to contain a number of measures designed to achieve a good environmental status. The directive did not define what a good environmental status was, or give a description of it. Rather, it attempted to let the regional conventions' structures take care of, elaborate and monitor the future programmes, limiting itself largely to providing for reporting provisions. It is significant that common measures for assessing the quality of marine waters were only adopted in 2017.[125] Aspects other than marine *water* aspects – for instance, the fauna and flora or marine natural parks – were barely covered at all.

Under the directive, a common implementation strategy was developed, though it not published; this work was led by the Member States' administrations, and the work of different groups, sub-groups and conferences was only very selectively made publicly available. The Commission published several progress reports, which reported on activities and problems rather than on results.[126] Generally, though, reporting by Member States on the implementation of the directive was poor.

The remarkably frank implementation report[127] stated that only some of the 4700 measures[128] which Member States adopted under the directive were considered to be adequate. The work on the common implementation strategy had not led to a common understanding of what 'good environmental status' meant.[129] Just half of the submitted programmes addressed the pressures on the Union's marine environment, and the concept of an ecosystem approach was only partially realised. The Commission identified the lack of human resources and lack of political will as the main factors impeding a proper implementation of the directive; these causes were aggravated by the slow recovery of the marine environment in cases of impairment.

The two specific problems which Directive 2008/56 intended to address – marine litter and underwater noise – did not lead to any legally relevant proposal or measure. In contrast, the surface of marine protected areas grew to 10.8 per cent of the total surface of Union marine waters.[130] As mentioned in the previous chapter, the Commission's biodiversity strategy intends to have 30 per cent of the water surface protected by 2030.

Overall, the state of implementation[131] of Directive 2008/56 rather conveyed the message that business as usual was the dominant approach to managing the Union's marine waters.

[124] Commission, 'Implementation Report of Directive 2008/56' COM(2020) 259, 3.

[125] Commission Decision 2017/848 (n 123).

[126] Commission, SWD(2014) 49; Commission, SWD(2017) 1; Commission, COM(2018) 562; Commission, SWD(2018) 393; Commission, SWD(2019) 510.

[127] Commission, COM(2020) 259. Section 4 of this report contained a rather negative description of the state of the Union's marine environment.

[128] Commission, SWD(2020) 60, 33. This figure included measures taken under existing Union or national law, such as Directives 2000/60, 2006/7 and 91/271.

[129] See Commission, SWD(2020) 60, 15: 'there was no shared EU understanding of what constitutes "good environmental status", even at a (sub)regional level. There are 23 different "good environmental status" determinations across the EU, and therefore no common or comparable goals.'

[130] ibid 38.

[131] See also Commission, 'Review of the Status of the Marine Environment of the EU' SWD(2020) 61, which gave the trends and results for each of the descriptors of Commission Decision 2017/848 (n 123).

7-31 In 2014, the Union adopted a Directive establishing a framework for maritime spatial planning, based on Articles 43, 100, 192 and 194 TFEU.[132] Under this directive, the Member States had to establish integrated plans for their marine waters by 2021, and to update them every 10 years; consequently, the directive did not apply to landlocked Member States (Austria, Czechia, Hungary, Luxembourg, Slovakia). The necessity for such plans was explained with the multiple activities which were taking place in marine waters and which were likely to increase in future. In this regard, Recital 1 mentioned installations for the production of energy from renewable sources, oil and gas extraction and exploitation, maritime shipping and fishing activities, ecosystem and biodiversity conservation, the extraction of raw materials, tourism, aquaculture installations, underwater cultural heritage and the pressures on coastal resources.

The directive gave some rather vague and general indications of what a plan should contain, but did not impose any other obligations on Member States. In my opinion, this is not compatible with the principle of subsidiarity.

A progress report by the Commission of 2022 explained that nine Member States – Bulgaria, Croatia, Cyprus, Estonia, Greece, Italy, Portugal (for the Azores), Romania and Spain – had, by 2021, either not adopted plans or not adopted complete plans.[133]

7-32 The Union adhered to the following international conventions concerning the marine environment, most of which having been completed by a number of protocols to which the Union normally also adhered:

- Paris Convention on the Prevention of Marine Pollution From Land-Based Sources;[134]
- Barcelona Convention on the protection of the Mediterranean Sea Against Pollution;[135]
- Bonn Agreement for Co-operation in Dealing With Pollution of the North Sea by Oil and Other Harmful Substances;[136]
- Co-operation Agreement for the Protection of the Coasts and Waters of the North-East Atlantic Against Pollution;[137]
- Helsinki Convention on the Protection of the Marine Environment of the Baltic Sea Area;[138]
- Helsinki 1992 Convention on the Protection of the Marine Environment of the Baltic;[139]
- Paris Convention for the Protection of the Marine Environment in the North-East Atlantic (OSPAR);[140] and
- Montego Bay Convention on the Law of the Sea.[141]

The Union did not join the International Convention for the Prevention of Pollution From Ships of 1973, as that convention is only open to states, not to regional integration

[132] Directive 2014/89 establishing a framework for maritime spatial planning [2014] OJ L257/135.
[133] Commission, COM(2022) 185.
[134] Decision 75/437 [1975] OJ L194/5.
[135] Decision 77/85 [1977] OJ L240/1.
[136] Decision 84/358 [1984] OJ L188/7.
[137] Decision 93/550 [1993] OJ L267/20.
[138] Decision 94/156 [1994] OJ L73/1.
[139] Decision 94/157 [1994] OJ L73/19.
[140] Decision 98/249 [1998] OJ L104/1.
[141] Decision 98/392 [1998] OJ L179/1.

organisations. For the same reason, the Union is also not a member of the International Maritime Organization.

With the Union signing up to the international conventions, their legal provisions became part of EU law. Nevertheless, for each negotiation of a protocol to a convention or any other amendment, the Commission needs a mandate from the Council in order to negotiate in the name of the Union; for the signing of such a protocol, the same procedure applies.[142] 7-33

The reasons why Member States object to EU directives or regulations on environmental problems facing the sea have never been expressly specified. They are presumed to be the following:

1. International agreements are normally adopted unanimously. It is true that, during the last few years, public international law has developed the habit that amendments may, under certain conditions, be adopted by majority decisions; however, this possibility remains largely theoretical. Instead, the principle of international agreements remains based on consensus. Each contracting state thus has the right to veto decisions. In contrast, EU environmental measures are normally adopted by a qualified majority, which allows measures to be taken against the will of an objecting Member State.
2. The initiative for measures at international level is, jointly or severally, in the hands of contracting states. This allows a fairly direct influence on the international agenda. For the Commission to negotiate, in the name of the Union, at international conventions, a mandate is necessary under Article 218 TFEU. In contrast, initiatives for measures at EU level are taken by the Commission, which has the monopoly on this.
3. At international level, media attention and the participation of environmental organisations is normally relatively limited. At EU level, the increasing importance of the European Parliament and its co-decision function make quasi-confidential discussions and decisions practically impossible.
4. For years, France and the UK have both discharged radioactive materials, stemming from military or private activity, into the sea. In the name of national sovereignty, such activities were always considered to remain outside the area of EU competence. This attitude has probably caused these two countries, but also other Member States where the situation was similar – though not necessarily concerning radioactive matters – not to accept EU environmental initiatives to protect seas. Generally, a number of Member States continue to consider the seas as a big sewer system, where discharges are all too often allowed to take place.

The statement that the international agreements become, with the adherence of the Union, part of EU environmental law is legally correct. It is, however, rather theoretical, since the monitoring of these agreements is ensured not by the Commission, but by the secretariats of the different agreements. At no time has the Commission tried, with regard to the different decisions incorporating the agreements into EU law, to 'ensure the application of the Treaties and of measures adopted by their institutions pursuant to them',[143] and thus to control the effective implementation and enforcement of these agreements. Unless there is 7-34

[142] For details, see Art 218 TFEU.
[143] Art 17 TEU.

a specific EU directive or regulation that reproduces the content of the international agreement, it is left to Member States to decide if and to what extent they transpose the provisions of the agreements into their national legal order and apply them. The Commission has never explained why it applies this self-restraint.

In Case C-213/03, the CJEU confirmed the interpretation given here. It declared that France had infringed EU law, because it did not apply a protocol to the Barcelona Convention; this protocol had been ratified by the European Union, but not by France.[144] However, this is the only case to date where the Commission has taken action under Article 258 TFEU against a Member State for infringement of provisions of an international environmental agreement which had become part of EU law. The reason for bringing this case before the CJEU was that a French court had submitted a preliminary question to the Court and the Commission did not wish to be seen as remaining passive.

The present practice by the EU institutions leads to different legal situations and, hence, to different pollution situations for the different seas. To give some examples: OSPAR took decisions to reduce the discharge of radioactive substances into the North East Atlantic (Decision 2000/1), on the use of organic-phase drilling fluids (Decision 2000/3), on a control system for use and discharge of offshore chemicals (Decision 2000/2), on carbon dioxide streams in the water column, on the seabed or in geological formations (Decisions 2007/1 and 2) or on maritime protected areas (Decisions 2010/1–5). The EU was passive with regard to all these activities.

7-35 Most, if not all, of these measures, which concern the North-East Atlantic, have an impact on the functioning of the Union. However, it is highly unlikely that, in the context of the Barcelona Convention on the Mediterranean Sea, similar subjects will be raised at all, not to mention the taking of binding decisions.

At the same time, this list of subjects indicates the impact that OSPAR decisions have or might have on the Union. Indeed, the ban of products or processes will impinge on the free circulation of goods and the competitive situation of undertakings.

For example, in the case of hexachloroethane, a substance which a decision by the OSPAR Convention had phased out, the potential conflict was solved, not without complications, by the adoption of an EU directive which took over the OSPAR decision to phase out that substance.[145] Another approach was taken in the Brent Spar incident: while the Commission had first considered making a proposal for an EU directive on offshore installations, it finally rejected this approach with legally unconvincing arguments and left the decision to OSPAR, which took a decision in 1998.[146] The Commission then proposed

[144] CJEU Case C-239/03 *Commission v France* ECLI:EU:C:2004:598; see also Case C-213/03 *Pêcheurs de Berre* ECLI:EU:C:2004:464.

[145] Directive 97/16 [1997] OJ L116/31.

[146] OSPAR, Decision 98/3 on the disposal of disused offshore installations. See also Commission, 'Communication on Removal and Disposal of Disused Offshore Oil and Gas Installations' COM(1998) 49, para 6.2: 'The disadvantage of this approach [a directive] is that only EC and EEA Member States would be bound to the common approach whereas other third countries with which we share the Seas concerned would not be bound to implement the same or similar measures without the Community taking the initiative to negotiate and adopt such rules in the relevant regional seas Conventions. Although this approach would have the advantage of applying to all EC Member States immediately, ie also to those Member States outside OSPAR – namely Austria, Greece and Italy – it would only apply to Norway after a Decision of the EEC Joint Committee. It could also be interpreted as prejudicial to Community interest in other OSPAR policies if the Commission were to be seen to press ahead separately for action via EC legislation rather than via the newly ratified OSPAR Convention. Furthermore it could be seen as an attempt to exclude Norway from negotiations on any final policy.'

approving this decision by OSPAR by way of a decision, without, however, proposing an amendment of EU law, in order to introduce provisions on offshore installations that were binding on all EU Member States.[147] However, the proposal to take over the OSPAR decision was never adopted by the Council.

It must be assumed that the Commission definitely abandoned its plan for a directive on the decommissioning of offshore installations[148] because any such proposal would have been rejected in the same way as the proposal for a directive on the dumping of waste at sea. However, de facto, this development also risks leading to a loss of the Commission's right of initiative for EU action. Neither rules on subsidiarity nor rules on deregulation can solve the problem of decisions being taken by the regional marine conventions which have an impact on the Union as a whole. 7-36

The Commission also submitted proposals to approve other OSPAR decisions, for example on a new annex V to the OSPAR Convention[149] concerning the disposal of radioactive waste,[150] and on emission limit values from the production of vinyl chloride monomers.[151] However, these proposals were, again, not adopted.

In November 2002, the tanker *Prestige*, which was single-hulled and had loaded 77,000 tonnes of heavy fuel oil, had an accident off the coast of Galicia (Spain) and sank. A large quantity of fuel oil was released which polluted in particular the Spanish and French coast. The damage caused by the accident and the subsequent coastal and marine pollution was estimated to be more than €1 billion. The accident prompted strong activity from the EU to improve the safety of maritime transport of fuel oils and other dangerous substances, and generally to improve maritime transport safety.[152] Similarly increased legislative activities had already taken place after the accidents of the ships *Braer* in the Shetlands in 1993 and *Erika* in France in 1999. The *Erika* accident led to the setting up of the European Maritime Safety Agency,[153] which had been given the task of ensuring 'a high uniform and effective level of maritime safety and prevention of pollution from ships' and from offshore oil and gas installations (Article 1); the regulation was based on the present Article 100(2) TFEU. 7-37

B. Rivers

The Union is a member of the following international agreements regarding rivers: 7-38

- Bonn Convention for the Protection of the Rhine Against Chemical Pollution;[154]
- Regensburg Agreement on Co-operation on Management of Water Resources in the Danube Basin;[155]

[147] Proposal for a Council decision [1999] OJ C158/10.

[148] See also Directive 2013/30 on the safety of offshore oil and gas operations [2013] OJ L178/66. This directive was a follow-up of the accident of an offshore installation in the Gulf of Mexico and is almost entirely limited to accident prevention and restoration measures. See also para 4-57ff.

[149] [1999] OJ C158/1.

[150] [1999] OJ C158/8.

[151] [1999] OJ C158/19.

[152] Commission, 'Report to the European Council on Action to Deal With the Effects of the *Prestige* Disaster' COM(2003) 105 of 5 March 2003.

[153] Regulation 1406/2002 [2002] OJ L208/1.

[154] Decision 77/586 [1977] OJ L240/35.

[155] Decision 90/160 [1990] OJ L377/28.

- Magdeburg Convention on the International Commission for the Protection of the Elbe;[156]
- Sofia Convention on Co-operation for the Protection of the Danube;[157]
- Wroclaw Convention on the International Commission for the Protection of the Odra Against Pollution;[158] and
- Helsinki Convention on the Protection and Use of Transboundary Watercourses and International Lakes.[159]

7-39 The legal situation as regards rivers is similar to that of oceans. While the different agreements became, with the EU decisions to adhere to them, part of EU law, they are de facto treated, by both the Union and the Commission, as instruments of public international law. In particular, the Commission does not monitor the adoption of measures to incorporate the agreements into national law and their application in practice, the discharge of pollutants or the abstraction of waters. Thus, the question that was put some years ago, particularly by Dutch lawyers, 'Who shall clean up the Rhine river – the Rhine Commission or the European Community?', is in reality answered for the Rhine and for the other rivers that are the subject of agreements: it is not the Union, but the different secretariats of the agreements, which are in charge of combating river pollution. The question of water resources goes beyond river water, since it might also apply to groundwater resources. To date, though, there has not been a single provision in EU water law which deals with quantitative aspects of water resources.

The above-mentioned Directive 2000/60 also requested the elaboration of river basin management plans for the Rhine, Danube, Elbe and Oder. Member States have largely used the administrative structures existing for these rivers to fulfil their obligations under Directive 2000/60. The Commission's role in monitoring the application of the river basin management plans for these rivers – ie leaving the monitoring to the structures of the different agreements and not really caring about the practical results – did not change, though.

[156] Decision 91/598 [1991] OJ L321/25.
[157] Decision 97/825 [1997] OJ L342/18.
[158] Decision 1999/257 [1999] OJ L100/20.
[159] Decision 95/308 [1995] OJ L186/44.

8

Air Pollution and Noise

I. Air Policy and Law

The first environmental action programmes of the Union mentioned air pollution, its causes and its effects on the environment, but actions were dispersed, incoherent and limited to specific pollution sources, in particular to emissions from passenger cars. The turning point came at the beginning of the 1980s, when the state of the forests, particularly those in Germany and Central Europe (*Waldsterben*, forest dieback), raised considerable concern. The subject of air pollution was discussed, in 1983, by the Heads of State and Governments, who suggested effective action against acid rain and air pollution.[1] This led, in the same year, to proposals for a general directive on air pollution from industrial installations,[2] for a directive on large combustion plants[3] and for a directive for quality objectives for nitrogen oxides (NO_x).[4] Other measures concentrated on the introduction of a catalytic converter for cars, which had been discussed since 1984 and had been progressively introduced since 1988 for new cars; since 1993, all new cars have had to be equipped in this way. 8-01

Since the mid-1980s, the depletion of the ozone layer and climate change entered increasingly into the foreground of discussions. These aspects will not be dealt with here, but in a separate chapter.[5]

EU legislative measures on air emissions from industrial installations were based, in the early 1980s, on the concept of emission limit values, which was in use mainly in legislation in Germany.[6] Large industrial installations in specific sectors were to operate on the basis of a permit which was to impose the best available technology not entailing excessive costs. EU-wide emission limit values were to be elaborated.[7] This concept led to the elaboration of directives for large combustion installations[8] and waste incinerators.[9] However, the 8-02

[1] (1993) 3 *Bulletin of the European Communities* para 1.5.2.

[2] Commission, Proposal for a directive on air emissions from industrial installations [1983] OJ C139/5.

[3] Commission, Proposal for a directive on large combustion plants [1984] OJ C49/1.

[4] Commission, Proposal for a directive on air quality objectives for NOx [1983] OJ C258/3.

[5] See ch 9 below.

[6] Directive 84/360 on the combating of air pollution from industrial plants [1984] OJ L188/20.

[7] ibid Art 8.

[8] Directive 88/609 on the limitation of emissions of certain pollutants into the air from large combustion plants [1988] OJ L336/1; this directive has since been replaced by Directive 2001/80 [2001] OJ L309/1 and, in 2010, by Directive 2010/75 on industrial emissions [2010] OJ L334/17.

[9] Directive 89/369 on new installations for the incineration of municipal waste [1989] OJ L163/32; Directive 89/429 on the incineration of municipal waste from existing plants [1989] OJ L203/50; Directive 94/67 on the incineration of hazardous waste [1994] OJ L365/34. All these directives were replaced by Directive 2000/76 on the incineration of waste [2000] OJ L332/91. In 2010, the provisions on waste incinerators were integrated into Directive 2010/75 (n 8).

Union diverged from this concept and more or less implicitly – at least, silently – took the decision that emission standards for industrial installations within the Union should not be harmonised.[10] This policy found its expression in Directive 96/61 – since replaced by Directive 2008/1 and later on by Directive 2010/75[11] – which was based on the principle that the emission limits for an industrial installation were to be fixed on a case-by-case basis in the permit which was issued for the installation. Directive 96/61, which repealed Directive 84/360, affected the quantity of air emissions greatly. Three days after the adoption of Directive 96/61, a new framework directive was adopted,[12] which established the legal frame for setting quality standards on air pollution and which was progressively put into operation via daughter directives.

8-03 Under the Sixth Environmental Action Programme,[13] the Commission submitted, in 2005, a thematic strategy on air pollution[14] which intended to provide for a long-term integrated air policy strategy.[15] The non-binding strategy established targets on the reduction of air pollution for sulphur dioxide (SO_2; 82 per cent reduction), NO_x (60 per cent), volatile organic compounds (51 per cent), ammonia (27 per cent) and fine particulate matter ($PM_{2.5}$; 59 per cent) by 2020, compared to the year 2000. As the binding concentration limits in particular for $PM_{2.5}$, which had been laid down in a daughter directive, were not respected by the majority of Member States, a new Directive 2008/50, which replaced Directive 96/62, was adopted which brought the different daughter directives back into a single legal text,[16] but took away with the reduction percentages. The two other legal steps to reach the objectives of the 2005 strategy were a strengthening of the Union legislation on national air emission ceilings and the setting of emission limit values for point sources (industrial installations, motor vehicles).

In 2021, the Commission adopted a new strategy, with the aim that, by 2050, 'Air, water and soil pollution are reduced to levels no longer considered harmful to health and ecosystems and that respect the boundaries our planet can cope with, thus creating a toxic-free environment'.[17] The plan fixed ambitious intermediate targets for 2030.[18]

8-04 Policies, strategies and measures concerning air pollution were strongly influenced by a number of basic factors which need to be borne in mind.

First, air emissions stem in particular from the combustion of fuels, and the energy policy within the Union on the use of energy – nuclear energy, energy from oil, gas,

[10] For the background to this shift in policy, see A Héritier, C Knill and S Mingers, *Ringing the Changes in Europe. Regulatory Competition and Redefinition of the State. Britain, France and Germany* (Berlin, 1996).

[11] Directive 96/61 on integrated prevention and pollution control [1996] OJ 257/26; in 2008, this directive was replaced by Directive 2008/1 [2008] OJ L24/8, and in 2010 by Directive 2010/75 (n 8); see also para 4-45 above.

[12] Directive 96/62 on ambient air quality assessment and management [1996] OJ L296/55.

[13] Decision 1600/2002 laying down the Sixth Community Environmental Action Programme [2002] OJ L242/1.

[14] Commission, 'Thematic Strategy on Air Pollution' COM(2005) 446.

[15] See also Commission, 'The Programme Clean Air for Europe (CAFÉ): A Thematic Strategy on Air Quality' COM(2001) 245.

[16] Directive 2008/50 on ambient air quality and cleaner air for Europe [2008] OJ L152/1. For more details, see para 8-07ff below.

[17] Commission, 'Pathway to a Healthy Planet for All. EU Action Plan "Towards Zero Pollution for Air, Water and Soil"' COM(2021) 400.

[18] ibid s 2.1. The targets were: (1) reduce by more than 55% the health impacts (premature deaths) of air pollution; (2) reduce by 30% the share of people chronically disturbed by transport noise; (3) reduce by 25% the EU ecosystems where air pollution threats biodiversity; (4) reduce by 50% nutrient losses, the use and risk of chemical pesticides, the use of the more hazardous ones, and the sale of antimicrobials for farmed animals and in agriculture; (5) reduce by 50% plastic litter at sea and by 30% microplastics released into the environment; (6) significantly reduce total waste generation and by 50% residual municipal waste.

coal and lignite and, more recently, energy from renewable sources – varied considerably, depending on the national availability of energy sources. Second, air emissions cannot be regarded separately from other environmental problems; while, for instance, nuclear energy does not emit significant quantities of air pollutants, it has numerous environmental and other disadvantages, such as the technological risk, waste treatment and disposal problems, the location and decommissioning of installations, their vulnerability to terrorist attacks and their acceptance by the population. Also, nuclear energy is not economically competitive within the Union – except in France, where investments in the past were heavily subsidised by state aid. Third, air emission quantities largely depend on the level of economic development, which continues to vary considerably between Member States and makes common solutions difficult. Fourth, and perhaps foremost, there seems to be no readiness in Western European society seriously to question present lifestyles, particularly private passenger and truck transport. The words used in the early 1990s by a President of the USA that the American way of life was not negotiable appear also to be true for the European way of life – at least in the eyes of many citizens. Renewable energies have only recently become the subject of concentrated attention.[19] Since about the year 2000, climate change and the awareness that fossil fuels constitute an exhaustible source of energy have led to a gradual strengthening of the policy on renewable energies, though its role in the overall concept of EU energy is still unsatisfactory.

At international level, EU participation in discussions on long-range transboundary air pollution, which have intensified over the years, well illustrate the global nature of environmental (air pollution) problems. Furthermore, co-operation with the World Health Organization (WHO) – mostly represented by its European Centre for Environment and Health – led to a situation where the Union oriented its air quality standards on recommendations of the WHO, though not completely complying with them.[20]

It is difficult to assess existing provisions, in particular the scientific, economic, math- 8-05
ematical, technical and political conditions of the different standards, the measuring mechanisms, the monitoring of the standards and of the measures which Member States, regions, local authorities and individual emitters were taking in pursuance of Union law, as these measures are highly complex, only perceptible to initiated experts and not sufficiently transparent. One practical consequence of this situation is that EU air pollution legislation is hardly enforceable: where a Member State is determined to reduce emissions, improve air quality and work intensively with clean-up programmes or reduction measures that are provided for in EU legislation, Union legislation is a useful yardstick with which the different measures may be aligned, co-ordinated, structured, monitored and assessed. Where, in contrast, a Member State attaches less importance to air pollution or where its environmental policy ranks lower in its political priorities, EU legislation will only be capable with difficulty, if at all, of leading to a continuous reduction of emissions and an improvement in air quality. This same problem with regard to the enforcement of quality standards had already been observed with regard to discharges into water.[21]

[19] Commission, 'Green Paper: Energy for the Future: Renewable Sources of Energy' COM(96) 576; Commission, 'White Paper for a Community Strategy and Action Plan' COM(97) 599.

[20] See in particular WHO, *Air Quality Guidelines for Europe*, 2nd edn (Copenhagen, 2000).

[21] See ch 7 above.

8-06 Ultimately, air quality directives cannot really be enforced. It is true that the Court of Justice of the European Union (CJEU) paved the way for an enforcement of air quality directives by individual persons, by providing that whenever the exceedance of the limit values could endanger human health the persons concerned must be in a position to rely on mandatory rules in order to be able to assert their rights.[22] However, the large discretion for administrations in the fixing of the number and location of measuring stations, of measuring methods, the frequency of measuring, the average values, etc, and the publication of data only months or years later leads de facto to the situation where EU air quality values constitute policy guidance standards rather than legal instruments; the individual citizen hardly ever has enough information to claim that the Union's quality standards were not respected. And the CJEU has rejected the possibility of a citizen, whose health had been impaired by air pollution, asking for compensation.[23] This lack of civil society support also explains the very low number of infringement cases under Article 258 of the Treaty on the Functioning of the European Union (TFEU) against Member States, which for a long time were limited to cases of non-transposition of EU directives or the absence of reporting.[24] The Commission has only started since about 2015 to bring Member States before the CJEU for not complying with the air quality provisions of Union law.[25]

In 2005, the Commission estimated that its proposed measures would still cause the annual premature death of 272,000 people in the Union, plus 21,000 premature deaths caused by ozone.[26] In 2013, it declared:

> In 2010 [air pollution] caused over 406,000 premature deaths as well as substantial avoidable sickness and suffering including respiratory conditions (such as asthma) and exacerbated cardiovascular problems. The overall external costs of these impacts ranged from between €330–940 billion, including labour productivity losses and other indirect economic damages varied at €23 billion per year in 2010. Ecosystems are also suffering, with algal blooms, fish die-off and other ecosystem disruptions driven by nutrient nitrogen pollution ('eutrophication'). This problem is particular acute in Europe's richest and most diverse natural zones, more than three-quarters of which are under threat'.[27]

[22] CJEU Case C-361/88 *Commission v Germany* ECLI:EU:C:1991:224; Case C-237/07 *Janecek* ECLI:EU:C:2008:447.

[23] CJEU Case C-61/21 *Ministère de Transition écologique* ECLI:EU:C:2022:1015.

[24] The following CJEU cases concerned the transposition of Union acts into national law: Case C-92/79 *Commission v Italy* ECLI:EU:C:1980:86; Case C-186/91 *Commission v Belgium* ECLI:EU:C:1993:93; Case C-320/99 *Commission v France* ECLI: ECLI:EU:C:2000:650; Case C-417/99 *Commission v Spain* ECLI:EU:C:2001:645. The following cases concerned the transposition of Union acts into national law by non-binding instruments: Case C-58/89 *Commission v Germany* ECLI:EU:C:1991:391; Case C-361/88 (n 22); Case C-13/90 *Commission v France* ECLI:EU:C:1991:309; Case C-14/90 *Commission v France* ECLI:EU:C:1991:359; Case C-64/90 *Commission v France* ECLI:EU:C:1991:360.

[25] CJEU Case C-488/15 *Commission v Bulgaria* ECLI:EU:C:2017:267; Case C-336/16 *Commission v Poland* ECLI:EU:C:2018:94; Case C- 635/18 *Commission v Germany* ECLI:EU:C:2021:437; Case C-636/18 *Commission v France* ECLI:EU:C:2019:900; Case C-637/18 *Commission v Hungary* ECLI:EU:C:2021:92; Case C-638/18 *Commission v Romania* ECLI:EU:C:2020:334; Case C-644/18 *Commission v Italy* ECLI:EU:C:2020:895; Case C-286/21 *Commission v France* ECLI:EU:C:2022:319; Case C-573/19 *Commission v Italy* ECLI:EU:C:2022:380; Case C-730/19 *Commission v Bulgaria* ECLI:EU:C:2022:382; Case C-125/20 *Commission v Spain* ECLI:EU:C:2022:1025; Case C-342/21 *Commission v Slovakia* ECLI:EU:C:2023:87; Case C-633/21 *Commission v Greece* ECLI:EU:C:2023:112; Case C-220/22 *Commission v Portugal* ECLI:EU:C:2023:521.

[26] Commission, COM(2005) 446 (n 14) 3.

[27] Commission, 'A Clean Air Programme for Europe' COM(2013) 918, 5. See also the detailed analysis in SWD(2013) 531.

In 2022, finally, the Commission declared:

> 'Approximately 238,000 premature deaths are attributed to fine particulate matter ($PM_{2.5}$) in the EU, 49,000 to nitrogen dioxide and 24,000 to acute exposure to ozone.'[28]

These data do not show significant progress.

The emissions stemming from fossil fuel consumption in traffic are the main cause of air pollution in the Union, but in its defence before the CJEU, the French government argued that town and country planning, infrastructure construction and other planning methods had been based on the existence of (fossil-fuel-using) cars and could not easily be changed.[29] This is presumably the reason why the Commission is more than reluctant to start court proceedings under Article 260 TFEU against Member States,[30] though the CJEU had found in several cases that the non-respect of Union air quality legislation dated back to 2010 and extended over more than five years.[31]

A significant improvement in air quality in the Union will probably only be reached when electrical vehicles more or less completely replace the existing fossil-fuel-using cars, which is not likely to occur before 2035.

II. Air Quality Requirements

The basic EU instrument on air pollution is – leaving aside Directive 2010/75,[32] which only applies to some large industrial installations – Directive 2008/50.[33] This directive dealt with SO_2, nitrogen dioxide (NO_2), benzene, carbon monoxide, lead, particulate matter (PM_{10}), $PM_{2.5}$ and tropospheric ozone. 8-07

Member States had to divide their territory into zones and agglomerations, and 'ensure that throughout their zones and agglomerations, levels of sulphur dioxide, PM_{10}, lead and carbon monoxide do not exceed the limit values' (Article 13). A limit value was defined as a value that had to be attained within a given period and not to be exceeded thereafter.[34] However, the directive provided for 'margins of tolerance', within which the limit values may well be exceeded; also, the definition of 'limit value' itself provided that it may not be exceeded for more than a certain number of days per calendar year, which means that it is not an absolute limit. Furthermore, when limit values were exceeded, Member States were obliged to draw up a clean-up plan, which means that they may delay respecting the limit values until the end of this – or even a second – plan. Finally, the locations where the Member States were requested to measure the concentration of pollutants were fixed by

[28] Commission, 'The Third Clean Air Outlook' COM(2022) 673, s 2.1. In s 6, methane is identified as responsible for having caused 24,000 premature deaths in 2020.

[29] CJEU Case C-636/18 (n 25).

[30] The only case under Art 260 TFEU until the end of 2022, which was decided by the CJEU, was Case C-730/19 against Bulgaria (n 25), which was held inadmissible by the Court for formal reasons.

[31] In all cases mentioned in n 25 except Case C-730/19, the CJEU found that the air quality values had been 'systematically and persistently' exceeded.

[32] Directive 2008/1 (n 11); Directive 2010/75 (n 8).

[33] Directive 2008/50 (n 16).

[34] ibid Art 2.5.

the Member States themselves. Directive 2008/50 established criteria; however, these criteria were very general and allowed all sorts of measures which might significantly influence the measuring of results.[35]

In appropriate cases, alarm thresholds – these are values 'beyond which there is a risk for human health from brief exposure and at which immediate steps shall be taken by Member States' – were to be fixed; where such values were exceeded, the population had to be alerted. No limit value was fixed for tropospheric ozone.[36] A limit value for $PM_{2.5}$ has applied since 2015.[37]

8-08 The limit values established are presented in Table 8.1.[38]

Table 8.1 Air quality limit values

Pollutant	**Time**	**Limit value ($\mu g/m^3$)**	**Number of days per year where exceeding is allowed**	**Margin of tolerance**
Sulphur dioxide	Hour	350	24	150 $\mu g/m^3$
	Day	125	3	
Nitrogen dioxide	Hour	200	18	
	Year	40		
Benzene	Year	5		5 $\mu g/m^3$
Carbon monoxide		10		60%
Lead	Year	0.5		100%
Particulate matter, PM_{10}	Day	50	35	50%
	Year	40		20%
Fine particulate matter, $PM_{2.5}$	Year	25		

Member States were allowed to postpone the application of the limit values for benzene and NO_2 in a given zone or agglomeration by five years, provided they set up an air quality plan for those pollutants which had the objective of enabling them to respect the limit values at a later stage. The same possibility existed for PM_{10},[39] though the respect of the directive's limit value had to be ensured by June 2011.[40]

[35] For example, the sampling point 'shall be between 1.5 m (breathing zone) and 4 m above the ground' – as if children could not be affected by air pollution (annex III); 'traffic-oriented sampling probes shall be at least 25 m from the edge of major junctions and no more than 10 m from the kerbside' (annex III). In earlier EU legislation, the requirement was that the measuring station should be placed where pollution was thought to be the worst.

[36] The reason given for this was that tropospheric ozone is not emitted, but is formed by reactions of different precursor substances, in particular under the influence of sunlight.

[37] Directive 2008/50 (n 16) Art 16 and annex XIV, s E.

[38] Directive 2008/50 (n 16) annexes XI and XIV. These limit values have been in force since the beginning of 2010. The value for $PM_{2.5}$ was to be revised by the Commission in 2013, but this was not done. Thus, since 2020, an indicative value of 20 $\mu g/m^3$ continued to exist (annex XIV, s E). The proposal for amending Directive 2008/50, COM(2022) 542, suggested to fix the daily level at 25 $\mu g/m^3$, which was not to be exceeded during 18 days per year, and 10 $\mu g/m^3$ for the calendar year.

[39] Particulate matter 10 (PM_{10}) is a particulate with a diameter of less than 10 µm.

[40] The limit value for PM_{10} had already been fixed by Directive 1999/30 [1999] OJ L163/41; Member States were obliged to ensure that, as of January 2005, it was not exceeded during more than 35 days per calendar year. However, numerous cities had not taken measures to reach this result and thus were, from 2005, in open breach

In the zones and agglomerations designated by them, Member States had to monitor ambient air quality. In particular, they had to establish measuring systems for air quality and to assess air quality. These systems vary according to the air pollution in question: in certain places, measurement from fixed stations is required; in other areas, where the limit values are not exceeded, modelling or indicative measurements are sufficient. Member States then have to make a list of those zones and agglomerations where the limit values were exceeded. Such exceedance is based on average concentrations, not on the fact that, for example, the limit values were exceeded in only one street. Where exceedances occurred, Member States had to elaborate an air quality plan in order to keep the period of non-compliance as short as possible (Article 23). These plans had to be sent to the Commission by, at the latest, two years after the discovery of the exceedance. The Commission was given no possibility to influence the content of the plan or to monitoring progress in respecting the limit values. Its only course of action would be to start legal proceedings under Article 258 TFEU – a very hypothetical option. It is true, though, that Member States are obliged to inform the Commission of details of their national compliance situation (Article 27). 8-09

The difficulties of enforcing compliance with Directive 2008/50 became apparent in a case brought against the UK.[41] The UK had divided its territory under the directive into 43 zones. In 2010, when the limit values for NO_2 were to be complied with, the UK found that these values were exceeded in 40 of the 43 zones. It elaborated clean-up plans for 28 zones, of which the Commission accepted nine outright, accepted three under conditions and objected to 16. Compliance for these zones was to be achieved by 2015. For 16 zones, the UK did not submit clean-up plans to the Commission for approval because it was of the opinion that the deadline for compliance of Article 22 of Directive (five years) could not be reached anyway. The plans it drew up for these 16 zones provided for compliance by 2025. The CJEU held that under Article 23 of Directive 2008/50, the UK was obliged to comply with the NO_2 parameter 'as soon as possible'. It did not itself pronounce on whether the deadline of 2025 complied with this requirement; rather, it left this question to the national court. Nor did it state that any non-compliance by 2015 constituted a breach of Directive 2008/50. This meant that Member States have, de facto, a very large amount of discretion as to whether and by when they comply with the directive's limit values.

In its 2013 strategy, the Commission had declared that compliance with Directive 2008/50 would be reached by 2020, and that by 2030 the premature deaths would be reduced by 40 per cent;[42] in the European Green Deal, this reduction was increased to 55 per cent. This means that there will still be some 140,000 premature deaths per year in 2030, a figure which is almost 10 times higher than the number of premature deaths in road accidents. In 2022, the Commission indicated that it had opened procedures under Article 258 TFEU against 17 Member States for not complying with the requirements of Directive 2008/50.[43] It admitted that compliance with Directive 2008/50 was far away.[44]

of EU law. This was the main reason for the EU to replace Directive 96/62 and its different daughter directives by Directive 2008/50 – which delayed the requirement to respect the limit values until 2010/11. On this, see Commission, COM(2005) 446 (n 14).

[41] CJEU Case C-404/13 *ClientEarth v United* Kingdom ECLI:EU:C:2013:2382.

[42] ibid 5.

[43] Commission, COM(2022) 637, s 2.2; Commission, 'Environmental Implementation Review 2022' COM(2022) 438, fn 54. The Member States in question were Austria (NO_2), Belgium (NO_2), Bulgaria (PM_{10}), Czechia (NO_2 and PM_{10}), Greece (NO_2 and PM_{10}), Spain (NO_2 and PM_{10}), France (NO_2 and PM_{10}), Germany (PM_{10}), Croatia (PM_{10} and $PM_{2.5}$), Hungary (NO_2 and PM_{10}), Italy (NO_2, PM_{10} and $PM_{2.5}$), Lithuania (NO_2), Poland (NO_2 and

Annex XVI of the directive required the provision of extensive information on air quality values to the public concerned, in part even information for each half of a day. However, that annex was not enforced, and public information is often nonexistent in large parts of the Union. The Union is far away from, for example, information on air pollution in Beijing (China), where such information is provided to the public via electronic means on their smart phones and updated, if necessary, several times a day.

The CJEU also held that a citizen whose health was affected by air pollution in excess of the requirements of Directive 2008/50 had no right to claim compensation.[45] This judgment confirms the general impression that the right of the citizen to clean air – or the right to see their health effectively protected – is not ensured by this directive.

8-10 Directive 96/62 had set the framework for the elaboration of limit values for 13 explicitly enumerated pollutants. Eight of them had been covered by three daughter directives[46] and later by Directive 2008/50. A fourth directive covering the remaining pollutants from the list of Directive 96/62 – cadmium, arsenic, nickel, mercury and polcyclic aromatic hydrocarbons – should have been proposed by the end of 1999, but was only submitted in 2003 and adopted at the end of 2004.[47] The problem with these substances was that Directive 96/62 required the fixing of binding limit values and these substances are, at least as regards their compounds, known carcinogens. The industries which would be most affected by the provisions – oil refineries, cement producers, waste incinerators, chlor-alkali and glass producers, iron and steel processors, non-ferrous metal processors and combustion processors – successfully argued that the economic costs for complying with limit values were high, while the advantages for human health and the environment would be limited; they could not assume obligations beyond the non-binding provisions which were laid down in the different BREF (best available technique reference) documents under Directive 2008/1.[48]

Directive 2004/107 diverged from the Council decision only eight years after this decision had been laid down in Directive 96/62, to fix binding limit values, and limited itself to fixing target values which were defined as 'a concentration … to be attained where possible over a given period' (Article 2(a)). The justification given in Recital 3 was in diplomatic language, yet clear: 'With a view to cost-effective measures, ambient air concentrations of arsenic, cadmium, nickel and polycyclic aromatic hydrocarbons which would not pose a significant risk to human health, cannot be achieved in specific areas.' For mercury, not even a target value was fixed, with the argument that there would be a general strategy to reduce mercury in the environment; in the meantime, this strategy and subsequent legislation were published, but without limiting industrial air emissions of mercury.[49] This turn in policy approach with regard to heavy metals emissions was rightly considered to be a 'victory

PM_{10}), Portugal (NO_2), Romania (NO_2 and PM_{10}), Slovenia (PM_{10}), Slovakia (PM_{10}) and Sweden (PM_{10}). It should be noted that there were relatively few procedures for non-compliance with the $PM_{2.5}$ values, considering the Commission had indicated for the greatest number of premaure deaths this pollutant; see the text to n 28.

[44] See also Commission, 'Fitness Check for the Ambient Air Quality Directives' SWD(2019) 427; European Environment Agency (EEA), *Air Quality in Europe 2022, Report 5/2022* (Copenhagen, 2022).

[45] CJEU Case C-61/21 (n 23).

[46] Directive 1999/30 [1999] OJ L163/41; Directive 2000/69 [2000] OJ L313/12; Directive 2003/2 [2003] OJ L67/14.

[47] Directive 2004/107 [2005] OJ L23/3.

[48] Directive 2008/1 (n 11); for more detail on this directive, see ch 4.

[49] Regulation 2017/852 on mercury [2017] OJ L137/1.

for industry'.[50] Indeed, as the different substances are labelled 'human genotoxic carcinogens' in Directive 2004/107, Recital 3, their presence in the environment should be limited as far as possible. And as Directive 2008/1 only covered some industrial installations, a reference to the non-binding provisions of the BREF documents was not likely to lead to significant emission reductions. There was no public discussion on this change of policy. The Commission proposal of 2022 to amend Directive 2008/50 suggested fixing binding air quality levels for arsenic, cadmium and nickel in the new text.[51]

There are no other air quality values for pollutants that are fixed at EU level. In 2022, the Commission considered regulating pollution by methane and black carbon, but preferred, for methane, voluntary commitments and did not act at all on black carbon.[52] Article 32 of Directive 2008/50 provided that the Commission should review, by 2013, the situation of $PM_{2.5}$ and other pollutants and make appropriate proposals for legislation. The Commission complied with this requirement and proposed legislation for medium combustion plants and for national emission ceilings, both of which were adopted, but proposed changing the limit values for $PM_{2.5}$ from EU level to national emission ceilings.[53] Thus, the quality standards of Directive 2008/50 for $PM_{2.5}$ are the only Union-wide quality standards for that pollutant. 8-11

III. National Emission Ceilings

In 1979, an international convention on long-range transboundary air pollution was concluded in Geneva, to which the Union adhered.[54] In 1999, a protocol under that convention to combat acidification, eutrophication and ground-level ozone was adopted, which was amended in 2012 (Decision 2012/2). The amended protocol (the Gothenburg Protocol) fixed reductions, limited the emissions 'until 2020 and beyond', expressed in absolute quantities and in percentages, for SO_2, NO_x, volatile organic compounds (VOCs), ammonia (NH_3) and $PM_{2.5}$, as well as emission limit values for a number of stationary sources (installations) and fuels. The Union transposed the 1999 protocol as Directive 2001/81,[55] which was subsequently replaced by Directive 2016/2284.[56] Directive 2016/2284, based on Article 192(1) TFEU, transposed the reduction quantities of the amended protocol into Union law. However, it did not take over the sections on emission limit values, as the Union Directive 2010/75 was based on the concept of best available techniques, a concept that was not compatible with emission limit values. The decision to approve the amended protocol 8-12

[50] See *ENDS Daily*, 20 December 2001, 2; Environmental Issue Manager (Brussels), *Issue Tracker*, January 2003, 9.

[51] Commission, COM(2022) 542; Commission, SWD(2022) 545.

[52] Commission, COM(2022) 673, s 6.

[53] Commission, COM(2013) 919 and 920. For the general strategy, see also Commission, COM(2013) 917.

[54] Decision 81/462 [1981] OJ L171/13.

[55] Directive 2001/81 on national emission ceilings for certain atmospheric pollutants [2001] OJ L309/22.

[56] Directve 2016/2284 on the reduction of national emission ceilings of certain atmosspheric pollutants [2016] OJ L344/1. An attempt by Poland to have the directive annulled because it should have been adopted unanimously (Art 192(2)(c)TFEU) was unsuccessful, see CJEU Case C-128/17 *Poland v European Parliament and Council* ECLI:EU:C:2019:194.

passed this partial transposition in silence, mentioning only in general terms the existence of several Union legislative acts on air pollution.[57]

8-13 As mentioned, Decision 2012/2 under the Geneva Convention had established, for each contracting party, absolute emission data for the year 2005 and had then indicated by what percentage these quantities had to be reduced. Directive 2016/2284 did not refer to the absolute values of 2005,[58] but only provided for the reduction of emissions by a certain percentage compared to emissions of 2005, following in that the bad example of Directive 2001/81. As no legally precise and binding provision exists anywhere on the different emission quantities by Member States in 2005,[59] the percentage reduction of Directive 2016/2284 'hangs in the air'. This makes the enforcement of the reduction percentages of Directive 2016/2284 impossible.

Apart from the obligation to reduce the air emissions of certain pollutants by 2029 'and from 2030 onwards' by a certain percentage (Article 4), Directive 2016/2284 required Member States to draw up a national inventory of pollutants' emissions into the air, transmit it to the Commission and update it annually (Article 8). The inventory had to cover the above-mentioned pollutants, as well as cadmium, mercury and lead, some persistent organic pollutants and particulates PM_{10}. Member States were also required to adopt a national air pollution control programme, transmit it to the Commission and update it every four years (Article 6).

There was no obligation for Member States to publish the inventory or the control programme. Rather, the directive referred to the possibility of the public having access to information, and laid down an obligation of the Commission to ensure the active dissemination of the necessary information (Article 14).

The Commission Implementation Report 2022[60] was not very informative, as Member States had not yet had to report on actual reduction commitments. Nor did the report inform on the existence and content of the national inventories, and was rather general on the content of the national air pollution control programmes. It indicated that, according to the programmes, there was a high risk that numerous Member States would not reach their reduction commitments for 2029 and beyond 2030 – though the commitments actually made in the national legislation were not yet known.[61] The Commission saw a particularly high risk for ammonia reductions in agriculture.[62]

The percentage reductions of the Gothenburg Protocol which were to be reached by the contracting parties were not explained or justified anywhere, yet were apparently taken over by Directive 2016/2284. An attempt by Poland to have the directive annulled because its impact on Member States had not been examined in sufficient detail failed.[63] Yet, the

[57] Decision 2017/1757 [2017] OJ L248/3.

[58] It can only be supposed that the absolute figures were not taken up in the Commission proposal because they conflicted with the Commission's own data, which it had assembled during the lifetime of Directive 2001/81.

[59] The absolute emission quantities of the Gothenburg Protocol cannot serve as a basis for the calculation of the percentage reduction of the EU Member States as these quantities were expressly marked as being 'for information purposes only' and contracting parties were invited to update them regularly (annex II, no 4 to the protocol). Also, Directive 2001/81 gave in annex I absolute figures 'to be attained by 2010' for SO_2, NO_x, VOCs and NH_3, but did not indicate the quantities that were emitted.

[60] Commission, COM(2022) 266.

[61] See also Commission, COM(2022) 438 (n 43) 10.

[62] ibid.

[63] CJEU Case C-128/17 (n 56).

technocratic construction of the directive, its lack of transparency, its work with percentage projections until 2029 and beyond and the absence of information on the actual pollutant emissions of Member States make it a directive which is difficult to monitor. It can only be hoped that this form of legislation, which is everything but legislation that is 'as open as possible and as close as possible to the citizen' (Article 1 TEU), is corrected the near future.

The WHO published in 2021 updated air quality guidelines as a 'response to [the] real and continued threat' to human health.[64] A comparison with the actual Union air quality standards shows the distance between the Union standards and those of the WHO (Table 8.2).[65] 8-14

Table 8.2 Union air quality standards versus those of the WHO

Pollutant	EU requirement	WHO recommendation
Fine particulates, $PM_{2.5}$ (μg/m³)		
Annual	25	5
24 hours	–	15 (3–4 days exception)
Fine particulates, PM_{10} (μg/m³)		
Annual	40	15
24 hours	50 (35 days exception)	45 (3–4 days exception)
Tropospheric ozone, O_3 (μg/m³)		
8 hours	120 (25 days exception)	100 (3–4 days exception)
Sulphur dioxide, SO_2 (μg/m³)		
24 hours	125 (9 days exception)	40 (3–4 days exception)
Nitrogen oxides, NO_x (μg/m³)		
Annual	40	10
Hourly	200 (18 hours exception)	200 (3–4 hours exception)
Carbon monoxide, CO (mg/m³)		
8 hours	10	4 (3–4 days exception)

The Commission proposal for amending Directive 2008/50[66] examined three options of alignment with the WHO guidelines: a full alignment, a closer alignment and a partial alignment. It found the benefit–cost ratio for full alignment to be between 6:1 and 18:1, for close alignment between 7.5:1 and 28:1 and for partial alignment between 10:1 and 28:1. The Commission opted for a partial alignment, which indicated there would be 55 per cent fewer premature deaths by 2030, with the prospect of full alignment with the WHO guidance by 2050. If one takes the figures mentioned in paragraph 8-09 above, this means that there will still be 139,950 annual premature deaths in the Union in 2030. How the

[64] WHO, 'Air Quality Guidelines 2021' who.int/news-room/feature-stories/detail/what-are-the-who-air-quality-guidelines.

[65] Commission, 'Impact Assessment Report' SWD(2022) 545, s 5.2, Table 2; WHO (n 64).

[66] Commission, COM(2022) 542.

Commission calculated the economic value of a prematurely dead person is not known; the calculations, though, are close to being cynical.

IV. Air Emissions from Products

8-15 Pollution emission limit values from products were the first measures the EU took on air pollution. The purpose of these first provisions, however, was not to combat air pollution, but to ensure the free circulation of products.[67] The efforts undertaken by the Union to reduce air emissions from products, in particular from means of transport, were not at all systematic. They concentrated on cars, since it became increasingly obvious that individual passenger transport was the main generator of air emissions. Measures to combat air emissions from trucks, trains, aeroplanes and ships were much less intense and less systematic. As regards the air polluting substances contained in fuels – eg lead in petrol and sulphur in diesel fuel – see paragraph 6-11.

A. Air Emission from Cars

8-16 EU measures to reduce air emissions from cars started in 1970. These measures concentrated on emission limit values and, since the early 1980s, when the dying forests signalled the need for more stringent measures, on the fuels used by cars. Consequently, they were based on Article 100 of the Treaty on the European Economic Community, and since 1987 on Article 95 of the Treaty on the European Community (now Article 114 TFEU).

8-17 Measures to reduce air emissions from cars have, since the early 1990s, been prepared by the Commission's so-called Auto/Oil Programme (Auto/Oil I), which set up working groups where the European associations of the car and petrol industries were invited to 'make available their considerable know-how and expertise'.[68] Auto/Oil I tried to find combined solutions concerning the emission from cars, the quality and composition of fuels, and new emission control technologies on a 'cost-effective'[69] basis. Proposals for fixing emission limit values by the Commissions were based on the results of this programme. These proposals were criticised for being based not on an objective assessment, but rather on an assessment which conformed with the interests of two industrial sectors, ie the car industry and the petrol industry. In any case, the Commission did not develop policies and proposals which would constitute an alternative to the interests of these two industrial sectors.

[67] See Directive 70/220 on measures to be taken against air pollution by emissions from motor vehicles [1970] OJ L176/1, Recitals 2 and 3: 'a regulation of 31 March 1969 on the composition of exhaust gases emitted from petrol engines of motor vehicles was published in France … those provisions are liable to hinder the establishment and proper functioning of the common market … it is therefore necessary that all Member States adopt the same requirements.'

[68] Commission, COM(96) 248, 44; this remark referred to the Auto/Oil Programme, which started in 1992 and had the task of developing an 'objective assessment of the most cost-effective package of measures to reduce emissions'.

[69] See the criticism of the European Parliament on the way in which this cost-effectiveness was calculated without taking into consideration social and environmental costs: Resolution of 18 February 1998 [1998] OJ C80/92.

Auto/Oil II started in 1997 and looked in particular at the development of the air quality measures to be adopted or implemented at EU level by 2010, including in sectors other than the road transport sector. In contrast to Auto/Oil I, all interested stakeholders, and also Member States, the European Parliament and non-governmental organisations, were invited to participate in the discussions.[70] The discussions of Auto/Oil II considerably influenced not only proposals and legislations in the transport sector, but generally all air pollution measures suggested by the Commission and adopted at EU level.

Directive 70/220 set, in 1970, limit values for carbon monoxide and unburned hydrocarbon emissions.[71] In 1977, limit values for nitrogen oxides were established.[72] The values for these three pollutants were progressively reduced by different directives.[73] In 1989, more stringent emission limit values for gaseous pollutants were introduced and progressively extended to all passenger cars. Emissions from diesel engines were fixed in 1972 and progressively reduced.[74] All emission limit values were the subject of almost permanent review discussions. 8-18

The present emission limit values for new passenger cars are presented in Table 8.3[75] 8-19

Table 8.3 Emission limit values (mg/km) for new passenger cars (Euro 6)

Carbon monoxide, CO	Hydrocarbons, HC	Non-methane hydrocarbons, NMHC	Nitrogen oxides, NO_x	HC + NO_x	Mass of particulates
Petrol 1000	Petrol 100	Petrol 68	Petrol 60	Petrol –	Petrol 5.0/4.5
Diesel 500	Diesel –	Diesel –	Diesel 180	Diesel 230	Diesel 5.0/4.5

The fixing of a generous emission limit value for joined HC and NO_x emissions was a hidden concession to diesel cars, as no limit value was fixed for HC emissions alone from such cars. The Commission made another concession to diesel cars by allowing, for a transitional period, increased NO_x emissions and declaring this amendment of Regulation 715/2007 as an adaptation to technical progress.[76] Court actions to denounce this procedure as illegal failed for procedural reasons.[77]

There is no emission limit value for carbon dioxide (CO_2), the gas which is primarily responsible for climate changes. In 1990, CO_2 emissions from passenger cars accounted for about 45 per cent of transport CO_2 emissions and about 12 per cent of total CO_2 emissions in the Union. In 1993, the Commission had announced a proposal for a directive on an emission limit value for CO_2 for cars,[78] in which it was supported by the European

[70] Commission, COM(96) 248 (n 68).

[71] Directive 70/220 (n 67).

[72] Directive 77/102 [1977] OJ L32/32.

[73] Directive 74/290 [1974] OJ L159/61; Directive 78/665 [1978] OJ L223/48; Directive 83/351 [1983] OJ L197/1; Directive 88/76 [1988] OJ L36/1; Directive 89/458 [1989] OJ L226/1; Directive 91/441 [1991] OJ L242/1; Directive 94/12 [1994] OJ L100/42.

[74] Directive 72/306 [1972] OJ L190/1; Directive 88/77 [1988] OJ L36/33; Directive 91/542 [1991] OJ L295/1.

[75] Regulation 715/2007 on type approval of motor vehicles with respect to emission for light passenger and commercial vehicles (Euro 5 and Euro 6), as amended [2007] OJ L171/1, annex I.

[76] Commission Regulation 2016/646 [2016] OJ L109/1.

[77] General Court Case T-339/16 *Cities of Bruxelles, Paris and Madrid v Commission* ECLI:EU:T:2018:927; CJEU Case C-177/19P *Germany v cities of Bruxelles, Paris and Madrid* ECLI:EU:C:2022:16.

[78] Commission, 'Legislative Programme 1994' COM(93) 588, para 241.

Parliament.[79] This approach was heavily opposed by the car industry, which found some support in Member States, in particular in France, Italy and Germany. In 1996, the Commission suggested it would not legislate, but would instead introduce financial incentives to lower fuel consumption, introduce a labelling scheme for fuel consumption of cars, conclude a voluntary environmental agreement with the car industry to reduce CO_2 emissions from cars and promote research and development;[80] at the same time, it started discussions with car manufacturers on a voluntary agreement. It is not clear what particular reasons existed for having an environmental agreement just for CO_2[81] but not for the other above-mentioned pollutants.

8-20 In 1998, the Commission announced[82] that it was ready to accept an offer by the ACEA (Association des Constructeurs Européens d'Automobiles, Association of European Car Manufacturers), which grouped together European and US car manufacturers to limit the CO_2 emissions for new cars which were brought into circulation in the EU from 2008 onwards to 140 g/km. This offer was different from what the Council had wished to see reached (120 g/km by 2005 or, at the latest, by 2010). The agreement that was subsequently made consisted, in legal terms, of: a commitment by the ACEA;[83] a recommendation by the European Commission, addressed to the ACEA;[84] and an exchange of letters between the Commission and the ACEA.

The commitment stated that as long as the ACEA's promises were kept, the ACEA assumed 'that this commitment provides [a] complete and sufficient substitute for all new regulatory measures to limit fuel consumption or CO_2 emissions, and for any additional fiscal measures in pursuit of the CO_2 objectives of this commitment'.

This expressed the expectation that the EU legislature – possibly also the national legislature – would not take regulatory measures to reduce CO_2 emissions from cars during the lifetime of the agreement. The commitment was, furthermore, based on several assumptions – amongst others, that non-ACEA car manufacturers would commit themselves to equivalent CO_2 reduction efforts. The agreement was made with the ACEA, not with the car manufacturers themselves. Later, similar agreements were concluded with the Japanese and Korean car manufacturers' associations.[85] The agreements referred to the EU market, not to cars which were marketed in other parts of the world.

8-21 The Commission published a number of progress reports on the implementation of the voluntary agreements. In 2006, it became obvious that all three associations would not comply with their commitment by 2008. The Commission then made proposals for legislating which were adopted in 2009.[86] As of 2013, the average emissions per car fleet of a car producer were progressively limited to 130 g/km, with considerable transition periods. This

[79] European Parliament Resolution of 27 October 1993 [1993] OJ C315/160.

[80] Commission, COM(95) 689; Commission, 'Communication on Transport and CO_2' COM(1998) 204.

[81] European Parliament Resolution of 19 February 1998 [1998] OJ C80/227, pt 14.

[82] Commission, COM(1998) 495.

[83] Published as annex to Commission, COM(1998) 495.

[84] Commission Recommendation 1999/125 on the reduction of CO_2 emissions from passenger cars [1999] OJ L40/49.

[85] Commission Recommendation 2000/303 on the reduction of CO_2 emissions from passenger cars (KAMA) [2000] OJ L100/55; Recommendation 2000/304 on the reduction of CO_2 emissions from passenger cars (JAMA) [2000] OJ L100/57.

[86] Regulation 443/2009 [2009] OJ L140/1.

solution mainly favoured expensive cars with high CO_2 emissions. The rules applied only to new cars which were marketed within the Union. Overall, the introduction of mandatory provisions was thus delayed by more than 15 years.

In 2019, Regulation 2019/631 replaced Regulation 443/2009.[87] It fixed from 2020 onwards EU fleet-wide targets of 95 g/km for new passenger cars and of 147 g/km for new light commercial vehicles. Further reductions were foreseen as of 2025 and 2030. And in 2021, the Commission proposed to provide for zero CO_2 emissions of new passenger cars and of light commercial vehicles as of 2035.[88] A political agreement between the European Parliament and the Council on that proposal still needed to be formalised in 2023 or 2024.

For heavy-duty vehicles (more than 2610 kg), Regulation 595/2009 did not fix any CO_2 emission limit values, but only regulated emissions of NO_x and hydrocarbons.[89] A regulation of 2019 addressed for the first time CO_2 emission reductions, providing for percentage reductions in 2025 and 2030 compared to baseline emissions of 2019.[90] These projected reductions would, however, lead to only 14 per cent less emissions by heavy-duty vehicles in 2030 and 70 per cent less emissions by 2050.[91] For this reason, the Commission suggested, in 2023, further percentage reductions of emissions by the years 2025, 2030 and 2035; urban buses should reach zero emissions by 2030.[92]

Thus, during the last 15 years, the Union completely revised its policy with regard to 8-22
air emissions by motor vehicles, moving from a policy of legal approval of technological developments in the industry to taking into consideration climate change and the health of individual citizens. However, these measures also demonstrate the earlier absence of measures taken to protect the climate and health. Thus, the Union never considered applying the principle that environmental impairment should best be tackled at its source (Article 191(2) TFEU), eg by imposing the construction of cars that do not exceed a maximum speed limit (eg 100 km/h) or which do not consume more than a certain amount of fuel per 100 km.[93] Directive 2009/125 on ecodesign requirements would give legal competence to the Union to impose such construction requirements.[94] However, this directive explicitly excluded means of transport from its field of application; the Commission proposal of 2022 to replace the directive by a regulation finally also covered means of transport.[95]

The Union also did not take measures to introduce taxes or charges for cars according to their environmental emissions. Nor did it take any measures for Union-wide tax incentives in order to promote the marketing or purchase of less-polluting cars, though it knew

[87] Regulation 2019/631 setting CO_2 emission performance standards for new passenger cars and for new light commercial vehicles [2019] OJ L111/13.

[88] Commission, COM(2021) 556.

[89] Regulation 595/2009 on emissions from heavy duty vehicles (Euro VI) [2009] OJ L188/1.

[90] Regulation 2019/1242 setting CO_2 emission performance standards for new heavy-duty vehicles [2019] OJ L198/202.

[91] Commission, SWD(2023) 88, s 2.1.1.

[92] Commission, 'Proposal for Amending Regulation 2019/1242' COM(2023) 88.

[93] See, however, European Parliament Resolution of 10 April 1997 [1998] OJ C132/170, where the Parliament requested that new cars do not consume more than 5 litres of petrol (4.5 litres of diesel) per 100 km as of 1 January 2005 and not more than 3 litres of petrol or diesel as of 1 January 2010.

[94] Directive 2009/125 establishing a framework for the setting of ecodesign requirements for energy-related products [2009] OJ L285/10.

[95] Commission, 'Proposal for a Regulation Establishing a Framework for Setting Eco-design Requirements for Sustainable Products' COM(2022) 142.

that such measures could have positive effects.[96] A Commission proposal to fix the taxes for individual cars according to their CO_2 emissions, made in 2005, was not adopted by the Council and was withdrawn in 2015.[97] Since the late 1980s, the Union had accepted that Member States granted tax incentives for less polluting cars, albeit under very restrictive conditions:[98] only temporary incentives for new cars were allowed, during the transition period of the Union act that reduced air emissions. Furthermore, the Union was not able or willing to consider a limitation to the CO_2 emissions of each individual car, but recurred to the fleet-wide reduction approach. It did not provide for a mandatory check, in the periodic roadworthiness test of cars, of the compliance of each individual car with all the emission limit values mentioned above, or with CO_2 emissions.[99] And no measures, or at least incentives, were adopted to achieve the retrofitting – be it at least for greenhouse gas emissions – of other than new cars.

As cars have an average lifetime of 12–15 years, air emission reductions will only be significantly accelerated after the massive arrival of electric cars on the market.

B. Air Emissions from Aeroplanes, Ships and Machines

8-23 There are no EU emission limit values for ships and aeroplanes. Both sectors are, in part, regulated by global organisations (cartels), the International Maritime Organization and the International Civil Aviation Organization (ICAO).

In 1998, the Commission submitted, for the first time, a proposal on the limitation of polluting emissions from civil subsonic aeroplanes.[100] The proposal only concerned nitrogen oxides and did not contain an emission limit value, only a formula for calculating such emissions. The proposal had been submitted because the ICAO had not been able to agree on suggestions for reductions which had been proposed to ICAO bodies and discussed there. The EU proposal was based on the present Article 100(2) TFEU, which was a surprising legal basis since all emission limit values for cars and commercial vehicles had been based on Article 114 TFEU. When the ICAO finally agreed new limit values which would apply to new engine designs after 2003, the Commission's proposal became obsolete and was no longer pursued.

Attempts by the EU to indirectly reduce the CO_2 emissions from aeroplanes by including them in the CO_2 emissions trading scheme of Directive 2003/87[101] were only partly successful: a directive which provided for such an inclusion as of 2012[102] met with very strong resistance from third countries, including the USA, Japan, India, China and Russia.

[96] See Commission, 'Review of the Auto-Oil II Programme' COM(2000) 626, point 6.2: 'well-targeted, differentiated taxes are considered to be an effective tool to influence consumer behaviour, and can therefore confidently be expected to provide an effective means of accelerated improved performance in the transport sector, with a very low societal cost'.

[97] Commission, COM(2005) 261.

[98] See now Regulation 715/2007 (n 75) Art 12.

[99] See Directive 2014/45 on permanent roadworthiness tests for motor vehicles and their trailers [2014] OJ L127/51, annex I, no 8.

[100] [1998] OJ C108/14.

[101] Directive 2003/87 [2003] OJ L275/32.

[102] Directive 2008/1 (n 11) 3.

Though the CJEU considered the EU measures to be compatible with public international law,[103] the political pressure was so strong that the EU adopted Decision 377/2013,[104] which 'temporarily' suspended the application of the scheme to third countries, justifying this approach with ongoing discussions on CO_2 emission reductions at international level. In 2014, a further regulation exempted flights from and to airports outside the European Economic Area from the application of Directive 2003/87.[105] This exemption was limited to the end of 2016, but was prolonged and continues to apply in 2023.

The ICAO did not adopt measures to limit air emissions by aeroplanes. A resolution of 2021 promoted an 'aspirational global fuel efficiency improvement of 2% per annum from 2021 to 2050', but hastened to add that this was a voluntary agreement that contained no obligations.[106] Thus, any state or company that would build another supersonic aeroplane like Concorde would not be hampered by international air emission requirements.

There has been, to date, almost no EU provision to regulate air pollution emissions, 8-24
including greenhouse gas emissions, from ships.[107] Internationally, the pollution from ships is discussed in the context of the Convention for the Prevention of Pollution From Ships (MARPOL), to which the Union is not a signatory; annex VI of that convention deals with air pollution from ships. MARPOL introduced emission control areas, where only the use of fuels with a maximum SO_2 content of 0.10 per cent in mass was allowed; this concerned, as regards Union waters, the Baltic Sea (since 2006) and the North Sea (since 2007), as well as ships on berth in Union ports; there are ongoing efforts to have the Mediterranean Sea declared an Emission Control Area for SO_2 and particulate matter as of 2025. In all other Union waters, the maximum allowed SO_2 content of marine fuels has been 0.50 per cent in mass since 2020.[108] In 2017, MARPOL also designated the Baltic Sea and the North Sea as 'Nitrogen Oxides Emission Control Areas', which will lead to restrictions in NO_x emissions from ships in these two areas; so far, the Union has not taken any measures to transpose this MARPOL decision into EU law. Discussions on the introduction of environmentally differentiated shipping charges according to their emissions have been discussed internationally, but have not led to any concrete action at EU level.

For internal navigation, Directive 2004/26 introduced emission limit values for inland waterways vessels with regard to CO (5.0 g/kWh), HC and NO_x combined (7.5–11.0 g/kWh) and particulates (0.4–0.5 g/kWh).[109] These values were replaced by slightly stricter values which were laid down in Regulation 2016/1628.[110] However, no retrofitting of existing vessels was prescribed and the useful lifetime of inland waterway vessels is very long. Thus, the effect of the new regulation will only become visible in time.

[103] CJEU Case C-366/10 *Air Transport Association of America* ECLI:EU:C:2011:864.

[104] Decision 377/2013 [2013] OJ L113/1.

[105] Regulation 421/2014 [2014] OJ L129/1.

[106] ICAO, Resolution A41-21, nos 4 and 5.

[107] As regards quantities of air emissions, see EEA, *European Maritime Transport. Environmental Report 2021* (Luxembourg, 2021) 37ff.

[108] Directive 2016/802 relating to a reduction in the sulphur content of certain liqud fuels [2016] OJ L232/88. In 2017, MARPOL decide that the 0,.50% level should be applied globally, see Commission, 'Implementation and Compliance with Directive 2016/802' COM(2018) 188 13.

[109] Directive 2004/26 [2004] OJ L146/1.

[110] Regulation 2016/1628 on requirements relating to gaseous and particulate pollutant emission limits for non-road mobile machinery [2016] OJ L252/53.

8-25 As regards machines, in 1997, the Union adopted for the first time a directive[111] which set air emission limit values for machines other than passenger and commercial vehicles, aeroplanes and ships; it thus concerned machinery such as compressors, forestry equipment, road-maintenance equipment, snow-plough equipment, aerial lifts, mobile cranes and ground support vehicles in airports. The directive was replaced in 2016 by Regulation 2016/1628, with the same field of application, but also covering inland waterway vessels.[112] The regulation was based on Article 114 TFEU and concerned new machinery; existing non-road mobile machinery was thus not affected. The emission limit values were established for CO, HC, NO_x and PM, and were differentiated according to the power of the engine, which led to a very high level of sophistication (annex I).

C. Emissions of VOCs and Methanes

8-26 Volatile organic compounds (VOCs) are generated from the handling of (motor) gasoline; this gasoline is stored before being distributed, which can be by pipeline, road truck, rail, barge or ship. After distribution, the gasoline is discharged into a storage tank. During all these stages of loading/unloading, the gasoline generates VOCs. VOCs are among the precursors of photochemical oxidants, such as tropospheric ozone, which is also a greenhouse gas. Some VOCs that are emitted are classified as toxic, teratogenic or carcinogenic. The biggest emitting sectors are road transport, solvent use and the extraction and distribution of fossil fuels.

Directive 91/441 and other directives on motor vehicle emissions[113] had already introduced a number of measures to reduce VOC emissions from motor vehicles, the main source of such emissions, without fixing emission limit values. It is estimated that these measures will reduce VOC emissions from road transport by about one-third.

8-27 Council Directive 94/63[114] followed the same line; it dealt with the VOC emissions resulting from the storage of petrol and its distribution from terminals to service stations, and required Member States to make sure that the conditions laid down in the directive and its annexes were complied with. The directive was based on Article 114 TFEU; it also applied to road transport, which is why it is mentioned in this chapter; yet it also applied to stationary sources and allowed Member States to fix more stringent provisions (Articles 3(3) and 4(3)). The discussion of limiting VOC emissions from other stationary sources will be discussed at paragraph 8-36 below. Contrary to what its title provided, Directive 94/63 did not contain any emission limit values, but rather laid down requirements for storage installations at terminals (stationary petrol tanks, annex I), for loading and unloading of mobile containers at terminals (annex II), for loading and storage installations at service stations and terminals, where the intermediate storage of vapour is carried out (annex III) and specifications for bottom-loading, vapour collection and overfill protection

[111] Directive 97/68 relating to measures against the emissions of gaseous and particulate pollutants from internal combustion engines to be installed in non-road mobile machinery [1998] OJ L59/1.

[112] Regulation 2016/1628 (n 110).

[113] Directive 91/441 [1991] OJ L242/1; Directive 91/542 [1991] OJ L295/1; Directive 93/59 [1993] OJ L186/21; Directive 94/12 (n 73).

[114] Directive 94/63 on the control of volatile organic compound (VOC) emissions resulting from the storage of petrol and its distribution from terminals to service stations [1994] OJ L365/24.

of European road tankers (annex IV). As mentioned, it was thus a measure that affected both mobile and stationary sources of VOC generation. The emission of VOCs from the charging of ships was only covered by a non-committing statement in a recital.[115]

The Commission indicated a reduction of VOC emissions under the directive between 1995 and 2020 from 339 kilotonnes to 129 kilotonnes.[116]

Methane (NH_4) is a greenhouse gas with a global warming potential of 86 in 20 years (28 in 100 years).[117] In the Union, methane is generated mainly from agriculture (53 per cent, principally livestock and manure management), energy (20 per cent, fugitive emissions of oil, gas and coal activities) and waste (19 per cent, landfills).[118] The Commission, having already adopted a methane strategy in 1996,[119] had tried to include methane emission reductions in Directive 2016/2284; however, Member States did not accept its proposal,[120] in particular due to pressure from the agricultural sector. Methane was also included in the regulatory obligation to reduce the Union's greenhouse gas emissions by 2030, but no concrete measures were laid down in that act.[121] In 2020, the Commission adopted a new methane strategy,[122] and in 2021 proposed a regulation on the measurement, reporting and verification of methane emissions in the energy sector as well as their reduction.[123] The proposal, based on Article 194(2) TFEU, is at present being discussed by the other Union institutions. It is intended, among other things, to prohibit the venting (releasing into the air) and flaring (burning) of methane under normal circumstances, and to stop the leakage of methane from oil and gas activities and the operating of abandoned coal mines. 8-28

Internationally, in 2021, the Commission and the USA launched a 'Global Methane Pledge', consisting in a voluntary commitment to reduce methane emissions by 2030 by at least 30 per cent compared to 2020. About 100 countries have joined this pledge, though not China, India or Russia (three of the highest emitters).

V. Air Emissions from Installations

A. Directive 2010/75

EU law contains very few provisions relating to installations, since it is thought that prod- 8-29
ucts that circulate within the Union should be subject to uniform rules, but that installations

[115] ibid Recital 6: 'On grounds of international standardisation and of safety during the loading of ships, standards must be drawn up at International Maritime Organisation level for vapour control and recovery systems to apply to both loading installations and ships, whereas the Community must therefore endeavour to ensure that the necessary provisions are introduced into the Marpol Convention during the current revision of Marpol due to be completed in 1996; whereas in the event that the Marpol Convention is not so revised, the Community, after discussion with its major trading partners, should propose appropriate measures to apply to ships and port installations servicing ships.'

[116] Commission, SWD(2017) 65. The data include the UK. The figure for 2020 is an estimation.

[117] Carbon dioxide (CO_2) has a global warming potential of 1.

[118] Commission, 'On an EU Strategy to Reduce Methane Emissions' COM(2020) 663, 2.

[119] Commission, 'Strategy Paper for Reducing Methane Emissions' COM(96) 557.

[120] Directive 2016/2284 (n 56).

[121] Regulation 2018/842 on binding annual greenhouse gas emission reductions by Member States from 2021 to 2030 contributing to climate action to meet commitments under the Paris Agreement [2018] OJ L156/26.

[122] Commission, COM(2020) 663 (n 118).

[123] Commission, COM(2021) 805.

do not circulate freely and therefore do not need uniform rules. This attitude ignored the fact that products which leave installations compete with each other and the knowledge that water discharges and air emissions from installations circulate and pollute transnationally.

Following the discovery of dying forests in the early 1980s, the Union discussed air pollution at a summit of Heads of State and Governments in 1983. In 1984, it adopted Directive 84/360, a framework directive on air emissions from larger industrial installations.[124] The intention was to elaborate emission limit values of a number of pollutants. However, apart from legislative acts on combustion plants and waste incinerators, no such measures were adopted, as policies preferred to stick with the concept of 'best available techniques', which was to be served, for different industrial sectors, by non-binding industry provisions. Directive 84/360 was replaced by new directives in 2007 and later, before Directive 2010/75 brought the legislative process to a standstill.[125]

According to Directive 2010/75, the permits which Member States give to industrial installations that come under the directive must contain emission limit values for a number of pollutants which are enumerated in annex II to the directive,[126] and pollutants 'which are likely to be emitted … in significant quantities' (Article 14). The actual emission limit values were fixed, for the different industrial sectors which were covered by the directive, in the BREF documents.[127] Member States shall report annually to the Commission on the implementation of the directive (Article 72), but the Commission provided that the information was made available to the Commission only;[128] whether a Member State makes the permit conditions and the actual emissions also available to the general public – an easy thing to do in the electronic age – was each Member State's own decision. The Commission's implementation reports did not indicate cases of non-compliance in concrete terms.[129] The Commission's proposal to amend Directive 2010/75 suggested making the permits publicly available, but not the actual emissions.[130]

B. Combustion Plants

8-30 In 2001, Directive 2001/80[131] on large combustion plants was adopted, replacing Directive 88/609.[132] However, the emission limit values for new installations and the overall emission ceilings of SO_2 and NO_x for existing installations (annexes I and II) were hardly amended or updated. Directive 2001/80, taking over the previous provisions, provided for

[124] Directive 84/360 (n 6).

[125] See also para 4-44ff.

[126] Annex II listed the following substances: SO_2 and its compounds, NO_x and its compounds, CO, VOC, metals and their compounds, dust, including fine particulates, asbestos, chlorine and its compounds, fluorine and its compounds, cyanides, carcinogenic or mutagenic substances or mixtures, polychlorinated dibenzodioxins and polychlorinated dibenzofurans.

[127] See, eg Commission Implementing Decision 2021/2326 [2021] OJ L469/1 on large combustion plants; Commission Implementing Decision 2022/2427 [2022] OJ L318/157 on chemicals.

[128] Commission Implementing Decision 2018/1135 [2018] OJ L205/40.

[129] Commission, 'Implementation Reports' COM(2017) 727 and COM(2021) 793.

[130] Commission, COM(2022) 156.

[131] Directive 2001/80 on the limitation of emissions of certain pollutants into the air from large combustion plants [2001] OJ L309/1.

[132] In this regard, see Commission Recommendation 2003/47 on the guidelines to assist a Member State in the preparation of a national emission reduction plan [2003] OJ L16/59.

emission limit values of SO_2, NO_x and dust for new installations. For existing installations, the directive introduced national emission ceilings for SO_2 and NO_2.

Directive 2010/75 replaced the provisions of Directive 2001/80; it maintained the emission limit values for such plants for SO_2, NO_x, CO and dust, as laid out in annex V. Derogations were foreseen for plants which burn indigenous coal that contains too much sulphur (Article 31), plants which form part of a 'transitional' (rather, derogatory) plan (Article 22), plants which were intending to stop operating after a certain time (Article 33), plants for isolated settlements (Article 34) and district heating plants (Article 35). New plants with more than 300 MW capacity were obliged to examine whether there was a possibility for the capture and underground storage of CO_2 (Article 36).

In 2015, the Union adopted a directive concerning the emissions of medium combustion plants (with a thermal input between 1 and 50 MW).[133] The directive fixed emission limit values for SO_2, NO_x and dust, differentiating between new and existing plants, the plant size and the fuel used. Long transition periods, exceptions and derogations – until 2030 – make an assessment of the directive's effects at present impossible.

C. Waste Incinerators

In 1989, the Union adopted two directives on municipal waste incineration plants and, in 1994, one on installations for the incineration of hazardous waste.[134] These three directives were replaced by a new directive at the end of 2000.[135] In 2010, this directive was then incorporated into the new Directive 2010/75 on industrial emissions.[136] 8-31

Directive 2010/75 concerned, like its predecessor Directive 2000/76, almost all waste incineration installations. It excluded installations which exclusively burn vegetal waste, agricultural waste, radioactive waste, animal waste or waste from oil platforms which is incinerated there, and finally installations for test or research purposes which burn less than 50 tonnes per year. The provisions of Directive 2010/75 also applied to installations, the principal objective of which is the production of goods or energy and which 'use waste as a regular or additional fuel or in which waste is thermally treated for the purpose of disposal' (Article 3, no 41) (co-incineration); to this category belong such installations as power plants, steel plants and cement kilns. The emission limit values which were fixed were less stringent for co-incineration installations[137] – as if the environmental impairment were less relevant in the case of co-incineration.

Installations need a permit for operation. Article 4 of Directive 2010/75 fixed the general conditions for such a permit. For example, the permit must indicate the type of (hazardous) waste which may be burnt, the sampling and measuring methods for air and water discharges or – for hazardous waste – the content of pollutants such as chlorides, pentachlorophenol, polychlorinated biphenyls, fluorides, sulphur or heavy metals in the waste. A number of other measures have the objective of minimising environmental impairment. 8-32

[133] Directive 2015/2193 on medium combustion plants [2015] OJ L313/1.

[134] Directive 2000/76 on the incineration of waste [2000] OJ L332/41.

[135] Directive 2010/75 (n 8).

[136] ibid.

[137] [1998] OJ C372/11.

The minimum temperature, including in cases of co-incineration, was 850°C, and, where hazardous waste was burned, 1100°C (Article 50). The installation must be equipped with an automatic system to stop the incineration process where this temperature was not reached, or where emission limit values were exceeded, due to a disturbance. The emission limit values were fixed in annex VI.

However, long transition periods, derogation possibilities, exceptions for small installations and differentiations according to new or existing installations and, for cement kilns, according to the fuel used were provided.

The directive also fixed emission limit values for discharges of waste water from the cleaning of waste gases into the water, in particular for heavy metals (annex VI, part 5). It detailed the measuring requirements and methods, and imposed in particular an automatic, continuous measuring of emissions into the air and the water (annex VI, part 6).

8-33 Overall, the requirements of Directive 2010/75 were strict, and were by far the most stringent requirements for any type of industrial installation laid down at Union level. The apprehension of the population against the pollution emissions from incinerators would therefore appear not to be completely justified – provided the installation would always function according to the legal requirements. However, breakdowns or deficiencies in the operation, the burning of hazardous materials and other circumstances may easily lead to emissions which are toxic or dangerous. This also applies to co-incinerators, though there is less public concern there. For this and other reasons, co-incineration and combined heat and power generation by incinerators are techniques which are being used increasingly, and attempts are continually made to find new names for the installations in order to avoid the negative image of 'waste incinerators'.

D. VOCs from Stationary Sources

8-34 In 1999, the Council adopted Directive 1999/13 on emissions of VOCs from solvent-using industries,[138] which was a follow-up to Directive 94/63.[139] In 2010, the directive was integrated into the new Directive 2010/75 on industrial emissions.

As in Directive 1999/13, Directive 2010/75, Article 56ff referred to installations and activities using organic solvents; so, in particular, coating processes, coil coating, dry cleaning, printing, surface cleaning, manufacturing of pharmaceutical products, fat extraction, rubber conversion, or wood and plastic lamination were covered. Thresholds and emission limit values were set for the different activities, based on the solvent consumption, the emission limit (mg of organic carbon per m^3) and the diffuse/total emission limit, expressed as a percentage of solvents input (annex VII, part 2). For vehicle-coating installations, no emission limit values were fixed; instead, a calculation formula was to be used by such installations (annex VII, part 3). The differentiation of limit values and their monitoring, as laid down in annex VII to the directive, is extreme, and it seems hardly possible to ensure serious compliance control.

[138] Directive 1999/13 on the limitation of emissions of volatile organic compounds due to the use of organic solvents in certain activities and installations [1999] OJ L85/1; Proposal [1997] OJ C99/32.

[139] Directive 94/63 (n 114). See para 8-28; as mentioned, that directive also partly covered stationary sources.

Instead of applying the emission limit values fixed by the directive, an installation could also recur to a 'reduction scheme specially designed for this installation', provided that comparable results were achieved (annex VII, part 5). When an individual operator was able to demonstrate that complying with the emission limit values was not 'technically and economically feasible', Member States were entitled to grant a derogation from the limit values, 'provided that significant risks to human health or the environment are not to be expected' and that the operator could demonstrate that they were applying the best available technique.[140]

In 2009, the Union adopted a directive on the recovery of petrol vapour during refuelling of motor vehicles at service stations.[141] An assessment by the Commission found that about 72 per cent of service stations in the Union were fitted with a vapour recovery system and that another 6 per cent of stations were likely to be so equipped by 2020; about 57 per cent of the Union's VOC emission reductions were attributable to Directives 94/63 and 2009/126.[142] 8-35

Overall, the air pollution reduction by Union measures has had mixed results. Undoubtedly, without the Union measures, air pollution reduction measures would not have been adopted by all Member States, and the national measures would have been different in content, duration and practical application. However, the following aspects concern the possibility of improving the present situation and reducing premature mortality and very significant damage to the environment: 8-36

- there should be a central Union inventory on all greenhouse gases, including the sources, which would be accessible to the public;
- the different Union measures deal with some air pollutants only and do not systematically tackle the pollutant at source. A percentage reduction as foreseen in particular in Directive 2016/2284 lacks transparency and effectiveness. The numerous legislative concessions to the car industry are not helpful; and
- compliance monitoring is the biggest problem for the Union. Zero tolerance is far from being practised.

VI. Noise and Electromagnetic Waves

A. General Aspects

Data on noise levels within the Union are limited and fragmented. Guiding figures on human exposure to noise have been issued by the WHO, which published, in 2018, recommendations for levels which should not be exceeded in order to avoid health problems (Table 8.4).[143] 8-37

[140] Directive 2010/75 (n 8) Art 59(2).

[141] Directive 2009/126 on stage II petrol vapour recovery during refuelling of motor vehicles at service stations [2009] OJ L285/36.

[142] Commission, SWD(2017) 65 14.

[143] WHO, *Environmental Noise Guidelines for the European Region* (Copenhagen, 2018). The figures were taken up by the Commission, 'Implementation Report of Directive 2002/49' COM(2023) 139, 3.

Table 8.4 WHO recommendations for noise levels which should not be exceeded in order to avoid health problems

	Noise during day, evening and night, L_{den}	Noise during night, L_{night}
Road	53	45
Rail	54	44
Aircraft	45	40

The Commission estimated in 1996 that almost 80 million people in the Union 'suffer from noise levels that scientists and health experts consider to be unacceptable' (above 65 dB(A)) and that an additional 170 million citizens were living in areas where the noise levels were such as to cause serious annoyance during the daytime (55–65 dB(A)).[144] The EEA estimated for the year 2000 that about 50 million people in the Union were exposed to traffic noise levels above 65 L_{dn}[145] and some 120 million to traffic noise levels above 55 L_{dn}. Traffic noise was the main source of outdoor noise, followed by neighbourhood and aircraft noise.[146] In 2014, the EEA indicated that the number of people exposed to more than 55 L_{dn} was 125 million; it mentioned 10,000 premature deaths due to noise and reported on other damaging factors of noise.[147] And a Commission study of 2021 found that 167 million people in the Union were exposed to noise levels above the maximum recommended by the WHO, 36 million to excessive railway noise and 15 million to excessive aircraft noise.[148] It was thus logical that the Commission stated in 2023 that noise exposure in the Union had not diminished during the last 20 years.[149]

8-38 An EU strategy to reduce noise levels within the Union was announced years ago, in the context of the different environmental action programmes.[150] In 1996, the Commission published a Green Paper, 'Future Noise Policy', where it identified noise as one of the principal local environmental problems.[151]

In the follow-up to that Green Paper, the Union in 2002 adopted a directive on environmental noise.[152] The directive was based on Article 192 TFEU. It intended to avoid, prevent or reduce environmental noise; such noise was defined as 'unwanted or harmful outdoor sound created by human activities, including noise emitted by means of transport, road traffic, rail traffic, air traffic and from sites of industrial activity … (Article 3(a))'.

The directive applied to environmental noise to which humans were exposed, in particular in built-up areas, in public parks or other quiet areas in agglomerations, in the open country, and near schools, hospitals or other noise-sensitive buildings and areas. Noise

[144] Commission, 'Green Paper on Future Noise Policy' COM(96) 540, 1a and 3.

[145] L_{dn}, a day–night level, is a descriptor of noise level based on the energy equivalent noise levels (L_{eq}) over the whole day, with a penalty of 10 dB(A) for night-time noise (22:00–07:00 hours).

[146] EEA, *TERM 2000, Are We Moving in the Right Direction?* (Copenhagen, 2000) 32.

[147] EEA, *Noise in Europe 2014. EEA Report 10/2014* (Copenhagen, 2014). See also the data assembled in Commission, COM(2011) 321.

[148] Commission, COM(2023) 139 (n 143) 3.

[149] ibid 6.

[150] See Second Environmental Action Programme [1977] OJ C139/1, pt 67 et seq; Fourth Environmental Action Programme [1987] OJ C328/5, pt 4.5.

[151] Commission, COM(96) 540 (n 144); see also European Parliament Resolution of 10 June 1997 [1997] OJ C200/28.

[152] Directive 2002/49 relating to the assessment and management of environmental noise [2002] OJ L189/12.

which was caused by the exposed person themself, noise from domestic activities and noise created by neighbours, at the workplace, by wind turbines or inside means of transport or in military areas was not covered.

Before 2007, Member States had to draw up strategic noise maps,[153] showing the noise situation in the preceding calendar year. These maps had to be made available to the Commission and the public, and be updated at least every five years. They referred to (figures applicable since 2012):

- agglomerations with more than 100,000 inhabitants;
- major roads which have more than three million passages per year;
- major railways which have more than 30,000 train passages per year; and
- major civil airports which have more than 50,000 take-offs or landings per year.

By 2008, Member States had to draw up, make publicly available and regularly update action plans to manage noise issues, if necessary. The measures taken were at the complete discretion of the Member States (Article 8(1)). No binding quality limit values or non-binding target values were set for noise levels.

1Directive 2002/49 provided for extensive reporting to and by the Commission,[154] for technical provisions concerning the measuring and assessing of noise, for minimum requirements for strategic noise planning and action plans, as well as for the data which are to be sent to the Commission. However, the Commission did not seriously monitor the operation of the directive by publishing, for example, the noise levels found, comparing action plans, sharing best practices or pushing for measures that reduced the noise levels.[155] The Commission's implementation reports[156] identified a considerable number of shortcomings in implementation, which were in part due to vague and unclear formulations in the directive. However, the Commission saw no reason to propose an amendment to the directive or take actions against Member States, but reflected on the elaboration of guidance documents (Second Report, 2017) and on local measures, such as the use of quieter tyres, establishing a low-noise road surface and speed limitations (Third Report, 2023).

EU measures to reduce noise levels so far have concerned noise emissions from certain 8-39
products. The main objective of these directives has been to ensure their free circulation within the Union and ensure that this circulation was not hampered by different noise standard levels at national level. For this reason, the directives set noise emission levels only for those products that were implicated in intra-EU trade; by contrast, Member States

[153] ibid Art 3: a strategic noise map is a map designed for the global assessment of noise exposure in a given area due to different noise sources or for overall predictions for such an area.

[154] EEA, *Noise in Europe 2014* (n 147) 13 reported that only 44% of the reporting obligations had been complied with.

[155] See, eg the report from the EEA, *Towards a Resource-Efficient Transport System. TERM 2009. Technical Report 2/2010* (Copenhagen, 2010), where the EEA reported (p 20) that 164 agglomerations were obliged to report on their noise levels; 102 had reported on road noise, 93 on railway noise, 76 on air noise and 94 on industry noise. A total of 82,576 reports were expected on major roads, but only 21,310 were delivered; 12,315 reports should have been made on major railways, but only 5310 were delivered; and of 78 airports, 66 reported.

[156] Commission, 'First Report' COM(2011) 321; Commission, 'Second Report' COM(2017) 159; Commission, COM(2023) 139 (n 143).

may set independent noise standards for products intended exclusively for the domestic market.[157] They may also provide for specific standards for the use of the products in sensitive areas.

All noise levels fixed in the specific directives were based on the work of international standardisation organisations. They fixed noise levels for products that were put on the market for the first time, but contained no provisions on noise emissions throughout the lifetime of a product.

B. Transport Noise

8-40 Motor vehicle noise emissions have been regulated since 1970, when noise emission limit values were introduced.[158] Directive 70/157 was based on the present Article 115 TFEU. Later amendments were introduced, mainly when technical progress had already led to a practical reduction of noise levels;[159] since 1987, such amendments have been based on Article 114 TFEU. The noise limits for cars were gradually made stricter.[160]

In 2014, a new regulation was adopted which repealed Directive 70/157.[161] It provided for new noise levels, which were to be applied progressively from 2016, 2022 and 2026 onwards. For passenger cars, the ordinary levels were 72, 70 and 68 dB(A) respectively; however, the more powerful the passenger car, the higher the permitted noise level; thus, a passenger car with an engine power between 150 and 250 kW only had to comply with levels of 78, 77 and 76 dB(A) respectively. The same system was applied for vehicles used for the carriage of goods (N group): the permitted levels ranged from 72, 71 and 69 to 82, 81 and 79 dB(A). In view of the fact that in the affluent societies of Europe, increasingly consumers buy big passenger cars, there are doubts whether these levels will lead to an overall decrease in noise from cars.[162]

For two- and three-wheelers, emission limit values have existed since a directive of 1978,[163] which was amended several times and provided for a reduction of around 3 dB(A). A regulation of 2014 fixed the noise levels for new two- and three -wheelers between 63 and 80 dB(A).[164]

[157] As regards noise emissions from cars, this so-called 'optional harmonisation approach' was abandoned by Directive 92/97 [1992] OJ L371/1, which introduced the total harmonisation approach: all vehicles which were put into circulation within the Union had to comply with the directive's requirements.

[158] Directive 70/157 [1970] OJ L42/16.

[159] See, eg Directive 77/212 [1977] OJ L66/33, Recital 2: 'whereas for the protection of the general public from noise nuisance, suitable measures are required to reduce the noise level of motor vehicles; whereas such a reduction has been made possible by the technical progress in motor vehicle construction'; similar observations are made in Directive 81/334 [1981] OJ L131/6, Recital 1; Directive 84/372 [1984] OJ L196/47, Recital 1; Directive 84/424 [1984] OJ L238/31, Recital 2.

[160] They were fixed at 82 dB(A) in 1972, 80 dB(A) in 1982, 77 dB(A) in 1988/90 and 74 dB(A) in 1995/96, see Commission, COM(96) 540.

[161] Regulation 540/2014 on the sound level of motor vehicles and of replacement silencing systems [2014] OJ L158/131.

[162] In this sense, see Commission, SEC(2011)1505 on the impact assessment for its regulation proposal.

[163] Directive 78/1015 [1978] OJ L349/21.

[164] Regulation 168/2013 on the approval and market surveillance of two- or three-wheel vehicles and quadricycles [2013] OJ L60/52, annex VI.

A directive concerning the admissible noise levels from new tyres was adopted in 2001,[165] but was replaced in 2009 by a regulation,[166] which, in turn, was replaced by new provisions in 2016 and 2019.[167] The permitted rolling noise level was fixed between 70 and 78 dB(A).

The Commission stated that electric cars would not be quieter than combustion engine vehicles at a speed over 30 km/h, without giving an explanation.[168]

Aircraft noise has been regulated since 1979 by a number of directives,[169] which were based on Article 100 TFEU and which applied, at EU level, standards set by the ICAO; the ICAO levels depend on the aircraft weight and number of engines. The EU directives did not fix emission limit values, but referred to the provisions laid down by the ICAO. Directive 92/14 provided for a ban, as of 1995, of civil subsonic aeroplanes which did not comply with the ICAO 'chapter 2' or 'chapter 3' requirements but were not more than 25 years old.[170] A number of aeroplanes from third-world airline companies were exempted from these provisions because European airlines had sold such planes to the third-world countries prior to 1995. A number of other derogations were also allowed. 8-41

In 1998, the Commission proposed a ban on the registration of aeroplanes which had been modified in order to comply with the 'chapter 3' requirements, the so-called 'hush-kitted' aircraft.[171] As this requirement hit, in particular, older aeroplanes that were used in the USA or by US companies, there were excited discussions as to whether this requirement de facto discriminated against the USA. Under political pressure from that country, which threatened retaliation measures and also argued that some hush-kitted aircraft were less noisy than modern aircraft such as Airbus, Council Regulation 925/1999, which finally adopted the proposal,[172] postponed the entry into effect of the measure so that from April 2002 onwards, hush-kitted aircraft were to be prohibited at EU airports unless they had operated at EU airports before May 2000.

The terrorist attacks on US cities on 11 September 2001 were used by the USA discreetly to suggest again a withdrawal of Regulation 925/1999. This time, the Union gave in, and in a record time of four months, a new directive, based on Article 100(2) TFEU, was prepared; it was adopted in March 2002 and repealed Regulation 925/1999.[173] In its place, the Union embraced the USA's concept that noise-induced restriction for aeroplanes had to be airport-specific and had to be limited to the necessary environmental objective, which had to be established for each airport (Article 4). Hush-kitted aeroplanes – which were not named as such, but were called 'marginally compliant aircraft' – received protection in the form of a phased restriction (Article 6), and hush-kitted aeroplanes registered in 'developing countries' which had used European airports before received a derogation for 10 years (Article 7). Urban airports – annex I listed them as being Berlin-Tempelhof, 8-42

[165] Directive 2001/43 [2001] OJ L211/25; legally, this directive was an amendment to Directive 92/23 [1992] OJ L129/95.

[166] Regulation 661/2009 [2009] OJ L200/1.

[167] UNECE Regulation 117 on uniform provisions concerning the approval of tyres with regard to rolling sound emissions [2016] OJ L218/1, s 6; Regulation 2019/2144 on type approval for motor vehicles including tyre requirements [2019] OJ L325/1, Art 4(2).

[168] Commission, COM(2023) 139 (n 143) 10.

[169] Directive 80/51 [1980] OJ L18/26; Directive 89/629 [1989] OJ L363/27.

[170] Directive 92/14 [1992] OJ L76/21, amended by Directive 98/20 [1998] OJ L107/4.

[171] [1998] OJ C329/98.

[172] Regulation 925/1999 [1999] OJ L115/1.

[173] Directive 2002/30 [2002] OJ L85/40.

Stockholm-Bromma, London City and Belfast City – were allowed to adopt more stringent provisions with regard to hush-kitted aeroplanes.

Instead of creating uniform conditions for aeroplane noise within the Union which would be normal under a uniform ('common') transport policy, this 'balanced approach' left it to each airport to impose its own noise restrictions. In view of competition problems – aircraft companies which are confronted with the possibility of such restrictions are likely to threaten to use the next airport, where no such restrictions exist[174] – noise rules for individual airports are not very likely. Measures on noise restrictions are therefore likely to follow the example of night-flight restrictions, which also can only in theory be introduced by each airport, but which are not introduced for competition reasons.[175]

Quite rightly, therefore, the aeroplane operators considered the directive first of all to constitute a 'protection against the use of operating restrictions',[176] while the Commission itself was satisfied about 'how well the objectives of the directive have been achieved'.[177] Nevertheless, in 2011, it suggested a new legislative act, which was adopted in 2014 and repealed Directive 2002/30.[178] This new regulation, based on Article 100(2) TFEU, harmonised and strengthened the conditions for the individual airports to introduce operating restrictions for noise reasons. Any such decision had to be preceded by a noise assessment and an assessment of the cost-effectiveness of the measure. Three months before its adoption, it had to be notified to the Commission, to the other Member States and to 'interested parties', accompanied by a written report which justified the intended measure (Article 8). A restriction decision had to be open to appeal, independent of existing judicial possibilities. The regulation provided for some exceptions for aeroplanes from developing countries in order to avoid 'undue economic hardship', and let existing restrictions continue. This regulation will make the taking of restriction measures by local authorities, such as night flight restrictions, even more difficult than before.

Though a Commission study found a number of inconsistencies between Regulation 598/2014 and Directive 2002/49,[179] the Commission did not see any reasons to amend the different acts.

8-43 No specific Union noise provisions exist for railways. A proposal for a directive, submitted in 1983, was withdrawn by the Commission in 1993.[180] The introduction of high-speed trains in the Union, also promoted by the rules on trans-European networks (Articles 170–72 TFEU) since the Maastricht Treaty of 1993, did not lead to a change in this situation. The Union was much more concerned with the free circulation of locomotives and wagons all over the Union ('interoperability') than with noise. Under Directive 2008/57, trains had to comply with essential requirements, which only specified that they

[174] See also Written Question E-1021/02 (Hortefeux) [2002] OJ C277/E/132; a good example is the case of the DHL company which had its EU headquarters at Zaventem airport (Brussels). Planes from overseas landed at night, and the freight was moved onto other planes and transported to different European countries. Following extended complaints from citizens over too much noise at night, the Belgian authorities negotiated with DHL on noise reduction measures. These negotiations remained unsuccessful and DHL moved its EU headquarters to Leipzig – with the loss of some 20,000 jobs in Brussels.

[175] Commission, 'White Paper on a Community Strategy on Sustainable Mobility' COM(92) 494.

[176] Commission, COM(2008) 66, 8.

[177] ibid 3.

[178] Regulation 598/2014 on the establishment of rules and procedures with regard to the introduction of noise-related operating restrictions at Union airports within a Balanced Approach [2014] OJ L173/65.

[179] Commission, *Study on Airport Noise Reduction* (Luxembourg, 2022).

[180] Commission, Proposal for a directive relating to noise emissions of rail-mounted vehicles [1983] OJ C354/4; withdrawal COM(96) 540.

had to respect existing legislation.[181] In 2006, non-binding technical specifications for interoperability (TSIs) were elaborated, which were amended in 2014 and which fixed maximum noise levels for stationary noise, starting noise and pass-by noise of trains; high-speed trains had extra high permitted noise levels granted.[182] The pass-by noise levels laid down were between 73 and 85 dB(A), and for a speed of more than 250 km/h between 95 and 99 dB(A). In view of the growing public concern of noisy freight wagons, Regulation 2019/774 introduced the possibility for Member States to designate 'quieter routes', on which the use of wagons that were not equipped with silencing brakes was prohibited.[183] The Commission stated that 'by far' the best solution for freight wagons would be to impose the retrofitting of wagons with cast iron blocks with silent (composite) brake blocks,[184] but dared not propose it. In 2020/2021, Germany and Switzerland prohibited the use of freight wagons with cast iron blocks on their territory, without the Commission interfering.

C. Outdoor Equipment and Machines

At the end of 2000, the Union adopted a directive on the noise levels of outdoor machinery, construction equipment, garden equipment (lawnmowers) and equipment used for specific vehicles.[185] The directive, which was based on Article 114 TFEU, replaced a number of previous directives. It applied to new machines and equipment, and intended, first of all, to ensure the free circulation of these machines within the EU. Member States may not prevent the placing on the market of machines that comply with the requirements of the directive, but are, of course, free to determine sensitive areas where the equipment may not be used or where it may be used during certain hours only. Noise emission limit values were fixed (Article 12) for a number of machines and equipment (about 10,000 models), and varied between 96 and 109 dB(A); new values have applied since 2006 which range from 84 to 106 dB(A).[186] Where an EU noise emission limit value was laid down, this had to be labelled on the machine; where no level was fixed (about 16,000 models), the machine only had to be labelled with its noise level (Article 13). The directive also determined the measuring standards. There was no requirement to maintain the noise level for new machines during the total service life of the machine, or at least for some years. 8-44

After the adoption of Directive 2000/14, some manufacturers had difficulties complying with the more stringent values; derogations were therefore introduced, as 'the intention was never to restrict the placing on the market of use … of equipment solely based on technical feasibility'.[187] In other words, the noise limit values were not meant to protect citizens or the environment.

[181] Directive 2008/57 on the interoperability of the rail system within the Community [2014] OJ L191/1.
[182] Commission Regulation 1304/2014 [2014] OJ L356/421.
[183] Commission Implementing Regulation 2019/774 [2019] OJI L 139/89.
[184] Commission, 'Rail Freight Noise Reduction' SWD [2015] 300, 5. See also European Railways Agency, *Full Impact Assessment of the Noise TSI* (Valenciennes, 2018) 5: 'Retrofitting of existing wagons with silent brake blocks would immediately and directly provide benefits to citizens (noise reduction), but at the same time it brings also considerable costs to the railway industry.'
[185] Directive 2000/14 relating to the noise emission in the environment by equipment for use outdoors [2000] OJ L162/1.
[186] Directive 2005/88 [2005] OJ L344/46.
[187] ibid Recital 2.

The Commission saw some reduction in the noise levels of outdoor equipment after the adoption of the directive, but admitted that the noise levels did not motivate public or private purchasers to buy quieter products.[188]

8-45 New household equipment was the subject of another framework directive, which left Member States the freedom to fix emission limit values but fixed a frame for those requirements.[189] No specific EU measures have subsequently been taken. Thus, Directive 86/594 was repealed; Member States were allowed to use the provisions of that directive until new measures were taken at EU level. The energy labels fixed for certain household appliances provided for an indication of the noise level.[190]

The Union has not so far fixed quality objectives for noise emissions in sensitive areas such as urban centres, residential areas or near airports, hospitals or schools.

Overall, compliance with the noise levels within the Union is highly inadequate and the EU measures protecting against excessive noise levels also seem inadequate. This protection, by fixing quality standards, tends to be left to Member States. Directive 2002/49 on environmental noise did not significantly change the situation in any way, all the more as there is hardly any attempt to enforce it.

D. Electromagnetic Waves

8-46 There are no EU provisions on electromagnetic waves from electrical power lines and other sources which are thought, sometimes, to cause problems to the health of people living next to such power lines. The Commission stated that there was no 'convincing scientific evidence' of electromagnetic fields causing cancer.[191]

Directive 2011/92 on the environmental impact assessment of certain projects requires an environmental impact assessment for electrical power lines of more than 15 km in length; however, the competent authorities remain free to decide on such projects, whatever the outcome of the assessment.[192]

In 1998, the Commission proposed a Council recommendation, based on the present Article 168 TFEU, on 'the limitation of exposure of the general public to electromagnetic fields',[193] where essentially Member States were invited to take action in order to limit exposures to electromagnetic fields. Electrical power lines were not specifically addressed. The Council adopted this recommendation in 1999.[194] Requests by the European Parliament to update this recommendation and to adopt other measures in order to reduce the risk from electromagnetic fields[195] were ignored. The Council and the Commission continue to argue that 'there is currently no well-established scientific evidence of a causal relationship'[196] between such waves and human illness.

[188] Commission, 'Evaluation of Directive 2000/14' SWD(2020) 266.

[189] Directive 86/594 [1986] OJ L344/24.

[190] See para 6-46.

[191] Written Questions E-1387/97 (Baldi) [1997] OJ C373/115; E-4190/97 (Caccavale) [1998] OJ C196/96; E-1788/98 (Sierra Gonzalez et al.) [1999] OJ C50/93.

[192] See generally para 4-33ff.

[193] Commission, COM(1998) 268.

[194] Recommendation 1999/519 [1999] OJ L199/59.

[195] European Parliament, Resolution of 2 April 2009 on health concerns assessed with electromagnetic fields [2010] OJ C137E/38.

[196] Directive 2013/35 on the minimum health and safety requirements regarding the exposure of workers to the risks arising from physical agents (electromagnetic fields) [2013] OJ L179/1, Recital 7.

9

Climate Change

I. General Remarks

Since the Lisbon Treaty came into force on 1 December 2009, climate change issues have been mentioned in the Treaties: Article 191 of the Treaty on the Functioning of the European Union (TFEU) fixes as one of the objectives of EU environment policy 'combating climate change'. This insertion is not particularly convincing, as climate change policy is a horizontal policy which requires numerous EU policies to reorient themselves in view of this objective; this refers in particular to energy policy, but also to transport, industry, trade, development, agricultural and competition policy. Thus, it would have been wiser to insert the fight against climate change at the beginning of the TFEU, for example in Article 11. 9-01

Action regarding climate change attempts to reduce anthropogenic interference with the climate in order to prevent a global temperature increase and greenhouse gas concentrations in the atmosphere that are significantly higher than pre-industrialised levels.[1] The appearance of climate change issues as a topic of EU environmental policy is of recent date. The fourth EU Environmental Action Programme, which covered the period 1987–92,[2] mentioned the 'greenhouse effect' of human activities and climate change only marginally,[3] and announced that the EU research programme would cover, among others, 'climatology and natural hazards, addressing long-term problems, such as potential climate changes due to an increase of the CO_2 [carbon dioxide] concentrations in the atmosphere'.[4] In 1989, the Commission submitted a first communication to the Council on climate change and its impact.[5] The Council was quick in reacting: in 1990, it

[1] See the definition of climate change in Art 1(2) of the UN Framework Convention on Climate Change of 9 May 1992, signed in New York: 'Climate change means a change of climate which is attributed directly or indirectly to human activity that alters the composition of the global atmosphere and which is in addition to natural climate variability observed over comparable time periods.'

[2] 4th EU Environmental Action Programme 1987–1992 [1987] OJ C328/5.

[3] See ibid s 2.3.20: 'Looking further ahead into the future it is clear that difficult problems could arise from the use of fossil fuels if the build-up of atmospheric carbon dioxide levels and the "Greenhouse effect" are shown (as certain scientists fear) to have serious impacts on climate and agricultural productivity worldwide. In case further scientific research should confirm the likelihood of such impacts, the Community should already be thinking about possible responses and alternative energy strategies. The Commission will continue its studies in this context.' See also s 7.2.3: 'Tropical forests … have a profound influence on climate and on global natural cycles. Because tropical forests benefit people in so many ways, the alarming rate of forest destruction is a matter of grave concern.'

[4] ibid s 6.3.

[5] Commission, 'The Greenhouse Effect and the Community' COM(89) 656.

committed itself in a non-binding resolution to stabilise CO_2 emissions by the year 2000 at their 1990 level.[6]

In the Fifth Environmental Action Programme (1993–2000), climate change issues played a considerably greater role: the programme dedicated a whole section to climate change. It identified CO_2, chlorofluorocarbon (CFCs) nitrous oxide (N_2O) and methane (CH) as the main agents for climate change,[7] and tried to fix objectives:

1. 'no exceeding of natural absorbing capacity of planet earth'; and
2. 'no emissions of ozone layer depleting substances' – and targets up to the year 2000 and announcement of a number of actions to be undertaken.

In 1994, the Union adhered to the UN Climate Change Convention[8] and has since pursued an active policy to address the issues of climate change.

9-02 Climate change is not a subject that is included in the list of policies and activities which are mentioned in Articles 3 and 4 TFEU. The legal basis for measures addressing climate change issues is, depending on the nature of the measure, Article 43 (agriculture), 91 or 100 (transport), 113 (taxation), 114 (internal market), 207 (trade), 194 (energy) or 192 (environment) TFEU. In the absence of a specific legal basis in the past, energy-related measures were normally based on the present Article 192 or 352 TFEU. In particular, Article 192 TFEU was of increasing importance in the area of energy policy measures. For example, the above-mentioned Decision 94/69 to adhere to the Convention on Climate Change was based on Article 130s of the Treaty establishing the European Community (EC Treaty), the predecessor of the present Article 192 TFEU. Furthermore, the decision to adhere to the Kyoto Protocol,[9] the different decisions on energy saving[10] and alternative energies,[11] the decision on a monitoring mechanism of greenhouse gas emissions[12] and the first Directive on the energy performance of buildings[13] were all based on Article 192(1) TFEU. Politically and legally, the competence of the Union to deal with climate change issues and to adopt EU-wide measures was not seriously disputed, it being understood that this competence was shared between the Union and the Member States.

9-03 In 1991, the Commission adopted a Communication on measures to combat global warming,[14] which suggested, essentially, three types of measures: energy conservation and improved energy technology; monitoring mechanisms for emissions; and fiscal

[6] (October 1990) *Bulletin of the European Communities* no 1.3.77.

[7] Commission, Towards Sustainability. A European Community programme of policy and action in relation to the environment and sustainable development [1993] OJ C138/5, pt 5.1.

[8] Decision 94/69 [1994] OJ L33/11; the Convention itself is published at 13.

[9] Decision 2002/358 concerning the approval, on behalf of the European Community, of the Kyoto Protocol to the United Nations Framework Convention on Climate Change and the joint fulfilment of commitments thereunder [2002] OJ L130/1.

[10] Decision 91/565 [1991] OJ L307/34; Decision 96/737 [1996] OJ L335/50; Decision 647/2000 [2000] OJ L79/6.

[11] Decision 93/500 [1993] OJ L235/41; Decision 98/352 [1998] OJ L159/53; Decision 646/2000 [2000] OJ L79/1.

[12] Decision 99/296 amending Decision 93/389 for a monitoring mechanism of Community CO_2 and other greenhouse gases [1999] OJ L117/35.

[13] Directive 2002/91 on the energy performance of buildings [2003] OJ L1/65; in 2010, this directive was replaced by Directive 2010/31 on the energy performance of buildings [2010] OJ L153/13.

[14] Commission, COM(91) 249.

measures. These measures were, in later years, prolonged and adapted, and, as regards the first group of measures, clarified to include the reduction of greenhouse gas emissions. Several conferences of Heads of State and Governments and environmental and energy councils dealt with climate change strategies. Following the signature of the Kyoto Protocol in 1997, where the obligations of the contracting parties were finally clarified, the Commission submitted, in 2000, a new draft for an EU strategy.[15] The European Climate Change Programme's objective was to identify and develop all those elements 'that are necessary for the implementation of the Kyoto Protocol'. This requires a comment on the objectives of a climate change strategy. The Commission stated that it followed a double concept: on the one hand, strengthening the EU policies and measures regarding climate change; and on the other hand, developing an emission trading scheme within the Union.

The Sixth Environmental Action Programme, adopted in 2002, stated that EU climate change policy should try to align to the 'long term objective of 2° Celsius over pre-industrialised levels and a CO_2 concentration below 550 ppm'.[16] In 2007, the European Council declared that global temperature should only rise by maximal 2°C and committed the Union to reducing its greenhouse gas emissions by at least 20 per cent below 1990 levels by 2020, and by 30 per cent provided that other developed countries committed themselves to comparable emission reductions and economically more advanced developing countries contributed adequately according to their responsibilities and respective capacities.[17] This commitment was inserted into a decision of 2009 which was based on Article 192(1) TFEU.[18]

However, at a conference in Copenhagen in December 2009, global negotiations on a follow-up agreement to the Kyoto Protocol failed, and neither industrialised countries nor developing countries made formal commitments as regards the reduction of greenhouse gas emissions for the time after 2012. Subsequently, the EU institutions did not increase the reduction commitment to 30 per cent, but decided to leave it at 20 per cent. No further progress was reached for a new global agreement at subsequent international discussions, though several countries made unilateral promises to reduce their greenhouse gas emissions. At a meeting in Doha in 2012, the EU committed to reducing its greenhouse gas emissions by 20 per cent by 2020 compared to its 1990 rates. Anticipating an important international meeting in Paris at the end of 2015, the EU adopted the objectives to reduce, by 2030, its greenhouse gas emissions by 40 per cent compared to 1990, and, on the same timescale, to ensure the share of renewable energies reached 27 per cent of the overall consumption of energy and improve its energy efficiency by 27 per cent.[19]

[15] Commission, 'Communication on EU Policies and Measures to Reduce Greenhouse Gas Emissions: Towards a European Climate Change Programme (ECCP)' COM(2000) 88.

[16] Decision 1600/2002 laying down the 6th Community Environment Action Programme [2002] OJ L242/1, Art 2(2).

[17] European Council, 'Meeting of 8–9 March 2007, President's Conclusions' Doc 7224/07 Rev.1 of 2 May 2007.

[18] Decision 406/2009 on the efforts of Member States to reduce their greenhouse gas emissions to meet the Community's greenhouse gas emission reduction commitments up to 2020 [2009] OJ L140/136.

[19] European Council, 'Minutes of the Meeting of 23–24 October 2014' Doc EUCO 169/14.

II. The Union's Commitments to Reduce Greenhouse Gases

9-04 The objectives of the Climate Change Convention of the United Nations were 'to achieve … stabilization of greenhouse gas concentrations in the atmosphere at a level that would prevent dangerous anthropogenic interference with the climate system'.[20]

The Union's Decision on the Sixth Environmental Action Programme[21] repeated this objective and then continued:[22]

> Thus a long term objective of a maximum global temperature increase of 2°Celsius over pre-industrial levels and a CO_2 concentration below 550 ppm shall guide the Programme. In the longer term this is likely to require a global reduction in emissions of greenhouse gases by 70% as compared to 1990 as identified by the Intergovernmental Panel on Climate Change (IPCC).

Thus, while it is clear that 'dangerous anthropogenic interference' with the climate system was to be avoided, it is not completely clear what is to be done to achieve this goal. Almost all depends on scientific data and assessment. In 1999, the Commission was of the opinion that CO_2 emissions had to fall 'by at least 35% by 2010, if long-term temperature increases are to be limited to 1.58 by 2100.'[23] Fourteen months later, it was of the opinion that 'a global reduction of 20–40% (depending on actual rates of economic growth and thus greenhouse gas emissions as well as the success of measures taken to combat climate change) over 1990–2020 will need to be aimed at', and that 'global emissions of greenhouse gases need to be reduced by approximately 70% over 1990 levels in the longer term'.[24] As mentioned, the Council cautiously took up the second figure only.

9-05 In 1997, the Kyoto Protocol, a protocol under the Climate Change Convention, was concluded.[25] It covered six greenhouse gases, CO_2, CH_4, nitrous oxide (N_2O), hydrofluorocarbons (HFCs), perfluorocarbons (PFCs) and sulphur hexafluoride (SF_6). Those contracting parties which were listed in an annex to the Kyoto Protocol – all industrialised countries – committed themselves to reducing the emissions of these six gases[26] 'in the commitment period 2008 to 2012' (Article 3(1)) to a percentage of the 1990 values that was laid down in that annex. For the Union, which was expressly mentioned in the annex, and its – at that time – 15 Member States, this figure was fixed at 92 per cent, so the Union had to reach a reduction of greenhouse gases by 8 per cent. As the Union decided to approve

[20] United Nations Framework Convention on Climate Change (n 1) Art 1.

[21] Decision 1600/2002 (n 16).

[22] ibid Art 2(2).

[23] Commission, 'Europe's Environment: What Directions for the Future? The Global Assessment of the European Community Action Programme of Policy and Action in Relation to the Environment and Sustainable Development' COM(1999) 543, s 3.1.

[24] Commission, 'Communication on the Sixth Environmental Action Programme of the European Community – Environment 2010: Our Future, Our Choice' COM(2001) 31, pt 3.2.

[25] The protocol is published at [2002] OJ L130/4.

[26] The different gases have different global warming potentials (GWPs). This potential is calculated on the basis of CO_2, the most widespread greenhouse gas. The GWP for CO_2 is 1, that for methane 24.5, for nitrous oxide 320, for HFC between 97 and 12,000, for PFC 5700–11,900 and for SF 22,200. See Regulation 842/2006 [2006] OJ L161/1, annex I. There are some scientific uncertainties about these figures.

the Kyoto Protocol and adopted Decision 2002/358 in this regard, there was thus a legal obligation to reduce greenhouse gas emissions within the Union by 8 per cent by 2012 at the latest.

However, the Kyoto Protocol should, according to its Article 25, only enter into force once 55 Parties to the Climate Change Convention, 'incorporating Parties included in Annex I which accounted in total for at least 55 percent of the total carbon dioxide emissions for 1990 of the Parties included in Annex I', had agreed to it. The USA signed the protocol under the Clinton administration, but recalled this signature under the Bush administration and declared that they would not ratify the protocol. As the USA was the biggest generator of greenhouse gas emissions worldwide, the complicated calculation method under the protocol led to the necessity that most of the other industrialised countries that were listed in annex I had to adhere to the protocol before this could enter into effect. This led to a lot of horse-trading, in particular with Japan and Russia. Finally, Russia adhered to the protocol at the end of 2004, so that it entered into effect on 16 February 2005, more than seven years after its adoption. 9-06

The Union's strategy prior to 2005 consisted of deploying enough international activity to make the Kyoto Protocol effective. Worldwide, no party was prepared to play a leading role in the attempt to promote the Kyoto Protocol other than the UN Secretariat; the Secretariat was, however, hardly able to take on such a function, as it lacked the most elementary financial and human resources to do so. Similarly, the Union was hardly equipped to be the driving force for the promotion of the Kyoto Protocol either. In its external relations with other countries, trade questions predominated. Its climate change department lacked the human resources to play an active role worldwide. And many of the measures needed to make the Kyoto Protocol operational – measuring methods, frequencies and stations, legislative and administrative infrastructural measures, identification of sources, introduction of new technologies, etc – required considerable technical and scientific know-how, as well as the financial means to ensure smooth transition periods, allow the taking into consideration of local specificities or sector problems and the approval of policy-makers, parliaments and public opinions in the different countries. The few persons working on climate change issues within the Commission's climate change department were hardly able to assume such work for the whole of the Union, though they had very great personal, financial and administrative support from EU Member States; they were not equipped to be in the driving seat worldwide, all the more as – mainly due to the 'mixed agreement' character of the Climate Change Convention and the Kyoto Protocol – Member States appeared autonomous at international level, and did not rally behind the EU institutions or the Commission to speak and act with one voice internationally.[27] 9-07

Within the Union, the Commission tried, prior to the negotiations which led to the 1997 signing of the Kyoto Protocol, and in particular after that signature, to reach an EU-wide 9-08

[27] Confirmation of this point might be seen in the fact that the EU Commission did not even ask for a negotiation mandate for the global climate change negotiations in Copenhagen, December 2009, which had the consequence that the UK, France, Germany and the other EU Member States all spoke for themselves and the EU as an organisation did not play any significant role during the negotiations. This situation also existed in subsequent international meetings.

consensus on the strategy to follow.[28] This was only partly successful, as Member States did not wish to see, at that time, a complete and coherent EU climate change policy. Therefore, Member States agreed among themselves – without a corresponding Commission proposal – how they would organise themselves with regard to the commitment under the Kyoto Protocol. Based on existing emissions, economic development and technical possibilities, they politically agreed to a burden-sharing, which allowed some Member States to increase their greenhouse gas emissions while others had to reduce them. This burden-sharing was made legally binding in 2002 by Decision 2002/358,[29] and provided for the percentages which were to be respected by 2012 (1990 = 100).[30]

Decision 2002/358 was based on Article 192(1) TFEU. A number of Member States had favoured the use of Article 192(2) TFEU, which would have provided for unanimity; the reason was not that they opposed the decision, but that they wanted to keep a veto right for future decisions on climate change. However, as the Commission threatened to have the question of the correct legal basis clarified by the CJEU, and there was a strong political interest for the Union to show, at the Johannesburg World Summit which took place in September 2002, that it had complied with its commitments under the Kyoto Protocol and was able to take the global lead in climate change matters, Article 192(1) was finally accepted as the appropriate legal basis.

9-09 In 2009, a new burden-sharing was agreed for all 27 Member States for the period 2013–20.[31] The decision, again based on Article 192(1) TFEU, requested each Member State to reduce its greenhouse gas emissions in a linear manner by a percentage fixed in an annex, but changed the reference year from 1990 to 2005. Where the annual emissions exceeded the required emissions, increased reduction quantities for the following year were to be achieved, multiplied by an abatement factor of 1.08; the state was required to develop a corrective action plan; and there was a temporary suspension of the possibility of transferring part of its emission allocations to another Member State. In contrast, the decision neither mentioned what would happen when a Member State continuously delayed reducing its emissions nor what would happen if a Member State did not reach the required reduction by 2020. The decision concerned emissions from fuel combustion, fugitive emissions from fuels, industrial processes, solvent and other product use, agriculture and waste, but excluded emissions from installations that were covered by Directive 2003/87 on emission trading (Article 1 and annex 1).[32] The reduction quotas were fixed, according to Recitals 8 and 9 of the decision, on the principle of solidarity between Member States, the objective to reach a fair distribution between the Member States and the gross domestic product of each Member State. However, the use of the year 2005 as the baseline was arbitrary.

[28] Commission, 'Climate Change – Towards a European Union Post-Kyoto Strategy' COM(98) 353; see also Commission, 'Communication – Climate Change – the EU Approach for Kyoto' COM(97) 481.

[29] See Decision 2002/358 (n 9) annex II.

[30] The percentage changes compared to 1990 were: Belgium, –7.5%; Denmark, –21%; Germany, –21%; Greece, +25%; Spain, +15%; France, 0%; Ireland, +13%; Italy, –6.5%; Luxembourg, –28%; the Netherlands, –6%; Austria, –13%; Portugal, +27%; Finland, 0%; Sweden, +4%.

[31] Decision 406/2009 (n 18).

[32] Directive 2003/87 establishing a scheme for greenhouse gas emission allowance trading within the Community [2003] OJ L275/32.

In 2015, the Union again committed itself to reducing its greenhouse gas emissions by 2020 by 20 per cent compared to 1990 levels.[33] In 2014, the European Council stated that the Union's overall greenhouse gas emissions by 2030, compared to 2005, should be reduced by an average of 40 per cent: by 30 per cent for those sectors which were covered by Directive 2003/87 and by 43 per cent for the other sectors. The European Council referred to a 'binding' commitment, though, according to Article 15 TEU, its positions are not binding. Its statement was taken up in 2018 by Regulation 2018/842.[34] The effort-sharing among Member States was agreed in a form whereby Member States had to reduce their emissions by 2030 by a certain percentage which varied between 0 per cent for Bulgaria and 40 per cent for Luxembourg and Sweden (annex I). 9-10

In 2015, the Paris Agreement was formally adopted as another protocol to the United Nations Framework Convention on Climate Change. The agreement was concluded by the Union[35] on the basis of Articles 192(1) and 218(6) TFEU. It fixed as an objective keeping greenhouse gas emissions within limits that did not cause a temperature increase by more than 2°C compared to pre-industrialised periods, and to endeavour to limit the increase to 1.5°C.[36] This led the Commission, which had in the meantime launched the European Green Deal.[37] to propose, and the European Parliament and the Council to adopt, a European Climate Law.[38] That regulation, based on Article 192(1) TFEU, fixed as the Union's objective the reduction of greenhouse gas emissions to net zero by 2050 and to maintain it thereafter. An intermediate target of a 55 per cent reduction by 2030 was fixed; the year of comparison was no longer 2005, but 1990. The regulation did not contain any specific reduction obligations for Member States. 9-11

The development of greenhouse gas emissions in Member States was quite diverse. Central and Eastern European countries showed particularly large reductions. In Western Europe, Greece, Spain, Portugal and Ireland had been allowed, in 2002, to increase their emissions, and this showed even in 2021 (Table 9.1).

In 31 years (1990–2021), the EU reduced its greenhouse gas emissions by, on average, one per cent per year. Reaching the target of 55 per cent reduction by 2030 and then climate neutrality by 2050 will mean more than doubling the effort. The reductions, the information on which stems from Member States, were reached without any monitoring sanction by the European Commission. For Member States which acceded to the Union since 2004, most of the reductions were reached before 2005, which means that the reductions mainly concerned low-hanging fruit.

[33] Decision 2015/146 [2015] OJ L26/1.

[34] Regulation 2018/842 on binding annual greenhouse gas emission reductions by Member States from 2021 to 2030 [2018] OJ L156/26. Reference to the European Council is made in Recitals 1 and 2.

[35] Decision 2016/1841 on the conclusion, on behalf of the European Union, of the Paris Agreement adopted under the United Nations Framework Convention on Climate Change [2016] OJ L282/1. The text of the Agreement was attached to the decision.

[36] Paris Agreement, Art 2: '[It is the objective of the Agreement] holding the increase of the global average temperatre to well below 2°C above pre-industrialised levels and pursuing efforts to limit the temperature increase to 1.5°C above pre-industrialised levels.' Art 4 no 2 and 3: 'Each Party shall prepare, communicate and maintain successive nationally determined contributions that it inttends to achieve … [which] will … reflect its highest possible ambition.'

[37] Commission, COM(2019) 640.

[38] Regulation 2021/1119 establishing a framework for reaching climate neutrality (European Climate Law) [2021] OJ L243/1.

Table 9.1 Member States emissions since 1990 and reductions/increases by 2021

Member State	Quantities emitted in 1990 in million tonnes	Quantities emitted in 2021 in million tonnes	Quantities emitted in 2005	Quantities emitted in 2010	Reduction/ increase by 2021 compared to 1990 in percentage
Austria	67.7	68.4	76.1	67.0	+0.9
Belgium	146.1	115.2	147.2	137.5	-21.1
Bulgaria	83.4	45.3	45.6	48.1	-45.6
Croatia	25.6	18.9	22.2	21.6	-26.1
Cyprus	6.2	9.1	9.9	10.1	+45.7
Czechia	192.8	127.8	142.8	135.0	-33.7
Denmark	80.2	47.5	75.6	69.6	-40.7
Estonia	36.7	15.6	16.5	15.7	-57.4
Finland	46.5	49.2	42.6	51.3	+5.8
France	531.0	406.2	515.6	482.5	-23.5
Germany	1299.4	782.7	1016.0	958.2	-39.8
Greece	104.2	74.5	135.8	118.4	-28.5
Hungary	92.1	57.4	71.8	62.4	-37.7
Ireland	67.7	70.8	81.3	72.4	+12.8
Italy	522.3	388.1	567.2	490.7	-24.4
Latvia	13.9	13.4	5.3	10.2	-3.8
Lithuania	43.2	14.4	18.5	13.7	-66.7
Luxembourg	13.1	10.7	13.7	13.3	-18.8
Malta	2.8	2.4	3.3	3.3	-15.4
Netherlands	233.6	179.3	231.9	230.1	-23.2
Poland	447.0	382.3	354.2	376.3	-14.5
Portugal	68.2	92.5	92.5	65.8	+23.0
Romania	229.3	66.4	118.2	89.9	-71.0
Slovakia	64.6	33.7	46.1	40.7	-47.8
Slovenia	14.5	13.0	13.5	12.7	-9.9
Spain	258.6	252.6	406.0	323.7	-2.3
Sweden	26.5	7.1	25.3	16.2	-733.2
EU-27	**4.711**	**3.311**	**4296**	**3429**	**-29.7**

Source: European Environment Agency, 'Annual European Union Greenhouse Gas Inventory 1990–2021 and Inventory Report. Submission to the UNFCCC Secretariat' (Copenhagen, 2023) Tables ES 3v and ES 6viii.

The biggest emitters were Germany, followed by France, Italy and Poland. Germany, France, Italy and Romania were responsible for 67 per cent of the reductions since 1990. 9-12

The EEA also differentiated according to the source (and sinks) of the emissions (Table 9.2).[39]

Table 9.2 Greenhouse gas sources

Greenhouse gas source and sinks	1990 in million tonnes	2021 in million tonnes
Energy (including road transport)[a]	3747	2663
Industrial processes	495	318
Agriculture	485	382
Land use, land use change, forestry	–209	–241
Waste	184	111
Indirect emissions	6	3
International aviation	54	70
Total	4712	3311

[a] The emissions from road transport increased, between 1990 and 2021, by 16%.

Globally, the greenhouse gas emissions increased from 22,717.23 million tonnes in 1990 to 37,857.58 million tonnes in 2021, thus by about 67 per cent.[40] 9-13

Another picture appears when the greenhouse gas emissions per capita are considered, which is probably, in the long term, the only generally accepted global measuring method. This gives the following picture for the Union (2021, kg per capita):[41] Romania, 3.47; Malta, 4.62; Croatia, 4.85; Portugal, 5.08; Lithuania, 5.14; Spain, 5.33; Hungary, 5.91; Slovenia, 6.17; Slovakia, 6.18; Italy, 6.51; Bulgaria, 6.59; Sweden, 6.81; France, 6.82; Greece, 7.00; Latvia, 7.11; Cyprus, 7.31; Austria, 7.63; Denmark, 8.11; Finland, 8.82; Germany, 9.40; Belgium, 9.93; Poland, 10.12; Netherland, 10.22; Estonia, 11.72; Czechia, 12.10; Ireland, 14.06; Luxembourg, 16.71; EU-27, 7.40.

In the same year, China had per capita emissions of 8.73, India had 1.83, Japan 8.60, Russia 13.35 and the USA 14.24.[42]

[39] ibid Table ES 5 vii.i.

[40] Commission, EDGAR Emission database for global atmospheric research, https://edgar.jrc.ec.europa.eu/report_2022#data_download. China increased its emissions from 2425.65 million tonnes in 1990 to 12,466.31 in 2021, India from 600.03 million tonnes to 2648.78 tonnes, Japan decreased emission from 1171.76 to 1084.69 million tonnes, Russia from 2395.64 to 1942.54 million tonnes and the USA from 5067.48 to 4782.08 million tonnes. The EDGAR data are not completely aligned to the data published by the European Environment Agency (see Table 9.1).

[41] Own calculation. The data from Table 9.1 were taken and divided by the population of each Member State. The population figures stem from The World Bank, 'Publication Total – European Union (reference year 2021)' https://data-worldbank.org/indicator/SP.POP.TOTL?locations=EU.

[42] Commission (n 40). As mentioned, these data are not aligned to the data of the EEA; under the Commission's EDGAR publication (n 40), the EU had per capita emissions of 6.25 in 2021.

III. Emission Trading with Greenhouse Gases

9-14 In March 2000, the Commission adopted a Green Paper on greenhouse gas emissions trading,[43] which was followed a year later by a proposal for a directive establishing a scheme for greenhouse gas emission allowance trading within the Union. Without significant amendments, the proposal was adopted in 2003 as Directive 2003/87, based on Article 192(1) TFEU.[44] The directive which initially only covered carbon dioxide (CO_2) gas, established a legal framework for an emissions trading scheme, which was launched in 2005. The scheme was limited to installations which were mentioned in annex I and which concerned, essentially, iron and steel furnaces; glass manufacturing installations; oil refineries; coke ovens; smelters and cement kilns; and pulp and paper mills of a particular size. Later amendments widened the types of installations covered, to cover some 11,000 installations overall. Installations which came under Directive 2003/87 had to receive a permit for the emissions of greenhouse gases. Overall, some 45 per cent of all greenhouse gas emissions were covered by the directive.

In 2009, the directive was revised.[45] Flights which arrived at or departed from an EU airport were included – though they were mobile products and not installations! – and the number of installations covered was increased.[46] For specific types of installations, additional gases to CO_2 were also included. The proposal to include aeroplanes met with strong objections from non-EU airlines and their host countries (including USA, China, Russia, Japan, Brazil, India and Mexico). These countries threatened the EU with legal measures and economic sanctions. In view of these objections, the EU retracted the proposal. Instead, it used the ongoing negotiations within the International Civil Aviation Organisation to include the application of its provisions only to those flights which arrived at or departed from airports situated in the territory of a Member State to which the TFEU applied.[47]

In 2023, the Union decided to include emissions from maritime shipping (as of 2026), road transport and buildings in the directive's field of application;[48] the inclusion of road transport and buildings is expected to be decided in 2023 or 2024.

Applications for the permit had to contain specific information on the installation, in particular the materials the use of which was likely to lead to greenhouse gas emissions, the sources of emissions from the installation and the measures planned to monitor emissions (Article 3). Member States were obliged to draw up a national plan which indicated the total quantity of allowances that were intended to be allocated (Article 9). These plans had to be published and notified to the Commission. The Commission could reject the plan if it was

[43] Commission, 'Green Paper on Greenhouse Gas Emissions Trading Within the European Union' COM(2000) 87.

[44] Directive 2003/87 (n 32).

[45] Directive 2009/29 amending Directive 2003/87 so as to improve and extend the greenhouse gas emission allowance trading scheme of the Community [2009] OJ L140/63.

[46] In 2008, the CJEU had to decide whether the inclusion of the steel industry in the scheme without, at the same time, including the aluminium and plastic industries infringed the principle of equal treatment. The CJEU held that such different treatment was justified, CJEU Case C-127/07 *Arcelor* ECLI:EU:C:2008:728. In the meantime, aluminium production has been included in Directive 2003/87, and plastic production has partly been included.

[47] See Decision 377/2013 [2013] OJ L113/1; Regulation 421/2014 [2014] OJ L129/1.

[48] Directive 2023/959 amending Directive 2003/87 [2023] OJ L130/134.

incompatible with the directive. However, it was the Member States which determined the quantity of allocations and the calculation method, not the Commission.[49]

An undertaking could either invest in cleaner technologies in order to reduce its greenhouse gas emissions or, when it thought that it would incur less cost, buy allowances (emission rights) on the market. When it had more allowances than it needed, it could sell them on the market.

An amendment of 2009[50] provided that the allowances would have to be, as of 2013, in principle auctioned and would no longer be issued free of cost, as the free allocation had led to rather generous attributions of allowances to some Member States. The auctioning increased the price of allowances, which made it more attractive to invest in cleaner technologies than to buy emission allowances. The free allocations were thought to be allowed for a transitional period only in order to avoid too high financial costs for some industries; however, due to pressure from some Member States, which were afraid of too high a burden for their industry or feared the relocation of installations to third countries with lower greenhouse gas emission costs ('carbon leakage'), some free allocations were still foreseen to be granted until 2030, though in decreasing quantities.[51] 9-15

Allowances were transferable between undertakings within the Union without restrictions. Every year, the operator of an installation had to surrender a number of allowances that was equal to the total emissions from that installation; these allowances were then cancelled (Article 12). The directive also provided for sanctions in cases where the operators of installations did not correctly report on emissions or emitted more gases than allowed (Articles 15 and 16).[52] The 2009 amendment of the directive provided that the total EU-wide quantity of emission allowances be reduced, as of 2013, by 1.74 per cent per year, in order to reduce the excessive amount of emission allowances, which led to too low prices for them. As this reduction appeared still to be insufficient, the Union reduced the allowances by 2.20 per cent per year by 2021. An increased reduction of available allowances as of 2024 by 4.3 per cent annually was decided in 2023.[53]

Decision 2015/1814 established a stability reserve to take allowances from the market and to hold them in reserve.[54] That decision was based on Article 192(1) TFEU. Poland was of the opinion that Article 192(2) TFEU – which required unanimous Council decisions – would have been the correct legal basis, but was unsuccessful when it challenged the decision before the CJEU. The Court held that the objective and content of a legal act were the determining factors which decided on the correct legal bases; the effects of a measure were too unforeseeable to be taken into consideration.[55]

The Kyoto Protocol had not only provided for the introduction of an emission trading system, but also provided for two other instruments, the Joint Implementation and the 9-16

[49] See CJEU Case C-504/09P *Commission v Poland* ECLI:EU:C:2012:178; Case C-505/09P *Commission v Estonia* ECLI:EU:C:2012:179.

[50] Directive 2009/29 (n 45).

[51] Directive 2003/87 (n 32), as amended by Directive 2018/410 [2018] OJ L76/3, Arts 10a(11) and 10b(4).

[52] On such sanctions, see CJEU Case C-203/12 *Billerud* ECLI:EU:C:2013.664; Case C-113/19 *Luxaviation* ECLI:EU:C:2020:228.

[53] Directive 2023/959 (n 48).

[54] Decision 2015/1814 concerning the establishment and operation of a market stability reserve for the Union greenhouse gas trading scheme [2015] OJ L264/1; Directive 2023/959 (n 48).

[55] CJEU Case C-5/16 *Poland v European Parliament and Council* ECLI:EU:C:2018/483.

Clean Development Mechanism. Both these instruments concerned specific projects. Joint Implementation projects may be undertaken in developed countries or in countries with economies in transition. This method allowed an investment, eg by Denmark, in a clean technology project in Georgia or in Moldovia, which would be capable of being realised with less investment costs than in Denmark. The Clean Development Mechanism was intended to permit investments in developing countries which were not subjected to targeted reductions of emissions under the Kyoto Protocol.

In 2004, the Union adopted Directive 2004/101, which amended Directive 2003/87 and established 'a scheme for greenhouse gas emission allowance trading within the Community, in respect of the Kyoto Protocol's project mechanisms'.[56] This directive, based on Article 192(1) TFEU, enabled operators in the Union to use both the Joint Implementation and the Clean Development Mechanism. However, the latter broke down following the global financial crisis of 2007–10 and no longer played an important role. The Joint Implementation, which was mainly destined for measures in the countries of the former Soviet Union, lost its impetus with the accession of most of those countries to the Union. Its objectives are now largely integrated into the emission trading system of Directive 2003/87.

9-17 Directive 2003/87 concentrated the attention on the economic instruments in the area of climate change. However, it should be underlined that the directive does not as such lead to a reduction of greenhouse gas emissions; it only promotes cost-effective investments. The directive required high administrative costs for calculation, registration, transparency, reporting obligations, etc and has, since its adoption some 20 years ago, developed into an extremely complicated legal and administrative instrument.

The continued price increase for heating, hot water, electricity and products in general (food, mechanical instruments, chemicals, etc) which, during the coming years, will also affect the normal citizen and in particular those in the lower socioeconomic groups, is likely to create social unrest and political effects, and might require significant state aid and similar measures for undertakings and citizens alike.

The Union reacted by establishing, in 2018, a Modernisation Fund.[57] That fund was destined to support Member States with a gross domestic product per capita below 60 per cent of the Union's average, to modernise their energy sector. The actual beneficiaries were Bulgaria, Croatia, Czechia, Estonia, Hungary, Latvia, Lithuania, Poland, Romania and Slovakia, all from Central and Eastern Europe. The fund was established for the period 2021–30 and was equipped with approximately €48 billion.

The Union also established, on the basis of Articles 175 and 322(1)(a) TFEU, a Just Transition Fund (JTF).[58] The JTF was equipped with €17.5 billion and destined 'to provide support to people, economies and the environment of territories which face serious socio-economic challenges' to reach the 2030 and 2050 targets of the Union (Article 1). The main regions addressed were those where coal, lignite, oil shale and peat are produced; this was not explicitly expressed, but was reflected in the earmarking of the available funds, which provided 20 per cent for Poland, 12.8 per cent for Germany, 11.1 per cent for Romania, 8.5 per cent for Czechia, etc (annex I). The JTF was

[56] Directive 2004/101 [2004] OJ L338/18.
[57] Directive 2018/410 (n 51) new Art 10d.
[58] Regulation 2021/1056 establishing the Just Transition Fund [2021] OJ L231/1.

to run from 2021 to 2027, though it is likely that its application will be extended. An interesting sanction is found in Article 7: 'Where a Member State has not made a commitment to implement the objective of climate neutrality by 2050, only 50% of the annual allocation for that Member State shall be made available.' This provision was aimed in particular at Poland, which had, in the past, shown reservation to agreeing to the Union's targets.[59]

Furthermore, the Union established, in 2023, a Social Climate Fund, for the period 2026–32;[60] its legal bases were Articles 91(1), 192(1), 194(2) and 322 TFEU. The fund was equipped with a budget of €65 billion. Its objective was to mitigate the effects of the inclusion of buildings, transport and some economic sectors in the emission trading scheme of Directive 2003/87 and provided in that regard that it intended 'to benefit households, micro-enterprises and transport users which are vulnerable … in particular households in energy poverty and households in transport poverty'.[61] Energy poverty and transport poverty were defined.[62] Member States were asked to elaborate national social climate plans which were to address the impact of carbon pricing, in order to reach a more affordable heating, cooling and mobility situation (Article 4). The plans were to be assessed by the Commission; a negative decision by the Commission had to be taken into consideration by the affected Member State when it resubmitted the plan (Article 17).

The Member States had to finance 25 per cent of the costs of their national plan. Annex I to Regulation 2023/955 fixed the maximum amount which Member States could obtain from the fund; Poland (17.6 per cent), France (11.2 per cent), Italy (10.8 per cent), Spain (10.5 per cent), Romania (9.3 per cent) and Germany (8.19 per cent) were the main beneficiaries.[63]

To mitigate the effects for some undertakings, the Union also introduced a carbon 9-18
border adjustment mechanism (CBAM),[64] which was intended to prevent the emigration of undertakings to countries where energy and electricity were cheaper ('carbon leakage'[65]). This mechanism applied to cement, electricity, fertilisers, iron and steel, aluminium and hydrogen (annex I), which are produced in third countries. Their import into the Union may only be effected by authorised importers. These have to buy CBAM certificates from the public authorities, the price of which is fixed weekly by the

[59] See Europeaan Council, 'Conclusions of the Meeting of 12 December 2019' Doc EUCO 29/19.

[60] Regulation 2023/955 establishing a social climate fund [223] OJ L130/1. Poland had voted against the proposal, though it had voted in favour of the EU Climate Law (n 38).

[61] ibid Art 1.

[62] ibid Art 2(1): 'energy poverty means a household's lack of access to essential energy services that underpin a decent standard of living and health, including adequate warmth, cooling, lighting and energy to power appliances'; (2) 'transport poverty means individuals' and housholds' inability or difficulty to meet the costs of private or public transport or their lack of or limited access to transport needed for their access to essential socio-economic services and activities'. Recital 13 stated that 34 million people in the Union had declared that they could not afford to heat their home sufficiently.

[63] Annex I to Commission, SWD(2020) 900–27 contains a list of EU funds which are available for each Member State during the years 2021–27.

[64] Regulation 2023/956 establishing a carbon border adjustment mechanism [2023] OJ L130/52.

[65] ibid Recital 9: 'Carbon leakage occurs if for reason of costs related to climate policies, businesses in certain industry sectors or sub-sectors transfer production to other countries or imports from those countries replace equivalent products that are less intensive in terms of greenhouse gas emissions.'

Commission and aligned to the price of the auctioned emission rights under Directive 2003/87. The mechanism is intended to progressively replace the free allocation of emission rights under that directive. After a transition period, the regulation will be operational as of 2025.

IV. Energy Efficiency

9-19 In order to promote better energy conservation and use, the Union adopted Directive 93/76, which was based on the present Articles 192 and 352 TFEU and had as its objectives the improvement of energy efficiency in housing, cars and industrial installations, and the promotion of public investment schemes.[66] It requested Member States to draw up and implement programmes to improve the energy efficiency of buildings and to organise the billing of heating, air conditioning and hot water consumption on the basis of annual consumption. New buildings should be equipped with thermal insulation; boilers should regularly be inspected: undertakings with high energy consumption should regularly be audited. All details for the drawing up of such programmes were left to the Member States. The implementation of the directive was hardly controlled by the Commission.

Nine years later, the Union adopted Directive 2002/91 on the energy performance of buildings, based on Article 192(1) TFEU.[67] It asked Member States to apply a method of calculating the energy performance of buildings, based on criteria laid down in the directive. Member States had then to establish minimum energy performance requirements of buildings. New buildings had to comply with these requirements as of 2006; existing buildings with a used floor area of over 1000 m^2 had to upgrade their energy performance should they undergo major renovation and it was 'technically, functionally and economically feasible' (Article 5). Where a building was constructed, sold or rented out, an energy performance certificate had to be made available to the interested person. Regular inspections had to be made for boilers, other heating installations and air conditioning systems in order to reduce energy consumption and limit CO_2 emissions.

9-20 In 2010, this directive was replaced by Directive 2010/31, based on Article 194(2) TFEU.[68] The new directive applied to new buildings and to existing buildings which underwent major renovations, though the threshold of 1000 m^2 was deleted. It introduced a common method for calculating the energy performance and asked Member States to set minimum requirements for buildings and for building units (apartments). Such measures also had to include equipment and appliances which were installed in buildings; for these, Member States had to establish technical requirements. It allowed Member States to maintain or adopt more stringent national provisions, as a provision similar to Article 193 TFEU was lacking in Article 194 TFEU.

By 2018, all new buildings occupied and owned by public authorities and, by 2020, all new buildings had to be 'nearly zero-energy' buildings; a 'nearly zero-energy' building

[66] Directive 93/76 to limit carbon dioxide emissions by improving energy efficiency (SAVE) [1993] OJ L237/28.
[67] Directive 2002/91 on the energy performance of buildings [2003] OJ L1/65.
[68] Directive 2010/31 on the energy performance of buildings [2010] OJ L153/13.

was defined as a building that had a very high energy performance, as determined in accordance with criteria laid down in annex I to Directive 2010/31. The amount of energy required should be covered 'to a very significant extent' by renewable energies, including energy from renewable sources produced on-site or nearby.[69] Member States were asked to draw up national plans in order to increase the number of nearly zero-energy buildings. A system of certification of energy performance of buildings was to be established by Member States, which had to allow the comparison of the different energy performances of the buildings. The certificate had to be handed over to a buyer or a tenant of the building or building unit. The inspection requirements for equipment and appliances were repeated.

An amendment of the directive in 2018[70] introduced an obligation of Member States 9-21
to draw up a long-term renovation strategy for buildings and fixed minimum energy performance requirements for new buildings. The technical measures for buildings and the inspection requirements for heating systems and air conditioning became more detailed and fine-tuned. With the European Green Deal of 2019, the efforts concerning the energy performance of buildings intensified, as the Commission stated that buildings use about 40 per cent of the energy in the Union and were responsible for 36 per cent of the Union's emissions of greenhouse gases, but that the decrease in greenhouse gas emissions was only about 1 per cent per year;[71] the directive constituted an insufficient framework to achieve the Union's 2030 targets. This led the Commission to propose a new directive in 2021,[72] with the general objective of reaching a 'zero-emission building stock by 2050' (Article 1). The proposal repeated and further specified the obligation of Member States to draw up a building renovation plan, with milestones for 2030, 2040 and 2050. The plans had to be updated every five years, had to be transmitted to the Commission and had to contain an implementation chapter on the past implementation of the plan (Article 3). The proposal also provided, among others, that all public buildings had to be, as of 2027, zero-emission buildings. Other new buildings had to reach this requirement by 2030 (Article 7), existing buildings in cases of major renovations. For 'technical building systems' (heating and cooling, ventilation, hot water, lighting, on-site energy generation and storage, etc) and recharging points in non-residential buildings, Member States had to lay down provisions.

In 2022, the Commission proposed to provide for 'suitable solar energy installations' by the end of 2026 in all public and commercial buildings with more than 250 m^2 surface area, by the end of 2027 for existing public and commercial buildings with that surface area and by the end of 2029 for all new residential buildings.[73]

These far-reaching proposals are at present being discussed by the other Union institutions. As their provisions, if they were adopted, would constitute a significant interference with citizens' activities, there appears to be some reluctance by Member States and in the European Parliament to adopt them for fear of social unrest, especially as the inclusion

[69] ibid Art 2, no 2.
[70] Directive 2018/844 [2018] OJ L156/75.
[71] Commission, 'Impact Assessment Report of Directive 2010/31' SWD(2021) 453, 4 and 29.
[72] Commission, COM(2021) 802.
[73] Commission, COM(2022) 222.

of the building sector in the emission trading scheme of Directive 2003/87[74] is likely to increase consumer prices for heating, hot water, etc anyway.[75]

9-22 In 2012, the Union adopted a Directive on energy efficiency, based on Article 194(2) TEU.[76] The directive again allowed Member States to adopt more stringent national measures. It fixed an overall non-binding objective of saving, by 2020, 20 per cent of the Union's primary energy consumption, 'compared to projections'.[77] Member States were asked to fix a national indicative energy efficiency target, which should take into account the Union's or national energy and climate change measures.

Furthermore, the Member States were requested to:

- establish a long-term strategy for mobilising investments in the renovation of the national stock of residential and commercial public or private buildings (Article 4);
- make an inventory of central government buildings (Article 5);
- ensure that three per cent of the heated and/or cooled buildings which were owned and occupied by central government were renovated each year in order to meet minimum energy performance standards (Article 5);
- ensure that central governments only purchase products with a high energy efficiency performance (Article 6);
- set up an energy efficiency obligation scheme which ensured that energy distributors or retailers reach 'a cumulative end-use energy savings target' which was to be fixed by Member States on the basis of some provisions in the directive (Article 7);
- ensure the availability of independent energy audits (Article 8); small and medium-sized enterprises and private households should be persuaded of the benefits of such audits; for other enterprises, the energy audit was compulsory (Article 8(4));
- ensure that final consumers of electricity, natural gas, district heating or cooling and domestic hot water were provided with individual meters which accurately reflected the consumption (Article 9); however, this requirement was nuanced by the proviso that the obligation existed 'in so far [as] it is technically possible, financially reasonable and proportionate', which transformed the obligation de facto into a recommendation;
- assess the potential of cogeneration and efficient district heating and cooling (Article 14); and
- ensure that national energy regulators pay sufficient attention to energy efficiency issues (Article 15).

Member States were also encouraged to set up an Energy Efficiency National Fund to support national initiatives in this area (Article 20).

The directive established a good framework for those Member States that had the political will to promote energy efficiency. Where this was not the case, the enforcement of the directive proved difficult, as most of the provisions mentioned above contained derogations

[74] See para 9-14 above.

[75] See European Court of Auditors, *Energy Efficiency in Buildings: Greater Focus on Cost-effectiveness Still Needed* (Luxembourg, 2020).

[76] Directive 2012/27 on energy efficiency [2012] OJ l 315/1.

[77] ibid Recital 2. The 'projections' were studies that had been made in 2007.

and exemption possibilities. The 20 per cent target was thus more a wish than a commitment that could be measured and enforced.

The directive was amended seven times by 2019, thus on average once per year. The general objective of the directive was that the Union should not consume more energy than 1433 Mtoe (million tonnes of oil equivalent) of primary energy or 1086 Mtoe of final energy by 2020;[78] the 20 per cent target was increased to 32.5 per cent, to be reached by 2030.[79] The Commission stated in 2022 that the primary energy consumption in 2020 was 1236 Mtoe of primary energy and 907 Mtoe of final energy; no percentage result was published. The Commission considered that the objectives for 2020 were reached, though it admitted that they had been highly influenced by the COVID-19 pandemic.[80] A general evaluation of the directive showed mixed results.[81] 9-23

In 2021, the Commission proposed a new objective of energy consumption for 2030,[82] but less than a year later, reduced it further: the total primary energy consumption in 2030 should not exceed 980 Mtoe and final energy consumption 750 Mtoe;[83] the Commission justified this new proposal with a single phrase.[84] The objective should be a collectively binding Union target; national indicative targets should continue to exist. The public sector should assume a lead role in energy efficiency.

The proposal is at present being discussed by the other Union institutions. The compromise reached between the European Parliament and the Council[85] provided that the primary energy consumption in 2030 should not exceed 992.5 Mtoe (non-binding target) and the final energy consumption 763 Mtoe (binding target). Member States should promote energy-efficient measures ('energy efficiency first'). The public sector should take the lead in energy efficiency measures by annually reducing its energy consumption by 1.9 per cent and renovating about three per cent of its buildings per year.

V. Renewable Sources of Energy

In 1997, the Commission adopted a White Paper on renewable sources of energy, which suggested, among others, to increase the percentage of renewable energies from six to 10 per cent by 2010.[86] This was followed by the proposal for a directive, which was adopted in 2001.[87] The directive was based on the present Article 192(1) TFEU. It provided that Member States should encourage a greater consumption of renewable energies and fixed 9-24

[78] Directive 2013/12 [2013] OJ L141/28.

[79] Directive 2018/2002 [2018] OJ L328/210.

[80] Commission, '2022 Report on the Achievement of the 2020 Energy Efficiency Targets' COM(2022) 641.

[81] Commision, 'Evaluation of Directive 2012/27' SWD(2021) 625.

[82] Commission, 'Proposal for a Recast of the Directive on Energy Efficiency' COM(2021) 558.

[83] Commission, COM(2022) 222.

[84] ibid 3: 'given the high energy prices and a radical change in market conditions leading to an increased cost-effectiveness of energy efficiency measures and the need for the Union to overcome its dependency on fossil fuels and energy imports from Russia, it is necessary'.

[85] Council document 7446/23 of 23 March 2023.

[86] Commission, 'White Paper: Energy for the Future: Renewable Sources of Energy' COM(1997) 599.

[87] Directive 2001/77 on the promotion of electricity produced from renewable energy sources in the internal electricity market [2001] OJ L283/33.

indicative national targets for that purpose. The Member States had to publish a progress report every two years and to report whether the national targets were compatible with the overall EU indicative target of 12 per cent gross national energy consumption of renewable energies by 2010 and in particular with the 22.1 per cent indicative share of electricity produced from renewable energy sources in the total Union energy consumption by 2010 (Article 3(4)). Member States were allowed to give financial support to electricity producers in order to reach the objectives of the directive. Electricity from renewable sources did not have to be labelled; however, on request, a guarantee of origin had to be issued (Article 5). Member States also had to ensure that operators of transmission and distribution systems (grid systems) guaranteed the transmission and distribution of electricity from renewable sources (Article 7).

In 2003, Directive 2003/30 on the promotion of the use of biofuels for transport was adopted, on the basis of the present Article 192(1) TFEU.[88] It concerned liquid or gaseous fuels for transport that were produced from biomass. The directive set an indicative target for Member States which had to reach a two per cent share of total sales of petrol and diesel fuels by the end of 2005 and a 5.7 per cent share by the end of 2010. Member States were obliged to report annually on the total sales of transport fuels and the share of biofuels, as well as on measures to stimulate the production of biofuels. The environmental problems of biofuels – extensive land use, use of pesticides and other chemicals, monocultures, loss of biodiversity – were not addressed.

The Commission's compliance report of 2013, which reported on data until 2010, indicated that Member States had difficulties in reaching the directives' objectives.[89] This was true, reported the Commission, for wind and biomass energy, whereas the photovoltaic sector had developed positively. The biofuel sector for transport would need supplementary measures in order to reach the 10 per cent share by 2020, all the more as about one-third of all biofuels used in the Union were imported from third countries. The share of renewable energies in the Union in 2010 was 12.7 per cent, that in the transport sector 4.7 per cent.

9-25 Both Directives 2001/77 and 2003/30 were amended and progressively repealed by a directive of 2009.[90] Directive 2009/28 was based on the present Article 192(1) TFEU, except Articles 17–19, which dealt with biofuels and for which the present Article 114 TFEU was fixed as a legal basis. It set mandatory national targets for the overall share of renewable energies in the gross final consumption of energy, and also for the share of renewable energy in transport. The national targets together had to reach 'a target of at least 20 per cent share of energy from renewable sources in the Community's gross final consumption of energy in 2020' (Article 3). Furthermore, each Member State had to ensure that the share of renewable energy in all forms of transport in 2020 was at least 10 per cent of the final consumption of energy in transport (Article 3(4)). The different repartitioning among Member States was made, according to the explanation in Recital 15, based on the different points of departure of Member States, their past efforts, their gross domestic product, and the fairness and adequacy of the allocation; nevertheless, the final result remained relatively arbitrary.

[88] Directive 2003/30 on the promotion of the use of biofuels or other renewable fuels [2003] OJ L123/42.
[89] Commission, COM(2013) 175; Commission, SWD(2013) 102.
[90] Directive 2009/28 on the promotion of the use of energy from renewable sources [2009] OJ L140/16.

Member States were obliged to draw up national renewable energy action plans (Article 4), which had to contain an annual 'indicative trajectory'. When the trajectory was not respected within two consecutive years, an amendment of the action plan was required. Other provisions dealt with the calculation of the share of renewable energies, the co-operation between Member States and with third countries, access to and operation of the grids and reporting requirements. Directive 2009/28 also addressed in detail the production of biofuels and fixed sustainability criteria for them (Articles 17–19); these criteria were quite general and did not solve the environmental problems caused by the extensive use of land for the production of biofuels. Most of the measures to be taken were left at the discretion of the Member States. The directive did not provide for any sanctions in case of non-compliance, relying entirely on the procedures under Article 258 TFEU.

Member States were allowed and even encouraged to grant state aid to support renewable energy production. The CJEU had held in 2001 that it was compatible with Union law to restrict such measures to the national production.[91] It did not see any reason, in 2014, to change this opinion, despite the progress in setting up an EU-wide internal energy market.[92]

In 2022, the Commission published a report 'on the achievement of the 2020 renewable energies targets'.[93] It stated that in 2020 the share of renewable energies in the gross final consumption of energy had reached 22.1 per cent and in transport 10.2 per cent,[94] though it admitted that the COVID-19 pandemic had helped to reach the targets. Sweden (with a share of 60.1 per cent), Finland (43.8 per cent) and Latvia (42.1 per cent) were the most successful countries, while Malta (10.7 per cent) and Luxembourg (11.7 per cent) ranked last.

In 2018, Directive 2009/28 was replaced by Directive 2018/2001, which was based on Article 194(2) TFEU.[95] The new directive fixed a collective Union target of a share of renewable energies[96] of at least 32 per cent by 2030; Member States had to make 'contributions' to meet this objective collectively (Article 3). They were allowed to apply support schemes in order to meet the target (Article 5) and to include in that scheme electricity which was produced in other Member States (Article 5). The directive fixed maximum delays for some of the permit-granting procedures (Article 16), simplified the grid-connection procedures and established details for district heating and cooling and renewable energies in the 9-26

[91] CJEU Case C-379/98 *PreussenElektra* ECLI:EU:C:2001:160.

[92] CJEU Case C-573/12 *Aaland Vindkraft* ECLI:EU:C:2014:2037; Joined Cases C-204/12 to C-208712 *Essent* ECLI:EU:C:2014:2192.

[93] Commission, COM(2022) 639. The report carefully avoided to give details regarding all Member States.

[94] The share of bioenergy in the overall production of renewable energy was 58.1%, followed by windpower (14.3%), hydropower (12.4%), solar energy (6.9%), ambient heat (5.5%) and geothermal energy (2.9%).

[95] Directive 2018/2001 on the promotion of the use of energy from renewable sources [2018] OJ L328/82.

[96] ibid Art 2, no 1: renewable energy 'means energy from renewable non-fossil sources, namely wind, solar (solar thermal and solar photovoltaic) and geothermal energy, ambient energy, tide, wave and other oceanic energy, hydropower, landfill gas, sewage treatment plant gas and biogas'; no 24: '"biomass" the bodegradable fraction of products, waste andresidues from from biodegradable origin from agriculture, including vegetal and animal substances, from forestry and rrelated industries, including fisheries and aquaculture, as well as the biodegradable fraction of waste, including industrial and municipal wsste of biodegradable origin'. An action which argued that forestry biomass should not have been declared renewable energy was declared inadmissible, see CJEU Case C-297/20P *Sabo v European Parliament and Council* ECLI:EU:C:2021:24.

transport sector, which had to reach a minimum share of 14 per cent by 2030 (Article 25). Furthermore, many provisions in the directive and its annexes concerned the calculation of the share of renewable energies.

Following the strategy of the European Green Deal of 2019,[97] the Commission proposed, in 2021, to increase the share of renewable energies to 40 per cent in 2030,[98] and suggested a number of other amendments of Directive 2018/2001 which mainly specified the different provisions.[99] A year later, the Commission proposed another amendment of Directive 2018/2001, based on Articles 192(1) and 194(2) TFEU, now suggesting a share of renewable energy in the total consumption of energy of 45 per cent by 2030 and a number of provisions to accelerate and shorten the permit-granting procedures for renewable energy projects.[100] The proposal was based on the Commission's assumption that 'lengthy and complex administrative procedures are a key burden for investments in renewable energies and the related infrastructure' and that the 'bureaucratic burden, non-transparent processes and lack of legal coherence'[101] required[102] the fixing of the duration of permit-granting procedures at Union level.

Both proposals are presently being discussed by the other Union institutions. Their adoption was delayed because France wanted to have nuclear energy included in them.

9-27 In November 2022, the Commission made a third proposal on renewable energies[103] on the basis of Article 122 TFEU,[104] which the Council adopted one month later. The new Regulation 2022/2577[105] used the Russian war against Ukraine as justification for the urgency measures, without associating the European Parliament, the European Economic and Social Committee or the Committee of the Regions, and without providing for the participation of the public or an impact assessment. The regulation was limited to 18 months, but with a possibility to prolong its validity. It provided:

> The planning, construction and operation of plants and installations for the production of energy from renewable sources … shall be presumed as being in the overriding public interest and serving public health and safety, when balancing legal interests in individual cases for the purposes of Article 6(4) and 16(1)(c) of Directive 92/43, Article 4(7) of Directive 2000/60 and Article 9(1)(c) of Directive 2009/147.

Thus, the considerations of those three environmental directives[106] should be secondary when the realisation of a project on renewable energy is in question.

[97] Commission, COM(2019) 640.
[98] Commission, COM(2021) 557.
[99] The share of renewable energy in transport should, however be lowered from 14% to 13%.
[100] Commission, COM(2022) 222.
[101] ibid explanatory memorandum.
[102] ibid. The requirement was justified with one word, ie that it was 'necessary'.
[103] Commission, COM(2022) 591.
[104] Art 122(1) TFEU: 'Without prejudice to any other procedure provided for in the Treaties, the Council, on a proposal from the Commission, may decide, in a spirit of solidarity between Member States, upon the measures appropriate to the economic situation, in particular if severe difficulties arise in the supply of certain products, notably in the area of energy.'
[105] Regulation 2022/2577 laying down a framework to accelerate the deployment of renewable energy [2022] OJ L335/36.
[106] On the protection ensured by these directives, see para 5-10 et seq and para 7-05 et seq.

Furthermore, the regulation provided for an acceleration of the permit-granting process for solar energy projects, which should take no longer than three months (Article 4). Small solar projects were deemed to be approved if the public authorities did not react to an application within one month. Also the maximum duration of the installation of heat pumps was fixed at three months (Article 7); for other procedures, the provisions for making an environmental impact assessment according to Directive 2011/92[107] were considerably eased.

I doubt that the conditions necessary to apply Article 122 TFEU were complied with: the 'spirit of solidarity', which is mentioned in that provision, does not require an interference with the duration or other conditions of the permitting procedure. Whether the provisions of Regulation 2022/2577 will really lead to an acceleration of permit-granting procedures for renewable energy projects appears doubtful. The fixing of the maximum duration of a permit-granting procedure is thus hardly compatible with the subsidiarity principle; the Commission and the Council may too easily have listened to vested interest presentations.[108]

VI. Limiting Emissions of Greenhouse Gases

So far, the Union has been very reserved as regards limiting the emission of greenhouse gases or banning or restricting the use of certain gases. For industrial installations, the Union left, under Directive 2010/75, the decision to limit or prohibit the emissions of greenhouse gases to the national permitting authorities. For products, the most important limitations of emissions concerned the car sector. After the failure of the voluntary agreement with the car industry to limit CO_2 emissions – see paragraph 8-20 et seq above – the Union adopted provisions on CO_2 emissions by passenger cars and light commercial vehicles in 2009 in Regulation 443/2009.[109] This regulation was superseded in 2019 by Regulation 2019/631.[110] Following a Commission proposal of 2021,[111] the European Parliament and the Council agreed in 2023 that, as of 2035, new passenger cars should no longer emit CO_2, which paves the way for electric cars. No CO_2 emission limits had previously been set for trucks; but as of 2025, new trucks will have to reduce their CO_2 emissions by a certain percentage.[112] 9-28

For methane emissions, the Commission made a proposal limiting them from the energy sector,[113] but did not tackle such emissions from agriculture, despite the sector being responsible for about half of all methane emissions. The proposal is currently being discussed by the other institutions.

[107] Directive 2011/92 [2012] OJ l 26/1; see para 4-33 et seq.

[108] According to Commission, COM(2022) 222, the length of permitting procedures had only been raised by project promoters and associations as a barrier, not by public authorities.

[109] Regulation 443/2009 setting a performance standard for new passenger cars as part of the Commission's integrated approach to reduce CO_2 emissions from light duty vehicles [2009] OJ L140/1.

[110] [2019] OJ L111/13.

[111] Commission, COM(2021) 556.

[112] Regulation 2019/1242 [2019] OJ L198/202.

[113] Commission, COM(2021) 805.

9-29 For fluorinated gases, which have high global warming potential,[114] a directive of 2006 prohibited the use of certain greenhouse gases in cars.[115] It was based on the present Article 114 TFEU. A regulation of the same year, based on the present Articles 192(1) and (as regards its Articles 7–9) 114 TFEU, provided for the containment, prevention and reduction of the three fluorinated gases HFCs, PFCs and SF_6.[116] In 2014, the regulation was replaced by Regulation 517/2014, which was based on Article 192 TFEU alone and which covered a longer list of fluorinated gases.[117] As of 2015, the Commission had to allocate to each producer and importer a quota for the placing on the market of HFCs. The sum of these quotas for 2015 constituted 100 per cent and this was to be gradually reduced, to reach 45 per cent during the years 2021–23 and 21 per cent by 2030.[118]

Following the conclusion of the Paris Agreement on Climate Change and the European Green Deal, the Commission proposed, in 2022, a new regulation to replace Regulation 517/2014.[119] The new act intended to further discourage the use of fluorinated gases, prevent emissions, encourage the use of alternatives to those gases and restrict illegal trade in them. The proposal is at present being discussed by the other Union institutions.

VII. Fiscal Measures

9-30 In 1992, the Commission proposed a directive on the tax of fossil fuels; the amount suggested was 10 dollars per barrel of oil.[120] The proposal was based on the present Articles 113 and 192 TFEU, and thus had to be adopted by a unanimous Council decision. The proposal indicated that it would only become applicable if other OECD countries also introduced a similar tax or took equivalent measures (Article 1(2)). This made the proposal unrealistic, since neither the USA nor Japan, the economic competitors at that time, considered introducing an energy tax.

The negotiations in the Council showed that it was impossible to reach unanimity on the proposal; in particular, the UK and Spain opposed the taking of tax measures at Union level. The Commission thus amended its proposal.[121] Under the new proposal, Member States remained free to decide whether or not to introduce a carbon/energy tax. If they decided positively, they had to comply with certain structural requirements laid down in the proposal. The amended proposal also did not find approval in the Council and became obsolete.

In 2003, the Council adopted, on the basis of the present Article 113 TFEU, Directive 2003/96 on the (minimum) taxation of energy products, including coal, natural gas and electricity, as well as motor and heating fuels.[122] Energy-intensive industries and

[114] As regards the global warming potential of fluorinated gases, see annex I to the Commission, 'Proposal for a Regulation on Such Gases' COM(2022) 150.

[115] Directive 2006/40 relating to emissions from air conditioning systems in motor vehicles [2006] OJ L161/12.

[116] Regulation 842/2006 on certain fluorinated greenhouse gases [2006] OJ L161/1.

[117] Regulation 517/2014 on fluorinated greenhouse gases [2014] OJ L150/195.

[118] ibid Art 16 and Annexes V and VI.

[119] Commission, COM(2022) 150.

[120] Commission, Proposal for a directive [1992] OJ C314/11.

[121] Commission, COM(95) 12.

[122] Directive 2003/96 restructuring the Community framework for the taxation of energy products and electricity [2003] OJ L283/51.

agricultural, horticultural and forestry products could be exempted from the tax if they entered into national environmental agreements, participated in emission trading schemes or otherwise contributed to reducing energy consumption. Member States were allowed to introduce reduced tax rates for biofuels and electricity which was produced from renewable energies. Where biofuels were used for local public transport, the excise duty could be waived altogether.

Following an evaluation of Directive 2003/96[123] and the launching of the European Green Deal, the Commission proposed, in 2021, a recast of the directive.[124] It considered that Directive 2003/96 did not offer sufficient incentives to invest in clean technologies, de facto favoured fossil fuels and did not provide for lower tax rates for renewable energies. It suggested switching from the volume of a product to its energy content as the basis for taxation, and proposed to tax energy products according to their 'environmental performance': the highest tax rate should be applied to oil and gas. This should be followed by rates for fossil fuels that were less harmful, such as natural gas, hydrogen of fossil fuels origin and LPG. The next class would be constituted by sustainable, but not advanced, biofuels; the last category would be formed by electricity, advanced biofuels, hydrogen of renewable origin, etc. The Commission proposal is at present being discussed by the other Union institutions. 9-31

In 2005, the Commission proposed a directive on the taxation of passenger cars according to their CO_2 emissions.[125] The proposal again met strong opposition in the Council, as well as from the interested industry; the main argument from the Member States was that they did not want to see the introduction of Union-wide taxes and preferred to keep this residue of national sovereignty – the adoption of taxes – in their own hands. The Commission withdrew its proposal in 2014.[126]

Another fiscal measure which should be mentioned is the carbon border adjustment mechanism, introduced by Regulation 2023/956 and discussed above in paragraph 9-18.

In 2021, the total energy subsidies in the Union were €184 billion (among others €50 billion for fossil energies, €78.2 billion for renewable energies and €7.2 billion for nuclear energy); in 15 Member States, subsidies for fossil energies were higher than for renewable energies.[127]

VIII. Accompanying Measures

In 2007, the Commission started an initiative to assist vulnerable third countries in combating climate change.[128] The initiative intended to assist those countries in the development of programmes on climate change. Between 2007 and 2020, the Commission made 9-32

[123] Commission, 'Evaluation of Directive 2003/96' COM(2019) 329.

[124] Commission, COM(2021) 563.

[125] Commission, 'Proposal for a Directive on Passenger-Related Taxes' COM(2005) 261.

[126] [2014] OJ C80/17.

[127] Commission, 'Report on energy subsidies in the EU' COM(2022) 642. See also European Court of Auditors, *Energy Taxation, Carbon Pricing and Energy Subsidies* (Luxembourg, 2023).

[128] Commission, 'Building a Global Climate Change Alliance between the European Union and Poor Developing Countries Most Vulnerable to Climate Change' COM(2007) 540.

available €729 million and co-financed projects in some 80 countries. The programme was discontinued, though, because the Member States made only minor sums available from their side, the projects were unevenly distributed and they did not always meet the priorities and concerns of the receiving countries.[129]

In 2023, the Union adopted a regulation to stop deforestation mainly in third countries.[130] The regulation applied to cattle, cocoa, coffee, oil palm, rubber, soya and wood. It was based on Article 192(1) TFEU. It argued that deforestation and forest degradation were taking place at an alarming rate (Recital 2) and that 'climate change, biodiversity loss and deforestation are concerns of the highest global importance, affecting the survival of humanity and sustained living conditions on Earth' (Recital 6). Union consumption was a considerable driver of deforestation and forest degradation on a global scale, and risked causing the loss of 248,000 hectares of forest by 2030. One-third of the globally traded agricultural products that were associated with deforestation were imported and consumed by the Union (Recital 18). 'Drastically reducing deforestation and forest degradation and systematically restoring forests and other ecosystems is the single largest nature-based opportunity for climate mitigation' (Recital 4).

The regulation tried to establish a system under which operators and traders of concerned products have to submit a 'due diligence' statement, according to which they declare that their products are deforestation-free.[131] Control mechanisms shall ensure that these due diligence declarations are correct.

9-33 In order to get rid of CO_2, the Union adopted Directive 2009/31 on the underground storage of CO_2 (carbon capture and storage, CCS).[132] This directive was based on Article 192(1) TFEU; it entered into effect in 2011. It attempted to set a legal framework to allow the storage of CO_2, although the technique of such underground storage was not yet certain. It called the technique 'bridging technology', as it meant to give greenhouse gas-emitting industries the option, instead of reducing their emissions, of putting these emissions underground; for this purpose, new large combustion plants had to examine whether suitable sites for the storage of CO_2 were available and, if so, they had to set aside that space (Article 33).

Member States were given the freedom to allow or refuse the geological storage of CO_2 in all or parts of their territory. Each storage site needed a specific permit, for which an environmental impact assessment had to be made. The storage site had to be inspected regularly; when leaks appeared, an action plan would have to be applied which should stop the leak. After the closure of the site, the operator would normally remain responsible for the necessary post-closure measures for a period of 20 years. After that, the responsibility for post-closure measures would fall on the Member State in question. Stored CO_2 was not considered to be waste, with the exception of leaked CO_2.

All Member States transposed the directive into their national law, though a number of them – Luxembourg, Finland, Austria, Croatia, Estonia, Ireland, Latvia, Slovenia and some

[129] European Court of Auditors, *The Global Climate Change Alliance – Achievements Fell Short of Ambitions. Special Report 4/2023* (Luxembourg, 2023).

[130] Regulation 2023/1115 on the making available on the Union market and the export from the Union of certain commodities and products associated with deforestation and foresst degradation [2023] OJ L150/206.

[131] As to the definition of deforestation-free and other details of the regulation, see para 5-05 and n 42.

[132] Directive 2009/31 on the geological storage of carbon dioxide [2009] OJ L140/114.

German Länder – prohibited CCS altogether; other Member States introduced their own restrictions.[133] By 2023, no carbon capture and storage installation existed in any Member State. The Commission admitted that the storage of CO_2 in the Union had 'not yet taken off', though the Union's overall storage capacity was about 300 gigatonnes, while its annual CO_2 emissions were about 2.2 gigatonnes. The main reasons were the high costs for the installation and the risk of liability.[134]

In 2018, the Union tried to give a structure to its different initiatives and measures on climate change, by adopting, based on Articles 192(1) and 194(2) TFEU, Regulation 2018/1999 'on the governance of the energy union and climate action';[135] the main objective of the regulation was, though, the promotion of the energy union.[136] The regulation obliged Member States to draw up a draft integrated national energy and climate action plan and transmit it to the Commission. The Commission was to assess whether the plan was in conformity with the Union's climate change and energy union objectives, and could make country-specific recommendations to amend the draft. The Member State had to take 'due account' of those recommendations when it adopted the plan and to 'provide and make public its reasons' when it did not follow the recommendations (Article 9). The regulation contained detailed provisions on the content of the plans concerning decarbonisation, renewable energies, energy efficiency, energy security and the internal market for energy, and on research, innovation and competitiveness. The plans had to be adopted by a specific date and be updated every 10 years. Member States also had to adopt a long-term strategy of at least 30 years as regards climate and energy issues, make it public, transmit it to the Commission and update it every 10 years. On the basis of these national strategies, the Commission had to elaborate a long-term Union strategy (Article 15). 9-34

The regulation requested an avalanche of national reports on climate change and energy union issues, which largely replaced earlier reporting obligations. Member States had to report every two years on the implementation of the national energy and climate action plan (Article 17), on policies and measures in that area (Article 18) and on adaptation and financial measures, including support to third countries (Article 19). The report on the integrated national energy and climate action plan had to contain reporting sections on renewable energy, energy efficiency, energy poverty,[137] energy security, internal market energy issues and innovations. Annual reports had to submit information on crude oil stocks and on offshore oil and gas installations. And the Commission had to draw up an annual report on the state – not of the fight against climate change, but of the energy union (Article 34).

Finally, the regulation installed a Climate Change Committee and an Energy Union Committee, consisting of persons (officials) appointed by the Member States (Article 44).

[133] Commission, 'Report on the Implementation of Directive 2009/31' COM(2014) 99; Commission, COM(2015) 576, annex 2; Commission, COM(2017) 37.

[134] Commission, 'The Future of Carbon Capture and Storage in Europe' COM(2013) 180.

[135] Regulation 2018/1999 [2018] OJ L328/1. In 2023, the Union published 'Guidelines on Member States' Adaptation Strategies and Plans' for this Regulation [2023] OJ C264/1.

[136] ibid Recital 26.

[137] On energy poverty, see Commission Recommendation 2020/1563 on energy poverty [2020] OJ L357/35, Recital 1: 'Energy poverty is a situation in which households are unable to access essential energy services and products. With nearly 34 million Europeans unable to afford to keep their homes adequately warm in 2018, energy poverty is a major challenge for the EU.'

No specific tasks were attributed to these committees. They were to function independently of the EU Scientific Advisory Board on Climate Change, which was set up under Regulation 2021/1119,[138] consisted of 15 independent experts and should serve 'as a point of reference on scientific knowledge related to climate change'.

IX. Concluding Remarks on Greenhose Gases

9-35 Overall, the Union initiated a very considerable number of measures in order to reduce emissions from point sources, promote changes in the use of fuels and incite professionals and citizens to change their behaviour or their lifestyle in order to reach the objectives of the UN Climate Change Convention and its Kyoto and Paris Protocols. Not all of these measures, which also concern measures in the area of agriculture, fisheries, energy, transport, development policy, industrial policy, and competition, have been mentioned here. The Union reached the target of the Kyoto Protocol and reduced its greenhouse gas emissions by 2012 by 8 per cent compared to 1990; the further commitment to reduce the greenhouse gas emissions by 20 per cent by 2020 was also reached. The problem of the EU climate change policy lies first in the fixing of and complying with targets for 2030 and 2050, which do not require, within the Union, just 'measures as usual' to reduce emissions, but rather the putting into effect of efficient climate-change policies in the different sectors of energy, transport, agriculture, industry, etc. The present measures give the impression that the attitude of 'business as usual' continues in large parts of EU and national policies. The 20 per cent target for 2020 was hardly ambitious, and scientists appear to be increasingly in agreement that, from the point of view of climate change, it was not sufficiently ambitious. The target of a 55 per cent reduction by 2030 appears correct, but it is not certain that it will be reached. The political concessions which are constantly made for nuclear energy, coal, petrol and gas only slow down the necessary reconversion of the EU economy and society to a carbon-free status. Member States which are, at present, dependent on coal, such as Poland, heavily oppose measures which would lead to a reduced role of coal as an energy source. And the political shift of governments, also in Member States, to a policy of 'my country first' does not make a common climate change policy any easier.

The second problem is the global dimension of climate change. No successful global climate change policy can be made without the participation of China and the USA; these countries are too big, too influential and too often imitated by other countries to be left aside. Unless China drastically reduces its greenhouse gas emissions and the USA lowers its per capita emissions, too many countries will be tempted to follow their example and increase their own emissions, with whatever pretext.

9-36 The Union is not a global power and does not have the weight to lead the world towards a successful climate change policy. Its attempts to influence the climate change negotiations worldwide were rather harshly brushed aside at the global summit in Copenhagen 2009, by the USA and China, but also by Brazil, Australia, Canada, India and other countries. The inability to speak with one voice, paired with the ambition of the bigger Member States – Germany and France in particular, and the UK before Brexit – to speak for themselves and

[138] Regulation 2021/1119 (n 38) Art 3.

the lack of a strategy to advance the global discussions were the main reasons for this result. Initiatives such as the making of a new EU Treaty along the lines of the Euratom Treaty but for renewable energies or a concrete suggestion to conclude an international climate change agreement with the some 80 states parties to the Cotonou Agreement and test the co-operation between developed and developing countries in this format remained reflections by academics; no visionary or strategic initiative came from the Union, though everybody in the Union knows that the fight against climate change will never be won by measures within the Union alone.

The global summit in Paris at the end of 2015 led to self-commitments by the states to reduce their greenhouse gas emissions in a more or less distant future – without control and without sanctions. The target of not exceeding a 2°C increase in temperature and the effort to aim at an increase of only 1.5°C are laudable, but the measures adopted – the 'nationally determined contributions' of the Paris Agreement – are not likely to match this target, as is demonstrated by the almost doubling of greenhouse gas emissions since 1990[139] and by the continued increase of such emissions since 2015. It is thus more likely that a temperature increase of three, four or even more degrees by the end of the century will be reached.

X. Ozone Depletion

The depletion of the ozone layer was discovered at the end of the 1970s and was relatively 9-37
quickly attributed to a number of chlorine and bromine compounds which were of human origin. These substances are mainly used as coolants, aerosol gases, cleaning agents and fire extinguishers.

At the international level, ozone-depleting substances are regulated by the Montreal Protocol on some 200 substances that deplete the ozone layer, which was concluded in 1987, to which the Union adhered[140] and which is regularly updated. Regulation 1005/2009, which replaced earlier regulations,[141] transposed the provisions of the Montreal Protocol into EU law, though it went further than the protocol. The regulation was based on Article 192 TFEU, though Article 114 would have been the more correct legal basis as the regulation dealt with product-related standards.

The regulation banned the production, placing on the market and use of the substances which came under the Montreal Protocol, in particular CFCs, fully halogenated CFCs, halons, carbon tetrachlorides, 1,1,1-trichloroethanes, HFCs and hydrobromofluorocarbons. The production, placing on the market and use of methyl bromides was progressively phased out by 2010 (Article 12). The production of hydrochlorofluorocarbons (HCFCs) had to be progressively stopped by 2020.

The reason for the long transition period for HCFCs was that a number of producers had developed these substances as a substitute for CFCs and were not prepared to write off

[139] See text to n 42.

[140] Decision 88/540 [1988] OJ L297/8. The Montreal Protocol was elaborated in the context of the Vienna Convention of 1985 on the protection of the ozone layer. The EU also adhered to the Vienna Convention by Decision 88/540.

[141] Regulation 1005/2009 on substances that deplete the ozone layer [2009] OJ L286/1.

their investments; and they found support in this attitude from their national governments. The regulation limited the use of HCFCs in a number of substances such as aerosols, sprays, cooling systems and air conditioning, but provided for extensive derogations. Quantities which a producer does not use may be traded within the contracting parties to the Montreal Protocol.

Annex II to the regulation listed ozone-depleting substances which were included in the regulation but not (yet) in the Montreal Protocol. Also, with regard to trade and use of substances and equipment, the regulation went beyond the protocol.

9-38 The Union reserved the possibility to allow the production of banned or restricted substances for essential use where no substitutes or recycled substances were available. Detailed rules dealt with the import and export of ozone-depleting substances to and from third countries. The export of such substances to countries which had not adhered to the Montreal Protocol was prohibited, as were substances other than HCFCs to all countries (Article 11). The Commission issues licences for imports of ozone-depleting substances from third countries, where this is still legal; import of such substances from countries which are not party to the Montreal Protocol is forbidden (Article 8). Undertakings were obliged to inform the Commission in detail on the production, processing, recycling, uses and other data of ozone-depleting substances. The Commission may ask national authorities to make investigations as regards these substances. The regulation also dealt with the recycling of ozone-depleting substances, the monitoring, Member States' information obligations, controls and sanctions, which must be 'effective, proportional and deterrent' (Article 21).

The production and use of ozone-depleting substances in the Union have been considerably reduced during the last decades. The regulation is thus rightly considered to have been a successful piece of legislation.[142] Nevertheless, the Commission proposed, in 2021, to replace it by a new act which should further strengthen the restrictive measures for ozone-depleting substances, in particular as regards foam recovery at the end of its useful life.[143] Though the Montreal Protocol provided for less strict production and trade provisions for developing countries than for industrialised countries, it was considered that the ozone layer may recover around 2050 if the present measures continue to be applied.[144]

[142] Commission, SWD(2019) 407.

[143] Commission, COM(2022) 151.

[144] ibid Recital 5; see also European Environment Agency, *Environment in the European Union at the Turn of the Century* (Copenhagen, 1999) 99.

10

Waste

I. Waste Management Policy and Law

'Waste' is defined as any substance or object which the holder discards or intends to discard or is required to discard.[1] The Union generates about 2.15 billion tonnes of waste per year, approximately 5 tonnes per capita; each citizen generates half a tonne of municipal waste per year. Despite all Union and Member States measures, waste generation in the Union continues to grow.[2] 10-01

Waste management issues played a role in EU environmental policies from their very beginnings. The Commission's communication of 1972 mentioned the necessity of preventing waste generation and promoting waste recovery.[3] The first environmental action programme discussed the question of what action on waste management could usefully be tackled at EU level and announced the harmonisation of legislations.[4] The second action programme declared that a comprehensive waste management policy was necessary, which should include measures for prevention, reclamation and disposal of waste.[5] The third action programme repeated the intentions of the second programme in similar form and announced promotional measures for waste prevention and recovery.[6]

The EU dimension of waste management problems fully came into the open when the incident of the Seveso barrels occurred in 1982. Forty-one barrels containing highly toxic waste, which stemmed from a major industrial accident in Seveso in 1976, were shipped, with the consent of Italian public authorities but in contradiction to the provisions of Directive 78/319,[7] from Italy abroad, and disappeared. Numerous EU Member States were afraid that the waste might have secretly been brought to their territory.[8] The European Parliament set up, for the first time, an inquiry committee and in its final conclusions, it criticised the Commission for not having properly exercised its role as guardian of the Treaty

[1] Directive 2008/98 on waste [2008] OJ L312/3, Art 3, no 1. That directive was amended, up to the end of 2022, by Commission Regulation 1357/2014 [2014] OJ L315/89; Commission Directive 2015/1127 [2015] OJ L184/13; Regulation 2017/997 [2017] OJ L150/1; Directive 2018/851 [2018] OJ L150/109.

[2] Commission, 'A New Circular Economy Action Plan: For a Cleaner and More Competitive Europe' COM(2020) 98.

[3] [1972] OJ C52/1 12.

[4] First Environmental Action Programme (1973–1977) [1973] OJ C112/1, ch 7, s 1.

[5] Second Environmental Action Programme (1977–1982) [1977] OJ C139/1, paras 174–201.

[6] Third Environmental Action Programme (1983–1986) [1983] OJ C46/1, para 29.

[7] Directive78/319 on toxic and dangerous waste [1978] OJ L84/43.

[8] The wastes were later found back on a non-authorised storage site in France, transported to Switzerland and, it was reported, incinerated there.

and ensured the application of existing EU rules on waste management. It expressly asked for the elaboration of a consistent and coherent EU waste policy.[9]

10-02 The fourth action programme confirmed the previous policy objectives and underlined, in particular, the importance of promoting clean technologies and recycling of waste; it also announced a specific communication on a waste management strategy.[10]

This strategy communication was finally made in 1989.[11] It essentially fixed five strategic guidelines: (1) prevention of waste generation; (2) promotion of recycling and reuse; (3) optimisation of final disposal; (4) transport of waste; and (5) remedial action.

10-03 In concluding chapters, the Commission stated the objective that 'as far as possible waste is disposed of in the nearest suitable centres', but that the situation was 'different with waste to be recycled'. Furthermore, it confirmed that 'waste arising within the Community which cannot be recycled should be treated within the Community where possible and exported only in exceptional circumstances'. These statements constituted the basis of the proximity and self-sufficiency principles, which are now laid down in Article 16 of the Waste Framework Directive, Directive 2008/98.[12]

The Fifth Environmental Action Programme referred back to the 1989 strategy;[13] it repeated its guiding principles and announced rather ambitious waste management targets for the year 2000.[14] These targets were made somewhat less ambitious by the 1996 review of the waste management strategy of 1989,[15] which confirmed the hierarchy of principles while stating that, within the recovery principle, 'where environmentally sound, preference should in general be given to the recovery of material over energy recovery operations. This reflects the greater effect on the prevention of waste produced by material recovery rather than by energy recovery.'[16]

The Sixth Environmental Action Programme linked waste management to the sustainable use of natural resources. It proposed a significant reduction in the quantity of waste going to disposal and the volume of hazardous waste that was produced (Article 8), and suggested the development of quantitative and qualitative reduction targets of all relevant wastes.[17]

[9] European Parliament Resolution of 8 June 1983 [1983] OJ C184/50; Resolution of 16 March 1984 [1984] OJ C104/147; Resolution of 11 April 1984 [1984] OJ C127/67. See also Economic and Social Committee [1984] OJ C206/62.

[10] Fourth Environmental Action Programme (1987–1992) [1987] OJ C328/1, para 5.3.

[11] Commission, 'A Community Strategy for Waste Management' SEC(89) 934.

[12] Directive 2008/98 (n 1); this directive had replaced Directive 75/442 [1975] OJ L194/23, amended by Directive 91/156 [1991] OJ L78/32 and codified under the number 2006/12 [2006] OJ 114/9. Art 16 reads: 'Member States shall take appropriate measures … to establish an integrated and adequate network of waste disposal installations and of installations for the recovery of mixed municipal waste collected from private households. This network shall be designed to enable the Community as a whole to become self-sufficient in waste disposal as well as in the recovery of waste … and to enable Member States to move towards that aim individually … The network shall enable waste to be disposed of or waste to … be recovered in one of the nearest appropriate installations.'

[13] Fifth Environmental Action Programme [1993] OJ C138/5, para 5.4.

[14] Amongst others, a stabilisation of quantities of waste generated at 300 kg per capita and year; a recycling/reuse rate of paper, glass and plastics of at least 50%; markets for recycled materials; reliable EU data on waste generated, collected and disposed; a functioning system of liability for hazardous waste; and an inventory of risks for hazardous waste.

[15] Commission, COM(96) 399.

[16] See also Council Resolution of 24 February 1997 [1997] OJ C76/1; European Parliament Resolution of 14 November 1996 [1996] OJ C362/241; Economic and Social Committee [1997] OJ C89/2; Committee of the Regions [1997] OJ C116/74.

[17] Decision 1600/2002 laying down the Sixth Community Environment Action Programme [2002] OJ L242/1.

The Seventh Environmental Action Programme set out four key objectives to be reached by 2020:[18] 10-04

- waste should be considered and treated as a resource; this would 'open up new markets, create new jobs, and reduce dependence on imports of raw materials, while having lower impacts on the environment'. This objective was repeated and strengthened in a further Commission communication with the title: 'Towards a Circular Economy. A Zero Waste Programme for Europe';[19] under this strategy, waste would no longer be landfilled – 'wasted' – but, through recycling and recovery, reintroduced into the economic circle;
- total waste generation and waste generated per capita should decrease;
- landfilling should be limited to non-recyclable and non-recoverable waste;
- energy recovery should be limited to non-recyclable waste.

None of these objectives were reached.[20]

The Eighth Environmental Action Programme limited itself to the request that 'the waste hierarchy is applied'.[21]

The different policy statements at EU level have, to date, left open three basic policy decisions which very considerably influence waste management policy and legislation at EU level. 10-05

1. *Waste policy and product policy*. Waste prevention was, and continues to be, the first and most important objective in EU waste management policy, confirmed by all statements and repeated in the Waste Framework Directive.[22] However, before a material becomes waste, it was a good (product). Thus, preventing the generation of waste requires a product policy. Only very recently did the Commission start to develop measures in order to improve the reuse or the recyclability of products.[23] Since waste management is an end-of-the-pipe technique, its conception and implementation must necessarily be influenced by actions or omissions that are taken 'upstream'. And as long as there is no product policy, the concept of waste prevention remains a sort of wishful thinking.

2. *Waste as a renewable source of energy*. EU declarations since 1996 have proclaimed that, in principle, material recycling of waste should have priority over waste incineration with energy recovery.[24] This priority was also established in several EU directives, including 10-06

[18] Decision 1386/2013 on a General Union Environment Action Programme to 2020 'Living well, within the limits of our planet' [2013] OJ L354/171, paras 39, 40 and 43.

[19] Commission, COM(2014) 398.

[20] Commission, SWD(2019) 181, in particular annex V.

[21] Decision 2022/591 [2022] OJ L114/22, Art 2.2.c.

[22] See Council Resolution of 24 February 1997 (n 16) paras 16 and 17: 'waste prevention should be first priority for all rational waste policy, in relation to minimising waste production and the hazardous properties of waste; … efforts made in this respect need to be increased, inter alia, by improving the environmental dimension of technical standards, by reducing the presence of dangerous substances where less dangerous alternatives are available.' Directive 2008/98 (n 1) Art 4: 'The following waste hierarchy shall apply as a priority order in waste prevention and management legislation and policy: (a) prevention; (b) preparing for re-use; (c) recycling; (d)other recovery, eg energy recovery; and (e) disposal.'

[23] Commission, 'Proposal for a Regulation Establishing a Framework for Setting Ecodesign Requirements for Sustainable Products' COM(2022) 142; Commission, 'On Making Sustainable Products the Norm' COM(2022) 140.

[24] See para 10-03 above. See also Council Resolution, 24 February 1997 (n 16), which is, to say the least, ambiguous: '[The Council] recognises, as regards recovery operations, that the choice of option in any particular

Directive 2008/98.[25] In practice, however, the Union frequently takes measures to promote waste incineration (with energy recovery) rather than waste recycling. This manifests itself in several areas: as regards energy policy, waste is considered a source of energy which is sometimes available at a low price and used as a substitute for fossil fuels. An example is Directive 2010/75, which exempted certain installations that burn waste altogether from their field of application and which provided for extensive provisions on co-incineration – which is nothing other than the incineration of waste in production installations.[26]

In its policy on renewable sources of energy, the Commission went so far as to consider the incineration of municipal waste as a renewable source of energy.[27] The Council and Parliament were more restricted; they declared 'biomass' a source of renewable energy, which they defined as follows:[28]

> [T]he biodegradable fraction of products, waste and residues from biological origin of agriculture including vegetal and animal substances, from forestry and related industries including fisheries and aquaculture as well as the biodegradable fraction of waste, including industrial and municipal waste of biological origin.

As, however, the notion of 'biodegradable' is not defined anywhere in EU law and as there is also no obligation to separate biodegradable from non-biodegradable fractions of waste, one might well imagine how precise this definition is in practice and how easy it is to incinerate industrial waste of non-biological origin under this formula. Generally, agricultural policy is interested in seeing agricultural waste – called 'biomass' – recognised as a renewable source of energy, which allows the granting of tax relief or state aid for the generation of biofuels while at the same time seeing the considerable quantities of agricultural waste reduced by incineration. Furthermore, EU research policy has a tendency to promote high-technology and large-scale projects such as the incineration of (hazardous) waste rather than the small-scale technology of separation, sorting, material recycling or composting of waste.

The Union instruments to increase recycling and recovery contain numeric targets. However, such targets are neither enforceable nor enforced. In practice, they constitute policy orientations; their achievement depends on the policy which the different Member States develop and pursue.

10-07 3. *EU responsibilities and Member States' responsibilities.* A consistent EU waste management policy has also not been developed, because it is not clear to what extent waste management strategies, policies and measures are to be established at Union or national level. Member States generally prefer to keep responsibility for management options, including questions on investments into cleaner technologies, at national level, in part because the waste management infrastructure – waste collection and treatment, recycling and recovery

case must have regard to environmental and economic effects, but considers that at present, and until scientific and technological progress is made and life-cycle analyses are further developed, reuse and material recovery should be considered preferable where and insofar as they are the best environmental option.' See also the waste hierarchy in Art 4 of Directive 2008/98 (n 1).

[25] Directive 94/62 on packaging and packaging waste [1994] OJ L365/10; Directive 2008/98 (n 1) Art 4.

[26] Directive 2010/75 on industrial emissions [2010] OJ L334/17.

[27] [2001] OJ C153/81.

[28] Directive 2018/2001 on the promotion of the use of energy from renewable sources [2018] OJ L328/82, Art 2 no 24.

installations, the transporting of waste, etc – is set up and monitored by them, not by the Union.

The Court of Justice of the European Union (CJEU) decided, in 1992, that waste materials are, in the EU terminology, products, though of a specific nature, to which the present Article 34 of the Treaty on the Functioning of the European Union (TFEU) applied.[29] This judgment ended a long controversy as to whether waste issues came under the provisions of the free circulation of goods or the freedom to provide services, or were not covered by the EU Treaties at all. Since the CJEU declared, in 1993, that Directive 91/156, which amended Directive 75/442 on waste, was rightly based on Article 192 TFEU,[30] most waste measures have been based on that provision, except two product-related waste directives.[31] It is obvious, though, that Article 192 TFEU leaves Member States greater discretion for national measures, since Article 114 TFEU primarily aims at establishing the internal market, which requires uniform rules, while Article 192 TFEU primarily aims at protecting the environment; under Article 114, national measures are systematically controlled and eventually 'authorised' if they comply with the conditions laid down in that article, while Article 192 does not contain conditions. This leads, in practice, to measures which are adopted on the basis of Article 192 TFEU at a low common denominator, since Member States that wish to see higher provisions adopted can easily be referred to the provision of Article 193 TFEU, which allowed the taking of more protective national measures.

To give some examples of political divergence within the Union: a number of local authorities have set up installations for the incineration of waste; this has led to a clear interest to see the waste generated at local level also being treated in these installations, in order to use the available capacities,[32] but has restricted the circulation (shipment) of waste within the Union. 10-08

The preference for material recycling over incineration with energy recovery, which was laid down in the EU strategy, was discussed in Germany and the UK, but was ultimately not laid down in the relevant political and legal documents. Scandinavian Member States, the Netherlands, France and others strongly promoted the incineration of at least municipal waste.[33] The general scarcity of sites for landfill favours waste incineration, unless a very active waste prevention, reuse and recycling policy is pursued; this again presupposes a product policy, which predominantly comes into the realm of the EU.[34]

Other uncertain aspects and controversies concern the question of whether waste management measures are to be taken at EU or at national level, such as the treatment

[29] CJEU Case C-2/90 *Commission v Belgium* ECLI: ECLI:EU:C:1992:310: 'waste has a special characteristic. The accumulation of waste, even before it becomes a health hazard, constitutes a threat to the environment, because of the limited capacity of each region or locality for receiving it.'

[30] CJEU Case C-155/91 *Commission v Council* ECLI:EU:C:1993:98.

[31] Directive 91/157 on batteries [1991] OJ L78/38; Directive 91/157 was replaced, in 2006, by Directive 2006/66 on batteries and accumulators and waste batteries and waste accumulators [2006] OJ L266/1. This directive was based on Arts 114 and 192 TFEU. Directive 94/62 (n 25).

[32] This was the underlying situation in CJEU Case C-203/96 *Dusseldorp* ECLI:EU:C:199:316, though in particular German and Danish local authorities invested a lot in incineration installations.

[33] In addition to the Dutch situation which was described in Case C-203/96 (n 32), see the German situation underlying Case C-324/99 *Daimler-Chrysler* ECLI:EU:C:2001:682.

[34] On the EU product policy, see para 6-03 above.

and disposal of radioactive waste, the shipment of waste to third countries, the clean-up of contaminated land and old landfills, and provisions on liability and monitoring measures.

In 2015, the Commission adopted a circular action plan,[35] which it updated in 2020.[36] It started from the fact that only about 12 per cent of the raw material used by industry came from recycled waste materials.[37] 'Circular' meant that 'the value of products, materials and resources is maintained in the economy as long as possible and the generation of waste minimised'.[38] The 2020 plan also announced measures to prevent waste generation by promoting sustainable products, improving separate waste collection, increasing the recycling quota and reducing hazardous substances in products in order to facilitate recycling and create a well-functioning market for secondary raw materials.

II. Waste Installations

A. Siting

10-09 There are no EU provisions on the location of waste treatment or disposal installations. The Directive on industrial emissions,[39] which incorporated an earlier directive on the incineration of waste,[40] is silent on the question of siting. However, an earlier proposal for a directive on the landfill of waste stipulated that landfills had to be placed at a distance from residential areas, waterways, water bodies, etc of 0.5 km in the case of municipal landfills and 2 km from residential areas in the case of hazardous landfills.[41] The directive, adopted in 1999, deleted any precise minimum distance requirement and limited itself to requiring that the landfill should not pose a serious environmental risk.[42] Finally, no specific Union provisions exist for the location of installations for radioactive waste.

10-10 EU restrictions for the location of a waste installation flow from Article 4(4) of Directive 2009/147[43] and Article 6(2) of Directive 92/43,[44] where such installations could constitute a significant disturbance of habitats or of the species protected in them. Furthermore, a site may – at least de facto – not be chosen where the operation of the installation would, despite precautionary measures that are eventually taken, lead to a breach of the requirements of Article 13 of Directive 2008/98.[45] In extreme cases, the siting of an

[35] Commission, 'An EU Action Plan for a Circular Economy' COM(2015) 614.

[36] Commission, 'A New Economy Action Plan for a Cleaner and More Competitive Europe' COM(2020) 98.

[37] Commission, COM(2021) 708.

[38] Commission, COM(2015) 614 (n 35).

[39] Directive 2010/75 (n 26).

[40] Directive 2000/76 on the incineration of waste [2000] OJ L 332/91.

[41] [1997] OJ C156/19, annex I, para 1(1.1.a).

[42] Directive 1999/31 on landfills of waste [1999] OJ 182/1, annex I, para 1(1.1.a).

[43] Directive 2009/147 on the conservation of wild birds [2010] OJ L286/36.

[44] Directive 92/43 on the conservation of natural habitats and of wild fauna and flora [1992] OJ L206/7.

[45] Directive 2008/98 (n 1) Art 13: 'Member States shall take the necessary measures to ensure that waste management is carried out without endangering human health, without harming the environment and, in particular: (a) without risk to water, air, soil and plants and animals; (b) without causing a nuisance through noise or odours; and (c) without adversely affecting the countryside or places of special interest.'

installation may injure human rights,[46] which the EU institutions and national courts must also safeguard.

Before they are authorised, hazardous waste disposal installations must be the subject of an environmental impact assessment; the same requirement applies to incineration installations for the recovery or the disposal of non-hazardous waste that have a capacity of more than 100 tonnes per day.[47] For other waste installations, Member States must either examine case by case whether an environmental impact is necessary or fix thresholds beyond which such an assessment is necessary.[48]

B. The Choice of a Type of Waste Installation

The choice of the waste installation – landfill, composting plant, recycling plant, incineration plant with or without energy recovery – is at the complete discretion of Member States. It is true that Article 4 of Directive 2008/98 provides for a waste 'hierarchy'.[49] However, this hierarchy is, legally speaking, a recommendation ('encourage'); indeed, paragraph 2 of Article 4 asked Member States to consider, among others, the economic viability when deciding on a measure. The provision, seen in its general context, does not appear to oblige a Member State to close landfills and turn to recovery, recycling or waste prevention measures. This is a policy orientation, but it is unthinkable to bring the Member State in question to the CJEU for not respecting its obligations from Directive 2008/98, Article 4. Indeed, endless legal disputes could take place on the question of whether a Member State really has done enough as regards waste prevention. If waste prevention were a legal obligation, the Commission would be obliged, under Article 17 of the Treaty on European Union (TEU), to take legal action against Member States which did not do enough for waste prevention; the same would apply where a Member State favoured landfills over incineration of waste. In reality, such an action has never been taken or even considered by the Commission. 10-11

C. Permits

The permitting of waste treatment and disposal plants is, in general, subject to provisions of national legislations. For some[50] installations, Directive 2010/75[51] and its preceding directives have required a permit since 1999 to provide for the use of the best available 10-12

[46] See European Court of Human Rights, *Lopez Ostra v Spain*, judgment of 9 December 1994 (41/1993/436/515), where an installation had been built at a distance of 12 metres from a private home.

[47] Directive 2011/92 on environmental impact assessment [2012] OJ L26/1. CJEU Case C 486/04 *Commission v Italy* ECLI:EU:C:2006:732 clarified that an environmental impact assessment is also required for waste recovery installations of a specific size.

[48] As regards Directive 2011/92, see also para 4-33 above.

[49] Directive 2008/98 (n 1) Art 4.

[50] Essentially, installations for the recovery or disposal of hazardous waste with a capacity exceeding 10 tonnes per day, municipal waste incinerators with a capacity of more than three tonnes per hour, installations for disposal of non-hazardous waste (biological and chemical process) with a capacity of more than 50 tonnes per day, and landfills with a capacity of more than 25,000 tonnes or receiving more than 10 tonnes per day.

[51] Directive 96/61 [1996] OJ L257/26. See also para 4-45 above.

technique and the setting of specific conditions and, in particular, emission limit values for pollutants.[52]

While there are no specific provisions on facilities for the treatment, and in particular the incineration, of nuclear waste, specific requirements apply to (non-nuclear) waste incineration installations, which were laid down in Directive 2010/75.[53] The directive set emission limits for certain heavy metals and other pollutants, including dioxins and furans.[54] It also provided for detailed conditions on the operation of the incinerators, such as minimum temperature of the burner and measures for cases of operation disturbance.

10-13 Directive 2010/75 replaced earlier directives on the incineration of municipal waste because, from the point of view of the environment, it was considered irrelevant whether the dangerous emissions stemmed from one or another type of incinerator.

Directive 2010/75 does not apply to animal waste. Animal waste was regulated under Regulation 1069/2009,[55] as specific provisions had become necessary when the 'mad cow disease' (bovine spongiform encephalitis, BSE) broke out in the 1990s.[56] The regulation, based on the public health provision of the present Article 168(4) TFEU, laid down detailed provisions on the conditions under which animals and material that come under Regulation 1069/2009 may be incinerated. According to Directive 2008/98, products and by-products which come under Regulation 1069/2009 are treated as waste whether they are incinerated, co-incinerated, landfilled or go to a biogas or composting plant;[57] it follows from this that Directive 2010/75, which applies to waste incinerators,[58] and Directive 1999/31 on landfills[59] apply.

Installations that use waste as regular or additional fuel (waste co-incineration plants) – at present, in particular, power plants, cement kilns and steel plants – were regulated by the provisions of Directive 2010/75 on incinerators (Article 42ff). Where the main purpose of an installation was the thermal treatment of waste, the specific provisions of Directive 2010/75 apply, which differentiate between incineration and co-incineration plants.

D. Landfills

10-14 About one-third of all waste generated in the EU is landfilled.[60] The Commission submitted a proposal for a directive on landfills in 1991.[61] In 1996, the European Parliament

[52] Directive 96/61 became applicable to existing installations from 2007 onwards. See also para 4-45 above.

[53] Directive 2010/75 (n 26).

[54] For more detail, see para 8-30 et seq above.

[55] Regulation 1069/2009 laying down health rules as regards animal by-products and derived products not intended for human consumption [2009] OJ L300/1; this regulation replaced Regulation 1774/2002 [2002] OJ L273/1. See also para 10-55 below.

[56] Until then, the applicable directive was Directive 90/667 laying down the veterinary rules for the disposal of animal waste, for its placing on the market and for the prevention of pathogens in feedstuffs of animal or fish origin [1990] OJ L363/51.

[57] Directive 2008/98 (n 1) Art 2(2)(b).

[58] Directive 2010/75 (n 26).

[59] Directive 1999/31 (n 42).

[60] Commission, 'Eurostat, Waste Statistics' ec.europa.eu/eurostat/statistiques-explained, index.php?title=waste. statistices.

[61] [1991] OJ C190/1.

rejected the Council's common position on the proposal[62] with the argument that it contained too many derogations. The Commission then submitted a new proposal, which the Council adopted in 1999.[63] Directive 1999/31 had the same field of application as Directive 2008/98; thus, in law, it also applied to radioactive waste landfills, for which no specific EU provisions exist at present; in practice, though, Directive 1999/31 is ignored with regard to radioactive waste landfills. For high-level radioactive waste and spent fuels which are to be disposed of, no disposal facility exists at present in the EU.[64]

> Finland and France are the only Member States where the disposal capacities will be available for the [high-level and spent fuels] waste which is going to arise in the next two decades. Germany will only cover the needs for disposal from 2040, and Sweden from 2070. The disposal capacities are insufficient to cover the radioactive waste in the coming decades in the rest of the Member States with present or past programmes of nuclear power generation.[65]

Directive 1999/31 applies to all authorised or non-authorised landfills that are in operation; where existing landfills did not comply with its requirements, they had to be adapted by 2009 at the latest or be closed. In principle, any storage of waste on land or into land – thus also underground – is considered a landfill. However, temporary storage prior to disposal operations that does not exceed one year, or three years prior to treatment operations, was excluded from the definition of landfill. The directive introduced three classes of landfills: for hazardous waste, for non-hazardous waste and for inert waste. It laid down detailed provisions for the permitting of landfills and the conditions accompanying a permit, and in particular for water control and leachate management, the protection of soil and water, gas control, stability and barriers to free access, the necessity of a treatment of waste before landfilling and the closure of landfills. The criteria and procedures for the acceptance of waste at landfills were laid down in 2002.[66]

An amendment of Directive 1999/31[67] clarified that it was the Union's objective to reduce, and possibly even stop, the landfilling of waste (Article 1). Also, Member States should 'endeavour' to stop the landfilling of recoverable[68] waste in principle by 2030, and only 10 per cent of the municipal waste generated was to be landfilled in 2035; the original version of the directive had fixed this level at 55 per cent. A Commission amendment proposal of 2022 suggested providing for the establishment of 'best available technique' documents for landfills, according to the model of Directive 2010/75.[69]

Neither Directive 2008/98 nor Directive 1999/31 dealt in detail with unauthorised landfills. The CJEU clarified in a number of judgments that Member States not only had the obligation, from Article 36 of Directive 2008/98, to prohibit unauthorised landfilling,[70]

[62] [1996] OJ C59/1.
[63] Directive 1999/31 (n 42).
[64] Commission, 'Seventh Situation Report. Radioactive Waste and Spent Fuels Management in the EU' SEC(2011) 1007, 9.
[65] ibid 22.
[66] Decision 2003/33 [2003] OJ L11/27.
[67] Directive 2018/850 [2018] OJ L150/100.
[68] Recoverable waste includes recyclable waste and waste that is incinerated with energy recovery.
[69] Commission, COM(2022) 156.
[70] Directive 2008/98 (n 1) Art 36: 'Member States shall take the necessary measures to prohibit the abandonment, dumping or uncontrolled management of waste.'

but they also must clean up unauthorised landfills.[71] This raises the important question of differentiating between such clean-up operations and the cleaning of contaminated sites which are not covered by EU law. As EU law prohibited the unauthorised dumping of waste in 1977, when Directive 75/442[72] became applicable, it must be concluded that the legal clean-up obligation under EU waste law has existed since that time; for Member States which joined the EU after 1977, the borderline date was that of their accession to the EU. Contaminated sites, then, are sites which already existed in 1977 or at the moment of the accession. No publicly accessible inventory exists for them.

E. Decommissioning of Installations

10-15 There are no specific EU provisions on the decommissioning of waste installations or, indeed, other industrial installations, such as nuclear power plants. The demolition of buildings, structures or installations leads to the generation of (movable) waste, for which the general provisions apply. Where such installations contain asbestos, Article 7 of Directive 87/217[73] applies, which requires that the release of asbestos fibres does not cause 'significant asbestos pollution' – whatever that means. For the rest, the general provision of Article 13 of Directive 2008/98[74] also applies to decommissioning of installations.

The decommissioning of offshore oil platforms was the subject of a decision under the OSPAR Convention, taken in 1998,[75] which provided for a prohibition of putting such installations into the sea or maintaining them there after use; the decision allowed contracting parties to grant a derogation under certain conditions. The Commission proposed that the Union approve this decision.[76] However, the proposal was not discussed in detail by the Council and has since become obsolete.

There are no EU-wide rules on the decommissioning of nuclear installations. The Commission estimated the costs for decommissioning of about 15 per cent of the investment cost for the installation.[77] The EU structural funds do not co-finance the decommissioning of nuclear installations,[78] though the Union might still have some financial obligations in this regard which flow from the accession Treaties.

F. Contaminated Land

10-16 Directive 1999/31 on landfills does not deal with issues of contaminated land, such as closed landfills, unauthorised discharges or abandoned military or industrial sites. No EU

[71] CJEU Case C-196/13 *Commission v Italy* ECLI:EU:C:2014:2407; Case C-378/13 *Commission v Greece* ECLI:EU:C:2013:2405; see also Case C-137/07 *Commission v Italy* ECLI:EU:C:2007:250.

[72] Directive 75/442 (n 12).

[73] Directive 87/217 on the prevention and reduction of environmental pollution by asbestos [1987] OJ L85/40.

[74] See Directive 2008/98 (n 1) Art 13.

[75] OSPAR Decision 98/3 on the disposal of disused offshore installations [1998] OJ C158/11. As regards OSPAR in general, see para 7-35 above.

[76] [1999] OJ C158/10.

[77] Commission, 'Nuclear Safety in the European Union' COM(2002) 605, 3.

[78] Regulation 2021/1058 on the European Regional Development Fund and the Cohesion Fund [2021] OJ L231/60, Art 7.

inventory of such contaminated land sites exists,[79] but the majority of Member States set up national inventories,[80] though with different criteria. Thus, in Germany, the number of suspected contaminated sites registered is about 190,000; this figure does not include military sites or sites for the production of armaments. The total number is thought to be well over 240,000. Austria has a list of 2584, Finland has 10,400 contaminated sites, while France sometimes had quoted a figure of about 1000 contaminated sites.[81] The Commission estimated in 2021 that there were 2.8 million contaminated sites in the Union, of which 390,000 needed remediation and, as of 2018, only 65,500 sites had actually been remediated.[82] No official work is done at EU level concerning the identification of sites, classification, prioritisation and so on. However, in the context of its research policy, the Commission set up a 'concerted action on risk assessment for contaminated sites' (CARACAS) in 1996, and two other similar networks, NICOLE (1996) and CLARINET (1998).

In its proposal for a directive establishing a framework for the protection of soil of 2006, the Commission suggested the elaboration of an EU inventory of contaminated sites[83] and estimated that about 3.5 million sites in the Union were potentially contaminated. The proposal was rejected by a blocking minority in the Council;[84] in 2014, the Commission withdrew it. The cleaning up of contaminated sites thus remains the responsibility of Member States.

G. Port Reception Facilities

In 2000, the Union adopted a Directive on port reception facilities for ship-generated 10-17
waste and cargo residues.[85] Mainly because of the lack of adequate port facilities in parts of the Union, insufficient enforcement and a lack of incentives to hand over the waste to a reception facility,[86] the directive was replaced, in 2019, by Directive 2019/883, which was based on Article 100(2) TFEU.[87] EU Member States were required to ensure that there were 'adequate' facilities in ports for the reception of waste from ships, including from fisheries and recreational vessels; for that purpose, each port was obliged to establish a waste reception and management plan. All ships that use a port of a Member State shall deliver all ship-generated waste to a port reception facility. In order to avoid the waste being discharged at sea, the directive provided that ships have to pay an indirect fee for the port reception facilities, irrespective of the actual use of the facilities (Article 8).

[79] See also para 10-14 above.

[80] European Environment Agency, 'Progress in Management of Contaminated Sites (CSI015/CSI003) – Assessment Published in May 2014' (Copenhagen, 2014). According to that report, only Poland, Slovenia, Portugal and the UK had no inventory. In Belgium, Germany, Italy, Greece and Sweden, the inventories existed at regional level.

[81] See, eg *Le Monde*, 7 April 1998, 10: 'Le gouvernement relance l'inventaire des sites pollués … la France compte officiellement 896 lieux contaminés. En réalité, il en existe 200,000 à 300,000, de nature et d'impact différents.'

[82] Commission, 'Pathway to a Healthy Planet for All. EU Action Plan "Towards Zero Pollution for Air, Water and Soil"' COM(2021) 400, s 2.3. The figures might refer to some 39 countries, rather than to EU-27.

[83] Commission, COM(2006) 232.

[84] See para 5-05 et seq above.

[85] Directive 2000/59 on port reception facilities for ship-generated waste and cargo residues [2000] OJ L332/81.

[86] See Commission, 'Evaluation of Directive 2000/59' COM(2016) 168, s 3; Commission, 'Impact Assessment' SWD(2019) 21.

[87] Directive 2019/883 on port reception facilities for the delivery of waste from ships [2019] OJ L151/116.

III. Waste Materials

A. Framework Provisions

10-18 Eurostat, the Statistical Office of the EU, publishes data on waste generation and treatment on the basis of Regulation 2150/2002 on waste statistics.[88] According to these data, which are based on information from Member States, the Union generated, in 2020, 2153 million tonnes of waste. Construction and demolition waste made up 37.5 per cent of all wastes, mining and quarrying 23.4 per cent, waste water 10.8 per cent, manufacturing 10.7 per cent, household 9.4 per cent, services 4.4 per cent, energy 2.3 per cent and agriculture 1.0 per cent. Of the waste, 95.5 million tons was hazardous.[89]

Municipal waste – that is, waste which is collected by or for municipalities and treated or disposed by them – increased between 1995 and 2021 from 467 kg per capita to 530 kg per capita, with Austria (834 kg), Luxembourg (793 kg) and Denmark (786 kg) ranking top. The changes in treatment of municipal waste between 1995 and 2021 is presented in Table 10.1.

Table 10.1 Treatment of municipal waste between 1995 and 2021 (in million tons)

	1995	**2021**	**Increase/decrease (%)**
Landfill	121	54	−56
Incineration	30	62	+107
Material recycling	23	70	+213
Composting	14	45	+218
Other	10	5	−50

Source: Commission, 'Eurostat, Municipal Waste Statistics' ec.europa.eu/eurostat/statistics-explained/index.php?title=Municipal_waste_statistics.

As regards radioactive waste, the Commission generally differentiates between very low-, low-, medium- and high-level waste.[90] About 3,466,000 m^3 of radioactive waste was thought to exist within the Union (EU-28) in 2007, out of which 6000 m^3 was high-level waste.[91] Considerable quantities of radioactive waste, including all high-level waste and spent fuels for disposal, are placed in what is called 'interim storage', sometimes for years or decades, as no final disposal facility site for high-level radioactive waste has yet been established within the Union.

10-19 The basic legal instrument for waste materials is Directive 2008/98, which constituted a fundamental review of Directive 75/442, its review in 1991 and its codification in 2006.

[88] Regulation 2150/2002 on waste statistics [2002] OJ L332/1.

[89] Commission, 'Eurostat, Waste Statistics' (n 60).

[90] Low, medium and high refer to the concentration of radionuclides in the radioactive waste and hence to the intensity of the emitted radiation.

[91] Commission, 'Inventory of Radioactive Waste and Spent Fuels in the Community's Territory and the Future Prospects' SWD(2019) 435. The report is based on national data and reports. It is silent on exports of radioactive waste and also does not clarify that spent fuels are treated by some Member States as 'products', by other Member States as waste.

Directive 2008/98 is the framework instrument for waste legislation at Union level.[92] The directive defined waste; established a hierarchy for waste management (prevention – recycling–recovery – safe disposal) and basic requirements for all waste management activities; introduced a licensing requirement for all persons who are active in waste treatment, disposal and management operations; and requested that Member States draw up waste management and waste prevention plans and regularly report on the directive's transposition and implementation.

Unlike its predecessor Directive 75/442, Directive 2008/98, which was based on Article 192 TFEU, did not aim to obtain an alignment of waste management policies and provisions within the Union. Member States were keen to maintain their different national approaches to waste management, however successful these were. 10-20

Waste management policy within the Union – at EU level and within Member States – was, and still is, heavily influenced by the attempts, in particular from economic operators, to deregulate waste policy and submit waste production, treatment, trade and disposal to a minimum of rules only. In part, this goes hand in hand with efforts from administrations not to introduce an EU-wide waste management system, but to leave it to Member States – or regions or local authorities – to decide to what extent they want to allow wastes to be traded, treated and disposed of. These policy- and/or interest-driven concepts appear mainly in the discussions on the definition of waste on the one hand, and on the treatment of waste, the export–import restrictions and the shipment of waste on the other hand.[93]

The definition of waste, as laid down in Directive 2008/98, has been, and continues to be, used in numerous other EU waste acts. Directive 2006/12, Article 1 had requested the Commission to draw up 'a list of wastes belonging to the categories listed in annex I'. This list had been established in 1994.[94] In 2000, it was completely revised and merged with the EU list on hazardous waste which had been drawn up under Directive 91/689 and updated in 2014.[95] Article 7 of Directive 2008/98 referred to that list, though it conceded large discretion to Member States, such as the possibility to consider some hazardous wastes as non-hazardous, or to consider that materials which were on that list were in fact not waste. At present, the list contains some 650 entries. 10-21

The field of application of Directive 2008/98 is very broad, though the following exclusions are foreseen:[96] 10-22

- gaseous effluents emitted into the atmosphere; such emissions are excluded, obviously for the reason that air pollution provisions would apply;
- land (in situ), including unexcavated contaminated soil and buildings permanently connected with land;[97]
- uncontaminated soil and other material excavated in the course of construction activities;

[92] Directive 2008/98 on waste (n 1).
[93] For this last point, see para 10-36 et seq below.
[94] Commission Decision 94/3 [1994] OJ L5/15.
[95] Commission Decision 2000/532 [2000] OJ L226/3; Commission Decision 2014/955 [2014] OJ L370/44.
[96] For details, see Directive 2008/98 (n 1) Art 2.
[97] With this exclusion, a judgment in the CJEU Case C-1/03 *Van de Walle* ECLI:EU:C:2004:490 was reversed which had declared that the definition of waste also included unexcavated contaminated soil, as well as parts of buildings that were connected with land.

- radioactive waste;[98]
- decommissioned explosives;[99] and
- faecal matter and non-hazardous agricultural or forestry materials used in farming, forestry or the production of energy through non-dangerous processes.

The large exclusion of agricultural and forestry waste can only be explained by successful lobbying from those sectors. In particular, it is not clear why faecal matter should not be considered 'waste'. Should these forms of waste be seen as products?[100] As with nuclear waste, the exclusion is not rational, but is the outcome of the EU bargaining process.

Furthermore, some waste materials were excluded 'to the extent that they are covered by other Community legislation'.[101] This wording solved a problem of the previous Directive 2006/12, where the word 'Community' was lacking. The CJEU had then decided that 'other legislation' could also apply to national legislation.[102] The new wording made this interpretation impossible.

10-23 It is obvious that the definition of waste is a legal creation and is therefore open to criticism; like any definition, it contains an arbitrary element. Whether a corporal object is called a good, product, substance, residue, pollutant, discharge (of pollutants), emission or waste is a question of legal agreement. From the point of view of environmental protection, the name which is given to a specific object is not very relevant; what matters is the contamination or pollution which that object causes or risks causing.

The criticisms against the – unanimously agreed – definition of waste stem in particular from concepts that look at the difference between product and waste from an economic perspective. Under this concept, 'waste' should not be applied to objects that have an economic value and could thus be recycled or recovered; to such materials, product legislation should apply in full. It is no surprise that such concepts are in particular defended by economic vested interest groups. The main weakness of this concept is that every object has an economic value somewhere in the world.[103] If one were to follow this argument, there would be no waste from precious metals, from steel, copper, iron, etc as all these materials have an economic value and can be recycled or reused. The contradiction goes even further, as the incineration of material is generally, and rightly so, considered to be a recovery operation, where the energetic part of the material is used for heating purposes, to generate energy, etc. As such incineration with energy recovery gives economic advantages – the use of ordinary fuel is not necessary – all materials that burn and generate heat[104] would have to be considered 'products' and not 'wastes'.

[98] On radioactive waste, see Directive 2011/70/Euratom establishing a Community framework for the responsible and safe management of spent fuels and radioactive waste [2011] OJ L199/48; para 10-30 below. The main difference to general waste legislation currently is that nuclear waste which is recoverable or recyclable is not classified as 'waste', but as 'product'.

[99] Why decommissioned explosives are excluded from the scope of the directive is not clear. No explanation is offered in the recitals.

[100] See also CJEU Case C-416/02 *Vera pig farm* ECLI:EU:C:2005:511.

[101] For details, see Directive 2008/98 (n 1) Art 2(2).

[102] CJEU Case C-114/01 *Avesta Polarit Chrome Oy* ECLI:EU:C:2003:448.

[103] The notion 'economic value' cannot be limited to national frontiers, as economic questions per se are independent of administrative–political considerations and notions: international trade may take place in objects which have no value for one person but a high value for another. For example, in South Asia even parts of plastic bags are collected from landfills and sold.

[104] Technically, the generation of heat is feasible with a calorific value of 5000–6000 kjoule.

Whether such a definition of 'waste' could be viable is irrelevant. In any case, it is not the definition of EU legislation, and in particular not that of Directive 2008/98. Legally, there can be no doubt that the EU concept of waste also includes recoverable or recyclable material. The enumeration of recovery operations in annex II to Directive 2008/98 on waste – not on products! – would make no sense if material that is destined for a recovery operation were not covered by that directive.

In 1986, Germany had adopted legislation that declared, in essence, that recoverable items were not waste but secondary raw materials. It was only after the CJEU stated, nine years later, that this provision was incompatible with EU law[105] that Germany changed its legislation; the Court expressly found that the definition of waste under Directive 91/156[106] – which corresponds to the present definition of Directive 2008/98 – would not allow the exclusion of recoverable waste from the waste definition. A similar provision to the German one was then introduced by Italy in 1996, and this elicited the same verdict from the CJEU.[107]

Since the discussion on whether recoverable material should be classified as waste or 10-24
as products is not really promising, discussions subsequently concentrated on the concept of 'discard', which is not defined in EU law. All products become waste, which normally occurs at the end of their useful lifetime. This question has nothing to do with the economic value that the item ultimately retains: where a new television set is, after two months' use, thrown away or dumped on the street, it is considered discarded, even if a passerby takes the television and uses it for several years. Horse manure might be an excellent fertiliser for the garden: it remains true, however, that where it is left on the road, it constitutes a real production residue – waste.

Since recovery (recycling) is considered a waste management activity, it is logical that an item can be discarded even where it is collected or transported with a view to being recycled or recovered. This is, *de lege lata* and *de lege ferenda*, heavily argued about, in particular where residues of production are at stake.[108] Admittedly, the borderline between residues of production, which the Union considers waste and the generation of two products, is not always easy to make. Thus, where steel is cut to make the body of a car, gold is worked on to make a golden ring or wood is cut, the residues – steel scrap, gold dust and wood chips – are discarded and thus constitute waste. However, where chemical substances are processed to produce two chemical preparations, one of these cannot be considered the residue of the other; normally, they are both products. As with all borderline cases, the final decision is to be made on a case-by-case basis.

In the end, the CJEU will be the final arbiter, and it has started, in a number of judgments, to act as such.[109] However, it does not yet seem to have found the right balance

[105] CJEU Case C-422/92 *Commission v Germany* ECLI:EU:C:1995:125.

[106] Directive 91/156 (n 12).

[107] CJEU Case C-304/94 *Tombesi* ECLI:EU:C:1997:314. See also Case C-457/02 *Niselli* ECLI:EU:C:2004.707; Case C-113/07 *Commission v Italy* ECLI:EU:C:2004:116.

[108] A good example is the Resolution on (steel) scrap, adopted by the Consultative Committee of CECA on 10 October 1997 [1997] OJ C356/8.

[109] CJEU Joined Cases C-206/88 and C-207/88 *Vessoso and Zanetti* ECLI:EU:C:145; Case C-422/92 (n 105); Case C-304/94 (n 107); Case C-129/96 *Inter-Environnement Wallonie* ECLI:EU:C:1997628; Case C-192/96 *Beside* ECL:EU:C:1998:315; Case C-203/96 (n 32).

in all cases. Thus, in Case C-416/02 it stated that pig manure, which can be spread onto farmland, was not waste, but a product.[110] This contradicts the Court's earlier judgments, according to which a subsequent use of a material cannot be decisive for the question of whether it must be classified as product or as waste. Transferring this to industrial production, it means that production residues which *can* be used in another production process constitute products.

10-25 Directive 2008/98 tried to answer these questions politically, by introducing the concept of 'by-product' into EU waste legislation. Article 5(1) reads as follows:

> Member States shall take the appropriate measures to ensure that a substance or object resulting from a production process the primary aim of which is not the production of that substance or object is considered not to be waste but to be a by-product if the following conditions are met: a) further use of that substance or object is certain b) the substance or object can be used directly without any further processing other than normal industrial practice c) the substance or object is produced as an integral part of the production process; and d) further use is lawful, ie the substance or the object fulfils all relevant product, environment and health protection requirements for the respective use and will not lead to overall adverse environmental or human health impacts.

Decisions on whether these conditions are fulfilled will be taken by the comitology procedure at Union level (Article 5(2)).[111]

In my opinion, this provision will lead to the consequence that precious metal residues, metal residues in general and numerous other production residues will, in time, not be considered waste any more but by-products, to which product legislation applies. The 'normal industrial practice', which is not further specified, will lead to more pressure from economic operators to have production residues excluded from waste legislation. The notion of 'overall adverse impacts' is not really a limitation to the decision-making under this provision. And the (welcome) political side-effect is that the amount of waste will decrease.

10-26 Directive 2008/98 introduced another way of limiting the application of waste law. Article 6(1) of that directive reads:

> Member States shall take the appropriate measures to ensure that a substance or object which has undergone a recycling or other recovery operation is considered to have ceased to be waste if it complies with the following conditions: a) the substance or object is to be used for specific purposes; b) a market or demand exists for such substance or object; c) the substance or object fulfils the technical requirement for the specific purposes and meets the existing legislation and standards applicable to products; and d) the use of the substance or object will not lead to overall adverse environmental or human health exposure.

Decisions under this provision are again taken by the comitology procedure at Union level. However, in the absence of such decisions, Member States may take decisions at national level; they then have to notify the Commission and other Member States of their draft decision under Directive 2015/1535.[112]

[110] CJEU Case C-416/02 (n 100).

[111] See also CJEU Case C-113/12 *Brady* ECLI:EU:C:2013:627; Case C-212/18 *Prato Nevoso* ECLI:EU:C:2019.898: Case C-629/19 *Sappi* ECLI:EU:C:2020:824; Case C-238/21 *Porr Bau* ECLI:EU:C:022:885.

[112] Directive 2015/1535 [2015] OJ L241/1.

The Commission adopted provisions on the question when scrap metal,[113] copper scrap[114] and glass cullets[115] ceased to be waste. It failed to adopt provisions when recovered paper ceased to be waste.[116] The reason was, in simplified terms, that the Commission wished to see waste paper lose its status as waste when it was, according to CEN standard EN 643, sorted into different categories according to its humidity, contamination, quality, etc. The European Parliament, though, objected to that proposal, as it considered that the sorting of waste did not yet end its waste characteristics.

The differentiation is particularly relevant in the shipment and export of such materials, as the shipment of products is largely unregulated, whereas strict provisions apply to the shipment of waste. Hitherto, a material was classified as waste until the recycling or recovery process had finished – thus, for example, the sorted used paper had been transformed into new paper, so that the transport of used paper was classified as the transport of waste. The Commission proposal, influenced by strong lobbying from vested interests, tried to change this borderline.

Directive 2008/98 introduced the concept of extended producer responsibility (Article 8) 10-27
and repeated the polluter-pays principle (Article 14). The concept of extended producer responsibility, originally developed by Scandinavian countries, is based on the understanding that the responsibility of the producer does not end with the manufacturing of the product. When the product is on the market, the producer has labelling, information guarantee, warning and eventually take-back obligations. And when the product ends its useful lifetime and becomes waste, the producer has responsibilities as to the collection and treatment of this waste, having also had the profit from it. With this reasoning, producers and their associations (including importers) can be made responsible for organising and financing take-back systems, collect waste from consumers and users, and ensure that such waste is properly recycled, recovered and/or disposed of.

EU law already provided for such concepts in Directive 2000/53 on end-of-life vehicles[117] and Directive 2012/19 on waste from electrical and electronic products.[118] Directive 2008/98 only gave a framework to the concept, leaving it to Member States to decide to what extent they wanted to recur to it.

As regards the polluter-pays principle, Directive 2008/98, repeating the previously applicable EU law, imposed the application of this principle in national waste legislation. This has far-reaching consequences for national legislation. Thus, the CJEU held that a petroleum company could be held liable for damage caused by petrol that had spread into the environment following a shipping accident, though the company had excluded all such liability by way of contracts with the shipowner.[119] In another case, the Court held that municipalities in the Member States were not entitled to charge the cost for collecting waste according to the size of the ground from which the waste was taken; rather, the actual quantities of waste which were collected had to form the basis of charging the cost.[120]

[113] Commission Regulation 333/2011 [2011] OJ L94/2.
[114] Commission Regulation 715/2013 [2013] OJ L201/14.
[115] Commission Regulation 1179/2012 [2012] OJ L337/31.
[116] See Commission, COM(2013) 502.
[117] Directive 2000/53 on end-of life vehicles [2000] OJ L269/34.
[118] Directive 2012/19 on waste electrical and electronic equipment (WEEE) [2012] OJ L192/38.
[119] CJEU Case C-188/07 *Commune de Mesquer* ECLI:EU:C:2008:359.
[120] CJEU Case C-254/08 *Futura* ECLI:EU:C:2009:479.

The main instrument of the directive was the waste management plan which Member States shall have to establish and regularly update (Article 28). The directive gave a number of indications as to the content of such plans. The plans must be sent to the Commission, which, however, does not have any obligation to assess, compare or otherwise evaluate them. This is consistent with past experience. Indeed, since 1977, Member States have been obliged to elaborate and monitor waste management plans and to inform the Commission thereof. However, the Commission has never made any evaluation of those plans or drawn attention to omissions, inconsistencies or failures. Directive 2008/98 now 'invites' the European Environment Agency to annually review progress in the completion and implementation of the national waste management plans (Article 30(2)). This is an elegant way of complying with Article 17 TEU and ensuring that EU law is applied by Member States!

Directive 2008/98 provided that municipal waste should be recycled or prepared for reuse[121] by 50 per cent by weight in 2020, 60 per cent in 2030 and 65 per cent in 2035; the recycling or preparedness for reuse of construction and demolition waste had to reach 70 per cent by 2020. At least 50 per cent of weight of paper, metal, plastic and glass were to be recycled or prepared for reuse by 2020, and of textiles by 2025 (Article 11). These percentages are difficult to control, and it is not surprising that the Commission was silent as to the results in 2020; in 2017, it reported that the majority of Member States had already reached the 2020 targets by 2012,[122] but in 2022, it informed that Poland, Spain, Slovakia, Romania, Portugal, Malta, Latvia, Hungary, Greece, Finland, Estonia, Cyprus, Bulgaria and Croatia were at risk of missing the 2020 target.[123] Overall, the use of recycled material in the Union was only 12 per cent, while 16 per cent of generated waste was exported.[124]

B. Hazardous Waste

10-28 Council Directive 78/319 on toxic and dangerous waste[125] was substituted, in 1991, by Directive 91/689.[126] This directive defined hazardous waste, introduced a licensing requirement for installations which processed hazardous waste and requested management plans for hazardous waste to be drawn up and regular information on installations which handled hazardous waste. Directive 2008/98 repealed this directive and incorporated some provisions on hazardous waste into its own provisions.

As with the notion of 'waste', difficulties appeared as regards the concept of 'hazardous waste'. The 1978 directive gave a definition of dangerous waste[127] that was soon considered

[121] 'Prepared for re-use' is defined, in Art 3, no 16, as 'checking, cleaning or repairing recovery operations by which products or compoents of products that have become waste are prepared so that they can be re-used without any other pre-processing'.

[122] Commission, COM(2017) 88 3.

[123] Commission, COM(2022) 438, s 3.1.

[124] Commission, COM(2021) 708; Commission, COM(2022) 438. According to the Commission, the percentage of recycled material used was 1.3% in Romania and 30.9% in the Netherlands.

[125] Directive 78/319 (n 7).

[126] Directive 91/689 on hazardous waste [1991] OJ L377/20.

[127] Directive 78/319 (n 7) Art 1(b): '"toxic and dangerous waste" means any waste containing or contaminated by the substances or materials listed in the Annex to this directive of such a nature, in such quantities or in such concentrations as to constitute a risk to health or the environment'.

to be too vague. For that reason, it was replaced, in Directive 91/689,[128] by a 'listing approach': hazardous waste was listed in an EU list.[129] Directive 2008/98 changed this approach again and considered waste as 'hazardous' 'which display one or more of the hazardous properties listed in Annex III' (Article 3, no 2). This annex listed in general terms 15 hazard categories.[130] As regards the precise decision of whether (or which) one of the hazard categories applied to a specific waste, or the test methods to be used and the possible limit values, the annex to Directive 2008/98 referred to two EU directives on chemical substances and preparations,[131] without considering that these directives had, at the time of application, already been replaced by Regulation 1907/2006.[132] In order to somehow reach a uniform understanding of what constituted hazardous waste, Article 7 of Directive 2008/98 determined that the 'list of waste shall be binding as regards determination of the waste which is to be considered to be hazardous waste'.[133] Member States may, though, in specific cases consider a non-hazardous waste as hazardous, or a hazardous waste as non-hazardous; in both cases, they have to inform the Commission, so that the waste list may be updated.[134] They may also 'consider waste as non-hazardous waste in accordance with the list of waste referred to in paragraph 1 (of Article 7)'.[135] Thus, the principle has been maintained that a waste is hazardous when it is marked as hazardous in the EU list on waste.[136]

The main problems with the EU definition of hazardous waste are that it is not precise and 10-29
that Member States use different terminology in their national legislation, such as 'special waste', 'chemical waste' and 'specially controlled waste'. These different definitions make it possible to establish national waste lists that are different from the Union list. To complicate things further, the Basel Convention on the Shipment of Hazardous Waste and the

[128] Directive 91/689 (n 126); the word 'hazardous' was presumably preferred to 'dangerous', because the Basel Convention on the shipment of waste used this terminology; in substance, there is no difference between 'hazardous' and 'dangerous'.

[129] ibid Art 1(4): '"hazardous waste" means: wastes featuring on a list drawn up ... on the basis of Annexes I and II to this directive ... These wastes must have one or more of the properties listed in Annex III. The list shall take into account the origin and composition of the waste and, where necessary, limit values of concentration ... any other waste which is considered by a Member State to display any of the properties listed in Annex III. Such cases shall be notified to the Commission and reviewed ... with a view to adaptation of the list.'

[130] See, eg Directive 2008/98 (n 1): 'H 7: Carcinogenic: substances and preparations which, if they are inhaled or ingested, or if they penetrate the skin, may induce cancer or increase its incidence'; 'H8: Corrosive: substances and preparations which may destroy living tissue on contact'; 'H14: Ecotoxic: waste which presents or may present immediate or delayed risk for one or more sectors of the environment'.

[131] Directive 67/548 [1967] OJ 196/1; Directive 1999/45 [1999] OJ L200/1. It had already been mentioned in ch 6 that Directive 67/548 only provided for test methods on the effect of chemical substances on humans and the aquatic environment, but not on other parts of the environment, such as plants and animals.

[132] Regulation 1907/2006 [2006] OJ L396/1.

[133] As to the waste list, see Decision 2014/955 (n 95).

[134] See CJEU Case C-194/01 *Commission v Austria* ECLI:EU:C:2004:248, where the Court stated that Member States were not obliged to transpose the waste lists word by word into their national legal system. The consequence of that judgment is that the notions of waste and of hazardous waste will continue to vary from one Member State to another. While thus everybody between Stockholm and Madrid has the same notion of what a car is, there are differences with regard to waste.

[135] For details, see Directive 2008/98 (n 1) Art 7.

[136] See also Commission, COM(2018) 32, which identified four issues that made waste recycling difficult, due to the presence of substances of concern: (1) information on the presence of such substances is not available; (2) waste may contain substances which are no longer allowed to be used in new products; (3) the provisions on end-of waste are not coherent; and (4) some materials are differently classified as hazardous or non-hazardous in waste and in chemical legislation.

Organisation for Economic Cooperation and Development (OECD) have also established hazardous waste lists which are different from the EU list, a legal situation that generates difficulties, inconsistencies, grey markets and illegal practices.

Directive 2008/98 contained only a few provisions on hazardous waste. The general provision of Article 13 that waste shall be treated without harming human health or the environment also applied to hazardous waste. Article 18 stated that hazardous waste shall not be mixed with other hazardous or non-hazardous waste or materials and may not be diluted either. However, this provision did not apply to operators which have a licence, where the mixing or dilution corresponded to the best available technique or where the provisions of Article 13 were respected;[137] furthermore, the provision did not apply to hazardous household waste.

Provisions on the prevention of hazardous waste hardly exist, as this would require the taking of product-related measures. Also, few hazardous wastes are recycled, and only half of incinerated hazardous wastes are incinerated with energy recovery. About 46 per cent of hazardous waste is landfilled and attempts of illegally handling hazardous waste – by declaring waste electrical and electronic products and end-of-life vehicles as second-hand goods or by mixing hazardous with non-hazardous waste – are significant. Overall hazardous waste generation increased from 2004 to 2018 by 26 per cent (from 80.8 million to 101.7 million tons).[138]

10-30 In 2011, the EU adopted, for the first time, a directive on spent fuel and radioactive waste,[139] based on Articles 31 and 32 of the Euratom Treaty. Directive 2011/70/Euratom became applicable in 2013; the Commission had to start proceedings under Article 258 TFEU against Belgium, Germany, Spain, France, Cyprus, Italy, Croatia, Latvia, Lithuania, Austria, Poland, Romania and Sweden because these Member States had not transposed the directive into their national law in time.[140]

'Spent fuel' was considered either to be a usable resource or – when no further use was foreseen – a radioactive waste (Article 2.10 and Recital 20). This definition meant that recoverable radioactive waste is not considered to be waste, but a product.

The directive aimed at the protection of workers, the general public and future generations (Article 1); the environment, fauna and flora were not mentioned. The directive did not apply to authorised releases (Article 3), which meant that discharges of radioactive waste into waters would neither fall under Directive 2008/98 nor under Directive 2011/70. In substance, Directive 2011/70/Euratom essentially requested Member States to draw up and monitor management programmes for radioactive waste; it did not contain a fraction of the details which were laid down in Directive 1999/31 on landfills; and there was no word on whether radioactive waste may be disposed of in ordinary or hazardous waste landfills. The proposition in the proposal that Member States draw up a safety plan for radioactive waste was not retained in the directive.

Directive 2011/70/Euratom also did not contain any quality requirement as to the treatment or disposal of radioactive waste. In Recital 16, it mentioned the existence of

[137] See the wording of Directive 2008/98, Art 13 (n 45).

[138] On this assessment, see European Court of Auditors, *EU Actions to Address the Increasing Amount of Hazardous Waste* (Luxembourg, 2023).

[139] Directive 2011/70/Euratom (n 98).

[140] Written Question E001376/14 (Van Brempt) [2014] OJ C331/51; the CJEU found that only Italy lacked a national plan on radioactive waste, Case C-458/18 *Commission v Italy* ECLI:EU:C:2019:683.

international safety principles which were set up by the International Agency for Nuclear Energy. However, these principles were not laid down as such in the directive, nor were Member States requested to respect them.

In view of the very poor content of this directive, Recital 24 almost sounds cynical. It read:

> It should be an ethical obligation of each Member State to avoid any undue burden on future generations in respect of spent fuels and radioactive waste, including any radioactive waste expected from decommissioning of existing nuclear installations. Through the implementation of the Directive, Member States will have demonstrated that they have taken reasonable steps to ensure that that obligation is met.

C. Waste Prevention

Directive 2008/98 fixed the prevention of waste generation as the first priority for waste legislation and waste management (Article 4). The aim was 'breaking the link between economic growth and the environmental impacts associated with the generation of waste' (Article 29). It obliged Member States to set up waste prevention programmes (Article 29) and offered, in Article 9, a list of measures that could form part of such programmes. The programmes had to be regularly updated. 10-31

A closer look at the measures which were favoured by Article 9 and annex IV shows their vague and general, mainly promotional character.[141] Nowhere were Member States obliged to take binding measures to reduce waste generation. The basic error of the directive's provisions on waste prevention was that it does not recognise that in order to prevent waste generation, there must be a product policy, because before a material becomes waste, it is a product; a product policy which aims at the prevention of waste generation will have to address cleaner technologies and the ecodesign of products, and improve the eco-efficiency of production and consumption patterns.

However, before 2015, there was a basic decision by the Union not to pursue an active, integrated product policy and to limit itself, in the context of its product policy, to non-binding measures. Things started to change only with the first action plan on a circular economy,[142] and gained speed with the European Green Deal,[143] the (proposed!) measures on sustainable products and the second strategy on a circular economy.[144] The result of the past policy was that waste quantities have constantly risen in the Union, hand in hand with economic growth. No significant change in this evolution is yet visible.[145] Much will depend on the implementation of the letter and the spirit of the European Green Deal, and the subsequent proposed measures.

[141] Directive 2008/98 (n 1) Art 4 exclusively contained provisions which 'encourage', 'promote', 'reduce', etc. See also annex IV, no 1: 'The use of planning measures, or other economic instruments promoting the effective use of resources'; no 4: 'the promotion of eco-design'; no 9: 'the use of voluntary agreements, consumer/producer panels or sectoral negotiations, in order that the relevant businesses or industry sectors set their own waste prevention plans or objectives or correct wasteful products or packaging'; no 13: 'the promotion of creditable eco-labels'.

[142] Commission, COM(2015) 614.

[143] Commission, COM(2019) 640.

[144] Commission, COM(2020) 98.

[145] See para 10-18 above.

D. Waste Recovery

10-32 Waste recovery includes reuse, material recycling and incineration with energy recovery. Directive 2008/98 defined reuse as 'an operation by which products or components that are not waste are used again for the same purpose for which they were conceived'.[146] However, a material may also be reused where it had been discarded: for example, if a piece of furniture has been placed on the roadside to be taken away by the waste collection services but is taken instead by a person, its continued use constitutes a recovery operation. However, where an object is reused without having been discarded – a friend, visiting a home, discovers a pair of shoes in a corner which are disused, takes them and wears them – the object has never become waste, so no waste recovery operation is involved. The repair of a dress or the reuse of packaging, such as empty bottles, normally comes into the second category, so the classification of reusable packaging as products by Directive 94/62[147] is correct.[148]

In 2005, the Commission presented a thematic strategy for the recycling of waste.[149] The Commission suggested creating a 'European Recycling Society', but did not propose any concrete measures. The suggestion has since disappeared.

Directive 2008/98 enumerated a non-exhaustive list of recovery operations in annex II. It suggested practical measures to be taken by Member States in order to promote reuse, recycling and recovery. Where necessary, waste should be collected separately (Article 10). With regard to paper, metal, glass and plastic from households and equivalent waste streams, the directive prescribed separate collection; a recycling target of 50 per cent by weight was to be reached by 2020. For non-hazardous construction and demolition waste, the recycling target to be reached by 2020 was 70 per cent (Article 11). Details for the calculation methods were elaborated by the Commission.[150] The relationship with the separate collection requirement of packaging under Directive 94/62 is unclear, as it does not make sense to provide, for example, for separate collections of paper from packaging waste and of paper from other origins.

10-33 In the past, the greatest discussions have been provoked by the classification as a recovery operation of waste that is 'use[d] principally as a fuel or other means to generate energy'. Indeed, several Member States had established in their national legislation calorific values below which a waste could not be considered to come under this process. While it might be necessary to specify under what circumstances a waste principally serves as a fuel, it was obviously not legal to set these conditions at national level.

In a judgment of 2003, the CJEU clearly rejected, under Directive 2006/12, the possibility of using the calorific value of waste as a criterion for differentiating between recovery (recycling) and disposal operations.[151] The Court also clarified that the shipment of municipal waste to a waste incinerator could not *normally* – whatever that means – be regarded as a

[146] Directive 2008/98 (n 1) Art 3, no 10.

[147] See Directive 94/62 on packaging and packaging waste (n 25) Art 1(5)–(9), where reusable packaging is not considered to be waste.

[148] For the notion of reuse, see also CJEU Joined Cases C-307/00 to C-311/00 *Oliehandel* ECLI:EU:C:2003:108.

[149] Commission, 'Thematic Strategy on the Prevention and Recycling of Waste' COM(2005) 666.

[150] Commission Decision 2011/753 [2011] OJ L310/11.

[151] CJEU Case C-228/00 *Commission v Germany* ECLI:EU:C:2003:91.

shipment for recovery, even if the incinerator uses the energy from the incineration in part or in full.[152] The Court was of the opinion that in such a case, the waste was not substituting a fuel; rather, the objective of the incineration was the thermal treatment of waste, and not the making of products or the production of energy. These judgments played a considerable part in the discussion on the review of the Waste Framework Directive (see paragraph 10-06 above), as there were strong forces which would like to see all waste incinerators which burn waste and use the energy to be classified as recovery installations; this would facilitate waste shipments and increase the profitability of such incinerators. Environmental groups, in contrast, pleaded for such installations to be classified as disposal installations, as they prefer the composting, recycling and reuse of materials. Directive 2008/98 remained silent on incineration. In the follow-up of the European Green Deal and the turning to a circular economy, some Union texts declared waste incineration – in soft wording, it is true – to be harmful to the environment.[153] In any case, the incineration of waste has increased considerably since 1995.[154]

To date, the Union has not fixed provisions on the quality of recycling: where 10 kg of materials out of 1000 tonnes of waste are extracted and recycled, it is obviously not possible to consider the whole process – shipment, storage, extraction – to be a recycling operation. EU specifications are urgently required.

Since Directive 2008/98 was based on Article 192 TFEU, Member States are entitled, under Article 193, to identify recovery operations other than those listed in annex II. They are then obliged to notify the Commission. This leads to a decision by way of a committee procedure under Directive 2008/98 to adapt annex II to the new situation (Article 38).

E. Disposal of Waste

Directive 2008/98 limited itself to the statement that waste should be disposed of without harming human health or the environment; at the same time, it prohibited the abandonment or dumping of waste (Article 36). It also contained, in annex I, a list of operations that were classified as disposal operations.[155] The legal status of this list is the same as the list in annex II for recovery operations, so the reader is referred to the remarks above, in paragraph 10-18. The specific disposal operations are not often contested. Germany considered the placing of waste into old mines and other underground cavities as recovery operations, since this disposal would prevent the cavities from caving in.[156] This interpretation contradicted several operations in annex IIA of Directive 75/442.[157] 10-34

[152] CJEU Case C-458/00 *Commission v Luxembourg* ECLI:EU:C:2004:94.

[153] See, eg Regulation 2020/852 on the establishment of a framework to facilitate sustainable investment [2020] OJ L158/19, Art 17: according to that provision, an economic activity shall be considered to significantly harm the environment where it leads to a significant increase in the incineration of waste.

[154] See para 10-18 above.

[155] It should be noted that Directive 75/442 originally also included recovery and recycling operations in the word 'disposal'. The differentiation between the two notions was introduced into EU law by Directive 91/156 in 1991.

[156] Between 1994 and 2001, 1.5–2 million tons of waste were placed in old mines in Germany.

[157] Directive 75/442 (n 12), annex IIA, D1: 'Tipping above or underground (eg landfill, etc)'; D3: 'Deep injection (eg injection of pumpable discards into wells, salt domes or naturally occurring repositories, etc)'; D12: 'Permanent storage (eg emplacement of containers in a mine, etc)'.

When the CJEU established some conditions under which underground storage of waste could be considered to be a recovery operation,[158] Germany introduced legislation to better delimitate underground disposal and recovery operations. Under Directive 2008/98, 'backfilling' – the filling in of caves, mines, etc with waste – is not classified as a recycling activity.[159]

10-35 At present, EU law contains only a few limitations on the landfill of waste. Directive 1999/31 on landfills[160] banned the landfilling of liquid waste, explosive, corrosive, oxidising or flammable waste, infectious hospital waste and of whole and shredded used tyres; furthermore, the landfilling of biodegradable municipal waste will have to be considerably reduced. Apart from that, Directive 2008/98 prohibited the uncontrolled management of waste. Thus, there is no ban on, for instance, shipping the waste into outer space, burying BSE-infected cattle or providing for seabed insertions of waste. There are also no restrictions in EU law as regards the incineration of waste; annex I classifies incineration on land or at sea as disposal operations.

F. Shipment of Waste

10-36 Directive 78/319[161] had laid down some general requirements on the shipment of waste. Subsequent to discussions which took place within the framework of the OECD and which also concerned the shipment of waste between the USA and the Union, the Commission proposed, in the early 1980s, an EU directive on the shipment of waste.[162] This proposal introduced into waste law, for the first time, a differentiation between shipments in the Union that crossed the frontier of a Member State and other shipments, a clear departure from the concept of the single EU market and of the common transport policy, as laid down in Articles 3(f), 70 and 94 EC Treaty in its version applicable at that time. The Council adopted the proposal in 1984;[163] it was amended in 1986 to cover the shipment of hazardous waste to third countries, too.[164]

10-37 The adoption of the 1989 Basel Convention on shipments of hazardous waste[165] followed a number of serious incidents concerning illegal shipments from industrialised to developing countries; this convention and OECD measures on waste shipments adopted in reaction to the convention led the Union completely to review its provisions and to adopt, in 1993, a regulation that was based on the present Article 192 TFEU and concerned all waste shipments.[166] An important amendment in 1997 largely stopped the export of

[158] CJEU Case C-6/00 *Abfall Service Austria* ECLI:EU:C:2002:121.

[159] See Directive 2008/98 (n 1) Art 11(5): 'end-of-waste material to be … backfilled, shall not be counted towards the attainment of the recycling targets'.

[160] Directive 1999/31 (n 42).

[161] Directive 78/319 (n, 7).

[162] [1983] OJ C53/3.

[163] Directive 84/631 on the supervision and control within the European Community of the transfrontier shipment of hazardous waste [1984] OJ L326/31.

[164] Directive 86/279 [1986] OJ L181/13.

[165] Basel Convention on the Control of Transboundary Movements of Hazardous Wastes and Their Disposal 1989; the EU adhered to the convention by Decision 93/98 [1993] OJ L39/1.

[166] Regulation 259/93 on the supervision and control of shipments within, into and out of the European Community [1993] OJ L30/1; amended (export ban) by Regulation 120/97 [1997] OJ L22/14.

hazardous waste to third countries. A major change of legislation took place in 2006, when Regulation 1013/2006 on the shipment of waste was adopted.[167]

In 2013, the EU adopted a regulation to promote the sound elimination of end-of-life ships.[168] The underlying problem of ships was that, at the end of their useful lifetime, they were sailed to South Asia and sold there in order to be dismantled in ship recycling facilities in Bangladesh, Pakistan, India and China. The dismantling and recycling conditions in these countries (though to a lesser extent in China) are, from the social and environmental perspectives, appalling. The dismantling takes place in open air, with little or no protection for workers and almost no care for the environment. 10-38

End-of-life ships are legally classified as waste, and as they normally contain hazardous liquids (oil) and frequently contain asbestos or other hazardous substances, they are considered hazardous waste, the export of which for disposal or recycling is prohibited under EU law. This prohibition is based on a corresponding provision of the Basel Convention to which the EU adhered. In order to bypass this legislation, ships are sailed to South Asia with cargo, ie as 'products', and the dismantling/recycling decision is only taken in South Asia.

Regulation 1257/2013, anticipating a rather soft international convention (Hong Kong Convention 2009) which has not yet entered into force, provides for a number of measures in order to stop the present form of ship recycling. Among other things, an inventory of recycling facilities was set up which listed facilities worldwide that complied with minimum social and environmental standards.[169] In order to bypass the provisions of Regulation 1013/2006, Regulation 1257/2013 declared that Regulation 1013/2006 did not apply to ships which came under Regulation 1257/2013 (Article 27). This is not in compliance with the obligations under the Basel Convention, which considered ships to be hazardous waste unless they were cleaned of all hazardous substances, and which prohibited the export of hazardous waste. This export ban finally entered into force in 2019 but, under the Vienna Convention on the Law of Treaties 1969, the EU was bound by the export ban, as it had already signed up to it in 1997.

(i) Waste Shipments to and from Third Countries

With regard to waste shipments, the first distinction to be made was between hazardous and non-hazardous waste. This Union distinction did not follow the lines of Directive 2008/98 and the lists on waste and on hazardous waste that had been adopted at EU level.[170] Rather, due to historical reasons, the Council decided to largely follow a listing system which had been developed by the OECD. Therefore, the question of whether a waste is hazardous or not is decided by the lists in the annexes to Regulation 1013/2006 (see Article 36 of that regulation). In this way, EU law in practice has a list of hazardous wastes[171] and another list for the shipment of hazardous waste, though this is no longer called 'hazardous waste list'; this is a model of non-transparency. 10-39

[167] Regulation 1013/2006 on shipments of waste [2006] OJ L190/1.

[168] Regulation 1257/2013 on ship recycling [2013] OJ L330/1.

[169] The Commission Implementing Decision 2022/691 establishing the European list of ship recycling facilities [2022] OJ L128/84. The list includes 46 facilites (26 in the Union), but no facility from South Asian countries.

[170] See para 10-28 above.

[171] Decision 2000/532 as amended by Commission Decision 2014/955 (n 95).

A second distinction is made by the regulation about whether the shipment is made for disposal or for recovery purposes; for this, the definitions in Directive 2008/98 do apply.[172]

10-40 Imports of waste for disposal of any kind into the Union are prohibited, with the exception of imports from countries that are parties to the Basel Convention or where specific import agreements have been made either by the Union or by Member States (Article 41). The import of waste for recovery is prohibited, but such waste may be imported from countries which apply the OECD decision on waste shipment and from other countries with which specific agreements have been made.[173]

10-41 The export of waste to third countries for disposal purposes is prohibited (Article 34). An exception is made for European Free Trade Area (EFTA) countries which are also parties to the Basel Convention. Exports for recovery of wastes which are not hazardous – these are now listed in annexes III and IIIA, though these annexes are currently empty – are subject to a complicated procedure (Article 37). The Commission had to ask each third country, for all types of non-hazardous waste, whether it was ready to accept such waste and, if so, what kind of control procedure it wished to see applied. As there are more than 180 countries which had to be addressed, and as some of these countries did not answer at all, gave incomplete answers or subsequently changed their position, the different provisions which are now adopted by the Commission have constantly to be changed and adapted.[174]

Difficulties were also caused by the Commission basing its proposal on the trade provision of Article 207 TFEU[175] and had proposing that those third countries that had indicated that they did not wish to receive waste should nevertheless be able to obtain it, though under the prior informed consent procedure; the Commission had argued that some of these countries 'may not be fully aware of the significance of their decision for those parts of their industrial sector which can use "green" list waste for transformation and further processing'.[176] This question is now regulated by Article 37(2) of Regulation 1013/2006: where a third country does not answer a request, it has to be informed of the intended shipment, which may then only proceed where a written agreement by the third country is given.

All exports of *hazardous* waste for disposal are prohibited, except to EFTA countries which are also party to the Basel Convention. Furthermore, the Union decided[177] that, as of 1998, all shipments of hazardous waste for recovery to third countries were also prohibited, with the exception of industrialised countries.[178]

As regards the waste that comes under this export ban, Regulation 1013/2006 established its own lists of wastes (annex V), even though the management of these lists and their daily use are bound to create permanent problems for export controls, customs officers, etc.

[172] See para 10-18 et seq above.

[173] For details, see Regulation 1013/2006 (n 167) Art 43ff.

[174] See Commission Regulation 1418/2007 [2007] OJ L316/6.

[175] In Case C-411/06 *Commission v European Parliament and Council* ECLI:EU:C:2009:518, the CJEU clarified that the present Art 192 and not the present Art 207 TFEU was the correct legal basis for Regulation 1013/2006 (n 167).

[176] Commission, COM(94) 678, para 11.

[177] Regulation 120/97 (n 166).

[178] Formally, the exception was made for countries which apply the OECD decision of 30 March 1993 on the shipment of waste for recovery.

(ii) Shipments between and within Member States

Non-hazardous wastes that are destined for recovery may freely circulate between Member States; their shipment need not be notified. Regulation 1013/2006 allowed a Member State to take the necessary measures to prevent movement of wastes that were not in accordance with its waste management plans,[179] a provision that has so far not been used frequently. 10-42

Shipments of waste for disposal were subject to the principles of proximity and self-sufficiency,[180] principles that normally only applied to waste disposal, not to waste recovery shipments. However, Directive 2008/98 added to this the recovery of municipal waste. This means in practice that municipalities could prohibit the shipment of municipal waste to other places where they wanted to handle (incinerate) such waste themselves,[181] a provision which had been favoured in particular by Germany, as German municipalities have large over-capacities.[182] Directive 2008/98 also allowed Member States to object to shipments for recovery which went to waste incinerators, 'where it is established that such shipments would result in national waste having to be disposed of or waste having to be treated in a way that is not consistent with their waste management plan'.[183] Member States may prohibit generally or partially, or object systematically to, waste shipments for disposal; furthermore, they may also object to individual shipments.[184]

Subject to the changes which Directive 2008/98 introduced, shipments of hazardous waste for recovery may not be objected to systematically. Rather, the grounds for objection are laid down in Article 12 of Regulation 1013/2006 and may also not be extended by a Member State that invokes its right, under Article 193 TFEU, to set more stringent requirements.[185] Again, the details of the intended shipment must be notified to the competent authorities, which may, in the case of dangerous waste, give tacit consent, but must agree in writing to the shipment of listed hazardous waste. 10-43

Overall, these provisions are rather sophisticated and bureaucratic; the number of possibilities for Member States to object to a shipment for recovery has even increased from five to 100 causes. The provisions must be understood as a reaction to several abuses of previous provisions, in particular those under Directive 84/631, but also reflect the will of Member States *not* to have an internal EU market for shipments of waste, as well as of some Member States (Germany, the Netherlands, Denmark) to allow local monopolies for

[179] Regulation 1013/2006 (n 167) Art 12(1)(k).

[180] On the distinction between shipments for disposal and shipments for recovery, see CJEU Case C 292/12 *Ragn-Sell* ECLI:EU:C:2013:820.

[181] Directive 2008/98 (n 1) Art 16: '1. Member States shall … establish an integrated and adequate network of waste disposal installations and of installations for the recovery of mixed municipal waste collected from private households … 2. The network must be designed to enable the Community as a whole to become self-sufficient in waste disposal as well as in the recovery of waste referred to in paragraph 1, and the Member States to move towards that aim individually … 3. The network shall enable waste to be disposed of or waste referred to in paragraph 1 to be recovered in one of the nearest appropriate installations.'

[182] See also CJEU Case C-315/20 *Regione Friuli, Venezia, Giulia* ECLI:EU:C:2021:912, where a shipment of waste for recovery was successfully objected to in the name of the principles of proximity and self-sufficiency.

[183] Directive 2008/98 (n 1) Art 16(1).

[184] Regulation 1013/2006 (n 167) Art 4(3).

[185] See also CJEU Case C-203/96 (n 32). The Court did not allow the Netherlands to recur to Art 176 EC Treaty (now Art 193 TFEU) because the objections which were allowed under Regulation 259/93 were not applicable to the case.

municipal waste treatment. This is inexplicable, as the bureaucratic provisions introduced by Regulation 1013/2006 are strict enough to prevent abuses.

Shipments of waste within Member States are barely regulated at all. Regulation 1013/2006 stated in Article 1(5) that only Article 33 applies to such shipments. This provision only required Member States to set up a monitoring and control system which was coherent with EU law.

10-44 The export of waste to third countries increased by 75 per cent between 2004 and 2020, reaching 32.7 million tons in 2020. The EU also imported 16 million tons of waste; and the shipment of waste between Member States was 67 million tons in 2020.[186] Subsequent to its regular implementation reports[187] and an evaluation of Regulation 1013/2006,[188] the Commission made a proposal for revising the regulation.[189] The proposal addressed three main objectives: (i) to facilitate shipments of waste within the Union; (ii) to guarantee that waste which is exported is managed in environmentally and socially sound conditions; and (iii) to reduce and better address illegal shipments. The announcement made in the European Green Deal that the EU would stop waste exports altogether[190] was not followed up. The proposal is at present being discussed by the other Union institutions.

(iii) Shipment of Radioactive Waste

10-45 The shipment of radioactive waste is regulated by Directive 2006/117, which replaced Directive 92/3; it was based on Articles 31 and 32 of the Euratom Treaty. It only dealt with the shipment of radioactive waste and spent fuels which were to be disposed of.[191] Radioactive waste was defined as 'any material which contains or is contaminated by radio-nuclides and for which no use is foreseen', a definition which implies that recyclable or recoverable radioactive waste is – for shipment purposes – not waste.[192] This definition is not in line with that of Directive 2008/98.

10-46 Directive 2011/70 generally allows shipments of waste or of spent fuels to the other Member States or to a third country when there is an agreement between the two countries for such a shipment. The third country must ensure a high level of safety in general and with regard to the specific disposal facility. In a report of 2013, the Commission declared itself unable to control compliance with that provision.[193] No export is allowed to countries that are parties to the Cotonou Convention, to Antarctica or to countries that are not able properly to manage radioactive waste, the assessment of which is made by the authorities of the exporting Member State. Directives 2006/117 and 2011/70 do not contain any provision concerning the possibility of Member States adopting a partial or total ban on the import of nuclear waste, though 17 Member States banned the import

[186] Commission, COM(2021) 709.

[187] See Commission, COM(2023) 142.

[188] Commission, SWD(2020) 26.

[189] Commission, COM(2021) 709.

[190] Commission, COM(2019) 640, s 2.1.3: 'The Commission is of the view that the EU should stop exports of waste outside of the EU and will therefore revisit the rules on waste shipments and illegal exports.'

[191] Directive 2006/117/Euratom on the supervision and control of the shipments of radioactive waste and spent fuel [2006] OJ L337/1; Directive 92/3 [1992] OJ L35/24.

[192] See also Directive 2011/70/Euratom (n 98) Recital 20: 'The spent fuel can be regarded either as a valuable resource that may be reprocessed or as a radioactive waste that is destined for direct disposal.'

[193] Commission, 'Report on the Implementation of Directive 2006/117/Euratom' COM(2013) 240, 10.

of nuclear waste unilaterally.[194] In the period 2018–20, there were in total 1770 transfrontier shipments of radioactive waste (EU-28), of which 44 were to countries outside the Union and 70 were from third countries to a Member State.[195]

Overall, Directive 2006/117 is considerably less stringent than Regulation 1013/2006. Also, conditions for authorising an export to third countries are less stringent than those for a shipment between Member States. Finally, an export ban of radioactive waste to other than OECD countries, as exists for hazardous waste, is not foreseen.

IV. Specific Waste Streams

The Union has regulated a number of waste streams. The purpose of the provisions is to promote waste recycling and recovery and the safe disposal of waste, and to ensure that different national provisions on waste management do not unnecessarily affect the Union rules on the free circulation of goods. A useful assessment of five waste stream directives – on packaging, end-of-life vehicles, batteries, sewage sludge and polychlorinated biphenyls and triphenyls (PCB/PCT) – was made by the Commission in 2014.[196] 10-47

The Commission's circular economy strategy of 2020 mentioned a number of other waste streams,[197] though it is obvious that such a strategy paper does not yet have any legal value.

A. Packaging Waste

Packaging waste is thought to constitute 36 per cent of municipal waste; 40 per cent of plastics and 50 per cent of all paper used in the Union were used for packaging.[198] As early as the First Environmental Action Programme, it was announced that packaging issues would be looked at more closely; however, the Commission's initiative met with considerable hostility from economic operators, which were of the opinion that the Union would be better to abstain from this area. Directive 85/339, which the Union finally adopted in 1985, was based on Article 352 TFEU and was limited to liquid beverage containers.[199] It asked Member States to set up programmes for reducing the volume of liquid beverage containers. These programmes could even be implemented by voluntary agreements, which showed the directive's limited objective. 10-48

Implementation of this directive had only very limited success.[200] A number of Member States had adopted national measures on regulating packaging; attempts to

[194] Commission, 'Progress on Implementation of Directive 2011/70/Euratom' SWD(2019) 436, 35, Table 6. These Member States are: Bulgaria, Austria, Croatia, Cyprus, Czechia, Estonia, Finland, France, Greece, Ireland, Latvia, Lithuania, Malta, Poland, Portugal, Romania, and Slovakia. The remaining Member States did not inform on an eventual ban.

[195] Commission, '4th Implementation Report on Directive 2006/117' COM(2023) 77; Commission, SWD(2023) 43.

[196] Commission, SWD(2014) 209.

[197] Commission, COM(2020) 98.

[198] Commission, 'Proposal for a Regulation on Packaging and Packaging Waste' COM(2022) 677.

[199] Directive 85/339 on containers of liquids for human consumption [1985] OJ L176/18.

[200] In 1990, five Member States had not yet transposed the directive: see Commission, 8th report on monitoring application of Community law (1990) [1991] OJ C338/1 160. The CJEU gave judgments in the

have these measures declared void by the CJEU failed.[201] Since Germany, having been urged to do so by the Commission, introduced far-reaching measures on packaging, the Commission proposed a general directive on packaging waste, which was adopted in 1994.[202] The directive, based on Article 114 TFEU, tried to lay down uniform provisions on the free circulation of packaging as well as on the protection of the environment. It asked Member States to promote prevention, reuse and recycling of packaging, to set up collection systems for packaging waste and to established binding recovery and recycling targets for the different packaging materials.[203] Furthermore, the directive asked for standards for packaging, limited the content of heavy metals and requested Member States to draw up management plans for packaging and to report regularly on the implementation measures.

10-49 Most Member States were late in transposing the directive. As the recycling and recovery targets were fixed relatively low, a number of Member States made use of the possibility under Article 6(6) to get higher targets approved by the Commission. For the rest, the integration of the environmental and internal market requirements was only partly successful: imprecise drafting[204] and a loose reference to standards,[205] which did not fulfil the commitments of the directive, placed the responsibility of achieving the directive's objective on reducing quantities and promoting reuse and recycling of packaging back on to Member States, which were none too keen to venture into battle with the packaging industry and the retailers. While the directive allowed (national) environmental measures – for example, to restrict the use of PVC packaging, impose returnable bottles or tax packaging – it did not impose them; this favoured divergency among Member States, not harmonisation.

In two cases which dealt with the German system on packaging, the CJEU recognised that Germany was entitled to introduce a mandatory system for deposit and return in order to promote the use of returnable bottles.[206]

following cases: Case C-252/89 *Commission v Luxembourg* ECLI:EU:C:1991:321; Case C-192/90 *Commission v Spain* ECLI:EU:C:1991:465; Case C-255/93 *Commission v France* ECLI:EU:C:1994:366.

[201] CJEU Case C-302/86 *Commission v Denmark* ECLI:EU:C:1988:421, where a deposit and return system for packaging was attacked; Case C-380/87 *Enichem v Cinisello Balsamo* ECLI:EU:C:1989:318, where tax measures on non-biodegradable plastic packaging were in question.

[202] Directive 94/62 (n 25).

[203] ibid Art 6, provided that, by the year 2001, between 50 and 65% of packaging waste had to be recovered and 25–45% were recycled; the minimum percentage for each packaging material was 15%. Less stringent requirements were fixed for Greece, Ireland and Portugal.

[204] See, eg Directive 94/62 (n 25) Art 5: 'Member States may encourage reuse systems of packaging, which can be reused in an environmentally sound manner, in conformity with the Treaty'; the relationship to the recycling targets of Art 6 was not clear. Another example was Art 6 itself, which set targets but did not establish measuring methods.

[205] Under Directive 94/62 (n 25) Art 9, Member States had to admit only such packaging on their markets that comply with all essential requirements of annex II. Annex II provided that packaging shall be designed, produced and commercialised in such a way as to minimise its environmental impact when it is disposed of. Furthermore, packaging shall be so manufactured that the presence of noxious substances is minimised with regard to their presence in emissions, ash or leachate when packaging is incinerated or landfilled. This might easily lead to national measures as regards metal cans, aerosols, non-biodegradable or polyvinyl chloride (PVC)-containing packs, etc, with endless debates about whether such measures are permissible.

[206] CJEU Case C-309/02 *Radlberger* ECLI:EU:C:2004:799; Case C-463/01 *Commission v Germany* ECLI:EU:C:2004:787.

The target dates for recovery and recycling under Article 6 applied until 2001. Targets for the period 2001–06 were fixed by an amendment to Directive 94/62 in 2004[207] and extended until 2008.[208] Once more, the targets were fixed at a relatively low level. Consequently, the 2008 recycling targets were achieved in 2019 by all Member States except Croatia, Hungary, Malta and Poland,[209] with several Member States largely over-achieving them.[210] These results, though, did not take into consideration that packaging 'collected for recycling' and packaging which was actually recycled might give significantly different results.[211] The prevention of packaging waste generation (Article 4) had limited results, which were mainly due to the reduction in the weight of packaging; the 'essential requirements' laid down in Article 9 and annex II were too vaguely formulated to have any significant preventive influence.

In 2014, the Commission proposed new recycling targets for packaging,[212] without explaining how the different targets in Directives 2008/98 and 94/62 would be reconciled with regard to the payment for the separate collection systems by economic operators. This proposal was repealed in early 2015. In 2018, new targets for recycling and recovery of packaging were fixed for 2025 and 2030.[213] 10-50

In 2022, the Commission finally admitted that Directive 94/62 had failed to achieve its objectives of ensuring a level playing field within the internal market and ensuring sufficient protection of the environment. Based on a fitness check, an effectiveness study and an impact assessment,[214] it proposed to replace the directive with a regulation, which had three main objectives: to reduce the quantities of packaging, to provide better recycling and to promote the recycled content of materials in packaging.[215] The proposal is presently being discussed by the other institutions.

B. Batteries

A directive of 1991, based on the present Article 114 TFEU, regulated batteries and accumulators.[216] As it only referred to some batteries, Member States had difficulties 10-51

[207] Directive 2004/12 [2004] OJ L47/26.

[208] These targets for 2008 are (Art 6): a minimum of 60% of packaging material to be recovered, between 55% and 80% of packaging material to be recycled; recycling targets for glass and paper and cardboard: 60% each; recycling target for metals: 50%; recycling target for plastics: 22.5%; recycling target for wood: 15%.

[209] Commission, SWD(2022) 384, 8. The Commission itself, though, put some caution on this statement, as apparently a number of Member States considered that the quantities which are collected 'for recycling' are also actually recycled – which is not the case.

[210] ibid; see also Commission, SWD(2014) 209, 17.

[211] Commission, SWD(2022) 384, 11 quoted the example of plastic packaging, of which Member States declared 40.6% to be (collected for being) recycled, whereas it is estimated that only 14% of such packaging is actually recyced.

[212] Commission, COM(2014) 397.

[213] Directive 2018/852 [2018] OJ L150/141. By 2025, Member States had to reach the following recycling percentages (by weight): plastic, 50%; wood, 25%; ferrous metals, 70%; aluminium, 50%; glass, 70%; and paper and cardboard, 75%.

[214] Commisssion, 'Fitness Check of Directive 94/62. SWD(2014) 209; *Study on the Effectiveness of the Requirements for Packaging and Packaging Waste and Proposals for Reinforcement* (Brussels, 2020); Commisssion, 'Impact Assessment' SWD(2022) 384.

[215] Commission, 'Proposal for a Regulation' COM(2022) 677.

[216] Directive 91/157 on batteries and accumulators containing certain dangerous substances [1991] OJ L78/38.

in getting it off the ground, to elaborate plans and to set up effective collection systems. A revision was made in 2006, when Directive 2006/66 was adopted and Directive 91/157 repealed.[217]

The new directive declared that its primary objective was to minimise the negative impact of batteries on the environment, but that it also wanted to ensure the smooth functioning of the internal market. Therefore, it was based on Article 192(1) TFEU and, in relation to Articles 4 (prohibition to place certain batteries and accumulators on the market), 6 (batteries which comply with the requirements of the directive may circulate freely) and 21 (labelling requirements), on Article 114 TFEU. It applied to all batteries except for those used for security and military purposes and those that were sent into space (Article 2). It limited the mercury and cadmium content of batteries and provided for the separate collection of portable batteries. Producers had to bear the costs of the collection schemes (Article 16). Article 10 fixed binding collection targets for batteries – 25 per cent by 2012 and 45 per cent by 2016 – though export outside the collecting Member State or even outside the Union was allowed and counted for the target 'if there [was] sound evidence that the recycling operation took place under conditions equivalent to requirements of this directive' (Article 15). The disposal of industrial and automotive batteries in landfills and their incineration was prohibited (Article 14).

A Commission assessment of Directive 2006/66 was mildly critical of its operation,[218] but no significant measures were taken to ensure better compliance.[219]

Changes came with the transition to electromobility, which was thought to increase the need of batteries tenfold and which made the battery market strategically important. A Commission impact assessment report was highly critical of the application of the directive and its concentration on portable batteries, which accounted for only 12 per cent of the batteries market, against the 61 per cent of automotive batteries and the 27 per cent of industrial batteries.[220] It estimated that the directive had not ensured a sufficiently level playing field, was badly applied and did not help to establish a functional recycling market for batteries. Even the separate collection of portable batteries had only reached 45 per cent; Spain, Malta, Greece, Portugal, Estonia, Italy, Cyprus and Slovakia did not even reach this objective.[221] In July 2023, the Union then adopted a comprehensive regulation (96 articles) on the sustainability, safety, labelling, marking and information of all the batteries – portable, starting, lighting and ignition, transport, electrical vehicles and industrial (Article 1) – placed on the Union market, as well as on the management of waste batteries.[222] The regulation was based on Article 114 TFEU, except for the provisions on the management of waste batteries (Articles 54–76), which were based on Article 192 TFEU. Restrictions for mercury, cadmium and lead principally in portable batteries were maintained, and provisions on the recovery of cobalt, lead, lithium and nickel were introduced.

[217] Directive 2006/66 on batteries and accumulators and waste batteries and accumulators [2006] OJ L266/1; Directive 2013/56 [2013] OJ L329/5, amended Directive 2006/66, restricting in particular further the presence of cadmium and mercury.

[218] Commission, SWD(2014) 209, 29.

[219] Directive 2018/849 [2018] OJ L150/93.

[220] Commission, SWD(2020) 335, in particular annex 6; Commission, 'Implementation Report on Directive 2006/66' COM(2019) 166.

[221] Commission, SWD(2020) 335, 170.

[222] Regulation 2023/1542 on batteries and waste batteries [2023] OJ L191/1.

C. Used Oils

Directive 75/439, the very first environmental directive,[223] was based on Articles 115 and 352 TFEU; it provided for the safe collection, treatment, storage and disposal of waste oils. Member States had to give priority to the recycling (regeneration) of waste oils, 'where technical, economic and organisational constraints so allow'. The discharge of waste oils into waters and drainage systems was prohibited. Activities concerning the collection, treatment and disposal of waste were to be licensed. Waste oils may not contain more than 50 parts per million of PCB/PCT. 10-52

Member States all transposed the directive into national law, though in some cases with a considerable delay. Its application had only limited success: the recycling clause did not fulfil expectation; most waste oils were incinerated; and recycling remained a subordinate activity.

A CJEU judgment of 1999[224] clarified that Member States were obliged to give priority to the regeneration of used oils over incineration. As a consequence, the Commission introduced procedures under Article 258 TFEU against all Member States except Italy and France. However, this only increased the objections of Member States which had even introduced reduced tax rates for using waste oils as fuel. In particular, the cement industry was keen to use waste oils as fuels. In view of that, the Commission, based on contested studies, announced that the preference of material recycling was not cost-effective. Despite protests, it proposed to repeal Directive 75/439, which was successful: Directive 2008/98 repealed Directive 75/439.[225]

D. PCB/PCT

Directive 76/403[226] contained provisions to promote the recycling of and control the disposal of PCB/PCT – persistent organic pollutants that are carcinogenic and mutagenic. As recycling turned out to be impossible, the directive was replaced, in 1996 and after eight years of negotiations, by Directive 96/59,[227] which provided for the decontamination and disposal of all products containing PCB/PCT. The equipment used for this had to be inventoried, labelled and reported. Member States were obliged to formulate disposal plans by September 1999, and to ensure that PCB/PCT were removed from the environment by 2010 at the latest. 10-53

'The 31 December 2010 deadline for the complete decontamination or disposal has not been met by most Member States to a large extent. Conclusive inventories of PCB equipment are missing.'[228] The Commission admitted that no recent and sufficient data on the

[223] Directive 75/439 on the disposal of waste oils [1975] OJ L194/23.

[224] CJEU Case C-102/97 *Commission v Germany* ECLI:EU:C:1999:314. Germany was found to have breached EU law because it had not given priority to the recycling of used oils. Later on, similar judgments were given in Case C-201/03 *Commission v Sweden* ECLI:EU:C:2004:198; Case C-424/02 *Commission v United Kingdom* ECLI:EU:C:2004:452; Case C-92/03 *Commission v Portugal* ECLI:EU:C:2005:58; Case C-531/03 *Commission v Austria* ECLI:EU:C:2005:159.

[225] See Directive2008/98 (n 1) Art 41.

[226] Directive 76/403 on the disposal of PCB/PCT [1976] OJ L108/41.

[227] Directive 96/59 on the disposal of PCB/PCT [1996] OJ L243/31.

[228] Commission, SWD(2014) 209 13.

directive's application were available, but that it had not done anything to change that situation; in particular, it had not started proceedings under Article 258 TFEU.[229] In 2019, Regulation 2019/1021 provided that by 2025 Member States had to destroy or irreversibly transform all material containing PCB, so that the risks of PCB were eliminated.[230]

Directive 96/59 is thus another demonstration of the need to monitor compliance, as otherwise even legally binding obligations are ignored by Member States, with no pressure from the public, from non-governmental organisations or other interests.

E. Sewage Sludge

10-54 Directive 86/278, based on the present Articles 115 and 352 TFEU, dealt with the use of sewage sludge in agriculture.[231] The directive fixed maximum limit values for concentrations of heavy metals in the sludge and in soil, and defined conditions for the use of sewage sludge. Sludge and the soil on which it was used had to be regularly analysed in order to make sure that the heavy metal concentrations were not exceeded. Member States were expressly allowed to set more stringent requirements. Presumably in view of that, the values fixed by the directive were not too severe. Several Member States adopted more stringent requirements at a national level 'often way above' the limit values of the directive.[232]

The use of sewage sludge which may contain heavy metals and other hazardous substances in agriculture has met increasing objections from farmers and the food industry, who were afraid of food contamination. Several Member States prohibited the spreading of sludge altogether. The Commission did not comment on whether such a ban was compatible with EU law. In my opinion, such a ban is allowed under Article 12 of the directive and Article 193 TFEU. The free circulation of sludge – Articles 34–36 TFEU – cannot be invoked, as the trade in sludge is not prohibited and no discrimination of producers or traders of other Member States is visible. Nor is it obvious that such a ban would have to be considered disproportionate, as it must be left to each Member State to decide how far it wants to go in the preventive protection of its soil – which is a non-renewable source.

A review of Directive 86/278, required under the Sixth Environmental Action Programme[233] and favoured by most Member States, has never been proposed, and appears to have been abandoned. This directive is a further example of legislation which was not monitored by the Commission. The Commission admitted that the values fixed were clearly outdated, that new contaminants and substances appeared in sludge, that it never made a risk assessment as regards the (short- and long-term) risk of sludge for soil and food, that it never took any proceedings against Member States under Article 258 TFEU and that, 'in its present form, the Directive is clearly outdated'.[234] In

[229] ibid 32 and 69.

[230] Regulation 2019/1021 on persistant organic pollutants [2019] OJ L169/45, Art 7(2) and annex IV.

[231] Directive 86/278 on the protection of the environment, and in particular of the soil, when sewage sludge is used in agriculture [1986] OJ L181/6.

[232] Commission, SWD(2014) 209, 33; see as an example CJEU Case C-260/93 *Commission v Belgium* ECLI:EU:C:1994:182.

[233] Decision 1600/2002 [2002] OJ L242/1, Art 8(2.iv).

[234] Commission, SWD(2014) 209, 34.

2020, the Commission announced that it would 'consider reviewing Directive 86/278. A rather general assessment of the Directive identified in particular considerable data gaps for sludge management, but underlined that not less than 17 Member States had considered it necessary to adopt stricter national measures.'[235]

F. Animal Waste

Directive 90/667 laid down hygienic provisions for the disposal and processing of animal waste.[236] The directive was an early EU reaction to BSE; it introduced 'high-risk' and 'low-risk' animal waste, and stated that high-risk waste had to be adequately incinerated or buried in order to prevent environmental impairment. The directive was mainly targeted at ensuring disposal of BSE waste without causing problems for humans or the environment. 10-55

After the full outbreak of mad cow disease and some other EU-wide scandals linked to animal feed and animal waste, Directive 90/667 was replaced by Regulation 1774/2002, which was based on Article 168 TFEU; this regulation was in turn replaced by Regulation 1069/2009, which still applies today.[237] Regulation 1069/2009 almost entirely avoided the word 'waste', though many of the material regulated would come under the definition of 'waste' of Directive 2008/98; the regulation preferred the word 'animal by-product'.[238] The material was divided into three categories:

- category 1 was mainly high-risk material which was suspected or proven to be infected with diseases communicable to humans or animals;
- category 2 included material which did not belong to the other two categories and which appeared to present a certain risk; and
- category 3 concerned material which did not present risks.

Material from categories 1 and 2 may only be shipped to another Member State with the agreement of the latter (Article 48). Reasons for refusing such an agreement had not been given and were not laid down in the regulation. The disposal of category 1 material was differentiated according to the risk that was linked to it; some parts could only be incinerated, whereas other parts could also be landfilled or processed. Similar, but less strict conditions applied to material from category 2, whereas Article 13 of Directive 2008/98 applied for material from category 3; this meant that it must be treated or disposed of without risk to humans or the environment.

The regulation further contained relatively summary provisions on the approval of intermediary plants, storage plants, processing, oleochemical, biogas and composting plants, and in particular rather detailed provisions for EU controls in Member States, including inspections, on-the-spot checks and audits. Its relationship to Directive 2008/98

[235] Commission, COM(2020) 98, s 3.7; Commission, SWD(2023) 157.
[236] Directive 90/667 (n 56).
[237] Regulation 1774/2002 (n 55); Regulation 1069/2009 (n 55).
[238] Regulation 1069/2009 (n 55) Art 3.1: '"animal by-products" means entire bodies or parts of animals, products of animal origin or other products obtained from animals, which are not intended for human consumption, including oocytes, embryos and semen'.

is not quite clear.[239] Though, in theory, the scope of application of both texts is clearly defined, in practice, the Commission hardly deals with questions of animal waste under Directive 2008/98, and considers that all animal waste is excluded from that directive's provisions.

G. End-of-Life Vehicles

10-56 A directive of 2000 dealt with end-of-life vehicles,[240] of which about 15 million per year are generated within the Union. The directive was based on Article 192 TFEU. It contained a number of provisions to prevent waste generation from cars by imposing restrictions on the manufacturing of new cars. Cars which were marketed after July 2003 were not allowed to contain lead, cadmium, mercury or hexavalent chromium (Article 4); a derogation clause in annex II, which was regularly updated, allowed some exceptions. The derogation clause was amended 10 times by 2021. The main effect of the amendments was to progressively reduce the number of exceptions. Furthermore, the directive contained recovery and recycling targets for cars which were gradually to be reached by 2015; new targets were to be set for the time beyond 2015 (Article 7(3)), but this never occurred.[241]

Member States had to establish take-back schemes for end-of-life vehicles which had to allow the last user to give back the car without having to pay costs (Article 5(4)). A car could only be deregistered – in particular, with the fiscal authorities – where its user presented a certificate of dismantling which was remitted to the user by one of the dismantling bodies. These provisions tried to establish the principle of producer responsibility which made the producer responsible for his products once they reached the end of their service life and become waste.

The directive contributed to considerably reducing the presence of heavy metals in cars. The intermediate targets for 2006 were reached by most Member States in 2011,[242] some[243] even reaching the 2015 targets at that time. The directive also had positive effects on dismantling, shredding and recycling activities.

Problems existed because the borderline between a used car and an end-of-life vehicle was not sharply enough defined. This allowed in particular the illegal export of end-of-life vehicles as used cars or their treatment by illegal operators: in 2008, 4.1 million end-of life vehicles thus 'disappeared' and were not treated in authorised treatment facilities; this number had not diminished 10 years later.[244] Other problems concerned the absence of influence of the design provisions on the actual design and production of cars, the electrical and electronic parts in electrical vehicles, for which the directive contains very little

[239] See also CJEU Case C-634/17 *ReFood* ECLI:EU:C:2019:469; Joined Cases C-21/19 to C-23/19 *Kamstra Recycling* ECLI:EU:C:2020:636.

[240] Directive 2000/53 on end-of-life vehicles [2000] OJ L269/34.

[241] Reuse and recovery of 95% of the car weight, reuse and recycling of at least 85%. The backfilling of end-of-life vehicle waste was classified by the directive as a recycling operation, Commission, SWD(2021) 60, 57.

[242] Commission, SWD(2014) 209, 24. The reuse and recycling targets were not reached by Estonia, France or Hungary.

[243] ibid 24. These Member States were Belgium, Bulgaria, Germany, Denmark, Latvia, Malta, Poland and Slovakia.

[244] ibid 26. Commission, 'Evaluation of Directive 2000/53' SWD(2021) 60, 29.

provisions, the growing use of plastics and other lightweight material, and the improvable conditions for extended producer responsibility.[245]

In 2023, the Commission proposed, on the basis of Article 114 TFEU, to replace this directive by a regulation on 'circularity requirements for vehicle design and on management of end-of-life vehicles'.[246] The new proposal specified the requirements for recyclability and recoverability of vehicles, the take-back obligation of manufacturers and the conditions for export of used vehicles; in order to be exported outside the Union, vehicles shall in future have to be roadworthy.

H. Waste Electrical and Electronic Equipment

Directive 2012/19 on waste electrical and electronic equipment (WEEE), which replaced Directive 2002/96, followed in its structure the model of Directive 2000/53.[247] It was based on Article 192 TFEU and intended to cover electrical and electronic waste, of which there was 8.3 million tonnes in 2005, with an estimation of 12 million tonnes in 2020. The directive contained a positive list of the categories of equipment which was covered.[248] 10-57

WEEE was to be collected separately; from the end of 2006, a rate of separate collection of at least 4 kg on average per inhabitant per year was to be reached; this obligation was replaced, in 2016, by an average collection of the products put on the market (45 per cent in 2016, 65 per cent in 2019, Article 7). Collection facilities had to be set up which enabled final holders and distributors to return WEEE free of cost. Normally, distributors which supply new equipment were obliged to take back the old equipment free of charge from private users or owners. Collected WEEE had to be brought to authorised treatment facilities; the disposal of collected WEEE was prohibited (Article 6).

Collected WEEE had to be treated, recycled or recovered, according to best available techniques. The above-mentioned collection targets of Article 7 are lower for all Member States which joined the Union since 2004 – except for Estonia and Cyprus. The directive tried to ensure that the collection from private households was free of charge for those households (Article 5). For the rest, detailed provisions dealt with the responsibility of producers to finance collection systems. Producers were also required to respect the recovery targets fixed in annex V (Article 11). These targets were different for different product groups and became stricter over time: they ranged from 50–75 per cent for recycling in 2015 to 55–80 per cent as of 2018, and from 70 –80 per cent of recovery in 2015 to 75–85 per cent as of 2018.

In order to inform consumers and users, electrical and electronic equipment had to be marked with a crossed-out wheeled bin (Article 15).[249] The directive contained a

[245] Commisssion, SWD(2021) 60.

[246] Commission, COM(2023) 451.

[247] Directive 2012/19 on waste electrical and electronic equipment [2012] OJ L192/38; this directive replaced Directive 2002/96[2003] OJ L37/24.

[248] Large and small household appliances, IT and telecommunications equipment, consumer equipment, lighting equipment, electrical and electronic tools, toys, leisure and sports equipment, medical devices, monitoring and control instruments and automatic dispensers.

[249] See para 6-52 above; that symbol is also used for batteries which must be collected separately, see para 10-51 above.

considerable number of other information obligations for producers and distributors, as well as reporting obligations for Member States and the Commission. As the directive covered new ground, adaptation of its provisions by Parliament and Council was foreseen, in particular as regards the quantified targets.

A particular concern which the directive tried to address was the large amount of electrical and electronic waste which was exported from the Union under the qualification of 'product'. Annex VI required detailed evidence from an exporter that it was actually products that were exported and not waste material: in particular, the responsible persons had to submit the contract and the invoice, which stated, among others, that the equipment was functional. They had to submit evidence of 'evaluating or testing … on each item' of the consignment which proved its functionality, and had to submit a declaration that 'none of the equipment' constitutes waste. When these conditions were not fulfilled, the consignment had to be considered a(n illegal) shipment of waste.

The directive did not contain provisions on the ban of hazardous substances in electrical and electronic equipment. Unlike for Directive 2000/53 on end-of-life vehicles, which included such provisions, the Council and the European Parliament accepted the Commission's proposal that such restrictions should be enshrined in a separate directive, which was adopted at the same time as the WEEE Directive.[250] The reason for this procedure was that this separation allowed Directive 2002/95 – later Directive 2011/65 – to be based on Article 114 TFEU. As a consequence, no Member State was allowed to maintain or introduce further bans or restrictions of dangerous substances in electrical and electronic equipment than those laid down in Directive 2011/65, except under the very strict conditions of Article 114(4) and (5) TFEU. The exception clause in Directive 2011/65 for certain uses of heavy metals was used, since 2004, to considerably increase the number of exceptions.

Member States had some difficulties setting up the collection, dismantling and recycling systems at local and regional level, as this required close co-operation with industry, for which both sides were not always well prepared. There is as yet (mid-2023) no assessment available on the effectiveness of Directive 2012/19.

I. Mining Waste

10-58 In 2006, the European Union adopted Directive 2006/21 on mining waste.[251] This directive was a consequence of the accidents of Aznalcóllar (Spain 1998) and Baia Mare (Romania 2000). When investigating these accidents, the Commission found that mining activities were largely exempted from existing EU environmental legislation and that the provisions of Directive 1999/31 on landfills did not always comply with practices in the mining industry.

[250] Directive 2011/65[2011] OJ L174/88; this directive replaced Directive 2002/95 [2003] OJ L37/19. It was amended by Directive 2015/863 [2015] OJ L137/10, which prohibited the use of four phthalates in electrical and electronic equipment: bis(2-ethylhexyl) phthalate (DEHP), butyl benzyl phthalate (BBP), dibutyl phthalate (DBP) and diisobutyl phthalate (DIBP).

[251] Directive 2006/21 on the management of waste from the extracting industries [2006] OJ L102/15.

Directive 2006/21 tried to lay down basic provisions for the storage and treatment of mining waste, the prevention of accidents and the permitting of mining activities, and for reducing the strict standards for landfills under Directive 1999/31 by accommodating the mining industry. In its implementation report, the Commission stated that the Member States' reports did not allow it to gain a clear, sufficiently detailed and reliable picture on the directive's application, as Member States reported mainly on the transposition, but not on the practical application, of the directive.[252] The Commission did not take any measures to improve this situation.

J. Other Waste Streams

With regard to plastics, the Commission stated that the Union generated 26 million tonnes of plastic waste per year; less than 30 per cent was recycled, 31 per cent was landfilled and 39 per cent was incinerated.[253] It voiced particular concern over plastics in the oceans and the effects of microplastics, and announced measures to improve the recycling of plastics, boosting the demand for plastic and improving its separate collection. 10-59

Directive 2019/904 reduced the placing on the market of some single-use plastic products (cutlery, plates, some food containers and beverage containers). For other single-use plastic products, Member States had to take 'ambitious and sustained reduction measures'. The directive provided for separate collection of plastic waste, extended producer responsibility and detailed labelling and reporting requirements. As Member States have discretion to comply with their obligations in part by 2026 and 2030, it is too early to assess the effectiveness of the directive. However, it did not address the numerous different plastics which are on the market and which make recycling all the more difficult.

The Commission adopted a separate strategy for textiles. It stated that about 5.8 million tonnes of textile waste were generated per year in the Union, approximately 11 kg per capita.[254] Apart from several soft law measures, it announced binding product-specific ecodesign requirements. Concrete measures have not yet been proposed.

No announcements have been made with regard to biodegradable waste,[255] including provisions on the composting of waste, though for a number of years a legislative initiative has been requested by Member States, economic operators and the European Parliament. As the Commission opposed a new directive, Directive 2008/98 only contained some general observation on bio-waste; the Commission was again invited to assess the situation and come up with a proposal – if it considered it appropriate (Article 22).

A Council recommendation from 1981 tried to promote the recycling of waste paper,[256] but remained largely unacknowledged. Its impact on economic or administrative practices was insignificant.

[252] Commission, 'Implementation Report of Directive 2006/21' COM(2016) 553.

[253] Commission, 'A European Strategy for Plastics in a Circular Economy' COM(2018) 28; Commission, SWD(2018) 16.

[254] Commission, 'A Strategy for Sustainable and Circular Textiles' COM(2022) 141.

[255] Directive 2008/98 (n 1) defined bio-waste as follows (Art 3, no 4): 'biodegradable garden and park waste, food and kitchen waste from households, restaurants, caterers and retail premises and comparable waste from food processing plants'.

[256] [1981] OJ L355/56.

11

Legal Aspects of Integration

I. General Remarks

11-01 Article 11 of the Treaty on the Functioning of the European Union (TFEU) requires that environmental protection requirements are integrated into other EU policies.[1] This message has been part of the EC Treaty since 1987, when provisions on environmental protection were incorporated into the primary law of the EC Treaty for the first time. Indeed, it was clear by then, and it is now even more evident, that the relatively few environmental regulations and directives which the Union has adopted since 1975 will, in themselves, neither reach a high level of environmental protection nor protect, preserve and improve the quality of the environment or avoid its deterioration, Union-wide or globally. Without specific environmental provisions, the Union environment would probably be in a much worse state; however, this does not necessarily mean that quality of life has improved in urban centres or elsewhere. The three global and Union-wide challenges of climate change, biodiversity loss and pollution have not yet been properly answered, either at global level or within the Union.

The concept of sustainable development, now also used in Article 3(3) and (5) and Recital 9 of the Treaty on European Union (TEU) and Article 11 TFEU, tries to assemble all the opposing interests between environmental protection and economic progress into one formula, in order to find a political compromise to which everybody can agree. This attempt is doomed to fail because the concept of sustainable development is void of sense and is given a political content according to the political actors who use it.[2]

11-02 The integration requirement of Article 11 TFEU is nevertheless the most important of the provisions which govern environmental policy,[3] since it constitutes the bridge between environmental policy and all the other policies at EU level. Since the present book does not try to examine policies themselves but tries to describe *legal* measures, its presentation of the other policies will necessarily remain limited and even rudimentary. Some indication as to the necessity of an approach to integration which combines political, legal, economic and strategic action might appear from the list of criteria which the European Environment Agency (EEA) established for assessing the integration of environmental actions into other Union policies:[4]

1. Is there qualitative identification of all environmental costs/benefits?

[1] Art 11 TFEU: 'Environmental protection requirements must be integrated into the definition and implementation of Union policies and activities, in particular with a view to promoting sustainable development.'

[2] See para 1-24ff.

[3] For this and the other requirements, see para 1-11.

[4] EEA, *Europe's Environment, the Second Assessment* (Aarhus, 1998) ch 14.

2. Is there quantification of environmental costs/benefits?
3. Are all external costs internalised into market prices (part of the polluter-pays principle)?
4. Are economic instruments designed to achieve behaviour change rather than just revenue raising?
5. Are environmentally damaging subsidies being withdrawn?
6. Is there an environmental impact assessment of projects before implementation?
7. Is there strategic environmental impact assessment of policies, plans and programmes at different spatial levels?
8. Is environmental procurement a cornerstone of purchasing strategy?
9. Are there environmental management measures within the sector and monitoring of their implementation?
10. Have eco-efficiency targets and indicators been developed and used to monitor progress?

Legal (binding or not binding) or political instruments for the application of these criteria have not yet been developed at Union level, with the exception of a directive on strategic environmental assessment of plans and programmes.[5] Thus, the EEA list is an accumulation of wishful thinking: neither energy nor transport policy, neither fishery nor agricultural policy ever tried to consciously follow the 10 points. For all policies, though, it should be clear that the integration of environmental issues must be conceived of as a process which might take decades to achieve and does not depend on whatever legal or political measure is adopted; examples would be changes in transport policy, the renouncing of nuclear energy or the transition to environmentally friendly agriculture, where organic farming would be the rule, not the exception. 11-03

The Commission tried, in 1993, to organise its internal administration in such a way as to allow it better to take into consideration environmental requirements;[6] these administrative measures were reviewed in 1997.[7] However, it is significant that it did not really attempt to give these decisions the widest publicity possible; thus, any serious control of their implementation by the other institutions, the media or the public was lacking.

The Commission measures provided mainly for the following actions:[8] 11-04

- All Commission proposals are assessed on their environmental effects. Where such effects are likely to occur, an environmental impact assessment is to be made.
- Proposals for new legal measures should, in the explanatory memorandum, describe and explain environmental effects and environmental costs and benefits.
- The Commission work programme identifies and flags those proposals that will have significant environmental effects.
- In all relevant Commission departments, contact persons for the integration of environmental requirements are designated.

[5] Directive 2001/42 [2001] OJ L197/30; see also para 4-37.
[6] Commission, SEC(93) 785.
[7] Commission, Press Release IP/97/636 of 11 July 1997.
[8] Written Question E-0649/97 (Diez de Rivera Icaza) [1997] OJ C367/33.

- An environmental network of director generals is set up, which is chaired by the director general for the environment and where the director generals of the most important departments are represented. The emphasis is on the total co-ordination of environmental questions and the interdependency between environmental policy and other political measures.
- A specific unit is created inside the environmental department, which is placed under the direct responsibility of the director general and which is charged with the implementation of the environmental action programmes and the integration of environmental requirements into other political measures.
- The Commission's annual report is partly modified; it now contains, for key political areas, an indication of which environmental considerations are taken into account.
- The Commission takes a number of measures for its recycling, waste management and purchase policy ('green accounting').
- Progress in better integrating environmental requirements into other policies are regularly assessed.

11-05 The overall effect of these measures on the orientation of the Commission's policy was insignificant. In particular, the administrative (re)structuring measures were bluntly rejected by the administration itself.

The Commission did not ensure the implementation of these measures, but has tried, since 2003, to make a new start for integration, by providing for an impact assessment for its major legislative proposals and important communications which defined future policies.[9] Under this policy, all such proposals were to be examined as regards their economic, social and environmental impact; furthermore, intensive consultations with stakeholders – government experts, trade and industry, environmental and consumer protection services – were to take place. This policy led to the elaboration of lengthy documents which accompany legislative and other major proposals. However, these impact assessments were generally written when the political decision to propose legislation had already been taken; they thus served as a supplementary explanation of the measures which were proposed, not as an objective assessment. Furthermore, the more important a measure politically was, the less precise was the assessment. Once a decision was taken, an impact assessment announced the environmental and human health benefits of that measure.

Economists have, so far, not managed to convincingly assess in economic terms – and this is almost the only argument that counts at Union level – the advantages or disadvantages of a specific measure for the environment. The diminution of bird species in Europe, the damage made to soil every day (soil erosion, sealing, pollution, compaction and the other elements which are mentioned in paragraph 5-06 above) or the particulates in the air which are believed to cause more than 300,000 premature deaths per year and an unknown number of sick persons in the Union – nobody ever has calculated the impact. In contrast, when the costs for industry are in question, each environmental measure leads to an outcry that it would cause the loss of jobs and of competitiveness, economic advantages for China

[9] See Commission, 'Impact Assessment Guidelines' SEC(2009)92; more closely, see also para 4-42.

and higher prices, and very precise figures are given to prove how dangerous this or that environmental proposal would be for economic operators. This is the reason why so many environmental proposals are repeatedly watered down even before the Commission presents them as official proposals. And this is the reason why, in practice, the Commission's idea of 'better regulation' is in conflict with the environmental policy and the concrete measures envisaged under that policy.[10]

So far, the impact assessment initiative of 2003, consolidated by the inter-institutional agreement of 2016, has not significantly contributed to the integration of environmental requirements into other sectors of EU policy. Quite the opposite, it has certainly contributed to the slowing down or blocking of environmental initiatives for reasons of industry or trade interests. This might in part be due not to the instrument of impact assessment itself, but to the fact that, in the first two decades of the twenty-first century, the Commission was more prepared to follow the ideas of new liberalism. The Commission seemed to see the Union more as a body of interstate co-operation than as a Union, and its own role more as a secretary than a policy institution. What lacked in the system, despite many good words in the Lisbon Treaty on European Union, were openness, transparency and accountability of the arguments which allow the policy-makers to make a fair balancing. There was also the lack of a reliable method of gauging the impacts of a given measure on the environment, but also on society as a whole. The Commission could, of course, make ex post evaluations of EU environmental measures in order to learn lessons – but it does not systematically do so. Ultimately, it remained that at the decision-making table – of the Commission, of the Union as a whole – the environment was poorly represented, as it neither votes nor has a voice.

The creation of the Directorate-General for Climate Action within the Commission in 2010 and the transfer of responsibilities such as biotechnology or animal testing to other (non-environmental) administrations within the Commission contributed somewhat to further marginalising environmental issues both administratively and politically. Increasingly, the needs of environmental protection were comparable to the role which religious issues play in general policy: nobody openly contests their importance, but in the daily work the requirements are all too often set aside.

The Fifth Environmental Action Programme (1993) had singled out five areas of activity 11-06
as target sectors where 'particular efforts' were to be made in order to integrate environmental requirements in those policies, namely the manufacturing industry, energy, transport, agriculture and tourism.[11]

The 'particular efforts' turned out to be purely on paper. No infrastructure was set up – such as a network inside the Commission, regular meetings between environmental and the specific ministers of Member States, Council meetings, public conferences or discussions – and no concrete joined actions were launched. The reason for this failure was that the action programme had been elaborated by the environmental commissioner and had later been discussed by the environmental working group and the environmental ministers in the Council – but the agricultural, transport and energy administrations and

[10] See Interinstitutional Agreement between the European Parliament, the Council of the European Union and the European Commission on better regulation [2016] OJ L123/1. Art 11 TFEU is not mentioned in that agreement.

[11] Fifth Environmental Action Programme [1993] OJ C138/1, 28 et seq.

policy-makers had not been associated with the work ('integrated'); they had other objectives and priorities, and did not pay attention to the words in the action programme.

11-07 The negotiations on and signing of the Amsterdam Treaty on European Union in 1997 led to the transfer of the provision on environmental integration into other EU policies from Article 174 to Article 6 EC Treaty.[12] The Commission prepared a report on the question[13] which the Heads of States and Governments used at a meeting in Cardiff 1998 to invite the different Council configurations to elaborate strategies for integrating environmental requirements into their sectors and reporting on it. Subsequently, different integration papers were submitted by the Commission[14] and 'approved' by the different Council configurations. However, these 'approvals' constituted at best a sort of political commitment for the different Councils; also, the Commission did not feel in any way legally bound by the Councils' resolutions or other statements. While the process of developing and discussing 'strategies' was never formally brought to a halt, it progressively turned more into political declamation than leading to a work programme with objectives, priorities and timetables. Following a Commission communication in 2004,[15] the Cardiff process was considered dead.

This integration process crossed with the 'sustainability process' which was started in Lisbon 2000 and promised to make the Union the most effective economy worldwide in 10 years, ensuring at the same time a high level of social protection. During the Swedish presidency, the Heads of State and Governments added an environmental dimension to the Lisbon process.[16] In 2010, the Commission adopted its strategy paper for 2020, 'Smart, Sustainable and Inclusive Growth'.[17] Environmental concerns were reduced to climate change and energy issues; the accent was, as in 2000, on growth and jobs, and the Juncker Commission (2014–19) did not change this priority.

11-08 The Von der Leyen Commission (2019–24) introduced the 'European Green Deal', which was called the new growth strategy of the Union,[18] identifying climate change, biodiversity loss and pollution as the main areas for environmental action. When the Union

[12] See also para 1-24ff.

[13] Commission, 'Partnership for Integration – a Strategy for Integrating Environment into EU Policies' COM(98) 333.

[14] See Commission, COM(98) 716 and COM(99) 640 (transport); Commission, COM(98) 571 (energy); Commission, COM(99) 22 and COM(2000) 20 (agriculture); Commission, COM(1999) 263 (internal market); Commission, COM(1999) 36 and COM(2000) 264 (development); Commission, COM(2001) 143 (fishery); Commission, COM(2000) 576 (economic questions); Commission, SEC(2002) 271 (external affairs).

[15] Commission, 'Integrating Environmental Considerations Into Other Policy Areas – a Stocktaking of the Cardiff Process' COM(2004) 394.

[16] Lisbon Statement: 'The Union is to become the most competitive and dynamic knowledge-based economy in the world, capable of sustainable economic growth with more and better jobs and greater social cohesion.' The European Council in Stockholm 2001 added to that: 'the European Union sustainable development strategy should complete and build on the Lisbon statement by including an environmental dimension'.

[17] Commission, 'Europe 2020: A Strategy for Smart, Sustainable and Inclusive Growth' COM(2010) 2020. Smart growth was described as 'developing an economy based on knowledge and innovation', sustainable growth as 'promoting a more resource efficient, greener and more competitive economy' and inclusive growth as 'fostering a high-employed economy delivering social and territorial cohesion'.

[18] Commission, COM(2019) 640: '[The European Green Deal] is a new growth strategy that aims to transform the EU into a fair and prosperous society, with a modern, resource-efficient and competitive economy where there are no net emissions of greenhouse gases in 2050 and where economic growth is decoupled from resosurce use. It also aims to protect, conserve and enhance the EU's natural capital, and protect the health and well-being of citizens from environment-related risks and impacts.'

adopted the Eighth Environmental Action Programme in 2022,[19] it mandated the Commission to publish a list of indicators which allowed the progress in environmental protection to be measured until 2030. The Commission published a list of 26 indicators and committed itself to publishing an annual progress report.[20]

The conclusion of this short description of past and present efforts is that any political and administrative effort to give life to Article 11 TFEU at EU level remains an objective to be reached. There are some tendencies of 'greening' the policy in the areas of fishery, agriculture and, in particular due to the climate change discussions, energy. However, these efforts are due to external pressure: the Union had to react to the problem that fish had disappeared because of overfishing; that the common agricultural policy (CAP) had become too expensive and too restrictive to imports; and that climate change raised the necessity to take energy-related measures at EU level.

The integration of environmental requirements into other policies, a legal requirement under Article 11 TFEU, will perhaps start to become a reality once the Court of Justice of the European Union (CJEU) annuls an EU regulation or directive because it did not respect Article 11. Whether the Court will ever give such a judgment is, of course, unknown. Until that time, Article 11 will remain an objective that is not taken too serious by the Union institutions and administrations.

II. Agricultural Policy

Since December 2009, when the Lisbon Treaty on European Union entered into effect, agricultural policy has been of shared competence between the Union and the Member States; before then, it had been a common policy, ie the Union had exclusive competence. Agricultural policy is based on Articles 38–44 TFEU. It pursues the objectives of Article 39,[21] which may, in general terms or in concrete measures, conflict with the environmental objectives of Article 191 TFEU. 11-09

The Commission's progress reports of 1999 and 2000, on integrating environmental requirements into the agricultural sector, mentioned above, remained relatively general, but recognised that the agricultural policy had not changed much. The EEA, in its different reports, identified the agriculture/forestry sector as a principal contributor to the environmental problems of climate change, chemicals, soil, waste, acidification, biodiversity, inland waters and marine and coastal zones.[22]

[19] Decision 2022/591 [2022] OJ L114/22.

[20] Commission, COM(2022) 357.

[21] Art 39(1) TFEU: 'The objectives of the common agricultural policy shall be: (a) to increase agricultural productivity by promoting technical progress and by ensuring the rational development of agricultural production and the optimum utilisation of the factors of production, in particular labour; (b) thus to ensure a fair standard of living for the agricultural community, in particular by increasing the individual earnings of persons engaged in agriculture; (c) to stabilise markets; (d) to assure the availability of supplies; (e) to ensure that supplies reach consumers at reasonable prices.' See also CJEU Case C-336/00 *Austria v Huber* ECLI:EU:C:2002:509, para 36, according to which environmental protection is another objective of the Union's agricultural policy.

[22] EEA, *Environmental Signals 2001* (Copenhagen, 2001); EEA, *The European Environment, State and Outlook 2005* (Copenhagen, 2005); EEA, *Integration of Environment Into EU Agricultural Policy. EEA Report 2/2006* (Copenhagen, 2007); EEA, *The European Environment, State and Outlook 2015* (Copenhagen, 2015); EEA, *The European Environment, State and Outlook 2020* (Copenhagen, 2020).

11-10 The objectives of agricultural policy, laid down in Article 39 TFEU, have not changed since the beginning of the Union (1958). Environmental considerations came only very slowly into perspective. A 1985 Green Paper devoted, for the first time, a special section to the environmental effects of agriculture.[23] In 1988, a communication on 'agriculture and the environment' followed, which was based on the assumption that the CAP was already under pressure anyway and did not need supplementary pressure from the environmental side.[24] The general problems of agricultural policy led in 1992 to a substantial reform of the CAP. Although environmental improvement was not among the main objectives of this reform, increased efforts were subsequently taken to ensure income to farmers by progressively considering them to be nature conservationists, thus giving them access to environmental money. In pursuance of this policy, measures were gradually introduced to grant financial aid for environmental services provided by agriculture, such as the production of energy, forest-fire prevention, water protection, stabilisation of carbon dioxide and other greenhouse gas emissions, recycling of organic waste, nature conservation and biodiversity management, tourism and recreation, soil conservation, landscape management, the setting aside of land and less intensive production methods or forestation. The principal objective remained, however, financial aid to farmers.

11-11 The European Green Deal, which was to orient Union policy until 2030, stated:[25]

> Food production still results in water, air and soil pollution, contributes to the loss of biodiversity and climate change and consumes excessive amounts of natural resources … [The national strategic plans adopted under the CAP] will need to reflect an increased level of ambition to reduce significantly the use and risk of chemical pesticides, as well as the use of fertilisers and antibiotics.

However, the subsequent measures concerning the CAP 2023–27 did not reflect this objective, but continued to follow the traditional orientations of the Union's agricultural policy.[26] Until 2027, €386.6 billion were to be made available to the agricultural sector, distributed by the European Agricultural Guarantee Fund (€291.1 billion, mainly in the form of direct payments) and the European Agricultural Fund for Rural Development (€95.5 billion).

Regulation 2021/2115 fixed nine specific agricultural objectives, among them 'to contribute to climate change mitigation and adaptation, including by reducing greenhouse gas emissions and enhancing carbon sequestration, as well as to promote sustainability energy'; 'to foster sustainable development and efficient management of natural resources such as water, soil and air, including by reducing chemical dependency'; and 'to contribute to halting and reversing biodiversity loss, enhance ecosystem services and preserve habitats and landscapes' (Article 6). It was left to Member States in the CAP strategic plans which they had to elaborate to make these objectives operational. Article 12 provided that Member

[23] Commission, 'Perspectives for the Common Agricultural Policy' COM(85) 333.

[24] Commission, COM(88) 338.

[25] Commission, 'The European Green Deal' COM(2019) 640, s 2.1.6.

[26] Regulation 2021/2115 establishing rules on support for strategic plans to be drawn up by Member States under the common agricultural policy [2021] OJ L435/1; Regulation 2021/2116 on the financing, management and monitoring of the common agricultural policy [2021] OJ L435/187. As regards the differences to the Commission proposals, see Commission, 'Analysis of Links Between CAP Reform and Green Deal' SWD(2020) 93.

States had to establish a system of conditionality, according to which farmers would have to pay an administrative penalty when they did not comply with core provisions of EU environmental law and policy. Such a system already existed in the past, but was not properly enforced.

Articles 31 and 70 of Regulation 2021/2115 provided for the possibility to financially support voluntary ecosystem or management measures by farmers. The Commission's proposal to make such eco-schemes mandatory was not retained.

The main impacts of agriculture on the environment are:[27]

- the emission of greenhouse gases (GHG). About 10.3 per cent of all such emissions come from agricultural activity in the Union, not included the emissions from imported food and feed.[28] Animal production – feed digestion and manure storage – is responsible for 70 per cent of GHG emissions. The Court of Auditors found that the GHG emissions had not decreased since 2010 and that, in particular, no reduction of livestock had been decided or was planned for the years ahead. And the polluter-pays principle was not applied to agricultural GHG emissions.

The Commission admitted the existence of the problem.[29] Its proposals for improving the situations, though, left the decisions to Member States, in the framework of the Shared Efforts Regulation.[30]

- chemical pollution. The use of chemical fertilisers had increased since 2010;[31] the Commission set the objective of reducing the use of chemical pesticides in agriculture by 50 per cent by 2030,[32] but without clarifying how this would be reached. Also, organic farming, which grew from 5.4 per cent of the farmed land in the Union to 6.7 per cent between 2015 and 2020, was to reach a share of 25 per cent by 2030,[33] without it being known how this increase would be achieved. The Commission's strategy on pollinators of 2018[34] did not show any significant results.[35]
- nutrients in water and over-abstraction of water. The Commission committed itself to reconsidering derogations under Directive 91/676, which it had granted very generously in the past. It did not allude at all to the basic decision of Directive 91/676, which was to reduce the number of animals. No general measure on agricultural waste water treatment exists at Union level. The Union also did not impose the use of reused water for

[27] See EEA, *Rethinking Agriculture* (Copenhagen, 2023).

[28] Commission, 'Farm to Fork Strategy' COM(2020) 381; European Court of Auditors, *CAP and Climate. Half of the Climate Spending but Emissions Are not Decreasing. Special Report 16/2021* (Luxembourg, 2021).

[29] Commission, SWD(2021) 554, s 2.1: ' Decreasing carbon removals in the land sector;. Insufficient integration of the land sector into climate policies.'

[30] Regulation 2018/841 on the inclusion of greenhouse gas emissions and removals from land use, land use change and forestry in the 2030 climate and energy framework [2021] OJ L156/1; Commission, 'Proposal to Amend This Regulation' COM(2021) 554.

[31] European Court of Auditors (n 28) 54.

[32] Commission, 'Biodiversity Strategy for 2030' COM(2020) 380, s 2.2.2.

[33] ibid.

[34] Commission, 'EU Pollinators Initiative' COM(2018) 395. The initiative had three main objectives: improve knowledge about pollinators, tackle the causes of their decline and raise awareness.

[35] European Court of Auditors, *Protection of Wild Pollinators in the EU. Commission Initiatives Have Not Borne Fruit. Special Report 15/2020* (Luxembourg, 2020).

irrigation under Regulation 2020/741,[36] but only offered this as an option for Member States and farmers.

- loss of landscape diversity and features, of soil health and fertility, and of biodiversity, including the decline in pollinators. The biodiversity strategy for 2030 pleaded for better implementation of existing provisions, announced a proposal for the restoration of nature[37] and for the protection of soils, but did not envisage a comprehensive Union legislation on biodiversity.

Overall, the CAP neglected environmental concerns for long decades and largely continues to do so even today. Environmental concerns were considered a disturbing factor to the smooth running of the CAP. The few existing legal provisions, such as on nitrates in water, the protection of fauna and flora species or the sustainable use of pesticides, were hardly enforced and were ignored as far as possible. The CAP appears to be unsustainable. Its conservative strength is demonstrated by the political objections to the reduction of the use of pesticides in agriculture and the proposal for the restoration of nature – two core proposals of the European Green Deal.

11-12 Article 39 TFEU provides that agricultural products shall reach consumers at reasonable prices. This could, in theory, also include the environmental costs which are caused by the production and distribution of agricultural products. However, agricultural prices, which have so far been fixed by the EU institutions, do not reflect environmental costs at all. For a number of years, political pressure tried to align these prices with global prices for agricultural products; however, it is implicitly accepted that a price system for agricultural products could not simultaneously reflect environmental costs and align to world market prices. Hence, the more the polluter-pays principle is applied in agriculture, the greater will be the need to avoid competition with agricultural products from the world market, since products from many regions in the world – quite apart from labour costs – do not take environmental concerns into account. As regards the political strategy, therefore, the Union should reflect on whether there is a need to export the environmental (and social) standards of the agricultural sector, instead of having global discussions almost exclusively centred on the import of agricultural products into the Union and on the price barriers which the Union has erected. There is very little evidence of such a policy at present.

III. Fisheries Policy

11-13 Under the Lisbon Treaty, the competence over fisheries is shared between the Union and the Member States (Article 4(2.d) TFEU), except as regards the 'conservation of marine biological resources under the Common Fisheries Policy' (Article 3(1.e) TFEU), for which there is an exclusive EU competence. The basic regulation concerning the Common Fisheries Policy is presently Regulation 1380/2013,[38] which replaced earlier provisions dated from 2002.[39]

[36] Regulation 2020/741, [2020] OJ L177/32.

[37] Commission, Proposal for a Regulation on Nature Restoration' COM(2022) 304.

[38] Regulation1380/2013 on the Common Fisheries Policy [2013] OJ L354/22.

[39] Regulation 2371/2002 on the conservation and sustainable exploitation of fishing resources under common fisheries policy [2002] OJ L358/99, replacing Regulation 3760/92 [1992] OJ L389/1.

Regulation 1380/2013 indicated as the main problems of fisheries overexploitation, the pressure on non-target organisms and on the physical environment, the excessive capacity of the European fleet, the negative impact of aquaculture – in particular as regards water quality, dissemination of diseases and parasites and the introduction of alien species – and unsatisfactory implementation of EU measures. It established an ecosystem-based approach to fisheries management and suggested a series of measures to come closer to this, in particular by the designation of protected areas and the possibility to restrict fishing. No mention was made of climate mitigation or adaptation measures. It did not refer at all to climate change and its impact on fisheries. And a Commission assessment of 2023 described in detail the impact of climate change on oceans, waters and fisheries, but was not able to indicate a single specific climate-related measure on fisheries, not even the replacement of fossil fuels by other sources of energy.[40]

For most commercial fish stocks, the Council fixes annually total allowable catches 11-14
and allocates to the Member States quotas within these fishing opportunities.[41] In contrast, concrete EU measures for protecting fish and other marine resources are rare. That said, provisions on the mesh size, the nets to be used and the minimum size of fish which may be landed all have some influence on the catches. The Union also decided on an almost complete ban on the use of drift nets.[42] No ban of bottom fishing, generally or at least in marine protected areas, has either been decided or even proposed by the Commission. Other measures prohibiting the use of certain fishing gear have also been adopted;[43] until the end of 2022, 14 technical regulations limited or prohibited certain fishing activities.[44] Fishing gear containing plastic material and waste fishing gear were to be collected separately, but could be brought to port reception facilities without costs.[45] Regulation 2022/1614 established a list of deep-sea fishing areas and vulnerable zones where fishing activities with certain gear were prohibited.[46] Multiannual plans were adopted for the Baltic Sea, the North Sea and the Western Mediterranean Sea to regulate fishing activities and avoid overfishing.

Generally, all measures to reduce ocean pollution are useful for the evolution of fish stocks and thus support the fisheries industry. Measures under Directive 92/43 to protect natural habitats,[47] the different measures on water policy and management[48] and the

[40] Commission, 'Common Fisheries Policy – State of Play' SWD(2023) 103, s 2.7.

[41] See, eg Regulation 2023/194 fixing for 2023 the fishing opportunities for certain fish stocks applicable in Union waters and, for Union vessels, in certain non-Union waters, as well as fixing for 2023 and 2024 such fishing opportunities for certain deep-sea fish stocks [2023] OJ L29/1.

[42] Regulation 1239/98 laying down certain technical measures for the conservation of fishery resources [1998] OJ L171/4; see now Regulation 2019/1241 on the conservation of fisheries resources and the protection of marine ecosystems through technical measures [2019] OJ L198/105.

[43] See, eg Commission Implementing Regulation 2017/117 on the prohibition of using bottom contacting gear in some restricted areas of the Baltic Sea [2017] OJ L19/1; Commission Implementing Regulation 2017/118 prohibiting the use of bottom contacting gear in some restricted zones of the North Sea, the Kattegat and the Skagerrak[2017] OJ L19/10.

[44] Commission, SWD(2023) 103 (n 40) s 3.8.

[45] Directive 2019/904 [2019] OJ L155/1, Art 8 and Recitals 23–28; Directive 2019/883 [2019] OJ L151/116, Art 8(c).

[46] Commission Implementing Regulation 2022/1614 determining the existing deep-sea fishing areas and a list of areas where vulnerable ecosystems are known to occur or are likely to occur [2022] OJ L242/1.

[47] Directive 92/43 [1992] OJ L206/7; see also para 5-13ff.

[48] See ch 7 of this book.

integrated management of coastal zones[49] have considerable, albeit indirect, influence on fisheries. As regards controls, the Council adopted a regulation to establish a control system applicable to the Common Fisheries Policy.[50]

Regulation 1380/2013 repeated much of the environmental language of the earlier Regulation 2371/2002 and introduced a number of new provisions, such as the obligation to land all catches (Article 15) or the regionalisation of the Fisheries Policy (Article 17). It did not follow the idea that the policy decision on allowable catches should be bound by the scientific advice on this matter.[51] Overall, it appears doubtful that the Council and the Member States are prepared to actually apply Regulation 1380/2013 according to its letter and its spirit.

The oversized EU fishing fleet is already – and will continue to do so in the future – fishing in third countries' waters, on the basis of so-called sustainable partnership agreements with third countries. Overfishing is thus now a global problem, rather than an EU problem alone. By the end of 2022, the Union had concluded 20 sustainable partnership agreements with third countries, which gave access to their fishing grounds against the payment of an amount to support local fisheries infrastructure.[52] The problem of competition with the local fleet has not yet been the subject of intensive discussions. Also, the application by Union vessels of local environmental rules instead of Union provisions was not seen as problematic, though the Union vessels apply Union social rules for their seamen.

In 2018, 67 per cent of the fish and shellfish stocks in Union waters were not of good environmental status, including 63 per cent in the North-East Atlantic and 93 per cent in the Mediterranean Sea; in the Mediterranean Sea, 85 per cent of the stocks were overfished.[53]

11-15 Generally, the opinion prevails that the Common Fisheries Policy did not integrate environmental requirements very well, in particular due to overfishing and the lack of providing for sufficient protection measures for sensitive species, the seabed and marine protected areas.[54] In contrast, the Commission saw the Common Fisheries Policy as a success,[55] arguing, among other things, that in 2009 only five fish stocks were harvested sustainably, whereas in 2020 there were 62 such fish stocks. It admitted that overfishing had not

[49] Recommendation 2002/413 concerning the implementation of Integrated Coastal Zone Management in Europe [2002] OJ L148/24.

[50] Regulation 1224/2009 establishing a Community control system for ensuring compliance with the rules of the common fisheries policy [2009] OJ L343/1.

[51] A first regulation adopted under the system of Regulation 1380/2013 showed that the Council continued to deviate from the opinion of its scientific adviser, the International Council for the Exploration of the Seas ICES; see, on the one hand, Commission, COM(2014) 552 with the ICES proposals; on the other hand, see Council Regulation 1221/2014 [2014] OJ L330/16.

[52] These countries and regions are Greenland, Mauretania, Morocco, Guinea Bissau, Cabo Verde, Cook Island, Côte d'Ivoire, Gambia, Gabun, Marshall Island, Sao Tomé et Principé, Senegal and Seychelles. An agreement was concluded for Equatorial Guinea, Liberia, Kiribati, Micronesia, Madagascar, Mozambique and Solomon Island, but the necessary implementing protocol is still missing.

[53] EEA, *Marine Fish Stocks* (Copenhagen, 2018); this was the most recent Union publication concerning fish stocks.

[54] See European Court of Auditors, *Marine Environment: EU Protection Is Wide but Not Deep. Special Report 26/2020* (Luxembourg, 2020); EEA, *Status of Marine Fish and Shellfish Stocks in European Seas* (Copenhagen, 2019).

[55] See the Commission's answer to Report 26/2020 of the European Court of Auditors (n 54) in the annex to that report.

fully stopped, and that fishing in the Mediterranean Sea and the Black Sea continued to be problematic.[56]

In 2023, the Commission adopted a Marine Action Plan,[57] which mainly relied on soft law measures. Even when the Commission described the negative impact of fisheries on sensitive species or on marine protected areas and deplored, for example, the widespread practice of bottom fishing – 'one of the least selective fishing methods'[58] – it appealed to Member States to take action, rather than to announce regulatory measures itself. Nor did the Commission announce plans to restrict or prohibit fishing in marine protected areas. As such, the action plan is not likely to change the state of fish stocks and fishing practices significantly.

IV. Transport Policy

With the Lisbon Treaty, the EU Transport Policy (Articles 90–100 TFEU) became a policy sector of shared competence (Article 4(2.g) TFEU), whereas, up to the end of 2009, it had been a sector of exclusive EU competence. However, this construction by the EC Treaty has never been realised; national transport policies continued to exist and for the large part were much more relevant than EU transport policy. For a long time, the EU transport policy was targeted towards realising the four Treaty freedoms for goods, services, capital and labour. The introduction of an environmental chapter into the Treaty in 1987 has not yet fundamentally changed this situation.[59] 11-16

Transport policy contributes to the environmental problems linked with climate change, acidification, tropospheric ozone, biodiversity, congestion, technological and natural hazards, as well as to land use, noise, waste generation and marine pollution. Subsequent to the different environmental action programmes, which mentioned the problems of the environment, the Commission first issued in 1992 a Greenbook on environmental problems linked to transport,[60] which was quite quickly followed by a White Paper.[61] In 1995, the Commission adopted an action programme on transport for 1995–2000[62] and a Green Paper on fair and efficient prices in the transport sector.[63] In 1998, the Commission adopted communications on sustainable transport, on transport and CO_2, and on the environment and heavy goods vehicles;[64] 1999 saw a communication on air transport and the 11-17

[56] Commission, 'The Common Fisheries Policy Today and Tomorrow' COM(2023) 103. A Commission proposal of 2018 to strengthen the provisions concerning the allowed catches in the Western Mediterranean and the Adriatic Sea was rejected by the European Paliament and the Council.

[57] Commission, 'EU Action Plan: Protecting and Restoring Marine Ecosystems for Sustainable and Resilient Fisheries' COM(2023) 102.

[58] ibid s 2.

[59] See, however, CJEU Case C-440/05 *Commission v European Parliament and Council* ECLI:EU:C:2007:625, para 60: '[in view of the present Art 11 TFEU, environmental] protection must be regarded as an objective which also forms part of the common transport policy'.

[60] Commission, 'Greenbook on the Impact of Transport on the Environment' COM(92) 46.

[61] Commission, 'White Paper on a Community Strategy on Sustainable Mobility' COM(92) 494.

[62] Commission, COM(95) 302.

[63] Commission, COM(95) 691.

[64] Commission, COM(98) 716; for transport and carbon dioxide, Commission, COM(98) 204; for the environment and heavy goods vehicles, Commission, COM(98) 444.

environment,[65] in 2001 there was a White Paper,[66] in 2006, 2008 and 2009 other communications, and in 2011 another White Paper.[67] Overall, there was thus an impressive number of opinions, statements, resolutions and other political measures on the environmental impact of transport that were adopted by the different EU institutions.

The Union only rather slowly managed to introduce economic instruments, such as fees for the use of motorways.[68] EU rules on fees for the use of roads or airports, incentives for the use of less-polluting vehicles, fiscal advantages for public transport, the promotion of bicycle use and bicycle lanes or even simply the comprehensive promotion of electric cars do not exist.[69] Also, the recurrence to eco-points, used in the agreement with Austria on the Alpine transit,[70] was never used as a model for measures within the Union. Between 1990 and 2019, greenhouse gas emissions from transport rose by 33 per cent, demand for transport increased, as did congestion in cities, and the dependency on carbon-intensive fuels did not diminish significantly.[71]

11-18 The European Green Deal[72] announced a sustainable and smart mobility strategy, with less greenhouse gas emissions – a 90 per cent reduction by 2050, compared to the 60 per cent target of the 2011 White Paper – the active pursuit of a modal shift in favour of rail and inland waterway transport, serious measures to fight air pollution and congestion, especially in urban agglomerations, and a serious internalisation of environment-related external costs.

The Commission's new transport strategy of 2020,[73] however, continued first of all to proclaim targets until 2030 and 2050, and to depict the future of the Union transport system in very rosy colours.[74] It did not explain how it meant to progressively internalise the €388 billion environment-related external costs. It admitted that the change from road transport to other forms of transport ('modal shift') had not brought significant results; noise issues, congestion problems and land use were not discussed, nor were the possibilities for bicycle transport in urban agglomerations; the strategy mentioned deaths from road traffic – about 22,000 per year in the Union – but did not mention the some 300,000 premature deaths due to air pollution, mainly from transport emissions. Not even the upcoming replacement of vehicles with electrical vehicles and the interrelationship with energy questions were discussed.[75]

[65] Commission, 'Air Transport and Environment' COM(99) 640.

[66] Commission, 'White Paper – European Transport Policy for 2010: Time to Decide' COM(2001) 370.

[67] Commission, COM(2006) 314; Commission, (2008) 433; Commission, (2009) 279; Commission, 'White Paper: Roadmap to a Single European Transport Area. Towards a Competitive and Resource-Efficient Transport System' COM(2011) 144. See also the evaluation of this White Paper, Commission, SWD(2020) 410.

[68] Directive 1999/62 on the charging of heavy goods vehicles for the use of certain infrastructures [1999] OJ L187/42. This directive was updated nine times before the end of 2022, last by Directive 2022/362 [2022] OJ L69/1.

[69] See European Parliament Resolution of 22 January 1993 [1993] OJ C42/256.

[70] See Regulation 3637/92 [1992] OJ L373/1; Decision 92/577 [1992] OJ L373/4.

[71] EEA, *Transport and Environment Report 2021. EEA Report 02/2022* (Copenhagen, 2022).

[72] Commission, COM(2019) 640, s 2.1.5.

[73] Commission, 'Sustainable and Smart Mobility Strategy. Putting European Transport on Track for the Future' COM(2020) 789.

[74] The European Court of Auditors called these objectives the 'unrealistic' 4, see European Court of Auditors, *Special Report 8/2023: Intermodal Freight Transport. EU Still Far From Getting Freight off the Road* (Luxembourg, 2023). The greenhous gas emissions from transport increased by 24% between 1990 and 2019, ibid 8.

[75] Most of the issues mentioned were discussed in Commission, SWD(2020) 331.

Overall, the strategy showed a very limited political determination to openly enlarge the discussion on transport and the environment to all environmental facets and to introduce the necessary changes in the form of a coherent strategy and legally binding acts. 'Sustainable' was the key word, which allowed the promotion of increasingly intensive traffic. However, sustainability is a magic word which covers everything and means nothing.

Only a minority of Member States pursue a national transport policy that integrates environmental requirements. Attempts to increase car production and to create a more efficient transport infrastructure – motorways, roads, railway lines, ports, airports, etc – are at the centre of transport policy practically everywhere; the necessity of building the corresponding infrastructure reduces the efficiency of environmental measures, where they are taken.

In 1996 and 2011, the Commission concluded that transport in the Union was not 11-19
sustainable.[76] The same conclusion must be drawn from the 2020 strategy. Transport policy is thus a good example of (not) integrating environmental requirements in other policies: the analysis of what could and should be done is made, but the concrete actions bluntly ignore the environmental requirements. No serious will exists at EU level to elaborate and implement an environmentally sound transport policy.

V. Energy Policy

As mentioned, EU energy policy operated, until the entry into force of the Lisbon Treaty 11-20
(2009), without an express legal basis in the Treaty; Article 3 EC Treaty only allowed the taking of (some) 'measures' in the area of energy. The lack of an express Treaty competence on energy did not prevent Articles 154–56 EC Treaty (now Articles 170–72 TFEU) from providing for the creation, under the EC Treaty, of trans-European networks, amongst other things, in the area of energy infrastructure.

According to the new Article 194 TFEU, EU energy policy has the following main objectives:

1. ensure the functioning of the internal energy market;
2. ensure the security of energy supply;
3. promote energy efficiency and energy saving;
4. promote the development of new and renewable forms of energy; and
5. promote the interconnection of energy networks.

Article 194 TFEU explicitly stated that these objectives shall be pursued while taking into consideration the protection of the environment. Thus, the environment has at least been identified as one of the elements which influence EU energy policy measures, which is not the case in any other EU policy.

Within the framework of the Union's energy objectives, the Commission had already identified in 1997 three vital points on which EU energy measures must act: reduce

[76] Commission, COM(96) 624, 32; Commission, COM(2011) 144, 2.

dependence on supplies from energy sources outside the Union; ensure more competitive prices for energy products; and make energy markets more compatible with environmental objectives.[77] One reason for slow progress in reaching these objectives was that Member States relied heavily on national sources of energy – gas in the Netherlands, nuclear energy in France and Belgium, coal in Germany and Poland, for example – and wished to keep national responsibility for energy policy measures, including the responsibility for determining the price of energy.

11-21 The EC Treaty, the Coal and Steel Treaty and the Euratom Treaty all provided for energy measures. The Euratom Treaty was designed to promote the peaceful use of nuclear energy, but very largely lost its political raison d'être when, in the 1960s, France refused to integrate nuclear policy into the EU mechanisms and Germany also went its own way. The Treaty of Lisbon did not include the Euratom Treaty; the Euratom Treaty is thus a Treaty that stands on its own – an odd construction, as the main institutions (Commission, Council, European Parliament) are identical under the Treaty on European Union and the Euratom Treaty, and the different policies are, of course, closely interlinked. The construction finds its explanation in the different nuclear energy policies pursued by the Member States and in the determination of the 'nuclear countries' not to suffer any interference from the Union on their national policies and measures.

At present, about half of the 27 EU Member States do not have nuclear energy production on their territory, mainly for environmental reasons. Sweden, Germany and Belgium took a political decision to phase out nuclear energy, though future national policy changes might reverse these decisions. As the nuclear energy industry is extremely influential – backed also by governments – EU decisions on nuclear matters, including those relating to the climate,[78] frequently took nuclear energy and its continuity for granted. Nobody dared even to raise at EU level a discussion on the environmental impact of nuclear installations, the risk of accidents or terrorist attacks, nuclear wastes, decommissioning of nuclear installations or the overall energy balance of nuclear energy. Energy decisions which were based on the Euratom Treaty, in particular on Articles 30, 31, 34 and 37 thereof, did not discuss the impact of nuclear energy on the environment in any significant way; they mainly considered effects of nuclear energy on human health, but not on fauna and flora or other environmental assets, and even there the approach was not consistent.[79] The nuclear industry treated nuclear matters as a closed shop and succeeded in adopting only minimal provisions at EU level.[80] The dilemma that Article 192 TFEU allows the restriction of nuclear energy activities also for environmental reasons but that the Euratom Treaty provisions are interpreted as being *leges speciales* to the TFEU provisions[81] and are aimed

[77] Commission, COM(97) 167.

[78] For climate change issues, see also ch 9.

[79] See, eg Commission Opinion on the discharge of radioactive substances from Sellafield (UK) [1997] OJ C291/5. The Opinion, based on Art 37 of the Euratom Treaty, did not discuss at all the impact of such discharges on the Irish Sea, on the UK, on the environment or on marine fauna and flora. When the Commission examined the effects of French nuclear tests in Mururoa, it looked at their effects on people in other states (the Pitcairn Islands, UK), but not on French citizens in Mururoa or on the environment.

[80] See para 4-52 on nuclear installations and on the prevention of nuclear accidents, para 10-30 on nuclear waste and para 7-18 on radioactive substances in drinking water.

[81] See, eg CJEU Case C-48/14 *European Parliament v Council* ECLI:EU:C:2015:91.

at the promotion of nuclear activities has been largely ignored by the EU institutions – and the public.

The Treaty on Coal and Steel entered into effect in 1952 and ended in 2002. Its functions were taken over by the Union. It mainly provided for measures on coal, though measures on lignite could also be taken under certain conditions. The use of coal as the main energy resource in the Union – which had taken over from wood in the nineteenth century – had already been replaced by oil by the end of the 1950s. The serious adaptation problems caused by this change continue to exist and have contributed to reducing the discussions on environmental problems linked to coal. 11-22

All energy resources, with the exception of nuclear energy, are thus subject to the provisions of the EU Treaties. Energy use is considered to contribute significantly to climate change and air pollution, acidification, tropospheric ozone creation, waste generation, soil degradation, marine and coastal zone problems and technological hazard issues, as well as land use by installations and networks, water pollution and light pollution. As some of these environmental problems do not occur with the use of nuclear energy, the ongoing discussion on climate change led to certain attempts to promote nuclear energy, although this energy is not economically competitive – except perhaps in France, where it has been subsidised for decades – and neither the problems of disposal of nuclear waste nor those of decommissioning of nuclear installations have been solved. Furthermore, the population in the EU is divided as regards nuclear technology, in particular since other options may likewise be costly, but also in view of the energy discussions following the invasion of Ukraine by Russia and the attempts of the Union to become independent from gas, oil and coal supplies from Russia.

The proponents of nuclear energy certainly were supported by a regulation of 2022, which declared investments in nuclear energy to be investments in 'green' technology.[82] However, openness, transparency, accountability and public participation are notions that cannot be attributed to the nuclear sector. EU measures on the safety of nuclear installations, nuclear waste and its shipment are completely insufficient and not comparable to the measures which have been adopted for non-nuclear installations and waste.[83]

As regards environment-related energy measures, most provisions were based, in the past, on Articles 192 or 352 TFEU. Article 192(2) TFEU expressly maintained a veto right for Member States in important energy matters by providing for unanimous decisions in such cases.[84] Since the end of the 1980s, a number of political, non-legally binding statements have been made on the relationship between energy and the environment,[85] including the statement to stabilise carbon dioxide emissions by the year 2000 at the level of 1990 in order to combat the greenhouse effect.[86] 11-23

[82] Commission Delegated Regulation 2022/1214 as regards economic activities in certain energy sectors [2022] OJ L188/1.

[83] See Directive 2009/71/Euratom on nuclear safety of nuclear installation [2009] OJ L172/18; Directive 2011/70/Euratom on spent fuels and radioactive waste [2011] OJ L199/48; Directive 2006/117 on the shipment of radioactive waste [2006] OJ L337/1.

[84] Art 192(2) TFEU: '[The Council shall unanimously adopt] … measures significantly affecting a Member State's choice between different energy sources and the general structure of its energy supply.' See also para 2-92.

[85] Commission, COM(88) 174; Commission, 'Energy and the Environment' COM(89) 369.

[86] Commission (1990) 10 *EC Bulletin* 1.3.77; this commitment was made in a form of Council conclusions, ie in a political and unpublished form.

Since 1991, the Union has made available (modest) financial means to promote energy saving and renewable sources of energy.[87] The discussion on climate change progressively led to the promotion of biofuels as a source of energy and, more generally, to the promotion of renewable energy sources.[88] The Union succeeded in fixing binding targets for the share of renewable energies in the total energy consumption. However, the attempt to fix binding targets on energy efficiency failed, as the Member States claimed that this was a question of national competence (subsidiarity). Only in 2012 was a directive on energy efficiency adopted which fixed an indicative target of 20 per cent increase in energy efficiency – without giving a base year of comparison.[89]

11-24 As regards taxes, the Commission proposed, in 1992, a tax on carbon dioxide emissions and energy.[90] The proposal was intended, in particular, to combat the greenhouse effect. It provided for an exception of renewable energies and stated that:

> in order to safeguard the competitiveness of Community industry, the tax arrangements cannot be applied in the Member States until such time as other member countries of the OECD have brought in a similar tax or measures having an equivalent financial impact.

This announcement condemned the proposal, since Japan and the USA, in particular, clearly indicated that they had no intention of introducing a similar tax. The amended proposal,[91] which has since also become obsolete, provided for some conditions for the introduction of the tax, but left it entirely at the discretion of Member States whether they wished to introduce an emission/energy tax.

In 2003, the Council adopted a directive on the taxation of energy products.[92] This directive repealed earlier directives; it imposed minimum tax rates on all energy products. Energy-intensive industries and the agricultural, horticultural, aquacultural and forestry sectors could request to be exempted from the tax, provided they entered into national environmental agreements, participated in emission trading schemes or in equivalent agreements. The minimum levels of taxation were fixed at the levels shown in Table 11.1. follows (in euro):[93]

Table 11.1 Minimum levels of taxation on energy products as per Directive 2003/96 (in euro)

For industrial and commercial use		**Heating fuels and electricity**	
Petrol (1000 l)	421		
Unleaded petrol	359		
Heavy fuel oil		15	
Diesel	330	21	21

(continued)

[87] Decision 91/565 [1991] OJ L507/34 (energy saving); Directive 93/76 [1993] OJ L273/28 (energy efficiency); Decision 93/500 [1993] OJ L235/41 (alternative sources of energy); Decision 96/737 [1996] OJ L335/50 (energy saving).

[88] Directive 2009/28 on the promotion of the use of energy from renewable sources [2009] OJ L140/16.

[89] Directive2012/27 on energy efficiency [2012] OJ L315/1.

[90] [1992] OJ C196/1; see also para 9-30.

[91] Commission, COM(95) 172.

[92] Directive 2003/96 restructuring the Community framework for the taxation of energy products and electricity [2003] OJ L283/51.

[93] For details, see annex I to Directive 2003/96.

Table 11.1 ***(Continued)***

For industrial and commercial use		Heating fuels and electricity	
Kerosene	330	21	0
LPG (1000 kg)	125	41	0
Natural gas (gigajoule)	2.6	0.3	0.3
Electricity (MWh)	1.0		

As can be seen, Table 11.1 does not show any favouring of renewable energy or the promotion of biofuels. The subvention of diesel fuel in comparison to petrol cannot really be explained by environmental considerations. And, like its predecessors, Directive 2003/96 contained numerous transition periods, derogations and exceptions. A Commission proposal of 2021 to amend Directive 2003/96 suggested removing the differential between petrol and diesel fuels and taxing fuels from renewable sources at half the minimum rate for petrol and diesel.[94] That proposal needs unanimity for its adoption (Article 113 TFEU).

Directive 2009/28 fixed, for 2020, a binding target of 20 per cent share of renewable energy in the total energy consumption, with 10 per cent of biofuels in transport.[95] And in 2015, the Juncker Commission adopted a new strategy paper for an energy union[96] which fixed five objectives: energy security; an integrated energy market; energy efficiency; decarbonising the economy; and research, innovation and competitiveness. 11-25

These different legislative and non-legislative measures were completely superseded by three events since 2015: first, the adoption of the Paris Agreement on climate change, which clarified the 'existential threat'[97] posed by climate change to the planet and called for action to limit greenhouse gas emissions so that the temperature on earth did not exceed 1.5°C beyond pre-industrial levels.[98] Second, the European Green Deal,[99] launched by the Von der Leyen Commission in 2019, which was approved by the other institutions and which proclaimed in particular increased ambitions for the Union to become climate-neutral by 2050; this meant in particular a departure from the use of fossil fuels. Third, the war which Russia started against Ukraine in 2022, which led to numerous measures by the Union and by the Member States to become independent of oil and gas supply from Russia.

The Union adopted a Climate Law, which proclaimed 'a binding objective of climate neutrality in the Union by 2050' and as 'a reduction of net greenhouse gas emissions by at least 55% compared to 1990 levels by 2030'.[100] Directive 2009/28 on renewable energies was replaced by Directive 2018/2001, which required Member States to ensure that the share of energy from renewable sources[101] was at least 32 per cent 11-26

[94] Commission, COM(2021) 563.

[95] Directive 2009/28 (n 88).

[96] Commission, 'A Framework Strategy for a Resilient Energy Union With a Forward-Looking Climate Change Policy' COM(2015) 80.

[97] Regulation 2021/1119 establishing a framework for achieving climate neutrality [2021] OJ L243/1, Recital 1.

[98] For more details, see ch 9.

[99] Commission, COM(2019) 640.

[100] Regulation 2021/1119 establishing the framework for achieving climate neutrality (European Climate Law [2021] OJ L243/1, Arts 1 and 4.

[101] 'Renewable energy sources' were defined as energy from renewable non-fossil sources, namely wind, solar (solar thermal and solar voltaic) and geothermal energy, tidal, wave and other ocean energy, hydropower, biomass,

by 2030.[102] This target was a binding overall target for the Union; no national target was fixed for the Member States, which had to set national contributions in their 'integrated national energy and climate plans' in order to allow the Union to reach its target. These national plans were mandatory according to Regulation 2018/1999[103] and had to be established for a period of 10 years. Should the Commission consider a national ambition to be insufficient, it could address a recommendation to the Member State in question, which had to duly take into consideration the Commission's view. Of course, the Commission could also resort to its powers under Article 258 TFEU, but this is a purely hypothetical possibility. De facto, it has no power to enforce compliance with the binding Union target.

Directive 2012/27 on energy efficiency was also amended.[104] Member States were in particular asked to contribute to reaching the 2020 Union target of 20 per cent improvement in energy efficiency and the 2030 Union target of at least 32.5 per cent; for that purpose, they had to establish indicative national energy efficiency targets. Again, the Commission powers to enforce compliance with the Union target appear theoretical. A large number of other Union acts were proposed to be amended in order to allow the Union to reach its target of a 55 per cent reduction in greenhouse gas emissions by 2030. All these proposals are presently under discussion by the other institutions of the Union.

11-27 The Union further adopted, on the basis of Article 122 TFEU,[105] Regulation 2022/2577.[106] This regulation laid down temporary rules of an emergency nature to accelerate the permit-granting process applicable to the production of energy from renewable energy sources. It declared that such projects 'shall be presumed as being in the overriding public interest and serving public health and safety when balancing legal interests in the individual case' for the purpose of applying Directive 92/43 on habitats and wild fauna and flora, Directive 2009/147 on birds and Directive 2000/60 on water.[107] Furthermore, for solar energy equipment, a screening to determine whether an environmental impact assessment had to be made under Directive 2011/92[108] was no longer necessary. Permit procedures were normally limited to six months; for private projects on solar equipment, the permit was even deemed to be granted when the authorities had not reacted to an application within one month.

landfill gas, sewage treatment plant gas, and biogas (Art 2, no 1). See also CJEU Case C-297/20P *Sabo v European Parliament and Council* ECLI:EU:C:2021:24 (forest biomass was rightly classified as renewable energy source); Case C-402/20P *Santiga v Commission* ECLI:EU:C:2021:872 (the question whether palm oil was rightly classified as not being a renewable source of energy was held to be inadmissible).

[102] Directive 2018/2001 on the promotion of the use of energy from renewable sources [2018] OJ L328/82. In 2021, the Commission proposed to fix this share at 40%, Commission, COM(2021) 557.

[103] Regulation 2018/1999 on the governance of the energy union and climate action [2018] OJ L328/1.

[104] Directive 2018/2002 [2018] OJ L328/210. In 2021, the Commission proposed to reach, by 2030, a reduction of energy use by 9% compared to 2020, 'so that the Union's final energy consumption [in 2030] amounts to no more than 787 Mtoe and the Union's primary energy consumption amounts to no more than 1013 Mtoe in 2030', Commission, COM(2021) 558, Art 4.

[105] Art 122(1) TFEU: 'Without prejudice to any other procedures, provided for in the Treaties, the Council, on a proposal from the Commission, may decide, in a spirit of solidarity between Member States, upon the measures appropriate to the economic situation, in particular if severe difficulties arise in the supply of certain products, notably in the area of energy.'

[106] Regulation 2022/2577 laying down a framework to accelerate the deployment of renewable energy [2022] OJ L335/36.

[107] Directive 92/43 [1992] OJ L206/7; Directive 2009/147 [2010] OJ L20/7; Directive 2000/60 [2000] OJ L327/1.

[108] Directive 2011/92 [2012] OJ L26/1.

It is too early to assess whether this regulation really accelerated the permitting procedures, as much depends on the reaction of the national permitting authorities. The regulation was initially limited to 18 months, but may be prolonged. Such a prolongation is more than likely, as economic operators – and, in part, Member States – have long viewed the environment protection provisions of the above-mentioned four environmental directives as barriers to economic development.

Overall, the Union's energy policy has the objective of replacing fossil fuels by alternative sources of energy. This is, as such, a welcome objective, though the aspiration of giving priority to onshore or offshore energy projects over environmental considerations, as laid down in Regulation 2022/2577, appears too simplistic. It is remarkable, though, that all environment-related energy measures which the Union has adopted on the basis of Article 192 or 194 TFEU, were adopted by majority decisions. In no case was there any decision based on the unanimity provisions of Article 192(2)(c) TFEU – 'measures significantly affecting a Member State's choice between different energy sources and the general structure of its energy supply' – or Article 194 TFEU. Poland was twice unsuccessful in its request to have Union energy-related measures annulled because they had not been adopted unanimously.[109]

VI. Tourism Policy

The Lisbon Treaty enabled the Union to carry out actions 'to support, coordinate or supplement' measures of the Member States in the area of tourism (Article 6(d) TFEU). Article 195 TFEU specified this possibility, excluding 'any harmonisation of the laws and regulations of Member States'. 11-28

Tourism contributes in particular to land, energy and water use, waste generation, biodiversity loss and, via land, sea and air travel, to air pollution and greenhouse gas emissions. Tourism has developed into the largest service industry in the Union. Particular areas of concern because of negative impact on the environment are coastal zones, the Mediterranean, the Alps and cities such as Florence, Barcelona, Dubrovnik, Venice or Nice.

While the integration of environmental requirements into tourism policy was considered, under the Fifth Environmental Action Programme (1993), to be one of five priority policy areas, this approach changed rapidly. The Sixth Environmental Action Programme (2002) mentioned tourism in half a phrase,[110] the Seventh Environmental Action Programme (2013) mentioned it not at all[111] and the Eighth Environmental Action

[109] CJEU Case C-5/16 *Poland v Euroean Parliament and Council* ECLI:EU:C:2018:483. The case concerned Decision 2015/1814 concerning the establishment of a market stability reserve for the Union's greenhouse gas emissions trading scheme [2015] OJ L264/1; Case C-128/17 *Poland v European Parliament and Council* ECLI:EU:C:2019:194. The case concerned Directive 2016/2284 on the reduction of national emission ceilings for certain atmospheric pollutants [2016] OJ L344/1. A third case is pending (Case C-675/22) concerning Regulation 2022/1369 on coordinated demand-reduction measures for gas [2022] OJ L206/1; that regulation was based on Art 122 TFEU.

[110] Decision 1600/2002 [2002] OJ L242/1, Art 6(2): '[Priority actions should be] promoting the integration of conservation and restoration of the landscape values into other policies including tourism, taking into account relevant international instruments.'

[111] Decision 1386/2013 [2013] OJ L354/171.

Programme mentioned it in another non-committing phrase.[112] The Commission has made a number of communications on tourism[113] and announced, in 2007, an agenda for sustainable European tourism, without defining 'sustainable tourism';[114] however, it concentrated on increasing the number of tourists and was not concerned with environment-related measures. Thus, generally, environmental integration requirements into tourist policy became a negative priority for the Union.

11-29 Legal matters on tourism are affected by the lack of an explicit competence on tourism. Hence, objectives on tourism are not fixed at Union level – except for the statement that tourism should be or become sustainable. No legal instruments have so far been adopted or proposed to concretise this vague idea. A Council document concerning a 'European Agenda for Tourism 2030'[115] limited itself to invoking, in 22 paragraphs, a sustainable, innovative and resilient tourism industry, stressing the economic aspects and again omitting to address environmental aspects. In the same way, the European Court of Auditors concentrated on funding opportunities for tourism.[116] Overall, the Union action on tourism almost completely concentrated on financial assistance to pilot or demonstration projects; ecotourism is not yet a priority for assistance, financial support or explicit promotion.[117]

The idea for eco-labels for hotels, restaurants, beaches, villages or other holiday resorts did not lead to Union-wide initiatives. An eco-label for tourist accommodation was introduced in 2003 and later updated;[118] it was granted to some 500 accommodations – out of some 600,000 – and paid particular attention to water use and energy efficiency. In contrast, an eco-label for camping sites[119] expired in the meantime and was not renewed. Decision 1194/2011 introduced a European heritage label[120] to mark natural or cultural sites of particular interest; the label had very limited success: by 2023, 60 sites had received the label, too few to influence tourism.

There was no attempt to address the problems of tourism in coastal and mountainous areas. The Union adhered to the Convention on the Alps and its protocols on mountain farming, tourism and soil conservation, but not to its protocols on landscape management and mountain forestry. The protocol on tourism[121] was drafted in very general terms. It allowed for measures, for example, on ski lifts, ski slopes or quiet areas, but no such action was undertaken by the Union. It appears that the negative impact which mass tourism has had on the alpine environment is, with delay and more slowly, being repeated in other mountainous regions of the Union, such as the Pyrenees and the Carpathians.

[112] Decision 2022/591 [2022] OJ L114/22, Art 2(2)(f).

[113] Commission, 'Basic Orientations for the Sustainability of European Tourism' COM(2003) 716; Commission, 'A Renewed EU Tourism Policy. Towards a Stronger Partnership for European Tourism' COM(2006) 134; Commission, 'A European Strategy Form on Growth and Jobs in Coastal and Maritime Tourism' COM(2014) 86.

[114] Commission, 'Agenda for a Sustainable and Competitive European Tourism' COM(2007) 621.

[115] Council, Document 15441/22 of 1 December 2022.

[116] European Court of Auditors, *EU Support for Tourism. Need for a Fresh Strategic Orientation and a Better Funding Approach. Special Report 27/2021* (Luxembourg, 2021).

[117] See also the study by Interreg Europe (European Regional Development Fund), *For a New EU Integrated Tourism Policy* (Brussels, 2019), which again promoted better funding for touristic 'jobs and growth'.

[118] See last, Decision 2017/175 [22017] OJ L28/9; amended by Decision 2023/705 [2023] OJ L92/19.

[119] Decision 2005/338 [2005] OJ L108/67; Decision 2009/564 [2009] OJ L196/36.

[120] Decision 1194/2011 establishing a European Union action for the European heritage label [2011] OJ L303/1. The decision was based on Art 167(5) TFEU.

[121] Decision 2006/516 concluding the protocol [2006] OJ L201/31; the protocol is published at [2005] OJ L337/43.

12

Union Environmental Law at the International Level

I. Sustainable Development Goals

Internationally, the environmental discussion is largely marked by concerns on climate change – in particular, the Paris Agreement of 2015[1] – and the United Nations' Sustainable Development Goals (SDGs) of 2015, which were adopted by a Resolution of the UN General Assembly.[2] The 17 goals read as follows: 12-01

1. End poverty in all its forms everywhere.
2. End hunger, achieve food security and improved nutrition and promote sustainable development.
3. Ensure healthy lives and promote well-being for all at all stages.
4. Ensure inclusive and equitable quality education and promote lifelong learning opportunities for all.
5. Achieve gender equality and empower all women and girls.
6. Ensure availability and sustainable management of water and sanitation for all.
7. Ensure access to affordable, reliable, sustainable and modern energy for all.
8. Promote sustained, inclusive and sustainable economic growth, full and productive employment and decent work for all.
9. Build resilient infrastructure, promote inclusive and sustainable industrialization and foster innovation.
10. Reduce inequalities in and among countries.
11. Make cities and human settlements inclusive, safe, resilient and sustainable.
12. Ensure sustainable consumption and production patterns.
13. Take urgent action to combat climate change and its impacts.
14. Conserve and sustainably use the oceans, seas and marine resources for sustainable development.
15. Protect, restore and promote sustainable use of terrestrial ecosystems, sustainable manage forests, combat desertification and halt and reverse land degradation and halt biodiversity loss.
16. Promote peaceful and inclusive societies for sustainable development, provide access to justice for all and build effective, accountable and inclusive institutions at all levels.
17. Strengthen the means of implementation and revitalize the Global Partnership for Sustainable Development.

These goals were completed by more than 150 sub-goals and targets.

[1] For climate change questions, see ch 9 of this book.
[2] UN General Assembly, Resolution 70/1 of 25 September 2015: the 2030 agenda for sustainable development.

12-02 The Union, which is not a member of the UN, did not formally take over these 17 SDGs, as it has developed its own sustainable development strategy since 2001,[3] and had the objective of a sustainable development anchored as Union objectives in Articles 3 and 21 of the Treaty on European Union (TEU). However, the Commission set up a multi-stakeholder platform on the implementation of the SDGs in the Union.[4] And though there is no Union commitment to report to the UN (and no comprehensive Union report to the UN exists yet), the biennial progress report of the Statistical Office on sustainability has been aligned to the SDGs since 2017 in order to demonstrate the willingness of the EU to follow the UN orientation;[5] this was all the easier as the 17 SDGs were formulated in a rather vague form which left a lot of room for implementation measures. It is evident that the environmental SDGs, in particular nos 6, 7 and 11–15, received particular EU attention after the adoption of the 'new growth strategy of the EU', the European Green Deal.[6]

In its secondary legislation, the Union tries increasingly frequently to demonstrate its compatibility with the SDGs.[7]

II. The Union and its Neighbours

12-03 In 2021, the Union adopted Regulation 2021/947, which attempted to assemble the different international commitments, including financial commitments, for the years 2021–27 in a single legal instrument.[8] The regulation was based on Articles 209, 212 and 232(2) of the Treaty on the Functioning of the European Union (TFEU). The 'neighbourhood' countries, for which specific provisions were introduced, did not include the Western Balkan countries, but did include North African and Arabian countries, which have no serious prospect of ever becoming members of the Union. The regulation aimed at promoting, among others, environment and climate protection, and laid down the principles, values and objectives of Union action. The financing of measures which could have adverse negative effects on the environment of the climate was, in principle, not allowed (Article 4). The budget for the years 2021–27 was fixed at €79,462,000,000 (Article 6). Details for co-operation are to be elaborated in bilateral agreements.

12-04 The Union concluded an agreement with Norway, Liechtenstein and Iceland (the European Economic Area Agreement, the Agreement), according to which these countries take part in the EU internal market.[9] Decisions by the Union, including environmental

[3] See Commission, 'Towards a European Strategy for Sustainable Development' COM(2001) 264. European Council, 'Renewed EU Sustainable Development Strategy' Document 10917 of 26 June 2006.

[4] Commission Decision C(2017) 2941.

[5] Compare, eg Commission, *Statistical Office: Sustainable Development in the EU. 2009 Monitoring Report on the EU Sustainable Development Strategy* (Luxembourg, 2009) and Commission, *Statistical Office: Sustainable Development in the EU. Monitoring Report on Progress Towards the SDGs in the EU. 2023 Report* (Luxembourg, 2023). See also European Court of Auditors, *Reporting on sustainability. A stocktaking of EU Institutions and Agencies* (Luxembourg, 2019).

[6] Commisssion, COM(2019) 640.

[7] See, eg Directive 2020/2184 on drinking water [2020] OJ L435/1; Regulation 2023/1115 on deforestation-free products [2023] OJ L150/206.

[8] Regulation 2021/947 establishing the neighbourhood, development and international cooperation instrument – global Europe [2021] OJ L209/1.

[9] Agreement on the European Economic Area [1994] OJ L1/3. This agreement was amended 351 times before the end of 2022.

decisions, which are relevant for the free circulation of goods and services must be taken over for the European Economic Area by an explicit decision of a joint committee of the EU and the three countries. Environmental decisions by any contracting party are to be taken according to Articles 73–75 of the Agreement, which mirrors Articles 191–93 TFEU. Disputes on questions about whether an EU legislative act has to be taken over and is properly applied by the three countries are decided by the European Free Trade Area (EFTA) Court of Justice, seated in Luxembourg.[10] In practice, the application of the Agreement to environmental matters has not led to any difficulties or controversies between the contracting parties.

The relations between the Union and Switzerland are regulated by a set of sectoral agreements, for example on the free movement of persons, public procurement, trade in agricultural products, civil aviation, participation in the European Environment Agency, education or police co-operation. No such agreement exists for environmental measures, not even where they are of a transboundary nature. Thus, environmental problems have to be solved in a bilateral context, such as the noise level from Zurich airport (Switzerland–Germany), or by an ad hoc EU–Switzerland agreement. 12-05

Relations with the Western Balkan countries – Albania, North Macedonia, Montenegro, Serbia, Kosovo and Bosnia Herzegovina – are marked by the fact that these countries try to become members of the Union; with Serbia and Montenegro, Albania and North Macedonia, accession negotiations have already been decided. As it is a principle of EU law that a country which accedes to the EU has to take over all existing legislation – the *acquis communautaire* – including provisions on the environment, the EU has granted technical and financial support – paying experts – since about 2005 in order to allow all these countries to gradually align their environmental legislation to Union requirements. The Commission reports annually on progress in the accession preparations[11] and does not hesitate to make critical legal–political assessments on the progress on alignment. Generally, it deplores no or slow progress in implementation, but important omissions in legislation are also mentioned. 12-06

Turkey has been a candidate country for decades, but accession negotiations have advanced very slowly for political reasons. The Commission has also published progress reports and found, in the 2022 report, there had been no progress in the alignment of environmental legislation with Union law requirements.[12]

The association agreement which the Union concluded with Moldova was in the traditional style:[13] there was no specific section on the protection of the climate or the 12-07

[10] See, eg EFTA Court of Justice, Case E6/06 *EFTA Suveillance Authority v Liechtenstein* judgment of 3 October 2007 on the transposition of the Noise Directive 2002/49; Case E-8/11 *EFTA Surveillance Authority v Iceland* judgment of 14 December 2011 on the application of the Noise Directive 2002/49; Case E-5/14 *EFTA Surveillance Authority v Iceland* judgment of 24 September 2014 on the application of the Waste Directive 2008/98; Case E-3/15 *Liechtensteiner Gesellschaft für Umweltschutz* judgment of 2 October 2015 on the transposition and application of Directive 2011/92 on environmental impact assessment; Case E-7/15 *EFTA Surveillance Authority v Norway* judgment of 2 October 2015 on the application of Directive 2008/50 on air pollution; Case E-35/15 *EFTA Surveillance Authority v Norway* judgment of 2 August 2015 on the application of Directive 2008/15 on port reception facilities.

[11] See the environmental sections in the latest reports on Albania, Commission, SWD(2022) 332, 105ff; Kosovo, Commission, SWD(2022) 334, 115–16; Montenegro, Commission, SWD(2022) 335, 111ff; Bosnia Herzegovina, Commission, SWD(2022) 336, 105ff; North Macedonia, Commission, SWD(22022) 337, 95ff; Serbia, Commission, SWD(2022) 338, 122ff.

[12] Commission, SWD(2022) 333, 114ff.

[13] Association Agreement with Moldova [2014] OJ L260/4.

environment. In the chapter on trade and sustainable development (Article 363ff), general reference was made to compliance with international environmental agreements; some general remarks addressed biodiversity and management, as well as trade in forest and fish products. In contrast, the association agreement which the Union concluded with Georgia included provisions on co-operation in environmental and climate change matters.[14] Georgia undertook to approximate its legislation to key Union legislative acts on environmental and climate change within a specific time.[15] With Armenia, the Union concluded an agreement[16] under which Armenia also committed itself to approximate its legislation to key pieces of Union legislation on environmental and climate change.[17] These legislative acts, together with a precise indication of the timetable for the approximation, were laid down in annexes III and IV to the agreement. There is no compliance control, though, with regard to these provisions.

Besides this more formalised relationship, there are a number of regional environmental programmes of the Union in the water and waste management sectors which specifically addressed these and other Eastern European countries, Turkey or the Western Balkan countries mentioned above.

The environmental provisions concerning the relations with Russia, Ukraine and Belarus are not presented here. Indeed, the war between Russia and Ukraine which started in February 2022 has strongly politicised all those relations and it is not currently possible to anticipate what developments might follow.

III. International Environmental Agreements

12-08 Three types of international environment-related agreements which the Union concluded need separate mentions. The first is the so-called Cotonou Agreement, which the EU concluded with 79 countries from Africa, the Caribbean and the Pacific (ACP) – essentially, former colonies from EU Member States – in 2000.[18] The agreement intended to promote partnership, development, trade and investments, but also the protection of the environment and, since 2010, the fight against climate change. The above-mentioned budget under Regulation 2021/947 also covers financial support under the Cotonou Agreement. Concrete commitments were not laid down. The taking of joint measures with the contracting parties was difficult, because of diverging political and economic interests. The Union did not take concrete initiatives under the Cotonou Agreement to activate the different environmental provisions. Rather, co-operation with individual ACP countries or regional groups of countries prevailed. The general commitments in the Cotonou Agreement to promote environmental protection were not monitored and did not bring added value to the different national environmental policies of the 79 states.

[14] Association Agreement with Georgia [2014] OJ L261/4, Art 301ff.

[15] ibid, Arts 306 and 312, together with annexes XXVI and XXVII.

[16] Comprehensive and enhanced partnership agreement with Armenia [2018] OJ L23/4.

[17] ibid Arts 45 and 56.

[18] ACP–EU Partnership agreement [2000] OJ L387/3; amended [2005] OJ L209/27 and [2010] OJ L287/3. A further amendment is under discussion.

As mentioned in chapter seven, the Union concluded sustainable fisheries partnership agreements with a number of development countries. These countries granted European fishing vessels access to their fishing grounds against the payment of a certain sum.[19] The environmental law provisions – on fishing gear, the protection of spawning grounds and of vulnerable zones, and others – are those of the developing country; this is environmentally doubtful where the developing country has no or only weak provisions in force and has enforcement difficulties. Also, the competition aspect between the highly industrialised EU fishing vessels and the vessels of the developing country are not considered in the agreements, which are thus primarily agreements to ensure access of the EU to third-world fishing markets.

The Union is party to a considerable number of international environmental agreements.[20] Within the context of most of these conventions, protocols were adopted, which also require formal conclusion; the Union adhered to many of them. Perhaps the best example is the Paris Agreement on Climate Change of 2015, which is, formally, a protocol under the 1992 Framework Convention on Climate Change.

As the Union is not a state, accession to an international convention or a protocol is 12-09 only possible where there is a specific clause in the respective legal instrument according to which regional economic integration organisations – this term includes the Union – may also become a party. Not all international agreements contain such a clause, in particular not the agreements adopted under the auspices of the International Maritime Organization, which deals with the marine environment, or the International Civil Aviation Organization, which deals with air and noise pollution caused by air traffic. Thus, formally, only the EU Member States are, at best, members of the different legal instruments adopted by an international organisation to which the Union is not a party. However, according to the Court of Justice of the European Union (CJEU), provisions of such an international agreement may nevertheless be applicable in the Union provided that all EU Member States are party to the agreement, that the general nature and broad logic of the agreement do not preclude its application within the Union and that the provisions of the agreement which are in question are unconditional and sufficiently precise that they may be relied upon by natural or legal persons.[21] When only some Member States are party to an international agreement which had not been concluded by the Union itself, the Union is not bound by it unless the legal provisions are part of customary international law.

[19] See, eg Sustainable fisheries partnership agreement EU–Mauritania [2021] OJ L439/3.

[20] The most important conventions to which the Union is party are: the Framework Convention on Climate Change; the Rio Convention on Biodiversity; the Stockholm Convention on Persistent Organic Pollutants; the Rotterdam Convention on the Export and Import of Dangerous Chemicals; the Basel Convention on Trade in Waste; the CITES Convention on Trade in Endangered Species; the Barcelona Convention on the Protection of the Mediterranean; the OSPAR Convention on the Protection of the North-East Atlantic; the Helsinki Convention on the Protection of the Baltic Sea; the Convention on Long-Range Transboundary Air Pollution; the Convention on the Protection of the Alps; the Aarhus Convention on Access to Information, Public Particiption in Decision-Making and Access to Justice in Environmental Matters; the Bern Convention on the Protection of European Wildlife and Natural Habitats; the Bonn Convention on Migratory Species; the Vienna Convention on the Protection of the Ozone Layer; the Conventions on the Protection of the Rhine, the Protection of the Danube, the Protection of the Oder and the Protection of the Elbe; the Convention on the Prevention of Industrial Accidents in a Transboundary Context; and the Convention on Desertification.

[21] CJEU Case C-366/10 *Air Transport Association of America* ECLI:EU:C:2011:864; Case C-308/06 *Intertanko* ECLI:EU:C:2008:312. The CJEU also included the customary international law in 'international law'.

When the Union concludes an international environmental agreement, the provisions of this agreement form an integral part of the Union's legal order. They prevail over Union regulations or directives because they bind not only the Member States, but also the Union institutions and bodies.[22] Thus, the provisions of international agreements have to be respected and complied with by all public authorities of the Union and of the Member States.

12-10 It depends on the content of the provisions of international environmental law whether they have to be transposed into Union law or not. The list of agreements which have been concluded by the Union but where no Union provisions were adopted in order to implement the agreement is unfortunately not short, especially when the numerous protocols of the agreements are included. This would be less problematic if the Commission fully complied with its obligations under Article 17 TEU, according to which it 'shall ensure the application of the Treaties and of measures adopted by the institutions pursuant thereof. It shall oversee the application of Union law under the control of the Court of Justice of the European Union.' The Commission does not ensure the application of international environmental agreements, but ignores those provisions unless they were explicitly transposed by a regulation or a directive into Union law.[23] And neither the European Parliament nor a Member State has ever taken the initiative to have this understanding of Article 17 TEU checked by the CJEU.

The position of the Union in the meetings of international environmental agreements – normally the Conference of the Parties – consists first of all in defending the Union *acquis*. Whatever the subject matter of the agreement, the Union brings 27 votes to the voting table, and this position always has a considerable weight. During the negotiations at international meetings, the Union and the Member States continuously co-ordinate their positions during on-the-spot meetings, so that a Union reaction may also be possible when unforeseen initiatives are tabled which need an immediate reaction.

Normally, the Council adopts decisions on the position which the Union shall take at international meetings, having discussed the initiative beforehand in the Council (Article 218(4) TFEU).[24] This, however, has the reverse side, that at international meetings the EU has difficulties in proposing new, innovative measures as, before such a proposal is made, there would have to be an agreement within the Council on such an initiative – and the 27 Member States may not all find it a good idea to go beyond the existing Union law provisions.

12-11 As environmental policy is the shared competence between the Union and its Member States, a Member State may also propose regulatory measures to an international organisation. However, this possibility has limits. First, a Member State may not propose measures which would be contrary to Union law, for example, the lowering of standards. Second,

[22] Art 216(2) TFEU: 'Agreements concluded by the Union are binding upon the institutions of the Union and on its Member States.'

[23] Since 1976, there has been a single case where the Commission brought a Member State before the CJEU, because that state had not complied with provisions of an international agreement which the Union had concluded, CJEU Case C-239/03 *Commission v France* ECLI:EU:C:2004:598.

[24] See, eg Decision 2022/997 on the position to be taken by the EU during a meeting of the Stockholm POP Convention [2022] OJ L168/63: 'The position to be taken … shall be to support [the amendment of annex A] … Refinement of the position may be agreed upon during on-the spot coordination meetings without a further discussion of the Council.'

where the Union has developed a co-ordinated common strategy with regard to a specific issue, the principle of 'sincere co-operation' means that a Member State may not deviate from this common strategy and unilaterally make a proposal to the international body.[25]

IV. Trade Measures

The question of whether a specific legislative environmental measure adopted by the Union is trade-related and thus comes under Union and international rules on trade is highly controversial. Any permit requirement or other restriction for chemicals, pesticides, biocides etc, but also for imports of waste,[26] makes imports into the Union more complicated. Yet, such measures are generally accepted as being part of the Union environmental and human health policy and thus prevail over trade provisions. Greater uncertainties exist when Union provisions directly or indirectly deal with production methods in third countries. Examples are the sustainability criteria for the production of biofuels which were laid down in Directive 2009/28[27] or the deforestation-free requirements laid down for operators and traders in third countries – and, it is true, also in Union Member States – for certain products.[28] Such Union measures appear to be non-discriminating and proportionate; however, they might have to be tested as to their compatibility with free trade rules. For example, Indonesia and Malaysia both brought a complaint against the Union because they considered the Union's exclusion of palm oil for the production of biodiesel unjustified. The cases are pending.[29] 12-12

The Council and Member States interpreted the provisions on the common commercial policy narrowly and accepted the Union's exclusive competence only where no matters other than commercial issues concerning with products and services were part of the agreement. This considerably limited the area of exclusive EU competence, because most international agreements also concern other issues of foreign economic policy, such as economic co-operation, investments, financial and technical assistance, and the exchange of advisers or experts; according to the Council, agreements that include such aspects do not come under Articles 206–07 TFEU. This matter was highly controversial until the CJEU issued an Opinion in 2017 with regard to a free trade agreement that the EU negotiated with Singapore.[30] The CJEU clarified that the Lisbon Treaty had significantly influenced the common commercial policy. In particular, 'sustainable development', which was mentioned in Article 21 TFEU, formed part of the objectives of the EU's commercial policy and thus came under the exclusive competence of the EU.[31] The CJEU did not see any problem in the fact that environmental protection was a shared competence. It held that the parties to the 12-13

[25] CJEU Case C-246/07 *Commission v Sweden* ECLI:EU:C:2010:203.

[26] See Regulation 1013/2006 on shipments of waste [2006] OJ L190/1, Arts 41–45.

[27] Directive 2009/28 on the promotion of energy from renewable sources [2009] OJ L140/16, Arts 17–19; this directive was repealed by Directive 2018/2001 [2018] OJ L328/82, which generalised the criteria in Arts 29 and 30.

[28] Regulation 2021/1115 establishing rules on support for strategic plans to be drawn up by Member States under the common agricultural policy (CAP Strategic Plans) [2021] OJ L435/1.

[29] WTO Cases DS 593 and DS 600 *Indonesia and Malaysia against European Union* pending. The CJEU held an action against the exclusion of palm oil inadmissible, Case C-402/20P *Santiga v Commission* ECLI:EU:C:2021:872.

[30] CJEU Opinion 2/15 *Free Trade Agreement between the EU and Singapore* ECLI:EU:C:2017:376,.

[31] ibid paras 139–67.

agreement kept the right to determine the level of environmental protection within their own territory; no harmonisation was intended. The commitment to comply with obligations flowing out of international environmental agreements was not any supplementary commitment; obligations to prevent illegal logging and unfair fishing practices were so closely linked to trade in wood and in fish that they were to be understood as trade-related rather than as environment-related measures.[32]

This Opinion revealed that the term 'sustainable development' is void of an enforceable environmental content. Indeed, what sense is there in declaring that the trade agreement is to pursue the objective of sustainable development when no joint environmental measures – the CJEU's reasoning also referred to social matters – may be taken and the reference to international environmental agreements is merely declarative? From an environmental point of view, it was much more logical to consider such agreements as mixed agreements with shared competence. In a political decision, the Commission accepted, with regard to the EU–Canada Comprehensive Economic Trade Agreement (CETA), that the agreement constituted a mixed agreement, where the competence was shared between the EU and its Member States.[33]

12-14 EU decisions to adhere to international environmental agreements which contain trade elements are normally based on Article 192, not Article 207 TFEU. Examples are the decisions to adhere to the Montreal Protocol on Ozone-Depleting Substances[34] and the Basel Convention on the Shipment of Hazardous Waste;[35] also Decision 2015/451 to adhere to the CITES Convention on trade in endangered species of fauna and flora was based on Article 192.[36] This last decision was adopted after an amendment of 1983 to the CITES Convention which allowed the adhering of the Union had entered into force in 2013. Following a judgment of the CJEU, the adhesion to the Rotterdam Convention on the Export and Import of Dangerous Chemicals was based on Articles 207 and 192 TFEU jointly.[37]

EU environmental measures are affected increasingly by the globalisation of economies. In 1994, the World Trade Organization (WTO) was set up, which replaced the General Agreement on Tariffs and Trade (GATT) and had the objective of promoting international trade.[38] The WTO took over the GATT rules, which had been drafted in 1947 and did not expressly address environmental issues; it followed the primary objective of promoting free international trade; environmental measures were mainly seen and treated as being barriers to trade. In a half-hearted attempt to discuss ways for reconciling trade and environmental issues, the WTO set up a Committee on Trade and Environment to discuss environmental and trade aspects, though it did not have any power to set up rules or provide for concrete proposals; this committee has not managed to play any significant role in WTO policy. The WTO statutes also provided for a dispute settlement system to solve conflicts between,

[32] The CJEU ignored that Regulation 995/2010 laying down the obligations of operators who place timber and timber products on the market [2010] OJ L295/23 was based on the environmental provision of Art 192(1) TFEU.

[33] Comprehensive Economic and Trade Agreement (CETA) Canada – EU and its Member States [2017] OJ L11/23.

[34] Decision 88/540 [1988] OJ L297/8.

[35] Decision 93/98 [1993] OJ L39/1.

[36] Decision 2015/451 [2015] OJ L75/1.

[37] CJEU Case C-178/03 *Commission v Council* ECLI:EU:C:2006:4; on the double legal basis, see para 2-71ff.

[38] The EU adhered to WTO by Decision 94/800 [1994] OJ L336/1.

amongst others, environment and trade; decisions by the WTO in this area are binding upon the contracting parties and financial sanctions are foreseen in the case of non-compliance.

As in the case of the relationship between the Union and its Member States,[39] the questions concerning whether the EU environmental measures affect the rules of free international trade have to differentiate between situations where no international environmental measures have been taken and those where international agreements on the protection of the environment exist. 12-15

Where no international environmental agreements exist, an EU measure which endeavours to protect the environment is, in principle, compatible with GATT/WTO rules if it does not constitute a means of arbitrary or unjustifiable discrimination and where it is 'necessary', amongst other things, 'to protect human, animal or plant life or health' (GATT Agreement, Article XX(b)) or relating 'to the conservation of exhaustible natural resources' (Article XX(g)). Different GATT/WTO panels used the word 'necessary' in Article XX to introduce a proportionality test into measures by contracting parties. This thus makes the WTO provisions similar to those of Article 36 TFEU – except that the CJEU's interpretation of Article 34 TFEU, which also allows legitimate national environmental protection measures to restrict trade, has no counterpart in the WTO provisions as yet.

Of particular concern is the discussion as to whether WTO rules allow contracting parties to take trade-restricting environmental measures which protect the environment outside their own jurisdiction. Such measures may concern the environment in other contracting states, such as tropical forests, endangered species (tigers, elephants) or the so-called 'global commons' that do not belong to the jurisdiction of anybody, such as the high sea and its resources and fauna, the climate or the ozone layer. 12-16

In 1991 and 1994, two different GATT panels considered US restrictions on imports of tuna fish caught with so-called purse seine nets, which also trapped and killed large numbers of dolphins. The USA had prohibited the use of those nets and had, furthermore, banned the import of tuna that was caught using methods which did not correspond with the US legislation. The first panel denied that the measures were compatible with Article XX(b), since they had extraterritorial effects;[40] the second panel expressly stated that GATT also allowed extraterritorial measures,[41] but was of the opinion that the measures were disproportionate. Neither finding has been approved by the relevant WTO/GATT Council and has therefore remained unofficial.

In 2006, a WTO panel decided in a dispute between the USA, Canada and Argentina against the EU.[42] The dispute concerned the question of whether the de facto moratorium on the authorisation for the placing on the market of new genetically modified products – on which see paragraph 6-39 above – constituted an unjustified barrier to international trade. The panel held that the moratorium constituted a 'measure' and that it could not be justified. To the extent that it continued to exist, the Union was asked to take measures to 12-17

[39] See ch 3 of this book.

[40] 'The record indicates that the concerns of the drafters of Article XX (b) focused on the use of sanitary measures to safeguard life or health of humans, animals or plants within the jurisdiction of the importing country.'

[41] 'The panel further observes that, under general international law, states are not in principle barred from regulating the conduct of their nationals with respect to persons, animals, plants and natural resources outside of their territory …'.

[42] WTO, DS 291 *USA against European Union* Panel Report of 29 September 2006.

restore free trade; the EU argued that it had already amended its legislation by adopting Directive 2001/18 and Regulation 1829/2003,[43] and ended its moratorium.

It is doubtful whether this dispute really concerned an environmental matter. However, the case shows the potentially large impact which the WTO rules – including those on dispute settlement – may have on the EU policy.

In 2009, the Union adopted a regulation that banned the trade in seals products.[44] Canada and Norway brought a case before the WTO, arguing that this was an unjustified barrier to free trade. However, the WTO accepted that the EU measure was justified on grounds of public morals (Article XX GATT Agreement) and only requested some minor corrections,[45] which the Union adopted.[46]

This WTO decision clarified that animal welfare considerations may justify the restrictions of international trade. The basic justification of this is that life, health and natural resources – which are a short formula equivalent to the environment – are not available in unlimited quantities and cannot really be regarded as constituting trade barriers. Where measures are taken to protect the environment which are neither discriminating nor disproportionate, such measures are also allowed, under WTO rules, to restrict international trade; and the differentiation between product and production standards cannot really lead to different results in this regard. It seems clear to me that, for instance, the US measures in the above-mentioned tuna–dolphin case contained an element of protectionism (discrimination).

By the end of 2022, there was only one pending dispute before the WTO concerning the Union's environmental measures: the above-mentioned case which considered the exclusion of palm oil for the production of biodiesel to be unjustified.[47]

12-18 The problem with weighing the interests between trade and environment at international level lies in the fact that economic interests prevail quantitatively and qualitatively in international discussions, particularly in developing countries.[48] There is hence all the more need for tribunals or dispute-settlement bodies where environmental considerations are given the same amount of attention as trade matters – which does not seem to be the case at present. Indeed, if one looks at the different reactions of GATT and WTO panels where environmental and/or health matters were discussed, environmental matters do not have the same weight as economic or trade matters. In international discussions, outside concrete cases, even the Union has a tendency to let trade interests prevail over environmental interests, for instance by arguing that measures to protect the environment outside the jurisdiction of the acting state should only be allowed where they are in conformity with internationally agreed measures.[49] The necessity of avoiding, on the one hand,

[43] Directive 2001/18 on the deliberate release into the environment of genetically modified organisms [2001] OJ L106/1; Regulation 1829/2003 on genetically modified food and feed [2003] OJ L268/1. However, see now Directive 2015/412 on the restriction of cultivating GMO plants within the EU [2015] OJ L68/1.

[44] Regulation 1007/2009 [2009] OJ L286/36.

[45] WTO, 'Norway and Canada v European Union', Docs WT/DS400 and 401/AB/R of 29 April 2014; see also para 5-33.

[46] Regulation 2015/1775 [2015] OJ L262/1.

[47] See text to n 29.

[48] This is a matter of human behaviour which goes beyond environmental issues: 'Ventre affamé n'a pas d'oreille' (J de la Fontaine); 'Erst kommt das Fressen und dann die Moral' (B Brecht).

[49] Commission, COM(96) 54; see also the reproach by the European Parliament, Resolution of 24 May 1996 [1996] OJ C166/260.

protectionist measures that take the formal appearance of environmental protection (green protectionism) and of allowing, on the other hand, legitimate environmental protection measures is likely to find some compromise solutions only gradually; it is not surprising that legal writers look particularly to regional solutions, such as the Union or the United States–Mexico–Canada Agreement (USMCA), in order to find solutions for the problems of integrating environmental requirements into international trade rules. Article 114(7) TFEU shows a possible future solution: much of the pressure on dolphins, sea turtles and other environmental assets would be avoided if the world community were willing and able to adopt worldwide measures to ensure adequate protection of turtles, dolphins or marine mammals in general.

Even when environmental measures have been taken at international level, their compatibility with WTO/GATT rules may nevertheless be contested. In particular, there is considerable discussion as to whether the three above-mentioned conventions on trade in endangered species, on ozone-depleting substances and on hazardous waste are in conflict with the general WTO rules. The WTO panel on the genetically modified organism (GMO) moratorium in the Union, which gave its report in September 2006, touched on these questions, albeit in a more general form. It held that the rules of the WTO prevailed over other conventions, unless all WTO Member States had adhered to the other convention. This opinion appears to be in conflict with rules of public international law (the Vienna Convention) and can be better explained by motivations to let trade rules prevail than by an attempt to balance diverging interests. The legal question as to which international agreement should prevail – the WTO agreement or the specific environmental convention – will have to be decided politically. Under the existing rules of international law, it is not possible to solve this question. Since all three environmental conventions have been elaborated under the auspices of the United Nations, it appears to be only logical to assume that measures which are adopted by states or by the European Union and which are in compliance with these international conventions cannot be tackled under WTO rules. The fact that such trade restriction measures are also to be applied against states which have not ratified these specialised conventions is not decisive. 12-19

The Montreal Protocol, the Basel Convention and the CITES Convention all allow the contracting parties to adopt more stringent provisions than those of the conventions in order to protect the environment;[50] and the Union has, in the different areas coming under those three conventions, made use of this possibility. The question then is whether such additional domestic measures that are taken at EU or national level are also compatible with WTO rules. The problem has not yet been discussed in detail in the legal literature. My own opinion is that such measures are also compatible with WTO rules, since they rest on an explicit authorisation of the conventions which expresses the wish to improve environmental protection as far as possible. It is self-evident, though, that, here again, a careful examination has to take place in order to avoid such measures being discriminating or disproportionate. 12-20

[50] Basel Convention on the control of transboundary movement of hazardous wastes and their disposal [1993] OJ L39/3, Art 3(11); CITES Convention [1982] OJ L384/1, Art XIV. The Montreal Protocol is formally a protocol of the Vienna Convention; the EU became a party to the Vienna Convention and the Montreal Protocol in 1988 (Decision 88/540 [1988] OJ L297/8); Art 2 of the Vienna Convention allows additional domestic measures.

12-21 The Union has concluded a large number of bilateral, and sometimes also multilateral, trade agreements, some of which are only provisionally applied, pending final ratification by all partners. The environmental dimension of these agreements largely followed the Singapore Agreement: parties committed themselves to respect their obligations which came from international conventions, including the Paris Agreement on Climate Change. Also, they aimed at a high level of environmental protection, but recognised that each party had the right 'to establish its own level of domestic environmental protection'.

The Canadian agreement goes further. Thus, a dispute settlement procedure under CETA provides that investors may, before an arbitration tribunal, claim compensation from the EU or EU Member States when measures impair their investments.[51] Such a provision does not appear to be compatible with Articles 268 and 340 TFEU, which give exclusive competence to the CJEU to decide on extra-contractual damages against the EU. Further worries are that the arbitrators are not necessarily independent, that the procedure is largely confidential and that the arbitrators' interpretation of EU law might differ from that of the CJEU.

For the environment, the setting up of a regulatory committee, foreseen in CETA, is even more dangerous. This committee is intended to discuss any regulatory project which one side – thus the EU and its Member States or Canada and its states – intend to adopt and which might impair the free trade between the two regions. One might easily imagine how measures on the restriction of chemicals, the cultivation of GMOs or emission limit values, once they are based on the precautionary principle, will meet objections from the Canadian side, as the precautionary principle is not fully recognised in Canada. The preventive effect of interventions from the regulatory committee will most likely affect in particular measures on the protection of health, the environment, consumers and workers.

The CJEU considered the setting up, in CETA, of a tribunal to be compatible with Union law.[52] It was of the opinion that such a tribunal would be exclusively competent to decide on the compatibility of measures with CETA itself, but would have no competence to go any further. Furthermore, it quoted Article 8.9.2 CETA, according to which measures taken by one side to protect the environment – including measures to strengthen existing provisions – which negatively affected an investor or the expectations of an investor – did not constitute a breach of the CETA provisions[53] and did not normally constitute a form of expropriation.[54]

A member of the European Commission indicated in 2013 that the agreement with Canada and the envisaged trade agreement with the USA would establish a big transatlantic internal market. The problem is that the EU does not only have to realise an internal market, but must also achieve a high level of environmental protection within the EU according to Article 3 TEU and Articles 11, 114 and 192 TFEU. Such an obligation is lacking entirely

[51] There are considerable sums at stake in such claims: after the Fukushima nuclear accident, Germany decided to step out of nuclear power. In 2012, the Swedish company Vattenfall brought a case to an arbitration tribunal, claiming compensation. In a settlement of 2021, Germany paid Vattenfall a compensation of €1.4 billion. In 2011, the Regional Government of Quebec decided to restrict fracking in the region. The company Lone Pine Resources then filed a claim of 250 million Canadian dollars for damages caused by that regional legislation which was ultimately (at the end of 2022) unsuccessful.

[52] CJEU, Opinion 1/17 *EU–Canada CET Agreement* ECLI:EU:C:2019:341.

[53] ibid para 154.

[54] ibid para 157.

in the 'transatlantic internal market', which might thus lead to negative integration – all environmental, health and social measures being perceived as barriers to free trade which should be avoided as far as possible. 'Between the strong and the weak, legislation makes free and the freedom suppresses', indicated the French philosopher Lacordère back in the nineteenth century.

The war in Iraq of 2003, the policy in the USA since 2016 and the Russian war against Ukraine in 2022 all led to a diminishing interest in multilateral measures which fairly balance between trade and environmental interests; the Paris Agreement of 2015 raised, to some extent, the concern for climate change, but not for the protection of the environment in general. Bilateral trade agreements are perceived more as a chance to promote economic development than as a chance to raise the level of environmental protection, even as regards the environmental aspects of the UN sustainable development goals.[55] The Union would have the chance to export, via such trade agreements, its own environmental standards, which, seen from a global perspective, are rather advanced. It did not do so, though, in its measures under the Cotonou Agreement, under the Fisheries Partnership Agreements or under CETA or other trade agreements. Rather, it kept to the position that each side of an agreement should take care of its own environmental measures. With regard to loss of biodiversity, pollution, water and waste management, dangerous substances and products, preventive impact assessments and other aspects, this attitude is too conservative: indeed, why conclude a 'comprehensive economic trade agreement' such as that with Canada when the 'comprehensive' part is limited to trade aspects? The conclusion must be that the Union is not very active in exporting its environmental standards to third countries. 12-22

[55] These environment-oriented sustainable development goals are no 3 (good health and well-being), no 6 (clean water and sanitation), no 7 (affordable and clean energy), no 11 (sustainable cities and communities), no 12 (responsible consumption and production), no 13 (climate action), no 14 (life below water) and no 15 (life on land).

13

UK and EU Environmental Law after Brexit

I. Introduction

13-01 Since the UK joined the European Economic Community in 1973, the UK has followed EU law (previously known as Community law). Section 2 of the European Communities Act 1972 (ECA) gave effect to all directly applicable EU law and also domestic effect to general principles of EU law, including but not limited to the principles of supremacy and direct effect.

The supremacy of EU law has long been politically controversial in the UK. Nevertheless, as stated by Lord Bridges in *R (Factortame (no 2)) v Secretary of State for Transport* [1991] 1 AC 603, 658 and 659:

> If the supremacy within the European Community of Community law over the national law of member states was not always inherent in the E.E.C. Treaty … it was certainly well established in the jurisprudence of the European Court of Justice long before the United Kingdom joined the Community. Thus, whatever limitation of its sovereignty Parliament accepted when it enacted the European Communities Act 1972 was entirely voluntary. Under the terms of the Act of 1972 it has always been clear that it was the duty of a United Kingdom court, when delivering final judgment, to override any rule of national law found to be in conflict with any directly enforceable rule of Community law. Similarly, when decisions of the European Court of Justice have exposed areas of United Kingdom statute law which failed to implement Council directives, Parliament has always loyally accepted the obligation to make appropriate and prompt amendments. Thus there is nothing in any way novel in according supremacy to rules of Community law in those areas to which they apply.

EU law has also been implemented domestically through supporting or implementing domestic legislation by virtue of section 2(2) of the ECA, which provided for a general implementing power to allow for domestic regulations to implement EU obligations.

13-02 Following Brexit, the landscape has changed entirely. After the referendum on 23 June 2016, in which 51.9 per cent of votes were cast in favour of the UK leaving the EU, the UK government proposed, in 2017, a 'Great Repeal Bill' intended to repeal the ECA. This immediately presented difficulties. In the 2017 White Paper, 'Legislating for the United Kingdom's Withdrawal From the European Union', updated on 15 May 2017, the UK government made the following observations:

> 1.13 If the Great Repeal Bill did not convert existing EU law into domestic law at the same time as repealing the [ECA], the UK's statute book would contain significant gaps once we left the EU. There are a large number of EU regulations and many other EU-derived laws which form part of

> our law which, if we were to repeal the [ECA] without making further provision, would no longer apply, creating large holes in our statute book.
>
> 1.14 Simply incorporating EU law into UK law is not enough, however. A significant amount of EU-derived law, even when converted into domestic law, will not achieve its desired legal effect in the UK once we have left the EU. For example, legislation may refer to the involvement of an EU institution or be predicated on UK membership of, or access to, an EU regime or system. Once we have left the EU this legislation will no longer work. Government must act to ensure that the domestic statute book continues to function once we have left the EU.

The result was the European Union (Withdrawal) Act 2018 (EUWA). Originally designed for a 'hard Brexit', where no deal was reached between the UK and the EU, the EUWA preserved EU-derived domestic legislation as it had effect in UK domestic law, imported direct EU legislation, so far as operative, into part of UK domestic law and preserved rights, powers, liabilities, obligations, restrictions, remedies and procedures recognised in UK domestic law as a consequence of direct effect, allowing them to be enforced, allowed and followed in UK domestic law.

However, the UK and the EU did ultimately agree on a withdrawal agreement, includ- 13-03
ing a transition period during which the UK agreed that it would continue to follow almost all of EU law, on the same basis as a Member State would, until 31 December 2020. Accordingly, many of the effects of the EUWA were postponed until the end of the transition period (known in the legislation as the 'IP [implementation period] completion day') by virtue of the European Union (Withdrawal Agreement) Act 2020 (EUWAA).

The EUWAA repealed the ECA on 31 January 2020 whilst at the same time saving its effect in UK domestic law for the transition period.

The EU–UK Trade and Co-operation Agreement (TCA) governs the relationship between the EU and the UK. The TCA was concluded after eight months of negotiations and sets out preferential arrangements in areas such as trade in goods and services, aviation and road transport, energy, fisheries, social security co-ordination and participation in EU programmes. The TCA was signed on 30 December 2020, was applied provisionally as of 1 January 2021 and entered into force on 1 May 2021. The effects of the EUWA (as amended), as well as the TCA (largely implemented by the European Union (Future Relationship) Act 2020) are considered in detail below.

The next legislative step for the UK was to introduce and pass the Retained EU Law (Revocation and Reform) Act 2023 (REUL Act), which was granted royal assent on 29 June 2023.

II. The 2019 Political Declaration

The UK and the EU reached an agreement on the UK's withdrawal from the EU, with 13-04
a revised Withdrawal Agreement and a Political Declaration considered and agreed at European Council on 17 October 2019.

The Political Declaration was agreed on the basis that Article 50(2) of the Treaty on European Union 2017 (TEU) provides for the negotiation of an agreement setting out the arrangements for the withdrawal of a departing Member State. Central to the Political Declaration was an agreement that the future relationship should be underpinned by shared values such as the respect for and safeguarding of human rights and fundamental freedoms, democratic principles, the rule of law and support for non-proliferation.

It was a central objective of the Political Declaration that the parties retain their autonomy and the ability to regulate economic activity according to the levels of protection each deems appropriate in order to achieve legitimate public policy objectives in a range of areas, including public health, animal health and welfare, and the environment, including climate change.

13-05 Specific recognition was given to the following areas relevant to environmental issues:

- *Global co-operation* – whilst preserving their decision-making autonomy, the parties should co-operate in international fora (eg the G7 and G20) where it is in their mutual interest, including in the areas of climate change, sustainable development, cross-border pollution, public health and consumer protection, financial stability and the fight against trade protectionism. The future relationship should reaffirm the parties' commitments to international agreements to tackle climate change, including those which implement the United Nations Framework Conventions on Climate Change, such as the Paris Agreement.
- *Open and fair competition* – the parties were to uphold common high standards in the areas of the environment and climate change to allow open and fair competition. There was to be commitment to maintaining a robust and comprehensive framework for competition and state aid control to prevent undue distortion of trade and competition, as well as committing to the principles of good governance in the area of taxation and to the curbing of harmful tax practices so as to maintain environmental, social and employment.
- *Fishing* – it was hoped that there would be bilateral and international co-operation to ensure fishing was carried out at sustainable levels to promote resource conservation and foster a clean, healthy and productive marine environment. Regulatory autonomy was to be preserved, but the parties agreed to co-operate on the development of measures for the conservation, rational management and regulation of fisheries in a non-discriminatory manner. A new fisheries agreement was to be reached to deal with access to waters and quota shares with a target date of 1 July 2020.
- *Nuclear safety and non-proliferation* – any future relationship between the parties should include a Nuclear Cooperation Agreement between the European Atomic Energy Community (Euratom) and the UK. There was to be an exchange of information in areas of mutual interest, such as safeguards, safety and co-operation, with the International Atomic Energy Agency. The UK signalled an intention to participate as a third country in EU systems for monitoring and exchanging information on levels of radioactivity in the environment.

The Political Declaration sought to carve out an exception whereby the future relationship should address the possibility for a party to activate temporary safeguard measures that would otherwise be in breach of its commitments in case of circumstances of significant economic, societal or environmental difficulties.

III. The 2019 Withdrawal Agreement

The UK and the EU reached an agreement on the UK's withdrawal from the EU, with a revised Withdrawal Agreement being considered and agreed at the European Council on 17 October 2019, before it entered into force on 1 February 2020. The Withdrawal Agreement required domestic legislation to be implemented in the UK. On 23 January 2020, Parliament passed the EU (Withdrawal Agreement) Act 2020, which gave effect to the Withdrawal Agreement in UK law. 13-06

Under the Withdrawal Agreement, the UK's exit from the EU on 31 January 2020 was followed by a time-limited implementation period, which lasted until 11pm on the IP completion day. During the implementation period, common rules remained in place, with EU law (including new law) continuing to apply to the UK under the terms set out in the Withdrawal Agreement.

At the end of the implementation period, sections 2–4 EUWA, as amended by the 2020 Act, saved, and incorporated into domestic law, that EU law which applied in the UK at the end of the implementation period. The effect of the agreement is set out in Article 4 of the Withdrawal Agreement, which reads:

> Article 4
>
> Methods and principles relating to the effect, the implementation and the application of this Agreement
>
> 1. The provisions of this Agreement and the provisions of Union law made applicable by this Agreement shall produce in respect of and in the United Kingdom the same legal effects as those which they produce within the Union and its Member States.
> 2. Accordingly, legal or natural persons shall in particular be able to rely directly on the provisions contained or referred to in this Agreement which meet the conditions for direct effect under Union law.
> 3. The United Kingdom shall ensure compliance with paragraph 1, including as regards the required powers of its judicial and administrative authorities to disapply inconsistent or incompatible domestic provisions, through domestic primary legislation.
> 4. The provisions of this Agreement referring to Union law or to concepts or provisions thereof shall be interpreted and applied in accordance with the method and general principles of Union law.
> 5. The provisions of this Agreement referring to Union law or to concepts or provisions thereof shall in their implementation and application be interpreted in conformity with the relevant case law of the Court of Justice of the European Union handed down before the end of the transition period.
> 6. In the interpretation and application of this Agreement, the United Kingdom's judicial and administrative authorities shall have due regard to relevant case law of the Court of Justice of the European Union handed down after the end of the transition period.

Part Two of the Withdrawal Agreement provides protections for citizens' rights, including entitlements to work, study and access public services and benefits, insofar as these entitlements have derived from UK membership of the EU.

By Article 164,a Joint Committee, comprising representatives of the UK and the EU, was established to oversee and monitor the application of the Withdrawal Agreement. If either party took issue with the compliance of the other, for instance in respect of Part Two 13-07 rights, they must first attempt to resolve the dispute through the Joint Committee. If the Joint Committee could not help the parties reach an agreed solution, then the matter should be arbitrated by a panel administered by the Permanent Court of Arbitration. Any ruling is then binding on the parties, and non-compliance can lead to the imposition of financial penalties and the suspension of obligations under the Withdrawal Agreement. To date, the EU has launched proceedings under the dispute settlement mechanism on two occasions, on 1 October 2020 and 15 March 2021.

IV. The Northern Ireland Protocol

13-08 The Protocol on Ireland/Northern Ireland (the Protocol) in the Withdrawal Agreement provides arrangements that ensure that the UK (including Northern Ireland) does not remain in a customs union with the European Union. The Protocol cites as objectives the avoidance of a hard border and the protection the 1998 Good Friday Agreement.

In addition to protections of rights of individuals (Article 2), confirmation that Northern Ireland is part of the customs territory of the UK (Article 4) and hence prohibiting customs duties in respect of goods brought into Northern Ireland from another part of the UK by direct transport (Article 5), the Protocol set out environmental protections.

The Protocol was to be implemented to ensure continued North–South co-operation in, inter alia, the areas of environment, agriculture, transport, energy and inland fisheries (Article 11). Furthermore, by Article 5(4), multiple provisions of EU law (set out in annex 2) will continue to apply to and in the UK in respect of Northern Ireland.

V. The Trade and Cooperation Agreement

A. Chapter 7

13-09 Chapter 7 of the TCA is entitled 'Environment and Climate' and is the key part of the agreement capable of having an impact on environmental law.

The TCA is a free trade agreement between the UK and the EU. It was signed on 30 December 2020, provisionally applied from 1 January 2021 and formally came into force on 1 May 2021. The agreement was implemented into UK law by the European Union (Future Relationship) Act 2020, which was approved by the European Parliament on 27 April 2021 and approved by the Council of the European Union on 29 April 2021.

Both the EU and the UK has the right to set its policies and priorities in the areas of 'environment and climate' to determine the environmental levels of protection and climate level of protection the party deems appropriate and to adopt or modify its law and policies in a manner consistent with both parties' international commitments.

B. Article 390 – Definitions

Article 390 reads:

ARTICLE 390

Definitions

1. For the purposes of this Chapter, 'environmental levels of protection' means the levels of protection provided overall in a Party's law which have the purpose of protecting the environment, including the prevention of a danger to human life or health from environmental impacts, including in each of the following areas:
   (a) industrial emissions;
   (b) air emissions and air quality;
   (c) nature and biodiversity conservation;
   (d) waste management;
   (e) the protection and preservation of the aquatic environment;
   (f) the protection and preservation of the marine environment;
   (g) the prevention, reduction and elimination of risks to human health or the environment arising from the production, use, release or disposal of chemical substances; or
   (h) the management of impacts on the environment from agricultural or food production, notably through the use of antibiotics and decontaminants.
2. For the Union, 'environmental levels of protection' means environmental levels of protection that are applicable to and in, and are common to, all Member States.
3. For the purposes of this Chapter, 'climate level of protection' means the level of protection with respect to emissions and removals of greenhouse gases and the phase-out of ozone depleting substances. With regard to greenhouse gases, this means:
   (a) for the Union, the 40% economy-wide 2030 target, including the Union's system of carbon pricing;
   (b) for the United Kingdom, the United Kingdom's economy-wide share of this 2030 target, including the United Kingdom's system of carbon pricing.

Both parties must attain the same standards of environmental protection, but in the case of the EU the applicable standard is that which is 'common to all Member States'.

C. Article 391 – Non-regression

Article 391 reads: 13-10

ARTICLE 391

Non-regression from levels of protection

1. The Parties affirm the right of each Party to set its policies and priorities in the areas covered by this Chapter, to determine the environmental levels of protection and climate level of protection it deems appropriate and to adopt or modify its law and policies in a manner consistent with each Party's international commitments, including those under this Chapter.
2. A Party shall not weaken or reduce, in a manner affecting trade or investment between the Parties, its environmental levels of protection or its climate level of protection below the levels that are in place at the end of the transition period, including by failing to effectively enforce its environmental law or climate level of protection.

> 3. The Parties recognise that each Party retains the right to exercise reasonable discretion and to make bona fide decisions regarding the allocation of environmental enforcement resources with respect to other environmental law and climate policies determined to have higher priorities, provided that the exercise of that discretion, and those decisions, are not inconsistent with its obligations under this Chapter.
> 4. For the purposes of this Chapter, insofar as targets are provided for in a Party's environmental law in the areas listed in Article 390, they are included in a Party's environmental levels of protection at the end of the transition period. These targets include those whose attainment is envisaged for a date that is subsequent to the end of the transition period. This paragraph shall also apply to ozone depleting substances.
> 5. The Parties shall continue to strive to increase their respective environmental levels of protection or their respective climate level of protection referred to in this Chapter.

13-11 This section deserves some consideration. First, although this purports to amount to a non-regression clause, environmental and climate protection is explicitly linked to trade or investment between the parties. Furthermore, no definition is provided by the TCA of what is meant by 'a manner affecting trade or investment between the Parties'.

Second, the section explicitly recognises that implementation and enforcement of environmental law is as important as the existence of such law on the statute book. The monitoring of the implementation of environmental law was a key element of the role of the European Commission, a role now replaced (at least in part) by the Office for Environmental Protection (OEP).

Third, the relevant levels of protection were those that were in place as of 1 January 2021. There is no requirement within Article 391 for the UK to maintain a level of 'equivalence' with developments in EU environmental protection after this date.

(i) 'In a Manner Affecting Trade or Investment'

As identified above, there is no definition or guidance to assist with the meaning of this phrase. It is a phrase that can be seen in other trade agreements; for example, Article 16.2.1(a) of the Dominican Republic-Central America-United States Free Trade Agreement, which came into force on 1 January 2005, explicitly uses the phrase 'in a manner affecting trade between the Parties' in the context of labour laws, and the same phrase is used in the context of environmental laws in Article 17.2.1(a).

The word 'manner' does not, on the face of it, appear to present too many difficulties, likely equating to the way in which something is done or the way in which something happens.

More problematic is the term 'affecting'. Two potential interpretations come to mind as to how a party may try and demonstrate that the other party has 'affected' trade. First, this could be established through demonstrating a tangible 'trade effect', for example a change in the price or volume of internationally traded goods. However, the same term may be satisfied if one party can demonstrate a change in potential conditions of trade (that may not have manifested itself yet in a tangible effect). One key question is whether a modification of the conditions of competition is sufficient to pass the threshold of 'affecting trade' or whether there must be an actual effect on prices or trade flows in particular goods and services?

13-12 An example might be a failure to enforce environmental requirements that fall to be imposed on a business. One area where this may happen is in extended producer responsibility. It is unclear what the position would be if there were a failure by the UK to enforce end-of-life recycling requirements on an organisation such that the organisation gained a competitive advantage over its European competitors, who were required to comply with those requirements at a cost to their business. This, in turn, could incentivise other businesses not to comply with the law. A snowball effect could then affect international trade to the extent that the failure to enforce provided a competitive advantage to a business engaged in export or competing with imports, thereby affecting conditions of competition in international trade.

Adopting the above example, one potential interpretation is that a failure to enforce through a sustained or recurring course of action in a way that results in a 'competitive advantage' in trade to one of the parties could be deemed to meet the requirement of 'affecting trade' for the purposes of the TCA. This interpretation, if adopted, would apply in spite of the fact that the competitive advantage may not result itself in an effect on price (for example, increased profits made by the non-compliant organisation may be retained as profits, rather than translated into price reductions). Furthermore, to focus solely on price effects would appear to be highly limiting: there are a myriad of factors that can feed into international prices, not least currency fluctuations. Further, it may be evidentially very difficult to quantify the impact of a failure to enforce environmental law by reference to or attribution to any particular price reduction or increase in sales volumes.

In this way, the phrase 'in a manner affecting trade between the Parties' can legitimately be construed to be engaged when a competitive advantage has been conferred as a consequence of a weakening of or reduction in standards of environmental protection.

Nonetheless, a competitive advantage does not result from every failure to enforce environmental law or from a weakening of standards. The principled approach would appear to be to: (i) identify the factual circumstances that demonstrate the engagement in competitive trade between the parties; (ii) identify the effects of a particular weakening of standards or failure to enforce environmental law; and (iii) identify whether these effects are sufficient to confer a competitive advantage on one of the parties. It is submitted that the extent of competitive advantage is irrelevant to the wording of the TCA, provided that it can be demonstrated that the advantage is a material one and not insignificant or negligible.

The intention of the parties would appear to be irrelevant. Indeed, a failure to enforce may simply be a consequence of poor regulation, rather than an intended course of action to achieve a competitive advantage.

(ii) 'Between the Parties'

Another unanswered question is what happens in circumstances where divergence 13-13
improves trade with a third party? On its face, the application of the non-regression clause of the TCA is limited to trade between the UK and the EU. Consequently, a trade advantage gained, for example, by the UK over a third country as a result of a weakening in environmental protection would appear to fall outside of the ambit of this part of the TCA. Similarly, if a weakening of environmental standards led to trade being diverted to the UK rather than the EU from a third country (for example if the UK chose to lower environmental standards below that of the EU to attract US imports), that could negatively impact on the EU's trade with the USA but not necessarily impact trade between the UK and the EU themselves.

D. Article 392 – Carbon Pricing

13-14 Article 392 reads:

ARTICLE 392

Carbon pricing

1. Each Party shall have in place an effective system of carbon pricing as of 1 January 2021.
2. Each system shall cover greenhouse gas emissions from electricity generation, heat generation, industry and aviation.
3. The effectiveness of the Parties' respective carbon pricing systems shall uphold the level of protection provided for by Article 391.
4. By way of derogation from paragraph 2, aviation shall be included within two years at the latest, if not included already. The scope of the Union system of carbon pricing shall cover departing flights from the European Economic Area to the United Kingdom.
5. Each Party shall maintain its system of carbon pricing insofar as it is an effective tool for each Party in the fight against climate change and shall in any event uphold the level of protection provided for by Article 391.
6. The Parties shall cooperate on carbon pricing. They shall give serious consideration to linking their respective carbon pricing systems in a way that preserves the integrity of these systems and provides for the possibility to increase their effectiveness.

The UK Emissions Trading Scheme (UK ETS) went live on 1 January 2021, replacing the UK's participation in the EU Emissions Trading Scheme (EU ETS), although UK operators were still bound to comply with the EU ETS until April 2021, the end of the EU ETS scheme year. Under the Northern Ireland Protocol, electricity generators in Northern Ireland remained within the EU ETS.

In broad terms, under the UK ETS, the UK government sets a maximum level for total emissions, and every unit of emissions up to this maximum is party to a system of tradable allowances. In practice, a certain quantity of emissions, known as a free allocation, is allowed before a sector will start to pay for carbon. Free allocations are intended to reduce over time as overall emissions reduce.

The UK ETS and the EU ETS work in very similar ways, although the UK scheme is presently more ambitious than that of the EU. At the time of the scheme's launch, the UK emissions cap was 5 per cent lower than that of the EU.

13-15 On 25 March 2022, the UK government consulted on 'Developing the UK Emissions Trading Scheme' in order to seek views on proposals to meet a 'net zero consistent cap' for the scheme and to review the free allocation policy, as well as expanding the use of the emissions trading across the economy. On 3 July 2023, the government published its response to that consultation, which contained a number of decisions.

In respect of net zero, the UK ETS cap will be set to be consistent with net zero (at the top of the net zero consistent range). This change is to be implemented for 2024. The transition to the net zero will be smoothed by the release of additional allowances between 2024 and 2027 to ensure that there is no sudden drop in allowance supply.

The industry cap is to be set at 40 per cent of the overall cap, which is an increase from 37 per cent. This change is intended to permit the continued provision of free allowances to those sectors most at risk of carbon leakage. 'Carbon leakage' is a concept to quantify an increase in emissions in other countries because of the imposition of stringent targets: the UK ETS cap may add a premium to domestically produced fuels or commodities, which may cause a drop in demand in lieu of internationally produced items, which may lead to a change within the market and negate any benefit derived from the UK ETS cap. Carbon leakage is typically calculated as a percentage to reflect the increase in emissions outside the UK divided by the reduction in the emissions of the UK.

Conversely, free allocations are to be phased out in respect of the aviation sector. In addition, it has been decided that the UK ETS will be expanded into other sectors (subject to further consultation, but likely to include domestic maritime, energy from waste and waste incineration) and allowances are to be put aside for future market management, equivalent to 3 per cent of the overall cap. Finally, and again subject to further consultation, greenhouse gas removal technologies may be incorporated.

The UK has decided to reset the UK ETS cap for 2021–30 at the top of what it considers to be the net zero consistent range, 936 million allowances, a drop of 30 per cent over the course of this phase. The cap will require further adjustment following the addition of any new sectors to the UK ETS. It has been indicated that any change will retain the same level of ambition.

The EU level of ambition appears similar. In order to meet EU targets, EU ETS emissions will have to drop by 35 per cent compared to 2022. This is distinct from the overall EU reduction commitment of greenhouse gas emissions of 55 per cent compared to the emissions of 1990.

Despite the wording of Article 392(6), the prices of the two schemes are not linked, and on the horizon is the prospect of the EU carbon border levy. From 2026, the EU is expected to impose fees on imports of emissions-heavy goods, including steel, aluminium and cement, unless the exporting country has equivalent CO_2 pricing policies. This has the potential to impact on the UK, as the UK CO_2 price has fallen from approximately £97 per metric ton in August 2022 to approximately £51 per metric tonne in May 2023. In contrast, the price of emissions allowances reached a record high of €100.34 per metric tonne in February 2023. Clearly, there is a significant disparity between the carbon prices, which has the potential to be impacted in due course.

E. Article 393 – Environmental and Climate Principles

Article 393 reads: 13-16

ARTICLE 393

Environmental and climate principles

1. Taking into account the fact that the Union and the United Kingdom share a common biosphere in respect of cross-border pollution, each Party commits to respecting the internationally recognised environmental principles to which it has committed, such as in the Rio Declaration on Environment and Development, adopted at Rio de Janeiro on 14 June 1992 (the '1992 Rio Declaration on Environment and Development') and in multilateral environmental agreements, including in the United Nations Framework Convention on Climate Change, done at New York on 9 May 1992 ('UNFCCC') and the Convention on Biological Diversity, done at Rio de Janeiro on 5 June 1992 (the 'Convention on Biological Diversity'), in particular:
   (a) the principle that environmental protection should be integrated into the making of policies, including through impact assessments;

> (b) the principle of preventative action to avert environmental damage;
> (c) the precautionary approach referred to in Article 356(2);
> (d) the principle that environmental damage should as a priority be rectified at source; and
> (e) the polluter-pays principle.
>
> 2. The Parties reaffirm their respective commitments to procedures for evaluating the likely impact of a proposed activity on the environment, and where specified projects, plans and programmes are likely to have significant environmental, including health, effects, this includes an environmental impact assessment or a strategic environmental assessment, as appropriate.
> 3. These procedures shall comprise, where appropriate and in accordance with a Party's laws, the determination of the scope of an environmental report and its preparation, the carrying out of public participation and consultations and the taking into account of the environmental report and the results of the public participation and consultations in the consented project, or adopted plan or programme.

Article 393 commits the parties to respecting five specific internationally recognised environmental principles:

1. the principle that environmental protection should be integrated into the making of policies, including through impact assessments;
2. the principle of preventative action to avert environmental damage;
3. the precautionary approach referred to in Article 356(2);
4. the principle that environmental damage should as a priority be rectified at source; and
5. the polluter-pays principle.

Article 356(2) reads:

> The Parties acknowledge that, in accordance with the precautionary approach, where there are reasonable grounds for concern that there are potential threats of serious or irreversible damage to the environment or human health, the lack of full scientific certainty shall not be used as a reason for preventing a Party from adopting appropriate measures to prevent such damage.

The UK has chosen to commit to these principles through the adoption of a policy statement, pursuant to section 17 of the Environment Act 2021, that, as of 1 November 2023, should be interpreted and proportionately applied by Ministers of the Crown when making policy. The policy statement and the means by which that is to be taken into account in the creation of UK policy is considered in detail in section VIII of this chapter.

The same Article also commits the UK to environmental impact assessments or strategic environmental assessments, as appropriate.

F. Article 394 – Enforcement

13-17 Article 394 reads:

> ARTICLE 394
>
> Enforcement
>
> 1. For the purposes of enforcement as referred to in Article 391, each Party shall, in accordance with its law, ensure that:

> (a) domestic authorities competent to enforce the relevant law with regard to environment and climate give due consideration to alleged violations of such law that come to their attention; those authorities shall have adequate and effective remedies available to them, including injunctive relief as well as proportionate and dissuasive sanctions, if appropriate; and
>
> (b) national administrative or judicial proceedings are available to natural and legal persons with a sufficient interest to bring actions against violations of such law and to seek effective remedies, including injunctive relief, and that the proceedings are not prohibitively costly and are conducted in a fair, equitable and transparent way.

This Article emphasises the need for 'adequate and effective remedies' to be available to the domestic authorities that enforce the relevant law, as well as 'effective remedies' to be available to natural and legal persons in administrative or judicial proceedings.

The same Article requires that proceedings are not prohibitively expensive, reflecting Aarhus Convention requirements, as well as the need for fairness, equity and transparency.

G. Article 395 – Cooperation on Monitoring and Enforcement

ARTICLE 395 13-18

Cooperation on monitoring and enforcement

> The Parties shall ensure that the European Commission and the supervisory bodies of the United Kingdom regularly meet with each other and co-operate on the effective monitoring and enforcement of the law with regard to environment and climate as referred to in Article 391.

The Environment Act 2021 established the Office for Environmental Protection, a new independent regulator that is intended, amongst other functions, to scrutinise all government policy and to provide scrutiny and advice to public bodies. It is intended that the OEP will replace the role of the European Commission and ensure that there is no governance gap in environmental regulation.

The extent to which the OEP achieves this, together with its powers and functions, is the subject of detailed review in section IX of this chapter.

At the time of publication, the authors are not aware of any meeting between the OEP and the European Commission.

H. Article 396 – Dispute Settlement

ARTICLE 396 13-19

Dispute settlement

> 1. The Parties shall make all efforts through dialogue, consultation, exchange of information and cooperation to address any disagreement on the application of this Chapter.
> 2. By way of derogation from Title I of Part Six, in the event of a dispute between the Parties regarding the application of this Chapter, the Parties shall have recourse exclusively to the procedures established under Articles 408, 409 and 410.

If one party believes that the other side is not complying with their environmental obligations under the TCA, it can refer the dispute to consultations and arbitration by a panel of experts. If the panel of experts finds that a party has breached the agreement, the parties will discuss which measures should be taken to address the breach. If the two sides disagree, they can ask the panel to provide recommendations.

I. Article 411 – Rebalancing

13-20 Article 411(1) and (2) read:

> 1. The Parties recognise the right of each Party to determine its future policies and priorities with respect to labour and social, environmental or climate protection, or with respect to subsidy control, in a manner consistent with each Party's international commitments, including those under this Agreement. At the same time, the Parties acknowledge that significant divergences in these areas can be capable of impacting trade or investment between the Parties in a manner that changes the circumstances that have formed the basis for the conclusion of this Agreement.
> 2. If material impacts on trade or investment between the Parties are arising as a result of significant divergences between the Parties in the areas referred to in paragraph 1, either Party may take appropriate rebalancing measures to address the situation. Such measures shall be restricted with respect to their scope and duration to what is strictly necessary and proportionate in order to remedy the situation. Priority shall be given to such measures as will least disturb the functioning of this Agreement. A Party's assessment of those impacts shall be based on reliable evidence and not merely on conjecture or remote possibility.

Inclusion of Article 411 in the TCA and the consequential creation of a bespoke dispute resolution scheme demonstrates, on one view, that the general dispute settlement mechanism of the TCA was considered insufficient in respect of a level playing field.

Central to the TCA is the principle of autonomy of the parties and their right to determine future policies in key areas, including environmental or climate protection. However, rebalancing measures stand somewhat against this as they can be imposed unilaterally by the party concerned.

13-21 The process of rebalancing is far from clear: 'rebalancing measures' are not defined within the TCA, nor indeed are phrases such as 'significant divergences', 'material impacts' or 'reliable evidence'.

In the government's 'The UK–EU Trade and Cooperation Agreement: Level Playing Field' research briefing it was said they could include 'temporary suspension of parts of the Agreement or [the imposition of] tariffs'.

The phrase 'significant divergences' does not specify the direction of the divergence, ie the rebalancing mechanism could be triggered if one party dropped standards in a particular area, giving them a competitive advantage over the other party, but equally if one party raised standards where the other party did not make reciprocal improvements. In both cases, there would be a divergence within the meaning of the TCA.

For a party to make the decision to engage with the rebalancing mechanism is not likely to be one quickly taken. There is a need for reliable evidence (this surely must at least be something that is empirical and testable) and, in order for the resulting measures to be compliant with the scheme, they must be 'strictly necessary and proportionate', which can only be assessed if there is a clear understanding of the nature of the alleged breach and its impact.

This is a novel mechanism – it is understood that the EU originally wanted a kind of equivalence mechanism, but that morphed into the rebalancing mechanism during the negotiating process – and its operation is reliant upon interpretation. Indeed, the lack of certainty of the phrases referred to above is responsible for the relatively strict deadlines built into the process.

In a situation where there are 'significant divergences' that result in 'material impacts on trade or investment', the parties may enter consultation upon notification by the party concerned. Should no mutually acceptable solution be reached, the party concerned may adopt those 'rebalancing measures' that are strictly necessary and proportionate to remedy the 'material impacts' unless the notified party requests the establishment of an arbitration tribunal in accordance with Article 739(2) (if so, the rebalancing measures are not applied whilst the tribunal considers the alleged breach). The arbitration tribunal will assess whether there is a breach and whether the measures are proportionate to remedy the situation. If a breach is confirmed, then further sanctions (eg fines) may be applied to the notified party.

As an alternative to the arbitration tribunal, a party may refer the suspected non-compliance with labour or environmental standards to consultations and arbitration by a panel of experts. In contradistinction to the findings of the arbitrational panel, the breaching party does not have to abide by recommendations of the panel of experts. However, if it does not abide by the recommendations, in some circumstances the complaining party may be able to take temporary remedial measures in response.

There is a separate dispute settlement mechanism in respect of fisheries issues, which is different principally because retaliatory measures, including the suspension of access to fishing waters, the imposition of tariffs or the suspension of trade, may be used before arbitration. Any measure must be commensurate with the purported impact of the alleged breach.

J. Article 355 – Sustainable Development

A commitment to sustainable development is reflected in Article 355(1) and (2): 13-22

ARTICLE 355

Principles and objectives

1. The Parties recognise that trade and investment between the Union and the United Kingdom under the terms set out in this Agreement, require conditions that ensure a level playing field for open and fair competition between the Parties and that ensure that trade and investment take place in a manner conducive to sustainable development.
2. The Parties recognise that sustainable development encompasses economic development, social development and environmental protection, all three being interdependent and mutually reinforcing, and affirm their commitment to promoting the development of international trade and investment in a way that contributes to the objective of sustainable development.
3. Each Party reaffirms its ambition of achieving economy-wide climate neutrality by 2050.
4. The Parties affirm their common understanding that their economic relationship can only deliver benefits in a mutually satisfactory way if the commitments relating to a level playing field for open and fair competition stand the test of time, by preventing distortions of trade

> or investment, and by contributing to sustainable development. However the Parties recognise that the purpose of this Title is not to harmonise the standards of the Parties. The Parties are determined to maintain and improve their respective high standards in the areas covered by this Title.

It is clear that the phrase 'sustainable development' provides for a wide concept. When trying to understand its constituent parts, one can consider a number of factors. First, there is no definition given for 'social development' (and indeed it appears as a phrase only twice within the TCA), but one might reasonably infer that it links to quality and standard of living. Second, there is inclusion of explicit reference to climate neutrality in Article 355(3), which could be said to elevate the importance of environmental protection.

This Article outlines a long-term view towards sustainable development both by reference to 2050 and the wording of Article 355(4). The use of 'however' is an interesting disjunctive in this regard.

VI. The European Union (Withdrawal) Act 2018

13-23 Save for provisions listed in the Northern Ireland Protocol, EU law ceased to apply in the UK with effect from 11pm on 31 December 2020. However, in order to avoid the substantial gaps in the UK's legal framework, the EUWA created a new concept known as retained EU law.

A. Retained EU Law

Retained EU law started its life as all EU law that was in force and applicable in the UK at the end of the transition period. Following the end of the transition period, the UK legislated to remove or amend certain parts of retained law that the UK did not want to hold on to or which needed to be altered to reflect the fact that the UK was no longer part of the EU.

'Retained EU law' is defined by section 6(7) EUWA as: 'anything which, on or after IP completion day, continues to be, or forms part of, domestic law' by virtue of sections 2, 3, 4 or 6(3) or 6(6) of the European Union (Withdrawal) Act 2018'.

In real terms, sections 2–4 include the following, and each section is subject to certain exceptions provided by section 5 and Schedule 1 EUWA:

- By section 2, EU-derived domestic legislation, as it had effect in domestic law immediately before IP completion day, continues to have effect in domestic law on and after IP completion day. An example is the Working Time Regulations 1998, adopted under section 2(2) of the ECA.
- By section 3, direct EU legislation (as defined by section 3), so far as operative immediately before IP completion day, forms part of domestic law on and after IP completion day. Direct EU legislation means:
    - (i) any EU regulation, EU decision or EU tertiary legislation, as it has effect in EU law immediately before exit day other than those that are exempt EU instruments, decisions addressed to a Member State other than the UK, and its effect is not reproduced in EU-derived domestic legislation;

(ii) any annex to the Agreement on the European Economic Area (EEA Agreement), as it has effect in EU law immediately before exit day (other than whether such a provision would be caught within (i) above or is reproduced in EU-derived domestic legislation); and

(iii) Protocol 1 to the EEA Agreement.

It should be noted that the direct EU legislation is adopted as it exists on IP completion day: amendment or modification of such legislation made by the EU does not form part of retained law.

When considering the status of retained direct EU legislation, for the purposes of the Human Rights Act 1998, it is to be treated as primary legislation, as is minor EU legislation insofar as it amends other primary legislation, pursuant to paragraph 30(2) of Schedule 8.

- By section 4, any rights, powers, liabilities, obligations, restrictions, remedies and procedures ('rights, etc') which, immediately before IP completion day, are recognised and available in domestic law by virtue of section 2(1) of the ECA and are enforced, allowed and followed accordingly, continue on and after IP completion day to be recognised and available in domestic law (and to be enforced, allowed and followed accordingly). There is an exception in respect of those rights, etc that arise under an EU direction and 'are not of a kind recognised by the European Court or any court or tribunal in the United Kingdom in a case decided before exit day'. The phrase 'of a kind' is open to interpretation, but *Harris v Environment Agency* [2022] EWHC 2264 (Admin), [91] may be said to support a broad interpretation (see below).

When considering the retention of EU law, section 5 provides that the principle of the supremacy of EU law does not apply to any enactment or rule of law passed or made on or after exit day, but it continues to apply so far as relevant to the interpretation, disapplication or quashing of any enactment or rule of law passed or made before exit day. In addition, the Charter of Fundamental Rights is not retained as part of domestic law on or after exit day, although fundamental rights that exist irrespective of the charter are unaffected. 13-24

Schedule 1 contains further provision about exceptions to savings and incorporation, and it deals with three key issues:

1. There is no right in domestic law on or after exit day to challenge any retained EU law on the basis that, immediately before exit day, an EU instrument was invalid unless the European Court had made such a finding before exit day or the challenge is permitted by regulations made by a Minister of the Crown. Such regulations are permitted to provide for challenges against public authorities in the UK where, prior to exit day, challenge would have been brought against an EU institution.
2. No general principle of EU law is part of domestic law on or after exit day if it was not recognised as a general principle of EU law by the European Court in a case decided before exit day. Moreover, there is no right of action in domestic law on or after exit day based on a failure to comply with any of the general principles of EU law.
3. There is no right in domestic law on or after exit day to damages in accordance with the rule in *Francovich* (ECLI:EU:C:1991:428), ie where there is a failure to implement a European directive.

More recently, the UK has passed the REUL Act. The intention of this Act is to remove EU retained law from the UK statute book, save for where it is explicitly intended that such law should be exempt or reproduced. This Act is considered in detail later in section VII of this chapter.

B. The TEU

13-25 Hardly any of the TEU Articles have been retained in any form in the UK. The key exception to this is in the context of retained EU law. Where an TEU Article created a right that an individual or an organisation could rely on directly in domestic courts, that right is retained by virtue of section 4 EUWA.

C. EU Directives

The application of EU directives ended in the UK with effect from 31 December 2020. Directives are required to be implemented in domestic legislation through national legislation, and so the UK already had, at this point, measures that ensured that areas covered by EU directives were part of domestic law.

Many changes have therefore largely been technical, for example replacing references to the European Commission with references to UK ministers or regulators, and removing obligations that required EU or European Economic Area persons to be treated in the same way as UK citizens.

D. EU Regulations

As identified above, section 3 EUWA was intended to bring the entirety of EU regulations into the UK statute book as they were at the end of the transition period. In practice, this has largely been achieved through statutory instruments.

E. EU Decisions

Section 3 EUWA brought EU decisions onto the UK statute book, for the moment preserving their validity.

F. Construing section 4 of the European Union (Withdrawal) Act 2018

13-26 This issue was considered in *Harris v Environment Agency* [2022] EWHC 2264 (Admin). In this judicial review, the court found that the UK Environment Agency had acted unlawfully in relation to the investigation of licences to abstract groundwater from wetlands in special areas of conservation and that it had breached Article 6(2) of Directive 92/43 (the Habitats Directive) on the conservation of natural habitats and of wild fauna and flora, which remained enforceable in the UK, as well as the Conservation of Habitats and Species Regulations 2017.

Critically, the court held that Article 6(2) of the Habitats Directive was enforceable by a UK court. Section 4(3) EUWA did not require that a particular provision had been previously held to have direct effect, only that it was 'of a kind' that had been held to have direct effect. The Court of Justice of the European Union (CJEU) had already held that Article 6(3) had direct effect in domestic proceedings and that it has a very close relationship with Article 6(2): both required the national authorities to take steps to achieve the directive's aims and, in particular, to avoid deterioration of habitats and significant disturbances of species in Special Areas of Conservation. Consequently, the court held that Article 6(2) was of a kind that had been recognised as having direct effect. Furthermore, there was a requirement to recognise and enforce the precautionary principle that was inherent in Article 6(2). Accordingly, by reason of section 4 EUWA, Article 6(2) continued to be recognised and available in domestic law, and it had to be enforced accordingly.

The conclusion might be considered a little surprising as neither the CJEU nor any domestic court had actually ruled that Article 6(2) had direct effect in domestic proceedings. The answer lies in the wording of section 4(2)(b) EUWA, which specifically permits obligations that arise under an EU directive that are 'of a kind recognised by the European Court or any court or tribunal in the United Kingdom in a case decided before IP completion day (whether or not as an essential part of the decision in the case)' to be recognised and available in domestic law.

The court was then required to determine what, if any, remedy was appropriate following the claimants' successful application for a judicial review. 13-27 It was held that the claimants were presumptively entitled to an order providing an effective remedy, it having been established that the UK Environment Agency had acted unlawfully. There was also a statutory right, given that the UK Environment Agency had breached the 2017 Regulations and the Habitats Directive. The court was required to enforce the provisions of the directive and the 2017 Regulations under section 4(1)(b) EUWA.

Under section 6(3)(a) EUWA, the effect of the provisions had to be determined in accordance with retained general principles of EU law, including the right to an effective remedy (applying Article 19(1) TEU, which states 'Member States shall provide remedies sufficient to ensure effective legal protection in the fields covered by Union law'.

There was nothing objectionable in requiring the UK Environment Agency to formulate a plan as to how it would discharge its obligations. Although difficult scientific and technical assessments would be needed, the UK Environment Agency had known about the concerns of the claimants since 2010 and the need for remedial steps since it had lost the judicial review a month previously. Eight weeks was considered appropriate in those circumstances.

Applying the principle of an effective remedy, it was necessary for the UK Environment Agency to disclose the plan to the claimants, even where there was no requirement in the regulations or the directive to publish the steps to comply with its obligations. Once again, the court drew on European case law:

> The European Court of Justice has held that effective judicial review presupposes, in general, that the court may require the competent authority to notify its reasons for a contested decision. Where there is an issue about the ability to enforce a protected right, those who might wish to enforce

> that right should have 'the best possible conditions and have the possibility of deciding, with a full knowledge of the relevant facts, whether there is any point in their applying to the courts'. This means that the competent national authority must, on request, disclose its reasons for refusing the right in question: *Union Nationale des Entraineurs et Cadres Techniques Professionnels du Football v Heylens*, Case 222/86 [1987] ECR 4097 at [15].

Applying this principle, disclosure of the plan was the only means by which the claimants would know the practical outcome of these proceedings.

13-28 How might this be different following the REUL Act and the sunset provisions? The High Court could have made a reference to the Court of Appeal asking for a binding decision on whether or not Article 6(2) had direct effect in domestic proceedings. Section 4 EUWA would have been repealed following the coming into force of the REUL Act and the operation of the sunset provisions. There is no power to exempt all or part of the law that is currently retained by section 4 EUWA. Consequently, unless the legal effects had been reproduced by way of regulations after 2023, there would be no means by which the effects of Article 6(2) of the Habitats Directive could be held to have direct effect.

What will be the effect on *Harris* as a precedent? The Habitats Directive provisions on which *Harris* was determined would cease to have direct legal effect in domestic proceedings in the absence of regulations reproducing their effect. In such circumstances, *Harris* cannot continue to be considered good law and the particular circumstances would need to be redetermined.

In practical terms, this opens up the prospect of the regression of environmental protection, where effects have not been reproduced.

G. Retained EU Case Law

13-29 'Retained EU case law' is defined by section 6(7) EUWA as 'any principles laid down by, and any decisions of, the European Court, as they have effect in EU law immediately before IP completion day' so far as they relate to anything to which section 2, 3 or 4 EUWA applies and are not excluded by section 5 or Schedule 1 EUWA.

Any question as to the validity, meaning or effect of any retained EU law is to be decided, so far as that law is unmodified on or after IP completion day and so far as they are relevant to it, in accordance with any retained case law and any retained general principles of EU law, having regard (among other things) to the limits, immediately before IP completion day, of EU competences.

This will change with the coming into force of the REUL Act.

H. The Role of CJEU Judgments (at Present)

13-30 Until the REUL Act comes fully into force, CJEU judgments made on or before 11pm on 31 December 2020 are binding, as are CJEU judgments on matters that were referred to it from UK courts before the end of the transition period.

CJEU judgments made after this date are not binding, but UK courts are free to have regard to them. However, section 6(4) EUWA expressly provides that the UK Supreme Court is not bound by any retained EU case law.

In addition, a relevant court is bound by retained EU case law only insofar as there is post-transition case law which modifies or applies that retained EU case law and which is binding on the relevant court (Regulation 4 of the European Union (Withdrawal) Act 2018 (Relevant Court) (Retained EU Case Law) Regulations 2020/1525, in force from 31 December 2020).

Until the REUL Act comes fully into force, in deciding whether to depart from any retained EU case law, a relevant court must apply the same test as the Supreme Court would in deciding whether to depart from the case law of the Supreme Court (Regulation 5 and section 6(5)).

The relevant courts are the Court Martial Appeal Court, the Court of Appeal in England and Wales, the Inner House of the Court of Session, the High Court of Justiciary (when acting as a court of appeal in a devolution or compatibility issue), the Registration Appeal Court in Scotland, the Land Valuation Appeal Court and the Court of Appeal in Northern Ireland.

Until the REUL Act comes fully into force, any question as to the validity, meaning or effect of any retained EU law is to be determined in accordance with key European principles, such as proportionality, equivalence or effectiveness, insofar as retained EU law is unmodified after 31 December 2020, and insofar as the principles themselves are retained (section 6(3)).

I. The Charter of Fundamental Rights

The Charter of Fundamental Rights is excluded from the definition of retained EU law (section 5(4)).

VII. The Retained EU Law (Revocation and Reform) Act 2023

The REUL Act received royal assent on 29 June 2023. The REUL Act may be seen as the successor of the proposed Great Repeal Bill, which was heralded by the government to be a major new piece of constitutional legislation, which aims to end the supremacy of EU law in the UK. 13-31

In broad terms, the REUL Act will result in the following changes by the end of 2023:

- 587 legislative instruments of EU-related origin will be revoked in full or in part.
- All retained directly effective EU law (eg rights and obligations formerly conferred directly under EU treaties or directives) will be revoked.
- The modified principle of supremacy of EU law, which governs the hierarchy of laws passed before the end of the transition period, will be revoked.
- The retained general principles of EU law (which govern the interpretation of the REUL Act) will be revoked.
- The concept of 'retained EU law' will be renamed 'assimilated law'.

Beyond these revocations which will take effect by the end of 2023, the REUL Act will confer temporary (until 23 June 2026) broad delegated powers to restate, replicate, revoke and replace assimilated law, and permanent powers to update the REUL Act and assimilated law in light of technological or scientific developments. In addition, the REUL Act will permit and encourage lower courts to depart more often from legacy case law of the CJEU.

A. Government Investigation

13-32 The REUL Act is a product of a number of different governmental investigations.

In 2021, the Prime Minister tasked the Rt Hon Sir Iain Duncan Smith MP, Rt Hon Theresa Villiers MP and George Freeman MP to constitute a Taskforce on Innovation, Growth and Regulatory Reform (TIGRR) with a brief to identify and develop proposals for post-Brexit market regulation. In May 2021, TIGRR published its findings in a report. In the view of TIGRR, the EUWA 2018 'severely restricted the ability of the lower courts to depart from EU case law relating to unmodified retained EU law'. TIGRR invited changes to retained EU law, with a view to allowing lower courts the 'freedom' already enjoyed at the level of the Court of Appeal.

In June 2021, the government created the Brexit Opportunities Unit, which was tasked with capitalising on the UK's new freedoms following its exit from the EU. The unit was established at the request of Lord Frost to support him in changes to policy, law and regulations.

On 9 December 2021, Lord Frost made a statement in respect of his review of retained EU law. He concluded that there were seven areas in which EU law concepts continued to impact the UK.

B. Passage of the REUL Act

13-33 The House of Lords repeatedly tried to amend the Great Repeal Bill to try to increase parliamentary oversight of the expiry and replacement of retained EU law. There were several government defeats in the Lords on scrutiny mechanisms for delegated powers, both in general and with a particular focus on environmental standards. However, these amendments were repeatedly rejected by the House of Commons and do not form part of the final Act.

The original intention was to bring about a wholesale revocation of legislation at the end of 2023, affecting most retained direct EU legislation and EU-derived secondary legislation. At the Lords report stage, a major change of approach was announced, whereby a schedule to the Bill would set out a list of those legislative instruments that the government considered were no longer needed, leaving the remainder of retained EU law in place but susceptible to repeal under the new delegated powers through to June 2026.

Section 1 and Schedule 1 of the Bill deal with the revocation of legislative instruments of both UK and EU origin (originally retained under sections 2 and 3 EUWA).

Section 2 concerns the revocation of law that has been retained under section 4 EUWA (directly effective rights and obligations). It achieves this by repealing section 4 itself, targeting the retaining section, rather than referring to specific treaty provisions or directives.

There is no power to exempt all or part of the law currently retained by section 4 EUWA from expiry at the end of 2023. However, section 12 REUL Act provides a power to reproduce, to any extent, the effect of anything that was retained by virtue of section 4.

Section 3 abolishes the EU principle of supremacy of EU law, removing that principle from the UK statute book, even in the modified form found in the original section 5 EUWA.

Section 5 renames 'retained EU law' as 'assimilated law', a largely symbolic name change.

C. The Treatment of Legacy CJEU Case Law

Section 6 REUL Act amends section 6 EUWA, confirming in primary legislation that specific appellate courts can depart from legacy CJEU case law, and introduces a statutory test for higher courts in deciding whether to depart from CJEU case law. 13-34

The explanatory notes to the REUL Act indicate that the case of *TuneIn Inc v Warner Music UK Ltd* [2022] 2 All ER 35 had inspired the statutory criteria. In that case, the Court of Appeal identified a number of reasons why it was not considered appropriate in that particular case for the court to depart from the CJEU's jurisprudence:

1. there had been no change in domestic legislation post Brexit;
2. there had been no change in the international legislative framework;
3. the issue in question was a difficult one to interpret and the CJEU had unrivalled experience in confronting the issue in a variety of factual scenarios;
4. academic commentary went both ways;
5. care had to be taken not to give undue weight to legal interpretations outside of the EU, where the statutory framework differed and there was a lack of consistent guidance on the questions under consideration; and
6. departing from the CJEU case law would create 'considerable legal uncertainty'.

The statutory test now found in section 6(5) EUWA requires the higher court concerned to have regard to:

(a) the fact that decisions of a foreign court are not (unless otherwise provided) binding;
(b) any changes of circumstances which are relevant to the retained EU case law; and
(c) the extent to which the retained EU case law restricts the proper development of domestic law.

There is a question mark over the extent to which there is much of a meaningful link between the *TuneIn* case and the statutory test. In particular, (a) and (c) bear little resemblance to the reasons from the judgment stated above. Although not explicit, the statutory test appears to be implicitly predicated on a view that CJEU case law is likely to be restrictive to the development of domestic law.

A related statutory test is also set out for higher courts to decide when to depart from retained domestic case law, now found in section 5ZA EUWA.

The task of the courts will be to judge the extent to which retained EU case law is compatible with the UK's developing legislative framework as it will emerge post-Brexit, in particular given that it is likely that future UK law will diverge from that of the EU. There is consequently the prospect of this leading to a patchwork of decisions departing from legacy EU case law.

D. Lower Courts

13-35 This risk is arguably heightened by the prospect of first instance courts and tribunals being able to refer points of law arising in retained case law to higher courts for determination.

The amendment to the EUWA follows comments of the House of Lords Constitution Committee on section 6(5)(a) EUWA (as amended):

> We do not believe it is appropriate for courts other than the Supreme Court and the Scottish High Court of Justiciary to have power to depart from the interpretations of EU case law. Allowing lower courts to reinterpret EU case law risks causing significant legal uncertainty that would be damaging to individuals and companies. It would also increase court workloads as judgments involving departures are contested on appeal.[1]

The consequent approach of the legislation is to provide no opportunity to make a reference to the ECJ but to create an opportunity to make a reference to a domestic appellate court, which will then make a binding decision about whether lower courts should depart. This is an unusual development for domestic law, where the normal course has been for a first instance court to determine a legal dispute, then for that dispute to be appealed. The ordinary course of action allows for decisions to be made against the background of a clear factual matrix, rather than as an academic issue of law.

Where the lower court or tribunal considers that it is bound by retained case law and that the point(s) of law in issue are of general public importance, the court itself may make a reference or a party to the proceedings can make an application for a reference. The higher court may accept the reference if it considers that the point of law is relevant to the proceedings and is of general public importance. Any decision that is subsequently made by the higher court is binding on the lower court. An appeal from the decision of the higher court may, with permission, be made to the Supreme Court, although there is no right of appeal against a decision to make or not to make a reference or to accept or refuse a reference.

13-36 This leaves open the issue of appeals following a binding reference. Although there is a power to appeal to the Supreme Court, the question left open is where a binding decision is not appealed but subsequently the loser at first instance wishes to appeal the final determination. The status of the referred decision is not explicitly set out in the legislation.

Section 6 REUL Act also permits law officers (senior legal advisors to the UK government and devolved administrations) to make a similar type of reference within six months of lower court proceedings coming fully to a conclusion. If a law officer believes that a relevant point of retained case law should have been referred, they can refer it to a distinct set of proceedings.

Although the outcome of the reference would not impact the original decision (section 6B(6)), it would be binding on the point of law for future cases. There is no discretion on the higher court about whether or not to accept a law officer's reference.

[1] https://publications.parliament.uk/pa/ld5801/ldselect/ldconst/5/5.pdf.

VIII. The Environment Act 2021

The Environment Act 2021 is the most significant UK environmental law for a generation in terms of both scope and substance, subject only to the Climate Change Act 2008 (CCA 2008). It is, importantly, the first major Act concerning the environment since the UK left the European Union. 13-37

In essence, there are two main areas that interrelate to EU law, despite Brexit. The first is the introduction into UK policy-making of a requirement to have due regard to specific environmental principles that notably derive from European law.

The second lies in the creation of the OEP, an independent environmental watchdog designed to fill the environmental governance gap left by Brexit and the removal of the European Commission as the guardian of implementation and enforcement of EU environmental law.

A. Section 17

Section 17 of the Environment Act 2021 requires the Secretary of State to prepare a policy statement on environmental principles (EPPS). This is intended to explain how the specific environmental principles should be interpreted and proportionately applied by Ministers of the Crown when making policy. 13-38

The approach taken by the UK government rejects the notion of an overarching objective to protect or improve the environment, nor does it result in the carrying across of Article 191(2) TEU, requiring domestic policy on the environment to contribute to the achievement of specific objectives. In many ways, therefore, the adoption of a policy statement that may be the subject of amendment without significant scrutiny might be considered to be underwhelming. Nevertheless, section 17 does give some legal effect, for the first time in UK domestic legislation, to certain specific environmental principles, all of which are European in origin (even if the policy statement itself refuses to refer to that fact).

The specific environmental principles are:

- The integration principle
- Preventative action
- The precautionary principle
- Rectification at source
- The polluter-pays principle

In this way, the EPPS aims to achieve the purpose of Article 393 TCA, set out above.

Under section 19 of the Environment Act 2021, a Minister of the Crown must, when making policy, have due regard to the policy statement on environmental principles currently in effect. Whilst there are extensive references in the Environment Act 2021 to the need to have regard to something, this is the only section in the Act to impose a duty to 'have due regard to'. This was the result of a conscious government amendment, and a court would be entitled to consider that the wording was intended to impose a stronger test than simply to 'have regard to'.

(i) Have Due Regard

13-39 There is no definition in the legislation of the phrase 'have due regard'. However, there is a clear parallel with human rights law, not least due to the explicit reference of the then Secretary of State for the Environment, Food and Rural Affairs to the relevance of the Equality Act 2010 during the passage of the Bill through Parliament.

Principles from case law were helpfully summarised by McCombe LJ in *R (on the application of Bracking) v Secretary of State for Work and Pensions* [2013] EWCA Civ 1345, paragraph 25:

> (1) As stated by Arden LJ in *R (Elias) v Secretary of State for Defence* [2006] 1 WLR 3213; [2006] EWCA Civ 1293 at [274], equality duties are an integral and important part of the mechanisms for ensuring the fulfilment of the aims of anti-discrimination legislation.
>
> (2) An important evidential element in the demonstration of the discharge of the duty is the recording of the steps taken by the decision maker in seeking to meet the statutory requirements: *R (BAPIO Action Ltd) v Secretary of State for the Home Department* [2007] EWHC 199 (QB) (Stanley Burnton J (as he then was)).
>
> (3) The relevant duty is upon the Minister or other decision maker personally. What matters is what he or she took into account and what he or she knew. Thus, the Minister or decision maker cannot be taken to know what his or her officials know or what may have been in the minds of officials in proffering their advice: *R (National Association of Health Stores) v Department of Health* [2005] EWCA Civ 154 at [26–27] per Sedley LJ.
>
> (4) A Minister must assess the risk and extent of any adverse impact and the ways in which such risk may be eliminated before the adoption of a proposed policy and not merely as a 'rearguard action', following a concluded decision: per Moses LJ, sitting as a Judge of the Administrative Court, in *Kaur & Shah v LB Ealing* [2008] EWHC 2062 (Admin) at [23–24].
>
> (5) These and other points were reviewed by Aikens LJ, giving the judgment of the Divisional Court, in *R (Brown) v Secretary of State for Work and Pensions* [2008] EWHC 3158 (Admin), as follows:
>
> i) The public authority decision maker must be aware of the duty to have 'due regard' to the relevant matters;
> ii) The duty must be fulfilled before and at the time when a particular policy is being considered;
> iii) The duty must be 'exercised in substance, with rigour, and with an open mind'. It is not a question of 'ticking boxes'; while there is no duty to make express reference to the regard paid to the relevant duty, reference to it and to the relevant criteria reduces the scope for argument;
> iv) The duty is non-delegable; and
> v) Is a continuing one.
> vi) It is good practice for a decision maker to keep records demonstrating consideration of the duty.
>
> (6) '[G]eneral regard to issues of equality is not the same as having specific regard, by way of conscious approach to the statutory criteria.' (per Davis J (as he then was) in *R (Meany) v Harlow DC* [2009] EWHC 559 (Admin) at [84], approved in this court in *R (Bailey) v Brent LBC* [2011] EWCA Civ 1586 at [74–75].)
>
> (7) Officials reporting to or advising Ministers/other public authority decision makers, on matters material to the discharge of the duty, must not merely tell the Minister/decision maker what he/she wants to hear but they have to be 'rigorous in both enquiring and

reporting to them': *R (Domb) v Hammersmith & Fulham LBC* [2009] EWCA Civ 941 at [79] per Sedley LJ.

(8) Finally, and with respect, it is I think, helpful to recall passages from the judgment of my Lord, Elias LJ, in *R (Hurley & Moore) v Secretary of State for Business, Innovation and Skills* [2012] EWHC 201 (Admin) (Divisional Court) as follows:

(i) At paragraphs [77–78]

> '[77] Contrary to a submission advanced by Ms Mountfield, I do not accept that this means that it is for the court to determine whether appropriate weight has been given to the duty. Provided the court is satisfied that there has been a rigorous consideration of the duty, so that there is a proper appreciation of the potential impact of the decision on equality objectives and the desirability of promoting them, then as Dyson LJ in Baker (para [34]) made clear, it is for the decision maker to decide how much weight should be given to the various factors informing the decision.
>
> [78] The concept of 'due regard' requires the court to ensure that there has been a proper and conscientious focus on the statutory criteria, but if that is done, the court cannot interfere with the decision simply because it would have given greater weight to the equality implications of the decision than did the decision maker. In short, the decision maker must be clear precisely what the equality implications are when he puts them in the balance, and he must recognise the desirability of achieving them, but ultimately it is for him to decide what weight they should be given in the light of all relevant factors. If Ms Mountfield's submissions on this point were correct, it would allow unelected judges to review on substantive merits grounds almost all aspects of public decision making.'

(ii) At paragraphs [89–90]

> '[89] It is also alleged that the PSED in this case involves a duty of inquiry. The submission is that the combination of the principles in Secretary of State for Education and Science v Tameside Metropolitan Borough Council [1977] AC 1014 and the duty of due regard under the statute requires public authorities to be properly informed before taking a decision. If the relevant material is not available, there will be a duty to acquire it and this will frequently mean than some further consultation with appropriate groups is required. Ms Mountfield referred to the following passage from the judgment of Aikens LJ in Brown (para [85]):
>
> … the public authority concerned will, in our view, have to have due regard to the need to take steps to gather relevant information in order that it can properly take steps to take into account disabled persons' disabilities in the context of the particular function under consideration.'

Importantly, although the duty to have due regard cannot be lightly ignored, the environmental principles do not dictate the final content of policy.

(ii) Meaning of 'Policy'

'Policy' can be broadly understood as an intended course of action adopted to achieve an objective. 13-40

Examples of policy include:

- Proposals that lead to legislation
- National policy statements, strategies and frameworks

- Ministerial statements setting out the government's formal position on an issue
- Documents, strategies and frameworks prepared by public bodies that ministers are required by statute to approve
- Any other document that sets out a substantial change in approach to an established position

The definition of 'policy' is fantastically broad. On its face, it includes high-level strategy documents, such as the Food Strategy or the Road Investment Strategy. It would include proposals that lead to legislation; for example, proposals adopted by the Secretary of State in reaching a decision pursuant to his duty under section 13 CCA 2008 to prepare a package of 'proposals and policies' that will enable the carbon budgets set under the CCA 2008 to be met are highly likely to fall within this definition of policy.

The broad nature of the definition is in stark contrast to the Supreme Court's definition of 'Government policy', found in section 8 of the Planning Act 2008, in *R (Friends of the Earth Limited) v Secretary of State for Transport* [2021] PTSR 190, [105]–[106]:

> In our view the phrase is looking to carefully formulated written statements of policy such as one might find in an NPS, or in statements of national planning policy (such as the National Planning Policy Framework), or in government papers such as the Aviation Policy Framework. For the subsection to operate sensibly the phrase needs to be given a relatively narrow meaning so that the relevant policies can readily be identified.

The reasoning as to why the EPPS has taken the exact opposite approach is unclear. The sheer breadth of the definition raises practical issues, as it leaves little by way of decision-making that would not engage the EPPS.

(iii) Meaning of Environmental Effect

13-41 The policy statement defines an environmental effect as

> a change to the environment which can be:
> - A primary effect or secondary
> - Occurring once, repeatedly or cumulative
> - Local, regional, national or transboundary
> - Short-term, medium-term or long-term
> - Permanent or temporary
> - Positive or negative

In *R (on the application of Finch) v Surrey CC* [2022] EWCA Civ 187, the Court of Appeal held, in the context of an application for planning permission for an oil extraction and production project, that although downstream greenhouse gas emissions resulting from future combustion of refined oil were capable of being an environmental effect requiring assessment as part of an environmental impact assessment, impacts on the environment had to have a sufficiently close connection to the proposed development to be at least indirect effects of it. In this case, the planning authority had a reasonable and lawful basis for deciding that the environmental effects of downstream emissions could reasonably be seen as far removed from the proposed development itself, and not causally linked to it because of a series of intervening stages between the extraction of the crude oil and the ultimate generation of those emissions.

The case was appealed to the Supreme Court and heard on 21–22 June 2023. At the time of writing, the Supreme Court had yet to publish its judgment. The scope of environmental impact assessment is an important environmental topic, capable as it is of stretching into issues of climate litigation as well as purely domestic environmental issues. It is not difficult to anticipate that, in the event that the Supreme Court determines that Scope 3 emissions are legally required to be assessed and considered in the context of planning decisions capable of impacting on the environment, rather than being dismissed as too far removed, this is perfectly capable of leading to further litigation across Europe.

The term 'secondary', set out above in the policy statement, is as yet undefined. There is therefore the potential for a contrast between the line of reasoning in *Finch* on 'indirect' effects and the approach that should be taken towards 'secondary' environmental effects caused as a consequence of a specific policy decision. The definition of an 'environmental effect' in the policy statement is quite clearly intended to be extremely broad, and it would be unsurprising if that were later construed to include the environmental impacts of emissions that can be directly linked to a policy decision even where those emissions occur at some downstream point, even potentially abroad.

(iv) Proportionality

Ministers are not required under section 19 to take action or refrain from taking action 13-42 if there would be 'no significant environmental benefit, or the action would be disproportionate to the environmental benefit'. Consequently, where policy has no potential environmental effects, or where the environmental effects are negligible, policy-makers do not need to take action.

In taking a proportionate approach, the EPPS requires policy-makers to balance social, economic and environmental considerations when making policy. This includes the potential environmental effects and any mitigations, but also provides the context for the consideration of the costs and benefits to society of the primary objectives of any particular policy.

(v) Relevance of EU Case Law

The most striking omission from the EPPS is any reference to case law in the context of 13-43 the principles themselves. Despite the fact that these principles derive from EU environmental policy and have largely been tested on numerous occasions at European level, case law does not feature in the EPPS itself.

(vi) The Integration Principle

As defined in the EPPS, policy-makers should look for opportunities to embed environmental protection and/or enhancement across fields of policy, not just those directly related to the environment.

Article 11 of the Treaty on the Functioning of the European Union (TFEU) requires that environmental protection requirements be integrated into the definition and implementation of the Union's policies and activities, in particular with a view to promoting sustainable development. There is, therefore, an arguable difference between the two versions of the principle, namely that Article 11 is a mandatory obligation whereas the EPPS only requires due regard to be had to 'look for opportunities' to embed environmental protection. It is unclear whether this will make any difference in practice. It is worth comparing this with the definition of the integration principle found in section 17(5) of the Environment Act 2021, namely 'the principle that environmental protection should be integrated into the making of policies'.

(vii) The Principle to Take Preventative Action

13-44 As defined in the EPPS, government policy should aim to prevent environmental harm. Its application involves: (in summary)

- Understanding the potential environmental harm of the policy
- Considering the extent to which environmental harm can be prevented based on the scale of the harm
- Exploring the ways in which the harm could be prevented and the costs and benefits of either preventing or not preventing the damage

This reflects the EU requirement that, under Article 191 TFEU, Union policy shall be based on the principle that preventative action should be taken. The need for a cost–benefit analysis is more explicit in the EPPS that in Article 191.

(viii) Rectification at Source

Environmental damage should, as a priority, be addressed at its origin to avoid the need to remedy its effects later.

Policy-makers should: (in summary)

- Understand what the environmental damage (or potential environmental damage) is. This damage could relate to any aspect of harm to the natural environment.
- Understand where the damage originates from.
- Consider the feasibility of rectifying the issue at source versus other options, and the costs and benefits of doing so. Efforts should be made to pursue solutions at source, where proportionate.

(ix) The Polluter-Pays Principle

13-45 Where possible, the costs of the pollution should be borne by those causing it, rather than the person who suffers the effects of the resulting environmental damage or the wider community.

Policy-makers should consider: (in summary)

- What is the driver for the pollution being caused and who is responsible?
- How does the allocation of responsibility for the pollution cause the most benefit?
- Who is it fair to expect to pay for the pollution?

The principle should be applied proportionately, both to the environmental damage and to the wider costs and benefits to society of the activity in question. In some cases, full costs recovery may not be possible or proportionate.

The polluter-pays principle is already established with regard to environmental liabilities within the insolvency regime in Scotland – see *Re Doonin Plant Hire Ltd (in liquidation)* [2018] CSOH 89, in which it was held that there was a continuing liability for companies in liquidation to be mandated by the polluter-pays principle, requiring principle of environmental protection to trump the expectation that the property of an insolvent company should be divided equally amongst unsecured creditors.

There is the prospect that the polluter-pays principle will become highly relevant to carbon budgets in the future. The government is required, under section 13 CCA 2008, to prepare such proposals and policies as will enable carbon budgets to be met. As various proposals and policies are developed and implemented, it will be entirely consistent with the polluter-pays principle to consider how the principle is to be applied in practice to polluting activities. The EPPS itself makes it very clear that the application of the principle does not create an obligation on Ministers to create a tax on polluting activities, but nevertheless there is the potential for the polluter-pays principle to have a considerable role in deterring activities that give rise to environmental damage.

(x) The Precautionary Principle

The policy statement records that the precautionary principle assists the decision-making process in the face of a lack of scientific certainty. The principle helps policy-makers deal with risks which may not be precisely calculable in advance. 13-46

This requires:

1. Identifying the risk of serious or irreversible environmental harm. Where there are gaps in the scientific evidence base, this should not be used as a reason for inaction if there is a plausible risk of serious or irreversible harm. However, in all cases, there must be sufficient evidence that the risk of serious or irreversible damage is plausible and real, and where choices are considered to prevent or reduce the environmental degradation in question, they should be cost-effective. The precautionary principle should not be applied speculatively.
2. In managing the risk of serious or irreversible environmental harm, policy-makers must take a holistic approach. There may be an occasion where the policy-maker might judge that the likely environmental, economic or social harm or the opportunity cost of the established practices is greater than the risk of facilitating a cautious deployment of new technology and new innovations.

In *R v Secretary of State for Trade and Industry, ex p Duddridge* [1995] 10 WLUK 71, the Court of Appeal upheld a decision of the Divisional Court that Article 130r of the Treaty of Rome did not place any obligation on any organ of national government. Consequently, the Secretary of State was not under a duty to adopt and apply the precautionary principle when deciding whether to exercise his power to make regulations.

At first instance [1994] 10 WLUK 7, the Divisional Court had made the following observation:

> [The obligation to apply the precautionary principle] would entail the need to conduct cost–benefit analyses in respect of every known risk of damage to the environment and every known risk to human health from the environment. [Government departments] would then be obliged to legislate in every case in which the cost–benefit analysis showed that action would be reasonable. All this would be obligatory as a matter of national initiative, in the absence of any definition of the precautionary principle and before any formulation of a coherent policy on the environment. I find quite remarkable the proposition that each state should be obliged to act alone on the basis of so general a statement of objectives and considerations.

13-47 The introduction of the policy statement on environmental principles clearly alters the legitimate application of the precautionary principle on the development of future policy. However, there is little specific guidance on the application of a cost–benefit analysis to the precautionary principle, save for the requirement that damage prevention or reduction choices must be 'cost-effective'. The overarching requirement for a cost–benefit analysis can be found in the explanation in the policy statement of proportionality and in the application of the prevention principle.

The UK Innovation Strategy, published by the Department for Business, Energy and Industrial Strategy in July 2021, states:

> When applied disproportionately the precautionary principle can err too much on the side of caution, reversing the burden of proof and placing it on the Innovator to demonstrate no possible harm from an innovation … The precautionary principle can be interpreted in ways that can produce more harm than good. In some cases, the precautionary principle has become a policy of blocking all potential harms, even a possibility of harm, without a balanced analysis of likely benefits.

In order to counter this observation, the policy statement reads:

> The precautionary principle incentivises innovation by encouraging development of alternative policy options that reduce risk and uncertainty. New or innovative technologies should not be held to a higher standard of safety than existing ones where the level of risk is comparable, otherwise their potential to deliver benefits will be lost. The principle should not unnecessarily hinder innovation due to novelty, without plausible evidence of a risk of serious or irreversible harm, and it should only prevent or defer an innovative development where that risk outweighs the benefits, including potential benefits.

IX. The Office for Environmental Protection

13-48 The Office for Environmental Protection was established under section 22 of the Environment Act 2021.

Unlike bodies such as the Environment Agency or Natural England, the Secretary of State has no power to issue directions, either general or specific, to the OEP, but does have the power to issue guidance on its enforcement strategy. Paragraph 17 of Schedule 1 to the Environment Act 2021 provides that, in exercising any functions relating to the OEP, the Secretary of State must have regard to the need to protect the OEP's independence.

The OEP's jurisdiction formally covers the whole of the UK, but, given that most environmental matters are devolved, the majority of the OEP's operations will relate to England and Northern Ireland.

The principle objective of the OEP in exercising its functions is to contribute to environmental protection and the improvement of the natural environment.

Prior to Brexit, the European Commission oversaw the implementation of EU environmental law and policy by the UK government. Where necessary, the European Commission brought enforcement cases in the CJEU, which provided rulings on the interpretation of EU environmental law in order to ensure that it was applied correctly by Member States. The European Commission was also supported in its environmental governance functions by the European Environment Agency (EEA), a statutory body of the EU tasked with providing sound independent information and conducting assessments on a wide range of issues relating to the environment.

Analysis from the Institute for Government in 2017[2] identified that around half of the European Court of Justice cases found by the Commission against the UK between 2003 and 2016 concerned the environment, with the Commission winning the majority.

The European Commission carried out its monitoring using information from UK 13-49
submissions and reports, as well as the Commission's own assessments and those of other EU bodies. The EEA operated as a major information source for those involved in developing, adopting, implementing and evaluating environmental policy, as well as for the general public. It published findings on a wide range of topics, including progress on the EU's environmental policy framework and objectives as set out in Environmental Action Programmes (themselves multi-annual strategies setting environmental priorities for EU institutions and Member States).

The OEP was intended to provide a domestic replacement for the scrutiny function of the European Commission and the EEA. This is achieved through a number of specific statutory provisions in the Environment Act 2021. The OEP is required by section 28 of the Environment Act 2021 to monitor progress in improving the natural environment in accordance with the current UK environmental improvement plan, as well as meeting any targets or interim targets set by the Act. The OEP must report to Parliament by way of an annual progress report. In addition, the OEP must monitor the implementation of environmental law, by virtue of section 29 of the Environment Act 2021, and may report on any matter concerned with the implementation of environmental law, again arranging for its reports to be laid before Parliament. The OEP is also required by section 30 to give advice to a Minister of the Crown about any proposed change to environmental law, or any other matter relating to the natural environment, on which the Minister requires it to give advice. That advice must be published and the Minister may lay that advice before Parliament. Outside of the scrutiny function that lay with the European Commission, there are very few occasions where UK environmental law requires regular assessments and reviews of implementation. The scrutiny functions of the OEP are therefore highly significant.

The OEP has also been given specific enforcement powers against public authorities for failures to comply with environmental law. In many ways, the core procedures are designed to replicate and replace the processes used by the European Commission. There is a stepped process, consisting of the service of an Information notice, service of a decision notice and

[2] https://data.parliament.uk/writtenevidence/committeeevidence.svc/evidencedocument/environment-food-and-rural-affairs-committee/prelegislative-scrutiny-of-the-draft-environment-principles-and-governance-bill/written/95735.html.

referral to court by way of an environmental review. Although a failure to comply with information notices and decision notices does not lead immediately to sanctions, there are statutory duties to co-operate and respond, and not doing so can ultimately lead to court action. This compares with the TFEU processes under Articles 258 and 259, namely an infringement letter, a reasoned opinion and ultimately a referral to the European Court of Justice. As with the European Commission, the OEP's enforcement functions are aimed at the government, local authorities and other public bodies such as the Environment Agency or Natural England. Also as with the European Commission, there is a public complaint system, which allows for anyone to make a complaint to the OEP about potential breaches of environmental law.

13-50 One key element of European Commission engagement was the fact that it was able to settle the vast majority of enforcement disputes by negotiation with the Member States. The Institute for Government analysis noted that the ECJ judgments represented less than a third of the Commission's environmental enforcement action against the UK. Most infringement cases were resolved before they reached the court stage. This is replicated with the OEP. It is clear that the OEP does not view itself simply as a watchdog. The OEP's real strength lies in the fact that it has been set up to keep environmental issues front and centre, particularly in Parliament. Environmental reviews are, consequently, likely to be rare. Much more emphasis has been placed on co-operation with public authorities and on information gathering. This was emphasised by evidence given by Dame Glenys Stacey, Chair of the OEP, to the Environmental Audit Committee on 8 February 2023, making it clear that the OEP wants to be strategically important and focus its efforts on where it believes it can make a material difference, not simply enforcement.

Where the EU processes and the new UK approach may diverge is likely to be in environmental reviews. The CJEU has generally adopted an approach to litigation based on proportionality. Judicial review has largely considered the principle of irrationality and has shown a large degree of deference to the expert nature of regulatory bodies such as the Environment Agency. It is not the role of UK courts concerned with judicial review to consider the merits of the decision at issue, only the lawfulness of that decision. On an environmental review, section 38 of the Environment Act 2021 makes it clear that the court must determine whether the authority has failed to comply with environmental law, applying the principles applicable on an application for judicial review. The intensity of any review may, consequently, be at a level that falls below the degree of intervention that the ECJ has historically deployed.

X. The Impact of Brexit

13-51 In the years since the UK left the EU and the conclusion of the Trade and Co-operation Agreement, the Office for Budget Responsibility has stated that the latest evidence showed that Brexit had had 'a significant adverse effect on UK trade', cutting trade volumes and relationships between British and EU companies. Paul Johnson, director of the Institute for Fiscal Studies, stated: 'Very clearly Brexit was an economic own goal.'[3] A YouGov poll

[3] www.ft.com/content/9c288c28-835c-4bcc-96c7-b9b120205927.

recently found that public support for Brexit had fallen to a record low of 32 per cent, compared with 56 per cent who thought Brexit was wrong.[4]

It pays to consider a few specific areas.

A. Farming

According to the Department for Environment, Food & Rural Affairs (Defra),[5] in 2021 the contribution made by agriculture to the UK economy was £11,222 million or 0.51 per cent of GDP. It follows that even if there were to be a major increase in productivity, this would make a 'negligible difference to overall GDP performance'.[6]

In a speech to the National Farmers Union on 23 February 2022, Emma Howard Boyd, Chair of the Environment Agency, referenced the 'opportunities' of Brexit[7] and using public money to 'unlock more productive agriculture, long term food security, increased biodiversity, viable infrastructure and thriving places'.

In contrast to potential growth opportunities, the same speech recognised that agricultural diffuse pollution is one of the biggest contributors to poor water quality in England and the primary cause for 40 per cent of water bodies failing to achieve good ecological status. Undermining environmental law through poor farming practices damages the natural resources needed to grow food, harms the economic viability of farming and diminishes the public perception of farming. Every effort needs to be made to avoid circumstances where famers are effectively being paid to emit and pollute.

Agricultural productivity growth in the UK has been weak for many years. It is intended, according to the Growth Plan 2022,[8] that the government will rapidly review frameworks for regulation, innovation and investment that impact farmers and land managers in England. Plans were intended to be set out in autumn 2023, but to date these have not materialised.

Post-Brexit improvements have consequently yet to reach fruition. Even a concrete achievement like the UK's flagship post-Brexit trade deal with Australia is 'not actually a very good deal', according to former Environment Secretary George Eustice.[9] Australia and New Zealand have full access to the UK market to sell beef and sheep, while Australia still bans the import of British beef. There is clearly an environmental incentive for greater food production in the UK, not least when considering the carbon footprint of imported food or national food security, but this is not supported in post-Brexit trade deals.

[4] https://yougov.co.uk/topics/politics/explore/issue/Brexit?content=surveys.

[5] www.gov.uk/government/statistics/total-income-from-farming-in-the-uk/total-income-from-farming-of-the-united-kingdom-2021-provisional-estimate.

[6] D Helm, 'Going Backwards – the Retreat From Environmental Commitments' (October 2022).

[7] www.gov.uk/government/speeches/farming-and-the-environment-agency.

[8] www.gov.uk/government/publications/the-growth-plan-2022-documents/the-growth-plan-2022-html#:~:text=The%20Growth%20Plan%202022%20makes,a%20period%20of%20high%20inflation.

[9] www.theguardian.com/politics/2022/nov/14/flagship-post-brexit-australia-trade-deal-not-actually-very-good-george-eustice.

B. The Zero Emissions Vehicle Mandate

13-52 Following the announcement of the UK adopting a 'zero emission vehicle mandate' in the Net Zero Strategy[10] in October 2021, the government ran a technical consultation on zero emission vehicle mandate policy design between April and June 2022.

The government had committed to end the sale of new petrol and diesel cars by 2030 and for all cars to be fully zero emissions capable by 2035. In contrast, the EU's target is for all new vehicles sold from 2035 to be zero emissions, with an interim target of reducing emissions from new cars by 55 per cent by 2030.[11] The government has now postponed that ban, aligning itself with the EU's 2035 date.

C. The UK Emissions Trading Scheme

The UK ETS replaced the UK's participation in the EU ETS on 1 January 2021. The UK ETS has a similar scope to the EU ETS, although the cap has been set 5 per cent below the notional level that the UK would have had if it had stayed in the EU ETS. There does not appear to be any tangible data on the difference this may have made.

The Committee on Climate Change (CCC) has warned that the scheme risks low liquidity in the long term unless sectoral coverage is expanded.[12] In January 2022, *The Guardian* reported on a 'significant competitive disadvantage' faced by UK industry compared to their European rivals, indicating that UK companies are paying the equivalent of €90 per tonne for the carbon they emit compared to €85 a tonne in the EU,[13] with the reason given being the lack of liquidity identified by the CCC.

D. Divergence in Effect and in Progress

13-53 Divergence, or the risk of it, is becoming more prevalent, without necessarily bringing with it an obvious concurrent environmental benefit.

In chemicals regulation, the UK no longer follows the approach of the EU to designating substances of very high concern (SVHC). Several substances have been added to the SVHC list in the EU since January 2021, but these do not appear to have been considered by the UK.[14] A recent report by the National Audit Office recorded[15] that the Health and Safety Executive considers it will be a further four years before it reaches the full capacity it has planned for its post-EU exit regulatory regime.

The European Union's 'Fit for 55' package includes a proposal for a new Energy Efficiency Directive and a revised Energy Performance of Buildings Directive, which together would

[10] www.gov.uk/government/publications/net-zero-strategy.

[11] https://ec.europa.eu/commission/presscorner/detail/en/IP_22_6462.

[12] 'The Future of Carbon Pricing in the UK' (August 2019).

[13] www.theguardian.com/environment/2022/jan/09/brexit-decision-left-uk-firms-paying-10-more-than-eu-rivals-for-emissions.

[14] https://chemtrust.org/uk-reach-lacks-capacity/.

[15] www.nao.org.uk/reports/regulating-after-eu-exit/?slide=1.

require the renovation of public building floor space and targets for the reduction of emissions from public buildings and increasing annual energy savings.[16] The government's Heat and Buildings Strategy[17] and British Energy Security Strategy[18] place considerable importance on energy efficiency but do little to set out how this is to be achieved.

The European Union has proposed a 'deforestation-free' approach to reduce all deforestation, whether illegal or not, from its supply chains.[19] Section 116 and Schedule 17 of the Environment Act 2021 have provisions about the use of 'forest risk commodities in commercial activity', but the recent Defra consultation on the topic focused heavily on just the 'illegal' element of deforestation in UK supply chains.[20]

The EU has largely banned the export of plastic wastes, including mixed plastic wastes to, non-OECD countries. In contrast, the UK uses a system of prior informed consent which can permit the export of contaminated plastic wastes and numerous other plastic wastes and mixtures of plastic wastes.[21]

The Genetic Technology (Precision Breeding) Act 2023 includes an amendment to the definition of a 'genetically modified organism' (GMO) for England that, in contrast to the approach of the EU,[22] would allow for GMOs produced by gene editing. This is achieved by removing plants and animals produced using modern biotechnologies, and the food and feed derived from them, from GMO regulation if those organisms could have occurred naturally or been produced by traditional methods.

[16] www.ey.com/en_gl/tax-alerts/european-commission-proposes-legislative-package-including-environmental-tax-measures-to-support-eu-climate-ambitions.

[17] www.gov.uk/government/publications/heat-and-buildings-strategy.

[18] www.gov.uk/government/publications/british-energy-security-strategy/british-energy-security-strategy.

[19] https://environment.ec.europa.eu/publications/proposal-regulation-deforestation-free-products_en.

[20] www.gov.uk/government/consultations/tackling-illegal-deforestation-in-uk-supply chains.

[21] See the International Waste Shipments (Amendment of Regulation (EC) No 1013/2006) Regulations 2020.

[22] Case C-528/16 *Confédération paysanne and Others v Premier ministre and Ministre de l'agriculture, de l'agroalimentaire et de la forêt* ECLI:EU:C:2018:583.

14

Implementation and Enforcement

I. Obligations of Member States

A. Treaty Provisions

14-01 The Union provisions on implementation and enforcement are unique in international environmental law. There is no other independent body like the Commission which is charged to ensure the application of the law which is able to bring cases to a court and even impose financial sanctions for continued non-compliance. The different compliance committees which were set up under international environmental and other agreements – with the notable exception of the Aarhus Convention Compliance Committee – depend too much on the contracting parties, act in non-public meetings, accept non-compliance complaints only from contracting parties, do not let civil society participate in the procedure and hardly publish their findings, in order not to disturb the non-complying party too much. The limitation of national sovereignty in the Union's implementation and enforcement mechanism is one of the most striking features of Union (environmental) law. And despite all omissions, deficiencies and lacunae in the application of Union environmental law, the implementation and enforcement of the Union's environmental provisions remains a success story.

The Lisbon Treaties themselves did not contain environmental provisions which Member States would have to transpose into, or to apply in, their national legal order. Article 4(3) of the Treaty on European Union (TEU) stated that Member States shall assist the Union in carrying out its tasks and facilitate achieving them.[1] However, this does not mean that they would have to place in their national legislation the objective of attaining a high level of environmental protection or the aim that environmental requirements were incorporated into other policies pursued at national level. In contrast, Article 4(3) TEU required Member States to abstain from any measures at national level which would make it more difficult or impossible for the EU to move towards a high level of environmental protection or to make the different EU policies 'greener', ie environmentally more friendly. Article 19(2) TEU requested Member States to 'provide remedies sufficient to ensure effective legal protection' of EU (environmental) law, and Article 47(1) of the Charter of Fundamental Rights of the

[1] Art 4(3) TEU: 'Pursuant to the principle of sincere cooperation, the Union and the Member States shall, in full mutual respect, assist each other in respect, assist each other in carrying out tasks which flow from this Treaty. The Member States shall take any appropriate measure, general or particular, to ensure fulfilment of the obligations arising out of the Treaties or resulting from the acts of the institutions of the Union. The Member States shall facilitate the achievement of the Union's tasks and refrain from any measure which could jeopardise the attainment of the Union's objective.'

European Union[2] stated that 'Everyone whose rights and freedoms guaranteed by the law of the Union are violated has the right to an effective remedy before a tribunal'.

The environmental provisions of the Treaties are not formulated in such a way that they are self-executing or, in EU terminology, directly applicable. While Article 34 of the Treaty on the Functioning of the European Union (TFEU) prohibited creating or maintaining barriers to trade within the Union, Article 101 TFEU prohibited trade-distorting agreements between undertakings, Article 102 prohibited abuses of dominant positions and Article 107 TFEU prohibited state aid, no corresponding provision exists in environmental law, for instance forbidding significant environmental pollution. National enforcement bodies or courts therefore do not have to align Member States' laws to instructions that come from EU primary law.

B. Secondary Legislation

The situation is completely different as regards secondary EU environmental law. Under Article 192(4) TFEU, it is, in principle, the Member States that have to implement the different measures which have been adopted in pursuance of EU environmental policy. This provision is somewhat superfluous, since in other EU policies, too, where no such provision exists, the implementation of measures is an obligation for Member States which follows from Article 4(3) TEU. EU directives and decisions address Member States; EU regulations apply in all Member States without even any transposing act (Article 288 TFEU). In no case is there any decision required by the national constitution or of similar rank according to which EU secondary legislation shall be accepted or not; this question was solved by the accession to the Union and Article 4(3) TEU. 14-02

Regulations are directly applied in each Member State (Article 288(2) TFEU); and while environmental regulations frequently contain specific provisions that require Member States to take action – such as the appointing of responsible authorities, the publication of reports or even the taking of executive provisions – their general attribute of being directly applicable remains unchanged; the specific provision then has the characteristics of a directive and needs to be implemented, unless it is, in substance, a recommendation. Similar observations apply to decisions, which normally deal with a specific, concrete situation; where a specific provision in a decision is, in substance, that of a directive, it would require implementation as if it were a directive.[3]

'A directive shall be binding, as to the result to be achieved, upon each Member State to which it is addressed, but shall leave to the national authorities the choice of form and methods' (Article 288(3) TFEU). As EU legislation must be applied by Member States – this follows from Articles 4, 17 and 19(2) TEU[4] – Member States have two main obligations as regards EU environmental directives: they must transpose the provisions of the directive into their national law and they must ensure that these provisions are actually complied with. 14-03

[2] EU Charter of Fundamental Rights of the European Union [2000] OJ C364/1.

[3] See, more generally, para 2-39.

[4] Art 17 TEU: 'The Commission … shall ensure the application of the Treaties, and of measures adopted by the institutions pursuant to them. It shall oversee the application of Union law under the control of the Court of Justice of the European Union.'

(i) Transposition

14-04 Practically all[5] environmental directives contain a provision that requests Member States to transpose the directive's provisions into national law.[6] Generally, such a transposition into national law has to be done by an express binding legislative or regulatory provision, 'in order to secure full implementation of directives in law and not only in facts'.[7] The CJEU has, on numerous occasions, rejected Member States' attempts to transpose the requirements of an environmental directive into national law by means of a multi-annual plan, an administrative circular or a similar instrument.[8] Its main argument was the absence of legal certainty for individual persons and undertakings that was created by such a transposition, as it was not clear which rights and obligations followed out of an EU directive.[9] Since the Court of Justice of the European Union (CJEU) is of the opinion that directives which fix quality standards also give certain legal rights to individuals, most of the provisions of a directive will have to be transposed into national law by a binding provision. This applies even to the establishment of the requirement to set up clean-up programmes or waste management programmes; indeed, such programmes also contain information for individuals about future objectives, measures taken and envisaged, and so on.

14-05 Exceptions apply only to those provisions which provide for obligations of the Council, the Commission or other institutions and to provisions which exclusively concern the Member States' relations to the EU administration and ask them, for instance, to regularly send a report to the Commission. Even in such cases, though, the limits to Member States' obligations are not altogether clear: the CJEU held that a provision that requires regional or local authorities in border regions to consult with authorities from an adjacent Member State had to be transposed into national law.[10] The same applied to a provision where a Member State was allowed to grant a derogation under a directive but had to inform the Commission thereof; where that Member State delegated the right to grant derogations to regional or

[5] The exceptions are Directive 76/464 on pollution caused by certain dangerous substances discharged into the aquatic environment of the Community [1976] OJ L129/23, where this clause was probably forgotten; Directive 91/692 on standardising and rationalising reports on the implementation of certain directives relating to the environment [1991] OJ L377/48; and Directive 2015/412 on the cultivation of genetically modified organisms [2015] OJ L68/1. Directives 76/464 and 91/692 have in the meantime been repealed.

[6] See, eg Art 23 of Directive 92/43 on the conservation of natural habitats and of wild fauna and flora [1992] OJ L206/7: '1. Member States shall bring into force the laws, regulations and administrative provisions necessary to comply with this directive within two years of its notification. They shall forthwith inform the Commission thereof. 2. When Member States adopt such measures, they shall contain a reference to this directive or be accompanied by such reference on the occasion of their official publication. The methods of making such a reference shall be laid down by the Member States. 3. Member States shall communicate to the Commission the main provisions of national law which they adopt in the field covered by this directive.'

[7] CJEU Case C-131/88 *Commission v Germany* ECLI:EU:C:1991:87, para 8.

[8] CJEU Case C-96/81 *Commission v Netherlands* ECLI:EU:C:1982:192; Case C-131/88 (n 7); Case C-361/88 *Commission v Germany* ECLI:EU:C1991:224; Case C-13/90 *Commission v France* ECLI:EU:C:1991:309; Case C-58/89 *Commission v Germany* ECLI:EU:C:1991:391; Case C-262/95 *Commission v Germany* ECLI:EU:C:1996:427.

[9] See, eg C-131/88 (n 7) para 6: 'The transposition of a directive into domestic law does not necessarily require that its provisions be incorporated formally and verbatim in express, specific legislation; a general legal context may, depending on the content of the directive, be adequate for the purpose provided that it does indeed guarantee the full application of the directive in a sufficiently clear and precise manner so that, where the directive is intended to create rights for individuals, the persons concerned can ascertain the full extent of their rights and where appropriate, rely on them before the national courts.'

[10] CJEU Case C-186/91 *Commission v Belgium* ECLI:EU:C:1993:93.

local authorities, it had to ensure expressly that it was informed of the granting of derogations in order to be able to comply with its own requirements towards the Commission.[11] In the same way, it could also be argued that a Member State's implementation report to the Commission, where the Member State reports how a piece of EU legislation was transposed into the national legal order and how it was applied in practice, ensures transparency of implementation and compliance and allows individuals to take action themselves or otherwise orient their behaviour; it therefore has an external effect which requires its transposition into legally binding national legislation.

The necessity of transposing definitions in an EU directive into national law probably depends on the subject matter that is regulated: the more directly individual rights and obligations might be affected by a definition, the greater the need to transpose a directive's definition into national law. Good examples are the definitions of 'waste' and 'hazardous waste' under Directive 2008/98:[12] Member States' legislation often does not use the words 'hazardous waste' but, rather, 'specific waste', 'waste which is to be controlled', 'chemical waste', 'industrial waste' and other definitions. These linguistic differentiations have consequences as regards monitoring, surveillance, statistics, customs, police controls and other administrative matters, which impinge, in turn, on private agents, individuals or administrations. For this reason, the Commission has adopted the position that the definitions for waste and for hazardous waste had to be transposed literally into national laws. The CJEU required the transposition of a definition at least in those cases where an omission to transpose created doubts as to the meaning of the provisions.[13] 14-06

The transposition of an environmental directive, which contains mandatory requirements, cannot be made by non-binding national measures, in particular by administrative provisions, since it is settled case law of the CJEU that 'mere administrative practices, which by their nature may be changed at will by the authorities, cannot be regarded as constituting proper compliance with the obligation on Member States to which a directive is addressed'.[14] 14-07

For this reason, implementation of an environmental directive through an environmental voluntary agreement is not possible unless the EU directive expressly so provides;[15] such a possibility was foreseen, for the first time, by some provisions of some waste directives.[16] This practice appears to have been abandoned since about 2015. As environmental agreements only apply to contracting bodies, the equality of citizens with regard to the rights or obligations that a directive grants is not ensured. Transposition of a directive by environmental agreements that are not generally binding is therefore not possible.

[11] CJEU Case C-237/90 *Commission v Germany* ECLI:EU:C:1992:452.

[12] Directive 2008/98 on waste [2008] OJ L312/3.

[13] CJEU Case C-443/08 *Commission v France* ECLI:EU:C:2009:296; Case C-32/05 *Commission v Luxembourg* ECLI:EU:C:2006:749; Case C-120/09 *Commission v Belgium* ECLI:EU:C:2009:802; Case C-648/13 *Commission v Poland* ECLI:EU:C:2016:490.

[14] CJEU Case C-339/87 *Commission v Netherlands* ECLI:EU:C1990:119.

[15] In the same sense, Commission Recommendation 96/733 concerning environmental agreements implementing Community directives [1996] OJ C333/59.

[16] Directive 2000/53 on end-of-life vehicles [2000] OJ L269/34; Directive 2002/96 on waste electrical and electronic equipment [2003] OJ L37/24; Directive 2006/66 on batteries and accumulators [2006] OJ L266/1. Directive 85/339 on liquid beverage containers [1985] OJ L176/18, which is often quoted as allowing implementation of directives by environmental agreements, is not relevant: indeed, the directive required Member States to set up packaging reduction programmes and then allowed the implementation of such programmes by non-binding measures; it has since been repealed.

A transposition is also necessary in those cases where the Member State in fact already complies with the requirements of a directive. The legal certainty that economic operators and individuals are entitled to expect would be completely undermined if the local, regional or national administration could argue that the factual situation corresponds to the requirements of the directive and places the burden of proof that this is not the case on the person arguing that transposition is necessary.[17]

14-08 No obligation to transpose the requirements of a directive exists where it is physically impossible that the problem dealt with by the directive could ever occur in a Member State. Thus, Luxembourg or Austria would not be obliged to transpose requirements of a directive on coastal waters or (sea) port reception facilities.[18] In contrast, these Member States would normally be obliged to transpose the directive on (the sea discharge of) waste from the titanium dioxide industry,[19] even if they had no such industry on their territory, as this situation could change and, furthermore, titanium dioxide waste from other Member States might be transported to states that do not have such an industry.[20]

The transposition measures must cover the whole of the territory of a Member State. This observation sounds more trivial than it is. Indeed, in many Member States, responsibility for environmental issues lies at least partly with regional authorities; this is the case for Austria, Belgium, Germany, Italy and Spain. But in other Member States, too, environmental legislation is partially split; thus, in Finland, the Aaland Islands have a specific legislative status, and so have the Azores Islands in Portugal and French overseas territories. Finally, waste management plans in Sweden are traditionally set up at local level.

From the point of view of the Union, it is not relevant whether a provision of EU law is transposed by a single act at national level or by a number of regional regulations, as long as the transposition measures cover the whole of the territory.

14-09 It is much more difficult to comply with the second substantive requirement for the transposition measure; that is, that the EU environmental requirement is correctly transposed. First, a Member State may not rely on the wording in which a specific directive is drafted in the Member State's language – all EU languages have the same legal value (Article 55 TEU) and that wording may differ from one language to another. For that reason, the true sense of a provision has to be discovered, which may well vary between specific linguistic versions.[21] The CJEU refers to a teleological and systematic – sometimes even a historic – interpretation of a provision, unless the wording is entirely clear.

Secondly, EU law is autonomous and has to be interpreted without recurring to identical or similar notions that exist in national law. Thus, the same word might be used in EU

[17] CJEU Case C-339/87 (n 14).

[18] See, eg Directive 2008/56 establishing a framework for Community action in the field of marine environmental policy (Marine Strategy Framework Directive) [2008] OJ L164/19, Art 26(7), which provides that Member States without marine waters are only obliged to comply with Art 6 (regional co-operation) and Art 7 (designation of competent authorities).

[19] Directive 78/176 [1978] OJ L54/19.

[20] In this sense, see also CJEU Case C-435/99 *Commission v Portugal* ECLI:EU:C:2000:684. In practice, the Commission has accepted that Member States that do not have a titanium dioxide industry formally committed themselves to transposing the directive as soon as such an industry is established on their territory or where waste from such an industry is shipped into their country; for the reasons mentioned, this practice is not in compliance with EU law.

[21] CJEU Case C-36/98 *Spain v Council* ECLI:EU:C:2001:64; Case C-72/95 *Kraaijeveld* ECLI:EU:C:1996:404; the last case concerned the interpretation of Directive 85/337 on environmental impact assessment.

environmental law and in national law, yet the two meanings are quite different; this potential conflict is increased by the fact that EU law prevails over national law. However, since EU law stems from a source of law other than national law, it might carry different concepts, theories or structures that do not fit into the national legal or administrative infrastructure. An example is Article 9(2) of the Directive on the conservation of wild birds,[22] which provided that local nature protection authorities may give derogations from trading, hunting and other bans under the directive after having examined the local situation; however, such local nature protection authorities do not exist in Ireland.

Another complication is that EU environmental law provisions normally come up 14-10 against a structured and elaborate system of national rules that have been built up over years or decades, and into which the provisions then have to be integrated. The EU provision is then perceived – and all too often also treated – as an immigrant, if not as an intruder.[23]

Where the EU environmental law provision sets numerical values such as emission limit values, quality standards or targets, national legislation will have to adopt these numerical values. Economic operators and individuals must have the opportunity to find in the national statute books what these numerical values are.[24] The same applies to bans on substances or products. For other provisions, it is normally difficult to establish fixed rules, since it follows from Article 288 TFEU that a word-by-word transmission of the EU provision is not required. The recent trend in the Union's environmental law to establish percentage reductions of emissions or pollutants – in climate change laws, but also in waste legislation – does not, however, need transposing into national law. This applies to such percentage provisions which are binding Union-wide targets, such as in climate law. In contrast, when EU law fixes national targets – a collection of 60 per cent of packaging waste, for example – Member States will have to transpose this figure into their national law, so that households and economic operators are aware of their overall obligations.

A correct transposition also requires the establishment of sanctions for non-compliance 14-11 with the EU provisions.[25] It is true that EU directives contain no more than very general provisions on sanctions for non-compliance, and regulations also remain very general. The reason for this is that sanctions are understood in many countries as criminal or quasi-criminal sanctions, and the Union has, so far, abstained from providing for criminal sanctions in cases where the provisions of a directive or regulation are not respected; even where administrative sanctions could be used, there is considerable self-restraint used by the Union when addressing the details of sanctions. This also applies to environmental regulations, though it follows from Article 261 TFEU that regulations could contain penal sanctions.[26] The CJEU interpreted Article 4(3) TEU as meaning that national sanctions for non-compliance with EU law must be equivalent to sanctions for breach of national

[22] Directive 2009/147 on the conservation of wild birds [2010] OJ L20/7.

[23] Commission, 'European Governance – a White Paper' COM(2001) 428 [2001] OJ C287/1 21: 'the feeling persists that Community rules are "foreign laws"'.

[24] See CJEU Case C-361/88 (n 8): 'It is clear that legal certainty also requires the specific transposal of individual limit values, maximum permissible concentrations and emission values into national legislation. A general reference to Community legislation is not permitted.'

[25] CJEU Case C-68/88 *Commission v Greece* ECLI:EU:C:1989:339.

[26] Art 261 TFEU: 'Regulations … may give the Court of Justice of the European Union unlimited jurisdiction with regard to the penalties provided for in such regulations.'

law provisions; furthermore, they must be, according to its standard formula, effective, proportionate and dissuasive.[27] This or a similar formula is used in numerous EU environmental directives or regulations. The transposition of this formula in the different legal orders of Member States has, so far, not been the subject of any serious conformity check. EU environmental law has, furthermore, practically never made use of providing for administrative sanctions.[28]

(ii) Application

14-12 Finally, Member States are under an obligation to ensure the practical application of EU environmental law. The transposition itself is only a formal legal act, whereas the protection of the environment begins when emissions are reduced, substances are no longer put on the market or (the equivalent) into the environment, habitats are protected, etc. The practical application of environmental provisions is the most serious problem that national, EU and international environmental law faces. Even a piece of national legislation that copies a directive word for word will remain a mere piece of paper unless it is applied.

14-13 Some unique features which seriously affect the full application of EU environmental law in practice must be remembered. Since environmental provisions try to protect the general interests of the Union, they differ markedly from agricultural, transport or industry legislation, which primarily affect specific vested interests. Where vested interests are in question, law-making and law enforcement take place, in Western Europe, in constant public – and sometimes not so public – discussions with the representatives of those vested interests; this discussion also continues within the various administrations, parliaments and decision-making bodies. Vested interest groups are also used to ensure the transmission of knowledge on the specific legislation, and in this way contribute either to ensuring compliance with the legal rule or bringing about concerted action against that rule, often even preventing its generation. This lobbying function of vested-interest groups has become an integrated factor of decision-making at EU level and at the level of Member States.

The general-interest 'environment' has no vested-interest defender. Environmental organisations in Western Europe, despite being committed to promoting the general-interest 'environment', are structurally and financially too weak to defend environmental interests effectively over a long period of time. While there is consensus that the environment needs adequate protection and that economic development should be 'sustainable', the implementation of concrete, legally binding measures proves difficult wherever other, diverging interests appear. The environment, without a voice and without strong lobby groups, loses out in almost every specific conflict of interests. Since, furthermore, local, regional and national administrations in the 27 Member States are not all convinced to the same extent that EU environmental standards are to be enforced, complied with and applied in practice, practical application of EU environmental provisions, which are thought to be more or less uniform, varies very considerably within the Union.

General features also contribute to this situation. In a number of Member States, particularly those in the south and those which joined the Union since 2004, environmental

[27] CJEU Case C-68/88 (n 25).

[28] Exceptions were introduced for climate-change legislation in Directive 2003/87 on emissions trading [2003] OJ L275/32 and Regulation 443/2009 on CO_2 emissions from cars [2009] OJ L140/1.

problems are mainly perceived to be the problems of affluent society; hence, there is an attitude among economic operators, and also among administrations, that economic progress is of primary necessity and that environmental concerns should be tackled once the economic level of richer Member States has been reached. To this must be added the different enforcement cultures which exist in the Union, the traditional weaknesses of central government in some Member States, the lack of national environmental infrastructures such as adequate administrations at local, regional and national level, and a lack of environmental information and education, of general awareness, of environmental research bodies and laboratories, and of testing, monitoring or enforcement bodies. Also, for a number of years, neoliberal thinking in the Anglo-Saxon world has concentrated on economic growth, shareholder value and other ideologies which consider the environment to be a sort of *quantité négligeable*.

II. Monitoring Implementation

A. Implementation Reports

Almost all EU environmental directives have contained, since the mid-1970s, a provision asking Member States to report on the implementation of the directive. Typically, such reports had to be made every three years.[29] The Commission was charged with producing, on the basis of these national reports, an EU report on the implementation of the directive in question; the normal period for these reports was, similarly, every three years. 14-14

This system did not lead to the desired result, since neither the Member States' implementation reports nor the Commission's comprehensive reports were drawn up regularly; Member States' reports were not even regularly made public by the Member States or the Commission. Regular reports were only published for the Bathing Water Directive;[30] however, these dealt with the quality of bathing water rather than the implementation of the directive. Also, monitoring of a number of parameters was omitted, and the data transmitted from the Member States were, until recently, not comparable.

In order to improve the reporting system, the Council adopted, in 1991, a directive that restructured the reporting requirements.[31] This directive introduced the requirement for Member States to report, every three years, on the implementation of the different directives in a given sector (eg water, air or waste). The reports were to be based on questionnaires which were set up by committee procedure at EU level, in order to allow the national reports to address the same issues. The reporting period was three years. 14-15

The directive has not significantly improved the situation. The reports on water, waste and chemicals were published with considerable delay; and there was no report on air pollution at all. Also, those directives that have been adopted since 1991 have only partly aligned their reporting requirements to Directive 91/692. Where Member States submitted reports

[29] See, however, Directive 2006/7 on the quality of bathing water [2006] OJ L64/37, where Art 13 provided for annual reports by Member States and by the Commission.

[30] Directive 76/160 [1976] OJ L31/1. This directive is now replaced by Directive 2006/7 (n 29).

[31] Directive 91/692 (n 5).

to the Commission, these reports, together with the national implementing legislation, which is at the Commission's disposal anyway, allowed a relatively clear picture to be gained on the transposition of a directive into national law. However, such reports normally did not contain information on difficulties of practical application or cases of non-compliance, lacunae and omissions on the side of local, regional or national administrations, inspections and sanctions, or on specific interpretations of individual provisions. They reported on measures taken and legislation adopted, not on results achieved and the state of the environment.

14-16 Commission implementation reports have been very disappointing overall, apart from the reports on the quality of bathing waters, which continue to be published annually. Directive 91/692 did not lead to a systematic attempt to improve implementation reporting, despite other announcements.[32] Generally, the Commission's different reports on the implementation of the environmental directives were marked by the fact that the information contained therein came almost exclusively from the (central) administration of Member States. For that reason, the EU reports, like the national reports, gave a relatively reliable picture on the legal and administrative parts of implementing EU directives – for those Member States that did report. However, less information was found, for example, on monitoring frequency and intensity, practical non-compliance, gaps and omissions of the administrations and results achieved. In order to address this problem, part of the reporting on the implementation of EU environmental directives was delegated to the European Environment Agency (EEA), without the completeness and quality of the reports significantly improving. A review of the environmental reporting provisions led to the updating of reporting requirements of several waste-related legislative acts and the repeal of Directive 91/692, but was far from generally approaching the problem of environmental reporting.[33]

The Commission has, it is true, conducted some studies of its own on the practical implementation of environmental directives in the Member States, although inevitably only a limited number of these studies were undertaken. Their value was limited, though, by the fact that it proved extremely difficult to gain access to the data held by the national, regional or local authorities on the practical application – or non-application; no administration would be easily persuaded to release data showing that a directive was not properly monitored or applied in practice, whether the failure was found in the frequency and results of inspections, the attitude of economic operators that were controlled, the pollution levels recorded or the respect of the conditions laid down in the permits that the administrations had granted. And the Commission did not even make such transposition studies publicly available, but kept them confidential – for no legitimate reason. A decision by the CJEU incriminating this practice led to only limited improvements.[34] The Commission's practice increases administrative secrecy and makes research into the effects of EU environmental legislation significantly more difficult.

[32] Commission, 'Implementing Community Environmental Law' COM(96) 500, para 58: 'Through the most effective use of the Reporting Directive, and close co-operation with the European Environmental Agency, the Commission will ensure that the best possible information is available on the effectiveness of Community environmental measures and can be used in the formulation of its policies on environmental measures. The Commission will launch and co-ordinate case studies to evaluate the transposition, application and enforcement of selected provisions of Community environmental law.'

[33] Decision 2018/853 [2018] OJ L150/155.

[34] CJEU Case C-612/13P *ClientEarth v Commission* ECLI:EU:C:2015:486.

B. Monitoring by the Commission

The Commission has to ensure that EU environmental law is applied (Article 17 TEU).[35] This provision is the nucleus which has allowed the Commission to develop, over the years, a system of monitoring transposition, application and enforcement, which goes far beyond everything that is known in the relations between states. It is this monitoring task of the Commission that has caused the Commission to be called the 'guardian of the Treaty'. 14-17

It should not, however, be forgotten that it is Member States which have, according to Articles 4 TEU and 192(4) TFEU, the obligation to ensure the implementation of EU environmental law; this means that Member States have to ensure that EU environmental law is effectively applied. The establishment and functioning of the Union is also the task of Member States, and it is they which have to ensure that 'their' constitution – the Lisbon Treaties, including its environmental provisions – is properly functioning, ie that its provisions are actually applied.[36]

14-18 The Commission's task is to ensure that all EU primary and secondary environmental law is applied, in particular regulations, directives and decisions. As regards international agreements, it has already been stated that the Commission does not monitor their application within the Union, not even in cases where the Union adhered to them. This self-restraint has never been justified or reasoned in public. It is legally unjustifiable. Indeed, where the Union adheres to an international environmental agreement, the agreement becomes part of EU law (Article 216(2) TFEU). The Commission then has to ensure its application, as Article 17 TEU does not differentiate between different parts of EU law. By adhering to an agreement, the Union takes the commitment vis-à-vis the other contracting parties that it will ensure compliance with provisions of this convention throughout the territory of the Union. This obligation rests with the Union as such and pertains to the whole EU territory, even where a specific Member State has not ratified the international convention in question. Once the Union has adhered to the international convention, Member States are obliged, under Article 4 TEU, to take the necessary steps in order to allow the Union to respect its international commitments. This legal obligation was confirmed, in substance, by the CJEU in a case against France, which had not ratified an international agreement although the Union had. The Court found that France was thus obliged to respect the requirements of the international agreement.[37]

14-19 More generally, it is clear that the Commission has a particular responsibility for ensuring the application of EU environmental law, because the Union is the source of these legal provisions. The Commission does not have any specific structures to monitor application of environmental legal provisions; this is ensured, rather, by the general Commission administration. In particular, the Commission does not have any inspection bodies to examine

[35] See generally Commission, 'Enforcing EU Law for a Europe That Delivers' COM(2022) 518, which, however, lacks any self-criticism.

[36] Commission, 'Implementing Community Environmental Law' (n 32) para 25: 'The Commission simply cannot monitor the thousands of individual decisions taken each year … in the different parts and levels of authority within the Member States. The daily application and enforcement … must be fully ensured by the authorities in the Member States …'.

[37] CJEU Case C-213/03 *Etangs de Berre* ECLI:EU:C:2004:464; Case C-239/03 *Commission v France* ECLI:EU:C:2004:598.

whether and to what extent EU environmental law is actually complied with.[38] Discussions on green inspectors have been emotionalised as being an intrusion on national sovereignty and, furthermore, as being incompatible with the subsidiarity principle. This criticism omits to mention that there are Commission inspectors in the areas of competition, veterinary, food, customs, regional and fishery policy, without questions of interference or subsidiarity ever having been raised.[39] The Commission is very cautious in considering the setting up of EU inspectors.[40] The Council and Member States are clearly opposed to EU environmental inspectors.[41] The possibility to make fact-finding site visits, which is available to the Commission,[42] is hardly ever used, as the Member States do not like such visits either – so the Commission adapts.

Since 1983, the Commission has published annual reports on monitoring the application of EU law,[43] which include a chapter on environmental legislation; attempts in 1991/92 to produce a specific environmental report met with resistance from the Commission administration and failed. The reports publish some general data and trends on the application of EU environmental law, but do not provide complete transparency, do not establish data which are comparable over the years and are not always completely reliable; since about 2001, they have become increasingly general and vague, and principally report on cases which have been brought before the CJEU or where a reasoned opinion had been issued without giving details and without explaining where the application of a specific directive stands with regard to a specific Member State. The reports are therefore of rather limited informative value.

Following a rather general action plan on environmental compliance,[44] the Commission established an Environmental Compliance and Governance Forum, which consisted of national and international public authorities' representatives, without any civil society representatives.[45] The forum may only act at the request of the Commission's administration. Its influence on policy and practice appears insignificant.

Since 2017, the Commission has published every two to three years a so-called 'Environmental Implementation Review',[46] which is accompanied by Member State-specific reports. These reviews mention in general terms the Member States' compliance with the Union's environmental legislation, but carefully avoid going into too much detail; however, the reports on the individual Member States are more precise and would allow the taking of action before national courts. It appears, though, as if these national reports hardly ever give course to a public discussion in the different Member States, let alone give rise to judicial action against governments for non-compliance with legal obligations that flow from Union law.

[38] Recommendation 2001/331 [2001] OJ L118/41 recommended that Member States provide for inspectors in environmental matters; a corresponding recommendation for the Union institutions does not exist.

[39] See Regulation 2017/625 on official controls and other official activities performed to ensure the application of food and feed law, rules on animal health and welfare, plant health and plant protection products (Official Controls Regulation) [2027] OJ L95/1. Subsidiarity questions for inspecions were not discussed (Recitals 79 and 99).

[40] Commission, 'Implementing Community Environmental Law' (n 32) para 9: 'Further consideration would be given as to whether there might be a need for a limited Community body with auditing competencies.'

[41] Council Resolution of 7 October 1997 [1997] OJ C321/1.

[42] For an example of such site visits, see CJEU Case C-103/00 *Commission v Greece* ECLI:EU:C:2002:60.

[43] See Commission, 'Monitoring the Application of European Union law' COM(2022) 344 and SWD(2022) 194.

[44] Commission, 'Actions to Improve Environmental Compliance and Governance' COM(2018) 10.

[45] Commission Decision C(2018)10, not published.

[46] Commission, COM(2017) 63; Commission, COM(2019) 149; Commission, COM(2022) 438.

The Commission has also published (non-binding) guidance documents, notices etc as part of its monitoring function.[47] However, guidance documents are not monitored by the Commission, and are of limited value as regards implementation and enforcement.

C. Monitoring by Other Bodies

The European Parliament does not fulfil any significant function in the monitoring of EU environmental legislation. It is true that Members of the Parliament pose a great number of written or oral questions, which include issues of application of environmental legislation; however, these initiatives remain non-systematic, apart from the fact that they are difficult to find and are made public with considerable delays. Since the year 2000, the European Parliament occasionally organised debates in its Environmental Committee, where the Commission has to account for its monitoring of the application of environmental provisions. These debates have not yet led to any organisational consequences. 14-20

Where the European Parliament receives a petition on environmental issues from a citizen within the Union, it does not – contrary to the practice in most Member States – itself investigate the facts which underlie the petition, but leaves the investigation to the Commission, for which the national administration is the principal interlocutor, to clarify the facts. This is a dubious practice, because, for a number of years, the Commission has been quite selective in its handling of cases, petitions sometimes also complain on the Commission's passivity and, in particular, most of the petitions argue that the national public authorities did not comply with their obligations under Union environmental law.

The EEA, which was set up in 1990,[48] does not have any role in monitoring the application of EU environmental law. When the EEA was set up, the European Parliament had vehemently requested such a monitoring role, following the example of the US Environmental Protection Agency. However, it could not persuade the Council, which only conceded that a clause should be inserted in Article 20 of Regulation 1210/90 according to which the Council would check 'at the latest within two years' whether the EEA should be allocated tasks in the monitoring of application of EU environmental law. When the Commission submitted the corresponding proposal in 1997, it did not suggest giving monitoring tasks to the EEA;[49] the European Parliament had forgotten its previous insistence and the Council did not take the issue up either.[50]

The EU Ombudsman, set up under Article 228 TFEU, has the task of controlling complaints of maladministration in the activities of the EU institutions or bodies. This might include maladministration in the treatment of citizen complaints in environmental matters or general omissions in the monitoring of the application of environmental legislation. The Ombudsman's office has a staff of some 70 persons. Their control activities occasionally deal

[47] See Commission, SWD(2022) 194, 2; see also, eg Commission, *Note on Establishing Conservation Measures for Natura 2000 Sites* (Brussels, 2013); Commission, Notice Guidance providing a common understanding of the term 'environmental damage' under Directive 2004/35, Decision C/2021/1860 [2021] OJ C115/1.

[48] Regulation 1210/90 [1990] OJ L120/1; see also para 2-30.

[49] [1997] OJ C255/9, amended [1998] OJ C123/6.

[50] Regulation 933/1999 [1999] OJ L117/1 amending Regulation 1210/90 (n 48).

with environmental issues, but try to avoid becoming a complaint instance against decisions taken by the Commission.[51]

14-21 The Commission announced, in the Fifth Environmental Action Programme, that it would set up an implementation network which would aim 'primarily at exchange of information and experience and at the development of common approaches at practical level, under the supervision of the Commission'.[52] However, at that time, Member States had themselves already started to set up an informal implementation network. As they vigorously opposed any mechanism at EU level that would give the Commission more options to monitor the application of environmental provisions, they accepted the Commission as a member of that network but kept its nature informal, and, since 1993, have called it the European Union Network for the Implementation and Enforcement of Environmental Law (IMPEL).[53] At present, the network consists of representatives of the enforcement and monitoring bodies of Member States, and Commission representatives; however, since a number of Member States do not have such specific enforcement and monitoring bodies, officials from central or regional administrations also take part in the network. IMPEL mainly deals with the exchange of experience on practical application and enforcement issues, the exchange of staff and the elaboration of guidelines for different aspects of application. IMPEL is financed jointly by Member States and the Commission. Its impact on the actual application of environmental directives is very limited, since it concentrates on horizontal questions. In 2008, its structure was turned into that of a (private) association – which reveals all the more that its objective is not the monitoring of compliance of Member States with EU law.

D. Citizen Complaints

14-22 As the Commission does not have any inspectors, controllers or decentralised administrations which would inform it on the application of EU environmental law within the whole of the Union, its main source of information on possible omissions in the application of EU environmental provisions is the information that comes from outside the administrations, in particular from citizens.

In the late 1960s, the Commission instituted a complaint system for citizens, in order to obtain information on non-technical barriers to the free circulation of goods. The Commission offered to intervene with Member States' administration in order to eliminate border controls and other barriers. From the mid-1980s, the system developed considerably as regards environmental complaints. The fact that individuals were able to register a complaint with the Commission stimulated EU-wide awareness of the environment, demonstrated to the citizen that the Commission was also accessible to the person in the street and made it clear to the individual that they had some responsibility for their environment, that they could become active in contributing to the preservation and protection of the environment and that environmental impairment should not be taken as an Act of God, against which nothing can be done. This was particularly important for southern Member States.

[51] See European Ombudsman, Annual Report 1996 [1997] OJ C272/1.
[52] Commission, Fifth Environmental Action Programme [1993] OJ C138/5, ch 9.
[53] ibid para 54.

Environmental complaints to the Commission came – and still come – from individuals, environmental or professional organisations, national, regional or European deputies, local administrations, political parties, ambassadors and occasionally even environment ministers of Member States.[54] 14-23

The Commission considered as a complaint any written statement that invokes the breach of EU (environmental) law and asked the Commission to intervene to repair this breach. The formal requirements for such a complaint are very low; the reason for this lies in the fact that, under Article 17 TFEU, the Commission has the possibility of starting on its own initiative, without even having received a complaint, an inquiry into possible breaches of EU law by a Member State. Procedurally, such an official inquiry is treated in exactly the same way as a complaint. To facilitate the introduction of complaints, the Commission has even drawn up and published a form.[55]

A complaint is registered in a central Commission register. The Commission stated in 2002 that 'all complaints received are registered, without any selection'. A consequence of the registration was that the complainant was kept informed as to the evolution of the complaint and that only the Commission as an institution – not an individual official – could decide on the final outcome of it. 14-24

The Commission tries to obtain as much factual information from the complainant as possible, which often overburdens the person who has introduced the complaint. For the rest of the facts, the Commission seeks to obtain factual and legal information from the (central) administration of the Member State against which the complaint is directed. In rare cases, expert advice is taken. Hearings or witnesses' testimony are never taken in environmental cases. Also, inspections in Member States do not, as a rule, take place; in very rare cases, visits to the affected sites in the form of fact-finding missions have been organised, but no more frequently than once per year for the whole of the Union.

In the 1980s, the Commission committed itself – both on the complaint form and in different declarations to the public – to instructing each complaint; in 1999, it indicated that its administrations would decide according to the internal rules and priorities whether they would examine a complaint or not.[56] And in 2002, the Commission further reduced its commitment to examine each complaint. In 2017, the Commission repeated earlier statements, according to which it would examine complaints and petitions which argued: (i) there was an absence or incorrect transposition of Union law into the national law; (ii) there was an omission to follow a judgment of the CJEU; or (iii) the financial interests of the Union or its exclusive legislative competence were in question.[57] 14-25

Under the Barroso presidency, the Commission set up a pilot scheme whereby, when a complaint was received, it was registered in a special register.[58] The Commission then addressed the Member State in question to find out what the problem was and how it could

[54] The evolution of the number of environmental complaints went from 10 in 1982 to 697 in 2002. Since then, the number of complaints has fallen, in part because the Commission no longer registered all complaints it received, voiced its reluctance to instruct individual cases and instead tried to reach arrangements with Member States on breaches of EU environmental law. In 2021, 544 environmental complaints reached the Commission.

[55] [1989] OJ C26/1; reviewed [1999] OJ C119/5.

[56] See the different versions of the complaint forms (n 55).

[57] Commission, Better results through better application [2017] OJ C18/190: In COM(2007) 502, the third case had been the systematic neglect of applying EU law.

[58] Commission, 'A Europe of Results – Applying Community Law' COM(2007) 502.

be solved. The difference from the complaint system was that the Commission administration co-operated behind closed doors with the national administration in order to arrange things; as this was outside any public participation and no information was released, very often the national administration – which frequently was at the origin of the problem by granting permits, remaining passive or disregarding environmental law – got away with its practice. Also, this practice led increasingly to a refusal to register complaints where Commission officials felt that no breach of Community law was likely, or to similar abuses – a clear contradiction to the Commission's own commitment to register all complaints.[59] As an example, the figures from 2021 may be quoted:[60] the Commission received 544 environmental complaints. It opened 25 pilot cases and 52 infringement procedures under Article 258 TFEU.

The only sanctions that exist against an omission to instruct properly are disciplinary measures and, eventually, the intervention of the European Ombudsman. The complainant has no direct rights as regards the omission to examine a complaint or to treat it by way of the arrangement (pilot) procedure. Overall, this change in administrative practice by the Commission led, within five years, to a reduction in the number of instructed cases for example against Spain from some 480 to 30 – though no change in the Spanish environmental policy or practice occurred.

The Commission refused all requests to lay down, in a legal instrument, the procedures for examining potential breaches of EU environmental law. Such a legal instrument exists in competition law, where complaints by private persons or associations or media reports are taken by the Commission as valuable sources of information for examining potential breaches.[61] The difference in treatment between competition and environmental law is flagrant and has no justification.

At the end of the instruction period of a petition, a complaint or an own-initiative investigation – which shall not, according to the Commission's internal instructions, extend beyond one year – the Commission decides either to close the case or to open formal proceedings, under Article 258 TFEU, against a Member State.[62] Upon intervention of the European Ombudsman, the Commission changed its rules in 1997: now, before it decides to file a complaint, the complainant is heard and has the right to present observations.[63] This procedural guarantee, however, does not give any right to a complainant as regards the final decision which the Commission takes; the complainant can neither oppose the closing of the complaint nor oblige the Commission to start legal proceedings under Article 258 TFEU against a Member State. The complainant also does not have a right to ensure the Commission makes adequate use of its discretion or, in other words, to see that the Commission's decision is not grossly arbitrary, for instance compared to previous Commission decisions.

14-26 The CJEU, obviously motivated by political, not legal, considerations, rejected all attempts to oblige the Commission to start proceedings under Article 258 TFEU or not to

[59] See the Commission's own evaluations which are, of course, positive: Commission, COM(2010) 70; Commission, COM(2011) 930.

[60] Commission, SWD(2022) 194.

[61] Commission Regulation 773/2004 relating to the conduct of proceedings by the Commission pursuant to Articles 81 and 82 of the EC Treaty [2004] OJ L123/48.

[62] See para 14-30ff.

[63] Commission, 15th report on monitoring application of environmental law (1997) [1998] OJ C250/1 10.

close a file.[64] The Court argued that the decision under Article 258 was not a decision which could be tackled under Article 263 TFEU, since it formed an accessory part of a subsequent Court procedure.[65] Furthermore, a complainant was not in the position of a person entitled to take action before the European courts under Article 263(4)) TFEU, since a decision under Article 258 would not be addressed to the complainant. Finally, the Commission had a margin of discretion which could not be questioned by individual complainants.[66] In particular, the latter argument could hardly be called convincing, if one reads Article 258 TFEU ('the Commission … shall deliver …', in contrast to the fact that it 'may' bring a case before the CJEU).

Practice has shown that an environmental case, a complaint or a petition has a greater chance of leading to a positive result when the conflict between the environmental interests and the diverging economic interests is discussed in public. The mobilisation of public opinion constitutes an important element of ensuring that environmental interests are taken into consideration and demonstrates at the same time the – at least partly – political character of the complaint procedure; this political character also appears through the lack of control of the Commission's decisions, which facilitates policy interventions in the decision-making procedure.

Complaints procedures in environmental matters normally take a considerable time. Their lack of transparency, the obvious reluctance of the Commission to examine complaints and the overall limited results, in particular as regards large infrastructure projects, have not led to a situation where the Commission is perceived as a true complaints institution. This is strengthened by the fact that the Commission has tried, since about 2001, to do everything in its power to discourage complaints.

E. Direct Effect of Environmental Provisions

In an effort to make EU provisions fully operational for the individual citizen, the CJEU had, by the early years of the Union, already developed the doctrine of direct effect. It started with judgments which stated that provisions of the EC Treaty also had effects in favour of citizens, who were entitled to invoke those provisions before the courts. Later, the Court extended this doctrine to provisions of directives, which could also, under certain conditions, be invoked by citizens before national courts.[67] This constituted a deviation from the provision of Article 288 TFEU, which states that regulations, but not directives, are directly applicable and that directives must be transposed into national law in order to have legal effect. The Court justified its decision by the fact that a Member State should not be entitled 14-27

[64] See CJEU Case C-247/87 *Star Fruit Company* ECLI:EU:C:1989:58; Case C-72/90 *Asia Motors* ECLI:EU:C:1990:230; Case C-422/97 *Sateba v Commission* ECLI:EU:C:1998:395.

[65] General Court Case T-126/95 *Dumez v Commission* ECLI:EU:T:1995:189.

[66] CJEU Case C-247/87 (n 64); Case C-229/82 *Asia Motor France v Commission* ECLI:EU:C:1992:288.

[67] See, eg CJEU Case C-236/92 *Comitato di Difesa della Cava* ECLI:EU:C:1994:60: 'The Court has consistently held that wherever the provisions of a directive appear, as far as their subject matter is concerned, to be unconditional and sufficiently precise, those provisions may be relied upon by an individual against the State where the State fails to implement the directive in national law by the period prescribed or where it fails to implement the directive correctly.'

to take advantage of the fact that a directive was not, or was not correctly or completely, transposed into national law. For that reason, this doctrine was only applied in favour of individuals, but never – for instance, in criminal cases – against individual persons.[68] Furthermore, the Court did not apply this doctrine in cases where two individuals were in dispute.[69] This demonstrates that the direct effect of a directive is construed, by the Court, as a sanction against the deviating Member State.

14-28 The following conditions must be fulfilled for a provision of a legal act to be directly applicable:

- the period for transposing an act into national law has expired;
- a Member State has not, or has not correctly, transposed the provisions of an act;
- the provision of an act is unconditional, ie the provision 'is not subject, in its implementation or effects, to the taking of any measure either by the institutions of the Community or by the Member States';[70]
- the provision is sufficiently precise to be relied on by an individual and applied by the court; this is the case 'where the obligation which it imposes is set out in unequivocal terms';[71] and
- the provision explicitly or implicitly confers rights to an individual as against a Member State. In this regard, the CJEU held on several occasions that where a provision dealt with the relations between administrations, it did not give rights to individuals.[72] I am of the opinion that, for the test as to whether a provision of EU law grants rights to an individual, the provision has to be constructed in such a way as if it were contained in a regulation; then it would have to be checked as to whether in such a case the provision would confer an improved position, a legal advantage. It must be admitted, though, that the question of whether a provision confers a 'right' to a person is extremely difficult to answer.

As the CJEU constructed the direct effect as a sanction against a Member State which has not, or has not correctly, transposed a legislative act, it is only logical that it did not apply the doctrine of direct effect in favour of the Member State, for instance in a criminal procedure against a polluter, or in relations between a citizen and a polluting installation. These limitations and the general difficulties with the interpretation of when a provision has direct effect make this doctrine of rather restricted use.

[68] See, eg CJEU Case C-168/95 *Arcaro* ECLI:EU:C:1996:363: 'a directive may not by itself create obligations for an individual and … a provision of a directive may not therefore be relied upon as such against such a person … a directive cannot, of itself and independently of a national law adopted by a Member State for its implementation, have the effect of determining or aggravating the liability in criminal law of persons who act in contravention of the provisions of that directive'.

[69] CJEU Case C-91/92 *Dori* ECLI:EU:C:1994:292: 'The effect of extending that case-law [on direct effects] to the sphere of relations between individuals would be to recognise a power in the Community to enact obligations for individuals with immediate effect, whereas it has competence to do so only where it is empowered to adopt regulations.'

[70] CJEU Case C-236/92 (n 67).

[71] ibid.

[72] CJEU Case C-380/87 *Cinisello Balsamo* ECLI:EU:C:1989:318; Case C-194/94 *Security International v Signalson* ECLI:EU:C:1996:172.

The CJEU refused to give direct effect to Article 9(3) of the Aarhus Convention,[73] which had been ratified by the EU and was thus part of EU law.[74] It argued that it followed from the words 'if any' that Article 9(3) required the taking of implementing measures by the contracting parties; thus, it was not unconditional. In its reasoning, the Court did not (wish to) consider that the words 'if any' do not *require* the taking of implementing measures, but only *allow* such measures to be taken. No contracting party to the Aarhus Convention is obliged, under Article 9(3), to lay down (restrictive) criteria regarding access to justice in environmental matters. This might lead to an *actio popularis* situation in environmental matters. However, such an approach exists at present in Portuguese environmental law. It shows that the Court's reasoning is not legal, but political. 14-29

This position of the Court of Justice is all the more regrettable as the Court also refused to apply its concept of *effet utile* (useful effect) to Article 9(3) of the Aarhus Convention, concerning access to the EU courts: in Case C-240/09, the Court stated:[75]

> it must be observed that these provisions [Article 9(3) of the Aarhus Convention], although drafted in broad terms, are intended to ensure effective environmental protection … if the effective protection of EU environmental law is not to be undermined, it is inconceivable that Article 9(3) of the Aarhus Convention be interpreted in such a way as to make it in practice impossible or excessively difficult to exercise rights conferred by EU law. It follows that … it is for the national court, in order to ensure effective juridical protection in the fields covered by EU environmental law, to interpret the national law in a way which, *to the fullest extent possible*, is consistent with the objective laid down in Article 9(3) of the Aarhus Convention. (emphasis added)

The refusal to apply the same principle – to ensure 'to the fullest extent possible' access to the EU courts and without giving the slightest explication for this omission – demonstrates the double measure which the CJEU applies to access to the national courts and access to the EU courts.

III. Sanctions

A. Action under Article 258 TFEU

By far the most important instrument at the Commission's disposal when fulfilling its obligation under Article 17 TEU is Article 258 TFEU.[76] This provision provides for a three-stage procedure:[77] 14-30

[73] Aarhus Convention, Art 9(3): 'each Party shall ensure that, where they meet the criteria, if any, laid down in its national law, members of the public have access to administrative or judicial procedures to challenge acts and omissions by private parties and public authorities which contravene provisions of its national law relating to the environment'.

[74] CJEU Case C-240/09 *Lesoochranárske zoskupenie* ECLI:EU:C:2011:125.

[75] ibid paras 46–50.

[76] See wording of Art 258 TFEU: 'If the Commission considers that a Member State has failed to fulfil an obligation under the Treaties, it shall deliver a reasoned opinion on the matter, after giving the State concerned the opportunity to submit its observations. If the State concerned does not comply with the opinion within the period laid down by the Commission, the latter may bring the matter before the Court of Justice of the European Union.'

[77] The procedural provisions regarding Art 258 are not codified, in contrast to the competition provisions of Art 108 TFEU, see Commission Regulation 773/2004 (n 61). The Commission stated in Written Question E-2496/98 (Watson) [1999] OJ C142/18 that the provisions regarding Art 258 had been published in the introduction to the

1. formal notice of breach of obligations to the Member State;
2. issue of a reasoned opinion; and
3. application to the CJEU.

Steps 1 and 2 together constitute the prejudicial procedure, which has the objective of enabling the Member State to comply with its obligations under EU law or to present its arguments to the Commission on why there was no breach of EU law. For this reason, the Commission, which alone may initiate the procedure under Article 258, is obliged to specify clearly the object on which it considers the Member State's breach to have occurred (object of litigation).[78]

14-31 The formal notice to a Member State that is considered to be in breach of its obligation does not require a specific form. In practice, however, notice is always given in the form of a letter. The decision to send such a letter is taken by the Commission, after detailed preparation of the Commission's services. The formal letter is agreed word by word at administrative, legal and political level, before it is formally notified to the Member State. This careful preparation is also due to the view held by the CJEU that the Commission's letter defines the object of litigation for any subsequent Court proceedings.[79] Thus, the Commission cannot, in any subsequent part of the procedure under Article 258 TFEU, include any additional point of complaint against a Member State, since the Member State would not have had 'the opportunity to present its observations' on such points. Since, however, the factual side of the case is normally not completely clarified, changes in the legal assessment are, of course, possible. Normally, the Member State has two months to reply to the Commission's letter of formal notice. However, since, on average, the Commission discusses and decides on cases under Article 258 only once every six months, the time available to Member States for a reply is almost always much longer.

14-32 Where the Commission is not satisfied with the Member State's answer, it may decide to issue a reasoned opinion. The reasoned opinion is produced in the same form as the letter of formal notice. The facts of the dispute are supposed to have been clarified during the procedure preceding the decision to issue a reasoned opinion. The reasoned opinion gives a detailed and comprehensive description of the case as it presents itself in the opinion of the Commission, indicates the legal opinion and describes, in particular, in detail how EU environmental law has been breached. Should proceedings subsequently be initiated with the CJEU, the facts no longer need to be clarified and the dispute can normally be confined to legal issues. On average, the time span between the dispatch of the letter of formal notice and the judgment of the CJEU in environmental cases was 70 months in 2017, 67 months in 2018, 64 months in 2019, 64 months in 2020, 105 months in 2021 and 86 months in 2022. While the CJEU decided, on average, within 18 months, the pre-judicial phase (letters of formal notice and reasoned opinion) took on average more than four years, and even 77 months in 2021 and 65 months in 2022.

14-33 The Commission occasionally publishes general press releases on infringement decisions taken and occasionally even a press release on a specific dispute which it considers politically or environmentally important. The impact of such press releases is sometimes considerable,

Commission's 10th report on monitoring application of Community law (1992) [1993] OJ C233/1, and that later amendments were published in the successive annual reports. This is simply not correct.

[78] CJEU Case C-266/94 *Commission v Spain* ECLI:EU:C:1995:235.

[79] CJEU Case C-337/89 *Commission v United Kingdom* ECLI:EU:C:1992:456.

depending on the sensitivity of the media to the issue. However, the Commission does not make public either the letters of formal notice or the reasoned opinion. This practice, for which no explanation can be found in Article 258 TFEU, is justified with the argument that the confidentiality and mutual trust of the relations between Member States and the Commission would otherwise be disturbed and a smooth solution to the problem made more difficult. This attitude seems to be in the interests neither of the environment nor of the citizens, and it is not conducive to an open society; finally, it is also not compatible with Regulation 1049/2001 on access to documents held by EU institutions.

The Commission has very wide discretion to apply to the CJEU and, in practice, less than 10 per cent of cases where the procedure under Article 258 was initiated are actually submitted to the CJEU. There is no delay required in submitting the application to the Court, nor does the Commission need demonstrate a specific legal interest in order to obtain a judgment. In the last 15 years or so, the Commission has concentrated on cases of lack of or bad transposition of EU legislation into national law; cases where the existing law is badly applied are now the exception.[80]

The Court's decision under Article 258 TFEU states that there is a breach of EU environmental law unless the application is dismissed. The Court neither annuls the national measures that caused the breach of EU law nor does it declare what measures have to be taken; it is up to the Member State to comply with the judgment and take the necessary measures. 14-34

Between 1976 and 2022, the CJEU decided about 650 environmental cases under Article 258; since 2017, the average time span, including the prejudicial procedure, has been more than five years.

The Lisbon Treaties introduced Article 260(3) TFEU, according to which the Commission may, in a procedure under Article 258 TFEU, ask the Court to fix a lump sum or a penalty payment against a Member State 'which has failed to fulfil its obligation to notify measures transposing a directive adopted under a legislative procedure'; the Court may not go beyond the Commission's proposal, in contrast to Article 260(2) TFEU. In environmental measures, Article 260(3) TFEU has not yet been applied by the Court.

It is in particular arguable whether this provision also applies where a Member State has not transposed specific provisions of a directive, or where these provisions were incorrectly transposed. The CJEU has not yet decided on this issue. The Commission held that it was entitled to bring such cases to the Court under Article 260(3) TFEU[81] and started several procedures against Member States in this sense.[82] My own opinion is that Article 260(3)

[80] The main reason is probably that in cases of bad application, the factual side of the case needs to be clarified repeatedly before the CJEU, which is burdensome and time-consuming. And, although I cannot prove it, I would not exclude that the Court itself signalled to the Commission not to submit cases of bad application. The task of the Court is indeed much easier when it has to determine whether national legislation complies with EU law. In SWD(2022) 194, the Commission argued that the cases which were not investigated by it were 'individual and isolated cases'.

[81] Commission, SEC(2010)1371.

[82] CJEU Case C-663/13 *Commission v Austria* ECLI:EU:C:2015:323; Case C-236/14 *Commission v Ireland* ECLI:EU:C:2015:41; these two cases concerned the non-transposition of definitions and some provisions of Directive 2009/28 on renewable sources of energy [2009] OJ L140/16. See also Case C-302/14 *Commission v Belgium* ECLI:EU:C:2015:301; Case C-329/14 *Commission v Finland* ECLI:EU:C:2015:289; these two cases concerned the failure to transpose several provisions of Directive 2010/31 on the energy performance of buildings [2010] OJ L153/13.

TFEU aims at an accelerated compliance of a Member State with EU law. When there are questions regarding whether definitions need to be transposed into national law or whether national provisions in their context completely transpose an EU provision, this might lead to long and protracted discussions. Such procedures are better placed under Article 258 than under Article 260(3) TFEU, though the borderline between Article 258 and 260(3) TFEU can be very difficult to determine.

B. Action under Article 259 TFEU

14-35 Article 259 TFEU allows Member States to take judicial action against another Member State which has not fulfilled its environmental obligations under the EU Treaties. Until mid-2023, only two environmental cases were decided under this provision by the CJEU. In 2019, Austria won a case against Germany, which had introduced a road infrastructure use charge but had relieved German cars from this charge.[83] In 2021, Czechia introduced a case against Poland because it was of the opinion that an open-air lignite mining activity in a border region caused environmental damage. However, it withdrew its application after Poland paid it €45 million.[84] Generally, though, Member States rely on the Commission to take action.

C. Action under Article 260 TFEU

14-36 Where a Member State does not comply with a judgment by the Court, the Commission may, under Article 260 TFEU, start a new procedure. The justification for that is probably the continued non-compliance with EU law and, at the same time, the contempt of the Court that is enshrined in the non-execution of the judgment. Since the entry into force of the Lisbon Treaty, the procedure is no longer the same as under Article 258 TFEU. Indeed, the Commission only has to send out a letter of formal notice; if it is not satisfied with the Member State's answer or if the Member State does not answer, the Commission may go directly to the CJEU, without sending out a reasoned opinion (Article 260(2) TFEU). It shall specify the amount of the lump sum or[85] of a penalty payment to be paid by the Member State concerned. The Court may then impose a lump sum or penalty payment.

The Commission regularly issued a communication regarding the methods for calculating the penalty payments.[86] For each case, a basic amount of presently €2726 (penalty payment) and €909 (lump sum) is fixed. This figure is multiplied with a figure between 1 and 3 according to the duration of the infringement, and another figure between 1 and 20 according to the seriousness of the infringement. This sum is then multiplied by a

[83] CJEU Case C-591/17 *Austria v Germany* ECLI:EU:C.2019:504.

[84] CJEU Case C-121/21 *Czechia v Poland* ECLI:EU:C:2021:420 and ECLI:EU:C:2021:752 (orders under Art 279 TFEU).

[85] The word 'or' was interpreted by the CJEU in Case C-304/02 *Commission v France* ECLI:EU:C:2005:444 as allowing to impose a lump sum *and* a penalty payment. Since then, this became the general practice of the Commission and the Court.

[86] See Commission, Upgrading of data used to calculate lump sums and penalty payments to be proposed by the Commission to the Court of Justice of the European Union in infringement procedures [2022] OJ C74/2.

coefficient which is determined according to the ability of the Member State to pay the penalty (based on its gross domestic product) and the number of seats the Member State has in the European Parliament.[87]

By mid-2023, the CJEU had delivered a number of judgments under Article 260 in environmental cases, as shown in Table 14.1. 14-37

Table 14.1 Cases prosecuted by the CJEU under Article 260

Case	Member State	Reason for the penalty	Amount of the penalty (€)
C-387/97[a]	Greece	unauthorised landfill in the river valley of Kouroupitos (Crete)	20,000 per day
C-278/01[b]	Spain	bad quality of inland bathing waters	624,150 per year and per 1% of not complying waters
C-121/07[c]	France	incorrect transposition of Directive 2001/18 on genetically modified organisms	lump sum of 10 million
C-304/02[d]	France	no control of compliance with fisheries restriction measures	lump sum of 20 million; 57.6 million for every 6 months of non-compliance
C-279/11[e]	Ireland	incorrect transposition of Directive 85/337 on env. impact assessment	lump sum of 1.5 million
C-374/11[f]	Ireland	Directive 75/442 domestic waste waters may not go to septic tanks	lump sum of 2 million; 12,000 per day of non-compliance
C-533/11[g]	Belgium	incorrect transposition of Directive 91/271 on urban waste water in five municipalities	lump sum of 10 million; 859,404 for every 6 months of non-compliance
C-576/11[h]	Luxembourg	bad application of Directive 91/271 on two plants	lump sum of 2 million; 2800 per day of non-compliance
C-196/13[i]	Italy	unauthorised landfills	lump sum of 40 million; 42,800,000 penalty, minus 400,000 per closed and cleaned landfill
C-378/13[j]	Greece	unauthorised landfills	lump sum of 10 million; 14,520,000 penalty, minus 40,000 per closed and cleaned landfill
C-243/13[k]	Sweden	updating permits under Directive 2008/1 one installation in default	lump sum of 2 million; 4000 per day of non-compliance

(continued)

[87] This present co-efficient ('n-factor') varies between 0.080 for Malta and 5000 for Germany.

Table 14.1 ***(Continued)***

Case	Member State	Reason for the penalty	Amount of the penalty (€)
C-653/13[l]	Italy	waste management measures	120,000 per day of non-compliance; 20 million lump sum
C-167/14[m]	Greece	urban waste water treatment	3640 million every 6 months; 10 million lump sum
C-557/14[n]	Portugal	urban waste water treatment	8000 per day of non-compliance; 3 million lump sum
C-584/14[o]	Greece	landfill of waste	30, 000 perday of non-compliance; 10 million lump sum
C-328/16[p]	Greece	urban waste water treatment	3.276 million every 6 months; 5 million lump sum
C-251/17[q]	Italy	urban waste water treatment	30,112,500 every 6 months; 25 million lump sum
C-626/16[r]	Slovakia	landfill of waste	5000 per day of non-compliance; 1 million lump sum
C-205/17[s]	Spain	urban waste water treatment	10,950,000 every 6 months; 12 million lump sum
C-261/18t	Ireland	environmental impact assessment	15,000 per day of non-compliance; 5 million lump sum
C-298/19[u]	Greece	nitrates in water	3.5 million lump sum

[a]CJEU Case C-387/97 *Commission v Greece* ECLI:EU:C:2000:356.
[b]CJEU Case C-278/01 *Commission v Spain* ECLI:EU:C:2003:635.
[c]CJEU Case C-121/07 *Commission v France* ECLI:EU:C:2008:695.
[d]*Commission v France* (n 85).
[e]CJEU Case C-279/11 *Commission v Ireland* ECLI:EU:C:2012:834.
[f]CJEU Case C-374/11 *Commission v Ireland* ECLI:EU:C:2012:827.
[g]CJEU Case Cc-533/11 *Commission v Belgium* ECLI:EU:C:2013:659.
[h]CJEU Case C-576/11 *Commission v Luxembourg* ECLI:EU:C:2013:773.
[i]CJEU Case C-196/13 *Commission v Italy* ECLI:EU:C:2014:2407.
[j]CJEU Case C-378/13 *Commission v Greece* ECLI:EU:C:2014:2405.
[k]CJEU Case C-243/13 *Commission v Sweden* ECLI:EU:C:2014:2413.
[l]CJEU Case C-653/13, *Commission v Italy* ECLI:EU:C:2015:478.
[m]CJEU Case C-167/14 *Commission v Greece* ECLI:EU:C:2015:684.
[n]CJEU Case C-557/14 *Commission v Portugal* ECLI:EU:C:2016:471.
[o]CJEU Case C-584/14 *Commission v Greece* ECLI:EU:C:2016:636.
[p]CJEU Case C-328/16 *Commission v Greece* ECLI:EU:C:2019:98.
[q]CJEU Case C-251/17 *Commission v Italy* ECLI:EU:C:2019:358.
[r]CJEU Case C-626/17 *Commission v Slovakia* ECLI:EU:C:2018:525.
[s]CJEU Case C-205/17 *Commission v Spain* ECLI:EU:C:2018:606.
[t]CJEU Case C-261/18 *Commission v Ireland* ECLI:EU:C:2019:955.
[u]CJEU Case C-298/19 *Commission v Greece* ECLI:EU:C:2020:133.

In its judgments, the Court approved the Commission's general method of calculation, but underlined that it alone had the right to finally fix the penalty amounts to be paid. It may reduce or increase the financial penalty with regard to the Commission proposal or not fix a penalty at all. Its calculation is not specified in detail, but is much more general than that of the Commission.

In Case C-387/97, Greece paid €4.5 million. Then it fenced the unauthorised landfill and operated an interim landfill. The Commission closed the file. Later, the Court confirmed that EU waste law not only required the closing of an unauthorised landfill, but also that the waste had to be removed.[88] In Case C-278/01, Spain was ordered to pay some €624,000 per year and for each percentage of inland bathing waters that did not comply with the requirements of EU law.[89] The Commission later closed the case, in an obviously erroneous interpretation of the judgment.[90]

In Case C-121/21,[91] the CJEU confirmed that penalty payments could also be imposed on a Member State on the basis of Article 279 TFEU, which allows interim measures to be imposed. Poland introduced action contesting this possibility in the concrete case.[92]

D. State Liability

According to the CJEU, a Member State may also be liable for damages towards private individuals because it has breached EU law by failing to transpose an EU directive into national law.[93] The Court laid down a number of conditions for such a liability: there must be a serious breach of EU obligations; the EU directive must confer rights to individual persons; the content of these rights is identifiable by reference to the directive; and there exists a causal link between the Member State's obligations and the damage suffered by the person affected. Fault or negligence on the part of the Member State is not, however, required. In Case C-61/21, the CJEU decided that France was not liable to pay compensation to a citizen who had claimed that his health had suffered because France had not properly applied Directive 2008/50 on ambient air pollution.[94] The Court held that this directive intended to protect human health in general but not the health of individual citizens – a very unconvincing argument. As the Court itself considered that individuals also acquire rights from air quality objectives,[95] the construction of such damages could, in future, be considerable. 14-38

[88] CJEU Case C-196/13 *Commission v Italy* ECLI:EU:C:2014:2407; Case C-378/13 *Commission v Greece* ECLI:EU:C:2014.2405.

[89] CJEU Case C-278/01 (Table 14.1).

[90] Directive 76/160 on bathing water (n 30) required that 95% of all samples taken from bathing waters had to conform to the EU requirements. The Commission found that 94.7% of Spanish bathing waters complied with EU requirements and filed the case because the extra 0.3% were not relevant. It confounded the overall quality of the Spanish bathing waters with the compliance of the individual body of water.

[91] CJEU Case C-121/21 (n 84).

[92] General Court Cases T-200/22 and T-314/22 *Poland v Commission* pending.

[93] CJEU Case Joined C-6/90 and C-9/90 *Francovich v Italy* ECLI:EU:C:1991:428; Case C-48/93 *Factortame* ECLI:EU:C:1996:79.

[94] CJEU Case C-61/21 *Ministère de Transformation écologique* ECLI:EU:C:2022:1015.

[95] CJEU Case C-361/88 (n 8); Case C-131/88 (n 7).

E. Financial Sanctions

14-39 Financial sanctions for breach of EU environmental law exist in theory. Indeed, the different regulations for the EU Structural Funds and the Cohesion Fund provide that measures which are financed or co-financed by the Union must comply with the Union's objectives; the formula declaring that they had in particular to comply with EU environmental law was deleted in 2006.[96] According to this provision, measures could not be financed with EU funds if they failed to comply with all the provisions of EU environmental law. As a consequence of this, each measure which was undertaken in a Member State without respect to EU environmental law – for example, the construction of a motorway without an environmental impact assessment – could, before 2006, lead to a refusal of financial assistance or to the recuperation of the sums paid.[97] Subsequent to an obiter dictum by the General Court,[98] the Commission considered the procedures under Article 258 TFEU and under the provisions of the different funds that dealt with the recovery of the financial assistance to be independent from each other. Thus, the start of a procedure under Article 258 or even a judgment by the CJEU did not automatically lead to the Commission recovering the sums paid; rather, the Commission reserved the right to examine, in each individual case, what steps were to be taken. This evolution ended in 2006, when the new Regulations on the Structural Funds and the Cohesion Fund provided that non-compliance with EU law did not normally entitle the Commission to retain funds.[99]

When Germany delayed the designation of natural habitats under Directive 92/43,[100] the Commissioners for Regional Policy and Environment wrote, in June 1999, a letter to announce that financial means under the structural funds would not be able to be distributed to Germany, as the sums might serve to realise projects which would be realised within future habitats. This letter considerably accelerated the designation procedure in Germany.[101]

14-40 Since the Commission's decision to recover or not to recover its financial assistance cannot be attacked by any third person, and since the Commission does not publish details of cases where EU environmental law was not respected, nor any information as to how often it has suspended, refused or recovered financial assistance,[102] the main value of the provisions is likely to lie in a preventive effect: where a Member State is asked, prior to the financing of a project, whether it has complied with all EU environmental law provisions,

[96] See, eg Regulation 2081/93 [1993] OJ L193/5, Art 7; Regulation 1164/94 on the Cohesion Fund [1994] OJ L130/1, Art 8. The formula of Art 6 of Regulation 1303/2013 on the Structural Funds [2013] OJ L347/320 read: 'Operations supported by the European Structural and Investment Funds shall comply with applicable Union law and the national law relating to its application.'

[97] Regulation 2081/93 [1993] OJ L193/5, Art 24; see also Commission, 15th report (n 63) 76.

[98] General Court Case T-461/93 *An Taisce/WWF v Commission* ECLI:EU:T:1994:294.

[99] Regulation 1083/2006 [2006] OJ L210/25, Art 99ff.

[100] Directive 92/43 (n 6).

[101] The letter is mentioned in European Parliament, Resolution of 16 March 2000 [2000] OJ C337/333.

[102] The Commission's 14th and 15th reports on monitoring application of Community law (1996 and 1997) [1997] OJ C332/1, 70 and [1998] OJ C250/1, 76 contained for the first time a chapter on monitoring compliance under the Structural Funds. These chapters were virtually identical, though they concerned two different years and remained very abstract. For 1996, the Commission stated that EU environmental law was not respected in 23 cases, and for 1997 in 25 cases. There was neither an indication on the different cases nor any information on whether financial assistance was suspended, refused or recovered. Later Commission reports no longer gave such data.

this might lead to a more careful consideration of such provisions. From media reports, it is known that the Commission, in the past, has sometimes refused financial assistance, or has at least threatened to do so; however, no quantification can be given. I know of no case, and no publicly available document records any case, where financial assistance was ever definitely refused in an environmental case.

Article 16 of the directive on greenhouse gas emission trading[103] provides for penalties against companies. The provision reads:

> Member States shall ensure that any operator who does not surrender sufficient allowances by 30 April of each year to cover its emissions during the preceding year shall be held liable for the payment of an excess emission penalty. This excess emission penalty shall be EUR 100 for each tonne of carbon dioxide equivalent.

This provision may lead to quite important penalties and thus ensure compliance by operators.[104] Its importance, however, lies in its precedence for other EU legislation: nothing would oppose provisions in a directive which stipulate that Member States ensure that operators of industrial installations which, for example, emit too many emissions into the air or the water, which do not respect accident prevention measures or which do not comply with the best available technique pay a(n administrative) penalty for such non-compliance. So far, the EU has not made use of this possibility. However, such provisions would considerably increase the effectiveness of EU law, because they would give to national supervising authorities an instrument to enforce compliance. As the EU law does not foresee that such financial sanctions constitute criminal sanctions, there is also no risk of subsidiarity concerns being raised.

F. Criminal Sanctions

In 2001, the Commission made a proposal for a directive to protect the environment through criminal law[105] for a number of specific bans and prohibitions which had already been laid down in EU legislation. According to the proposal, Member States would provide criminal sanctions for cases of intentional or grossly negligent breach of the relevant requirements. Such cases would concern, for instance, the unauthorised disposal of waste, the deliberate discharge of solid or liquid waste into waters, or illegal trade in endangered species or ozone-depleting substances. Member States were to decide themselves on the kind of criminal sanctions which they wanted to introduce. 14-41

The proposal was based on Article 192 TFEU. Although the European Parliament approved of it, the Council was of the opinion that the EC Treaty did not allow for the provision of criminal sanctions and refused to discuss the proposal. Instead, the Council adopted, under Article 35 TEU, a framework decision on criminal sanctions in environmental cases.[106] The main difference between the two provisions was that there was no EU

[103] Directive 2003/87 establishing a scheme for greenhouse gas emission allowances within the Community [2003] OJ L275/32.

[104] See CJEU Case C-203/12 *Billerud* ECLI:EU:C:2013:664; Case C-113/19 *Luxaviation* ECLI:EU:C:2020:228.

[105] [2001] OJ C180/238.

[106] Decision 2003/80 [2003] OJ L29/55.

competence for monitoring the application of decisions under the third pillar of the Treaty on European Union, as a provision corresponding to Article 258 TFEU was lacking in that other Treaty. The framework decision is thus best compared with an international agreement. The CJEU declared in 2005 that the Treaty on European Union only applied where no provisions under the Treaty on the Functioning of the European Union applied. Therefore, it declared the Council's framework decision void, because legislation on criminal sanctions in the environmental sector could be based on Article 192 TFEU.[107] Then, in a later decision, the Court declared that, while the Union had competence to deal with criminal matters, the type and level of the criminal penalties were the competence of the Member States.[108] On this basis, Directive 2008/99 was adopted; this required a number of actions which the Member States must provide for criminal sanctions for actions that were unlawful and committed intentionally, or at least with serious negligence.[109] Such actions concern the emission or discharge of polluting substances which caused or were likely to cause harm to humans or damage to the environment; waste treatment or disposal which caused or was likely to cause harm to humans or damage to the environment; the shipment of waste in non-negligible quantities; the operation of a plant which caused or could cause harm to humans or damage to the environment; the damaging of fauna or flora; the deterioration of a protected habitat; trade in endangered species; and trade in ozone-depleting substances.

In 2020, the Commission evaluated the impact of Directive 2008/99.[110] It found considerable enforcement gaps in all Member States. The sanctions were too small to be dissuasive; cross-border co-operation was not systematic; there were deficiencies in resources, specialised knowledge, awareness, prioritisation and information; reliable accurate and complete statistical data were lacking; and Member States had no overarching strategy to combat environmental crime. Overall, declared the Commission, the directive did not have much effect on the ground. These findings caused the Commission to propose replacing Directive 2008/99 with a new directive,[111] based on Article 83(2) TFEU.[112] The proposal is presently being discussed by the other Union institutions.[113]

Environmental crime is a considerable growth industry, both within Europe and worldwide. The most important areas are illegal trade in endangered species and in ozone-depleting substances, illegal logging and trade in tropical timber and other wood, dumping of and trade in waste and, finally, illegal fishing. No concrete measures have yet been taken by the Union to combat organised environmental crime.

[107] CJEU Case C-176/03 *Commission v Council* ECLI:EU:C:2005:542.

[108] CJEU Case C-440/05 *Commission v European Parliament and Council* ECLI:EU:C:2007:625. It should be noted that the Court did not explain with even a single word *why* the type and level of sanctions was the exclusive competence of the Member States.

[109] Directive 2008/99 on the protection of the environment through criminal law [2008] OJ L328/28.

[110] Commission, SWD(2020) 259.

[111] Commission, COM(2021) 851; Commission, SWD(2021) 465; see also Commission, 'Stepping Up the Fight Against Environmental Crime' SWD(2021) 814.

[112] Art 83(3) TFEU: 'If the approximation of criminal laws and regulations of the Member States proves essential to ensure the effective implmentation of a Union policy in an area which has been subject to harmonisation measures, directives may establish minimum rules with regard to the definition of criminal offences and sanctions in the area concerned.'

[113] See Council, Document 16179 of 16 December 2022; European Parliament, Document A9-0087/223 of 28 March 2023.

G. Interim Measures

Article 279 TFEU provides that the CJEU may prescribe any necessary interim measure in cases before it. This provision does not state whether the Commission may also take interim measures as soon as it discovers a breach of EU law. However, it is now generally accepted that the Commission has no such powers and that the decision on interim measures can only be taken by the CJEU. The Commission may appeal to the Court to prescribe such measures, but this can only take place where a case is pending before the Court or where it is submitted to the Court together with the request for a decision. The Commission has then to demonstrate the urgency and necessity of the measure, in particular if there is a risk of serious and irreversible damage that might otherwise occur. 14-42

Attempts by the Commission to stop the construction of a dyke that would have destroyed a bird habitat were rejected, since the Commission was not able to show the urgency of such a measure.[114] An attempt by an environmental organisation to stop the construction of a tourist information centre in a natural habitat was rejected, because a national court had already stopped the project.[115] The attempt to stop, by way of interim measures, the French nuclear tests in Mururoa in 1995 was rejected as inadmissible, since the private applicants were not directly and individually concerned, and thus had no standing.[116] More recently, though, the Court stopped, by an interim decision, the application of a regional legislation on bird hunting in Italy and Malta, and the construction of a motorway in Poland which would have destroyed a Natura 2000 area.[117] In Case C-121/21, which had been brought by Czechia against Poland, the CJEU ordered, as interim measures, the closing of a Polish lignite mine and, since Poland had not followed this order, the payment of a financial penalty.[118] Czechia later withdrew its application, but the environmental impairment continued; the Commission did not take any action.

Generally, it can be said that it will hardly ever be possible to demonstrate the urgency and necessity of interim measures under Article 258 TFEU, since the pre-Court stage, during which no interim measures are possible, takes between four and five years.

H. Action by Citizens

EU environmental law does not provide for any active role for citizens or their organisations to ensure full application of EU environmental law. The role of monitoring the application of the law is given to the Commission, though it is obvious that the Commission is not the owner or the unique stakeholder of the environment; however, in that respect, EU environmental law is basically no different from law in most Member States – or, indeed, most other industrialised countries. It seems that only the USA ensures that there is the possibility for its citizens and private organisations actively to monitor the application of 14-43

[114] CJEU Case C-57/89R *Commission v Germany* ECLI:EU:C1989:334.

[115] CJEU Case C-407/92R *An Taisce v Commission* ECLI:EU:C:1993:261.

[116] General Court Case T-219/95R *Danielsson v Commission* ECLI:EU:T:1995:219.

[117] CJEU Case C-503/06 *Commission v Italy* ECLI:EU:C:2006:279; Case C-193/07 *Commission v Poland* ECLI:EU:C:2007:218; Case C-76/08R *Commission v Malta* ECLI:EU:C:2008/252.

[118] CJEU Case C-121/21 (n 84).

environmental law. Within the Union, the idea of having private citizens actively pursuing general interest matters such as the application of environmental law and, thereby, the protection of the environment is not strongly developed. Member States with a tradition of Roman law resist it, as the concept of an 'open society' and the activation of citizens as law enforcers has no tradition in law. In Scandinavian Member States, the concept of the modern welfare state seems to lead to the conclusion that it is best for public authorities to ensure the application of environmental law.[119] The complaint procedure, described in paragraph 14-22 above, does not give citizens the possibility of actively pursuing any lack of compliance with EU law.

Actions against Member States can only be taken by the Commission; its decision to act or not to act under Article 258 TFEU cannot be challenged by citizens. Where the Commission itself causes environmental impairment, there is hardly any possibility for a citizen to take action against the Commission, since that citizen is not directly and individually concerned. The jurisprudence by the CJEU, which grants citizens some 'rights' under EU environmental directives, has had no influence whatsoever on individuals' – and their organisations' – right of standing under EU law.[120]

14-44 In 1998, the Union and all Member States signed the Aarhus Convention on 'access to information, public participation in decision-making and access to justice in environmental matters', which had been elaborated under the auspices of the United Nations. This convention, which entered into force in 2001, was ratified by the Union in 2005;[121] it provided for access to justice[122] for 'members of the public concerned (a) having a sufficient interest or, alternatively (b) maintaining impairment of a right, where the administrative procedural law of a Party requires this as a precondition'. This provision included environmental organisations. In implementing the provisions of the Aarhus Convention, the Commission proposed, in 2003, a directive to give environmental organisations a right of standing in national courts.[123] Member States considered, however, that access to justice was their exclusive competence and did not adopt the proposal. In 2014, the Commission withdrew its proposal.[124]

In order to avoid being accused of measuring with two measures, the Commission also made a proposal for a regulation to improve access to the European Courts by the environmental organisations. The proposal was adopted in 2006, as Regulation 1367/2006.[125] It did not amend the present provisions of Articles 263 and 265 TFEU. Thus, the access to the European Courts has not been improved, which is incompatible with the requirements of the Aarhus Convention.

[119] See CJEU Case C-263/08 *Djurgaarden* ECLI:EU:C:2009:631; Sweden, one of the most advanced countries in environmental protection, had granted access to justice only to environmental organisations with more than 2000 members.

[120] Commission, Notice on access to justice in environmental matters [2017] OJ C275/1.

[121] Decision 2005/370 [2005] OJ L124/1.

[122] In the wording of Art 9(2) of the Convention, this means 'access to a review procedure before a court of law and/or another independent and impartial body established by law'.

[123] Commission, COM(2003) 624; see also para 4-20.

[124] Commission [2014] OJ C153/3.

[125] Regulation 1367/2006 on the application of the provisions of the Aarhus convention on access to information, public participation in decision-making and access to justice in environmental matters to Community institutions and bodies [2006] OJ L264/13; see also paras 4-14ff.

In a judgment of 2011, the Court declared Article 9(3) of the Aarhus Convention[126] to be, together with the Aarhus Convention itself, part of EU law. It held, however, that Article 9(3) did not have direct effect, because that provision only granted access to the courts once the conditions which were laid down by Member States were complied with. The Court encouraged the national courts to interpret Article 9(3) broadly and do their outmost in order to ensure, in environmental matters, wide access by private persons or environmental organisations to the national court.[127]

In March 2011 – confirmed in 2017 – the Compliance Committee of the Aarhus Convention held that the restrictive practice by the CJEU, to practically bar any access of environmental organisations to the EU Court, was incompatible with the provisions of the Aarhus Convention.[128] The Compliance Committee rejected in particular the argument raised by the Union that the possibility to address a national court which could then introduce, under Article 267 TFEU, a preliminary procedure before the CJEU was sufficient to satisfy the requirements of the Aarhus Convention.

Following long discussions on the Compliance Committee's findings, the Union amended its Regulation 1367/2006 on the possibility for individual persons and environmental organisations to ask for an internal review of any regulatory act of the Union other that a legislative act – but not to ask for an annulment of the incriminated act itself. The citizens or the environmental organisation had to be directly affected by the incriminated act or had to be impaired in their rights; in this latter case, the request for internal review had to be supported by 4000 citizens from at least five Member States (with at least 250 citizens per Member State). The internal review procedure left the original Union decision untouched; it was up to the competent Union institution to take steps in order to rectify the original decision, should the internal review be successful. As the rules of access to the CJEU – Article 263(4) TFEU – were not changed, this amendment continues, in my opinion, to be incompatible with the Aarhus Convention.

The extent to which an individual can address national courts and claim a breach of EU 14-45
law is governed by national law; no general EU provisions exist. A Commission communication of 1996 was silent in that respect;[129] the Council's resolution on that communication was no more explicit.[130] A proposal for a directive on access to justice in environmental matters was, as mentioned, withdrawn. Occasionally, Union directives provide that Member States shall, under certain conditions, allow access to justice in order to ensure compliance.[131] However, the Council rejected several other Commission proposals of this kind.

[126] Aarhus Convention [2005] OJ L124/3, Art 9(3): 'In addition and without prejudice to the review procedures referred to in paragraphs 1 and 2 above, each Party shall ensure that, where they meet the criteria, if any, laid down in its national law, members of the public have access to administrative or judicial procedures to challenge acts and omissions by private persons and public authorities which contravene provisions of its national law relating to the environment.'

[127] CJEU Case C-240/09 *Lesoochranárske zoskupenie VLK* ECLI:EU:C:2011:125.

[128] Aarhus Convention Compliance Committee, 'Findings and Recommendations of the Compliance Committee with Regard to Communication ACCC/C/2008/32 Concerning Compliance by the European Union, of 14 April 2011; Part II of 17 March 2017', Document ECE/MP.PP7C1/2017/7.

[129] Commission, 'Implementing Community Environmental Law' COM(96) 500 of 22 October 1996. The communication mainly addressed measures at national level and considered, at EU level, better information, co-operation and consultation.

[130] Council Resolution of 7 October 1997 [1997] OJ C321/1.

[131] See, eg Directive 2003/4 on access to environmental information [2003] OJ L41/26, Art 6; Directive 2004/35 on environmental liability [2004] OJ L143/56, Art 13; Directive 2010/75 on industrial emissions [2010] OJ L334/17,

Where a national court is seized with a litigation that involves EU environmental law, it has the possibility to submit to the CJEU a preliminary question on the validity or the interpretation of EU law; when it is a judgment of a national court 'against whose decisions there is no remedy under national law', that court is obliged to submit preliminary questions to the CJEU when these questions are relevant to the case before it.[132] For an individual person or an environmental non-governmental organisation, this provision is of limited value: the decision whether to submit a preliminary question to the CJEU depends on the national court. The national court also formulates the question. As, on average, preliminary cases before the Court of Justice take about 16 months, many national courts omit putting such questions for fear of delaying the litigation.

14-46 Overall, the provision of the Aarhus Convention that private persons and environmental organisations should have the right(!) to bring before EU courts actions against acts and omissions of the EU public authorities remains very largely a dead letter. Neither Article 263(3) TFEU nor the procedures under Article 267 TFEU offer an access to courts that corresponds to the requirement of Article 9(3) of the Aarhus Convention. It was thus quite correct that the Aarhus Convention Compliance Committee found that access to EU justice, as it is organised at present, is not in compliance with the Convention.[133] And it appears that the practice on access to justice is also not compatible with Article 47 of the Charter of Fundamental Rights.[134]

To what extent the monitoring of the application of EU environmental law should be ensured by the EU staff or should be, at least to some extent, externalised is a question of legal and institutional policy. It is obvious that Member States do not like to be checked as to their environmental performance – and actual or potential polluters even less so. The administrations, the governments and the EU institutions prefer to maintain the quasi-monopoly of the EU institutions and of national administrations to bring public and private polluters before the courts. Whether the environment can indefinitely survive the present monitoring practice, which is all too often influenced by political or administrative intervention or by private lobbying, is not a question to be dealt with here.

Art 25; Directive 2011/92 on the environmental impact assessment of certain projects [2012] OJ L26/1, Art 11; Directive 2012/18 on the control of major-accident hazards involving dangerous substances [2012] OJ L197/1, Art 23.

[132] See Art 267 TFEU: 'The Court of Justice of the European Union shall have jurisdiction to give preliminary rulings concerning: (a) the interpretation of the Treaties; (b) the validity and interpretation of acts of the institutions, bodies, offices or agencies of the Union. Where such a question is raised before any court or tribunal of a Member State, that court or tribunal may, if it considers that a decision on the question is necessary to enable it to give judgment, request the Court to give a ruling thereon. Where such a question is raised in a case pending before a court or a tribunal of a Member State against whose decisions there is no judicial remedy under national law, that court or tribunal shall bring the matter before the Court.'

[133] Aarhus Convention Compliance Committee (n 128).

[134] Charter of Fundamental Rights of the European Union [2000] OJ C364/1, Art 47: 'Everyone whose rights and freedoms guaranteed by the law of the Union are violated has the right to an effective remedy before a tribunal.' Obviously, all depends on the recognition of a 'right' to clean air, to clean water, etc.

15

EU Environmental Law and Policy

I. Introduction

EU environmental policy orientations were first formulated in 1971/72 and have progressively expanded since. They were anchored in the EC Treaty in 1987 by the Single European Act and further fine-tuned by the Treaty amendments of 1993 (Maastricht Treaty), 1999 (Amsterdam Treaty) and 2001 (Nice Treaty). In December 2009, the Lisbon Treaties on European Union entered into effect, after long negotiations on what constitutional basis the Union should rest. This last event only demonstrated that the Union does not enjoy the prerogatives of a state; in particular, it may act only where it has been expressly so authorised by the Lisbon Treaties. Any comparison with domestic environmental law in the Member States, of which there are 27 since the exit of the UK, or in the USA is therefore necessarily misleading. 15-01

This becomes obvious in the area of environmental law and policy, which is part of Union law and policy. It is difficult to determine what the European interest in environmental protection is, how far it goes in specific cases and which measures should be taken at what level in order to protect the environment in Europe. There are no European radio or television stations, no European press and, more generally, no European public opinion which would discuss the general environmental interest of the Union, and not just the French, German or Spanish interests in the Union. Lawyers very largely continue to perceive and discuss European environmental law from a national law perspective. One might find some consolation in the remark from Arthur Toynbee that the wheels of a car turn around themselves, yet move the car ahead; however, when the car is called 'European Union', which shall achieve ever-closer union among the peoples of Europe, there is some need to discuss the car's equipment, driving instruments and, most of all, the direction it shall take and is actually taking.

Law alone cannot answer these questions. Making environmental legislation for the 450 million or so people in the Union is possible. However, in view of the diversity of culture and education in the different parts of the Union, the differences in climate, geography and other environmental conditions, the differences in economic and social development and of policies within the 27 Member States and their regions, such European environmental legislation must necessarily be general in character and leave many details to the local, regional and national levels.

Also, law as a tool to protect the environment has its inherent limitations. The Union might adopt thousands more directives or regulations to protect the environment: if the mentality of humans to impair the environment is not reduced, and if the ecological footprint of everyone and of the European society is not reduced, all this environmental legislation constitutes food for lawyers but does not change the societal reality, which is marked by the simple fact that the European environment – and, more so, the global environment – is sick and is slowly but continuously becoming worse, not better.

15-02 There is a consensus, expressed in several Council political statements, declarations and resolutions, that the present lifestyle within the Union is not sustainable.[1] This consensus, though, has not yet led to significant steps in order to change the situation – and there are many reasons for this, among them considerations of competitiveness, economic growth, welfare and human greed. No politician at European level or within the 27 Member States has ever dared to declare, as President George HW Bush of the USA declared for his country in 1992, that 'our national lifestyle is not negotiable', meaning that significant changes in lifestyle are not acceptable. Yet, in practice, the Union behaves no differently from the USA, though there are differences between the two, as Europe has another history and culture, is less wealthy and has less geographical space. The emphasis which the Union puts on economic growth and the neglect of non-economic values – social, environmental and cultural – also progressively flatten such differences and make people forget that they cannot live from bread alone. Policies may influence and change trends, but then political leaders need vision, strategic thinking, leadership capacity and credibility. These are qualities which are rare throughout the world, including in Europe.

Policy risks of 'too much environmental protection' have already become visible. In almost every chapter of this book, new environmental legislative proposals by the European Commission have been presented which are awaiting adoption by the Union legislator. Objections against taking too many measures, interfering with people's private lives, increasing prices and reducing welfare are mounting, based on right-wing proponents ('my country first') and citizens who are afraid of the wind of change blowing too fiercely; and in rural areas, new forms of activity (renewable energy installations, animal welfare considerations, organic farming practices, etc) are appearing which threaten traditions, and which people who cannot get accustomed to the speed of change or oppose the fight against climate change, biodiversity loss and pollution consider unnecessary. The European Green Deal itself appears, in this year 2023, to be questioned, including all targets for 2030 and 2050.

II. Primary Law

15-03 The structure of the EU Treaties still reflects the preponderance of economic interests over environmental (and social) interests. The EU Treaties deal in detail with internal trade, the four freedoms (free circulation of products and services, capital and labour), transport, agriculture, etc. After some antecedents, the integration provision of Article 11 was inserted, in 1999, into the Union Treaty to ensure that the three environmental Articles 191–93 of the

[1] See, as an example, Counccil Resolution on the Fifth Environmental Action Programme [1993] OJ C138/1, no 3: 'The Council and the Representatives of Member States, meeting in Council, note that many current forms of activity and development are not environmentally sustainable … agree that the achievement of sustainable development calls for significant changes in current patterns of development, production, consumption and behaviour'. See also Commission Statistical Office, *Sustainable Development in the European Union. Monitoring Report on Progress Towards the SDGs in the EU Context. 2022 Report* (Luxembourg, 2022).

Treaty on the Functioning of the European Union (TFEU) influence all other EU policies and progressively 'green' them. This concept was to be completed by the overall objective of the Union to reach a sustainable development (Articles 3 of the Treaty on European Union (TEU) and 11 TFEU) and to aim at a high level of environmental protection (Articles 2 TEU and 114 and 191 TFEU).

However, this concept was and is based on the *political* decision to aim at integrating environmental requirements into other policies, to aim for a high level of protection and to aim for sustainable development. The legal provisions as such are not sufficient. And as the Court of Justice of the European Union (CJEU) never decided that Article 11 TFEU constituted a *legal* requirement, that a specific measure was not of *high* level of environmental protection or what the precise content of sustainable development was in a given context, the concept of the EU Treaties remains unfulfilled.

The weight of environmental law is different if one compares it, for example, with the economic provision of Article 34 TFEU, which stipulates that there should be no quantitative restrictions on the free circulation of goods or measures having equivalent effect. This provision was not only interpreted by the Commission – and confirmed by the CJEU – as prohibiting trade restrictions; it was also interpreted as giving individual persons and companies the right to invoke it in courts and have all measures which contradicted it declared void. The interpretation of Article 34 TFEU was thus not left to the Commission or to the public authorities alone, but could also be, and in fact was, influenced by citizens.

There is no provision in Articles 191–93 TFEU which prohibits environmental pollution or impairment. Formulating such a provision would not be too difficult, as the sole prohibition is no less precise than the original wording of Article 34 TFEU. Indeed, the Avosetta Group (a group of European environmental lawyers) once suggested a formula to be inserted into the Treaty: 'Subject to imperative reasons of overriding public interests, significantly impairing the environment or human health shall be prohibited.' However, inserting such a provision into the Treaty would have meant that citizens could tackle provisions or practices which contradicted this rule in courts – which would have broken the monopoly of the administration to decide, through action or inaction, what is good for the environment, what a high level of protection is and to what extent measures in other policy areas contradicted the environmental requirements. The Avosetta formula therefore has no chance of ever being included in any future Treaty. 15-04

The other big lacuna in the present Treaty provisions, from the point of view of environmental protection, concerns nuclear energy. Article 11 TFEU applies to the EU Treaties as such, not to the Euratom Treaty. It would have been easy to insert a provision similar to Article 11 into the Euratom Treaty. But this has not been done. And it is disappointing to see that nuclear energy policy, which has the biggest negative environmental potential of all industrial activities due to the longevity of radiation, risk of accidents, terrorist attacks, waste issues, etc, is not even contained in any environmental provision, while at the same time the European taxpayer – who has, in about half of the Member States, expressly rejected nuclear energy – pays huge amounts for nuclear research and infrastructure, nuclear installations, their decommissioning and their waste.

Is there the lack of any provision on an individual's right to a clean environment in the European Treaties? Human rights generally are formulated in the Charter on Fundamental Rights, which has, under Article 6 TEU, 'the same legal value as the Treaties'; 15-05 the environmental provision there resembles Article 11 TFEU.[2] This, thus, could plead in favour of an explicit human right to a clean environment. However, experience in Member States shows that not much is won with the insertion of such a human right into the constitution (or, for the Union, into the Lisbon Treaties), as almost all depends on the concrete, political organisation of protecting the environment – such as the environmental infrastructure and administration, the policy rank of environmental issues, the determination of local, regional and national administrations to take effective action in favour of the environment, and education of the population – including courts, media, academics, etc.

Member States which have an individual right to a clean environment in their constitution do not fare environmentally any better than those Member States where the protection of the environment is 'only' a constitutional policy orientation provision (*Staatszielbestimmung*). And the EU Treaties already include, in Articles 3 TEU and 11, 114 and 191–93 TFEU, such policy orientation provisions. What would be necessary is a change in the above-mentioned situation that, under the EU Treaties – including its Article 263(4) TFEU on access to the European courts – the Commission's and Member States' administrations have a de facto monopoly on enforcing the environmental provisions, including those of the EU Treaties themselves. In this regard, an individual right to a clean environment would be of use.

The environmental principles of Article 191(2) TFEU – the principles of precaution and prevention, the principle that environmental damage should be tackled at the source and the polluter-pays principle – have helped to justify specific legal measures, but were not interpreted as to require a specific solution to a specific problem or to prohibit this or that measure. To have such an effect, their precise content and their borders are too vague. These principles could be fulfilled by others, such as the substitution principle, though this would raise the same problems: the question of when a dangerous chemical substance should be replaced by another, less harmful substance can only be decided in view of the characteristics of both substances, their use, the availability of the substitute substance, cost elements and even legal considerations – where the use of a substitute substance would make the EU producers dependent on a third country patent holder, the policy decision on that substance will not remain uninfluenced. This proves that the insertion into the Treaties, for example, of a substitution principle would not change the present situation much.

Thus, the constitutional frame for the protection of the environment at EU level is satisfying overall. Some fine-tuning might be necessary or desirable in this or that provision; standing for citizens or environmental organisations could be introduced via secondary legislation. However, the Treaty enables the EU institutions and the EU Member States to develop an active, coherent and consistent environmental policy of and within the Union – if the political will to do so exists.

[2] Charter on Fundamental Rights [2000] OJ C364/1, Art 37: 'A high level of environmental protection and the improvement of the quality of the environment must be integrated into the policies of the Union and ensured in accordance with the principle of sustainable development.'

III. Law-Making and the Quality of EU Law

A. On Law-Making

When EU environmental law first appeared in the statute books in the mid-1970s, it met largely virgin ground at national level. Few environmental provisions existed at that time; and the progressive development of EU environmental legislation led several Member States – Greece, Ireland, Spain, Portugal, Luxembourg, Italy, and in part also France and Belgium – to take over that legislation rather than develop their own national rules on the basis of a national environmental policy. 15-06

Today, national environmental law consists, in numerous Member States in Southern Europe, as well as in all 13 Member States which joined the Union since 2004, virtually 100 per cent of the transposition and incorporation of EU environmental law. For most of the other Member States, this figure varies between 65 and 80 per cent. Thus, in theory, the conditions are very favourable for an intensive consensus building at Union level on the orientation of legislation, on its level of detail, on issues to address and on instruments to develop. To this has to be added, on the one hand, the three principal environmental challenges that were identified at global level and which plead in favour of the taking of measures beyond the nation-state level, namely climate change, biodiversity loss and pollution; and on the other hand, the overall umbrella provision of Article 193 TFEU, which allows Member States to maintain or introduce more stringent national provisions and to prevent a deterioration of their national environmental status quo. EU environmental law thus has the potential to be the foundation on which, according to the ecological, social and economic conditions in the different parts of the Union, national or regional supplementary environmental provisions are allowed to be built.

Practice, though, developed differently. As the national administration and policy had a de facto monopoly on protecting or not protecting the environment, legislation that was made at EU level was frequently perceived as interfering with this monopoly. And while, on the political level, Member States regularly agreed on EU environment action programmes, and on the objectives, principles and priorities of EU legislative activity, at the administrative level, this was not always followed – though it has to be admitted that the two levels cannot always easily be distinguished. As the devil of environmental protection is in the detail and not in great principles such as 'sustainable development', 'best technique' or 'the polluter shall pay', the making of environmental EU legislation gave ample opportunity to protect the national administrations' monopoly. The absence of environmental provisions at national level did not therefore mean that a Member State would be in favour of seeing such provisions imported from the Union. In concrete terms, this reluctance manifested itself in various forms, such as the stopping of new legislative initiatives,[3] the changes of approaches to tackle environmental pollution,[4] the watering

[3] Examples are the proposals for directives on the dumping of waste at sea, on a permit requirement for all industrial installations, on provisions on airport noise or on access to justice.

[4] Examples are the shift from emission limit values to quality standards in air and water legislation, the substitution of provisions for certain industrial sectors by best available technique reference documents or on the producer responsibility in waste management legislation.

down of Commission proposals[5] and the establishment of provisions which could alone be monitored and controlled by the national administration;[6] of course, the EU administration was not neutral in this effort, but often contributed to it, also according to the national provenance of the different EU officials. The efforts had the (welcome) side effect that the administrations' monopoly was also affirmed with regard to national environmental organisations, citizen groups and public opinion bodies.

The problem with this approach was that the individual national administration which pleaded for a reduced EU environmental legislation had its own national situation in mind; for example, it did not wish to see the Union interfere (this was frequently the attitude prevailing in Poland and Hungary); it wished to ensure its regional power (this was the prevailing motivation of the German *Länder*); or it was of the opinion that its own national environmental provisions were better anyway than those which could be generated at EU level (this last attitude was frequently found in the Netherlands). Nor did the national administrations pay much attention to the fact that the alternative to EU environmental provisions was not that there would be national provisions in the now 27 Member States; rather, the alternative was that some Member States would have national legislation on a specific item, but the large majority would not. This lack of a European perspective from national decision-takers has dominated the law-making process at Union level for decades, though it has never been openly discussed.

Despite this reluctance, EU environmental law achieved a number of quite remarkable results, in both quantity and quality. The following list of 10 pieces of EU environmental law which would, without the EU legislation, not have been subjects of national environmental legislation in the vast majority of both old and new Member States serves to illustrate this point (and the list could easily be lengthened): (i) environmental impact assessment; (ii) participation in decision-making (regarding climate change legislation); (iii) accident prevention; (iv) integrated pollution prevention and control; (v) drinking water; (vi) waste incinerators; (vii) end-of-life vehicles; (viii) packaging and packaging waste; (ix) habitat protection; and (x) bird protection.

The Commission's administration was and is not strong enough to ensure the adoption of environmental legislation at a high level against or without the support of national administrations. Its allies are not numerous: public opinion, the best ally of the environment, hardly exists at EU level; environmental scientists are barely organised at EU level; the European Parliament reacts, but hardly ever has the historic memory or the scientific support which would enable it to play an active role in environmental law-making; and European environmental organisations lack human and financial resources.

B. The Quality of EU Environmental Law

15-07 These imperfections of the law-making process affect the quality of environmental legislation. EU environmental law was developed ad hoc, without strategic thinking as to

[5] Examples are the Drinking Water Directive, Directive 2020/2184 [2020] OJ L435/1; the administrative obligation to clean up orphan damage in Directive 2004/35 [2004] OJ L143/56; the omission to fix quality standards for heavy metals in air in Directive 2004/107 [2005] OJ L23/3.

[6] Examples are the Water Framework Directive, Directive 2000/60 [2000] OJ L327/1; Directive 2006/7 on the quality of bathing water [2006] OJ L64/37; Regulation 1013/2006 on the shipment of waste [2006] OJ L190/1; Directive 2004/35 on environmental liability (n 5).

how to organise a specific sector (water, air, waste). Amendments were also made on an ad hoc basis, often as a follow-up to accidents or incidents. Where framework legislation was created, its basic orientations were questioned and changed after a few years, discrediting the nature of the framework legislation; examples are Directives 76/464 on water discharges,[7] 84/360 on industrial air pollution[8] and 96/62 on air quality standards.[9] More recent framework legislation – for example, for freshwater (Directive 2000/60[10]), marine waters (Directive 2008/56[11]), pesticide use (Directive 2009/128[12]) and flooding (Directive 2007/60[13]) – have no or very distant implementation deadlines and are so vague and general in their content that their added value to the protection of the environment appears limited. Indeed, where a Member State has the will to protect the environment in one of the areas mentioned, it may find useful orientation and support in such framework legislation; however, where this political will does not exist, the improved environmental protection will hardly ever be achieved, as the framework legislation mainly works with analysis, planning and reporting as EU instruments.

The codification of environmental legislation into one or several basic texts has never been seriously considered at Union level. After the Commission's somewhat populist announcement, in 2001, to reduce the volume of EU legislation by 25 per cent, efforts were undertaken to incorporate all amendments of a directive or a regulation into a single text, though without touching the substance. In this way, overlapping, contradictions and inconsistencies between different environmental pieces of legislation were not reduced, though this form of law-making also sailed under the name of 'codification'.[14] In some Member States, the putting together of environmental provisions in a single legal act or code has been successfully brought to an end. Such initiatives will not take place at Union level for a foreseeable time. 15-08

At EU level, there is also no instrument to measure the quality of environmental legislation. The only reasonable yardstick is whether the legislation has led to an improved permanent protection or not. On that, it is undoubtedly true that EU environmental legislation has contributed to the adoption of environmental legislation in all 27 Member States. Hence, it has led to the installation of environmental ministries, the creation of environmental structures – local and regional administrations, environmental groups, environmental education, discussion of environmental issues in the media, creation of specialised institutes, laboratories and others – and to the discussion of environmental issues in national policies. However, this alone does not yet protect the environment adequately. To illustrate this point, an example of a decision by the CJEU may be quoted. A citizen had applied to the Court because his private property had been inserted into the EU-wide list of habitats of European importance under Directive 92/43 and he was of the opinion that this Commission decision was wrong. The Court rejected his application as inadmissible,[15]

[7] Directive 76/464 [1976] OJ L129/23.

[8] Directive 84/360 [1984] OJ L188/20.

[9] Directive 96/62 [1996] OJ L296/55.

[10] Directive 2000/60 (n 6).

[11] Directive 2008/56 [2008] OJ L164/19.

[12] Directive 2009/128 [2009] OJ L309/71.

[13] Directive 2007/60 [2007] OJ L284/27.

[14] Examples are Directive 2010/75 on industrial emissions [2010] OJ L334/17; Directive 2008/50 on ambient air quality and cleaner air for Europe [2008] OJ L152/1.

[15] CJEU Case C-362/06P *Sahlstedt and others v Commission* ECLI:EU:C:2009:243; General Court Case T-150/05 *Sahlstedt and others v Commission* ECLI:EU:T:2006:172.

because he was not directly affected by the Commission decision. The Court held that the selection of habitats in a national list and the subsequent decision and publication of a Union list were all preparatory acts which did not affect the private property. This means that the existence of Directive 92/43 since 1992 – more than 30 years – has not led to the concrete protection of habitats; rather, this protection of the environment with regard to specific habitats will only begin once conservation measures by Member States have been taken.

15-09 The biggest merit of EU environmental legislation is that it exists, and that this existence has compelled all Member States to have equivalent provisions in their national statute books. Environmental policy can build on this set of rules where the political will exists.

EU environmental law has not prevented Member States from maintaining or introducing stringent provisions in national legislation. And nowhere has a Member State been prevented from protecting its national environment because of the existence of EU environmental legislation. One might think of the area of biotechnology as an exception: it is well known that countries such as Austria or Denmark would prefer not to have genetically modified seeds on their land, or fruit, vegetables or meat in their shops which contains genetically modified organisms (GMOs). However, it was explained in chapter six above that the Union deliberately based legislation on GMOs on the product-related Article 114 TFEU, not on the environment-related Article 192 TFEU. Member States agreed to that on several occasions. It is thus difficult for them to argue that they can no longer protect their environment in the way which they think best. Directive 2015/412 has since given some leeway to Member States in this area.[16]

In 2015, the Juncker Commission suggested that Member States, when transposing EU legislation into national law, should not go beyond the provisions that had been adopted at EU level (gold-plating).[17] As regards EU environmental law, this proposal is in contradiction which Article 193 TFEU, which expressly provides for such a possibility. Politically, the communication, and in particular the proposal to stop gold-plating, reveals the Commission's intentions: any legislation was perceived, in the communication, as a burden (for business) and should, whenever possible, not go beyond what the Commission – and later the EU – considered as adequate.

The proposal also fundamentally misunderstood the concept of environmental protection within the EU: the underlying concept of Articles 191–93 TFEU is not the harmonisation of (national) legislation; rather, the basic concept is to reach a high level of environmental protection. And this might *require* differentiation of environmental protection measures, according to the geography, the climate (wind, sunshine, tides and other factors), the constitutional and political structures in a Member State, citizens' awareness of the necessity and the possibility to protect the environment, etc. The proposal would be a little less disturbing if the Commission were indeed aiming at a high level of protection in its legislative proposals on the protection of the environment; then, stricter measures at the level of Member States would be less necessary. Unfortunately, however, a high level of environmental protection is not an objective which the Commission normally has in mind. Rather, it has a tendency to declare that *any* proposal which it makes is aimed at such a high level – which is, of course, simply incorrect.

[16] Directive 2015/412 [2015] OJ L68/1.

[17] Commission, 'Better Regulation for Better Results – an EU Agenda' COM(2015) 215, paras 8 and 9.

The impact of the Juncker Communication was reduced by the new strategy of the Von der Leyen Commission in 2019 on the 'European Green Deal', which explicitly recognised that environmental protection would contribute to and ensure economic growth.[18]

EU environmental legislation often lacks the necessary precision and details. Definitions of 'renewable energy' which include the 'biodegradable fraction of industrial and municipal waste',[19] of 'good environmental status' in Directive 2000/60 and Directive 2008/56 on marine waters – where the marine environment is practically reduced to the quality of the *waters* – and of 'participation' were loosely drafted and invite different interpretations and abuses. Environmental 'plans' and 'programmes', 'best available technique', reports and monitoring obligations are not defined with the necessary rigidity. More examples could be given. The oft-heard argument that this flexibility is inevitable in an enlarged Union of 27 Member States is simply misleading: between Stockholm and Sofia, Lisbon and Riga, everybody knows what a car is and understands the term in the same sense. Yet, there is no uniform definition of hazardous waste.[20] In contrast to that, the directive on three-wheel cars had 454 pages in the EU Official Journal,[21] and the number of large, very detailed CEN (European Committee for Standardisation) and CENELEC (European Committee for Electrical and Electronic Standardisation) standards is beyond 15,000 and rising. This demonstrates that a Union needs uniform EU definitions. Vague definitions in EU environmental law appear to be due more to the influence of British administrative law; they make law monitoring and application difficult, if not impossible. Article 193 TFEU, which allows Member States to better protect their environment, is not an excuse for not precisely defining what the EU legislation is about. 15-10

The greatest problem as regards the quality of environmental law are those pieces of EU environmental legislation which are, de facto, unenforceable. The issue also affects the quality of law. It had been argued in chapters seven (water) and eight (air) that EU quality standards are practically unenforceable against Member States. As the Commission has, in any case, the obligation to ensure that environmental law is not only transposed into national law, but also 'applied' (Article 17 TEU), it should think twice before it suggests setting quality standards at EU level. And if it does propose them, its proposals should contain provisions which address this enforcement problem. This has never been done in the past. The consequence is that quality standards are hardly enforced in the Union. And it should be remembered that nothing discredits the legislation in a society more than its non-application. 15-11

C. Better Regulation

For about 30 years, starting with the Edinburgh summit of the Heads of States and Governments in 1991, there have been efforts to deregulate environmental provisions that had been adopted at EU level. In order to hide their objective, these efforts sailed under the flag of 'better regulation'. While there were some efforts in the mid-1990s and by the 15-12

[18] Commission, 'The European Green Deal' COM(2019) 640.

[19] Directive 2009/28 [2009] OJ L140/16.

[20] Directive 2008/98 [2008] OJ L312/3.

[21] Directive 97/24 [1997] OJ L226/1.

Prodi Commission (1999–2004) in this regard,[22] the Barroso Commission (2004–14) made the subject of better regulation one of its central topics[23] and the Juncker Commission (2014–19) followed this line.[24] These two Commissions believed that deregulating the environment and other areas would create employment, make the European economy more competitive and would, overall, strengthen the Union, internally and globally (the Lisbon process).

15-13 This neoliberal policy orientation, which I consider wrong, is not discussed here. The Commission received part of an answer from the European citizens in the form of the negative answers to the referendums on the European Constitution in France and the Netherlands in 2004, in the continuously reduced number of voters in European elections and in the increase in anti-EU political parties and movements in the Member States. What should be mentioned here is that the Commission itself declared the following in 2001, when it presented its political environmental programme for the next 10 years:[25]

> Despite improvements on some fronts, we continue to face a number of persistent problems. Of particular concern are climate change, the loss of biodiversity and natural habitats, soil loss and degradation, increased waste volumes, the build up of chemicals in the environment, noise and certain air and water pollutants. We also face a number of emerging issues such as pollutants that affect the functioning of our hormone systems. Forecasts suggest that with current policies and socio-economic trends, many of the pressures that give rise to these problems, such as transport, energy use, tourist activities, land-take for infra-structure etc. will worsen over the coming decade.

The Juncker Commission never undertook to explain to the European citizen in detail how these trends could be reversed by the deregulation policy which it pursued.

There were several such basic contradictions. For example, under the 'Better regulation' policy, the Commission announced that it would try to promote the use of voluntary agreements with industry, including in the sector of environmental policy. In contrast, the Sixth Environmental Action Programme declared quite unambiguously that 'legislation remains central to meeting environmental challenges'.[26] No attempt was made to clarify this difference in approach. In 2002, the Commission announced that it would promote tripartite contracts between the European regions, the Member States concerned and the Union, in order to promote environmental protection;[27] there was no follow-up, but no explanation either. 'Governance', a central topic of the Prodi Commission, disappeared from the policy agenda of the Barroso and Juncker Commissions.[28] The Cardiff process, initiated by the European Council and which also should influence law-making and the quality of legislation, was buried in silence, without any explanation to the European citizen.

[22] See Commission, European Governance – a White Paper [2001] OJ C287/1.

[23] Commission, 'Communication: Better Regulation for Growth and Jobs' COM(2005) 97.

[24] Commission, COM(2015) 215 (n 17).

[25] Commission, COM(2001) 31, 10.

[26] See Decision 1600/2002 [2002] OJ L242/1, Recital 12. This statement constituted an answer to the Commission's 'Proposal for the Sixth Action Programme' COM(2001) 31, where the Commission stated: 'In some cases, non-regulatory methods will be the most appropriate and flexible means of addressing environmental issues. The Commission is currently examining new methods of governance, including alternative to traditional regulation such as voluntary commitments and agreements, which could improve the ability of enterprise to innovate and change.'

[27] Commission, COM(2002) 709.

[28] It came back on the political agenda in the follow-up to the Paris Agreement on climate change, see Regulation 2018/1999 on the governance of the energy union and climate action [2018] OJ L328/1.

The European Green Deal of 2019 reversed all of these approaches, though without explaining why there were errors in the past. It called itself the new growth strategy of the Union and returned to more classical legislative approaches in the different Union policies and regulations:[29]

> The European Green Deal … is a new growth strategy that aims to transform the EU into a fair and prosperous society, with a modern, resource-efficient and competitive economy, where there are no net emissions of greenhouse gases in 2050 and where economic growth is decoupled from resource use. It also aims to protect, conserve and enhance the EU's natural capital, and protect the health and well-being from environment-related risks and impacts.

It is to be hoped that the next Commissions will build on this Green Deal approach and not change the orientations again; after all, none of the climate change impact, the loss of biodiversity or the effects of environmental pollution will disappear in the next years and decades. Also, a significant new change in policy risks creating a credibility gap: how can the European citizen believe what the European institutions declare if this is no longer true a short time afterwards? The Commission is not a government which might change policies after elections have brought new political forces to power. Rather, the Commission has to act in the common European interest (Article 17 TEU), and it would be difficult to understand why and how this interest could change within short time.

IV. The Different Environmental Sectors

A look at the different sectors of EU environmental law has to start with the Seventh Environmental Action Programme itself. This was adopted in the form of an EU decision[30] and is thus legally binding. The programme contains a number of binding commitments to reach specific results in different sectors;[31] furthermore, it contains a number of instructions to the EU institutions, and in particular to the Commission, to tackle this or that aspect of environmental policy.[32] If the fact that the Seventh Programme was adopted by way of a decision had any sense, then the Commission was obliged to follow the mandates and instructions which the programme contained, and this for the lifetime of the programme – or at least until it had been amended. It makes no sense to elaborate a programme, proceed to extensive consultations with all stakeholders, discuss it at European level for more than two years, have it adopted by way of co-decision under active co-operation of the Commission and then ignore its content. However, this is more or less what happened between 2013 and 2019. 15-14

[29] Commission, COM(2019) 640, s I.

[30] Decision 1386/2013 [2013] OJ L354/171.

[31] See ibid annex, para 28: 'the 7th EAP shall *ensure* that by 2020' (emphasis added). The same wording is used in paras 43, 54, 65, 73, 84, 89, 95 and 106.

[32] See ibid annex: the paras quoted in n 31 contain 60 such instructions. As examples are quoted: 'increasing efforts to reduce soil erosion and increase soil organic matter, to remediate contaminated sites and to enhance the integration of land use aspects into coordinated decision-making involving all relevant levels of government, supported by the adoption of targets on soil and on land as a resource, and land planning objectives' (para 28 VI); 'developing measurement and benchmarking methodologies by 2015 for resource efficiency of land, carbon, water and material use and assessing the appropriateness of the inclusion of a lead indicator and target in the European Semester' (para 43 IV).

Other environmental *programmes* announced in a less binding form – as communications, thematic strategies, Green Papers, White Papers, strategies or framework legislation – suffered a similar destiny. They were often ignored by the administrative structures in the Commission, Parliament and Council and thus were not much more than an accumulation of good words. One principal reason for this is that the environmental programmes were elaborated by the environmental structure.[33] And while they were formally adopted by the Commission as a whole, the industry, agricultural, transport or energy departments, hardly having participated in their elaboration, did not feel committed to follow the programmes' objectives, principles and priorities, as they had, in their respective sector, to pursue their own objectives, principles and priorities. This pattern continued in the European Parliament and the Council. In other words: the integrative part of the EU institutions to make one coherent policy is limited. The different parts of EU policy – transport, industry, agriculture, consumer, environment, etc – are little integrated horizontally, but work vertically and rather autonomously.

Under the Green Deal, the Commission has adopted a considerable number of environment-related plans and programmes,[34] which extend up until 2030. It remains to be seen whether the specific proposals announced in these strategies will be submitted and adopted, and whether in particular the results expected in these strategies will be achieved.

15-15 As regards the *horizontal legislation*, which tries to follow the principles of an open society and give citizens more access to environmental information and more participation rights in decision-making, it is clear that the EU institutions do *not* try to be as open, transparent and accountable as possible. There are different cultures in the Union in this regard; the German, French and Spanish culture, which is far away from the openness of the Scandinavian culture, largely dominates the EU institutions and makes the wording of Article 1 TEU – that decisions are to be taken as openly and as closely to the citizen as possible – rather theoretical for the time being. At the level of Member States, the spirit of openness and participation which underlies the Aarhus Convention influences the daily practice in Scandinavian Member States and in the Netherlands. Elsewhere, and in particular in Central and Eastern Europe, but also in Spain, Portugal, Greece and Cyprus, much change in the mentality of the administration is still needed before openness, transparency and accountability will be the leitmotif of daily work.

Looking at *industrial installations*, it is understandable that the Union did not establish conditions for the emissions of all industrial installations; and it is a policy choice to opt for the best-technique approach in order not to have to establish the limitations for the different groups of installations and the pollutants by way of EU legislation. However, it is arguable that there should be a general provision which covers *all* industrial

[33] 'Environmental structure' is understood as being the environmental directorate general within the Commission, the environmental committee in the European Parliament and the environmental working group as well as the environmental ministers in the Council. Similar structures exist for agriculture, energy, etc.

[34] Commission, 'Circular Economy Action Plan' COM(2020) 98; Commission, 'Green Agenda for the Western Balkans' COM(2020) 223; Commission, 'Biodiversity Strategy' COM(2020) 380; Commission, 'Strategy From Farm to Fork' COM(2020) 381; Commission, 'Chemicals Strategy' COM(2020) 667; Commission, 'Strategy on Offshore Wind' COM(2020) 741; Commission, 'Strategy for Sustainable and Smart Mobility' COM(2020) 289; Commission, 'Industrial Strategy' COM(2021) 350; Commission, 'Sustainable Finance Strategy' COM(2021) 390; Commission, 'Zero Pollution Action Plan' COM(2021) 400; Commission, 'Forest Strategy' COM(2021) 572; 8th Environmental Action Programme, Decision 2022/591 [2022] OJ L114/22.

installations – 80 per cent are small- and medium-sized companies – and requires a permit for their emissions into the environment. Also, general requirements with regard to greenhouse gas emissions, resource management and waste handling could be imagined. On this, the Union currently relies on the Member States.

There is no comprehensive legislation on *biodiversity*. The two directives on birds (Directive 2009/147) and fauna, flora and habitats (Directive 92/43) are clearly not sufficient to protect EU nature. The latter even applies only to species and to habitats under threat. If it is correct that nature is slowly receding on the European continent, a more general legislation which also impacts on transport policy, agricultural policy, energy policy, the trans-European networks, etc would be needed. Such legislation could also usefully include considerations on wild animal welfare; indeed, animal welfare is a marked feature of differentiation of European values from other parts of the world. There seems to be a slow trend to also consider the protection of the welfare of other than wild animals as a topic of environmental law. Also, whether Member States will be able to make significant commitments as regards the restoration of nature[35] remains to be seen. 15-16

The absence of an environmentally oriented *product* policy was discussed in chapter six, and it is too early to assess whether, under the Green Deal, there will be a gradual change in this approach. Climate change considerations generated the adoption of a directive on the ecodesign of energy-related products,[36] and the Commission recently proposed to replace this act by a more general measure on the ecodesign of sustainable products.[37] This is, at last, consistent, as the Union's product safety legislation does not deal with environmental concerns.

In the *water* sector, the Union has largely given up its attempts to get a fixed set of minimum standards; it left the determination of 'good environmental status' to the different river basin management bodies and, for marine waters, to the European regional conventions. Also, the other EU directives in the water sector show this retreat from integrated standards. 15-17

Air pollution provisions from transport appear to be dictated more by the car industry than by environmental or human health concerns. The growing car fleet eats up reduction efforts made by the legislation, and the car industry's wish for planning security made it impossible to quickly introduce technical innovations such as the particulate filter for diesel cars. Emissions of point sources such as installations have diminished, though the overall air pollution, including its effects on soils, forests and human health, is still worrying. The statistic released by the Commission itself that more than 300,000 people die prematurely every year in the EU due to air pollution should have led to an outcry; instead, the reaction of the EU institutions is more or less a shrugging of the shoulders. The proposal to review existing legislation,[38] even when adopted, will not ensure clean air for Europe; improvement might rather come from the increasing number of electrical vehicles on the market.

As regards *noise*, a first directive of 2002 was not properly monitored by the Commission, and thus proved largely inefficient.[39] The Union is deficient in establishing noise reduction

[35] Commission, 'Proposal for a Regulation on Nature Restoration' COM(2022) 304.
[36] Directive 2009/125 [2009] OJ L285/10.
[37] Commission, 'Proposal for a Regulation on the Ecodesign of Sustainable Products' COM(2022) 142.
[38] Commission, 'Proposal for a Review of Directive 2008/50' COM(2022) 542.
[39] Directive 2002/49 [2002] OJ L189/12.

standards from transport vehicles (motorcycles, cars, trucks, aeroplanes). Here, legislation follows the technical evolution rather than driving innovation by legal standards that would have to be reached within a certain period. Compliance with standards throughout the lifetime of the product, and not only at the moment when it is first placed on the market, is another issue which would need to be addressed. Furthermore, noise around airports (night flight ban, noise levels) urgently requires an EU-wide solution; letting the individual airport find solutions is just inappropriate, since the airports in the Union are in strong competition with each other. As mentioned in chapter eight, the EU took the opposite way, to an EU-wide solution.

15-18 *Climate change* issues, started with the Paris Agreement and continued with the European Green Deal, have led to a fundamental rethinking of energy policy issues at EU level. The EU Climate Act and its objective to reach climate neutrality by 2050 at the latest are welcome signs of this new policy and EU leadership. At the same time, there is a growing conservatism felt within Member States ('my country first') which is likely to challenge these climate change targets. Furthermore, the global evolution of greenhouse gas emissions clearly demonstrates that the Union alone is not able to keep temperatures within the envisaged limits. In view of this situation, time works in favour of the return of nuclear energy and the continuation of the use of coal and lignite.

In the *waste* sector, the announcement of moving the Union towards a recycling society has not been followed by concrete action. Waste goes via the cheapest treatment or disposal path, and the EU instruments have not yet reoriented the majority of waste streams to economically more useful paths. Resource management, prevention of waste generation, recycling, the departure of the highly unpopular incineration of waste – all this would require an integrated and coherent product policy for which not even preliminary reflections have started at EU level – except the above-mentioned initiative on the ecodesign of products.

V. Assessment of the Process

A. The Monitoring Policy

15-19 It follows from Articles 5 TEU and 192(2) TFEU that Member States have to implement EU environmental law – which means its transposition into national law, its application and enforcement. This is often forgotten. Member States frequently implement and apply EU environmental law, because the Commission threatens with legal action under Article 258 TFEU, not because they perceive the need to ensure an adequate protection of the environment. This is particularly true of Member States which derive their national environmental legislation entirely from EU environmental law, as their environmental structure is normally not too well developed and not too influential in the political power game.

The Commission started to shift its monitoring policy and intends to concentrate on the *transposition* of environmental directives, much less on its actual *application*. It has not managed in the past to ensure a transformation of the Union's legislative acts in time by the majority of Member States, and the problem of incorrect and/or incomplete transposition continues to exist. With regard to the incorrect transposition, the Commission treats different Member States differently, due to unsystematically addressing problems and resource problems.

The Commission's policy of reducing or abandoning the monitoring of effective application of EU environmental legislation by Member States has some advantage, but also a number of strong disadvantages. The policy saves resources, avoids disputes and litigation with Member States on individual cases and allows the Commission to better concentrate on transposition questions. 15-20

A great legal disadvantage lies in the fact that Article 17 TEU is unambiguous: it requires the Commission to ensure that EU environmental law is not only transposed, but actually applied. The Commission is thus not entitled to ignore how the law is applied in practice.

The second disadvantage is perhaps even greater. As Member States have successfully prevented any green police, inspectors and other similar enforcement mechanisms in the area of the environment, the principal source of information for the Commission, when things go wrong, is the citizen complaint. Such a complaint demonstrates the citizens' interest in environmental as well as Union issues. Where this interest is frustrated, because the Commission does not investigate the complaint or arranges fake solutions with the Member State in question, the citizen might rightly ask why *they* should bother about the Union. They must then perceive the Union as a Union for big interests, but not for the person in the street. And where they get the feeling that the EU environmental law is something for the statute books but can in practice be breached without consequences, they will not bother about the environment either. The Union has considerable difficulties in explaining to European citizens why they should vote in European elections, what concrete advantage there is for the individual citizen in their daily life to belong to the Union and what all these costly institutions in Brussels and other places stand for. Environmental protection is popular with citizens all over Europe, and in particular with the young generation. Thus, the Union could improve its image in this area and show that it is down to earth and close to the citizen, not just committed to free trade and other policy areas – which mean little for the citizen in the street. The Commission's present approach to environmental issues contributes to alienating the young from the concept of the EU – probably the most disastrous long-term effect of the present policy.

B. Administrative Secrecy

Closely linked to these general considerations is the Commission's policy to consider that the whole implementation and enforcement policy, in particular the letters of formal notice and reasoned opinions in the environmental sector which are addressed to Member States, are not accessible to citizens. The reason given is that the confidentiality between the Commission and Member States would otherwise be disturbed. The underlying assumption is that the protection or lack thereof of the environment at national level is a matter between the Commission and the Member State in question – as if the Commission or the Member State or its administration were the owner of the environment. As the Commission decisions are the result of a long and detailed internal process, where all administrative, legal, technical and political arguments are weighed, this secrecy is neither comprehensible nor justified. And it is a poor consolation that the CJEU approved the Commission's practice in a number of judgments. 15-21

In policy terms, two observations need to be made. First, Member States with an 'open society' approach to administrative secrecy – the Netherlands, Sweden, Denmark, possibly also Austria and Finland – do make the letters of formal notice and reasoned opinions available to the public, apparently without any negative consequence. Second, in other areas, such as industrial, internal market, pharmaceutical, insurance, competition or transport and energy policy, letters of formal notice and reasoned opinions are systematically available to the interested trade and industry associations. There is not even a discussion on the necessity of keeping the Commission's opinion confidential. This shows that, overall, the system works with two measures: letters which are of interest to citizens are kept secret, while letters which are of interest to vested interest groups are accessible.[40] It is difficult to see how this policy increases the credibility of the Union in the eyes of the citizen in the street.

(i) Environmental Inspectors

15-22 It was mentioned that Member States did not accept the idea of environmental inspectors, which do not exist, at present, at EU level. Little public discussion has taken place on this during the last 15 years, though there is a need to explain: when a company makes an illegal merger with a company in another Member State and the Commission hears of it, the Commission may inspect the site, listen to witnesses, seize documents and ultimately pronounce fines against the company, against which the company may appeal to the General Court and then, if unsuccessful, to the CJEU. But when the same company exports hazardous waste, in breach of its EU obligations, and the Commission hears of that, the Commission may send a letter of formal notice to the Member State in question; it then has the Member State's answer as source of information. At the end of the procedure, the Commission may bring the *Member State* – not the company – before the Court of Justice, because the company has acted illegally. The judgment states the facts, but does not pronounce a fine.

This comparison of the procedure shows the doublespeak. Where the company wishes to increase its profits by concluding a merger, it may be fined; but where it wishes to increase its profits by exporting hazardous waste instead of having it treated properly, there is no sanction. This difference in treatment cannot be explained to either the citizen in the street or the law student. It just shows that environmental interests are ranked lower than economic interests. Why can the Commission send inspectors to examine the facts in the first example, but not in the second? Why are veterinary inspectors sent to 140 countries worldwide in order to check the sanitary conditions of slaughterhouses? Why are fishing boats equipped with a satellite system and, furthermore, have their landings inspected? The measuring with two different measures as regards inspections is obvious.

15-23 The Commission's own monitoring policy needs to be controlled. According to the jurisprudence of the European courts, the Commission's decision whether to open

[40] As long ago as in 1985, E Rehbinder formulated – in a more general context – on access to the EU decision-making process: 'Outside access to this process is generally limited to well organised industry groups', E Rehbinder and R Stewart, *Environmental Protection Policy* (Berlin, 1985) 334. This remark remains valid also with regard to the decision-making process under Art 258 TFEU.

proceedings under Article 258 TFEU cannot be controlled in court.[41] It is thus all the more necessary to have the Commission's practice audited, in order to see where it is inconsistent or contradictory, where it advantages some or disadvantages other Member States or industrial sectors, where the Commission omits to take obvious cases to court which, even under its own criteria, would be priority cases, etc. This has never happened so far. As a very first step, environmental organisations should systematically bring such cases of differentiated treatment of Member States – on air pollution in urban agglomerations, on waste treatment, on noise levels, on water management, etc – before the European Ombudsman.

(ii) International Agreements

It is the monitoring policy of the Commission – admittedly, not laid down in writing – not to monitor the transposition and application by Member States of international environmental agreements to which the EU has adhered. An exception is made in cases where the international agreement had been transposed into EU law by an environmental regulation or, less frequently, a directive; however, the Commission then monitors the transposition and application of this EU legislation, not of the international agreement itself. 15-24

Again, this policy is in conflict with the Commission's legal obligation under Article 17 TEU: as the international agreement becomes, by the adherence of the Union, part of EU law (Article 216(2) TFEU), the Commission has the legal obligation to ensure its application. Article 17 TEU does not differentiate between the different instruments of EU law. The CJEU's confirmation of this legal situation[42] has not yet led to any change in the Commission's practice.

C. Credibility

With the enlargement (and subsequent reduction) of the Union to 27 Member States, environmental law-making has undoubtedly become more difficult. It is thus all the more important to ensure that the existing legislation is actually applied. Numerous Council and European Parliament resolutions call on the Commission to ensure a full and complete application of existing environmental rules. The Sixth, Seventh and Eighth Environmental Action Programmes (for the periods 2002–10, 2013–20 and 2022–30, respectively), all adopted by formal European Parliament and Council decisions, made improvement of the implementation and enforcement of EU environmental legislation a top priority,[43] albeit with limited results. These decisions are contradicted by the practice of the Commission to drastically reduce the monitoring of effective application of environmental legislation in individual cases. 15-25

[41] General Court Case T-126/95 *Dumez v Commission* ECLI:EU:T:1995:189.

[42] CJEU Case C-239/03 *Commission v France* ECLI:EU:C:2004:598; Case C-213/03 *Pêcheurs des Etangs de Berre* ECLI:EU:C:2004:464.

[43] Decision 1600/2002 (n 26) Art 3; Decision 1386/2013 [2013] OJ L354/171, annex, para 57; Decision 2022/591 [2022] OJ L114/22, Art 3(a).

VI. Institutions

A. Commission

15-26 The Commission's mission to act in the common Union interest, its monopoly of making legislative proposals and the fact that it is the only institution whose members are permanently present at the seat of the Union (Brussels) gives it a very powerful position to steer environmental protection policy in the Union. The Commission has enough financial means to launch studies and research on environmental questions. And it has at its side the European Environment Agency (EEA), which supplies the necessary data.

The Commission is not well surrounded with environmental advisers. Leaving aside the very recently established European Scientific Advisory Board on Climate Change, which advises on climate change-related matters,[44] it has set up no scientific, academic, technical, ecological or socio-economic group of advisers which would advise – in particular, on its own initiative – on medium- and long-term trends in environmental issues, comment on actual problems from a point of view away from vested interests or draw attention to specific developments that are likely to affect the environment. A forum on the environment and sustainable development, which was to advise the environmental commissioner, was quickly dissolved and replaced by an industry-dominated round table group which advised the President of the Commission.[45] Environmental groups are not convened in a consultative group either. This structure is different from structures in agriculture, industry, transport or energy, where the Commission, often together with the Council, set up formal or informal consultative or advisory groups which discuss sector-related policies, trends and evolutions.

A politician who is all of a sudden elevated to the position of Environmental Commissioner or to the top of the administration is bound to listen to someone, as they simply cannot know all the environmental intricacies;[46] they will thus tend to turn either to persons from their home country or to networks which stem from their former activity – whatever that was. The result is less strategic thinking and less long-term reflection; also, the relay between top politicians is not ensured, when changes at the political level or top management occur, as each time a net has to be knitted anew.

As regards the staff levels of the Commission, the policy, introduced during the last 25 years, of seeing every official move around after three to five years increases mobility, but produces officials who think more of their career, do not really become experts in their area and are thus not always able to argue with Member States' officials or vested group representatives. This makes the European civil service too easily prone to adopting solutions which satisfy the interlocutors, without necessarily satisfying the needs of the environment.

[44] Regulation 2021/1119 [2021] OJ L243/1, Art 3.

[45] Commission Decision 93/91 [1993] OJ L328/33 (establishment of the committee); Decision 2001/704 [2001] OJ L258/20 (dissolution).

[46] A good example is Karmenu Vella (Malta), the member of the EU Commission in charge of the environment between 2014 and 2019. He had studied architecture and opened a private office on architecture. He served in the tourism, bank and financial business sectors, and was Minister for Public Works, Industries, Tourism and Finance in Malta. He appears to have never had any political or social connection with the environmental sector. The biography of Virinijus Sinkevicius (Lithuania), Commissioner for Environmental Affairs between 2019 and 2024, also does not indicate any previous activity in the field of environmental matters.

Within the Commission, the integration of administrations which would be required by the integration requirement of Article 11 TFEU is not a success. Administrations normally work vertically, ie with their administrative hierarchy, the respective parliamentary committee or the Council working group. There are no institutional or otherwise regular meetings between the environmental department and other departments within the Commission. One of the reasons for this situation is the fact that in such a meeting, when it is multilateral, the environmental official would regularly be confronted with a majority of officials who represent growth- and economy-interested departments (industry, transport, agriculture, fishery, regional policy, competition, fiscal matters, etc) and could hardly hope to see his point of view prevail. And there are not enough human resources for regular bilateral meetings. This pattern is found at all levels of the hierarchy: Commissioner, director-general, director, head of unit or desk officer. As there is enough work in all departments anyway, the temptation is great not to discuss environmental issues horizontally, except in concrete cases of necessity. 15-27

This incapacity of the Commission to discuss environmental issues in an integrated way is felt particularly strongly at sensitive points of policy. Examples are the problems of climate change on transport, which would, of course, require regular, intense discussions between the administrations of transport, but also those of agriculture, energy, industry, trade, regional policy, foreign relations and the environment, with a view to conceiving, adapting and implementing a strategy. The Sixth and Seventh Environmental Action Programmes developed some considerations in this regard and a number of measures to adopt, but without significant input from other vertical structures than the environment, such as agriculture, transport or energy; these considerations and the measures proposed have been very largely ignored since 2002, and were not taken up by the Eighth Action Programme. Another example is the question of environment and development policy, where the departments of development policy, economic policy, industry, trade, agriculture, fisheries, consumer protection and social affairs would be in need of developing an integrated strategy on the Union's policy with regard to the environment and development. This has not been done; therefore, the conclusion of the Court of Auditors of mid-June 2006–20 years after the insertion of the requirement to integrate environmental requirements into other EU policies! – was quite blunt: 'the environment has yet to be effectively mainstreamed into the Commission's development cooperation';[47] it remains valid. Similar descriptions could be made on agricultural policy, product policy and energy policy, and in other policy sectors.

As regards outside contacts, the Commission placed its work under the principles of openness, participation, accountability, effectiveness and coherence.[48] The question of openness and transparency has already been raised in paragraph 15-21 and will be further discussed below, in the section on citizens and the EU's environmental law and policy. As regards accountability, the Commission does not really explain why it takes certain measures or not. The following examples, taken at random, might explain the point: 15-28

- Almost all environmental directives require the elaboration, by Member States, of implementation reports and the elaboration, by the Commission, of EU-wide reports.

[47] European Court of Auditors, Special Report 6/2006 concerning the environmental aspects of the Commission's development cooperation [2006] OJ C235/1, no 84.

[48] Commission, European Governance (n 22) 7.

The Commission complies with this obligation in about one case out of two and normally with a considerable delay, which diminishes the value of its reports. The Commission does not explain its delays, change its approach or otherwise try to improve the situation. Member States' reports are normally not even made accessible, though, with the Internet, such access should be easy now.

- The implementation reports themselves normally report on legislative measures that have been taken by Member States, but almost never on results. However, from the point of view of the environment, it is the result that matters. There have been virtually no attempts made from the side of the Commission to explain what the state of the environment is before and after Union and national implementation measures have been taken. The reader of the reports thus learns about the legislation, while it may be assumed that they are interested in the protection of the environment; these two things are different.
- The Commission's practice, mentioned in paragraph 15-24 above, consists in not monitoring the application of international agreements.
- The Marine Strategy Framework Directive does not deal with the marine environment, but only with marine waters which had to reach a good environmental status by 2021.[49] There was no explanation given why the directive did not address issues of fauna and flora, air emissions from ships, noise, waste dumping and other aspects.
- The Sixth Environmental Action Programme requested the elaboration of a directive on biodegradable waste, which means essentially one on compost.[50] For once, there was a consensus among the majority of Member State, the European Parliament's environmental committee, and environment and industry organisations that EU-wide standards on compost and, more generally, on biodegradable waste were highly desirable, in particular for countries in Southern, Central and Eastern Europe, where the soil is in need of nutrients. Such a directive was never proposed by the Commission.
- The Commission might have good reasons not to make a proposal for a directive on biodegradable waste. The presentation of a proposal for a directive on the protection of soil would have been a good opportunity to explain its attitude. However, the Commission never explained if and why it considered such a proposal to be inadequate. Directive 2008/98 on waste charged the Commission again to examine the situation and to eventually come up with a proposal – without any follow-up or explanation from the side of the Commission as to why it remained inactive.

The list could go on. The impression is that of an administration which knows best what is good for the environment and does not consider it necessary to lay accounts on its acts and omissions.

15-29 The Commission's credibility problem was illustrated in paragraph 15-25ff above, in the area of monitoring the application of environmental law. This problem is not limited to application issues. Another example is that of the treating of sustainability issues. The question of whether the notion of sustainable development itself has not been given

[49] Directive 2008/56 (n 11).
[50] Decision 1600/2002 (n 26) Art 8.

an erroneous interpretation shall not be treated here. But it is difficult to understand why the Union adopts a strategy on sustainable development and establishes guiding principles for it[51] when, in daily practice, it adds 'sustainable' to almost all sectors of policy (sustainable energy, sustainable food law, sustainable chemicals, sustainable mobility, etc). This is an inconsistency which signals to the public that the strategy on sustainable development is pure rhetoric.

A similar rhetoric is found in the Commission's approach to transport problems. The different strategy papers duly mention that transport also causes environmental concerns and is not sustainable – and then move on to greater mobility, more traffic infrastructure and more aviation. There is simply no serious attempt to integrate environmental requirements into the elaboration and implementation of transport policy.

These examples could be multiplied for other sectoral policies.

B. European Parliament

The European Parliament has, in particular through its active environmental committee, constantly tried to strengthen legislative proposals on environmental issues which the Commission had submitted. This was and is more difficult when the majority in Parliament is conservative, as conservative parties are traditionally less committed to environmental questions. Yet, overall, the European Parliament has proved to side more with the environment than with vested interests. 15-30

Parliament's problems are structural. The deputies do not stay permanently in Brussels, but share their time between their constituency, Brussels (where the parliamentary committees work) and Strasbourg (where parliamentary plenary meetings are held). This results in contact between parliamentarians and the Commission or the Council being more rare than frequent.

The political parties in Parliament are not organised in the same way as at national level. They do not work on the same files as the Commission administration or, indeed, the national administrations in the capitals which then, later, meet in the Council working groups. Parliament's scientific and documentary service cannot rebalance this deficit. The results are that the Commission normally knows the environmental file better than the Parliament, and that Parliament has to react to Commission's initiatives, but cannot be proactive. This institutional deficit of the Parliament is particularly obvious in the conciliation discussions under Article 294 TFEU, where the deputies are confronted with the combined experts' know-how of all Member States – experts who have known the specific files often for decades. Their positions therefore regularly prevail.

The Parliament does not systematically control the implementation and application of the environmental legislation which it has co-decided. It cannot be argued that this is not Parliament's task, because the Parliament as co-legislator has a legitimate interest to know whether the European environmental legislation effectively works and if not, for what reasons. Also, the Parliament has to control the Commission's activity; this requires an active, systematic look at application questions. In this regard, the democratic system of checks and balances does not work properly.

[51] Council, 'Strategy on Sustainable Development' Document 10917/06 of 26 June 2006.

In its contacts with the public, Parliament is the most open European institution. Its members, in part due to some lack of detailed knowledge of the complex subjects which the Commission's environmental legislative proposals treat, normally recur to interest groups to receive briefings. The European environmental groups frequently find interlocutors in members of the environmental committee – and so do other interest groups with members of Parliament who are closer to their interests. Systematic consultations in the form of hearings could make the consultation process more transparent, but these are exceptional.

As, in general, the European Parliament is not yet a fully fledged Parliament comparable to national parliaments, its role in environmental law-making and in controlling the 'government' – if one may so call the Council and the Commission together – is not really efficient.

C. Council

15-31 The Council's environmental activity is very largely determined by the Commission's legislative proposals. These are discussed in working groups, where environmental attachés of the Permanent Representations of Member States and officials from central national administrations meet, together with Commission officials, who defend the proposal. Strategic discussions do not normally take place in these working groups, which limit themselves to finding concrete solutions on the basis of instructions from the Member States. The working groups do not have outside contacts; whether individual members have depends on their personal decision.

Strategic discussions may take place when action programmes are discussed, under 'other business' matters at formal Council meetings or when the environmental ministers meet at the two annual informal Council meetings, for which the presidency prepares a topic for discussion. As these informal ministerial meetings do not vote, adopt resolutions or other documents, their capacity for committing all members to future decisions, and thus their influence on long-term environmental policy, is limited.

The Council presidency is in regular contact with the Commission on matters that concern the organisation of the work on EU environmental policy. These contacts also include more general reflections on the different files, though they do not enter into the political area. As the presidency changes every six months, no long-term or more general discussions occur. Contacts with the European Parliament are much less frequent.

Outside opinions regarding the Council's work reach the Council via the capitals, not directly. This again contributes to the lack of forming a European public opinion.

If one looks at the institutions, the main motivation to develop strategic environmental thinking and long-term orientations, and to steer the Union's environmental policy, lies with the Commission, which itself is not sufficiently equipped to perform such a strategic task and, furthermore, does not feel bound by strategies such as action programmes. Since about 2005, the Commission has increasingly considered the protection of the environment as mainly being a question of climate change and moving towards a carbon-free economy, and has more or less ignored the other parts of the environment. It is too early to assess whether the European Green Deal of 2019 and the measures adopted to make it operational have really changed this situation and integrated environmental requirements into the majority of the Union's policies.

VII. Citizens and EU Environmental Law and Policy

EU environmental law and policy is popular with European citizens. The Eurobarometer's regular surveys on European citizens' opinions on EU issues have shown for three decades that a high percentage (80 per cent and more) of citizens rank environmental issues as very important and among the top three to five priorities for the Union. This result is not surprising if one considers that, for many people in the Member States, environmental legislation and the accompanying policy originate at EU level. The citizens in the street rather wish to see more EU environmental legislation and better protection of the environment, for which they feel responsible. As the objective of the Union is to be of service to its citizens and not just a free trade area, one would expect it to try to involve citizens more closely with the making and implementing of EU environmental law and policy. 15-32

It has already been mentioned that the Commission has not organised an environmental committee or forum with which it could consult. Communication activities by the Commission or by the different Commission offices in Member States are not targeted at informing or consulting citizens on environmental matters, or at making the administrative and political machinery of the EU institutions more transparent, comprehensible and accountable. The communication activity of the Commission in environmental matters is not impressive, and when the language is not diplomatic, it is unfortunately often closer to marketing or publicity concerns than to neutral information. The Commission's environmental reports and communications do not appear to reach the citizen in the street, for reasons of language, the complexity of the content and the fact that they are often not disclosed; also, very often the problem is not presented and the options for its solution are not discussed, but a specific solution is pushed forward as the right one. The presentation of environmental information and the education of citizens might not be the primary tasks of the Commission, but networking and deeper concern for the receiver of the information, including young receivers, might be worthwhile. And it is little consolation that the European Parliament and the Council do not fare any better in this area.

The access of citizens to environmental information remains difficult, even with the Internet. It was already mentioned that the EU institutions are not yet prepared for openness and transparency. Too much information is declared sensitive, including after the relevant decision has been taken. The Commission shows considerable sensitivity towards the interests of some Member States and of economic groups in keeping studies, surveys, findings and other issues confidential. Key examples are information on nuclear issues and on GMOs. Risk assessments, cost–benefit analyses, impact assessments, planning instruments, reports on meetings between members of the Commission and vested interest groups, communications on files, etc – there is a long list where a normal citizen has difficulties in obtaining access to documents. Regulation 1367/2006, which transposes the Aarhus Convention into EU law and applies it to the EU institutions,[52] did not really lead to any significant changes. And it is telling that the regulation excludes banking activities from its field of application, in order to exempt the European Investment Bank – a derogation which was not foreseen under the Aarhus Convention. 15-33

[52] Regulation 1367/2006 [2006] OJ L264/13.

Where the Commission receives a complaint from a citizen that access to environmental information was refused in a Member State, it refers that citizen to the national court. This is another way of disappointing citizens; indeed, Article 17 TEU constitutes an own obligation for the Commission to ensure that the law is applied; the general reference to a national court is not a way to comply with this obligation. Other factual difficulties in obtaining access to environmental information – unreasonably high costs, long delays for answers or receiving no answer at all, systematic refusals to grant access, etc – are not examined by the Commission, as it wishes to have as little to do with practical questions of applying EU environmental law as possible (see paragraph14-17ff). For the citizen, the Commission is perceived as the guardian of EU law; if, then, that same Commission does not take up issues of practical application, disappointment is inevitable.

15-34 Not much needs be said about citizen participation in environmental decision-making at EU and national level. The Commission appears to understand consultations as being synonymous with participation – which it is not. Internet consultations are not an equivalent to citizens' participation either. What is lacking in particular is the laying of accounts: the Commission does not explain why the opinions and comments from environmental groups or persons were not taken in or why it preferred a more economic-oriented approach to a more environment-oriented one.

As regards citizens' participation in the decision-making process at national level, the corresponding legislation is still too recent to be assessed. At present, the fact that there is such legislation at all is a positive element for citizens. Generally, the participation of citizens in the decision-making process on environmental issues is disappointing; the Aarhus Convention has not changed much in this regard. Whether there are questions on trans-European networks for transport or energy, infrastructure projects or nuclear energy, the larger the project is, the less the concerned population appears to be able to effectively participate in the decision-making process.

15-35 Giving citizens and/or environmental organisations the possibility to have environmental acts or omissions controlled by courts was one of the objectives of the Aarhus Convention to which the Union adhered. However, the Council was of the opinion that the present provisions of Article 263(4) TFEU were compatible with both the letter and the spirit of that convention and that no change was necessary with regard to access to the European Courts. Even if this were legally correct – in my opinion, the Aarhus Convention does require a change in the present state of affairs[53] – the political aspect remains: access to the European Courts on environmental matters is de facto impossible for individuals and for environmental organisations. A softening of the very dominant position of the Commission – more than 50 per cent of all environmental cases are brought by the Commission – would be of particular political importance, as it would also eventually hold EU institutions environmentally responsible.

15-36 A proposal for a directive to improve access to national courts was likewise not accepted by the Council, which invoked subsidiarity reasons. This means that Member States will decide on improved access to justice in environmental matters, and all indicators suggest

[53] See now, in the same sense, Aarhus Convention Compliance Committee, 'Draft Findings and Recommendations with Regard to Communication ACCC/C/2008/32 Concerning Compliance by the European Union', April 2011.

that the status quo will largely remain unchanged. Thus, for example, a company which is of the opinion that a piece of environmental legislation of a Member State – including legislation which is based on EU law – impedes the placing on the market of its products may go to court and challenge that legislation by virtue of Article 34 TFEU. However, an environmental organisation which is of the opinion that legislation allows too many emissions into the air or the water cannot appeal to a court.

The recent example of air pollution by particulate matter is a good illustration of this argument. The relevant national and EU legislation is not respected in a number of urban agglomerations. The CJEU had already declared in 1991 that air quality standards protect human health and therefore citizens must be allowed to demand their respect in court. This line of judgment was repeated in 2007.[54] However, the legislation continues not to be respected, and no applications from environmental groups have so far led even to the breach of EU law being acknowledged.[55]

Lawyers will explain the difference between the rights of a company and those of an environmental organisation in air pollution cases like this. Politically, this is more difficult, and it adds to the disappointment which European citizens must feel that the Union amended the existing legislation to grant Member States further delays in respecting their obligations which have existed since 1999.[56]

Similar examples could be given for the water, waste and noise sectors.

As one way of assisting citizens in contributing to protect the environment, the Commission had instituted the complaint procedure, being careful, however, to avoid formalising the procedural rules in any legal act. While, at the end of the 1980s, the Commission promised to examine each complaint as to its merits,[57] it has since diverged from this commitment and now only promises to register each complaint; it does, however, reserve the right to treat or not to treat complaints as to its own priorities; and, what is more, the registration takes place in a so-called pilot register and is submitted to a non-public procedure arranged between the Member State in question and the Commission. Instead of a formal examination of the complaint, the Commission thus looksto making an arrangement with Member States' authorities, though, in many cases, it is the national public authorities themselves which are disregarding the EU's environmental law.[58] Apart from the fact that, in the meantime, there are clear signs that environmental complaints are not even registered at all, this change in procedure – decided without any participation of citizens or the public – means that individual desk officers now decide on how to proceed with complaints. Seen from the point of view of the citizen, whether in Crete, Madeira, Bratislava or Tampere, the message which is sent from the Commission when their complaint is not examined is clear: 15-37

> It may be that the specific project on which you complain, is breaching EU environmental law. However, your Member State has correctly transposed the relevant EU legislation into national law. Therefore, we decided not to look into your specific case.

[54] CJEU Case C-237/07 *Janecek* ECLI:EU:C:2008:447.

[55] See also the saddening development in the air pollution case concerning the UK, CJEU Case C-404/13 *ClientEarth* ECLI:EU:C:2014:2382.

[56] Directive 2008/50 [2008] OJ L152/1.

[57] See the text which accompanied the complaint form issued by the Commission [1989] OJ C26/1.

[58] Commission, COM(2002) 725.

If one compares this with the Commission's message of the early 1990s, where the Commission committed itself to examine each complaint (see paragraph 14-24), the discrepancy becomes obvious. And it also becomes obvious why the frustration about the EU institutions is growing at local level, not diminishing.

Instead of taking complaints on individual cases as a way of sampling which allows it to gain an impression of how EU law works in practice, the Commission sees individual complaints as an undesirable practice which should best be abandoned. And the remark has to be made that neither in competition matters nor in internal market affairs is this handling of complaints practised.

In conclusion, it may fairly be stated that EU institutions put very little effort into bringing Union environmental matters closer to the citizen. Citizens are rather asked to take the initiative themselves – ask for access to information, file complaints – and often enough see their initiatives fail.

VIII. Member States and EU Environmental Law and Policy

15-38 The EU Treaties' concept of distributing responsibilities between the Union and the Member States is quite clear: there is shared responsibility for the European environment. Member States have the responsibility of protecting the environment, while certain measures are to be taken at EU level (Article 5 TEU).

The political reality is somewhat different. Member States rely heavily on the Union for environmental measures. It was already mentioned that for more than half of the Member States, 'environmental law' is more or less equivalent to 'EU-derived environmental law'. This means that where the Union does not take legislative measures, no legislative action will be taken in the majority of the Member States either. This contradicts the objective of the Union to ensure a more or less level economic, but also social and environmental, playing field – and this aspect is frequently overlooked by countries with a strong, though not necessarily pro-environmental, national policy, such as the Netherlands, Germany and the German *Länder* or France.

15-39 The result of this partitioning of responsibilities and political practice is that EU environmental policy is squeezed between two different orientations. On the one hand, Member States insist on the application of Articles 5 TEU and 193 TFEU, with the consequence that the Union should only regulate where this is absolutely necessary, and should not strive for an optimal solution of a problem, in order to leave Member States the possibility to maintain or introduce more stringent provisions. On the other hand, Member States do not themselves develop national measures to protect, preserve and improve the quality of the environment. Countries such as the Netherlands, Germany or Austria have even taken, in one or the other form, the decision not to adopt national environmental legislation which goes beyond the relevant EU measure (gold-plating), thus frustrating the concept of Articles 5 TEU and 193 TFEU.

There are numerous examples of this. The most obvious is the absence of environmental action programmes in Member States. The EU action programmes concern the EU level; the attempt of the Fifth Environmental Action Programme to also address targets and measures to be taken at national level[59] was a complete failure. However, protecting the European environment under the Treaties is also the task of Member States. From the point of view of the environment, it is not relevant whether it is protected through a local, national or EU measure, so long as it is protected. This simple truth is often forgotten in Member States which just rely on the Union to provide for the necessary protection. And no report on the state of the environment is published every three to four years by any of the 27 EU Member States, even though this is requested by the Aarhus Convention, which was ratified by all of them.

Other examples range from environmental liability via soil protection, permits for small and medium-sized companies, environmental impact assessments for smaller infrastructure projects, and marine water and groundwater protection, to contaminated site provisions, access to justice in environmental matters, coastal zone protection, fights against soil erosion and pollution emission registers. For most of these areas, there is some legislation in some Member States; however, the overall perspective for the territory of the Union, seen from a bird's eye view, is an unsatisfactory degree of protecting the environment. This reflects the different role which the protection of the environment plays in the political hierarchy of the individual Member States. While it ranks high in some, it ranks very low in others, especially in those where the environmental legislation is more or less completely EU-derived.

The objective of the high degree of environmental protection of Articles 3 TEU and 15-40
191 TFEU is normally ignored during the EU law-making procedure. The same applies to the principles that environmental damage should be rectified at source, that the polluter should pay or that environmental requirements should be integrated into the legislation of other policy areas. These principles of the EU Treaties are perceived as EU principles; but when Member States discuss a Commission proposal in the Council, they do not look at the Union's (environmental) interest, but at their own (environmental, economic and social). And this conflict of interest cannot easily be solved as, on the one hand, the Commission itself, which should have defined the EU's environmental interest, might have failed to do so due to pressure from vested interest groups or internal differences of opinion on the right approach, while, on the other hand, the Commission's representative, confronted with representatives of 27 Member States, would have to be superhuman to impose the Commission's point of view.

The Council environment working group does not normally wait for the European Parliament's opinion on a Commission proposal before discussing it. Rather, discussions in the working group run in parallel with Parliament's discussion. It is now normal for the working group to reach a political compromise on a Council position with regard to a proposal before the parliamentary opinion is delivered. This practice increases the Council's dominance in the legislative process, though it contradicts the objective of Article 294 TFEU. In the trilogue (between the European Parliament, the Council and the Commission) meetings, this approach has softened; however, in those meetings, the representatives of the European Parliament are normally already in a numerical inferior position, not to mention the accumulated expertise of the experts of the 27 capitals.

[59] Fifth Environmental Action Programme (n 1).

15-41 The monitoring of adopted EU environmental law varies considerably from one Member State to another. Again, this reflects the different degree of environmental awareness in Member States, though there is a secondary element. Member States' administrations perceive EU environmental law all too often as imported law, or immigrant law, which stems from an outside source and which is different from national law.[60] Such an attitude can be found, for example, in Germany, France or Italy. More generally, EU law is monitored because the Commission asks for such a monitoring, not because it corresponds to the own conviction of the Member State. Inevitably, the concept of imported law has practical consequences as regards the frequency and intensity of monitoring, sanctions for breaches, etc.

The national implementation reports which Member States send to the Commission report, as mentioned, on measures taken, not on results achieved. They practically never deal with lacunae, omissions, breaches of provisions, sanctions pronounced, etc. The implementation reports thus do not give an idea of an EU directive's effectiveness.

15-42 The enforcement of EU environmental law is entirely in the hands of Member States and practically no information is made public on that, nor in the previously mentioned implementation reports. The Commission does not monitor enforcement practices and the intensity of enforcement, in particular as regards pollution emissions, permit controls and water and soil contamination, and planning-related measures such as impact assessments or participation provisions vary considerably from one Member State to another. The Commission also hardly ever monitors the application of regulations; these are directly applicable, and thus Member States often do not feel obliged to monitor their application themselves.

It is difficult to identify different groups among Member States with regard to monitoring deficiencies. Some Member States make it a point of national honour to transpose EU environmental legislation in time. For others, delayed transposition is the rule. Some Member States consider that the provisions of EU law, once they are in the national statute books, have to be enforced; this includes the Scandinavian states and the Netherlands. Others do not see a problem in having contradictions between the law in the statute books and the law as it is applied; this attitude is not limited to environmental law.

It is too early to finally place the 13 Member States which joined the Union since 2004 into one of these categories. Generally, however, it can be said that under the former Communist system, the state which produced the environmental legislation and the state-owned companies were the biggest polluters of all. This created a certain cynicism in the citizens: why should a piece of legislation be respected if it is broken in particular by those who made it? This cynicism partly continues to exist and will be difficult to overcome. It adds to the point which is also true for the 14 'old' Member States, that the placing of environmental legislation into the statute books is easy, but that the real problems appear when these environmental provisions are to be applied. The application of environmental law remains, as in the new Member States, the biggest of all the legal and political problems.

[60] Commission, European Governance (n 22) 21: 'At the same time, the feeling persists that Community rules are foreign laws.'

IX. The Union as a Global Environmental Player

The Union does not play an active role at global level when it comes to the elaboration 15-43
of environmental standards. The jealously of Member States to appear on the international scene and be seen as a sovereign state is too big. Own initiatives from the Union would probably have to be classified as part of a foreign (environmental) policy and share all the difficulties of an EU foreign policy. The participation in international discussions on new environmental agreements is based, according to the Treaties (Article 218 TFEU), on a Council mandate. In practice, Member States are reluctant to give such a mandate, as then the Commission would normally represent the Union, and this would restrict Member States' possibilities for negotiation. It is therefore often the case that in such international negotiations, the Commission is present without a mandate, discusses and negotiates together with Member States and tries to co-ordinate the Member States' positions, in order to let the whole Union speak, as far as possible, with one voice, or at least take similar positions.

All this does not facilitate the role of the Union as such, but has to be accepted as part of international diplomacy. More relevant is the aspect that the USA, for more than 25 years, has proven to be incapable or unwilling to assume international leadership in environmental matters. As the Union, for the reasons sketched out above, is not in a state to assume leadership functions either, global environmental issues are at present not properly dealt with. Examples are issues of environmental crime (trade in timber, waste, exotic species, fish, etc), the provisions on biodiversity, the Convention on Hazardous Waste, the Arctic Area, the environmental behaviour of multinational companies, chemicals, access to water resources, soil erosion, desertification, the construction of dams and many others, and in particular the enforcement of existing rules.

The global discussions on climate change, where the Union played a very active role and 15-44
did assume global leadership, do not prove the contrary. In that case, the Union grew into a leading role due to a change in the USA's attitude towards climate change. However, the Union, whether as just the Commission or the Commission jointly with the Member States, is hardly equipped to assume a permanent global leadership function in climate change: fossil fuel energy responsibilities are too dispersed within the Union, human resources are too small, the scientific and technical data on the situation worldwide are too scattered, diplomatic services of the Union itself do not yet exist, the financial tools which such a leadership role requires are not available, etc.

In international negotiations which would require an integrated approach by the Union, such as combining agricultural questions with environmental ones, the Union negotiates under trade–agricultural perspectives alone, as it has not implemented Article 11 TFEU. Thus, for example, the proposal to open up EU agricultural markets on the condition that the environmental and health standards of the Union (pesticide residues, sanitary conditions, etc) are taken over internationally has apparently not even crossed the mind of the EU negotiators. The lack of integrating environmental requirements into the EU development policy[61] also makes the EU position in this area difficult on international forums.

[61] See the reference to Special Report 6/2006 of the European Court of Auditors (n 47).

Generally, the Union is much more interested in promoting exports of European products and services than having an international policy which effectively integrates environmental considerations.

15-45 The implementation of international environmental agreements within the Union has already been mentioned. Though the Union's monitoring mechanism regarding the application of law is quite impressive overall and could serve as a model for many a regional organisation – Mercosur, Nafta, the Asean Group, etc – the Union behaves internationally as the Member States behave with regard to the Commission: reports are submitted late, they report on measures, not on results, and they try to give a positive image of the Union and to hide imperfections.

Thus, at present, the Union has neither the internal structures nor the resources to assume a lead role as a global environmental player. This certainly also has consequences for the present state of the global environment – which is not good, if one thinks of climate change, poverty, biodiversity loss, chemicals, water problems, pollution, etc.

Strict EU environmental standards might incite companies to relocate their activities to third countries with less demanding requirements. This would lead to generating pollution problems in the third country, as well as effects such as deforestation, water abstraction or mining. Discussions within the Union have so far centred on such consequences in the climate change discussion ('carbon leakage'), where the Union has tried to mitigate such effects by its own measures, such as the free allocation of emission rights or a border tax adjustment. Generally, the impact of environmental measures adopted by the Union on third countries' production cannot be avoided, and it is perhaps not even desirable to avoid it: why, for example, should the import of a carcinogenic product into the Union be permitted when its production within the Union itself is not allowed? The WTO recognised that France was entitled to prohibit the import of asbestos from Canada because of the risks of asbestos.[62] It is true, though, that the specific decision-making, such as the narrow or wide interpretation of the precautionary principle, plays an important role in such discussions: while the Union restricted the use of hundreds of chemical substances under the REACH Regulation, the USA restricted barely a handful of such substances.

X. Perspectives

15-46 As the environment has no voice, there is a tendency to declare that things are slowly getting better. The EEA declared in 2001 that the state of the European environment showed some progress, but offered a poor picture overall;[63] this changed into the following statement in 2015:[64]

> Europe's natural capital is not yet being protected, conserved and enhanced in line with the ambition of the 7th Environmental Action Programme approach. Reduced pollution has

[62] WTO, Dispute DS 135/12, Canada/France and EC.

[63] European Environment Agency, *Environment in the European Union at the Turn of the Century* (Luxembourg, 1999).

[64] European Environment Agency, *The European Environment – State and Outlook 2015 – Synthesis Report* (Copenhagen, 2015) 11–13.

significantly improved the quality of Europe's air and water. But loss of soil functions, land degradation and climate change remain major concerns, threatening the flow of environmental goods and services that underpin Europe's economic output and well-being. A high proportion of protected species (60%) and habitats (77%) are considered to be in unfavourable conservation status, and Europe is not on track to meet its overall target of halting biodiversity loss by 2020, even though some more specific targets are met. Looking ahead, climate change impacts are projected to intensify and the underlying drivers of biodiversity loss are expected to persist.'

In its 2020 report, the Agency stated:[65]

> Europe faces persistent problems in areas such as biodiversity loss, resource use, climate change impacts and environmental risks to health and well-being … Europe needs to find ways to transform the key societal systems that drive environmental and climate change pressures and health impacts – rethinking not just technologies and production processes, but also consumption patterns and ways of living … The current trajectories of social and economic development are destroying the ecosystems that ultimately sustain humanity. Shifting onto sustainable pathways will require rapid and large-scale reductions in environmental pressures, going far beyond the current reductions.
>
> … it is clear that Europe is not making enough progress in addressing environmental challenges … policies have been more effective in reducing environmental pressures than in protecting biodiversity and ecosystems, and human health and well-being. The impacts of climate change on biodiversity and ecosystems are expected to intensify, while activities and such as agriculture, fisheries, transport, industry and energy production continue to cause biodiversity loss, resource extractions and harmful emissions. Full implementation of existing policies would take Europe a long way to achieving its environmental goals up to 2030 … Beyond implementation, Europe needs to address gaps and weaknesses, for example in land, soil and chemicals. Better integration of environmental goals into sector policies is also essential, as is improved policy coherence.
>
> … Europe will not achieve its sustainability vision … by simply promoting economic growth and seeking to manage harmful side-effects with environmental and social policy tools. Instead, sustainability needs to become the guiding principle for ambitious and coherent policies and actions across society.

The state of the environment in the Union is not satisfactory, the biggest challenges being climate change, the conservation of nature and biodiversity, the omnipresence of (polluting) chemicals and the problems of urban agglomerations. And the expectancy that there will be about nine billion people on earth by 2030 who all need food, shelter, water, energy and a job draws attention to the facts that the EU's problems are small compared to the global challenges which lie ahead, and that they are in part already the problems of today and require a credible leadership now.

The EU structures to adequately deal with the global and regional challenges could be improved. Active citizen involvement will be indispensable if the environmental policy is ever to produce results. And the Union will not be able to play an active and positive role on the evolution of the global environment unless it brings its own house in order.

Environmental legislation is not everything, but it is a very important factor in distributing justice in society, in determining rights and obligations, and in balancing diverging

[65] European Environment Agency, *The European Environment. State and Outlook 2020* (Copenhagen, 2019) 9ff.

interests. Western society has not found any other means to achieve these results than legislation, and I doubt that in modern society, where the role of economics is important, any other means could fulfil the same function. 'Between the strong and the weak, it is the law which makes free and the freedom which oppresses': these words of the French philosopher Lacordaire remain valid today and should warn against the hope that economic instruments can ensure justice in the society.

The Union will need, for a foreseeable time, environmental legislation and its effective application. More and more, this will become relevant also for the global level. It is hoped that decision-makers at all levels are aware of this and find the vision, the strategy, the will and the capacity to develop legal instruments which effectively protect, preserve and improve the quality of the environment, nationally, Europe-wide and globally. The environment can survive without humans, but humans cannot survive without the environment.

BIBLIOGRAPHY

Alaranta, J and Turunu, T, 'Drawing a Line Between European Waste and Chemicals Regulation' [2017] *Review of European Community and International Environmental Law* 163.

Amos, R, 'Assessing the Impact of the Habitats Directive' [2021] *Journal of Environmental Law* 365.

Bandi, G, 'The Role of Environmental Organisations in European Integration With Examples' [2018] *Hungarian Yearbook of International Law and European Law* 31.

Bogojevic, S, *Emissions Trading Schemes: Markets, States and Law* (Oxford, 2013).

Bogojevic, S and Rayfuse, R, *Environmental rights in Europe and Beyond* (Oxford, 2020).

Born, C-H and Schoukens, H, 'Biodiversity Litigation Before the Court of Justice of the European Union: A Promising Pathway for Better Enforcement of International Biodiversity Law' in G Futhazar et al (eds), *Biodiversity Litigation* (Oxford, 2022) 293.

Born, C-H et al (eds), *The Habitats Directive in Its EU Environmental Law Context* (London, 2015).

Boyle, A and Redgwell, C in Birnie, Boyle and Redgwell's *International Law and the Environment*, 4th edn (Oxford, 2021).

Brochet, A, et al, 'Preliminary assessment of the scope and scale of illegal killing and taking of birds in the Mediterranean' (2016) *Birdlife Conservation International* 4.

Brochet, A, et al, 'Illegal killing and taking of birds in Europe outside Mediterranean: assessing the scope and scale of a complex issue' (2019) *Birdlife Conservation International* 12.

Buonsante, V, 'Regulatory Coherence in the Transatlantic Trade and Investment Partnership Agreement; The Use of Chemicals' [2014] *Elmi Review* 39.

Cavoski, A, 'The Unintended Consequences of EU Law and Policy on Air Pollution' [2017] *Review of European Community and International Environmental Law* 255.

Clément, M, *Droit européen de l'environnement. Jurisprudence commentée*, 3rd edn (Brussels, 2016).

De Sadeleer, N, 'EU Law and Birds' in R Macrory (ed), *Reflections on 30 Years of EU Environmental Law* (Groningen, 2009) 369.

Epiney, A, *Umweltrecht der Europäischen Union*, 4th edn (Baden-Baden, 2019).

Epstein, Y, 'Favourable Conservation Status for Species: Examining the Habitats Directive's Key Concept Through a Case Study of the Swedish Wolf' [2016] *Journal of Environmental Law* 221.

Epstein, Y and Schoukens, H, 'A Positivist Approach to Rights of Nature in the European Union' [2022] *Journal of Rights and the Environment* 205.

Fermeglia, M and Pedrisa, K, 'Planning for Citizens' Health: Towards an Integrated Approach to Air and Noise Pollution in the EU' [2022] *Journal of European Environmental & Planning Law* 9.

Fogleman, V, 'Facilitating Enforcement of the ELD by Competent Authorities' (Brussels, 2022).

Garcia Ureta, A, *EU Biodiversity Law. Wild Birds and Habitats Directives* (Zutphen, 2020).

Hamlin, O, 'Sustainability and the Failure of Ambition in European Pesticide Regulation' [2015] *Journal of Environmental Law* 405.

Harb, AL, 'All Roads (Used to) Lead to Brussels. The Future of EU Created Environmental Law in Eastern Europe' [2015] *European Energy and Environmental Law Review* 144.

Hedemann-Robinson, M, 'Enforcement of EU Environmental Law: Taking Stock of the Evolving Union Legal Framework' [2015] 105 *European Energy and Environmental Law Review*.

Hendry, S, 'The EU Water Framework Directive – Challenges, Gaps and Potential for the Future' [2017] *Journal of European Environmental & Planning Law* 249.

Heritier, A, Knill, C and Minges, S, *Ringing the Changes in Europe. Regulatory Competition and the Transformation of the State: Britain, France and Germany* (Berlin/New York, 1996).

Jacobs, F, 'The Role of the European Court of Justice in the Protection of the Environment' [2006] *Journal of Environmental Law* 185.

Jans, J and Vedder, H, *European Environmental Law*, 4th edn (Groningen, 2011).

Karageorgeou, V, 'The EU Regulatory Framework to Deal With the Environmental Effects of Mining Activities – Assessing the Effectiveness' [2016] *European Energy and Environmental Law Review* 138.

Kingston, S (ed), *European Perspectives on Environmental Law and Governance* (Oxford, 2012).

Krämer, L, 'The EU Battle on the Last Word and the Environment' [2021] *Journal of European Environmental & Planning Law* 390.

Krämer, L and Orlando, E (eds), *Principles of Environmental Law* (Cheltenham, 2018).

Kouvaras, I, 'EU Confronting Wildlife Trafficking' [2016] *European Energy and Environmental Law Review* 76.

Leal-Arcas, R, Faktoufou, M and Kyprianou, A, 'Legal Exploration of the European Union Carbon Border Adjustment Mechanism' [2022] *European Energy and Environmental Law Review* 223.

Lee, M, *EU Environmental Law, Governance and Decision-Making*, 2nd edn (Oxford, 2014).

Lee, M, 'Environmental Pasts and Future: The European Union and the "British Way"' [2019] *Journal of Environmental Law* 559.

Macrory, R, (ed) *Principles of European Environmental Law* (Groningen, 2004).

Maître-Ekern, E and Dalhammar, C, 'Regulating Planned Obsolescence: A Review of Legal Approaches to Ensure Product Durability and Reparability in Europe' [2016] *Review of European Community and International Environmental Law* 378.

Marin Duran, G and Morgera, E, *Environmental Integration in the EU's External Relations. Beyond Multilateral Dimensions* (Oxford, 2012).

Misonne, D, 'The Emergence of a Right to Clean Air: Transforming European Union Law Through Delegation and Citizen Science' [2020] *Review of European Community and International Environmental Law* 34.

Möckel, S, '35 Years of the EU Birds Directive in the Light of the Court Practice of the European Court of Justice and the German Federal Administrative Court' [2014] *Journal of European Environmental & Planning Law* 392.

Moreno Molina, A, *El derecho del cambio climatico. Retos, instrumentos y litigious* (Valencia, 2023).

Ohler, A, Peeters, M and Eliantonio, M, 'How to Represent the Silent Environment? An Update of Germany's Struggle to Implement Article 9(3) of the Aarhus Convention' [2021] *Journal of European Environmental & Planning Law* 370.

Pagh, P, *Miljoeret*, 2nd edn (Copenhagen, 1996).

Pallemaerts, M, *Toxics and transnational law: an inquiry into the effectiveness of international and European Community environmental law* (Oxford, 2003).

Peeters, M and Uylenburg, R (eds), *EU Environmental Legislation. Legal Perspectives on Regulatory Strategies* (Cheltenham, 2014).

Peeters, M and Eliantonio, M (eds), *Research Handbook on European Environmental Law* (Cheltenham, 2020).

Rehbinder, E and Stewart, R, *Environment Protection Policy* (Berlin/New York, 1985).

Reid, E, *Balancing Human Rights, Environmental Protection and International Trade; Lessons From the EU Experience* (Oxford, 2015).

Sevenster, H, *Millieubeleid en Gemeenschapsrecht* (Deventer, 1992).

Sevenster, H, 'The environmental guarantee after Amsterdam: does the emperor have new clothes?' *The Yearbook of European Environmental Law 2000*, 291.

Squintani, L (ed), *Beyond Minimum Harmonisation: Gold-Plating and Green-plating of European Environmental Law* (Cambridge, 2019).

Tamisier, A, *Camargue milieux et payages. Evolution entre 1942 et 1984* (Arles, 1992).

Tegner Anker, H, 'Simplifying EU Environmental Legislation – Revising the EIA Directive' [2014] *Journal of European Environmental & Planning Law* 321.

Tegner Anker, H et al, 'Natura 2000 and the Regulation of Agricultural Ammonia Emissions' [2019] *Journal of European Environmental & Planning Law* 340.

Tegner Anker, H, de Graaf, K and Squintani, L, 'Coping with EU Environmental Legislation Transposition Principles and Practices' [2015] *Journal of Environmental Law* 17.

Thieffry, P, *Handbook of European Environmental and Climate Law*, 2nd edn (Brussels, 2021).

Trouwborst, A and Somsen, H, 'Domestic Cats (*Felis catus*) and European Nature Conservation Law – Applying the EU Birds and Habitats Directives to a Significant but Neglected Threat to Wildlife' [2020] *Journal of Environmental Law* 391.

Truilhé-Marengo, E, *Droit de l'environnment de l'Union européenne* (Brussels, 2015).
Turunu, T and Alaranta, J, 'The Role of the CJEU in Shaping the Future of the Circular Economy' [2021] *European Energy and Environmental Law Review* 81.
Van Calster, G and Reins, L, *EU Environmental Law* (Cheltenham, 2018).
Vanhellemont, A, 'Environmental Reporting by the EU Member States and the Commission – Current Practices, Legal Action and Ways Forward' [2020] *Journal of European Environmental & Planning Law* 189.
Vaughan, S, *EU Chemicals Regulation* (Cheltenham, 2015).
Verniers, E, 'One Health, One Welfare, One Right. Introducing Animal Rights in Europe' [2022] *Journal of European Environmental & Planning Law* 277.
Vijgen, J, *The Legacy of Lindane, HOH Isomere Production* (Amsterdam, 2006).
Woerdman, E, Roggenkamp, M and Holwerda, M (eds), *Essential EU Climate Law* (Cheltenham, 2015).
Zuleeg, M, 'Vorbehaltene Kompetenzen der Mitgliedstaaten der Europäischen Gemeinschaft auf dem Gebiet des Umweltrechts' [1987] *Neue Zeitschrift für Verwaltungsrecht* 280.

INDEX